Microsoft Project

B.A.S.I.C.S.®

Your Simple Guide for Building and Executing Project Schedules

JERRY REED, PMP, CSM, MCP
YOLANDA REED, CSM

B.A.S.I.C.S.®

Published by: B.A.S.I.C.S.®

Graphic images created by yolandareed.com or licensed

Cover design by yolandareed.com

Copyedit and layout by yolandareed.com

ISBN: 978-0-9979775-8-5

Print Run Number: 1

Author Reviews

Excellent course. Well-organized. Instructor Reed took a very difficult software program and broke it down into digestible bites, explaining the "why" behind each feature. I especially appreciate the practical approach, helping us understand when and why to use each feature and that the way we use MS Project will vary for each project environment. I came into this class with zero experience with MS Project. I feel I now have all the basic tools needed to successfully run projects using MS Project. Thank you, Instructor Reed!
— Student Feedback

Excellent knowledge of course topic; valuable real-world experience; well organized; clear communicator — **Student Feedback**

... it was nice to have someone who was working and applying what he knew in a real environment. Jerry had very good lessons learned from past experience that I will use with my teams — **Student Feedback**

"I feel I now have all the basic tools needed to successfully run projects using MS Project. Thank you, Instructor Reed! — **Student Feedback**

Excellent instructor. Really brings the information down-to-earth but is clearly incredibly knowledgeable of the software program and project management in general.
— Student Feedback

This course exceeded my expectations and provided me with very valuable professional skills.
— Student Feedback

Clearly you have provided your students with an outstanding learning experience and you have provided UCLA Extension with the quality of instruction that we seek in all our programs.
— UCLA Distinguished Instructor Award Committee

How to Get the Microsoft Project B.A.S.I.C.S.® On-Demand Course

This book includes a FREE 4-month subscription to the Microsoft Project B.A.S.I.C.S. on-demand course. This video rendition of the Microsoft Project B.A.S.I.C.S. book is a complete course on Microsoft Project, including a comprehensive Project for the Web tutorial. Like the book, you'll be introduced to software features in a meaningful and practical context. You'll also learn to build reliable schedules using the B.A.S.I.C.S. 6-step scheduling process.

It includes:

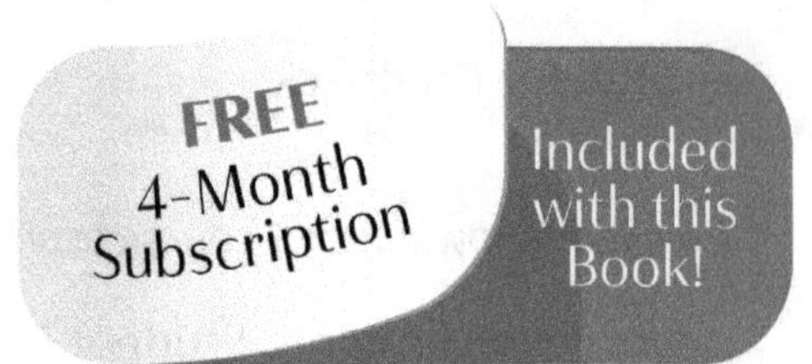

- A complete course on Microsoft Project
- A video for each chapter of the book
- Work-along software demonstrations
- A comprehensive Project for the Web tutorial
- Stunning, lively graphics

HOW TO GET YOUR 4-MONTH ACCESS LINK TO THE COURSE

If a postcard was included in the cover of your book, follow the instructions included on the postcard.

If your book did not include a postcard, follow the instructions below:

1. Go to **https://www.pmplicity.com/getvideos** to upload proof of purchase of this book. Acceptable forms of proof of purchase include Amazon receipts or screenshots of Amazon order details. Proof of purchase must reflect the Amazon order number, book title (or image) and delivery date. REMOVE ANY PERSONAL INFORMATION, such as your address.

2. Using the contact form, BE SURE TO PROVIDE AN EMAIL ADDRESS to send the access link. After acceptable proof of purchase is received, you'll be emailed a link to access the video course.
   Please note: an email address must be provided or we cannot send you the access link.

Companion Website

Visit **MSPBASICS.COM** — this book's companion website for solutions to the Practice Exercises, helpful videos, tips and tools for using Microsoft Project, and much more.

Preface

When I began developing a Microsoft Project course for the UCLA Extension Project Management certification program, Microsoft Project 2003 was the current version of the app. At that time, I had been using Project for several years to manage projects for AT&T. I was excited to develop and teach a Microsoft Project course based on the practical experience I had gained as a working project manager. My design approach was to reverse engineer many of the schedules I'd built over the years to build data centers, manage office relocation projects, and introduce new equipment into the AT&T wireless network. In the process, I uncovered the distinct project management fundamentals that contributed to effectively using Project to build reliable schedules. As I identified these fundamentals, I discovered other layers of knowledge beneath them. To streamline the lessons, I decomposed the key principles and organized them into a logical sequence that flowed into the natural steps for building a project schedule. My target learner was the absolute beginner. What emerged from this process was **B.A.S.I.C.S**, our six-step scheduling approach. The logical steps and practical context triggered active engagement, and lively discussions about scheduling problems students faced in the workplace. This applied approach effectively brought users, regardless of prior exposure, to an advanced–intermediate level of proficiency. I discovered that teaching the software features in a practical context and solving real problems faced in the field led to greater retention, and quicker mastery of the tool. Over the past 15+ years, my students, as well as experienced working project professionals have lauded this hand-on approach. Thanks to their feedback, the material is heavily vetted and reflects the changing needs of the workplace. Our text has also been adopted as the required text for several college and university courses and is now available in the Follett and E-campus book systems.

This newest edition of our Microsoft Project B.A.S.I.C.S. book and video series target an even wider audience of users - from the accidental project manager to the seasoned traditional or agile project manager. This version has some exciting additions, including exhaustive instruction on how to break down a project of any complexity into manageable parts, a tutorial on how to use Microsoft's Project for the Web and best use cases, how to use task relationships and lead time to complete projects faster, how to use the Agile features in Project Online Desktop, and an expanded tracking chapter that simplifies the concepts of Earned Value Management and teaches you how to configure Project to correctly calculate each metric.

Thank you for choosing our book. We're excited to guide you in learning Microsoft Project to build schedules you and your team can rely on!

Brief Contents

Table of Contents

TABLE OF CONTENTS

For an Overview of the On-Demand Course, go to:

www.pmplicity.com/about-basics-2

Practice Exercises

PRACTICE MAKES PROFICIENT! Some training requires hands-on experience to become adept. Learning Microsoft Project is no exception. Starting with Chapter 3 and throughout the book, you'll find "Challenge" practice exercises that reinforce the lessons and the software features covered in the respective chapters. The exercises include simple steps to strengthen learning and help you progress toward proficiency.

Solutions to the Practice Exercises, along with videos, and tips and tools for using Microsoft Project can be found on the companion website – **MSPBASICS.COM**.

TABLE OF CONTENTS

Introduction

Welcome to Microsoft Project **B.A.S.I.C.S**. With this book, you'll learn to build realistic and reliable schedules using Microsoft Project – the most widely used full-featured scheduling tool among professional schedulers and project managers around the world. The schedule is the most contentious document on any project. It's where the needs of the business collide with the capabilities of the business. Questions like *"When will we launch?"*, *"When is the release date?"* or *"When will we get the certificate of occupancy?"* can only be answered credibly by building real project schedules and using true scheduling apps, like Microsoft Project. A properly built schedule can help you set the right expectations from the start of the project – when things like budget and resource limitations are easiest to overcome.

To highlight this reality, consider the following scenario:

1. An organization needs a project completed in **six months** to exploit an emerging market opportunity.

2. Based on resource limitations, budget constraints, and competing priorities, the earliest the project can be delivered is **ten months**.

3. The project manager fails to build a proper schedule, and therefore doesn't know that there is a **4-month gap** between what the business needs and what the resources of the business can deliver.

4. Eager to meet the needs of the business and please the leaders, the project manager commits to doing in **6 months** what can only be done in **10 months**.

5. In time, the 4-month gap between business need and business capability becomes apparent and manifests in the form of project delays and high-level escalations.

6. Driven by the demands of senior leaders and frustrated stakeholders, the project manager and the project team scamper, circumvent processes, and work vigorously to improve the schedule.

7. Despite these efforts, the schedule only improves marginally.

8. Leadership presses the project manager and asks why the schedule has not improved.

9. The project manager struggles to offer a credible explanation.

The reason the schedule could not be improved is clearly stated in **point #2**.
The reason this project was doomed from the start is stated in **point #3**.

This type of slow train wreck plays out every day, in every industry, and in nearly every business. With a properly built schedule, the 4-month gap could have been discovered within the first few weeks of the project. Armed with this knowledge, the business leaders could have reallocated resources and funding to align the resources of the business with the priorities of the business. *Figure 1* below, adapted from *Figure 1-3 of the Standard for Project Management*, published by PMI, underscores this point.

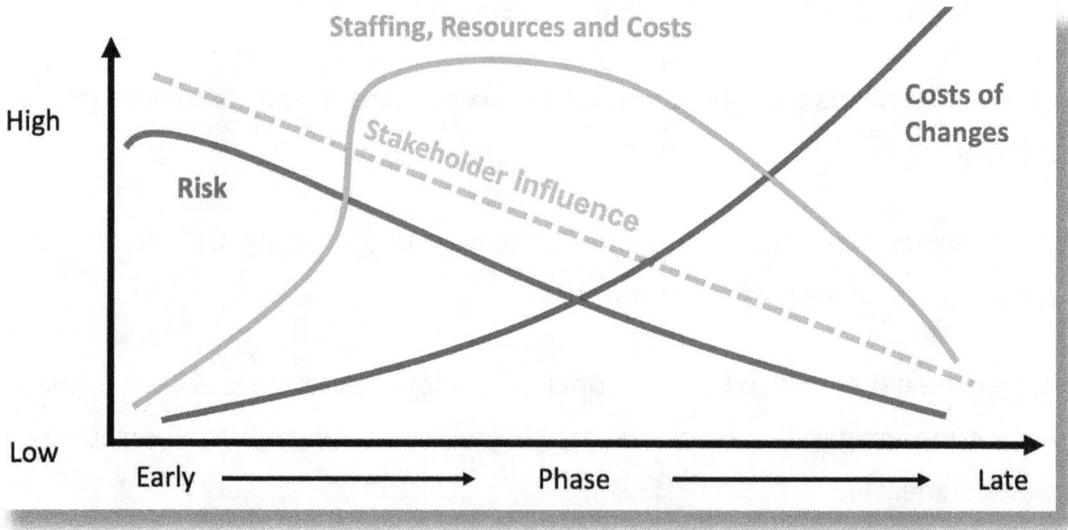

Figure 1 - PMI Standard for Project Management

It depicts that budget and resource limitations are much easier to overcome at the start of a project than at the end. The objective of this book is to enable you to use Microsoft Project to build reliable schedules and avoid such predictable clashes.

Scheduling Apps vs. Project Management Apps

Microsoft Project is one of the few apps that can help project managers forecast potential problems and set the right expectations from the start. The fact that effective scheduling apps are a critical business need is underscored by the sharp increase in the number of project management apps in recent years. Despite this notable rise, Microsoft Project's robust scheduling engine still has remarkably few contenders. In a modern workforce that is increasingly leaning toward cloud-based project management software, it is just as likely that many users will encounter the slow train wreck described earlier. This is because there is a popular assumption that "project management software" is the same as scheduling software. This is an incorrect assumption. Many popular project management apps sacrifice scheduling capability for ease of use and cloud-based collaboration features. Microsoft has joined this trend with its new, cloud-based, project management-rich, but project scheduling-poor **Project for the Web** app. Chapter 0 highlights this premise as we explore both the capabilities and limitations of this app.

The Schedule Maturity Model

To help you better understand the current landscape of project management software, we've developed a **Schedule Maturity Model™** shown in *Figure 2* below. Project managers in varying roles can use this model to determine the right type of schedule to build for each project and which scheduling capabilities they will need to build those schedules. Our model is based on the common denominator of all projects – tasks.

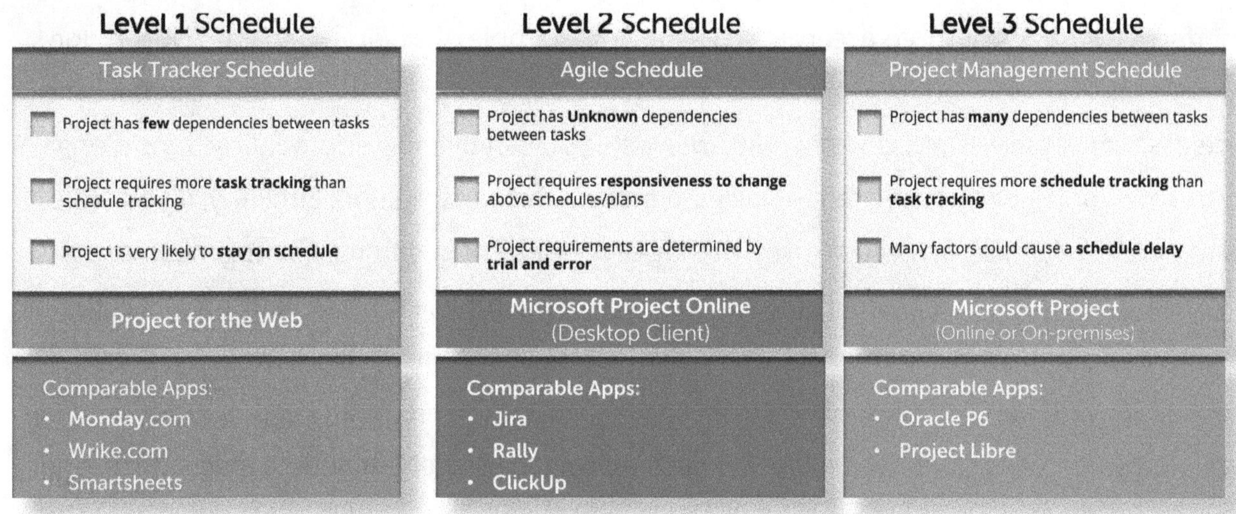

Figure 2 - Schedule Maturity Model

Whether you're managing an agile project, a waterfall project, or a classic project like a construction project, your project is based upon tasks. How granularly you need to keep track of those tasks and which methodology you're using to manage your project will determine what type of schedule you need to build. The type of schedule you need to build should determine which scheduling app you use.

The Microsoft suite of project management applications offers the best vantage point from which to understand the emerging world of project management apps. At the time of this publication, Microsoft features a project management app in every space of this evolving marketplace. Therefore, we've used it as a reference point to explain our Schedule Maturity Model™. To help place our model into your work context, we've also identified comparable scheduling apps from other providers in each scheduling category. The scheduling categories in our model are **Maturity Level 1** schedules (for Task Tracker schedules), **Maturity Level 2** schedules (for Agile schedules) and **Maturity Level 3** schedules (for Project Management schedules).

Scheduling Categories

Level 1 Schedules (Task Tracker Schedules)

Projects that are well-suited for Level 1 schedules will require more task tracking than schedule tracking. They will have few dependencies between tasks and the project requirements will be clearly identified. Level 1 schedules are like a print-out of turn-by-turn directions to a destination. They're a great tool for an unimpeded plan but can become ineffective if things don't go according to plan. For example, if several roads are closed due to construction, and you don't know the area very well, your printed directions can become useless. Conversely, if you do know the area well, you can use the printed directions along with your knowledge of the area to navigate around the construction. Similarly, if your role is to deliver a familiar project that you manage routinely, then you may simply need to track tasks and not track a complete project schedule. For example, suppose your project is to plan a 10K race event. You plan this race every year and know each task from memory. You're more concerned with keeping track of when each task gets completed, than keeping track of a full-scale project management schedule. For such a project, a Level 1 schedule may suffice, and using a full-featured scheduling app like **Microsoft Project** may be too robust.

Conversely, an app like **Project for the Web**, which features an intuitive interface and may be easier to learn, could provide all the scheduling functionality you need. We'll cover this type of lightweight schedule and the utility of this app in Chapter 0 – "Using Project for the Web".

Level 2 Schedules (Agile Schedules)

Level 2 schedules are for projects that are so dynamic that even the requirements are flexible. They're applicable to Agile projects which may be deployed in an iterative fashion (meaning in a repetitive cycle, such as every two weeks) and in an incremental fashion (meaning value is delivered in small chunks or increments).

For these types of projects, you must complete some portion of the work and get customer feedback before you can help define the scope of the project. Based upon this feedback, you may refine your next deliverable. You may also collaborate with your client to determine what that next deliverable should be. If this process sounds appropriate for your project, then it likely meets the threshold for an Agile schedule. Projects that are well-suited for Agile schedules will prioritize responsiveness to change over strict adherence to a project schedule. They will require that project requirements be refined by trial and error and require that dependencies between tasks be determined through experience and observation, rather than upfront planning. For example, suppose your project is to develop a scheduling app for your client. Your client knows the market is flooded but they think other apps fail to address an important user need. To help them define the scope of the project, you develop a product that features a small chunk of functionality, based on your extensive discussions.

In turn, they give you feedback on the product based on the ever-changing demands of the marketplace. You update the product based upon their feedback and help bring your client's vision to life one iteration at a time and one increment at a time. You don't necessarily know what the task dependencies are upfront, and you will only need to plan your work for the next two-week cycle (Sprint). Also, your estimations are performed using relative tools like story points and planning poker, which are decidedly simple and collaborative and would never require a robust scheduling engine. Your project would be better served by an app like the Online Desktop Client version of Microsoft Project, which includes agile features like Task Boards and Sprint Planning features. These features enable you to manage tasks using Kanban-style Task Boards and plan work using Sprints. Agile schedules are comprehensively covered in Part Four of this book.

Level 3 Schedules (Tracking schedules)

If your project includes many interdependent tasks, has a high risk of schedule delays, is under pressure to meet or beat the schedule forecast, and its success requires that you plan, execute, monitor, and control the schedule, then you are managing a classic project and will need to build a Level 3 schedule. Projects well-suited for Level 3 schedules will have clearly defined requirements at the start of the project. As such, there will be many known dependencies between tasks, and universal stakeholder expectations around your ability to build a reliable schedule forecast, control deviations from the plan, and publish updated schedules based upon the latest developments. For example, unlike agile projects, construction projects typically have fixed requirements, such as the number of floors, the location of the site and the required building material. There will also be known dependencies between tasks, such as the need to secure permits before beginning to build, the need to complete the foundation work before the plumbing or electrical work, and the need to process long lead procurements well ahead of the need-by date. As such, you will need an app that can capture every possible type of task dependency. Unlike a lightweight app, like Project for the Web, your scheduling app will need to manage a wide range of resources and task assignments, display slack between tasks, so you can identify options for delivering certain milestones earlier, capture extensive progress data and use that progress data to recalculate the schedule. To do these things, you'll need a more robust scheduling solution to build and track your schedule. Within the Microsoft suite of project management products, you'll need the **Microsoft Project Standard or Professional desktop client** (Online or On-premises). These options will give you the project intelligence you need to advise stakeholders on the least disruptive ways to cross the finish line faster.

We will review all versions of Microsoft Project and exhaustively cover the full-featured Online and On-premises desktop versions. **B.A.S.I.C.S.**, our six-step scheduling process was designed to support Level 3 schedules. It streamlines the schedule building process by organizing lessons around a simple acronym. It reflects the natural progression of a project and provides a real-world context for learning software features. The 6 steps of the **B.A.S.I.C.S.** scheduling process are listed on the right. As we delve into the features, we'll put each step into a practical context.

- **B**reak Down the Project
- **A**djust the Settings
- **S**tructure the Tasks
- **I**nitialize the Durations
- **C**onnect the Tasks
- **S**tart the Project

Now that we've explained our Schedule Maturity Model™, you may be tempted to build the type of schedule that sounds most intriguing. We recommend you base your decision on the needs of your project. Whichever schedule type you choose, this book is your comprehensive guide. And when you need a different type of schedule, the information you need will be right at your fingertips.

How This Book is Organized

This book is organized into four parts:

PART ZERO "Exploring Project for the Web"

In this section we'll explore Microsoft's newest cloud-based project management app - Project for the Web. We'll navigate the interface and learn to use the app to build lightweight Tracker schedules.

PART ONE "Laying the Foundation"

This section Introduces you to Microsoft Project and explains important scheduling fundamentals, like building a Work Breakdown Structure, working with task relationships and the two ways to build a schedule. You'll also learn to build your schedule outline using the key components of a schedule - tasks, summary tasks, project summary tasks, and milestones.

PART TWO, "Building Your Schedule"

In this section you'll learn to build schedules using the 6 steps in the **B.A.S.I.C.S.** scheduling approach and the key fundamentals supporting each step. You'll learn to build Simple schedules™ when you need to track time only, and Detailed schedules™ when you need to track both time and cost. You'll also learn how to create, level, and manage resources, how to compress your schedule to meet critical deadlines and how to use constraints to reflect real business restrictions, like delayed funding.

PART THREE "Executing Your Schedule"

This section focuses on executing your project and tracking it to completion. You'll learn key execution practices such as capturing your initial scheduling forecast in a baseline, inputting actual performance data, tracking costs and using Earned Value Metrics. You'll also learn to create dynamic status reports, and advanced features, such as how to create a Master schedule and establish dependencies between projects.

This section concludes with guidelines for closing your project and customizing Project to fit your personal workflow.

PART FOUR "Executing Agile Projects"

This section teaches you to use the Agile features included with the Project Online Desktop Client. You'll learn to use the Kanban-inspired Task Boards to build and track your agile user stories and tasks. You'll also learn to execute your agile projects using the Scrum-inspired Sprint features. In the final chapter, we'll put all these features to use in a real-world Agile software development project. We'll also review the business drivers behind the Agile movement and key Kanban and Scrum concepts. If you're fuzzy on Agile concepts, this section will sharpen the picture for you. Ideal learners include agile practitioners and anyone managing projects requiring a high level of responsiveness to shifting requirements.

How This Book Has Been Updated

The following summarizes the high-level additions to this book since the 2019 publication:

- A comprehensive overview of Project for the Web.
- Guidelines for identifying the capabilities of a true scheduling app.
- A more comprehensive introduction to the Project Interface, covering every command on each ribbon.
- Comprehensive instructions for breaking any project down into manageable parts.
- Thorough lessons and use cases for using the four task relationship types.
- Comprehensive lessons and use cases on Earned Value Analysis.
- Expanded FAQs to include questions relating to Project for the Web.

PART ZERO: Exploring Project for the Web

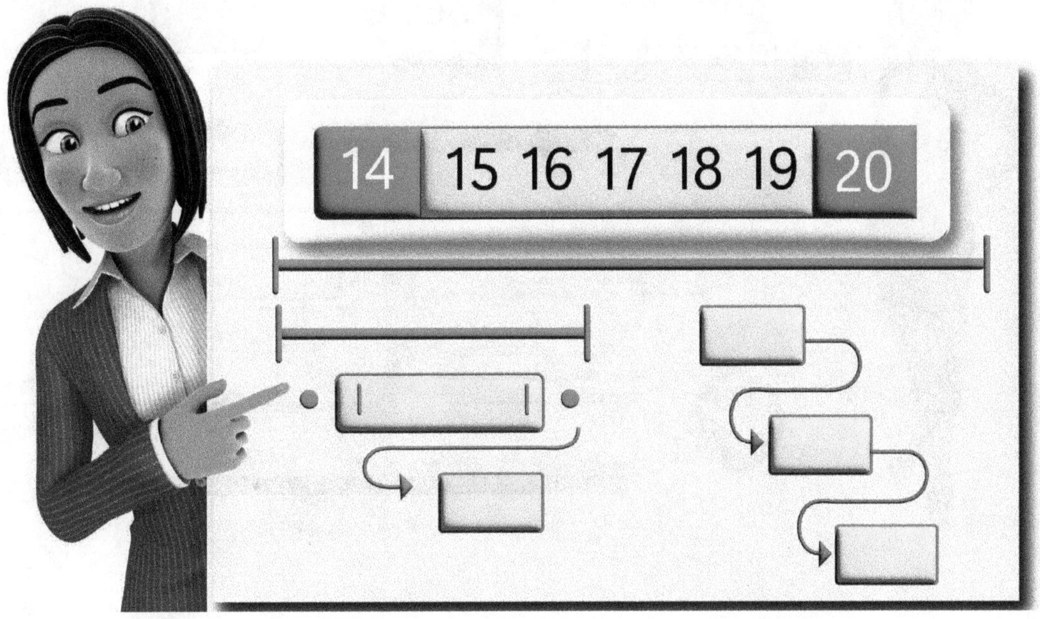

IN PART ZERO we'll explore Microsoft's newest cloud-based project management app – Project for the Web. We'll navigate the interface and learn to use the app to build lightweight Tracker schedules. The goal of this section is to provide a good working knowledge of both the capabilities and the limitations of Project for the Web, as it pertains to building schedules.

Chapter 0 Using Project for the Web

IN THIS CHAPTER we'll explore Microsoft's most recent cloud-based project management app, Project for the Web. Project for the Web is the newest addition to the Microsoft Project product family. We'll get to know this app and use it in a practical context.

The goal of this chapter is to provide a good working knowledge of both the capabilities and the limitations of Project for the Web, as it pertains to building schedules.

YOU'LL LEARN TO:

- Navigate the Project for the Web interface
- Use the Views to organize a project and work with tasks
- Apply the **B.A.S.I.C.S.** scheduling process to build a project schedule
- Use the Charts View to check project status
- Use the Timeline View to execute a project

The best way to learn **Project for the Web** – which we'll refer to as **PFW** in this chapter, is to get hands on and use it in a practical context. Because of its limited scheduling functionality, it's important to select an appropriate project candidate when using Project for the Web. The ideal project type is one that requires more task tracking than project management. In this chapter, we'll work on such a project. We'll apply our **B.A.S.I.C.S.** scheduling process to build a complete schedule using PFW and execute that schedule to completion. As we work with our project, we'll discuss each of the features and the limitations of PFW in context. You'll walk away with a general idea of whether PFW will suffice for your scheduling needs, or if you'll need a more complete scheduling app, like the full-featured versions of Microsoft Project.

Getting to Know Project for the Web

We'll begin by exploring the PFW interface and getting to know the features and views. *Figure 3* below shows the opening view you see when you log in to your PFW account.

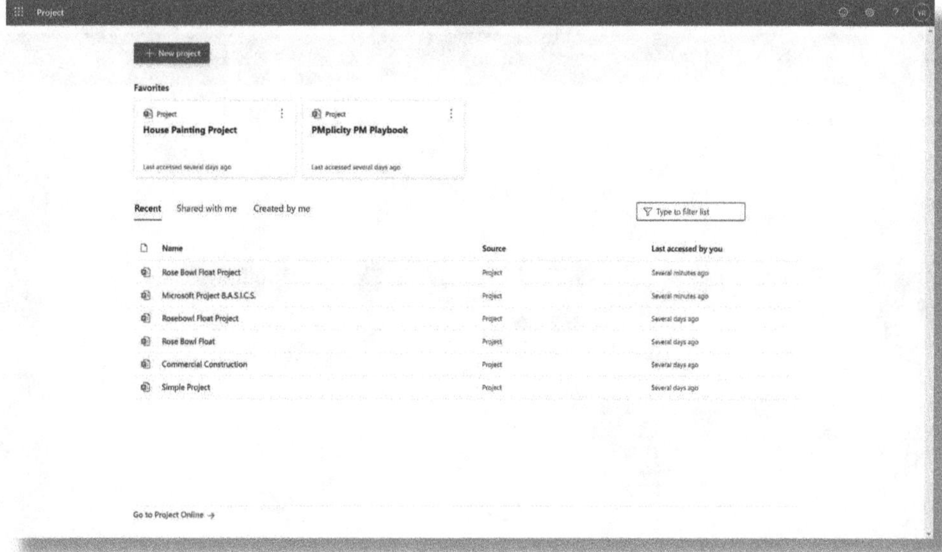

Figure 3 – The Opening View

In the top right corner of the screen, you'll find quick access icons to perform various functions. The smiley face icon allows you to send feedback to Microsoft about PFW. The gear icon takes you to the settings, where you can do things like select a theme for the interface, select a language and time zone, update your contact preferences, change your password, or configure the notifications so that Project will alert you when someone assigns a task to you or adds you to a project or roadmap. The question mark icon opens the Help panel, where you can search for help using PFW.

In the area at the top of the view, you'll find projects that you've starred as "Favorites". This area will be empty if you haven't identified any favorite projects. In the area beneath the Favorites, on the **Recent** tab (selected by default), you'll find a list of recent projects you've worked on. This area will also be empty if you haven't worked on any projects yet. To identify a Favorite project, hover in the area to the right of the project name you want, and select the star. The **Shared with me** tab shows projects that have been shared with you or Road Mapped. The **Created by me** tab shows a list of projects you've created.
Use the **Filter** command on the right to search for projects that fit the words you type in. At the bottom of the screen, beneath the recent projects list, you'll find a quick access link to Project Online, or Project Web App.

To start a new project, select the **New project** button, located at the top of the view on the left. This will take you to the **Create new project** screen (shown in *Figure 4* below), where you'll find several options for starting a new project.

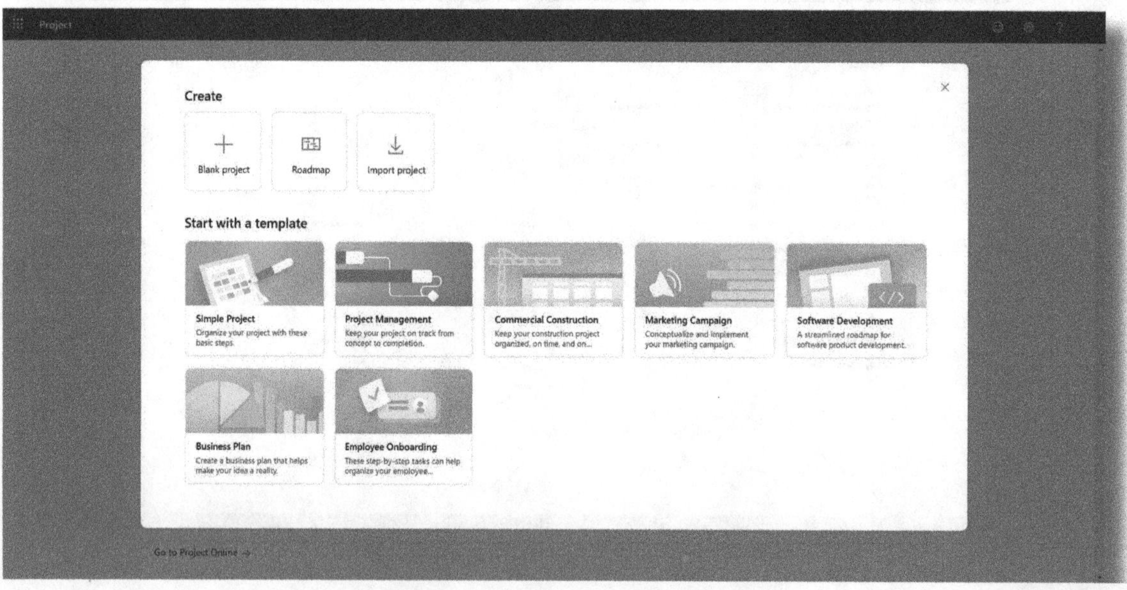

Figure 4 - Create New Project Screen

The **Blank Project** command is how you start a new project from scratch. The **Roadmap** command takes you to Microsoft 365 Roadmap, where you can create a view of your organization's projects and see multiple projects from multiple systems in one place. This is a handy way to customize a view and show stakeholders the big picture across several projects. To use this feature, you need a Microsoft Project Online Plan 3 or Plan 5 subscription.

The **Import** project command lets you import a project into Project for the Web from one of the desktop versions of Microsoft Project, starting with the 2016 version. It's important to note that many of the features available in the desktop versions of Microsoft Project aren't supported in Project for the Web. Things like resources, task deadlines, constraints, baselines, and cross-project dependencies don't migrate into Project for the Web. There are also limits on things like the number of tasks and levels a project can have, a maximum project duration, and other limitations. PFW has significantly less scheduling functionality than the desktop versions of Microsoft Project. If your project relies on these features, then PFW is not a good fit. In the bottom half of the screen, you'll find the option to use one of the built-in project templates. There are templates for Commercial Construction, Marketing, Software Development, and a few more. When considering a template, keep in mind that PFW only tracks tasks. Therefore, a project as robust as a Commercial Construction project, which requires more schedule tracking than task tracking is not a good candidate for Project for the Web.

If none of these Create options work for your project, you'll need to start from scratch, using the **Blank project** command. You'll be taken to the **Grid view**, shown in *Figure 5* below. This is where you'll enter your project's task list and build your project schedule.

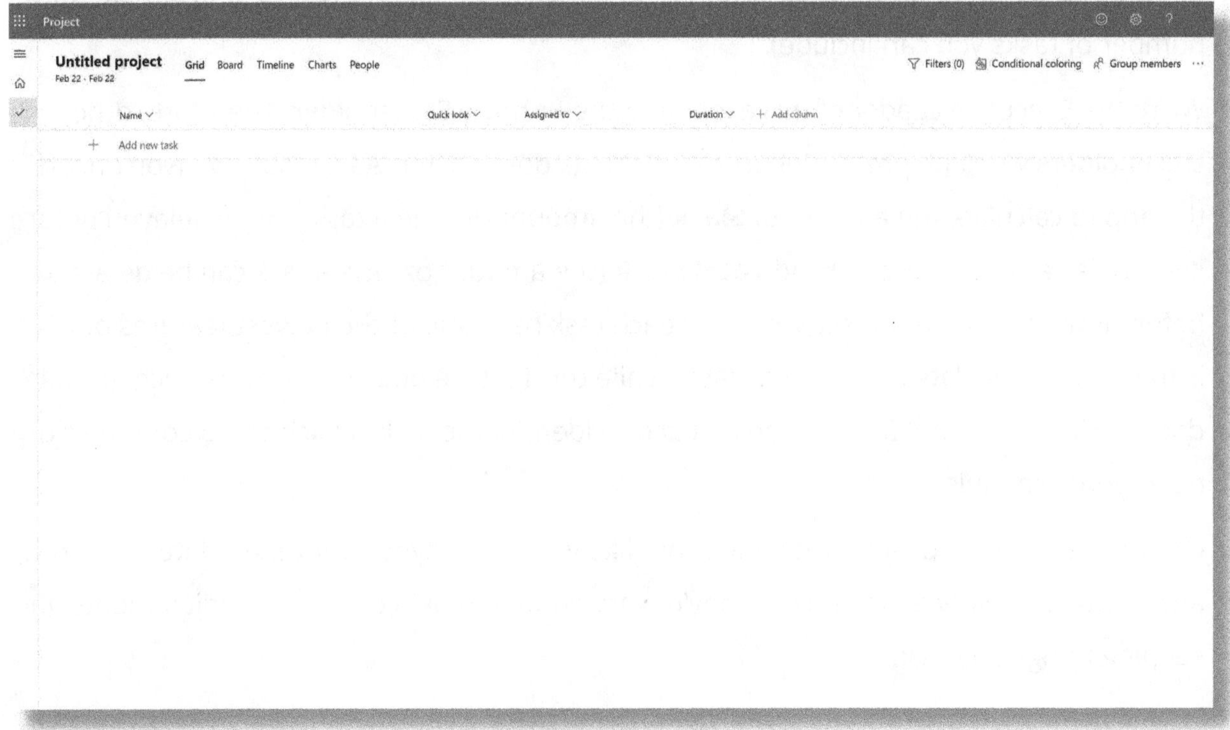

Figure 5 – Blank Project – Grid View

As mentioned earlier, the best way to learn Project for the Web is to get hands on and use the app in a practical context. We'll continue our tour of the interface by building and executing a schedule using the B.A.S.I.C.S. scheduling process. We'll work with a project that's ideal for the scheduling capabilities of Project for the Web.

OUR PROJECT: Build a winning float for the Pasadena Rose Bowl parade event.

This type of project is an excellent candidate for PFW. Here are some reasons why:

- We're very familiar with the schedule. We've entered a float for this event every year for the past ten years.
- Since we're very familiar with the schedule and when tasks should occur, we're not likely to need to apply constraints, or use lead and lag time between tasks to advance or delay a task's start date. (PFW doesn't include these features).
- We're more in need of a task tracker than a full-scale project management app.
- We simply need an app to help us be more organized and timelier as we move through the phases of the project.
- Our project has a limited number of phases and tasks. Our entire schedule will include five phases and no more than 30 tasks. (PFW has a maximum hierarchy level and a maximum number of tasks you can include).
- We're the Executive Leader of this event and the Primary Stakeholder. Therefore, other stakeholders won't be pressuring us to get things done faster. As a result, we won't need the app to calculate the amount of **Slack** (the amount of time a task can be delayed before it will delay a successor task) and **Total Slack** (the amount of time a task can be delayed before it will delay the project schedule) each task has. One of the newest features of PFW is that it now calculates the Critical Path. While this feature does not provide such granular data as Slack and Total Slack, it can be used to identify the tasks which could compress or delay your schedule.
- Our Rose Bowl float project schedule is not likely to be delayed. Our target dates are firm, and our team is very experienced. They're very good at making on-the-fly adjustments and keeping things on track.

One of the key benefits of full-featured scheduling software like the Online Desktop and On-Premise Desktop versions of Microsoft Project, is that it automatically recalculates the schedule when unforeseen delays occur or when resources are out sick or on vacation. Project for the Web doesn't have this capability. But since our team is experienced at keeping float projects on schedule, we won't need this capability. Based on the forgoing reasons, we're confident that we can manage our entire float project using PFW, applying the **B.A.S.I.C.S.** 6-step scheduling process.

Step 1 – Break Down the Project

Step 1 of the B.A.S.I.C.S. scheduling process is **Break down your project**. Breaking down your project is essentially creating your work breakdown structure. It's the process of decomposing your project scope statement, in this case "Build a Winning Float", into parts that you can manage. Since we've managed this type of project for a decade, we're familiar with the work that's needed to deliver the project. We know that the project is organized around five sequential phases:

- Phase 1 – the Approval Phase
- Phase 2 –the Sponsor Phase
- Phase 3 – the Construction Phase
- Phase 4 – the Painting Phase
- Phase 5 – the Floral Phase

We also know from experience that each phase will include two to five tasks. *Figure 6* depicts what the work breakdown structure for this project might look like.

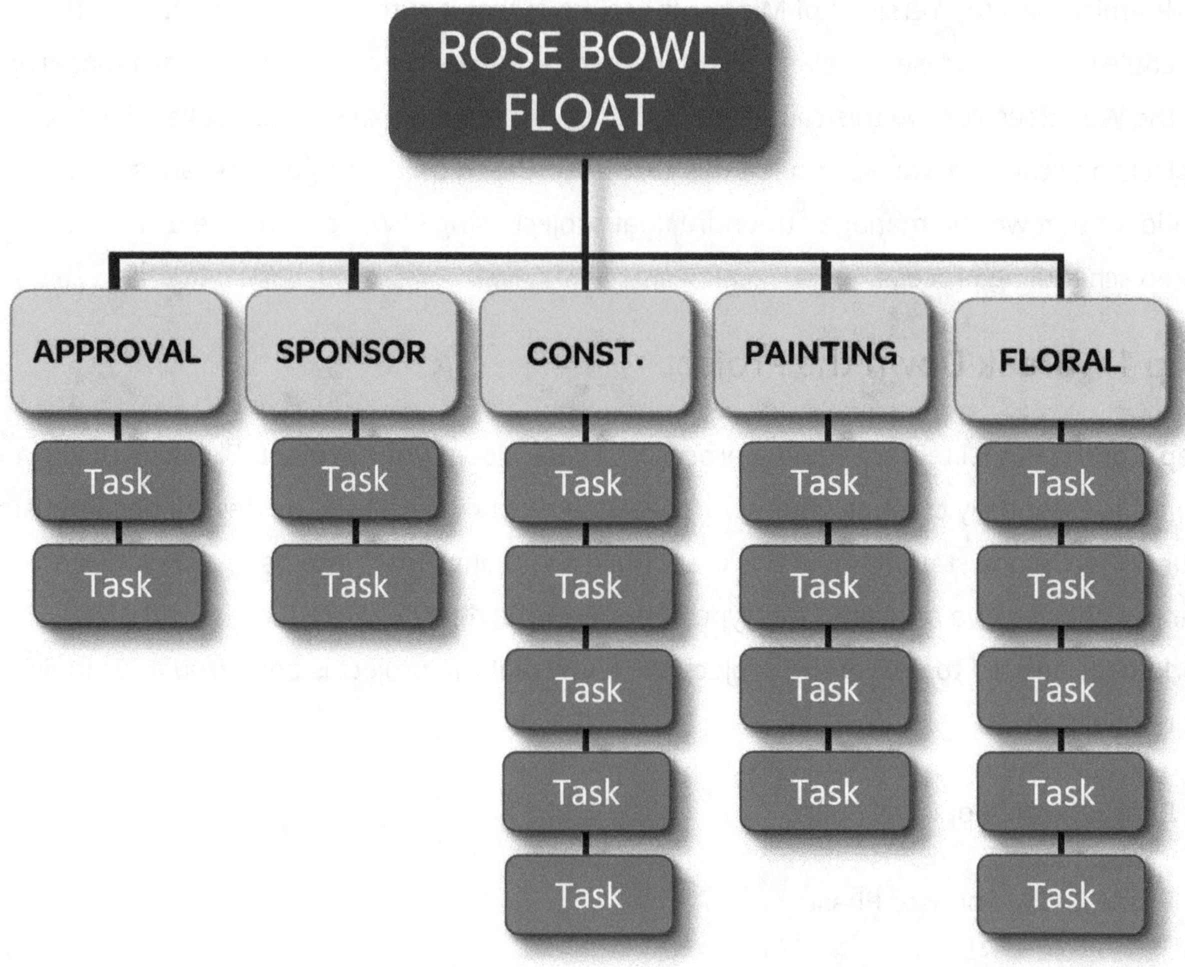

Figure 6 – Float Work Breakdown Structure

Step 2 - Adjust the Settings

Step 2 of the B.A.S.I.C.S. process is **Adjust the Settings**. The Online desktop versions of Microsoft Project allow you to adjust the settings to track task durations only or to track both durations and cost. PFW can only track tasks. Due to this limited scheduling functionality, there are no scheduling settings to adjust, so we're skipping step 2 for our Float project.

Before we begin step 3, we'll **name the project** and **set the start date**.

To name the project, in the top left corner of the screen, click the **Untitled project** text, to open the *Project details* panel (*Figure 7*).

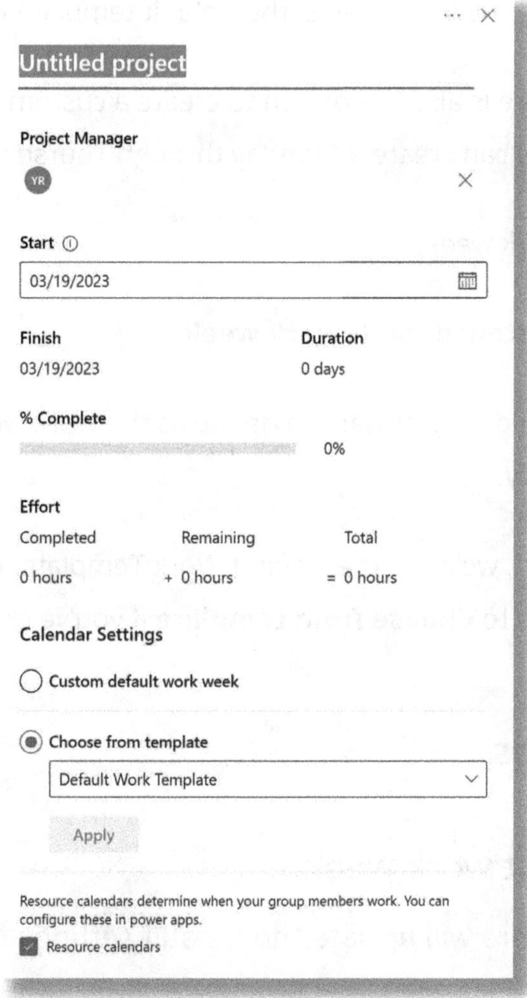

Figure 7 – Project Details Panel

Type over the **Untitled project** text with the project name – **Rose Bowl Float.** Next, we'll set the project start date. The start date is **1/15/24**. Enter the date into the **Start** field or use the calendar icon to select the date.

Next, we'll look at the **Calendar Settings**. A calendar template must be applied to all projects. The calendar template defines all working hours, start and end times, and working and non-working days for the project. By default, in the **Choose from template** field, the **default Work Template** is selected, which is based on the standard Monday through Friday work week.
If the standard work week doesn't work for your project, you can create a new work hours template. To create a new template, you must have access to the Microsoft PowerApps Project Resources page in the Dynamics 365 platform.

Using this platform, create the new template from the Resource page or from the Calendar Template page. Until you create new templates, the default template will be your only option.

In the *Project Details* panel, there is also the option to create a custom default work week for your project. For example, you can create a Monday through Thursday work week.

To create a custom default work week:

- Select the circle next to **Custom default work week**.
- Then, deselect or select the days you want to define as the work week for your project (*Figure 8*). Then, select **Apply**.

For our Rose Bowl Float project, we'll use the Default Work Template. If you're following along, be sure to select the circle next to **Choose from template** if you've clicked away.

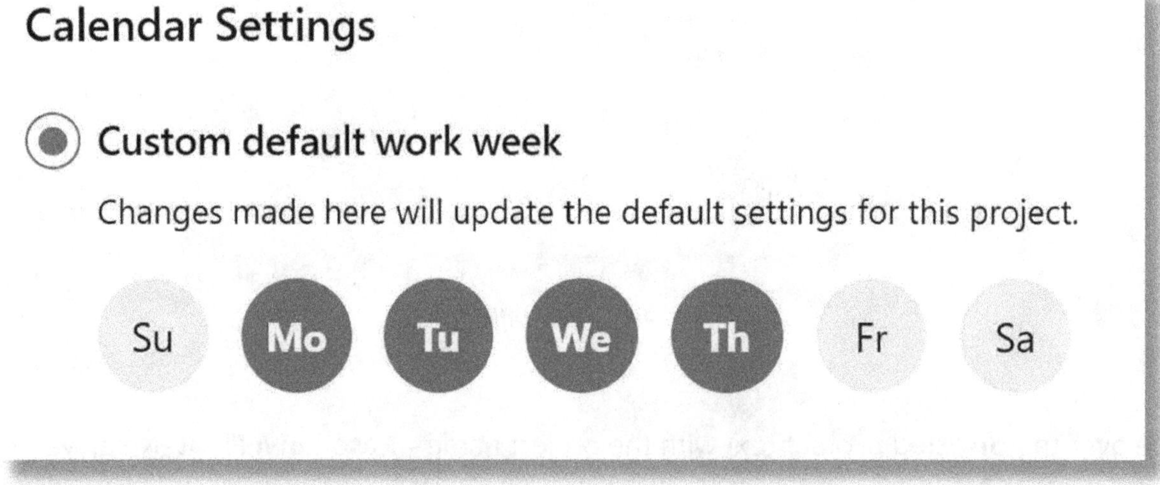

Figure 8 – Custom Default Work Week Example

The *Project details* panel also displays the project's Finish date, Duration, % Complete, and the total, completed and remaining Effort (work hours). Dy default, the Project Manager, will be the PFW account manager. Once you've named your project, set the start date, and made your calendar selections, close the *Project detail* panel, by selecting the **X** in the upper right corner. Your changes will be automatically saved.

Step 3 – Structure the Tasks

Since we've broken down our project, captured all the work, and organized the phases and tasks, we're ready for **Step 3** of the B.A.S.I.C.S. process – **Structure the Tasks**. To complete this step, we'll enter our task list into PFW, and structure the tasks to create the schedule outline. We'll do this in the **Grid** view. To confirm you're in the Grid view, in the view menu options next to the project name, the current view will have a green underline. The Grid view is a tabular view with columns and rows of task information. It allows you to add and view all the project information you want to work with as you build your schedule. The default columns in this view are **Quick look**, which will indicate when a task has a note or an attachment, **Assign To**, which shows who's assigned to a task, and **Duration**, which shows the task durations (the span of working time for a task). You can add new columns to the view using the **+ Add column** command. We will use this command to add the **Start** and **Finish** columns to the view, so we can see the task start and finish dates. This is good information to have at a glance as we build our schedule.

To add the **Start** column:

- Select the **+ Add column** command. Then, select **Start** from the options (Figure 9). Repeat these steps to add the **Finish** column.

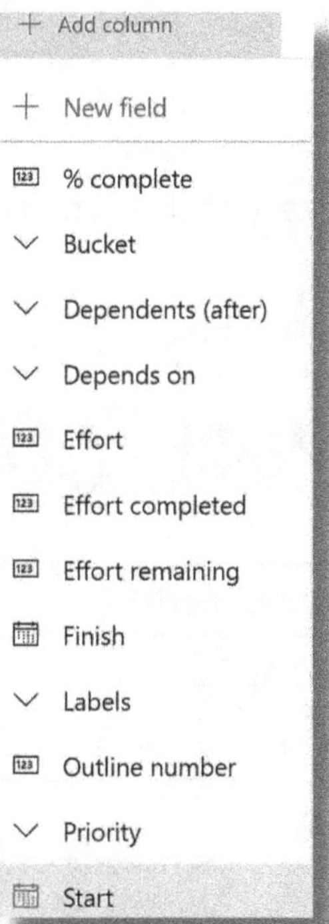

Figure 9 – Add New Columns

Now that we've added the Start and Finish columns to the view, we'll enter the task list. We'll start by entering the **Project Summary Task**. A project summary task is a task that displays summary information about the entire project and allows you to quickly confirm things like the total project duration and the finish date. It represents the highest level of your project outline, meaning that all the tasks in the schedule will roll up into it and collapse under it. It will be the parent task of every phase and task in the schedule.
Keep this in mind as we build the outline.

To create the Project Summary Task:

- Select the **Add new task** command to add a new task.
- Since this is the Project Summary Task, we'll give it the project's name. Click into the **Name** cell, and rename the task **Rose Bowl Float**, and press **Enter**.

Task ID 1 is now the Project Summary task (*Figure 10* below).

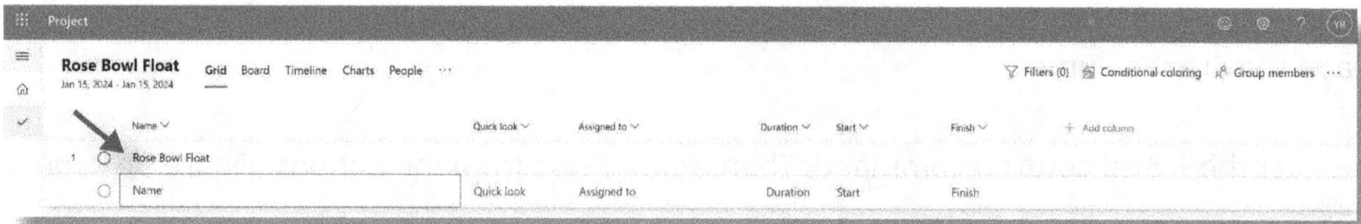

Figure 10 – The Project Summary Task

Next, we'll enter the tasks for **Phase 1** of the project – **The Approval Phase**.

Here's a list of the tasks that comprise Phase 1:

TASK ID #	TASK NAME
2	Phase 1 - Approval
3	Rose Bowl Theme Announced
4	Develop High-Level Float Design
5	Complete and Submit Entry Form
6	Entry Form Approved

To Enter the Tasks:

- Click inside the **Name** field beneath the Project Summary task (or select the **Add new task** command if applicable).
- Type the task name of task 2 **Phase 1 - Approval** into the field, and press **Enter**.
- Next, click inside the **Name** field beneath task 2. Type the next task name, and press **Enter**.
- Repeat these steps, to enter the remaining three tasks in Phase 1, pressing enter after each task name.

When you're done entering the Phase 1 tasks, your outline should look like *Figure 11*.

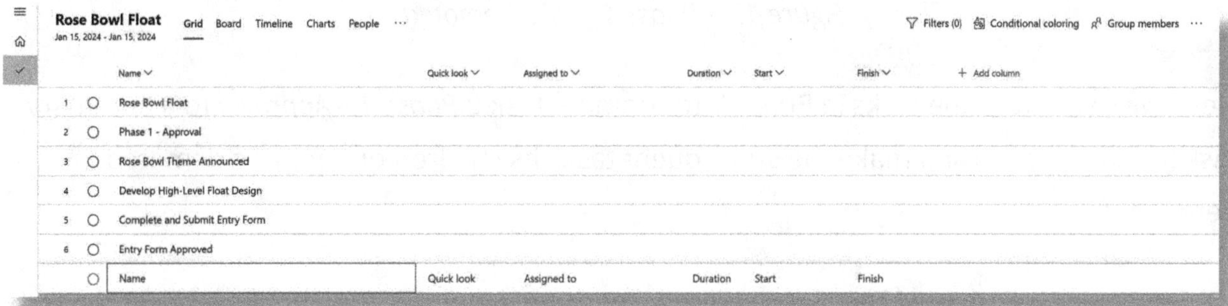

Figure 11 – Phase 1 Tasks Entered

Now that we've entered the Phase 1 tasks, we can perform the action of step 1 of the B.A.S.I.C.S. approach – **Structure the Tasks**, to create the schedule outline. We'll begin by demoting all the tasks in Phase 1 so that they become subtasks or children tasks of the Project Summary Task.

- First, select all the tasks by selecting task 2, *Phase 1 – Approval*. Then, while holding the Shift key, select the last task, task 6 *Entry Form Approved*. All the tasks should now be selected and highlighted (*Figure 12*).

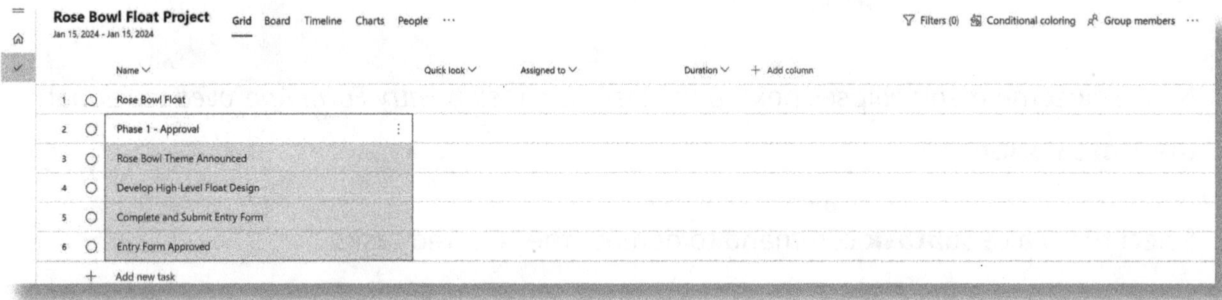

Figure 12 – All Tasks Selected

- To demote the Phase 1 tasks beneath the Project Summary task, select the menu ellipsis next to task 6 – *Entry Form Approved* to open the **More options** menu.
- Then, select **Make subtask** to demote the selected tasks.

The Phase 1 tasks should now all be subtasks of the Project Summary Task (*Figure 13*).

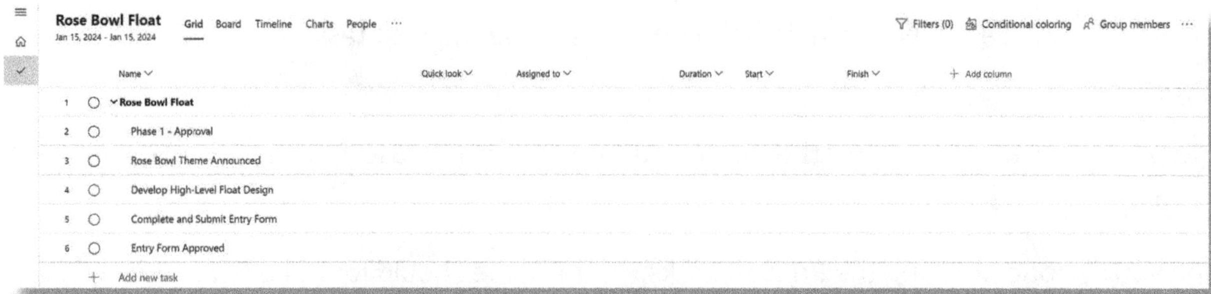

Figure 13 – Phase 1 Tasks Demoted

Next, we'll structure the tasks in Phase 1 to promote task 2 *Phase 1 – Approval* to a Summary task (or parent task) and make the subsequent tasks its children or subtasks demoted beneath it.

- Select task 3 *Rose Bowl Theme Announced*. Then, while holding the Shift key, select the last task in the list, task 6 *Entry Form Approved*. Tasks 3 through 6 should now be selected and highlighted (*Figure 14*).

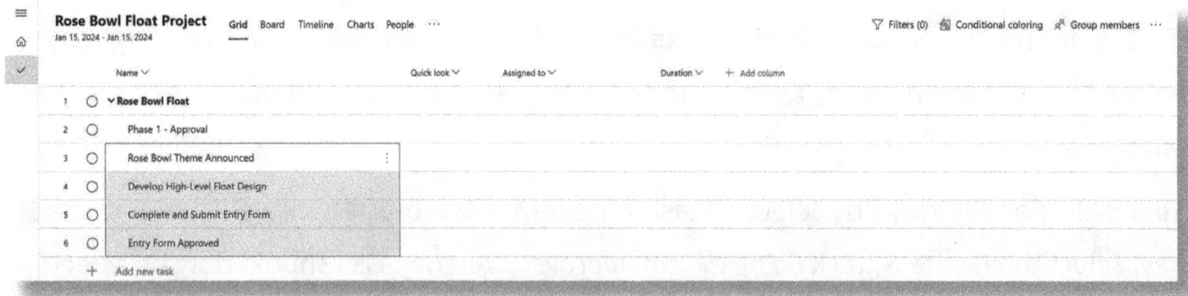

Figure 14 – Phase 1 Tasks Selected

- Now, select the menu ellipses next to the last task, task 6 *Entry Form Approved* to reopen the **More options** menu.
- Select the **Make subtask** command to demote the selected tasks.

Phase 1 of the schedule outline should now be structured (*Figure 15*).

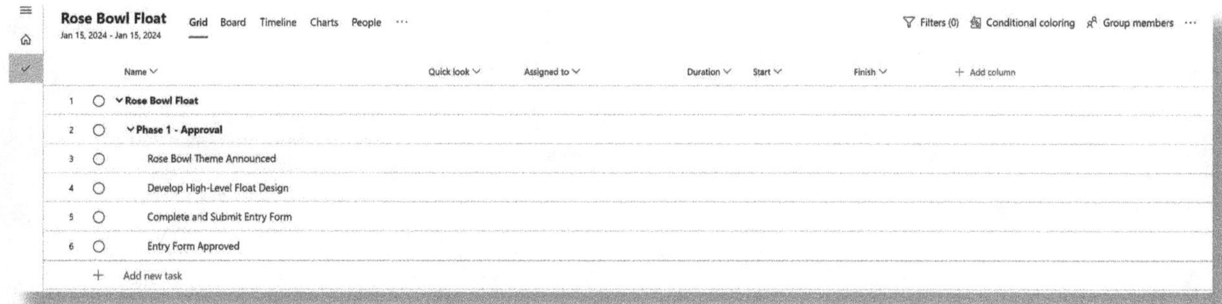

Figure 15 – Phase 1 Structured

Task 2 *Phase 1 – Approval* is now a summary task (or parent task), and the subsequent tasks are now its subtasks or children. Also, note that summary tasks are indicated with **bold** typeface – both the Project Summary task and the Phase 1 summary task. Next, we'll enter the tasks for **Phase 2** of the project, the **Sponsor Phase**.

Here is a list of the tasks that comprise Phase 2.

TASK 1D	TASK NAME
7	Phase 2 - Sponsor
8	Develop Detailed-Level Float Design
9	Submit Detailed Design to Potential Sponsors
10	Confirm Minimum Funding Interest
11	Construct Full-scale Model
12	Final Sponsor Review and Approval

To Enter the Tasks:

- Select the **Add new task** command beneath task 6.
- Then, click inside the **Name** field and type the name of task 7, ***Phase 2 – Sponsor***, and press **Enter**.
- Next, click inside the **Name** field beneath task 7. Type the next task name, and press **Enter**.
- Repeat these steps, to enter the remaining four tasks in Phase 2, pressing enter after each task name.

When you're done entering the Phase 2 tasks, your outline should look like *Figure 16 below*.

Rose Bowl Float — Jan 15, 2024 - Jan 15, 2024 — Grid | Board | Timeline | Charts | People | ··· — Filters (0) | Conditional coloring | Group member

		Name	Quick look	Assigned to	Duration	Start	Finish	+ Add column
1	○	**Rose Bowl Float**						
2	○	**Phase 1 - Approval**						
3	○	Rose Bowl Theme Announced						
4	○	Develop High-Level Float Design						
5	○	Complete and Submit Entry Form						
6	○	Entry Form Approved						
7	○	Phase 2 - Sponsor						
8	○	Develop Detailed-Level Float Design						
9	○	Submit Detailed Design to Potential Sponsors						
10	○	Confirm Minimum Funding Interest						
11	○	Construct Full-scale Model						
12	○	Final Sponsor Review and Approval						
	○	Name	Quick look	Assigned to	Duration	Start	Finish	

Figure 16 – Phase 2 Tasks Entered

Notice that all the Phase 2 tasks are demoted as subtasks under Phase 1. This is not what we want. We need to correct the outline to make task 7 *Phase 2 Sponsor* a summary task (or parent task), on the same level as task 2, the *Phase 1 Approval* summary task.

- Select task 7 *Phase 2 – Sponsor*.
- Then, select the menu ellipsis for this same task to open the **More options** menu.
- This time, select the **Promote task** command to promote task 7 *Phase 2 – Sponsor* to a parent summary task.

Phase 2 should now be structured (*Figure 17*). As indicated by the bold type, task 7, *Phase 2 – Sponsor* has been promoted to a parent summary task, with its five subtasks demoted beneath it.

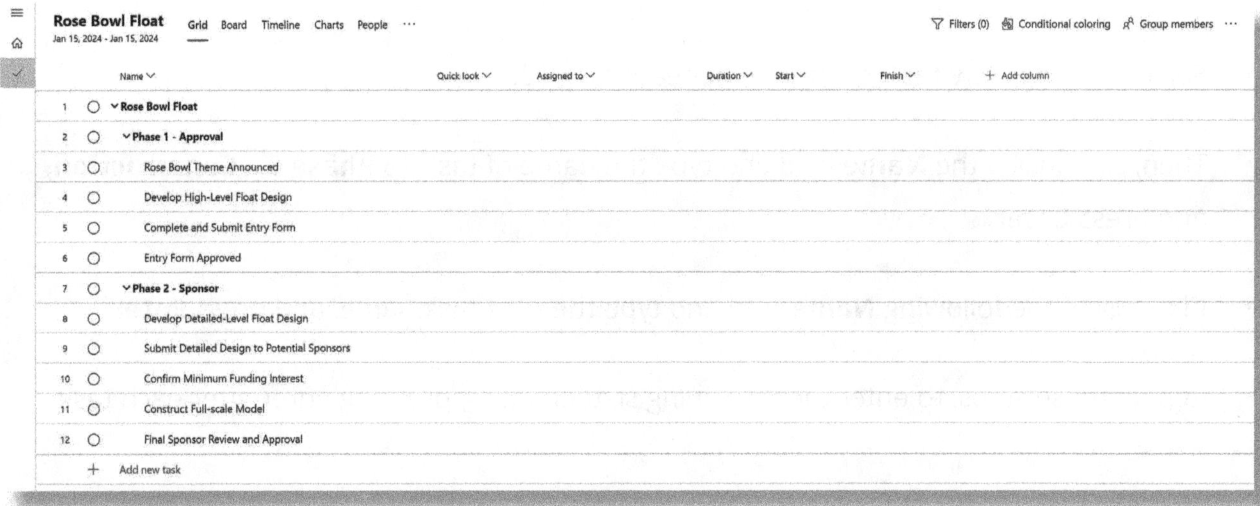

Figure 17 – Phase 2 Structured

Next, we'll enter the remaining tasks in our float project for **Phase 3** - the **Construction** Phase, **Phase 4** - the **Painting** phase, and **Phase 5** - the **Floral** phase.

Here's the list of the tasks that comprise phases 3, 4 & 5.

TASK ID #	TASK NAME
13	Phase 3 - Construction
14	Begin Heavy Construction
15	Complete Heavy Construction and Modular Component Build
16	Complete Electrical Work
17	Add Non-perishable Items to Float
18	Build Scaffolding for Decorations
19	Phase 4 - Painting
20	Paint Skins and Exteriors
21	Paint Small Areas
22	Phase 5 - Floral
23	Place Flower Order
24	Secure Volunteers (60 Minimum)
25	Construct Flower Tent
26	Receive Flowers on Site
27	Attach Flowers to Float
28	WINNERS ANNOUNCED
29	PARADE BEGINS

To Enter the Tasks:

- Select the **Add new task** command beneath task 12.
- Then, click inside the **Name** field and type the name of task 13 **Phase 3 – Construction**, and press **Enter**.
- Click inside the following **Name** field and type the next task name, and press **Enter**.
- Repeat these steps, to enter the remaining sixteen tasks, pressing enter after each task name.

When you're done entering the tasks, your outline should look like *Figure 18* below.

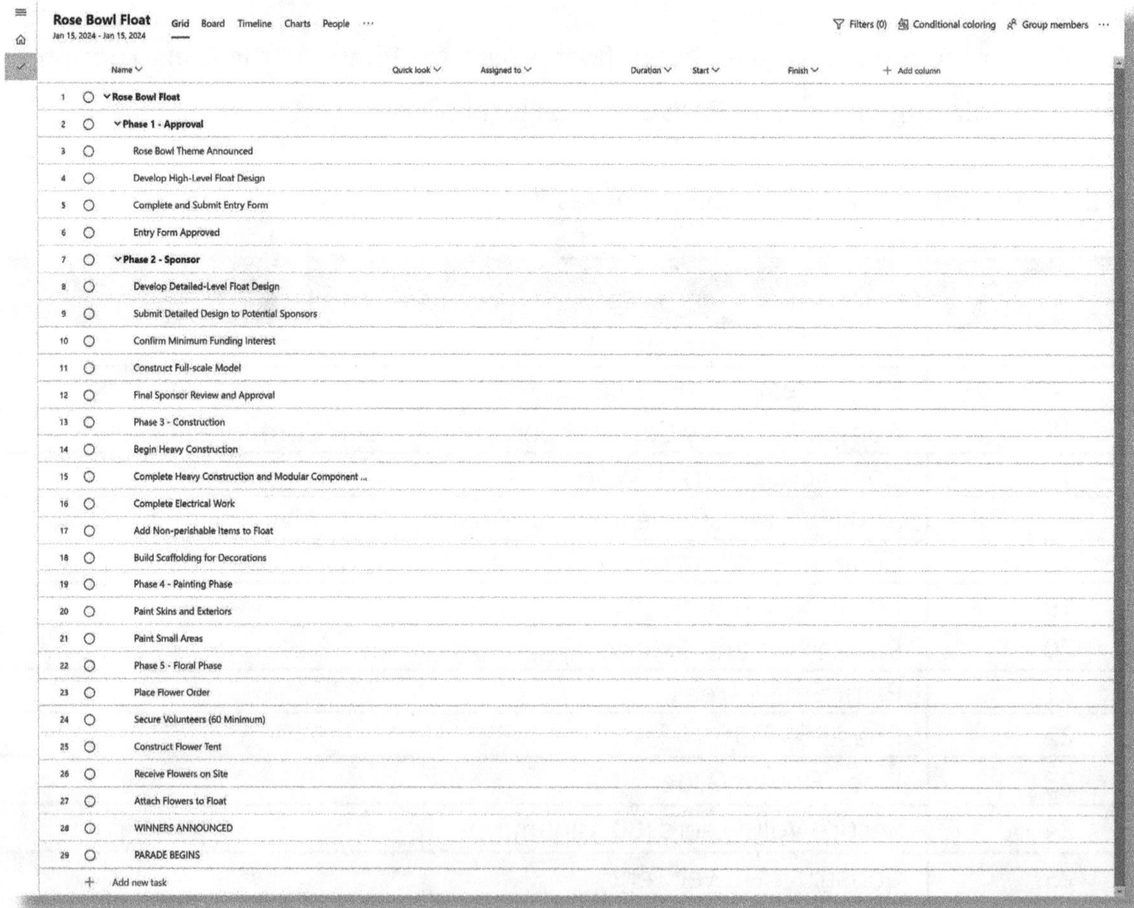

Figure 18 – Phases 3, 4 & 5 Tasks Entered

Notice that all the Phase 3, Phase 4, and Phase 5 tasks are demoted as subtasks under Phase 2. Again, this is not what we want.

We need to correct the outline to make task 13 *Phase 3 - Construction,* task 19 *Phase 4 - Painting* and task 22 *Phase 5 - Floral* summary tasks (or parent tasks), on the same level as summary tasks 2 & 7.

To structure the tasks for Phase 3:

- Select task 13 *Phase 3 - Construction*.
- Then, select the menu ellipsis for this same task to open the **More options** menu.
- Select the **Promote task** command to promote task 13 *Phase 3 - Construction* to a parent summary task.

Phase 3 should now be structured (*Figure 19*). As indicated by the bold type, task 13 *Phase 3 - Construction* has been promoted to a parent summary task, with its five subtasks, and all subsequent tasks demoted beneath it.

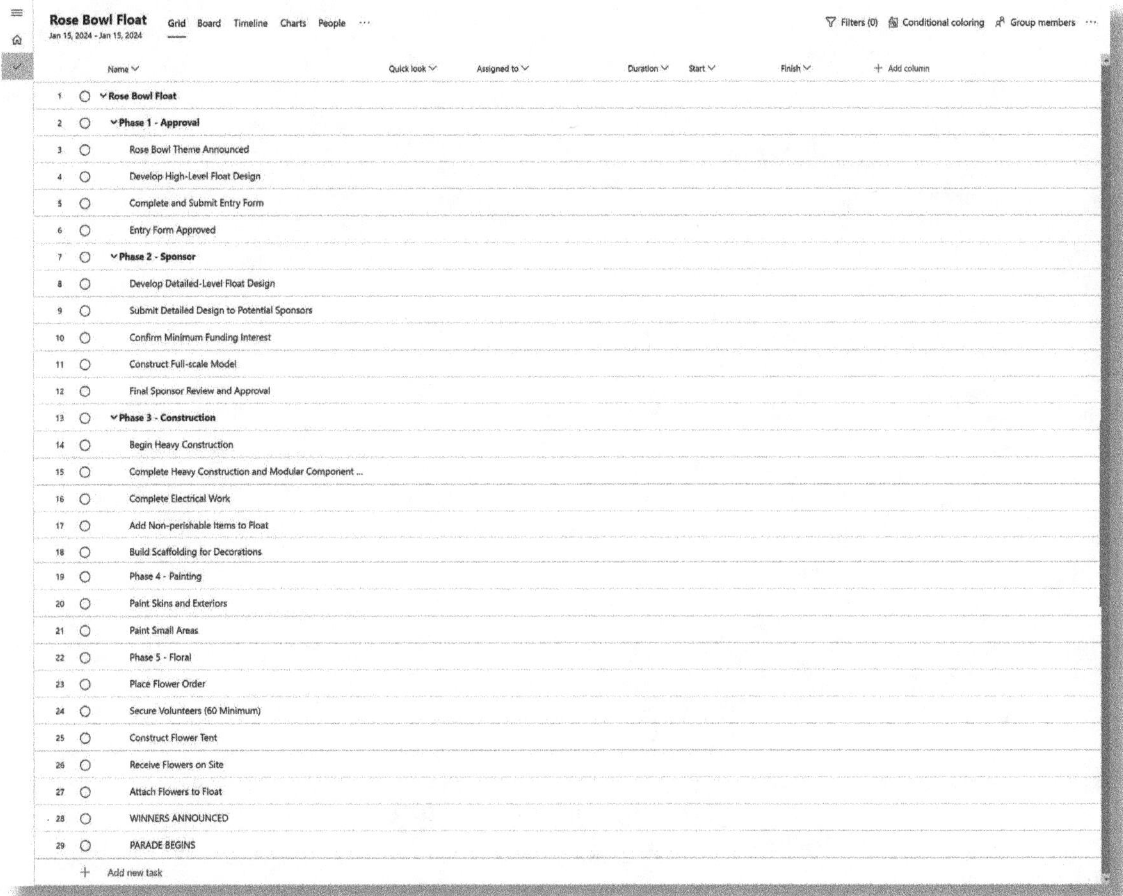

Figure 19 – Phase 3 Structured

To structure the tasks for Phase 4:

- Select task 19 *Phase 4 – Painting*.
- Then, select the menu ellipsis for this same task to open the **More options** menu.
- Select the **Promote task** command to promote task 19 *Phase 4 – Painting* to a parent summary task.

Phase 4 should now be structured (*Figure 20*). As indicated by the bold type, task 19 *Phase 4 – Painting* has been promoted to a parent summary task, with its two subtasks, and all subsequent tasks demoted beneath it.

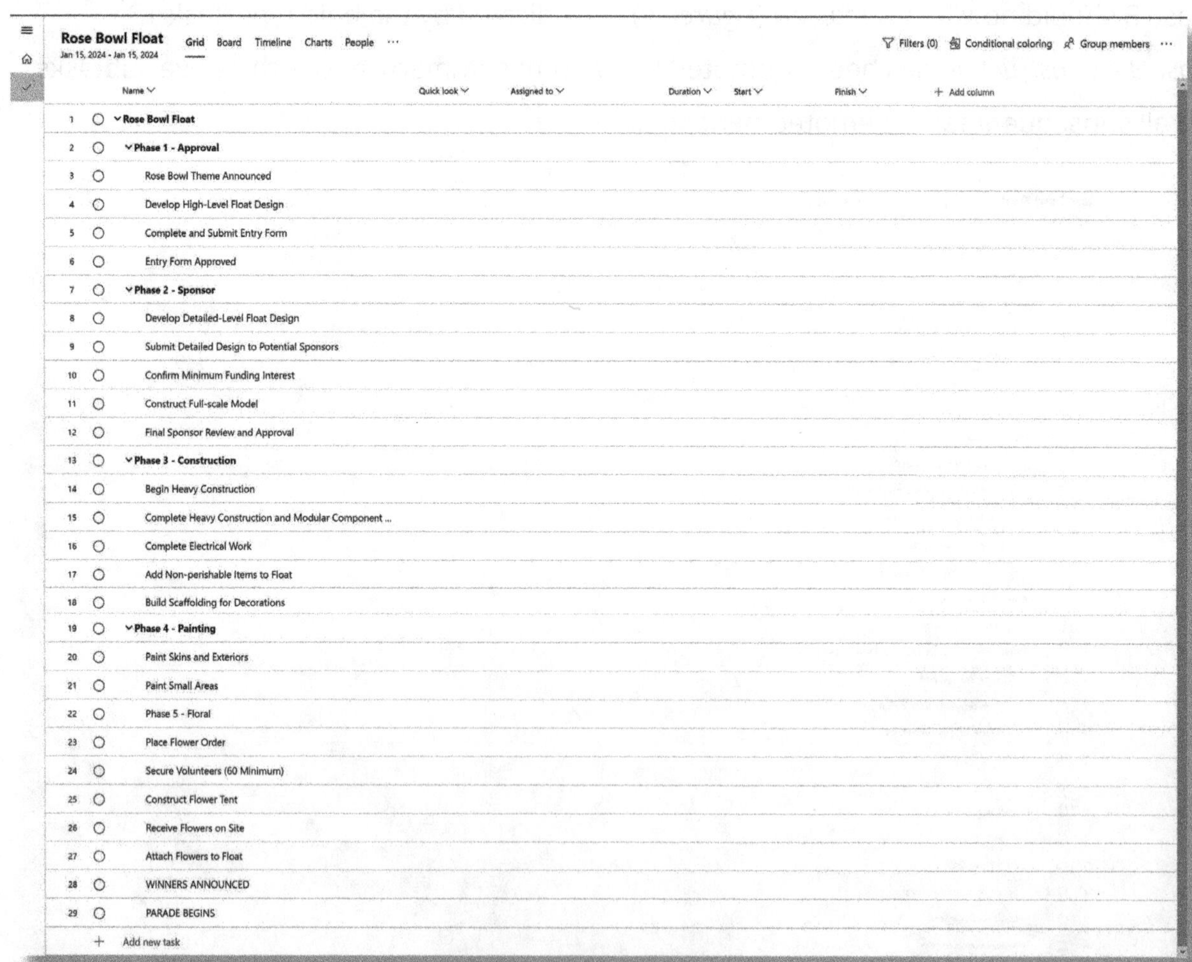

Figure 20 – Phase 4 Structured

To structure the tasks for Phase 5:

- Select task 22 *Phase 5 – Floral.*
- Then, select the menu ellipsis for this same task to open the **More options** menu.
- Select the **Promote task** command to promote task 22, *Phase 5 – Floral* to a parent summary task.

Phase 5 should now be structured (*Figure 21*). As indicated by the bold type, task 20 *Phase 5 – Floral* has been promoted to a parent summary task, with its seven subtasks demoted beneath it.

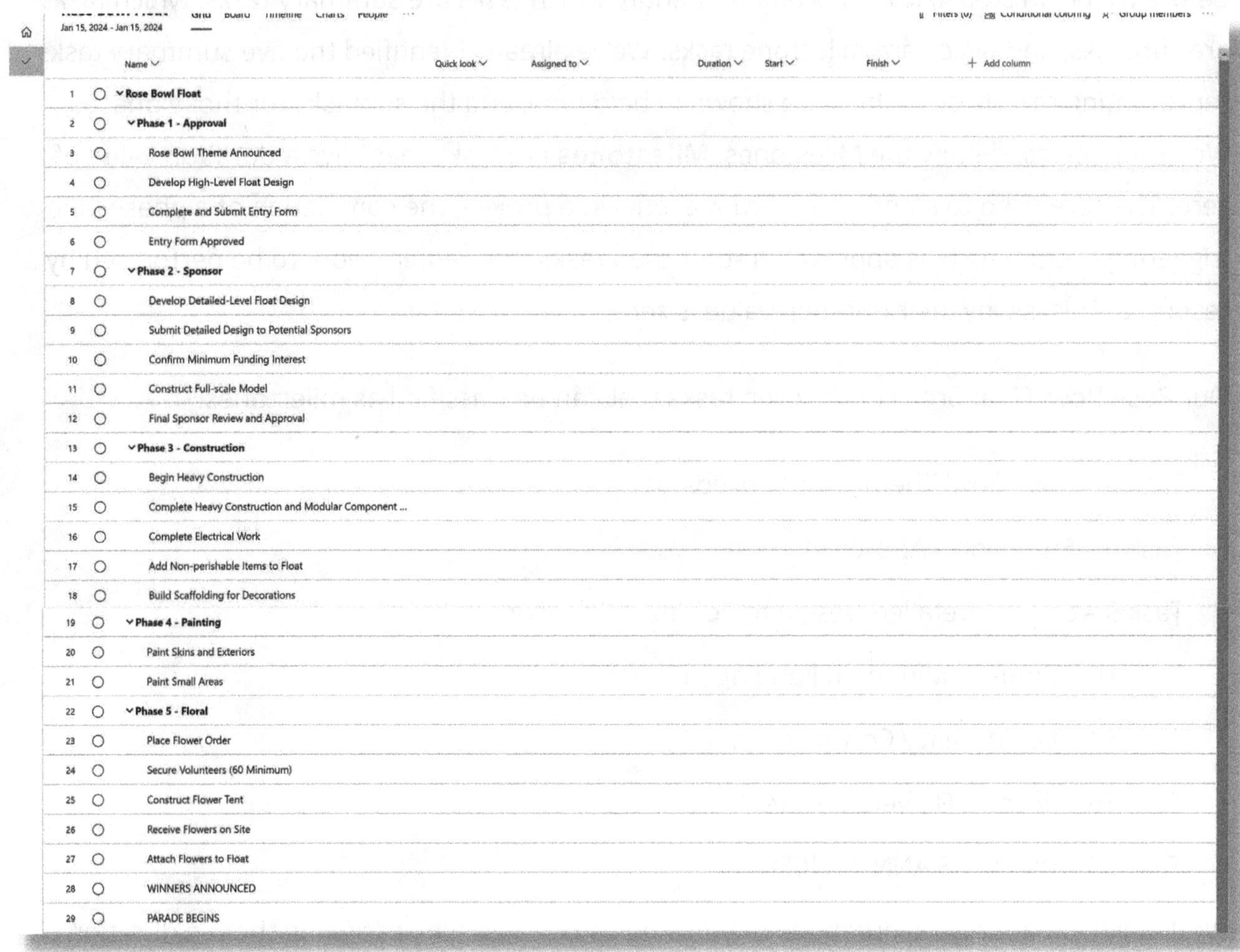

Figure 21 – Phase 5 Structured

We have now completed Step 3 of the B.A.S.I.C.S. scheduling process. We've structured the tasks to create the five phases and the schedule outline for our Rose Bowl Float project.

Step 4 – Initialize the Durations

We can now move on to **Step 4** of the B.A.S.I.C.S. process – **Initialize the Durations.** In practice, this step can vary in the way it's performed, depending upon the type of schedule you're building. The durations are initialized one way if you're tracking task durations only, and another way if you're tracking task durations and cost. This is where you can see the power of the scheduling engine of the Online Desktop and On-Premise Desktop versions of Microsoft Project. Project will automatically calculate duration and cost based upon things like work hours and resource availability. Since cost cannot be tracked using Project for the Web, for our Rose Bowl Float project this step will be as simple as entering the task durations.

Before we begin step 4, it's important to identify which tasks are summary tasks, which tasks are subtasks, and which are milestone tasks. We've already identified the five summary tasks representing the phases, which are shown in bold type, and the subtasks for those phases. We now need to identify the Milestones. **Milestones** are tasks that have a duration value of zero. They are used to identify significant events in a project, the completion of a phase, and triggering events, such as approvals, rather than tasks that require work to be performed by a resource. This is why their duration value is zero.

Our Rose Bowl Float project has seven tasks that can be classified as milestones:

- Task 3 – Rose Bowl Theme Announced
- Task 6 – Entry Form Approved
- Task 9 – Submit Detailed Design to Potential Sponsors
- Task 10 – Confirm Minimum Funding Interest
- Task 14 – Begin Heavy Construction
- Task 26 – Receive Flowers on Site
- Task 28 – WINNERS ANNOUNCED

We'll begin initializing the durations of these milestone tasks, by assigning them a duration value of zero. There are a couple of ways to enter task durations in PFW. The simplest way is to type the task durations directly into the **Duration** field. You can also enter the durations using the *Task Details* panel. This is the method we'll use for these seven milestones.

We'll start with milestone task 3 *Rose Bowl Theme Announced*.

To enter the duration:

- Select task 3 *Rose Bowl Them Announced*. Then, select the **Information icon** next to the task to open the *Task Details* panel.
- In the **Duration** field, enter zero to initialize the duration for this milestone, and press **Enter**.

Notice that when you enter a task duration, PFW automatically assigned the project start date, which is 1/15/24, as the Start and Finish dates for the task (*Figure 22*).

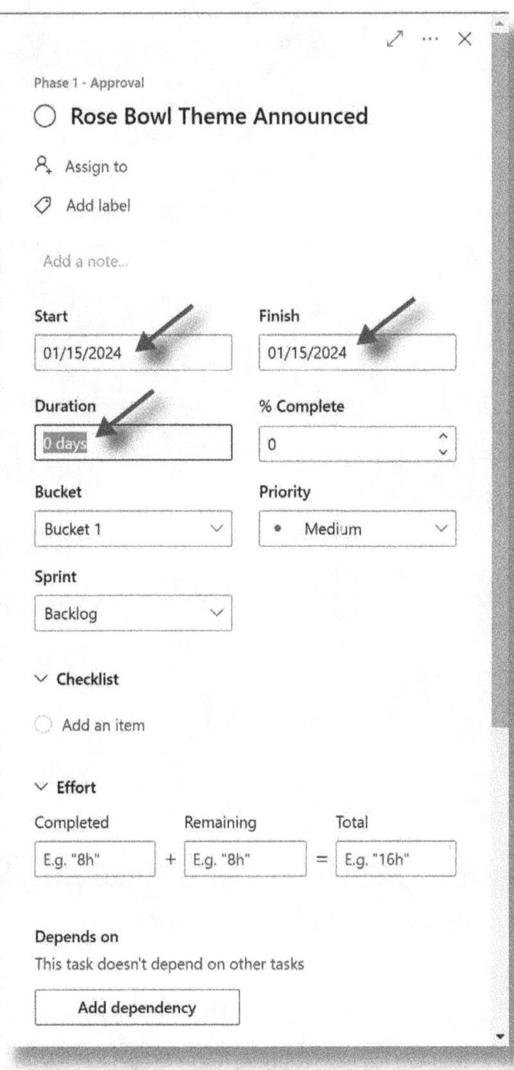

Figure 22 – Task Details Panel

Using the *Task details* panel, initialize the durations for each of the six remaining milestone tasks we identified earlier, starting with task 6 *Entry Form Approved*.

- Select the task. Then, in the *Task details* panel, enter zero in the **Duration** field, and press **Enter**.
- Repeat for each milestone task. Then, close the *Task details* panel.

When the seven milestone tasks are created, your schedule should look like *Figure 23* below. As mentioned earlier, by default the milestone tasks will been given the project start date of 1/15/24 as their Start and Finish dates.

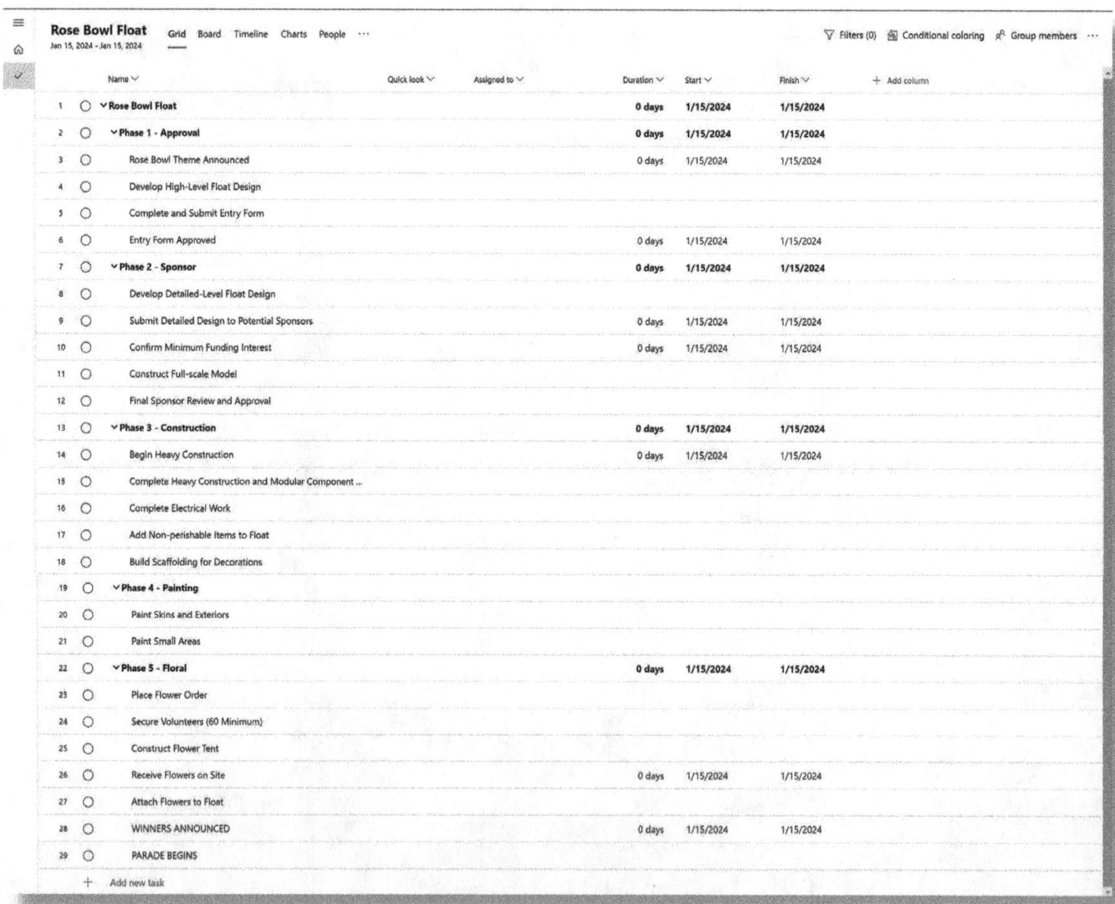

	Name	Quick look	Assigned to	Duration	Start	Finish
1	**Rose Bowl Float**			**0 days**	**1/15/2024**	**1/15/2024**
2	**Phase 1 - Approval**			**0 days**	**1/15/2024**	**1/15/2024**
3	Rose Bowl Theme Announced			0 days	1/15/2024	1/15/2024
4	Develop High-Level Float Design					
5	Complete and Submit Entry Form					
6	Entry Form Approved			0 days	1/15/2024	1/15/2024
7	**Phase 2 - Sponsor**			**0 days**	**1/15/2024**	**1/15/2024**
8	Develop Detailed-Level Float Design					
9	Submit Detailed Design to Potential Sponsors			0 days	1/15/2024	1/15/2024
10	Confirm Minimum Funding Interest			0 days	1/15/2024	1/15/2024
11	Construct Full-scale Model					
12	Final Sponsor Review and Approval					
13	**Phase 3 - Construction**			**0 days**	**1/15/2024**	**1/15/2024**
14	Begin Heavy Construction			0 days	1/15/2024	1/15/2024
15	Complete Heavy Construction and Modular Component ...					
16	Complete Electrical Work					
17	Add Non-perishable Items to Float					
18	Build Scaffolding for Decorations					
19	**Phase 4 - Painting**					
20	Paint Skins and Exteriors					
21	Paint Small Areas					
22	**Phase 5 - Floral**			**0 days**	**1/15/2024**	**1/15/2024**
23	Place Flower Order					
24	Secure Volunteers (60 Minimum)					
25	Construct Flower Tent					
26	Receive Flowers on Site			0 days	1/15/2024	1/15/2024
27	Attach Flowers to Float					
28	WINNERS ANNOUNCED			0 days	1/15/2024	1/15/2024
29	PARADE BEGINS					

Figure 23 – Milestone Tasks Created

Next, we'll enter the estimated task durations for the remaining subtasks (children tasks) in our Float project. This time, we'll enter the durations directly into the **Duration** column. We'll start with task 4 *Develop High-Level Float Design*. The estimated duration for this task is **10 days**.

- Click into the **Duration** field for task 4 *Develop High-Level Float Design*.
- Then, enter **10d** (for 10 days) directly into the **Duration** field and press **Enter**.

Notice the updates that automatically occurred (*Figure 24* below). In addition to the task 4 duration updating to 10 days, the Phase 1 summary task duration and the overall project duration were also updated to 10 days. Also, the finish date for task 4, the Phase 1 summary task finish date and the project finish date were updated to 1/26/24, which is 10 working days after the 10-day duration for task 4.

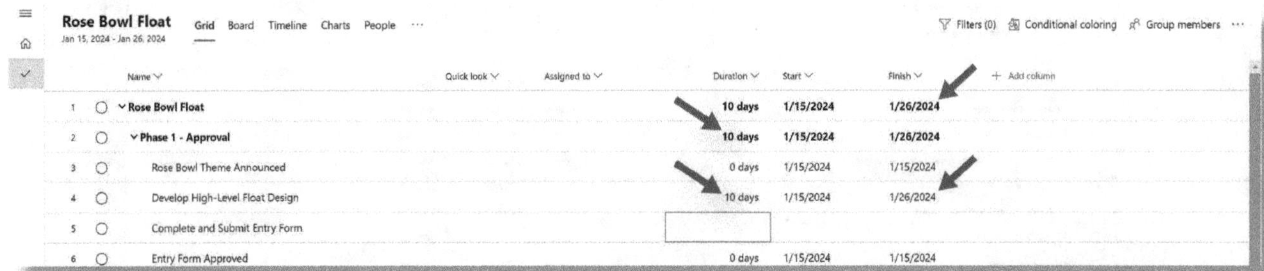

Figure 24 – Task 4 Duration Entered

Listed below are the durations for the remaining subtasks in our Float schedule. Enter the task durations directly into the Duration field for each task. Be sure to press Enter after each duration entry.

TASK ID	TASK NAME	DURATION
5	Complete and Submit Entry Form	2 days
8	Develop Detailed-Level Float Design	9 days
11	Construct Full-Scale Model	37 days
12	Final Sponsor Review and Approval	20 days
15	Complete Heavy Construction and Modular Component Build	74 days
16	Complete Electrical Work	20 days
17	Add Non-Perishable Items to Float	15 days
18	Build Scaffolding for Decorations	10 days
20	Paint Skins and Exteriors	5 days
21	Paint Small Areas	5 days
23	Place Flower Order	1 day
24	Secure Volunteers (60 Minimum)	30 days
25	Construct Flower Tent	12 days
27	Attach Flowers to Float	10 days
29	PARADE BEGINS	1 day

When all the task durations have been entered, your schedule should look like *Figure 25* below. The finish dates for each task, the summary tasks representing the phases, and the overall project finish date should be updated per the task durations.

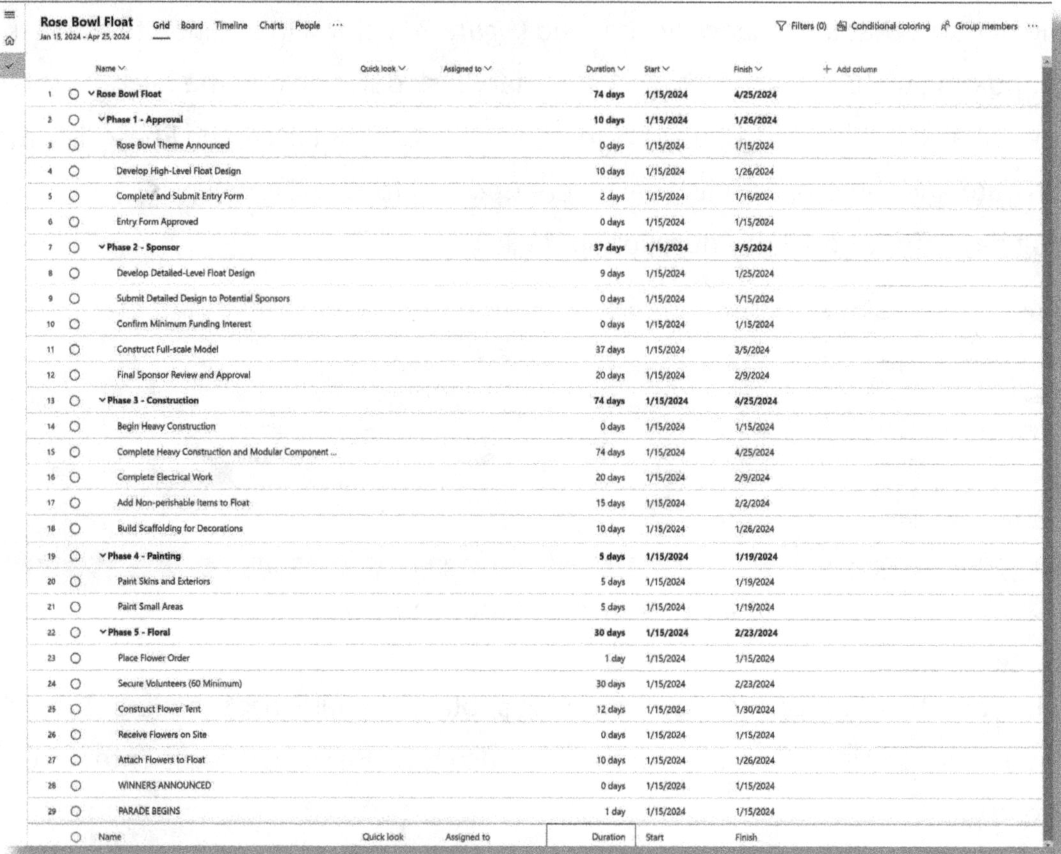

	Name	Quick look	Assigned to	Duration	Start	Finish
1	**Rose Bowl Float**			**74 days**	**1/15/2024**	**4/25/2024**
2	**Phase 1 - Approval**			**10 days**	**1/15/2024**	**1/26/2024**
3	Rose Bowl Theme Announced			0 days	1/15/2024	1/15/2024
4	Develop High-Level Float Design			10 days	1/15/2024	1/26/2024
5	Complete and Submit Entry Form			2 days	1/15/2024	1/16/2024
6	Entry Form Approved			0 days	1/15/2024	1/15/2024
7	**Phase 2 - Sponsor**			**37 days**	**1/15/2024**	**3/5/2024**
8	Develop Detailed-Level Float Design			9 days	1/15/2024	1/25/2024
9	Submit Detailed Design to Potential Sponsors			0 days	1/15/2024	1/15/2024
10	Confirm Minimum Funding Interest			0 days	1/15/2024	1/15/2024
11	Construct Full-scale Model			37 days	1/15/2024	3/5/2024
12	Final Sponsor Review and Approval			20 days	1/15/2024	2/9/2024
13	**Phase 3 - Construction**			**74 days**	**1/15/2024**	**4/25/2024**
14	Begin Heavy Construction			0 days	1/15/2024	1/15/2024
15	Complete Heavy Construction and Modular Component ...			74 days	1/15/2024	4/25/2024
16	Complete Electrical Work			20 days	1/15/2024	2/9/2024
17	Add Non-perishable Items to Float			15 days	1/15/2024	2/2/2024
18	Build Scaffolding for Decorations			10 days	1/15/2024	1/26/2024
19	**Phase 4 - Painting**			**5 days**	**1/15/2024**	**1/19/2024**
20	Paint Skins and Exteriors			5 days	1/15/2024	1/19/2024
21	Paint Small Areas			5 days	1/15/2024	1/19/2024
22	**Phase 5 - Floral**			**30 days**	**1/15/2024**	**2/23/2024**
23	Place Flower Order			1 day	1/15/2024	1/15/2024
24	Secure Volunteers (60 Minimum)			30 days	1/15/2024	2/23/2024
25	Construct Flower Tent			12 days	1/15/2024	1/30/2024
26	Receive Flowers on Site			0 days	1/15/2024	1/15/2024
27	Attach Flowers to Float			10 days	1/15/2024	1/26/2024
28	WINNERS ANNOUNCED			0 days	1/15/2024	1/15/2024
29	PARADE BEGINS			1 day	1/15/2024	1/15/2024
	Name	Quick look	Assigned to	Duration	Start	Finish

Figure 25 – All Task Durations Entered

You may have noticed that each task still currently begins on the project start date, which is 1/15/24. This, of course is not right, since these are subsequent tasks that cannot all begin on the same day. This is where **Step 5** of the B.A.S.I.C.S. process – **Connect the Tasks** comes in. Once we connect the tasks and establish dependencies, PFW will know that these tasks occur sequentially and will update their start and finish dates respectively.

Step 5 – Connect the Tasks

Connecting the tasks establishes the relationships and dependencies between the tasks in your schedule. There are several ways to connect the tasks in PFW. You can create dependencies in the **Timeline view**, which we'll review later in the chapter, you can also use the *Task details* panel or you can enter the dependencies directly into the **Depends on** column in the **Grid view**.

We don't currently see this column in the view because it isn't one of the default columns in the Grid view. We will need to add it using the **+ Add column** command, as we did with the **Start** and **Finish** columns.

To add the Depends on column to the view:

- Select the **+ Add column** command. Then, select **Depends on** from the options.

Below is a list of the dependencies for the tasks in our Rose Bowl Float project.
Note that the milestone tasks are not included, because in our schedule they depend on triggering events, like approvals, rather than on work performed by a resource. Also, the tasks noted as N/A don't require dependencies, because they're either the first task in a phase or their start dates are not driven by other tasks, but by other events.

TASK ID – NAME	DEPENDS ON
1 – Rose Bowl Float Project	N/A
2 – Phase 1 - Approval Phase	N/A
3 – Rose Bowl Theme Announced	N/A
4 – Develop High-Level Float Design	3
5 – Complete and Submit Entry Form	4
7 – Phase 2 - Sponsor Phase	N/A
8 - Develop Detailed-Level Float Design	6
9 – Submit Detailed Design to Potential Sponsors	8
11 – Construct Full-Scale Model	10
12 – Final Sponsor Review and Approval	11
13 – Phase 3 - Construction Phase	N/A
14 – Begin Heavy Construction	12
15 – Complete Heavy Construction and Modular Component Build	14
16 – Complete Electrical Work	N/A
17 – Add Non-Perishable Items to Float	16
18 – Build Scaffolding for Decorations	N/A
19 – Phase 4 - Painting Phase	18
20 – Paint Skins and Exteriors	N/A
21 – Paint Small Areas	20
22 - Phase 5 - Floral Phase	N/A
23 – Place Flower Order	21
24 – Secure Volunteers (60 Minimum)	23
25 - Construct Flower Tent	24
27 – Attach Flowers to Float	26
29 - PARADE BEGINS	28

We'll start with task 4 *Develop High Level Float Design*. The dependency for this task is task 3 *Rose Bowl Theme Announced*.

To Create the Dependency:

- In task 4 row, double-click inside the **Depends on** column. PFW suggests task 3 *Rose Bowl Theme Announced* for a dependency (*Figure 26* below). If you click the fly-out menu **|>**, you can also apply one of the four dependency types between these tasks.
  By default, the **Finish-to-Start** type is selected. Since all the tasks in our Float schedule occur in sequence, we will keep this default dependency type.

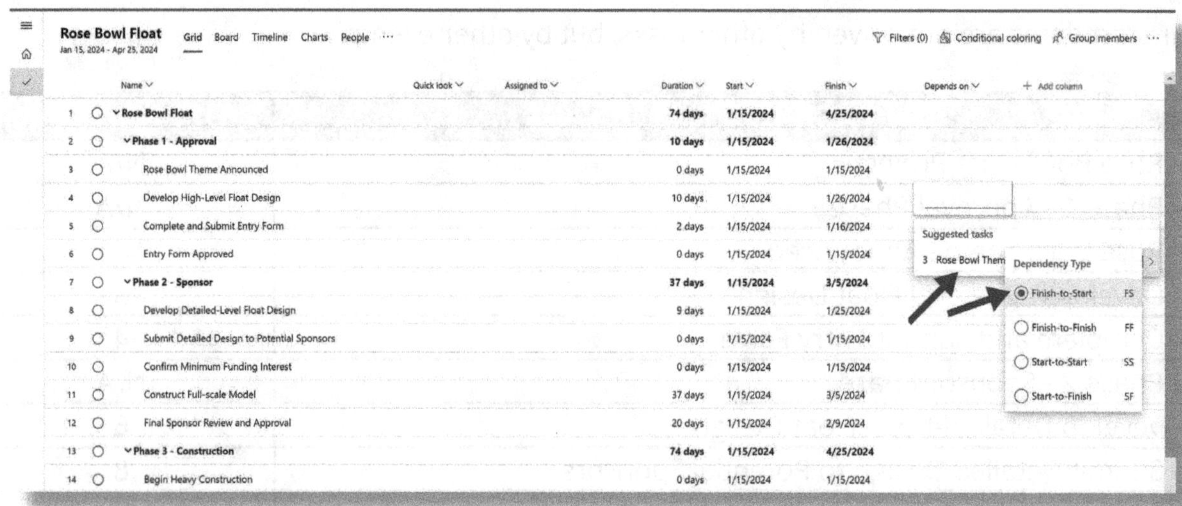

Figure 26 – Add a Task Dependency

- Select the suggested task 3 *Rose Bowl Theme Announced* for the dependency.

- Arrow down in the **Depends on** column to the next task on the list with a dependency, which is task 5 *Complete and Submit Entry Form*. This task depends on task 4 *Develop High-Level Float Design*.

- Click inside the **Depends on** column. Then, select task 4 from the suggested tasks.

- Arrow down to the next task on the list with a dependency and choose the correct dependency for each task.

- Press **Enter** after the last task dependency has been selected.

The dependencies will be indicated in the **Depends on** field with the predecessor task's ID and the two-letter acronym for the dependency type. When all the task dependencies have been selected, your schedule should look like *Figure 27 below.*

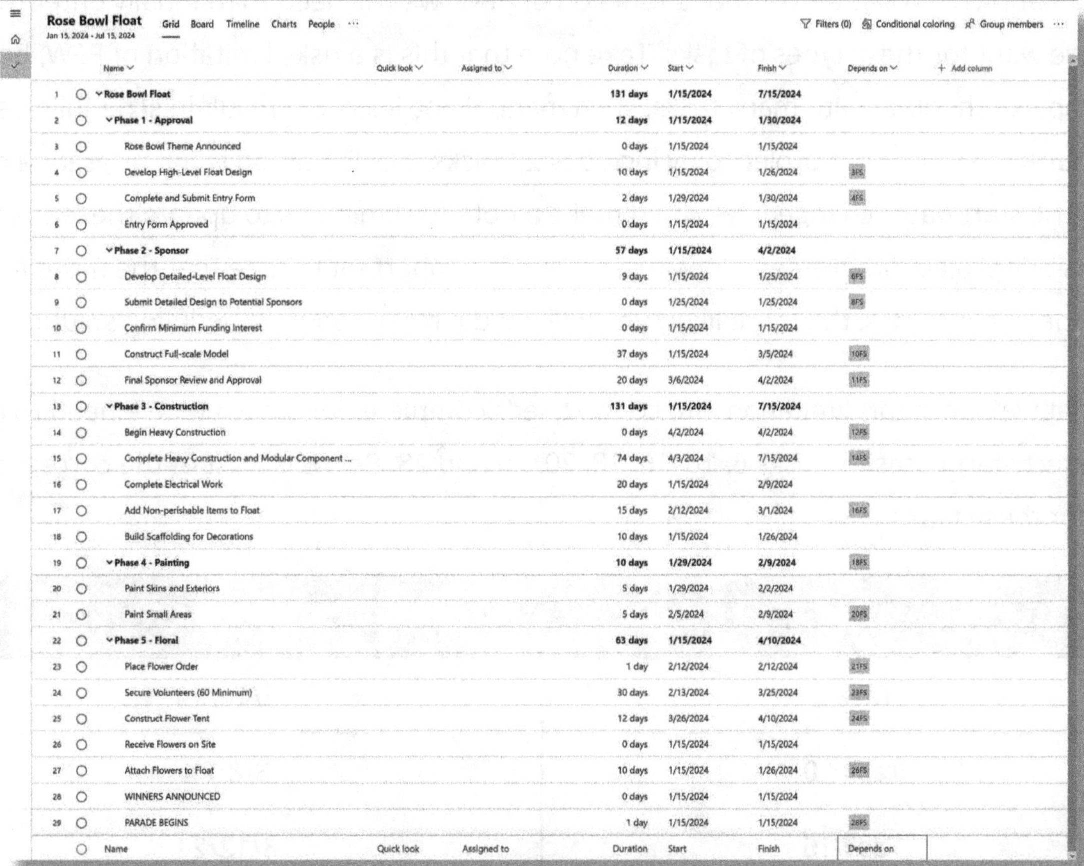

	Name	Quick look	Assigned to	Duration	Start	Finish	Depends on
1	**Rose Bowl Float**			**131 days**	**1/15/2024**	**7/15/2024**	
2	**Phase 1 - Approval**			**12 days**	**1/15/2024**	**1/30/2024**	
3	Rose Bowl Theme Announced			0 days	1/15/2024	1/15/2024	
4	Develop High-Level Float Design			10 days	1/15/2024	1/26/2024	3FS
5	Complete and Submit Entry Form			2 days	1/29/2024	1/30/2024	4FS
6	Entry Form Approved			0 days	1/15/2024	1/15/2024	
7	**Phase 2 - Sponsor**			**57 days**	**1/15/2024**	**4/2/2024**	
8	Develop Detailed-Level Float Design			9 days	1/15/2024	1/25/2024	6FS
9	Submit Detailed Design to Potential Sponsors			0 days	1/25/2024	1/25/2024	8FS
10	Confirm Minimum Funding Interest			0 days	1/15/2024	1/15/2024	
11	Construct Full-scale Model			37 days	1/15/2024	3/5/2024	10FS
12	Final Sponsor Review and Approval			20 days	3/6/2024	4/2/2024	11FS
13	**Phase 3 - Construction**			**131 days**	**1/15/2024**	**7/15/2024**	
14	Begin Heavy Construction			0 days	4/2/2024	4/2/2024	12FS
15	Complete Heavy Construction and Modular Component ...			74 days	4/3/2024	7/15/2024	14FS
16	Complete Electrical Work			20 days	1/15/2024	2/9/2024	
17	Add Non-perishable Items to Float			15 days	2/12/2024	3/1/2024	16FS
18	Build Scaffolding for Decorations			10 days	1/15/2024	1/26/2024	
19	**Phase 4 - Painting**			**10 days**	**1/29/2024**	**2/9/2024**	18FS
20	Paint Skins and Exteriors			5 days	1/29/2024	2/2/2024	
21	Paint Small Areas			5 days	2/5/2024	2/9/2024	20FS
22	**Phase 5 - Floral**			**63 days**	**1/15/2024**	**4/10/2024**	
23	Place Flower Order			1 day	2/12/2024	2/12/2024	21FS
24	Secure Volunteers (60 Minimum)			30 days	2/13/2024	3/25/2024	23FS
25	Construct Flower Tent			12 days	3/26/2024	4/10/2024	24FS
26	Receive Flowers on Site			0 days	1/15/2024	1/15/2024	
27	Attach Flowers to Float			10 days	1/15/2024	1/26/2024	26FS
28	WINNERS ANNOUNCED			0 days	1/15/2024	1/15/2024	
29	PARADE BEGINS			1 day	1/15/2024	1/15/2024	28FS

Figure 27 – All Dependencies Selected

Our schedule is almost complete. We just need to add a few finishing touches. Notice PFW has updated the task start dates to begin after the finish dates of the tasks they depend on.
As mentioned earlier, we didn't give every task a dependency, because not all the tasks depend on another task to finish before they can start. These tasks are driven by other circumstances that we're familiar with from having managed this project schedule many times before. By default, if you don't specify which task a task depends on, PFW will schedule it to begin on the project start date. This is the case for tasks 6, 10, 16, 18, 26 and 28. This does not always work, because although a task may not depend on another task, it still may not be able to start at the beginning of the project. This is where task relationship adjustments like adding **lead time** or **lag time** between tasks, or applying **constraints** to tasks comes in handy. This is a useful feature of the Online Desktop and On-Premise Desktop versions of Microsoft Project.

The task start dates would be automatically calculated based upon the contingencies you create using these features, such as "wait 2 days after a certain task ends, before starting the next task" or "start a task after a certain event occurs, like funding". Since adding lag and lead time and applying constraints is not a function of PFW, we will need to manually enter the start dates we want for these types of tasks. Take note that this is a risky limitation of PFW, because for complex schedules with many tasks, such manual entries could result in scheduling errors. Since our Rose Bowl Float project only includes 29 tasks, this limitation is not as great a risk. Even if the start dates changed, we could make a note to remind us to update these seven tasks as our project progresses. Notwithstanding, it's important to note that the more tasks your schedule includes, the more likely you will need a more robust scheduling solution.

Now that we've put this limitation into context, let's complete our schedule. We need to enter the correct start dates for tasks 6, 10, 16, 18, 20, 26 and 28. Below is a list of the correct start dates for these tasks.

TASK	START DATE
Task 6	2/14/24
Task 10	3/8/24
Task 16	8/12/24
Task 18	9/16/24
Task 20	9/30/24
Task 26	12/13/24
Task 28	1/1/25

Starting with task 6, *Entry Form Approved*, enter the start dates directly into the **Start** column. Simply, click into the field, enter the date, and press **Enter**. You can also select the dates using the calendar icon. After the start dates for these seven tasks have been entered, your schedule should look like *Figure 28*.

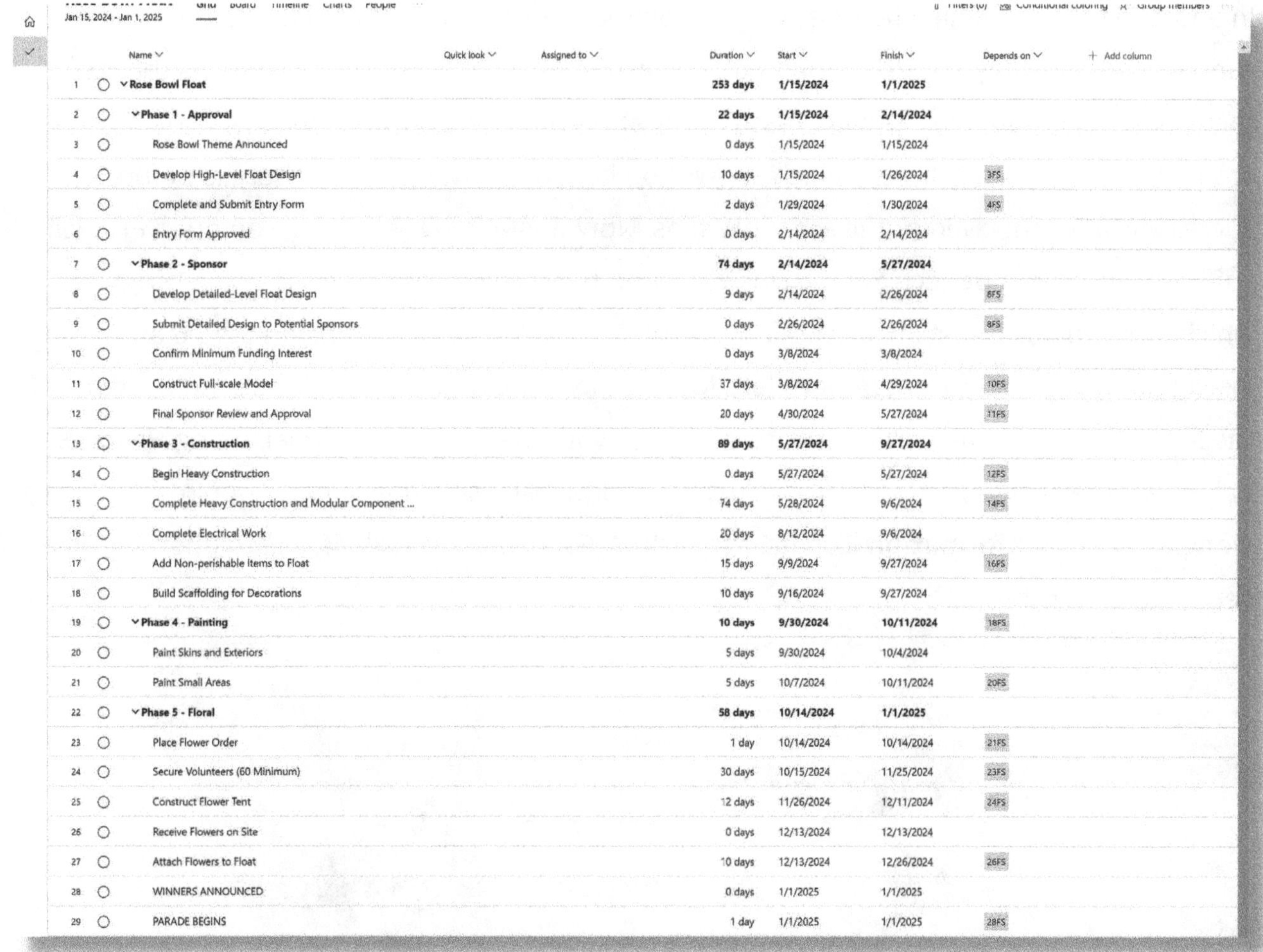

Jan 15, 2024 - Jan 1, 2025

	Name	Quick look	Assigned to	Duration	Start	Finish	Depends on
1	**Rose Bowl Float**			**253 days**	**1/15/2024**	**1/1/2025**	
2	**Phase 1 - Approval**			**22 days**	**1/15/2024**	**2/14/2024**	
3	Rose Bowl Theme Announced			0 days	1/15/2024	1/15/2024	
4	Develop High-Level Float Design			10 days	1/15/2024	1/26/2024	3FS
5	Complete and Submit Entry Form			2 days	1/29/2024	1/30/2024	4FS
6	Entry Form Approved			0 days	2/14/2024	2/14/2024	
7	**Phase 2 - Sponsor**			**74 days**	**2/14/2024**	**5/27/2024**	
8	Develop Detailed-Level Float Design			9 days	2/14/2024	2/26/2024	6FS
9	Submit Detailed Design to Potential Sponsors			0 days	2/26/2024	2/26/2024	8FS
10	Confirm Minimum Funding Interest			0 days	3/8/2024	3/8/2024	
11	Construct Full-scale Model			37 days	3/8/2024	4/29/2024	10FS
12	Final Sponsor Review and Approval			20 days	4/30/2024	5/27/2024	11FS
13	**Phase 3 - Construction**			**89 days**	**5/27/2024**	**9/27/2024**	
14	Begin Heavy Construction			0 days	5/27/2024	5/27/2024	12FS
15	Complete Heavy Construction and Modular Component ...			74 days	5/28/2024	9/6/2024	14FS
16	Complete Electrical Work			20 days	8/12/2024	9/6/2024	
17	Add Non-perishable Items to Float			15 days	9/9/2024	9/27/2024	16FS
18	Build Scaffolding for Decorations			10 days	9/16/2024	9/27/2024	
19	**Phase 4 - Painting**			**10 days**	**9/30/2024**	**10/11/2024**	18FS
20	Paint Skins and Exteriors			5 days	9/30/2024	10/4/2024	
21	Paint Small Areas			5 days	10/7/2024	10/11/2024	20FS
22	**Phase 5 - Floral**			**58 days**	**10/14/2024**	**1/1/2025**	
23	Place Flower Order			1 day	10/14/2024	10/14/2024	21FS
24	Secure Volunteers (60 Minimum)			30 days	10/15/2024	11/25/2024	23FS
25	Construct Flower Tent			12 days	11/26/2024	12/11/2024	24FS
26	Receive Flowers on Site			0 days	12/13/2024	12/13/2024	
27	Attach Flowers to Float			10 days	12/13/2024	12/26/2024	26FS
28	WINNERS ANNOUNCED			0 days	1/1/2025	1/1/2025	
29	PARADE BEGINS			1 day	1/1/2025	1/1/2025	28FS

Figure 28 – Start Dates Entered

We've now completed **Step 5** of the B.A.S.I.C.S. process – **Connect the Tasks** and our schedule is complete. The task start and finish dates now correspond with their durations, and task dependencies. The Project Summary Task (task 1), which displays the summary values for the entire project, displays our projected total project duration, which is 253 days.
The project finish date is 1/1/2025, which is the date of the Rose Bowl parade. If you recall, when we started, we chose the default work template for our project calendar, which is based on the standard Monday through Friday work week. This means that PFW tracks business days and not calendar days. This is why our year-long project has an overall project duration that is significantly less than a 365-day calendar year.

We've now built our winning Rose Bowl Float schedule from scratch using PFW! By definition, a schedule is a plan for carrying out a project within a projected time-frame. The operative question is always — can we execute on that plan? That's what **Step 6** in our B.A.S.I.C.S. scheduling approach is all about – **Starting (or Executing) a Planned Project**.

In addition to the planning features we've explored in PFW, the app includes some rudimentary tracking features. What makes these tracking features rudimentary is the fact that you cannot baseline a project, assign actual or remaining duration values, or view the amount of Slack each task has, which shows you how much wiggle room there is before a successor task is delayed or the schedule slips. Notwithstanding, what you can do in PFW will suffice for our Float project. You can indicate whether a task is complete or still in progress, which gives you an at-a-glance overall status of the project. Before we begin Step 6 and execute our Rose Bowl Float project, let's look at the some of the other views and functions of the interface that we haven't reviewed. We'll start with the *Task details* panel. Using *Figure 29* below, we'll review the actions you can perform for a task using this panel. If you're following along, select the **Information** icon next to task 11 *Construct Full-Scale Model*, to open the *Task details* panel for this task.

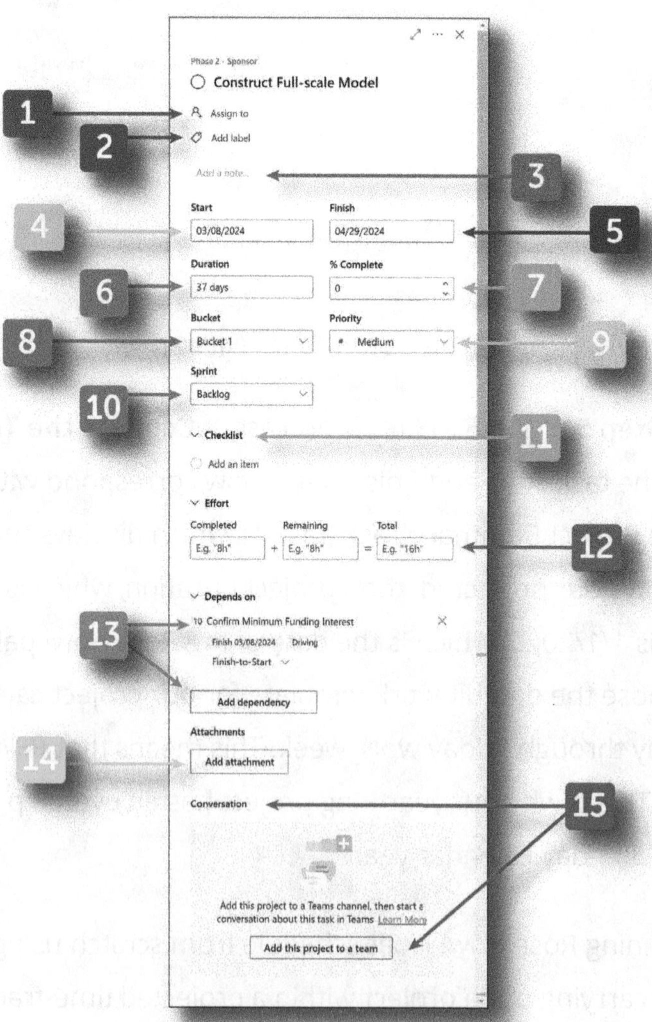

Figure 29 – Task Details Panel

The Task Information Panel

#1 - Assign to - Assign a resource to the task from an existing or new Microsoft 365 group.

#2 - Add label - Add a label to the task to sort tasks and keep them organized. The label names can be changed to whatever you like.

#3 - Add a note - Add a note to the task. Simply type the note into the field.

#4 - Start - Enter or update the start date for the task.

#5 - Finish - Enter or update the finish date for the task.

#6 - Duration - Enter or update the duration for the task.

#7 -% Complete - Enter or update the progress for the task, by entering a percentage of completion.

#8 -Bucket - Select a Bucket for the task. Buckets are created and used to organize tasks in the *Board* view.

#9 -Priority - Set a priority level for the task.

#10 -Sprint - Assign the task to a Sprint. Sprints must first be enabled in the *Board* view.

#11 -Checklist - Add an item to a Checklist for the task. This feature allows you to track smaller items of work in your project that are attached to tasks, but don't need to be scheduled on their own. Click inside the *Add an item* field to add a checklist item.

#12 - Effort - Enter the hours of Effort for the task. Effort is the number of hours a resource spends on a task. Note that PFW doesn't assume that 1 day equals 8 hours. You can enter whatever amount of effort you like in the Total field, and PFW will populate the other two variables of the equation (Completed + Remaining = Total). After that, if you change a task duration or an assignment, effort will adjust to fit.

Note also that these automations in PFW are limited to the effort hours - NOT Duration. The Duration value you enter for a task is Fixed. Meaning, Duration is never affected by changes in effort and assignment. For example, if you set a task duration as 2 days, and you add more effort than can fit in 2 days, PFW will not extend your duration beyond 2 days. Only the per-day hours will increase - NOT the amount of the task's duration days.

Also, assigning a task to one person will not affect effort or duration. However, when you assign a task to 2 people, while the duration will stay the same, the effort for that task will double. This is because PFW assumes when you add a second resource, that another set of the same amount of work for that second person will occur. If you meant to shorten the task's duration by adding a second person, you will need to manually reduce the duration accordingly. You'll also need to manually adjust the effort hours. Therefore, the Effort option in PFW does not affect your schedule. It is simply a place to log the hours a resource works on a task.

#13 - Depends on - Add or view the dependencies for the task. Select the *Add dependency* button to add a new dependency. Select a dependency from the suggested task(s).

#14 -Add attachment - Add an attachment from your computer or team files or add a link to a URL to the task.

#15 - Conversation - Integrate with the Microsoft Teams app to have conversations around the tasks. You must first add your project to a team.

Filter and Sort Tasks

In the top right corner of the view, you'll find commands to filter and sort tasks. The **Filters** command lets you filter tasks by a number of categories (Figure 30 below).

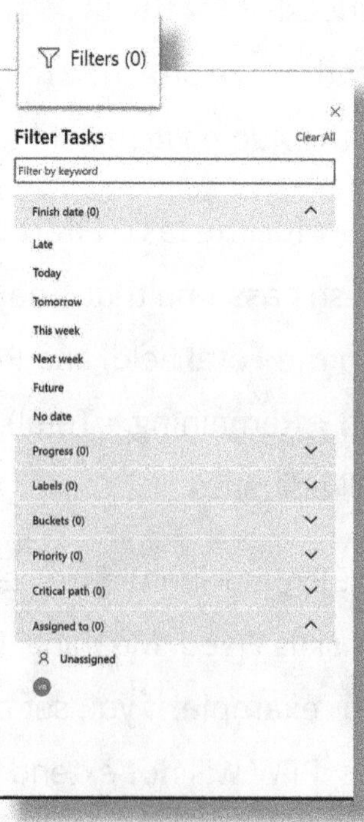

Figure 30 – Filter Tasks

Next to the Filters command, you'll find the **Conditioning coloring** feature. This feature allows you to highlight cells in selected fields if they meet certain conditions. For example, you could tell PFW to highlight tasks that exceed a certain duration, for instance 10 days.

How to use the Conditional Coloring feature:

- Select the **Conditional Coloring** command to open the dialogue box (*Figure 31 below*).
- In the **Field** cell, select the applicable column in which to set the condition. E.g. the *Duration* column.
- In the **Operator** field, select the appropriate condition. E.g. *is more than*.
- In the last field, which is the **Value** field, type the value you want, and press **Enter**. E.g. *10 days*.
- Last, choose the highlight color you want from the **color picker**.
- When you've selected your options, select **SAVE** to set the conditions.

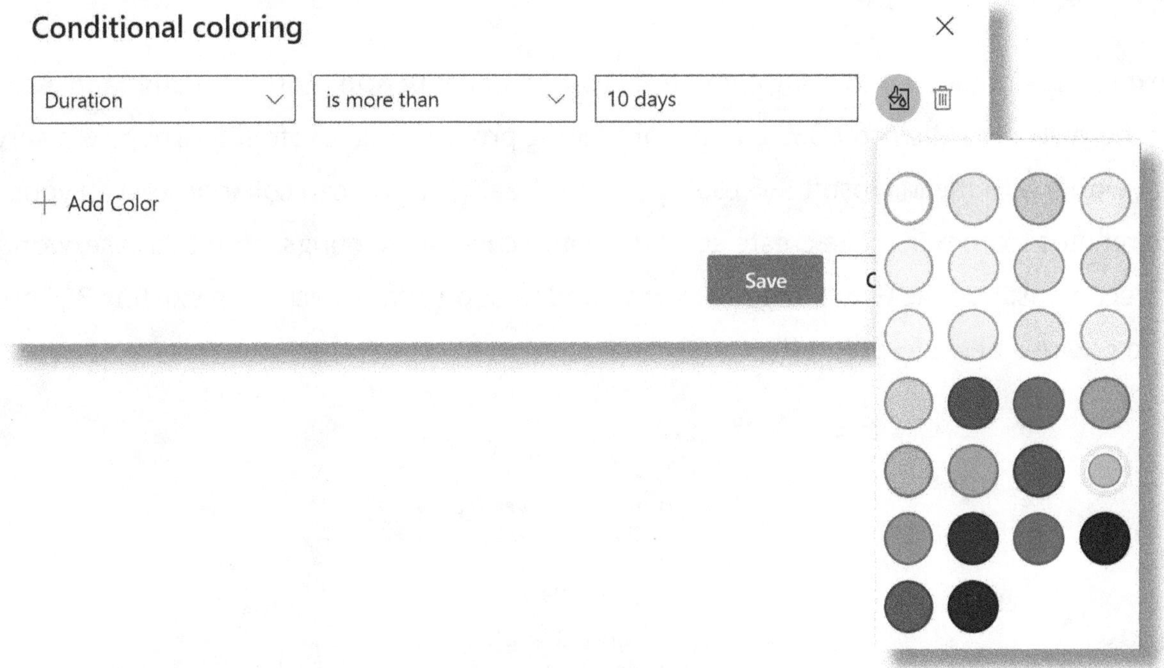

Figure 31 – Conditional Coloring Dialogue Box

After you save the conditions, PFW will highlight your schedule based on the conditions you set, as shown in *Figure 32*. In this example, we told PFW to highlight the tasks with durations more than 10 days with the teal color.

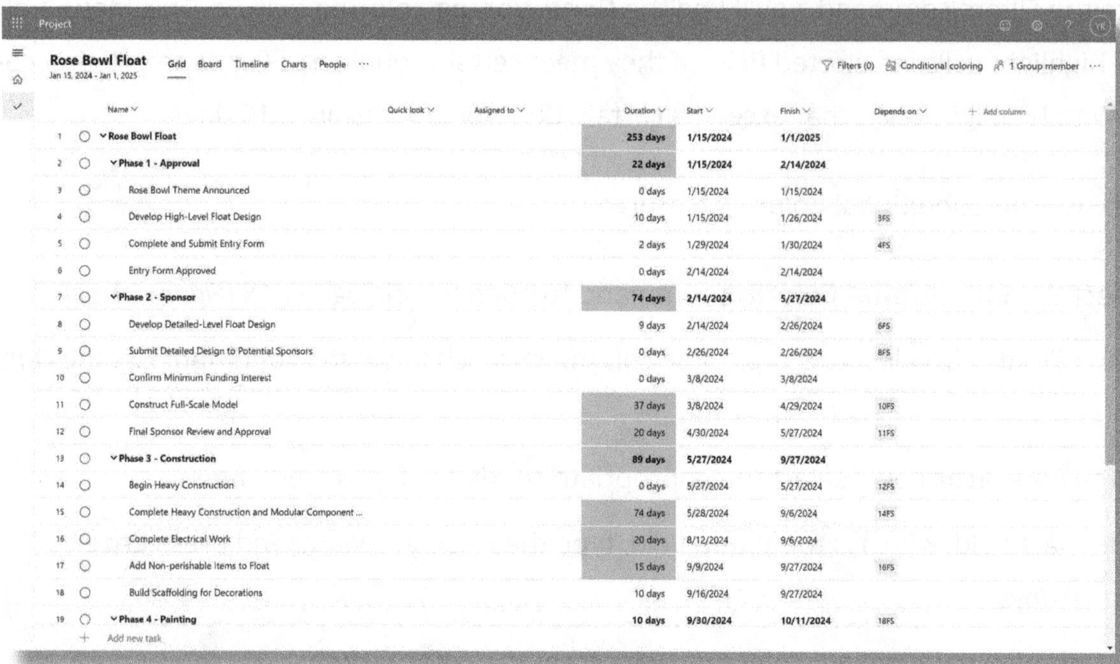

	Name	Quick look	Assigned to	Duration	Start	Finish	Depends on
1	**Rose Bowl Float**			**253 days**	**1/15/2024**	**1/1/2025**	
2	**Phase 1 - Approval**			**22 days**	**1/15/2024**	**2/14/2024**	
3	Rose Bowl Theme Announced			0 days	1/15/2024	1/15/2024	
4	Develop High-Level Float Design			10 days	1/15/2024	1/26/2024	3FS
5	Complete and Submit Entry Form			2 days	1/29/2024	1/30/2024	4FS
6	Entry Form Approved			0 days	2/14/2024	2/14/2024	
7	**Phase 2 - Sponsor**			**74 days**	**2/14/2024**	**5/27/2024**	
8	Develop Detailed-Level Float Design			9 days	2/14/2024	2/26/2024	6FS
9	Submit Detailed Design to Potential Sponsors			0 days	2/26/2024	2/26/2024	8FS
10	Confirm Minimum Funding Interest			0 days	3/8/2024	3/8/2024	
11	Construct Full-Scale Model			37 days	3/8/2024	4/29/2024	10FS
12	Final Sponsor Review and Approval			20 days	4/30/2024	5/27/2024	11FS
13	**Phase 3 - Construction**			**89 days**	**5/27/2024**	**9/27/2024**	
14	Begin Heavy Construction			0 days	5/27/2024	5/27/2024	12FS
15	Complete Heavy Construction and Modular Component ...			74 days	5/28/2024	9/6/2024	14FS
16	Complete Electrical Work			20 days	8/12/2024	9/6/2024	
17	Add Non-perishable Items to Float			15 days	9/9/2024	9/27/2024	16FS
18	Build Scaffolding for Decorations			10 days	9/16/2024	9/27/2024	
19	**Phase 4 - Painting**			**10 days**	**9/30/2024**	**10/11/2024**	18FS

Figure 32 – Conditional Coloring Applied

Sharing Your Project

Next to the Conditional coloring command, you'll find the **Group member** command. Project for the Web uses Microsoft 365 groups for sharing projects. Microsoft 365 Groups is a service that works with the Microsoft 365 tools you use already, so you can collaborate with your teammates to do things like create spreadsheets, schedule meetings, or in this case, work on project plans. Use the Group member command to add your project to an existing 365 group or to create a new 365 group (*Figure 33 below*).

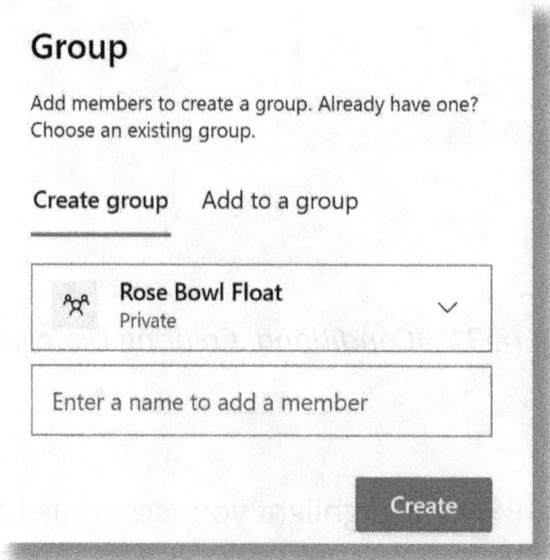

Figure 33 – Add Project to a Microsoft 365 Group

Once a 365 group has been added to your project, you can then add select group members to the project. Then, you can assign group members to tasks, share team files and other project activities. The number of members added to your project will display next to the Group members command title. If your project isn't added to a 365 group, you'll only see the option of adding the PFW account manger.

Next to the Group Member command, you'll find menu ellipses to view **More Actions** you can perform. When you select the menu ellipses you'll find the following actions you can perform (*Figure 34 below*):

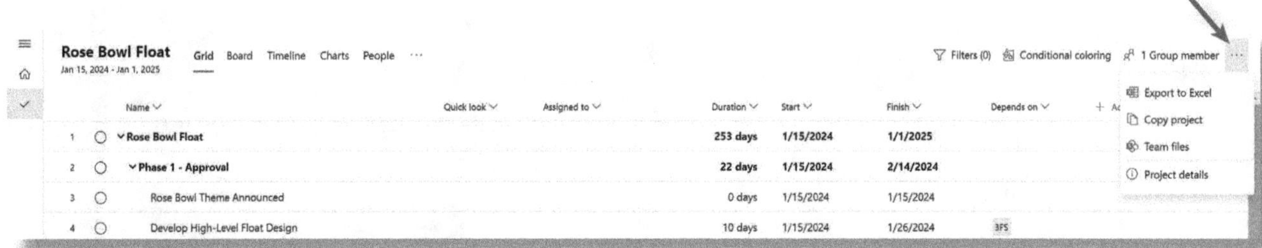

Figure 34 – More Actions Menu

- You can **Export** your project to Microsoft Excel.
- You can make a **Copy** of your project. The copy will be placed among the recent projects in the opening view.
- The **Project Details** action opens the *Project Details* panel, where you can view information about the project, such as the duration and the finish date. If you recall, this is where we entered the Project Start Date.
- If your project is connected to a 365 group, you can also access your **Team files.**

Views

In addition to the Grid view there are five additional views in which you can organize and manage your project — The **Board** view, **Timeline** view, **Charts** view, **People** view and **Assignments** view. The view menu with quick access links is located at the top of the current view next to the project name.

The Board view

In the **Board view**, you can create a visual view of your project and manage tasks in an agile way, on a Kanban-style task board. *Figure 35* below shows what the view looks like if you're staring a new project, and no tasks have been added.

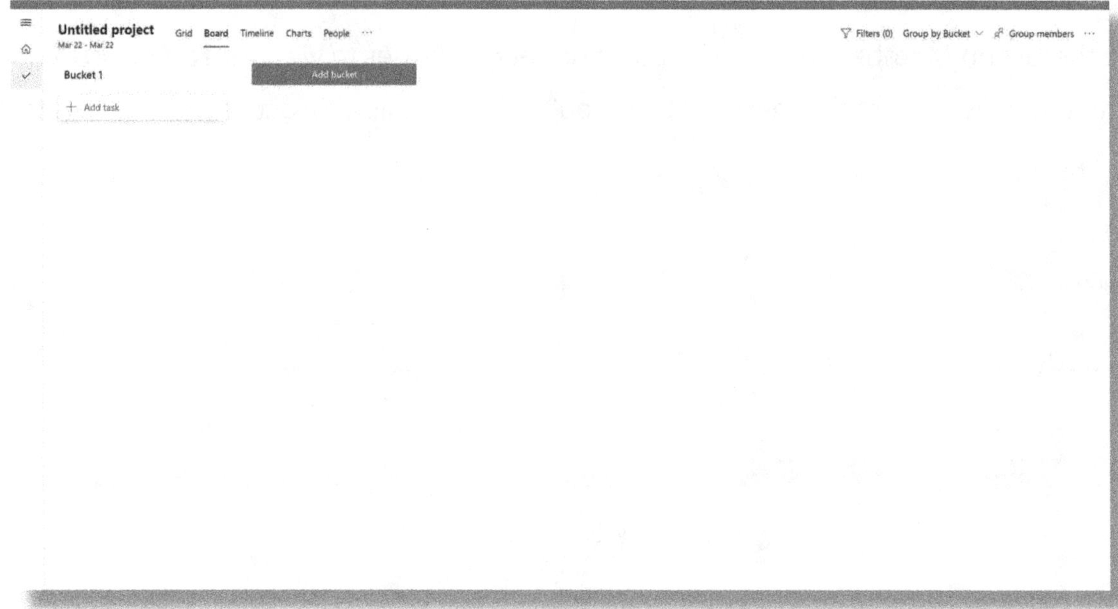

Figure 35 –The Board View

At the top of the view, on the right, you'll find commands for filtering and grouping tasks. We've already reviewed the Filters command in the Grid view. Next to the Filters command, you'll find the **Group By** command. This feature allows you to group tasks by various categories (*Figure 36* below). In the Board view, the default option is **Group by Bucket**.

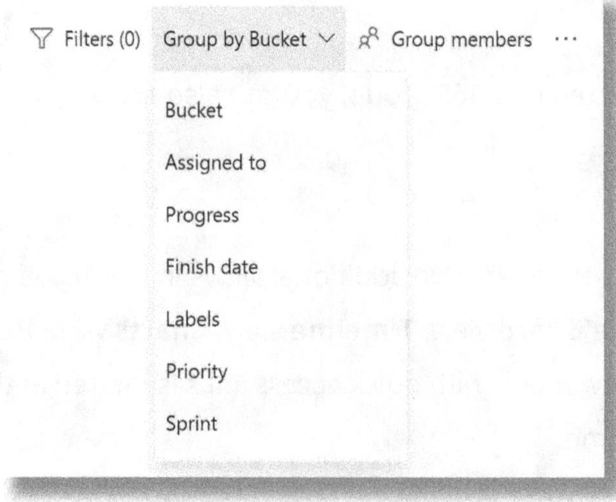

Figure 36 – The Group by Command

Once you add tasks to your project, they'll be organized into **Buckets**. **Bucket 1** is added to the view by default. When new tasks are added to your project in the Grid view, they'll be added to Bucket 1 by default. *Figure 37* below shows the tasks in the our Rose Bowl Float project in the Board view. The last task in the outline is placed at the top of the list, and the first task is at the bottom.

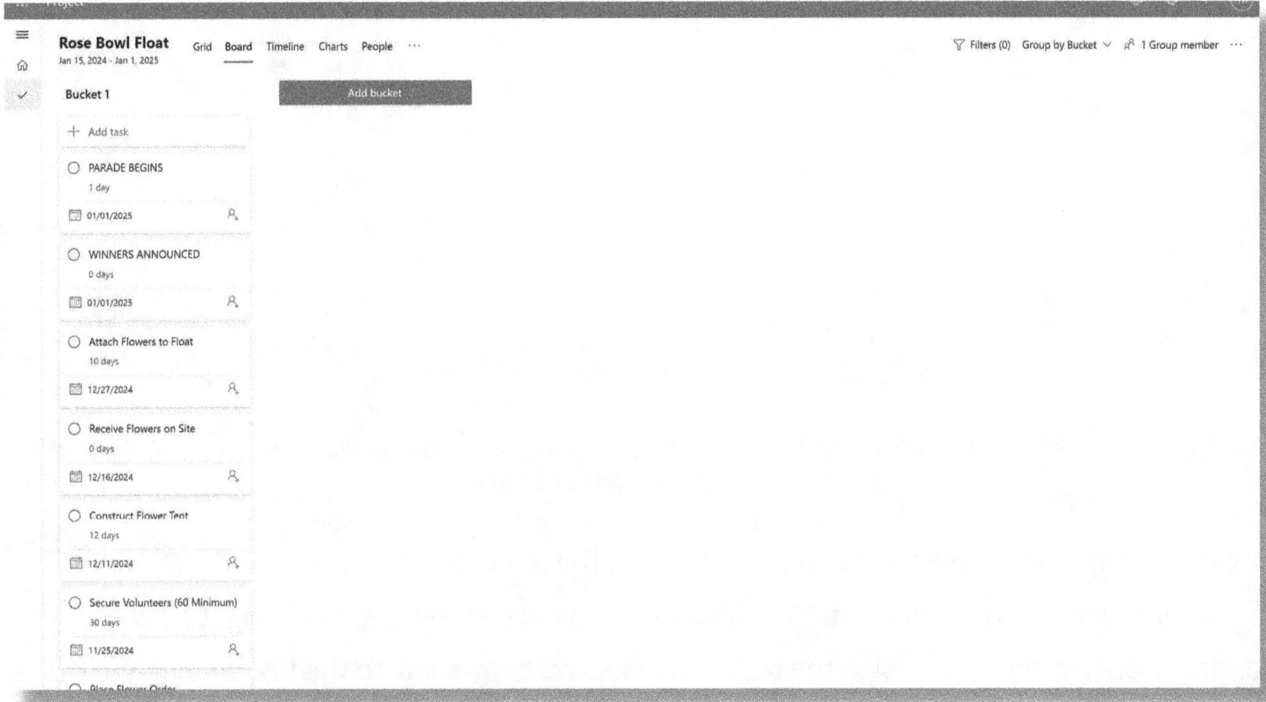

Figure 37 – The Board View - Float Project Tasks

You can rename the default bucket by simply triple-clicking the **Bucket 1** name, and typing over it with a new name. You can add additional buckets to the view using the **Add bucke**t command. Simply select the command, type the new name, and press **Enter**.

Think of the buckets as grouping categories to organize the tasks. Add and name them according to what suits your project. For example, for our Float project, we could name the buckets per the five phases of the project. You can also change the color of the buckets to help keep things organized. Hover over the bucket name, select the paint bucket icon to open the **Color Picker**, and choose the color you like. *Figure 38* shows our Rose Bowl Float project, with fives buckets created per the project phases.

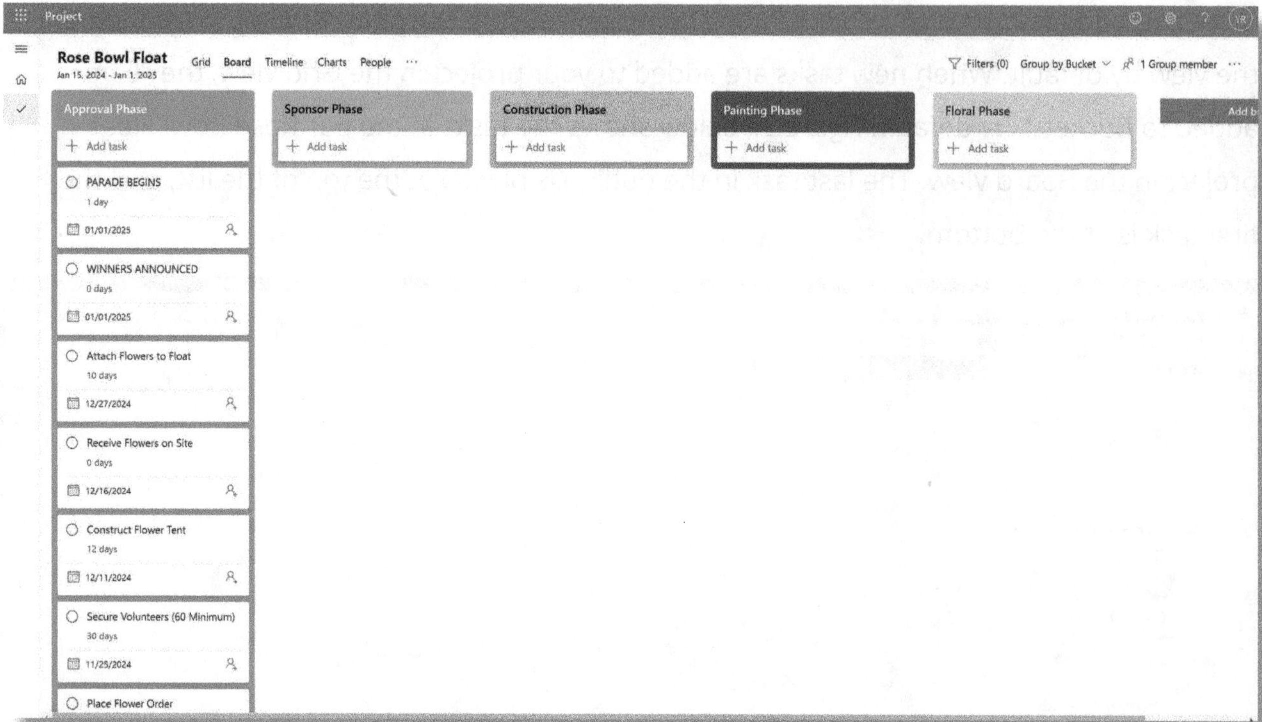

Figure 38 – Organize Tasks Using Buckets

Use the **+Add task** command to add new tasks to the buckets. Each task card displays the task's duration and the finish date. The **More options** menu ellipses on the right allow you to assign a label to the task, assign the task to a resource, copy a link to the task and delete the task. You can also click the circle next to the task name to mark the task complete.

To organize the tasks, simply click and drag them to move them within or across the buckets. Also, if you're working in another view, such as the Grid view, you can select a bucket for a task using the *Task details* panel. *Figure 39* shows the tasks in our Float project organized into their appropriate phases.

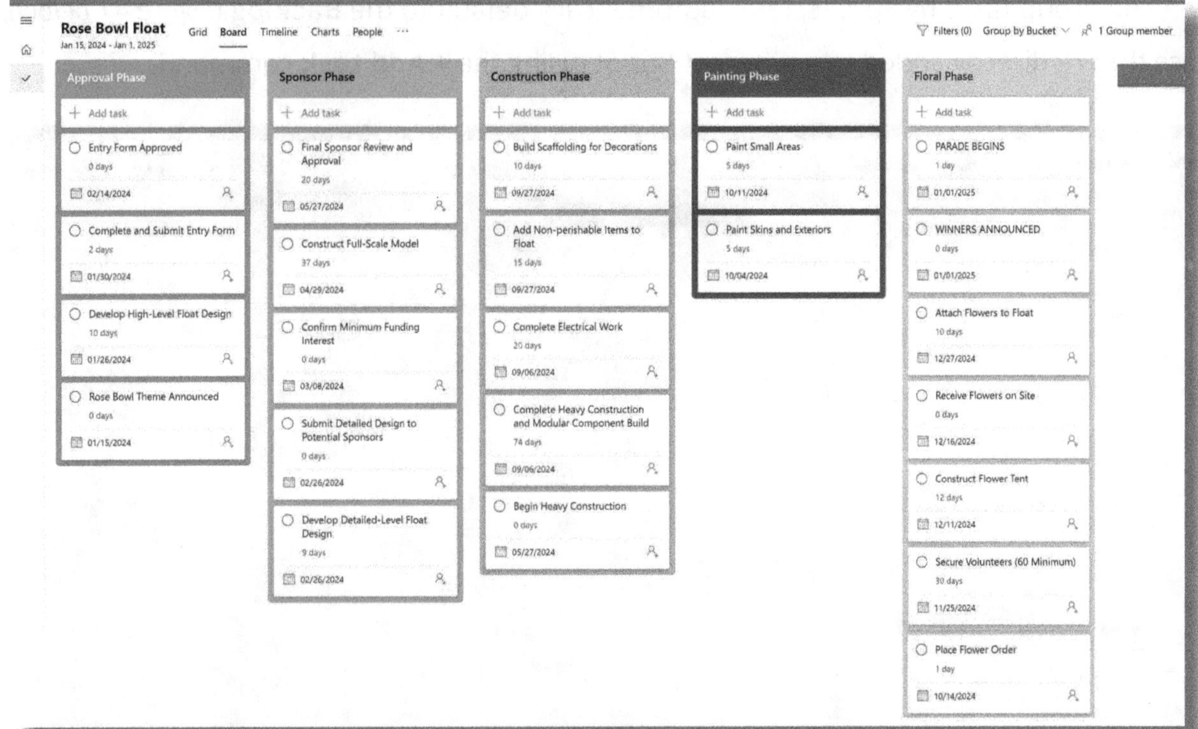

Figure 39 – Float Project Tasks Organized by Buckets

As you can see, this at-a-glance visual view of your project can be a handy way to help keep an Agile team on the same page about which task is being worked on at any given time. If you're planning your project based on Agile project management, you can also use the **Group by** command (in the top of the view, on the right) to group tasks by **Sprint** (*Figure 40*). You must be in the **Board** view to use this grouping option.

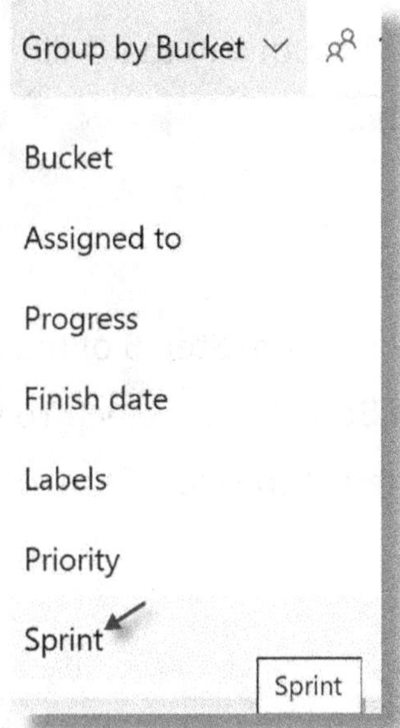

Figure 40 – Group by Sprint Command

When you group tasks by Sprints, tasks automatically default to the **Backlog** (*Figure 41 below*), unless they're directly added to a different Sprint, using the **+ Add task** command.

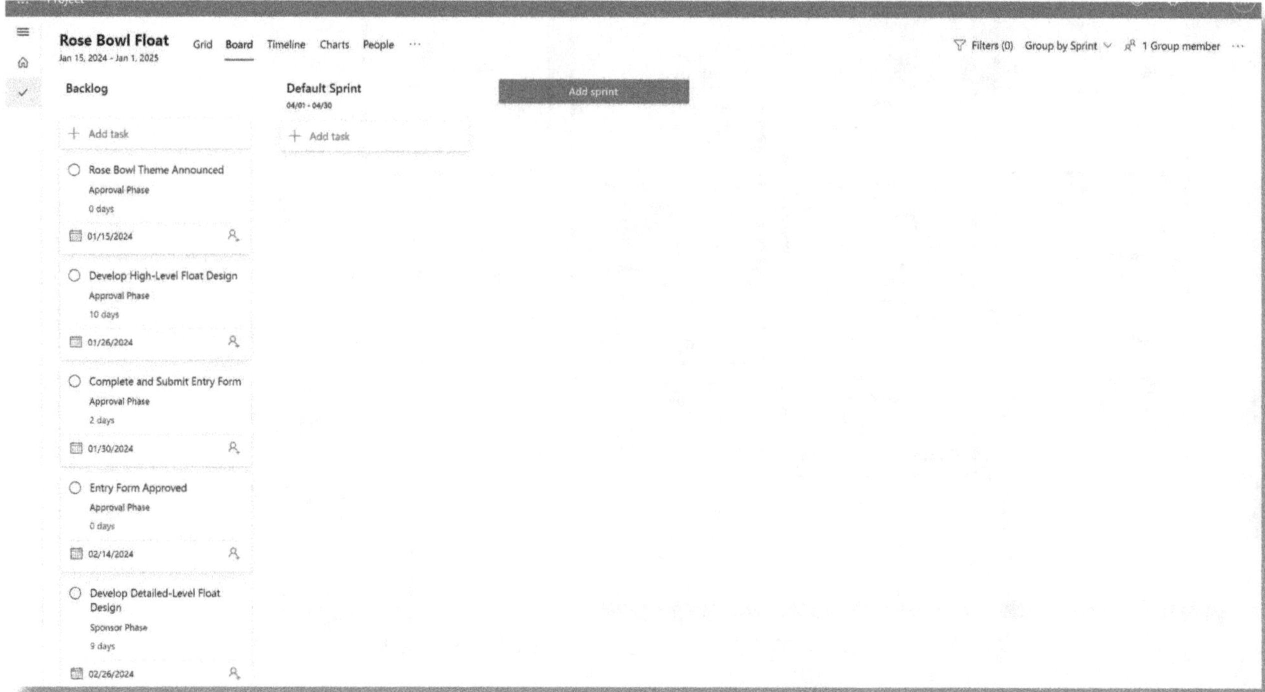

Figure 41 – Tasks Group by Sprint

The newest task displays at the bottom of the task list. While tasks can only be grouped by Sprints in the Board view, they can be added to a Sprint in either the Board view or the Grid view. The original Sprint template includes the **Default Sprint**. You can rename it and set the dates you like. Use the **Add Sprint** button to add a new Sprint. Name and Set the Date you like. We will cover the Agile features included in the Online Desktop Client version of Project exhaustively in Chapters 22 through 25.

The Timeline View

The **Timeline view** is where we will perform Step 6 of the B.A.S.I.C.S. process – **Start the Project**, and we'll execute our Rose Bowl Float project. To switch to the Timeline view, select the **Timeline** quick access link located at the top of the view, on the left.

Figure 42 below shows our Float project in the Timeline view.

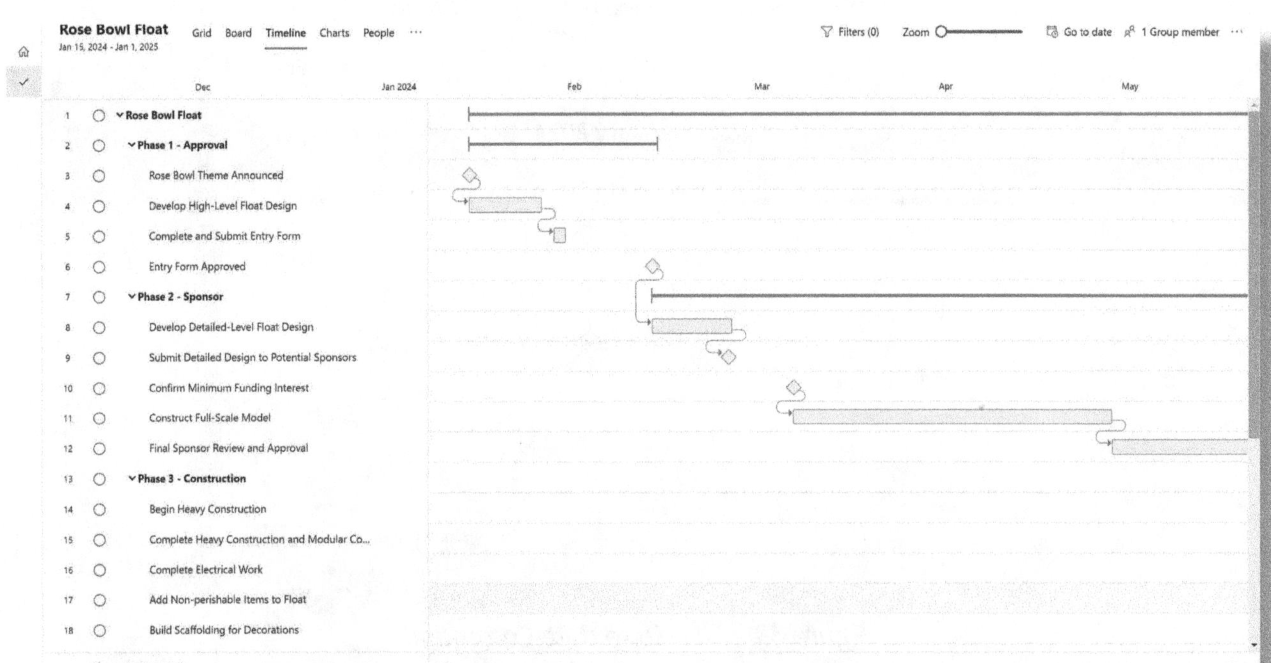

Figure 42 – The Timeline View

On the left side of the view, you'll find the task list and the schedule outline. This is what you also see in the Grid view. You may need to drag the gray line that splits the screen to the right, to better see the names of the phases and tasks.

On the right is a graphical depiction of the scheduled tasks in a Gantt chart. If you don't see anything on the right, you'll need to adjust the view. By default, the timeline for the current dates will be displayed. The current date is indicated by a vertical red line. Since current dates will vary, you may need to zoom in on the timeline to see the Gantt chart.

To zoom in on the timeline:

- Select the **Go to date** command (*Figure 43*) located in the top right corner of the view. Select **1/15/24**, which is the project start date. You should now see the Gantt chart.

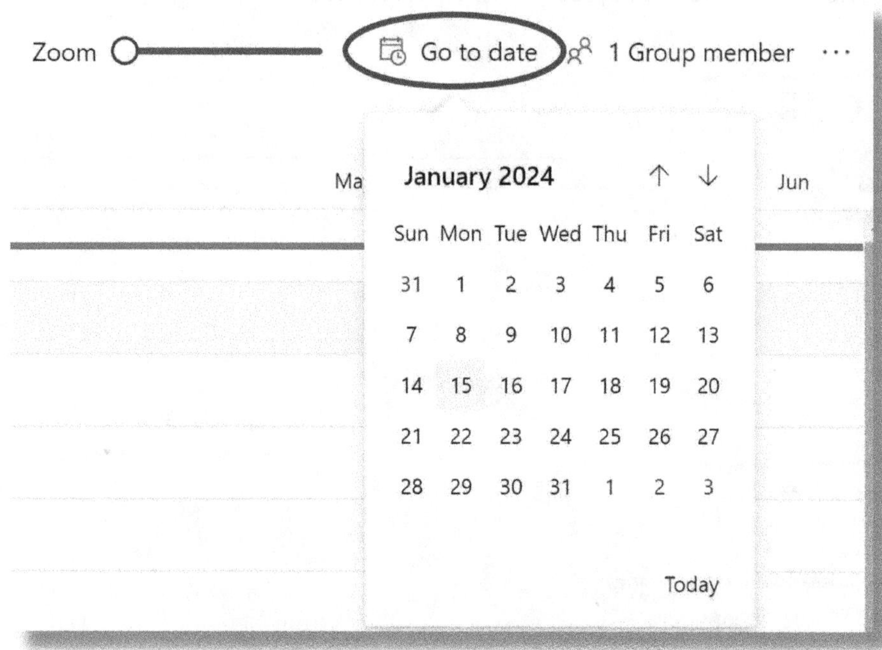

Figure 43 – The Go to date Command

- To zoom out further on the timeline, drag the **Zoom** slider (located next to the **Go to date** command) all the way to the left.

The bars in the Gantt chart are progress bars that represent the task durations. They span across the start and finish dates of the phases and tasks. The thin darker blue bars are summary bars representing the phases of the project. The thicker lighter blue task bars represent the tasks. Milestone tasks are indicated with a light blue diamond symbol. When zoomed in on the timeline, you'll see thick vertical gray lines, which represent non-working days, in this case weekend days. The gray arrows indicate the task dependencies. They're also indicated with the predecessor task's ID and the two-letter acronym for the dependency type. We created the dependencies earlier in the Grid view using the *Task details* panel. We could have also connected the tasks here in the Timeline view.

To create a dependency in the Timeline view:

- Hover over a task bar. A connector icon will appear at either end of the task bar (*Figure 44*).

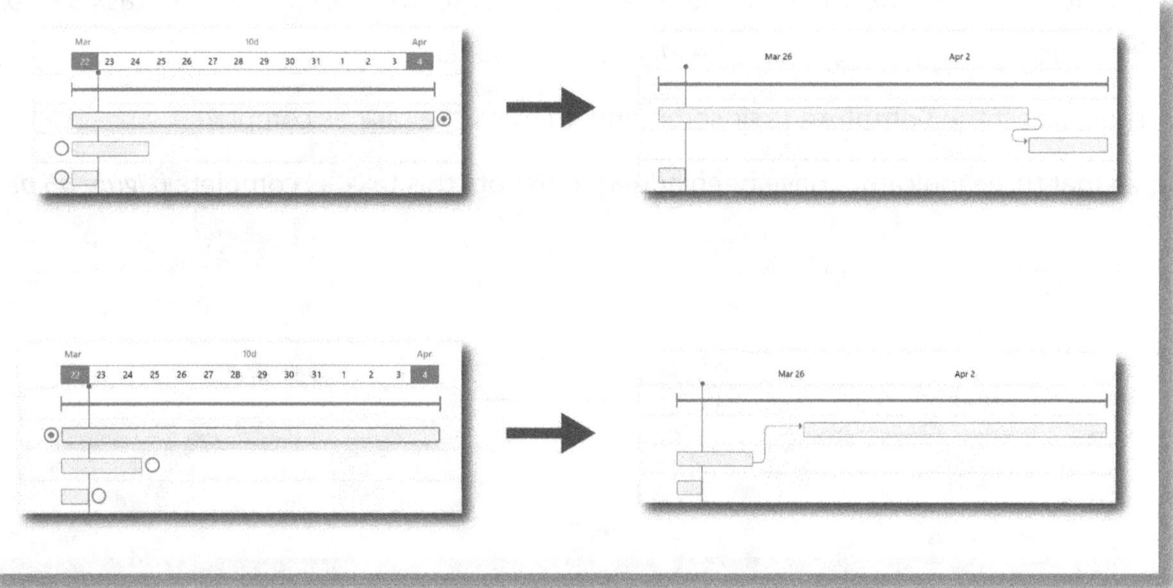

Figure 44 – Create Dependencies in the Timeline View

- **If you click the connector at the right end**, open connectors will appear at the left end of eligible task bars. This means that the finish date of this task will drive the start date of the task you connect it to. To create the dependency, drag the connector to the open connector of the task you want.
- **If you click the connector at the left end**, open connectors will appear at the right end of eligible task bars. This means that the start date of this task will be driven by the finish date of the task you connect it to. To create the dependency, drag the connector to the open connector of the task you want.

NOTE: In the Timeline view, using this click and drag method, you are only able to give tasks the *Finish-to-Start* dependency type. To assign any of the other three dependency types, you will need to use the *Task details* panel.

Step 6 – Start the Project

We will now execute our Rose Bowl Float project. The Timeline view is a handy view for making schedule updates because of its click and drag functionality. We'll start with **Phase 1 – the Approval phase**. The goal of this phase is to secure approval from the Rose Bowl committee to enter a float into the competition. The first task in this phase, task 3 - *Rose Bowl Theme Announced* is a milestone task. Since the Tournament of Roses committee announced the theme on schedule, we can mark this task as complete. We'll do this using the **More options** panel.

- On the left side of the screen in the task list, select the menu ellipsis next to task 3 – *Rose Bowl Theme Announced* to open the *More options* panel.
- Then, select the **Complete task** command, to mark the task as complete.

Notice that three indicators have been added to denote this task as complete (*Figure 45 below*).

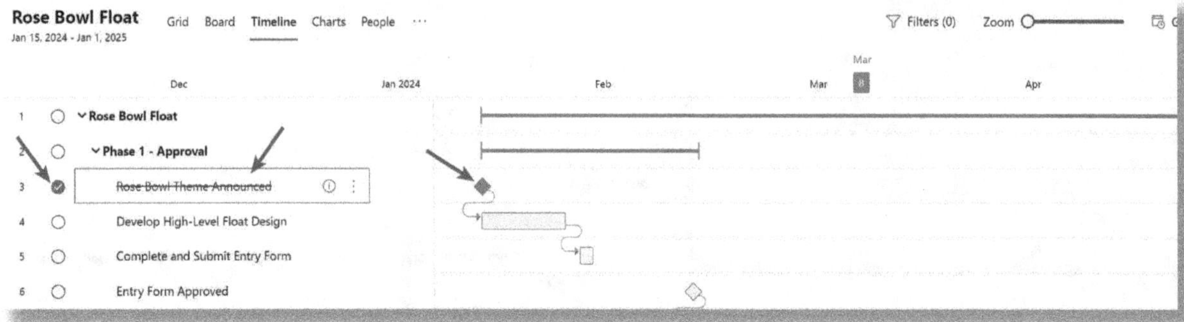

Figure 45 – Complete Task Indicators

A green check-mark was placed in the circle next to the task, the task name has been lined out, and the milestone symbol in the Gantt chart changed color, from a lighter blue to a darker blue. Also, depending on how you've configured the settings, you may have heard a bell chime indicating the task is complete.

The next task in Phase 1, task 4 – *Develop High-Level Float Design* is represented in the Gantt chart by the task bar beneath the task 3 milestone. This task didn't go according to plan. Our team had many questions about the theme and sent them to the Rose Bowl committee. They were slow to get back to us, and as a result, this task was delayed by two days. We'll need to update the schedule accordingly, so that the finish date for this task is 2 days later than we originally planned. If you hover over the task 4 task bar, an interactive timeline bar for this task will appear at the top of the view (*Figure 46 below*).

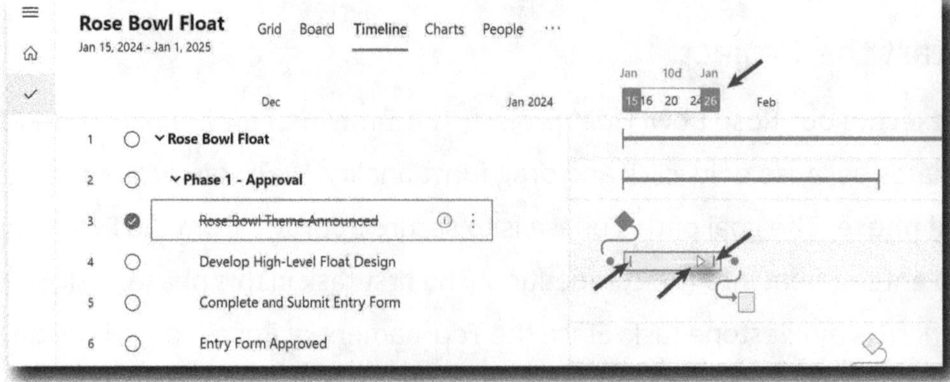

Figure 46 – Interactive Timeline

You can see from the interactive timeline that this task was expected to have a 10-day duration, starting on 1/15/24 and finishing on 1/26/24. Also, when hovering over it, the task bar has a slightly different appearance. There are two small vertical lines at the beginning and end of the task bar. The mouse cursor will also change to a two-headed arrow (*Figure 46*). You can click and drag either of these lines, to the left or to the right, to reschedule the task to an earlier or later date. In this case, task 4 needs to finish two business days later than it's currently scheduled.

- Using the interactive timeline as a guide, click and drag the line on the right of the task bar to the right, until the task finishes on 1/30/24 (two business days later). Task 4 will be updated and rescheduled to complete on 1/31/24. Its duration will also update from 10 days to 12 days.

PFW will alert you that dependencies were removed from this task to move it to the selected date. If you open the *Task details* panel, you will see that the dependency has been removed. Nonetheless, task 5 *Complete and Submit Entry Form*, which depends on this task, was automatically extended two days. It now finishes on 2/1/24. While the delay of task 2 was not welcomed, luckily, we had enough wiggle room in our schedule to accommodate this delay without delaying our project end date. We're still on track to finish on 1/1/25 - Parade Day. You can quickly confirm the project's finish and start dates in the top left corner of the view, beneath the project name. We know from experience, having managed this type of project for a decade, that this phase has a bit of cushion baked in to allow for the Entry Form to be approved. If we were using a full-featured Desktop version of Microsoft Project, we could add the Slack column to a tabular view, to determine how much wiggle room each task has before it will delay the schedule. Even though we don't have this feature available in PFW, we can still get a visual idea of how much wiggle room we have, here in the Timeline view. The period between the end of task 5 - *Complete and Submit Entry Form* and the start of Milestone task 6 - *Entry Form Approved* is the amount of Slack we have before our project would have suffered a delay because of the 2-day delay of task 4 (*Figure 47 below*).

Figure 47 –Slack

Fortunately, task 4 is the only trouble we encountered in Phase 1 of our Float project. The rest of the tasks went as planned. Therefore, we can mark the entire phase complete. This time, we'll use a quicker method to do this.

- Simply select the circle next to task 2 – *Phase 1 Approval.*

All the tasks in Phase 1 should now be noted with the complete task indicators.
Also, notice the task bars for task 4 and task 5 have been updated in the Gantt chart. They're now completely filled in with a darker blue color, indicating that they're 100% complete (*Figure 48*). As mentioned earlier, these bars are Progress Bars. If we had entered a percentage complete for this task, such as 50% complete, then only 50% of the progress bar would be shaded in the darker blue. The diamond symbol representing the task 6 milestone task has also been shaded in the darker blue.

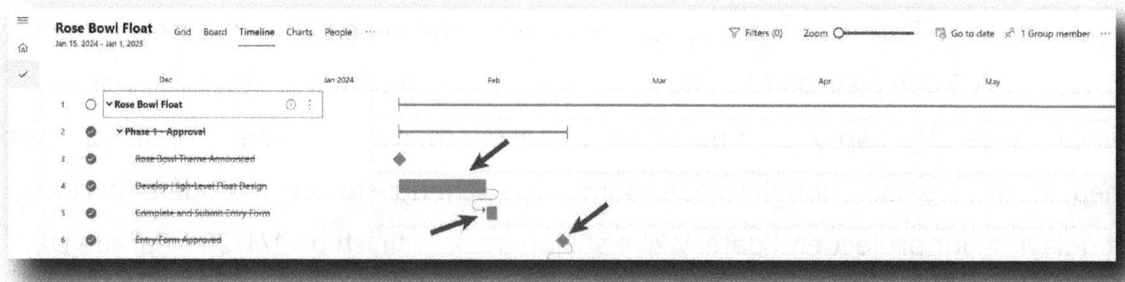

Figure 48 – Completed Task Progress Bars

We will now execute **Phase 2, the Sponsor phase**. The goal of this phase is to provide potential sponsors with enough information to get them excited about our chances of winning the float contest and to motivate them to fund our entry. This is the most important phase of our project as it serves to determine our funding limit and impose requirements that must be met to keep our sponsors happy, such as how their branding must be displayed on our float.

To better see the five Phase 2 task bars, we will adjust the view:

- Collapse the tasks in Phase 1, by selecting the collapse symbol next to task 2.

- Slide the Zoom slider all the way to the left to zoom out on the timeline. Your view should look similar to *Figure 49*.

Figure 49 – Phase 2 Task Bars

If you hover over the task 7 Summary Bar that represents Phase 2, the interactive timeline at the top of the screen will show that this phase is scheduled to start on 2/14/24 and finish on 5/27/24, with a 74-day duration. Since this phase is so important, we managed it very closely to ensure all tasks remained on schedule. Because of our diligence, this phase was executed according to plan.

- To update this progress in our schedule, simply select the circle next to task 7 – *Phase 2 Sponsor* to mark it complete. Your schedule should now look like *Figure 50 below*.

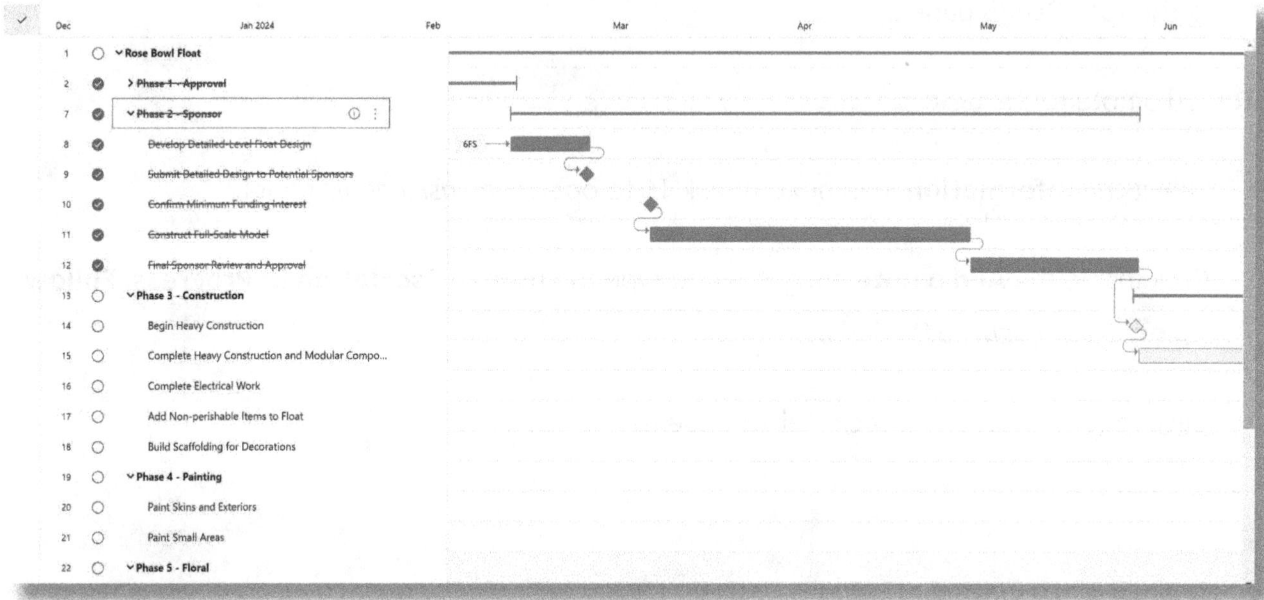

Figure 50 – Phase 2 Marked Complete

The next phase is the **Construction** phase, which is the longest phase in our project. Based on our years of experience managing float projects, we know that most of the delays occur in this phase. After applying lessons learned from prior years, we managed to start task 14 – *Begin Heavy Construction* on time. We've also managed task 15 – *Complete Heavy Construction and Modular Component Build* very tightly – and this task also completed on time.

- Mark tasks 14 and 15 complete by selecting the circles next to the task names.

Unfortunately, we've run into a bit of a problem with task 16 – *Complete Electrical Work*. While managing the Construction crew to keep tasks 14 & 15 on schedule, we failed to notice that the Electrical Contractor had fallen behind schedule. If you hover over the task 16 task bar, you can see that the Electrical Contractor was scheduled to complete their work in 20 days and finish on 9/6/24. They've informed us that they're currently running a week behind schedule. This delay is unacceptable because it will delay all subsequent phases. You can see by the Gantt chart that there is no slack between the subsequent tasks and phases. The 1-week delay is also a problem because one of our sponsors wants their logo to light up on our float. They've scheduled an inspection to approve the logo one week after the electrical work was scheduled to finish.

Since this delay is unacceptable, we've decided to escalate the matter to the owner of the Electrical Contractor's company. They've informed us that they need a week to investigate the matter and they'll get back to us. To remind ourselves to follow up, we'll add a note to task 16 using the *Task Details* panel.

To add a note to the task:

- Select the **Information** icon next to task 16 to open the *Task details* panel.
- Click inside the **Add a note** entry cell and type the note – **"Escalation in Progress. Follow up on 8/23"** (*Figure 51*)
- Click the **X** in the top right corner to close the panel.

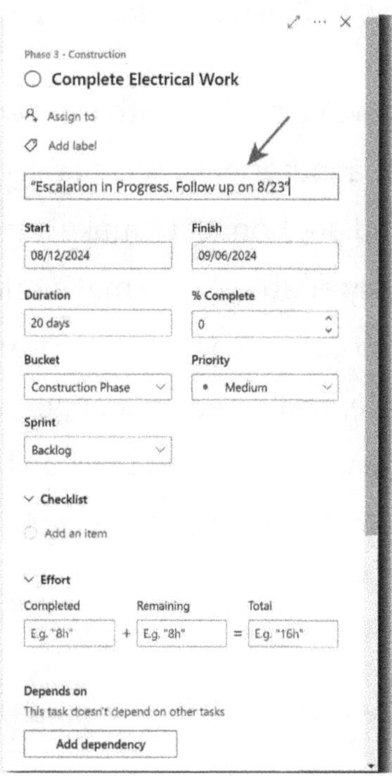

Figure 51 – Add a Task Note

To view the note, switch to the Grid view. You will see a note icon in the **Quick look** column, in the row for task 16 (*Figure 52 below*). If you select the icon, it will re-open the *Task details* panel where you can read the note.

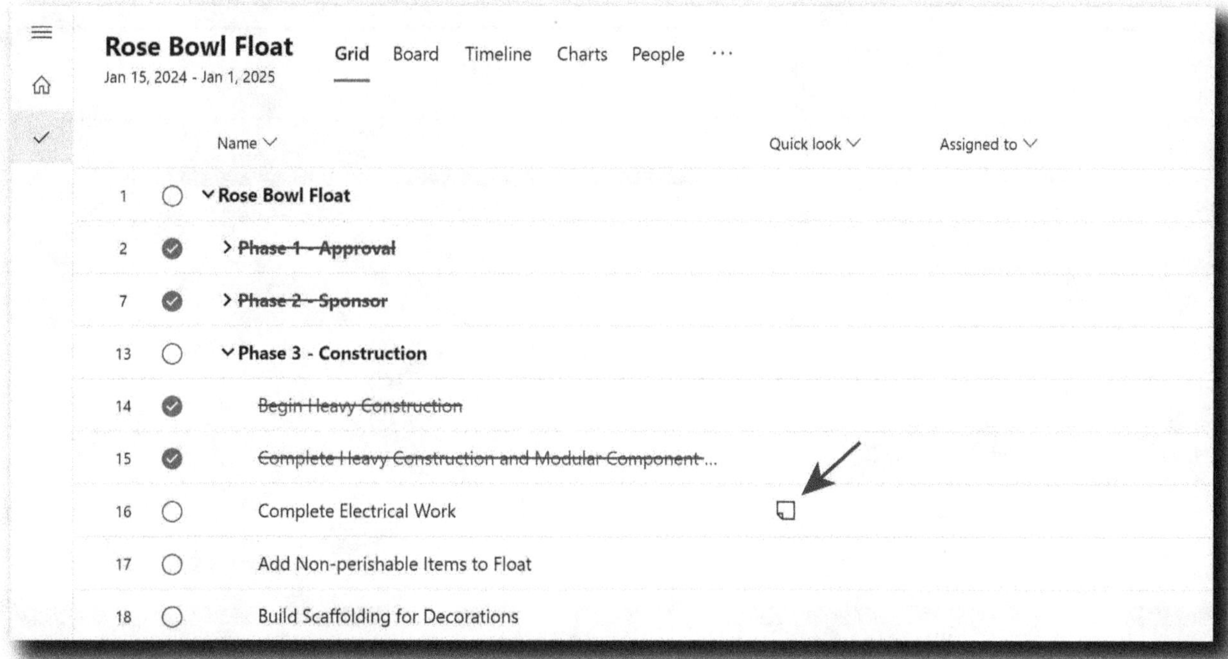

Figure 52 – Task Note Quick Look Column

- Switch back to the Timeline view to finish executing Phase 3 of our schedule.

Assume one week has passed and we've spoken with the owner of the Electrical contractor company. They've agreed to assign another electrician at no additional charge. They know we've won this event in the past and are hoping to make a good impression for future business opportunities. This not only enables us to make our sponsor's inspection date, but the Electrical contractors manage to complete their work early in 15 days instead of 20 days! To make this update in our schedule, we'll need to change the finish date of task 16 from 9/6/24 to 8/30/24, which is 5 business days earlier. We'll do this the same way we updated the finish date for Task 4. Except, this time, we'll slide the task bar to the left.

To update the task 16 finish date:

- Using the interactive timeline as a guide, click and slide the right line at the end of the task 16 task bar to the left to **8/30/24** on the timeline.

Task 16 should now be rescheduled to finish on 8/30/24. Your schedule should look like *Figure 53 below.*

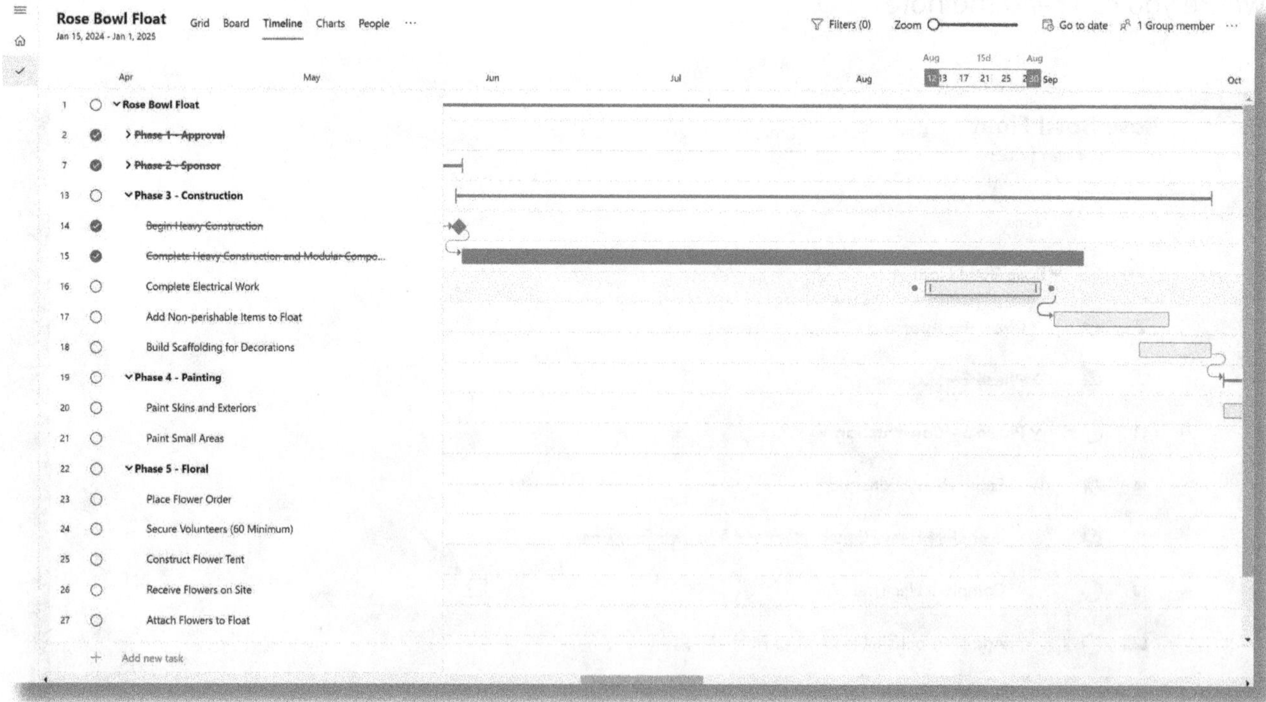

Figure 53 – Task 16 Updated

After the matter with the Electrical contractor was addressed, the remaining two tasks in this phase went according to plan. So, we can close out Phase 3.

- Mark task 13 – *Phase 3 – Construction* complete.

In Phase 4, we completed the **Painting** and in Phase 5, we completed the very important **Floral** phase. Based on our years of experience and lessons learned, we managed these phases very tightly. As a result, they also went according to plan and can be also closed out.

- Mark task 19 – *Phase 4 – Painting* complete.

- Mark task 22 – *Phase 5 – Floral* complete.

After marking Phase 3, Phase 4 and Phase 5 complete, your schedule should look like *Figure 54 below.*

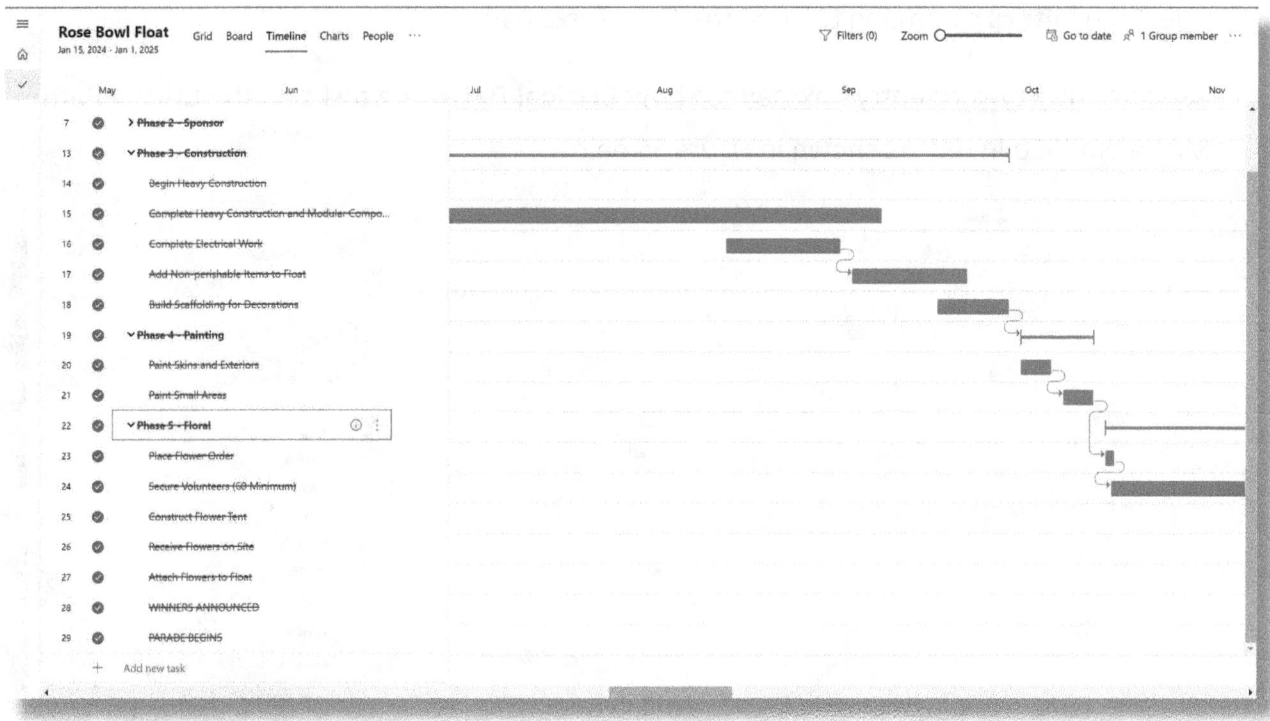

Figure 54 – All Phases Executed

Congratulations! We have now built and executed our Rose Bowl Float project using Project for the Web – applying the B.A.S.I.C.S. scheduling process. To finish our tour of the PFW interface, we will look at the remaining views and functions that we haven't reviewed.

Display Your Project's Critical Path

Microsoft is regularly adding features and updates to PFW to make the app more efficient for managing projects. One of the more recent and useful updates is the ability to display your project's **Critical Path**. The critical path directly affects the project finish date. It allows schedulers to know which tasks to focus on to execute faster, and which have the potential to delay the schedule if they're late. The critical path feature in PFW doesn't have the robust functionality as the feature does in the desktop versions of Microsoft Project. For example, in the desktop versions you can set up your project to display multiple critical paths. You can also change what shows up on the critical path. You can tell Project to include tasks with one or more days of slack, so you can forecast potential problems. In PFW, the **Filters** command is used to display the project's critical path. Although the Filters command is accessible in every view, you must be in the **Timeline** view to show the critical path.

To display the Critical Path:

- Select the **Filters** command to open the *Filter Tasks* panel.
- Beneath the keyword entry box, select **Show Critical Path**. The tasks on the Critical Path will be outlined in red, as shown in *Figure 55* below.

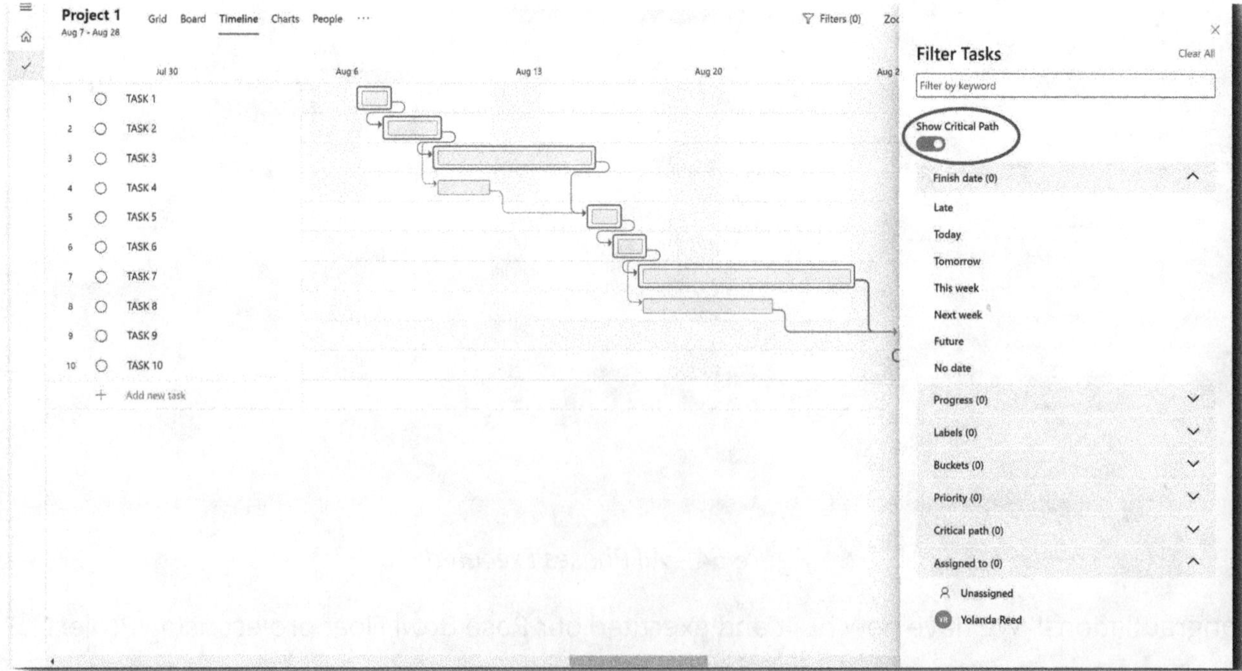

Figure 55 – Display the Critical Path

You can also filter the view to show only the tasks on the Critical Path:

- In the *Filter Tasks* panel, select **Critical path** from the list of filtering options. Then, select **Critical**.
- Select **Clear All** to clear the filter.

The Charts view

The **Charts view** shows you an at-a-glance graphical view of your project status. To switch to the Charts view, select the **Charts** quick access link, located at the top of the view, on the left. *Figure 56* below shows a Construction project in the Charts view.

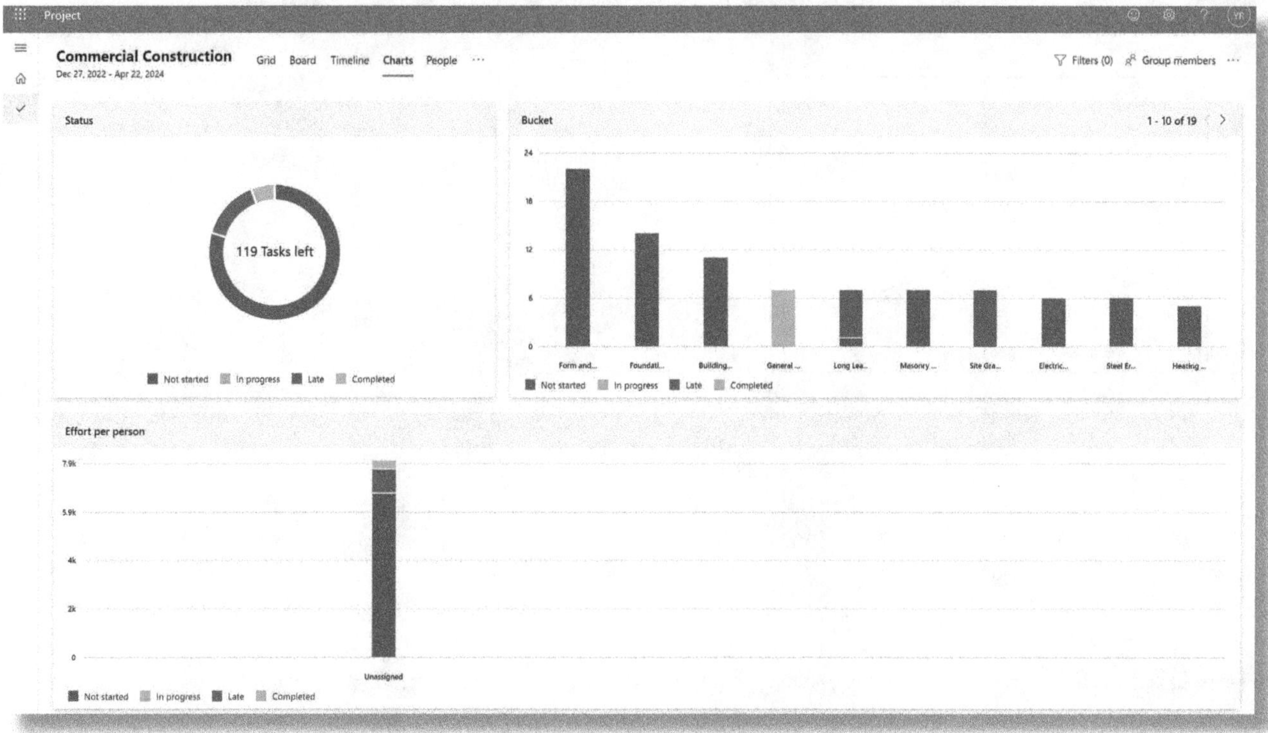

Figure 56 – The Charts View

In the top left area, you'll find the status of all the tasks in your project, depicted in a donut plot chart. The progress categories are – Not Started, In Progress, Late and Completed as shown in the legend below the chart.

In the center of the chart, you'll see the number of tasks that are left in the project. If you hover over a category in the chart or the legend, you'll see the specific number of tasks in that category.

In the top right area, you'll find a bar chart depicting the status of tasks, sorted by their Buckets. Recall that tasks are organized with Buckets in the Board view.

In the Bottom area, you'll find a bar chart depicting the Effort – or work hours – per person. If you hover over a category in the chart or the legend, you'll see the work hours for that category. The tasks in this project don't have resources assigned to them. So, the results are shown in the *Unassigned* category.

Figure 57 shows our Rose Bowl Float project in the Charts view. Since the project is fully executed, both charts show all tasks as complete. The bottom pane is empty because no effort has been entered for any of the tasks.

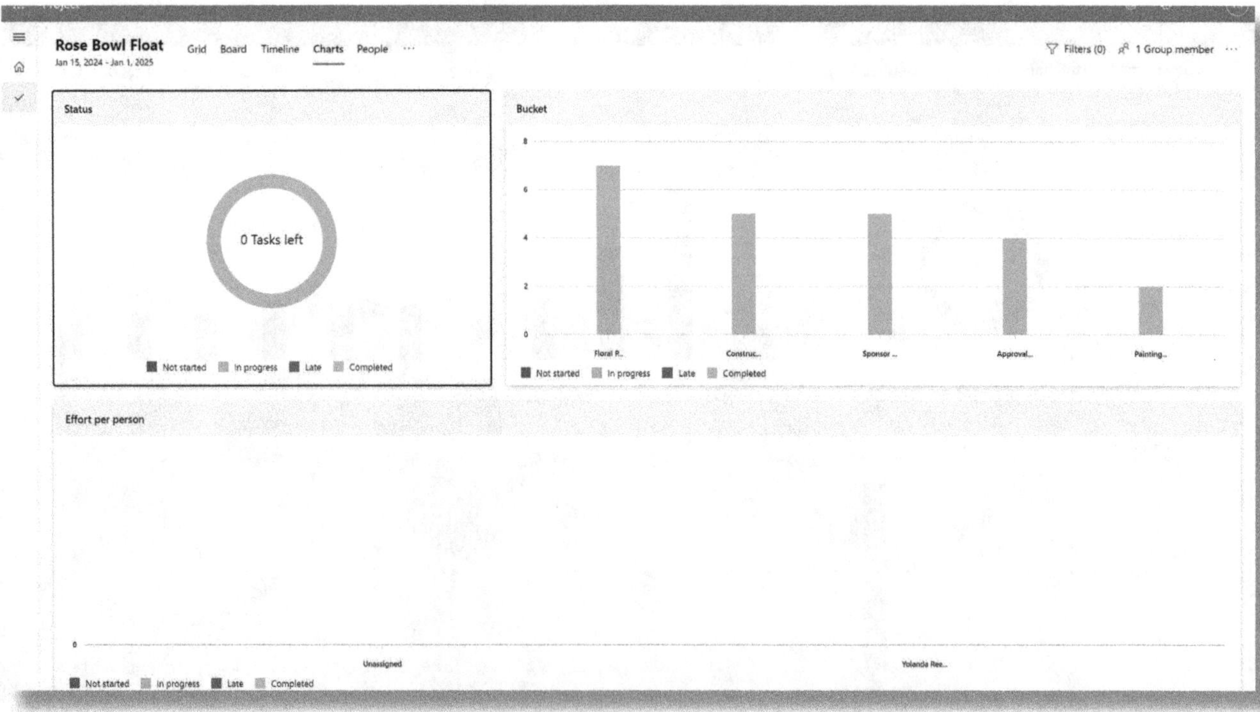

Figure 57 – Float Project in the Charts View

The People View

In the **People view** you can manage the task assignments for your project and quickly assess where team members may be over or under-allocated. Assigning resources to tasks isn't as streamlined in PFW as in the Desktop versions of Microsoft Project, where resources are created and assigned right in the app. To assign resources in PFW, you must first connect your project to a **Microsoft 365 group**. You can then assign group members to tasks and manage those assignments in the People view.

Each member with at least one task assigned to them will be represented with a **People card** which summarizes their assigned tasks (*Figure 58*).

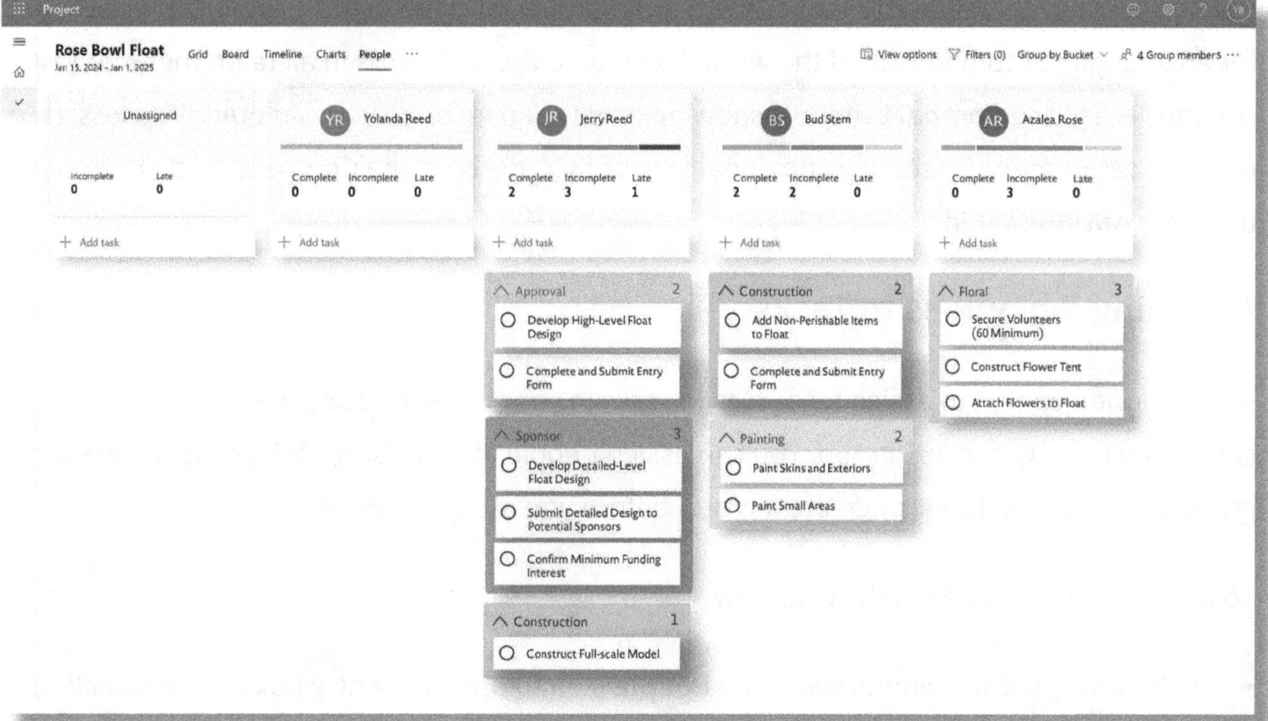

Figure 58 – The People View

The default People card view summarizes the person's current count of Incomplete and Late tasks. Below each card is a column containing additional information about the person's assigned tasks. You can enable PFW to also include Complete tasks on the cards. You can do this using the **View Options** settings (*Figure 59* below), located next to the Filters command in the top right corner of the view.

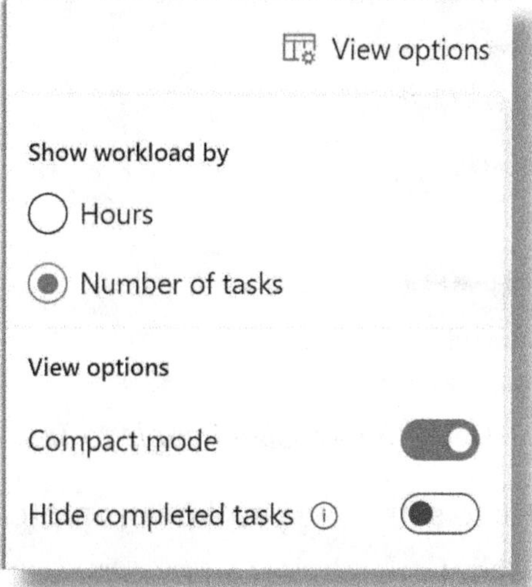

Figure 59 – The People View – View Options

You can also change the view to display the workload tallies by the number of tasks or by hours. *Number of tasks* is selected by default. The people-card tally bars indicate each person's task (or hour) count relative to that of the team member with the highest total. This is handy for an at-a-glance comparison of the work. By default, the task cards in all team member task columns are in the **Compact mode** – showing only task names, so you can quickly assess each person's assignment. To display additional task details, deselect the Compact mode button in the **View options** settings.

Assigning Resources to Tasks

As mentioned earlier, to assign resources to tasks in your project, your project must be connected to an Office 365 group. You can assign people to an existing 365 group, create a group as you assign tasks, or create a group before you assign tasks.

To assign people to tasks in the Grid view:

- In the **Assigned to** column, select the **People** icon to open the entry box (*Figure 60 below*). Select a person from the shown list or type a name in the search box.

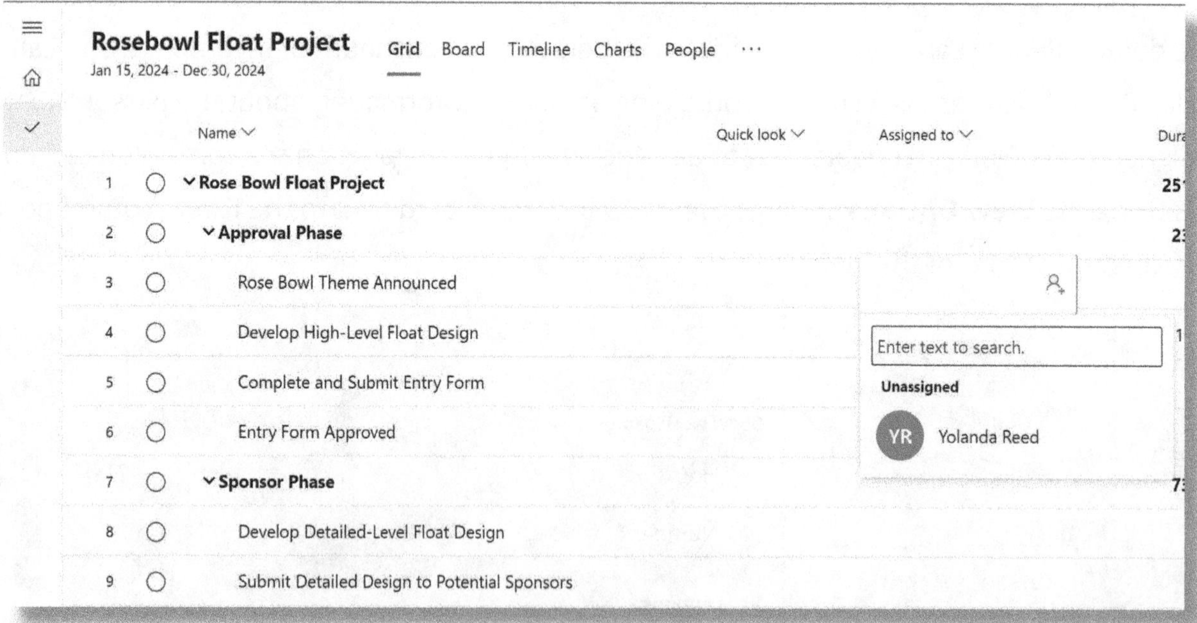

Figure 60 – Assign People to Tasks

The first time you assign a task to someone you'll be prompted to connect the project to a group (*Figure 61*). The group members you assign to tasks will become part of that group.

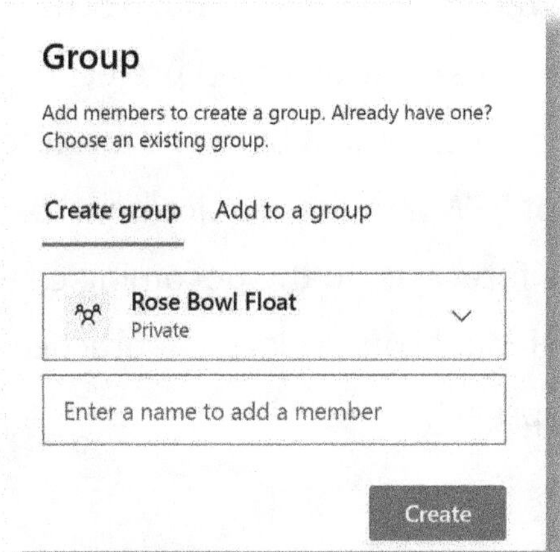

Figure 61 – Add or Create an Office 365 Group

- To create a new group, select **Create group** and then select **Create** and assign the group. A pane will appear on the right where you can name your project.

- To share the project with an existing group, select **Add to a group**, select the group, and then select **Add** and assign the group.

The Assignments View

To conclude our tour of the PFW interface, next to the People link on the Views menu, you'll find ellipses that take you to the **Assignments** view. This view displays a table of the task assignments in your project. The table includes the resources, the tasks they're assigned to, and their work hours (effort). This view is similar to the Resource Usage view in the Microsoft Project Desktop versions, but not as exhaustive. To use this view, you must first enter the effort values for the tasks using the *Task details* panel, as we reviewed earlier.

As you can see, Project for the Web includes just enough scheduling capability to manage a simple project that requires more task tracking than project management. If your project is more complex than the simple project we just built and executed, there's an increased risk that the scheduling limitations of PFW and the requirement for manual updates, will increase your risk of inaccurate schedule forecasts. In the upcoming chapters, you'll learn to use the full-featured desktop versions of Microsoft Project in a practical context – applying all six-steps of the B.A.S.I.C.S. scheduling approach.

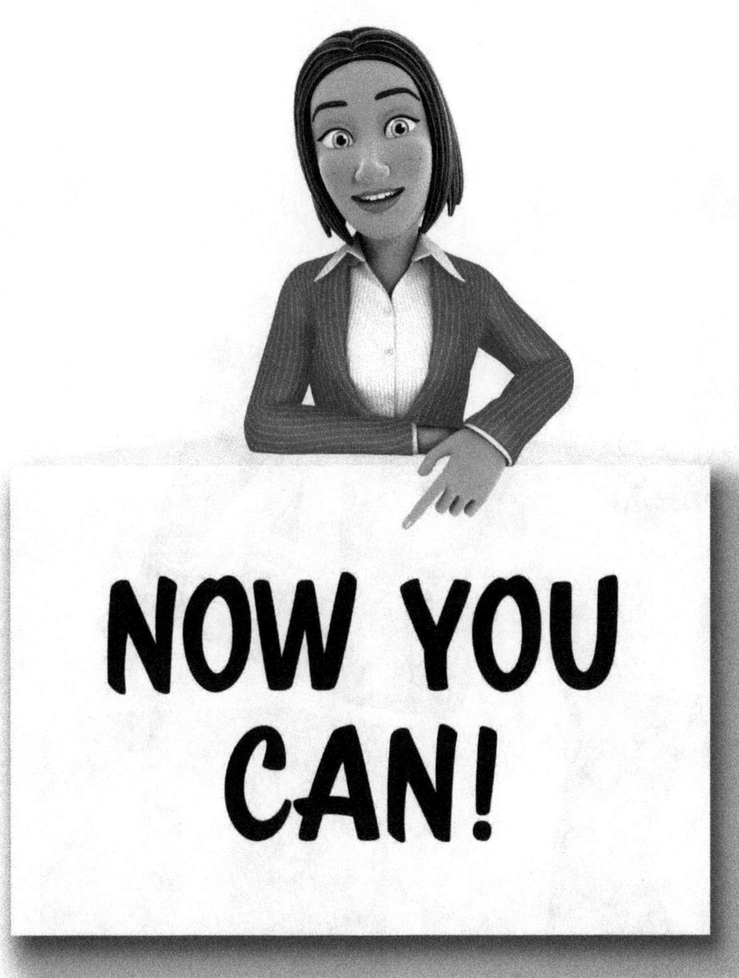

- ✓ Navigate the Project for the Web Interface
- ✓ Use the different Views to organize a project and work with tasks
- ✓ Apply the **B.A.S.I.C.S.** scheduling process to build a project schedule
- ✓ Use the Charts view to check project status
- ✓ Use the Timeline View to execute a project

A
B
C

PART ONE Laying the Foundation

PART ONE introduces you to Microsoft Project. You'll learn the advantages of scheduling with Microsoft Project over scheduling with Excel. You'll learn important scheduling fundamentals, like building a Work Breakdown Structure, working with task relationships and the two ways to build a schedule. You'll also learn to build your schedule outline using the key components of a schedule – tasks, summary tasks, project summary tasks, and milestones.

In **Part Two – Building the Schedule**, we'll put these fundamentals into practice.

Chapter 1 Why Not Use Excel for Scheduling

IN THIS CHAPTER we'll address the question – **Why Not Use Excel for Scheduling**? When you're done, you'll be able to explain the benefits of scheduling with Microsoft Project over Excel, what a true scheduling app is, why scheduling problems persist in modern Project Management environments, and the competitive advantages of using Microsoft Project.

WE'LL DISCUSS:

- Excel or Project?
- Microsoft Project in Project Management Practice
- Ten Criteria for a True Scheduling App
- Competitive Advantages of using Microsoft Project
- Microsoft Project and the Triple Constraints

Most project management environments don't require project managers to use full-featured scheduling software like Microsoft Project to build schedules. Many leaders believe that Project Managers should have the autonomy to use their tool of choice to build their schedules. I've observed this tendency while managing projects in the telecommunications industry, among my professional services clients, and with my students who work in various fields, such as oil, entertainment, health care, event planning, and defense. A notable exception has been the construction industry. Because their schedules can easily become the focus of legal disputes, they generally use more robust tools.

New project managers who take our courses are generally surprised to learn that full-featured scheduling apps like Microsoft Project are considered optional in professional project management environments. They frequently ask, *"How can project managers keep projects on track without a true scheduling solution?"* The answer is – they escalate and trade favors to pressure resources into prioritizing their projects ahead of operational needs and other projects. As you might imagine, these practices introduce risk, circumvent sound processes, and make inefficient use of company resources. The view that full-featured scheduling software is optional limits, rather than liberates, project managers. It results in schedules being imposed by business pressures when they should be built using realistic task durations and dependencies. Mandating that a project finishes on a specified date is like mandating that a potato be oven-baked in 15 minutes. Like a potato, every project has a minimum required duration. Full-featured scheduling apps like Microsoft Project are designed to help businesses determine what that minimum required duration is. This knowledge affords them the opportunity to balance the needs of the business with the constraints of the business.

Another consequence of project managers not using full-featured scheduling apps is that it undermines key aspects of the project manager's role, such as advising stakeholders on project dependencies, developing realistic options for compressing schedules, and clearly communicating the real trade-offs for getting a project back on schedule. The trade-offs typically include resource, risk, quality, and cost impacts. The goal of this chapter is to convey the real risks of using apps like Excel to manage schedules. Among these risks are unrealistic schedules and project delays. In the next section we'll demonstrate this premise, by comparing schedules built in both Excel and Project, and highlighting the differences.

Scheduling with Excel?

Figure 62 below shows a schedule for a House Painting project built in Excel. The schedule shows that if you started the project on 6/3/24, you'd finish in 20 days (not counting weekends) on 6/28/24. This schedule seems reliable enough.

So... why not use Excel for scheduling?

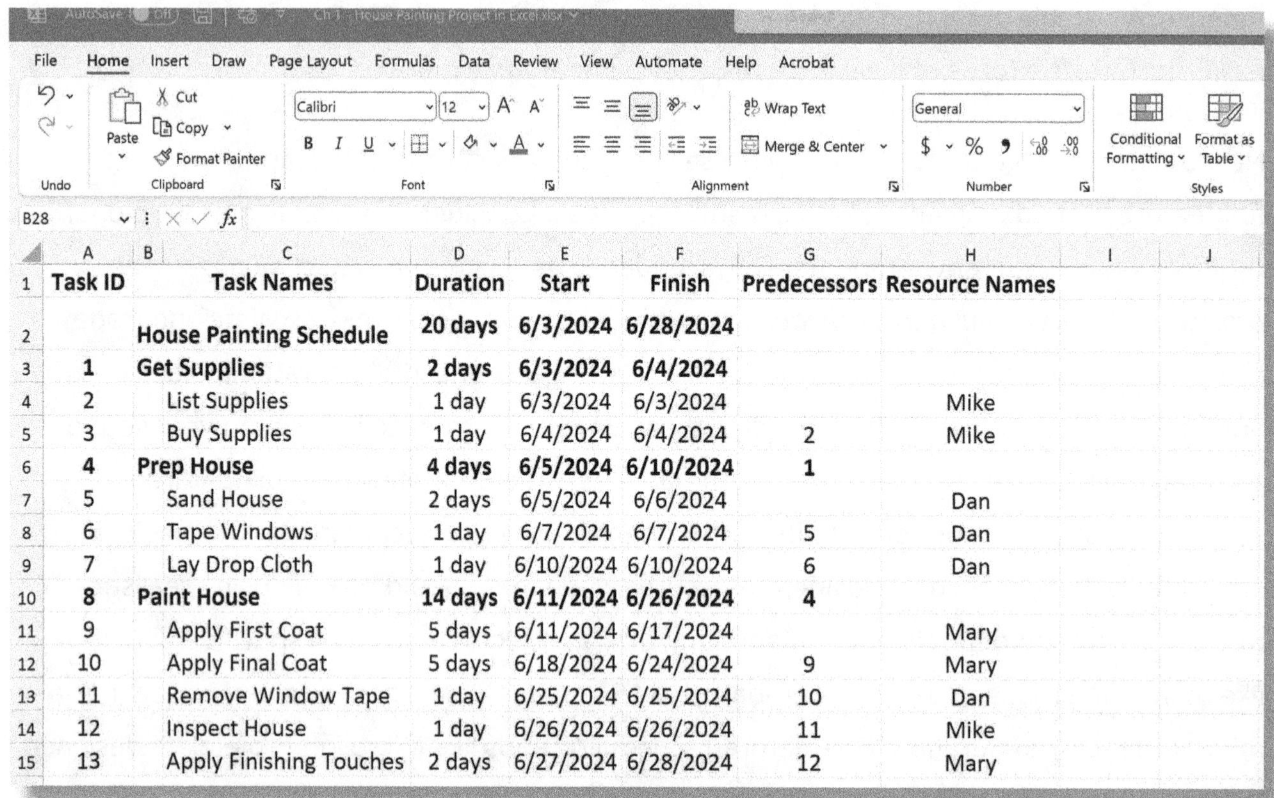

Task ID	Task Names	Duration	Start	Finish	Predecessors	Resource Names
	House Painting Schedule	**20 days**	**6/3/2024**	**6/28/2024**		
1	**Get Supplies**	**2 days**	**6/3/2024**	**6/4/2024**		
2	List Supplies	1 day	6/3/2024	6/3/2024		Mike
3	Buy Supplies	1 day	6/4/2024	6/4/2024	2	Mike
4	**Prep House**	**4 days**	**6/5/2024**	**6/10/2024**	**1**	
5	Sand House	2 days	6/5/2024	6/6/2024		Dan
6	Tape Windows	1 day	6/7/2024	6/7/2024	5	Dan
7	Lay Drop Cloth	1 day	6/10/2024	6/10/2024	6	Dan
8	**Paint House**	**14 days**	**6/11/2024**	**6/26/2024**	**4**	
9	Apply First Coat	5 days	6/11/2024	6/17/2024		Mary
10	Apply Final Coat	5 days	6/18/2024	6/24/2024	9	Mary
11	Remove Window Tape	1 day	6/25/2024	6/25/2024	10	Dan
12	Inspect House	1 day	6/26/2024	6/26/2024	11	Mike
13	Apply Finishing Touches	2 days	6/27/2024	6/28/2024	12	Mary

Figure 62 – House Painting Schedule in Excel

If no changes are needed and every task is executed exactly according to the plan, this Excel schedule will work fine. But in reality, schedules rarely, if ever, go according to plan. So, let's suppose that during execution, you discover that one of the tasks will take longer than expected. Since the house was last painted many years ago, Task 5 – *Sand House*, will take 3 days instead of 2 days. How would you make this schedule update in Excel?

To begin, the duration of Task 5 must be updated from 2 days to 3 days. The finish date must also be updated from 6/6/24 to 6/7/24. Then, you will need to manually update the start and finish dates of every task impacted by this change. This is where the Predecessors column is useful.

It shows which tasks will be affected if another task is updated. Since nearly every task in the schedule has a predecessor and occurs in sequence, changing the duration and finish date of one task will have a domino effect.

Figure 63 below shows the updated House Painting schedule. Each highlighted cell was impacted by the change.

Task ID	Task Names	Duration	Start	Finish	Predecessors	Resource Names
	House Painting Schedule	**21**	**6/3/2024**	**7/1/2024**		
1	**Get Supplies**	**2 days**	**6/3/2024**	**6/4/2024**		
2	List Supplies	1 day	6/3/2024	6/3/2024		Mike
3	Buy Supplies	1 day	6/4/2024	6/4/2024	2	Mike
4	**Prep House**	**5 days**	**6/5/2024**	**6/11/2024**	**1**	
5	Sand House	3 days	6/5/2024	6/7/2024		Dan
6	Tape Windows	1 day	6/10/2024	6/10/2024	5	Dan
7	Lay Drop Cloth	1 day	6/11/2024	6/11/2024	6	Dan
8	**Paint House**	**14 days**	**6/12/2024**	**7/1/2024**	**4**	
9	Apply First Coat	5 days	6/12/2024	6/18/2024		Mary
10	Apply Final Coat	5 days	6/19/2024	6/25/2024	9	Mary
11	Remove Window Tape	1 day	6/26/2024	6/26/2024	10	Dan
12	Inspect House	1 day	6/27/2024	6/27/2024	11	Mike
13	Apply Finishing Touches	2 days	6/28/2024	7/1/2024	12	Mary

Figure 63 – Updated House Painting Schedule in Excel

As you can see, twenty-two cells had to be manually updated to account for the delay of task 5. To determine which cells to update, it was imperative to include a Predecessors column. This surfaces an important question. Would every scheduler know to add a Predecessors column to their Excel schedule? If not, there's a good chance several cells would have been missed, resulting in an inaccurate schedule forecast. Moreover, the House Painting schedule includes only 13 tasks. Therefore, if we were careful, we might be able to account for each impacted cell. But what if this was a larger, more complex schedule? Imagine the number of impacted cells if this schedule included a typical number of project tasks, which could easily exceed 50 tasks. The chance of missing one of the impacted cells would increase significantly.

Excel power users might suggest creating formulas to automate the changes throughout the schedule. But note that the tasks in this schedule occur sequentially, which is not always the case. Therefore, creating formulas to account for each task dependency type would be time consuming, inefficient, and increasingly error prone as the number of tasks and manual updates increase. Microsoft's purpose statements for developing each of these apps support this point. Excel was designed for "data analysis and documentation". Microsoft Project was designed to "develop schedules, assign resources to tasks, analyze workloads, track progress, and manage project budgets". The intended function for these apps plainly supports the scheduling advantages of Microsoft Project over Microsoft Excel.

To place these advantages into context, *Figure 64* below shows the same House Painting schedule built in Microsoft Project.

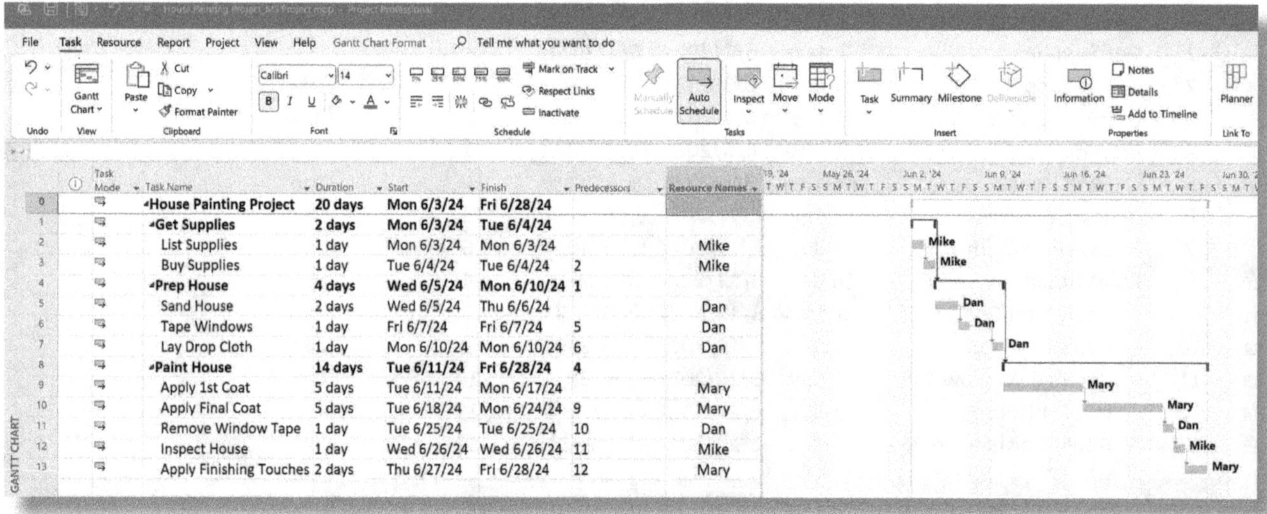

	Task Name	Duration	Start	Finish	Predecessors	Resource Names
0	**House Painting Project**	**20 days**	**Mon 6/3/24**	**Fri 6/28/24**		
1	**Get Supplies**	**2 days**	**Mon 6/3/24**	**Tue 6/4/24**		
2	List Supplies	1 day	Mon 6/3/24	Mon 6/3/24		Mike
3	Buy Supplies	1 day	Tue 6/4/24	Tue 6/4/24	2	Mike
4	**Prep House**	**4 days**	**Wed 6/5/24**	**Mon 6/10/24**	**1**	
5	Sand House	2 days	Wed 6/5/24	Thu 6/6/24		Dan
6	Tape Windows	1 day	Fri 6/7/24	Fri 6/7/24	5	Dan
7	Lay Drop Cloth	1 day	Mon 6/10/24	Mon 6/10/24	6	Dan
8	**Paint House**	**14 days**	**Tue 6/11/24**	**Fri 6/28/24**	**4**	
9	Apply 1st Coat	5 days	Tue 6/11/24	Mon 6/17/24		Mary
10	Apply Final Coat	5 days	Tue 6/18/24	Mon 6/24/24	9	Mary
11	Remove Window Tape	1 day	Tue 6/25/24	Tue 6/25/24	10	Dan
12	Inspect House	1 day	Wed 6/26/24	Wed 6/26/24	11	Mike
13	Apply Finishing Touches	2 days	Thu 6/27/24	Fri 6/28/24	12	Mary

Figure 64 – House Painting Schedule in Project

One notable advantage of Project is the Gantt Chart shown on the right side of the screen. Project uses the schedule information on the left and automatically generates this graphical depiction of the timeline. We'll review the Gantt chart more in Chapter 2, "Getting to Know Project". In Project, updating the entire schedule to account for the delay of task 5 – *Sand House*, is as easy as entering the new 3-day duration into the Duration field. *Figure 65* shows the results of the schedule update in Project.

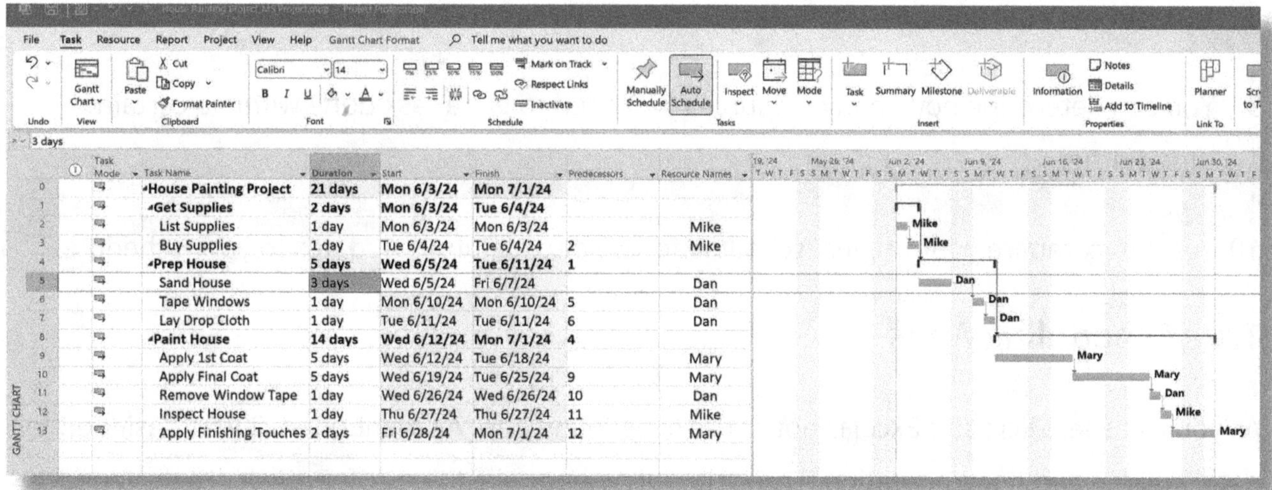

	Task Mode	Task Name	Duration	Start	Finish	Predecessors	Resource Names
0		**House Painting Project**	**21 days**	**Mon 6/3/24**	**Mon 7/1/24**		
1		**Get Supplies**	**2 days**	**Mon 6/3/24**	**Tue 6/4/24**		
2		List Supplies	1 day	Mon 6/3/24	Mon 6/3/24		Mike
3		Buy Supplies	1 day	Tue 6/4/24	Tue 6/4/24	2	Mike
4		**Prep House**	**5 days**	**Wed 6/5/24**	**Tue 6/11/24**	1	
5		Sand House	3 days	Wed 6/5/24	Fri 6/7/24		Dan
6		Tape Windows	1 day	Mon 6/10/24	Mon 6/10/24	5	Dan
7		Lay Drop Cloth	1 day	Tue 6/11/24	Tue 6/11/24	6	Dan
8		**Paint House**	**14 days**	**Wed 6/12/24**	**Mon 7/1/24**	4	
9		Apply 1st Coat	5 days	Wed 6/12/24	Tue 6/18/24		Mary
10		Apply Final Coat	5 days	Wed 6/19/24	Tue 6/25/24	9	Mary
11		Remove Window Tape	1 day	Wed 6/26/24	Wed 6/26/24	10	Dan
12		Inspect House	1 day	Thu 6/27/24	Thu 6/27/24	11	Mike
13		Apply Finishing Touches	2 days	Fri 6/28/24	Mon 7/1/24	12	Mary

Figure 65 – Updated House Painting Schedule in Project

After the duration for the *Sand House* task was updated, Project automatically updated the start and finish dates of each impacted task, using the task dependencies in the Predecessors field. Non-working times, like weekends and vacation days were also factored into the update. Project also automatically highlighted all updated cells in blue, so users know exactly what changes were made. This feature is called **Change Highlighting**. Because the scheduling updates are automated in Project, users can be confident that all changes are made.

Here are ten important scheduling tasks you can perform with Microsoft Project that you can't with Microsoft Excel:

1. You can create a schedule based on task relationships.

2. You can view your schedule's Critical Path (we will define this term later, but it's a BIG deal!)

3. You can provide realistic commitment dates.

4. You can provide realistic schedule compression possibilities.

5. You can easily create what-if scenarios to see the impact on your schedule.

6. You can automatically update the schedule when changes occur to a task.

7. You can receive notifications of entries that defy scheduling logic.

8. You can see how adding or removing resources will impact your schedule.

9. You can determine how many resources you need to get a task done within a certain time-frame.

10. You can compare your original schedule forecast to all future updates to your schedule.

True Scheduling Apps

As you can see, Microsoft Excel is not a true scheduling app. As mentioned, it was designed for data analysis and documentation. True scheduling apps like Microsoft Project are designed to help you build schedules, assign resources to tasks, analyze resource workloads, track scheduling progress, and manage project cost. Despite the usefulness and importance of these capabilities, there is a growing trend toward cloud-based project management apps, such as Wrike®, Monday.com®, and Project for the Web. These apps are great for collaboration and project administration, but lack the features required to manage and control project schedules. The makers of such apps are exploiting a little-known knowledge gap. There is a significant difference between a project management app and a scheduling app. To ensure you're using the right tool for the projects you manage, you should be clear about what constitutes a full featured scheduling app.

What True Scheduling Apps Should Do

Following is a list of the fundamental criteria all true scheduling apps are designed to address. You can use this list to justify the cost of a Microsoft Project license if your organization uses a solution that is project management-rich – but scheduling-poor. Here are ten things you must be able to do to build, manage and control your schedule from project initiation to project delivery. A capable scheduling app will include each of these fundamental features.

1. **THE ABILITY TO USE ALL FOUR TASK RELATIONSHIP (DEPENDENCY) TYPES**.
   The total duration of your project is not determined by how many tasks you must complete or the sum of their combined durations. It's determined by how those tasks depend upon one another. Some tasks must finish before others can start. Therefore, they required the Finish-to-Start (FS) relationship type. Others must at least start before others can finish, requiring the Start-to-Finish (SF) relationship type. Some tasks must start together, requiring the Start-to-Start (SS) relationship type.

Finally, some must finish together, requiring the Finish-to-Finish (FF) relationship. In a project of any size or complexity, you must have the ability to use all four task relationship types to accurately determine your project's duration. As you'll learn in Chapter 4, each task relationship type serves a unique scheduling function, and they are not interchangeable. Therefore, the needs of your project, and not the limitations of your app, should determine which task relationships you use.

2. **THE ABILITY TO ADD LAGS AND LEADS BETWEEN TASKS.** In conjunction with using the different task relationships, you may need to advance or delay a task's start date. For example, if task 1 is to paint a wall and task 2 is to hang a picture on that wall, how does one account for the time it takes the paint to dry before you can hang the picture? This is the type of issue that **Lag time** addresses. The time required for paint to dry is the lag time between the finish of task 1 (paint wall) and the start of task 2 (hang picture). **Lead time** addresses a different condition. It allows for a successor task to begin before its predecessor finishes. Suppose your task is to paint the broad areas of a house. Your friend's task is to paint the detailed areas after you finish. It will take you 3 days to paint your areas and 2 days for your friend to paint hers. Therefore, it will take 5 days to complete both areas. However, if your friend is able to begin painting her areas 1 day after you begin painting, you could then finish both areas in 3 days. In this case, your friend's task used 2-days of lead time, meaning the successor task started two days before the predecessor task finished. If your app does not allow you to create lag time and lead time, you will be unable to account for these types of common scheduling scenarios. We'll cover this important feature in Chapter 4.

3. **THE ABILITY TO ASSIGN RESOURCES TO TASKS.** Almost all cloud-based project management apps like Project for the Web and Monday.com® include the ability to assign resources to tasks. However, some require that you integrate with other services such as Microsoft 365 Groups. Also, you can only assign a resource to work on tasks the entire day and not part of the day. In most cases, your resources will only work on their assigned task for part of the day and not the whole day. Therefore, your scheduling app should include the ability to assign resources to tasks per their actual availability. We'll cover this important feature in Chapters 8 and 13.

4. **THE ABILITY TO AUTO-UPDATE THE SCHEDULE WHEN RESOURCES ARE ADDED OR REMOVED.** Most stakeholders expect that if they approve overtime or add more resources to a task, the duration of the task or project should decrease. Being able to forecast the schedule impacts of these additional resources would be useful for persuading stakeholders to provide them. This is a basic feature of true scheduling apps like Microsoft Project. In Project, this feature is called *effort-driven scheduling*. When this function is enabled, your task durations will automatically decrease or increase if you add or remove resources from tasks. This will allow you to set the right expectations based on the staff you have on hand to complete the work. We'll cover this important feature in Chapter 5.

5. **THE ABILITY TO ADD CONSTRAINTS TO OVERRIDE TASK DEPENDENCIES.** As mentioned in the first criterion, task relationships are the primary drivers of total project duration. Notwithstanding, there are times you will need to delay a task, even though the task it depends on is complete. Other business factors may prevent it from starting, such as delayed funding. In cases like this, you would need to use a **Constraint**. Constraints enable tasks to be scheduled based upon your business reality and not solely based upon task relationships. For example, sometimes you may need to force a task to start on a certain date, thereby requiring a *Must Start On* (MSO) constraint. Other times, a task may be able to start any time after a specific date, thereby requiring a *Start No Earlier Than* (SNE) constraint. Other times, you may allow your resources the flexibility to start a task whenever they have time, as long as it's started before a certain date. You would achieve this using a *Start-No-Later-Than* (SNL) constraint. As you'll discover in Chapter 11, there are eight such constraints available to use for building schedules. Which constraints you use should be determined by the needs of your project and not the limitations of your scheduling app.

6. **THE ABILITY TO BASELINE YOUR SCHEDULE.** No matter how skilled you become at managing projects, you will encounter scheduling delays. When you do, you'll need to assess the damage by referencing the original schedule. This record of the original schedule is called a **Baseline**. Although your schedule will change from week to week, your baseline will not. Therefore, when stakeholders ask whether you're ahead of schedule or behind schedule, they're really asking whether you're ahead of your schedule baseline or behind your schedule baseline. This is an important feature to have if you're expected to stick to your original schedule. We'll cover this feature in Chapter 15.

7. **THE ABILITY TO EXPLORE WHAT-IF SCENARIOS AND ASSESS POTENTIAL IMPACTS TO YOUR SCHEDULE**. Project managers should be able to accurately answer questions like, *"What must we do to recover the schedule?"* , *"How would this event impact the schedule?"*, and *"What resources do you need to bring this project in on time?"*. To accurately answer such questions, your scheduling app must have the ability to explore what-if scenarios and assess potential impacts to your schedule quickly and automatically. We'll cover this important feature in Chapters 8 and 15.

8. **THE ABILITY TO AUTOMATICALLY UPDATE THE SCHEDULE BASED ON ACTUAL PERFORMANCE DATA**. It's a little-known fact that building a schedule is a relatively minor function of full-featured scheduling apps. Schedules are like promises - easy to make and difficult to deliver on. Similarly, most of the robust features in scheduling apps are not focused on schedule building but on schedule tracking and execution. This would include capabilities like capturing how much work has been done on a task (and not simply whether it's complete or not), or auto-calculating the overall project completion percentage, or automatically updating the schedule when resources are out of the office. If your app can't perform these basic functions, then the limitations of your app can easily appear as your limitations as a project management professional.

   To underscore this point, consider that on a 10-month project in the real world, you will likely spend one month building your schedule and nine months updating your schedule based on actual performance data. If your scheduling app doesn't include this capability, then what will you spend those nine months doing? Unfortunately, you will likely spend them accounting for the limitations of your scheduling app by breaking scheduling promises and making new ones, with no record of the original promises you made. We'll cover this important feature in Chapter 15.

9. **THE ABILITY TO COMPARE PLANNED RESULTS TO ACTUAL RESULTS**. This feature speaks for itself. It's the practical application of criterion number 6. Your app should not only capture your schedule's baseline but enable you to pull reports that highlight variances between your planned results and your actual results. This would include variances like planned start date versus actual start date, planned finish date versus actual finish date, and planned cost versus actual cost. We'll cover this important feature in Chapter 16.

10. **THE ABILITY TO AUTOMATICALLY CALCULATE YOUR SCHEDULE'S CRITICAL PATH.** As mentioned in the first criterion, the total duration of your project is not determined by how many tasks you must complete or the sum of their combined durations. It's determined by how those tasks depend upon one another. This is because all tasks in a schedule do not happen in series. Some tasks start in parallel, some in series and some on specific dates. Therefore, you can't determine your schedule's duration by simply adding all the task durations together. This is where the **Critical Path** comes in. In simple terms, the sum of the durations of all the tasks that make up the critical path, is your total project duration. Your scheduling app should calculate it automatically in the background by plotting all your tasks on a network diagram and then determining the sequence (or network path) of tasks that make up your total project duration. This network path is called the critical path. So, why is this important? Because unless you know which tasks are on the critical path, you won't know which tasks to get done faster to get your project done faster. Conversely, you won't know which tasks have the potential to delay your project schedule. As a result, you will only discover such delays in real-time. And when you do, you will lack the project intelligence to know which tasks can be expedited to bring the project back on schedule and which ones will have no effect on your project's duration, no matter how much you expedite them. We'll cover this important feature in Chapter 11.

Competitive Advantages of Using Project

Because of the aforementioned capabilities, project management professionals who use Microsoft Project enjoy competitive advantages over their peers. Their project updates are more clear, reliable, and useful to decision makers. They appear well-informed about their projects and provide better status updates, better risk assessments, better budget assessments and more reliable scheduling forecasts. As a result, they build credibility faster with project teams and senior leaders.

Project and the Triple Constraints

Perhaps the best business case for using Microsoft Project in project management practice is its utility in balancing the **Triple Constraints** (project management jargon for the trade-off between scope, schedule and cost when managing a project). For example, if a project has a complex scope and must be delivered quickly, then the cost will be high. If the cost is too high, it can be reduced by changing the scope of the project or relaxing the timeline.

We'll conclude with an exchange between a project manager and client, which highlights the tradeoffs of the Triple Constraints and showcases how Microsoft Project can help you manage those tradeoffs.

Client: "We need 10,000 widgets in 10 weeks. Our budget is $10,000".

Project Manager: "I'm afraid that $10,000 can't pay for sufficient labor to build 10,000 widgets in 10 weeks. We'll need 20 weeks".

Client: "It has to be 10 weeks".

Project Manager: "We can do it in 10 weeks if you reduce the number of widgets from 10,000 to 5,000".

Client: "We absolutely need 10,000 widgets, and it has to be 10 weeks".

Project Manager: "If you increase the budget to $20,000, we can hire additional staff and deliver the 10,000 widgets in 10 weeks".

Client: "That's the thing. Our budget is frozen. Is there any way you can make this happen for us?"

Project Manager: "The only way we can make this happen is to use cheaper material, which would reduce the quality of the widgets".

Client: "Agreed. Quality is less of a concern in this case".

As you can see from this scenario, agreements are arrived at by managing tradeoffs between constraints such as scope, schedule, cost, and quality. But how did the project manager gather the project intelligence to advise the client on the precise cost increase? Or the exact number of weeks they would need based on the budget? Or precisely how many widgets they could build if the duration and budget were fixed? You guessed it – Microsoft Project!

Microsoft Project allows you to quickly assess the effects of scope, time, and cost restrictions. It's designed to measure these tradeoffs using the three parameters in its scheduling formula – Duration, Work, and Units. With Microsoft Project, you can negotiate better timelines and deliver projects faster than colleagues who use Excel for scheduling.

- ✓ Explain the benefits of scheduling with Microsoft Project over Excel
- ✓ Explain how Microsoft Project is used in Project Management Environments
- ✓ Identify Ten Criteria for a True Scheduling App
- ✓ Explain the Competitive Advantages of using Microsoft Project
- ✓ Explain how Microsoft Project works with the Triple Constraints

This chapter includes a **BONUS VIDEO** from the "Microsoft Project B.A.S.I.C.S." video course. The videos include tutorials of the information covered in the chapters, software demonstrations and other useful information.

To Watch this Chapter's Video:

- ✓ Visit mspbasics.com.
- ✓ Select **CheckPoint Images** from the menu.
- ✓ Select your version of the book.
- ✓ Select **Chapter 1**.
- ✓ Enjoy the video!

Chapter 2 Getting to Know Project

IN THIS CHAPTER you'll get to know the Project interface. When you're done, you'll be able to navigate the views to find the tools you'll need to build, analyze, and track your schedule.

YOU'LL LEARN TO:

- Use the seven Tabs on the Ribbon
- Explain the Gantt Chart View
- Access the Different Views
- Access the Status Reports

A QUICK NOTE:

The version of Microsoft Project being reviewed in this book is the **Online Desktop Client MSO** – which is one of Microsoft's cloud-based subscription options. At the time of this publication, the version is **2302** and the build is **16130.20332.**

Depending upon which version of Microsoft Project you're using, the interface and features you see may differ slightly from those shown in this book. If you're using a different version, don't worry. The differences are more cosmetic than functional.

This book is applicable to Microsoft Project Desktop versions 2013 forward.

Let's jump in and get to know Microsoft Project!

The Opening View

We'll start with the **Opening View**. *Figure 66* below shows what you see when you first launch Project. This is the **Home** screen.

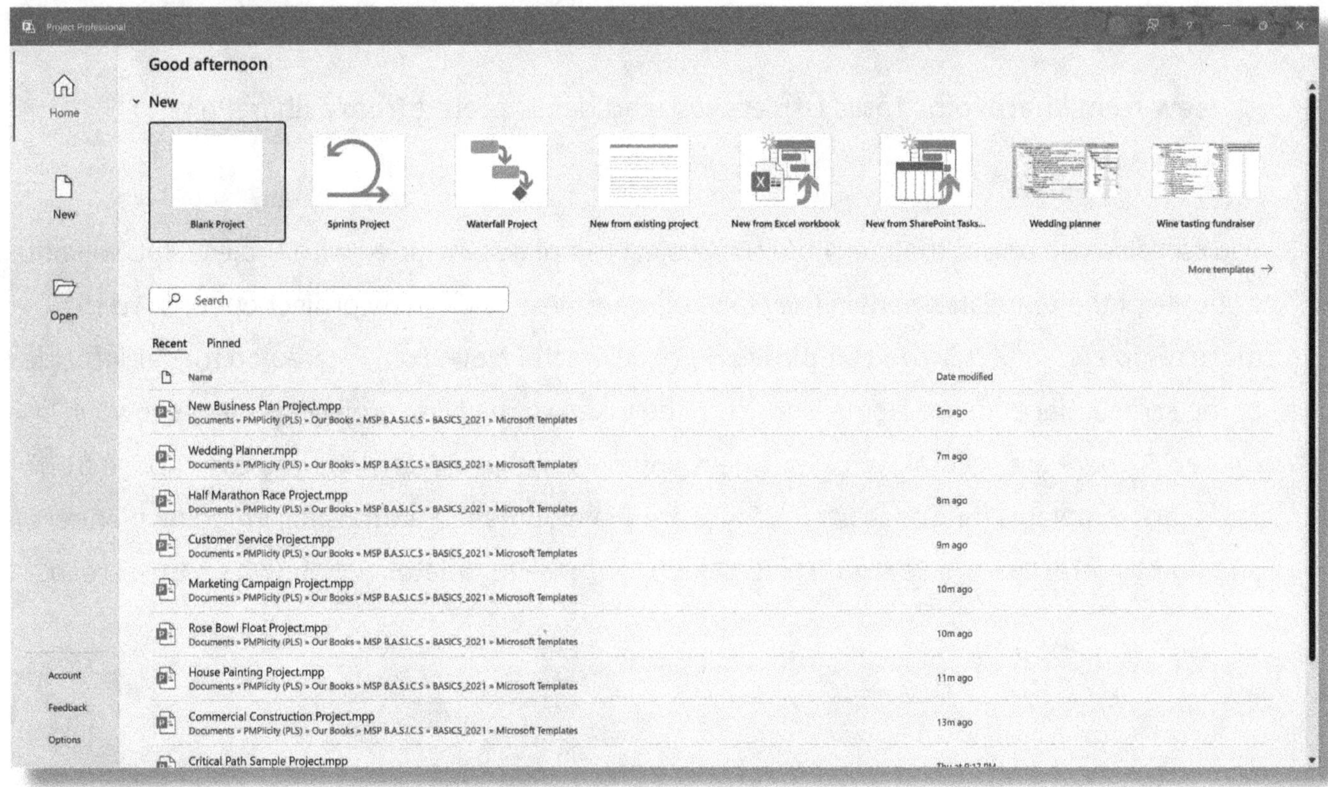

Figure 66 – The Opening View

In the bottom half of the view (or on the left, depending on the version you're using) you'll see a list of recent projects you've worked with. If this is the first time you're using Project, this area will be empty.

Starting a New Project

At the top of the screen (or on the right), you'll find your options for starting a new project:

- You can start from scratch using the **Blank Project** command.
- If you're a Project Online subscriber, you'll see the option to start a new Sprints-based project using the **Sprints Project** template. You can work with your projects in a more Agile way on Kanban-style task boards. We'll delve into the Agile features exhaustively in Chapters 23 and 24.
- With Project Online, you'll also see the option to start a new **Waterfall Project**. This is effectively starting a new traditional or predictive project from scratch.
- **New from existing project** lets you start a new project using an existing project plan.
- **New from Excel workbook** lets you start a new project from an Excel workbook.
- **New from SharePoint** Tasks List lets you start a new project from a SharePoint task list.

You can also use one of the many built-in project templates included with Project. You will find a couple of the templates here in the Opening view, next to the new project options. To see more templates, select **More templates →**, or select the **New** icon, located on the far left side of the screen, beneath the Home icon. You'll be taken to the New projects screen, shown in *Figure 67*. There are several typical business and personal projects plans you can choose from. There are templates for Construction, Software Development, Fundraising, Wedding planners and many more. Use the **Search** box to search for more templates not shown on the screen.

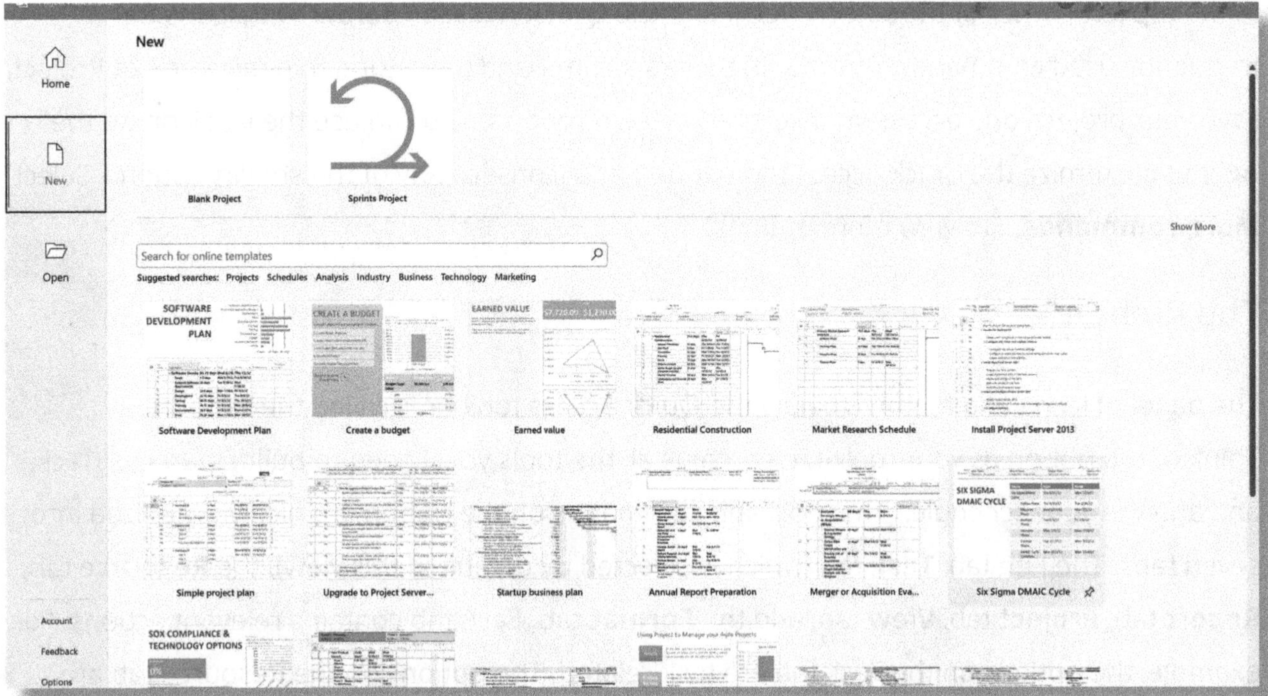

Figure 67 – Project Templates

If you don't find a template that fits your project, you'll need to build a schedule from scratch. To start a new project and build a schedule from scratch, select the **Blank Project** command. You'll be taken to the **Gantt Chart view**, shown in *Figure 68* below. This is the most commonly used view and it's where you'll build your schedule.

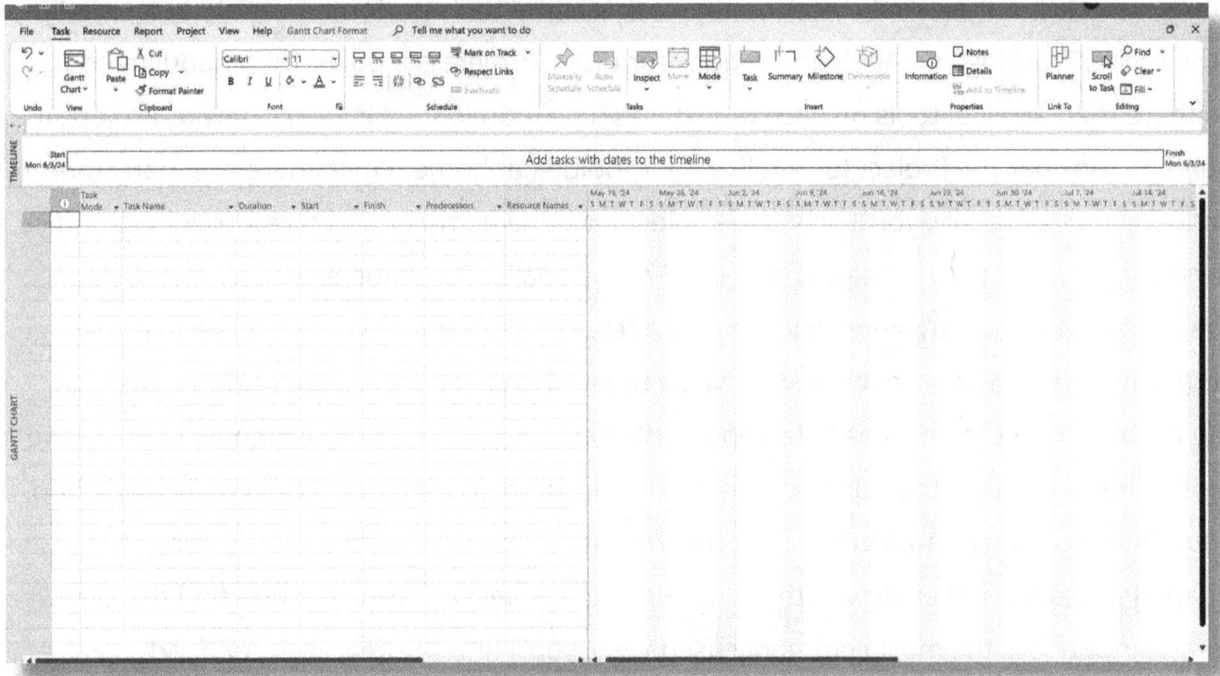

Figure 68 – The Gantt Chart View

In the top left corner of the screen, you'll find the **Quick Access Toolbar** with icons for frequently used commands. By default, there's a command to restore, minimize or exit Project, save your project, and access your recently viewed reports. You can use the last icon on the right to customize the Quick Access toolbar and add icons for any of the shown options. Select **More commands...** to view more options.

The Ribbon

The panel of icons and features below the Quick Access toolbar is called the **Ribbon**. Think of the ribbon as your toolkit. It contains all the tools you'll need to build, manage, track, and analyze your schedule. The tools and commands on the ribbon are nicely organized into seven tabs. The **File** tab, **Task** tab (which is selected by default in this view), the **Resource** tab, **Report** tab, **Project** tab, **View** tab, and the **Format** tab. Each tab contains relevant actions. For example, the options on the Task tab are task related. The options on the Resource tab are resource-related, and so forth. You can also hover over most of the icons to get a description of their function. The tools and commands on each tab are further organized into groups, which are separated by vertical, thin gray lines. The tool groups on the Task tab from left to right, are **Undo**, **View**, **Clipboard**, **Font**, **Schedule**, **Tasks**, **Insert**, **Properties**, **Link To** (only available with the Online Desktop version of Project; it allows you to link tasks to a plan in the Microsoft Planner) and the **Editing** group. Each group contains actions relevant to the tab you've selected. For example, here on the Task tab, the tools perform a variety of formatting, scheduling, Tracking and Analyzing actions for tasks. Project is a powerful scheduling tool, so there is an array of tools on each tab. This can be intimidating if you're new to Project. It helps to consider the Project toolkit, like your toolbox at home. While there are many tools to choose from, generally, you'll only use a select few. The hammer and screwdriver will suffice for most jobs, whereas the saw is only used occasionally. The same is true for the tools on the Project ribbon. You'll generally use only a few key tools on each tab to build and manage your schedule and use the more specialized tools when needed. Having said that, we'll go tab by tab and get to know each tab on the ribbon. Along the way, we'll identify some of the more frequently used tools and actions. We'll start here on the **Task** tab. In the **View** group, you'll find the **Gantt Chart view** short cut. This action allows you to quickly switch to the Gantt Chart view from another view, rather than having to select the View tab and find the view you want. Since this is the most commonly used view, you'll find this feature very handy.

You can also use the drop-down pick-list (*Figure 69 below*) to switch to other views from the Gantt chart view. We'll discuss the various views you can work in later in the chapter.

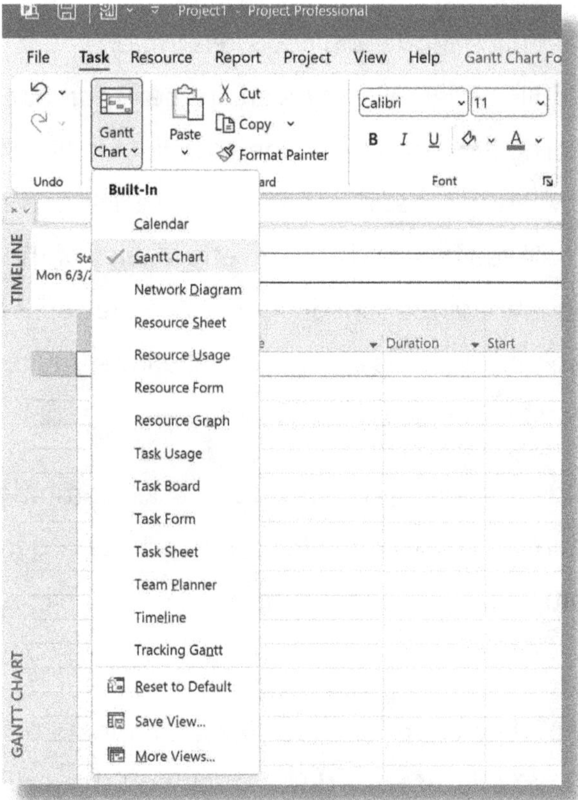

Figure 69 – Views Quick Access List

The tools in the **Clipboard** and **Font** groups are commonly used actions you'll find across other Microsoft applications. For example, the Font group contains the familiar options for formatting typeface.

In the **Schedule** group, you'll find actions you can perform to schedule or update the status of tasks. You can do things like quickly update task completion percentages, mark tasks as "on schedule" per the status date, tell Project to "respect links" and schedule tasks according to their task dependencies, inactivate a task, or split a task to interrupt the work and have it resume at a different time. Actions you'll commonly perform in this group are the **Outdent Task** and **Indent Task** functions – which you'll use to create your schedule outline. You'll also frequently use the **Link Tasks** command, which lets you quickly assign Finish-to-Start task relationships between tasks. You'll learn how to build your schedule outline and create task relationships in Chapter 4.

In the **Tasks** group, you'll find actions that affect how Project schedules tasks. For example, you can select the **scheduling mode** for a new or existing task. There are two scheduling modes to choose from, the **Automatic** mode and the **Manual** mode. The Manual mode is selected by default. The scheduling mode you choose is important. It determines the extent to which Project's robust scheduling engine is engaged. In the Automatic mode, Project calculates task dates and updates according to changes in the schedule. In the Manual mode, dates are not automatically updated when changes are made. We'll review the two scheduling modes in more detail in Chapter 5. You'll see the benefits and efficiencies of the Automatic scheduling mode, and why Project is an unmatched scheduling tool. In the Tasks group, you'll also find a shortcut to the **Task Inspector**, which is a feature that allows you to view factors in the schedule that determine a task's start date.

In the **Insert** group, you'll find actions to quickly insert Tasks, Summary Tasks, and Milestone Tasks into the schedule outline. The **Deliverable** command lets you track deliverables and dependencies between multiple projects. This command works in conjunction with Project Web App.

In the **Properties** group, you'll find commands to view and update task Information. You'll frequently use the **View Task Information** command, which allows you to view details about a task, such as resources and dependencies. The **Notes** command lets add or review notes for a selected task. The **Details** command lets you split the current view to see additional details about a selected task in a table called the Task Form. The **Add to Timeline** command, allows you to add selected tasks to the Timeline, which is the panel just below the ribbon.

If you're using an Online Desktop version of Project, you'll see the **Link To** group, with the **Planner** command. This command allows you to link tasks to a plan in the Microsoft Planner application.

The tools in the **Editing** group, allow you to search for and edit project information. The **Scroll to Task** command is another commonly used feature. It scrolls the view to show information pertaining to a selected task. For example, in the Gantt Chart view, it will scroll to the task bar of the selected task. The **Clear** command allows you to delete everything in a cell or clear its formatting. You can delete things you've added to tasks, like task notes or hyperlinks. The **Fill** command lets you continue a value in one or more adjacent cells. It works similarly to the Auto-fill function in Excel.

The next tab on the ribbon we'll review is the **Resource** tab. To confirm you're on the right tab, it will be underlined with a green line. The Resource tab contains actions you can perform for the resources assigned to your project. In the **View** group, you'll find a shortcut to the **Team Planner view**. This command works just like the Gantt view shortcut on the Task tab, with a drop-down list of shortcuts to built-in views.

The **Assignments** group contains actions to manage resource assignments. A command you'll frequently use in this group is the **Assign Resources** command, which is used to assign resources to tasks. The **Resource Pool** command allows you to share resources across multiple projects in a Resource Pool. You'll learn to work with Resource Pools in Chapter 18.

In the **Insert** group, the **Add Resource** command lets you add a new resource to the project. This command is active in certain views, like the Resource Sheet view, and allows you to manually create resources or add them from an address book or an active directory.

In the **Properties** group, the **Resource Information** commands allows you to view and update information for a selected resource. You can update information like pay rates or availability. The **Notes** command lets you add a note for a resource. These commands are grayed out because you must be in a Resource view to use them. The **Details** command works as it does on the Task tab – it splits the current view. In this case, you can view and update information about a selected resource, like their task assignments.

The **Level** group contains commands to level over-allocated resources. You can level a single resource or level all over-allocated resources using Project's Automatic leveling features. The **Leveling Options** command opens a dialogue box where you can control which actions Project can perform when you use the automatic leveling feature. We'll cover resource leveling in Chapter 13.

The next tab is the **Report** tab. On this tab, you can generate eye-catching reports to analyze and share project status, and other project data like cost overviews, Burn-down reports and resource reports. Project automatically creates these reports in the background as you develop your schedule. You can also create custom reports.

In the **Project** group, the **Compare Projects** command creates a comparison report that allows you to compare two versions of a project.

The report shows the differences between the two projects. This is a handy feature to use when you're closing a project and you want to compare your final project results to the planned estimates.

In the **View Reports** group, you can access a variety of built-in status reports. You'll find several Dashboard, Cost, Resource, and In-Progress reports. If you're using the Online Desktop version of Project, you'll also find the **Task Boards** reports, which are Agile reports from the Task Board views, like Sprint reports. The **Visual Reports** command in the **Export** group, lets you integrate with the Microsoft Excel and Visio applications to view your project data in Pivot tables and diagrams. We'll delve more into the reporting features in Chapter 17.

Next to the Report tab is the **Project** tab. The Project tab is used to perform actions that impact the entire project. The **Subproject** command in the **Insert** group allows you to insert project schedules into other schedules as sub-projects. This is a great feature if you're managing several interdependent projects at the same time. We'll learn about consolidating projects and creating Master schedules in Chapter 18. In the **Add-ins** group, you can browse for and insert Microsoft Office Add-ins that can simplify your workflow.

In the **Properties** group, you'll find several commands to work with to impact the entire project. The **Project Information** command in the **Properties** group is another command you'll frequently use. This is where you can update information like the project start date, or the status dates. The **Custom Fields** command lets you add a custom field to the view. This is handy when you want to display information that's specific to your organization, like cost codes. If you're using the Online Desktop version, you'll find the **Manage Sprints** command, which lets you manage sprint dates and names in the Sprints project views. The **Links Between Projects** command lets you view information about tasks that are linked between projects. The **WBS** command lets you define or renumber the Work Breakdown Structure number scheme for the tasks in your schedule. As you'll learn in the next chapter, WBS codes are numbers that identify the outline level of a task in the project outline. Project automatically applies the standard WBS scheme to tasks, but this command lets you create your own customized WBS scheme. Also, in the event you move or delete a task from your schedule, you can use this command to renumber the Work Breakdown Structure. Project won't automatically do this in case you're using them in documents or other systems that are not linked to your Project file.

The **Change Working Time** command is another frequently used action. This is what you'll use to specify non-working days in the schedule, like vacation days and special work schedules for resources.

In the **Schedule** group, the **Calculate Project** commands calculates your project after you make a change. Project does this automatically, so you would only need to do this if you've disabled calculations in the settings. The **Set Baseline** command is another key action. It allows you baseline or take a snapshot of your schedule to track changes in your project over time. In Chapter 15, you'll learn the importance of baselines in your schedule. The **Move Project** command updates the start and finish dates for all tasks, in the event your project is put on hold and must resume at a later date.. The **Update Project** command in the **Status** group, lets you quickly update tasks to a scheduled completion percentage. You can update progress information for the entire project or specific tasks up to a specific status date. In the **Proofing** group, you'll find a spell-checking command.

Project Views

Next to the Project tab is the **View** tab. On this tab you can work with subsets of your project information in various project views. A project view is the area you're working with on the screen. Project has several built-in views that display your project information in various tables, charts, diagrams, sheets, and forms. You can also create your own custom views. There are three types of project views: **Task** views, **Resource** views, and **Assignment** views. The Gantt Chart view is a Task view. It's comprised of a table on the left and a Gantt Chart on the right. We'll review these areas in detail in a later section.

The View tab contains quick access shortcuts to commonly used Task, Resource and Assignment views. Each view has tools and actions relevant to the view. In the **Task Views** group, a commonly used view is the **Task Usage view** (*Figure 70*), which is an Assignment view that displays the tasks in your project, the resources assigned to them and their work hours.

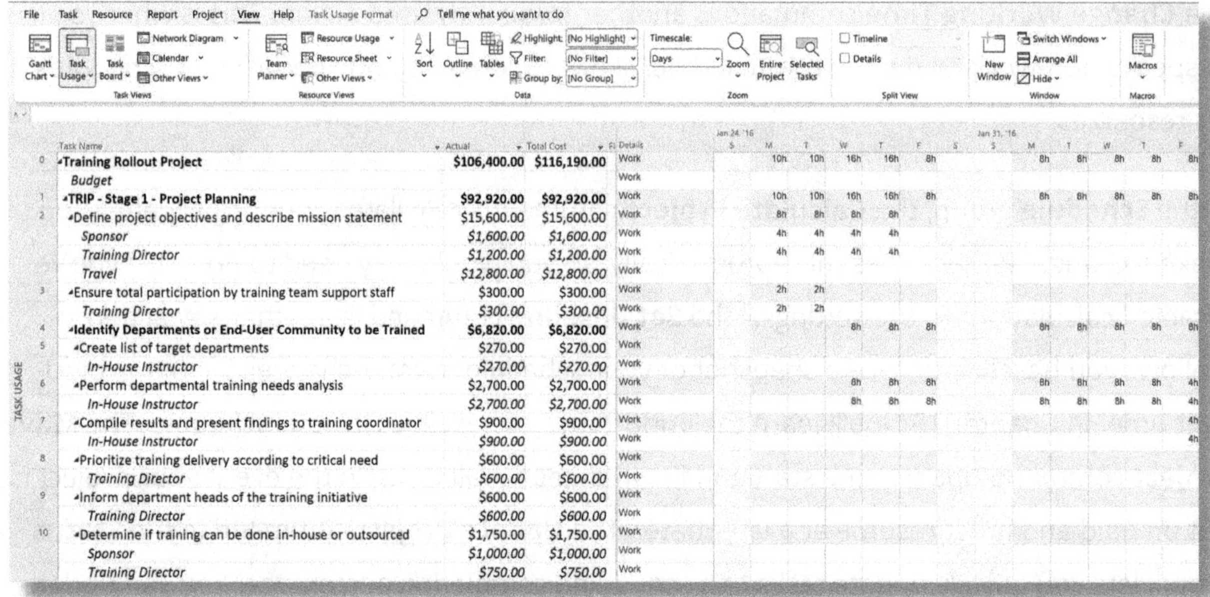

Figure 70 – The Task Usage View

If you're using an Online Desktop version of Project, you'll also have a shortcut to the **Task Board view** (*Figure 71* below), which allows you to view and update tasks in an agile way, using Kanban style Task boards.

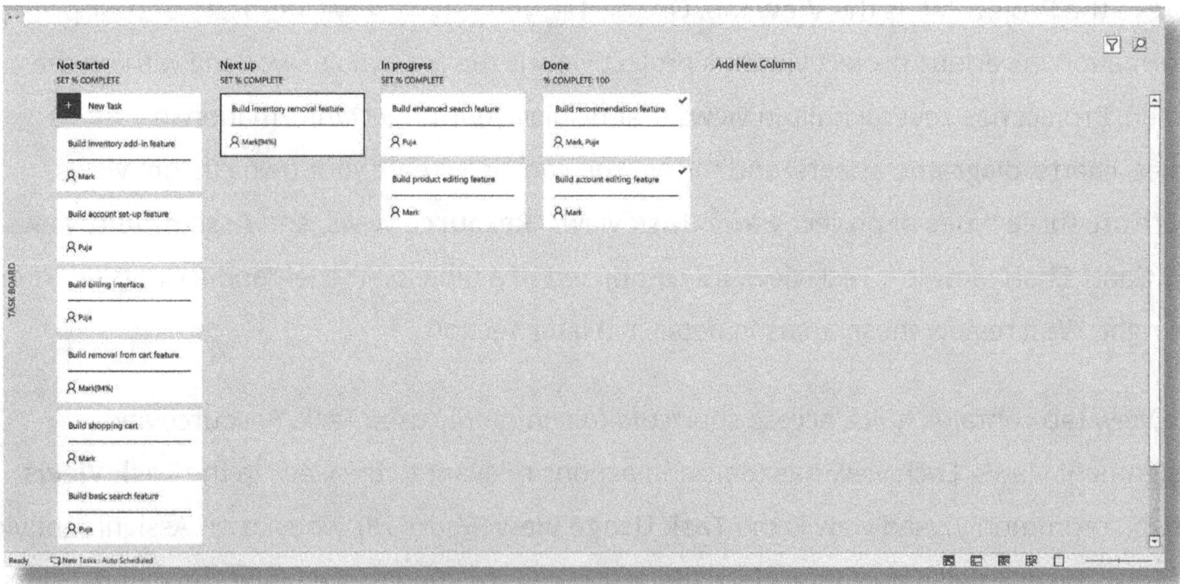

Figure 71 – The Board View

There's also a shortcut to the **Network diagram view** *(Figure 72)*, which displays tasks and task dependencies in a flowchart format.

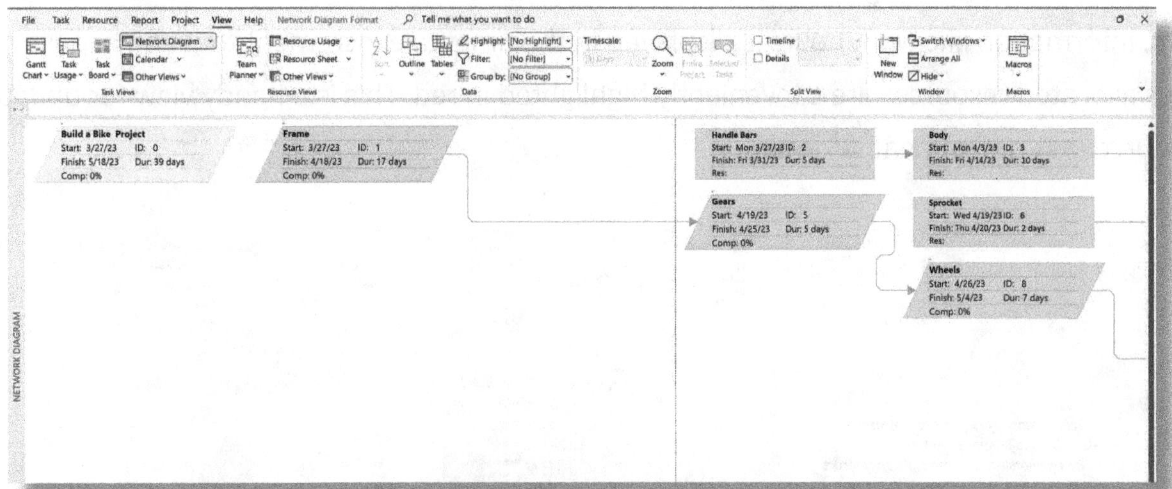

Figure 72 – The Network Diagram View

The last shortcut in the Task Views group is for the **Calendar view** (*Figure 73*), which displays tasks and task durations in a calendar format.

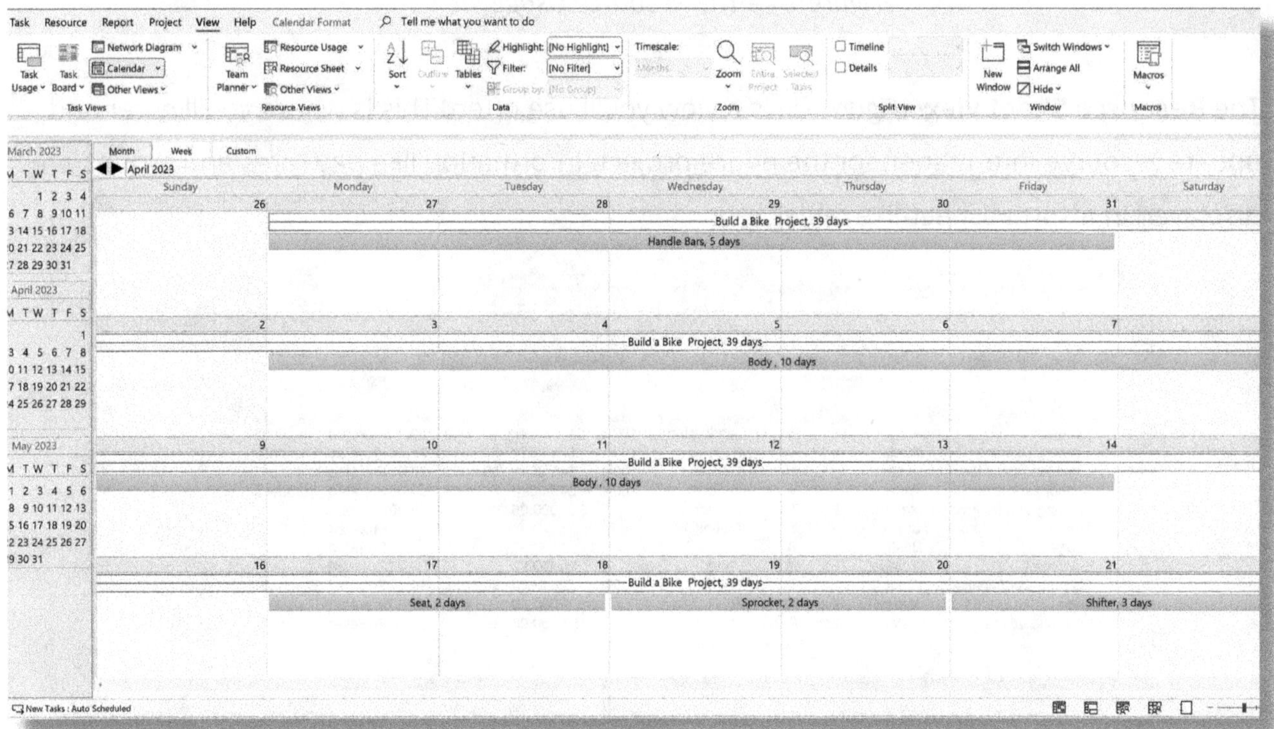

Figure 73 – The Calendar View

The **Resource Views** group contains shortcuts to some commonly used resource views. The **Resource Usage view** (*Figure 74* below) displays resource assignment information in a table. Resources, their task assignments, and cumulative work hours are listed on the left. On the right, information like work hours is displayed in the timescale increment that you choose. Over-allocated resources are conveniently highlighted in red. This is a handy view for updating resource task assignment information.

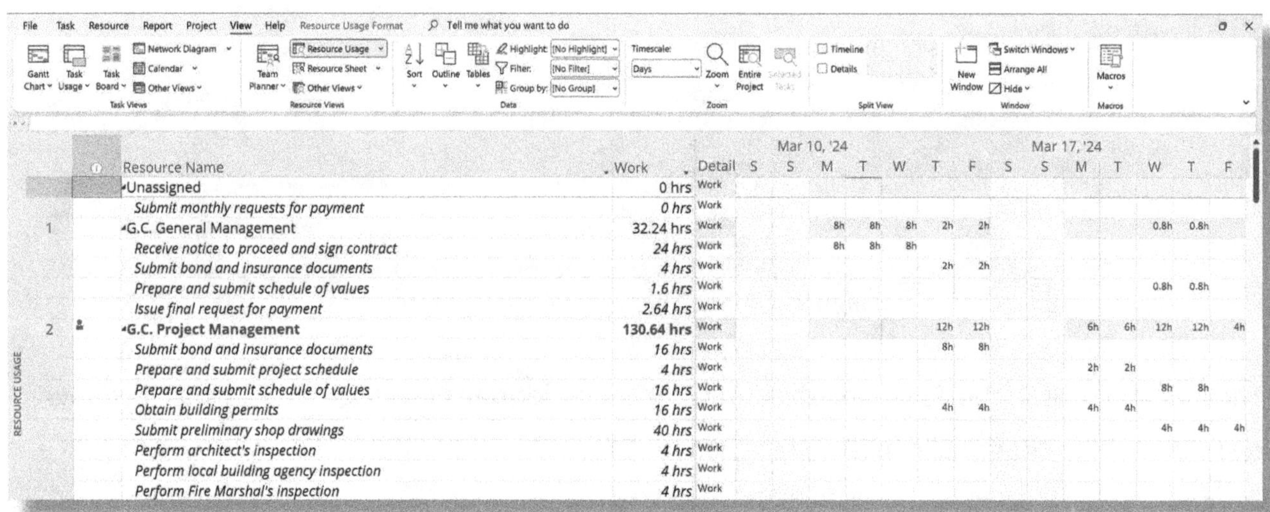

Figure 74 – The Resource Usage View

The **Resource Sheet view** (*Figure 75*) is a view you'll use often. This is where you'll enter and update resource information for the entire project. Information like pay rates and groups are displayed in a spreadsheet-like table.

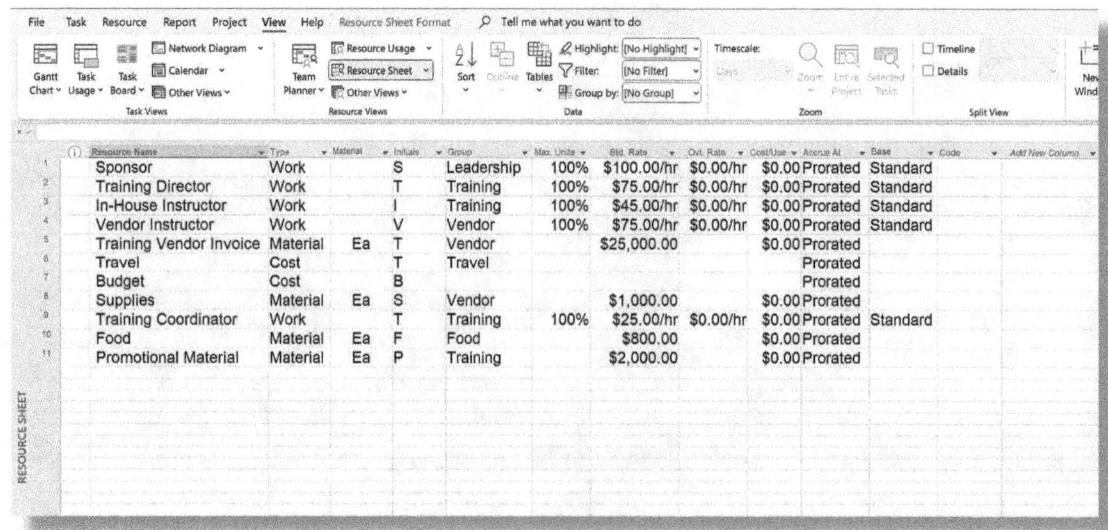

Figure 75 – The Resource Sheet View

The **Team Planner view** (*Figure 76 below*), like the Resource Usage View, displays resources, and their task assignments, but in a diagram format. Over-allocations are highlighted and outlined in red. What this view offers that the Resource Usage view doesn't, is a drag and drop option that allows you to quickly to quickly reassign work by dragging a task from one resource to another.

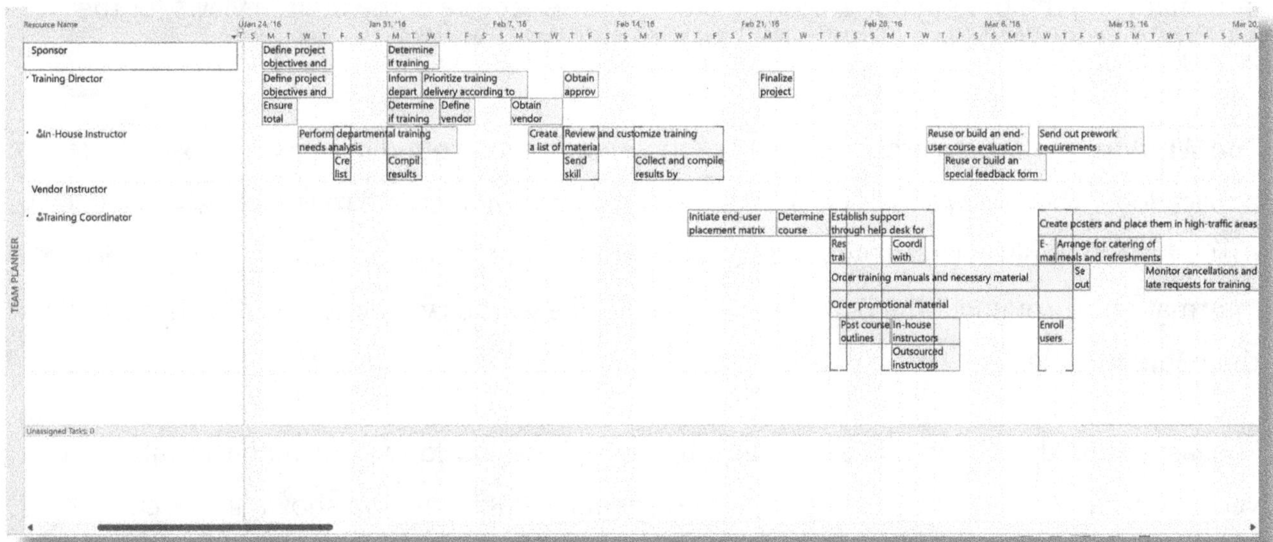

Figure 76 – The Team Planner View

The tools in the **Data** group allow you to sort, filter and group subsets of project information to work with the specific details you want to see. The **Show Outline** command is very helpful when working with large schedules. It allows you to collapse the outline to specific levels of the project and expand only the sections that you want to work with. It's also a handy way to check your task outline to ensure that task outline levels are correct. The **Tables** command lets you change the table in any view to display different project details, such as cost or tracking information. As mentioned earlier, many of the project views contain tables with project information. For example, by default, the Gantt chart view displays the Entry table, which contains Task information.

The **Zoom** group contains commands to zoom in or out of the view to see more or less project detail. A frequently used function on this tab is the **Zoom Entire Project** command which adjusts the view, so the entire project is shown on the screen. The **Timescale** command adjusts the time unit that appears on the timescale, in increments of hours to years.
The **Selected Tasks** command zooms in to see specific tasks.

In the **Split View** group, you'll find the option to toggle the **Timeline** panel on or off. The Timeline panel is located just below the ribbon. It you don't see it, check the check box. We'll review its function later in the chapter. The **Details** check box allows you to split the screen and create a combination view – one view in the top pane and another view in the bottom pane. For example, you can display task information in the top pane and resource information in the bottom pane. Use the pick-list to select one of the built-in views for the bottom pane.

The **Window** and **Macro** group actions are those commonly found in other Microsoft applications. They allow you to work in multiple windows and create macros to automate tasks that you repeatedly perform. As you see, there are many options for viewing your project information. Throughout the book, we'll work with the various views, tables and charts and put them into context.

The last tab on the ribbon is the **Format** tab. The actions you can perform on this tab allow you to format and customize the graphical elements and information shown in the current view. Almost all the views in Project are customizable. The Format tab is also a contextual tab – meaning, the tools and actions on this tab and the contextual label for this tab will vary depending on the view you're in, and which items are selected. In the Gantt Chart view, the tab is labeled *Gantt Chart Format* (or *Gantt Chart tools* depending upon your version of Project). If you're in a Resource view, like the Resource Usage view, the label would change to *Resource Usage Format* and the formatting tools would change to those relevant to the view. Here in the Gantt Chart view, in the **Format** group you'll find actions to customize the look and layout of many items in the Gantt chart and tables. The **Text Styles** command lets you format the text style of certain items shown in the view. For example, you may want milestone tasks to be shown in blue or bold typeface. The **Gridlines** command lets you change the look of certain gridlines in the view, such as the rows and columns, which by default are shown in light gray. Also, you can add or update progress lines, which show a visual depiction of what percentage a task is complete. The **Layout** option lets you customize the Gantt bars on the Gantt chart.

The commands in the **Columns** group allow you to align content, wrap text, insert more built-in data columns into the view or create your own custom field.

In the **Bar Styles** group, you'll find commands to highlight certain aspects of tasks, so they stand out. For example, you could show a bar to represent the baseline, or a line representing tasks that have slipped compared to the baseline projection. You can display **Slack** or highlight **Late Tasks**. A very helpful function in this group is the **Critical Tasks** check box. This will highlight your project's critical path in the Gantt chart. One of Project's most useful features is that it automatically calculates the critical path. This is very useful information to have in just one click, when you're trying to get work done faster.

The **Gantt Chart Style** group allows you to change the colors of the Gantt Chart Bars to one of the options shown.

The **Show/Hide** group let you display the **Summary Tasks** of the schedule, which generally represent phases of the project. You can also display the **Task Outline Numbers**, which is helpful with larger schedules. The **Project Summary Task** check box is one you'll commonly use. This will display a top-level task with summary information for the project, such as the project's duration or total cost.

The **Drawing** feature lets you add simple shapes to the view, which you can use to create simple diagrams or maybe highlight items in the schedule.

The ribbon also contains a **Help** tab that provides help using Microsoft Project. The help icon opens a panel where you can search for help on various features and topics. There's also a portal where you can take on-line training on using Microsoft Project. If you're using the Online Desktop version of Project, you'll see the **What's New** option, where you can learn about the latest features. You'll also see the **Feedback** option, which lets you offer feedback to improve Microsoft Office. You can also get help using the **Tell Me What You Want to Do** search box, which is found in other Microsoft applications. Just type in words or phrases that describe what you want to do and quickly get pointed to the right features or actions.

We have now reviewed the seven tabs on the Project ribbon and the tools and functions you'll need to build, manage, and track your amazing schedules. As we progress through the lessons, we'll work with the tools in context and realize their utility for building schedules.

The Timeline View Panel

The panel beneath the ribbon is called the **Timeline View**. As mentioned earlier, this panel can be toggled on off from the **View** tab. In the **Split View** group, check or uncheck the **Timeline** check box. Once your schedule has been built, you can customize the panel to show key milestones in your project (Figure 77 below).

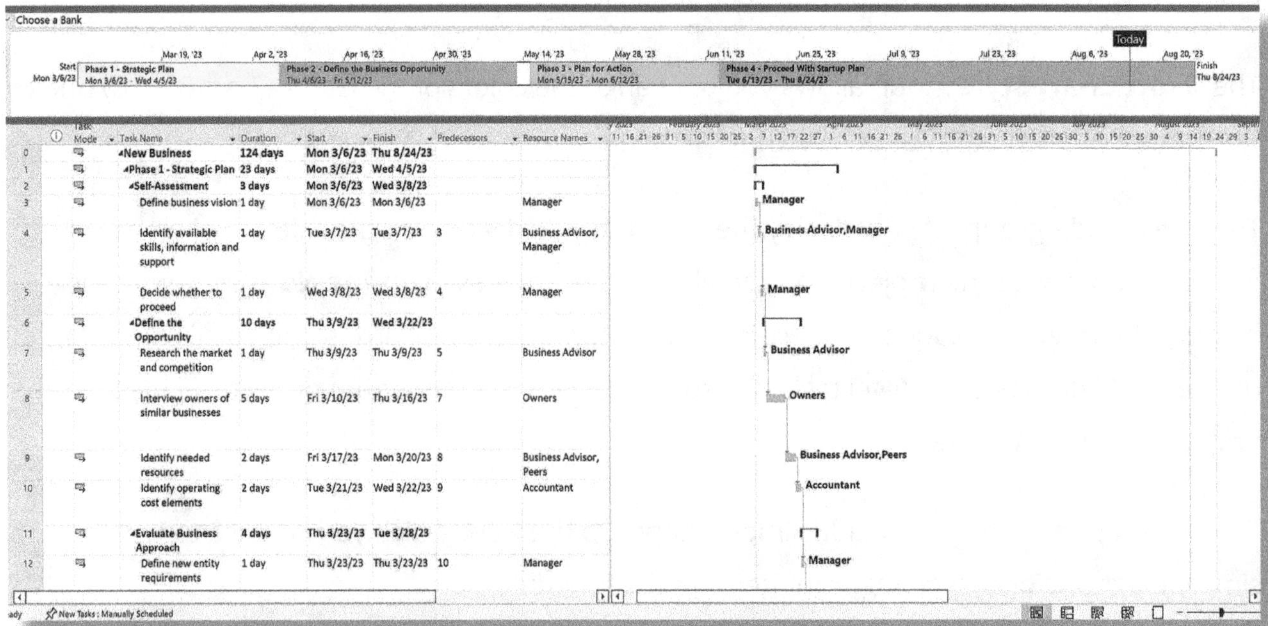

Figure 77 – The Timeline View Panel

This is a handy feature for reporting high-level project information. This view provides a vibrant snapshot of key tasks that can be easily exported into a PowerPoint slide or Word doc, printed, or emailed to stakeholders. You'll learn how to customize the Timeline view in Chapter 17.

The Gantt Chart View

Beneath the Timeline view panel are the table and chart that comprise the Gantt Chart View. Using *Figure 78*, we will review each section.

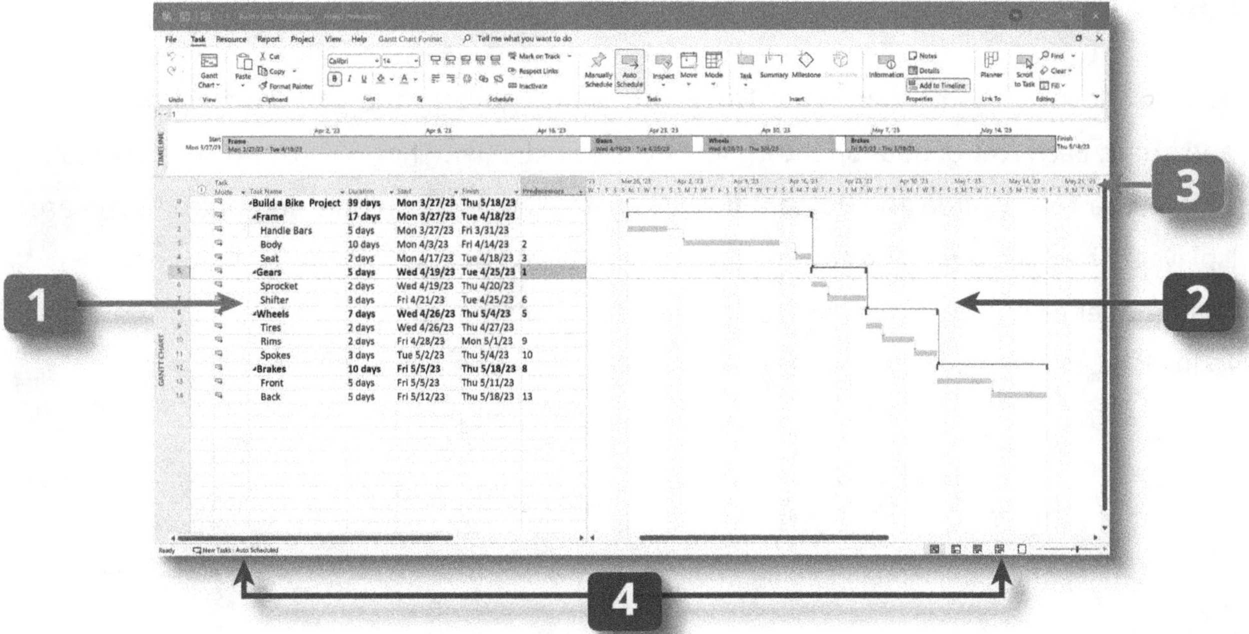

Figure 78 – The Gantt Chart View

Section 1

The table on the left side is called the **Entry Table**. This is the default table in the Gantt Chart view, and it's where you'll enter your task list and build your schedule outline.

Section 2

When you enter the task names into the Entry table, Project automatically generates a **Gantt Chart** on the right – hence the name of this view. When you enter scheduling details, like task durations and predecessors to create dependencies, the Gantt chart will depict your schedule across a timeline. For each task, the corresponding task bar spans across its start and finish date. The task dependencies are depicted by the arrows connecting the task bars. The thin black bars are called summary bars. They depict the duration of the summary tasks representing the phases. The vertical green line indicates the current date. By the way, this is one of the gridlines you can customize and make any color you like, using the *Gridlines* command we reviewed earlier on the Format tab, in the Format group. The thick vertical gray lines indicate non-working days. When using the default Standard calendar, weekends are non-working days and are grayed out.

Section 3

The area above the Gantt chart is the **Timescale**, which governs the time-frame shown in the Gantt chart. Each row of data on the Timescale is called a tier. There are three tiers available to display – the **Top**, **Middle** and **Bottom** tiers. By default, only the middle and bottom tiers are displayed. The middle tier currently displays the date and the bottom tier displays days.
For a broader or narrower view of the timeline, the timescale can be customized by double-clicking it (*Figure 79* below).

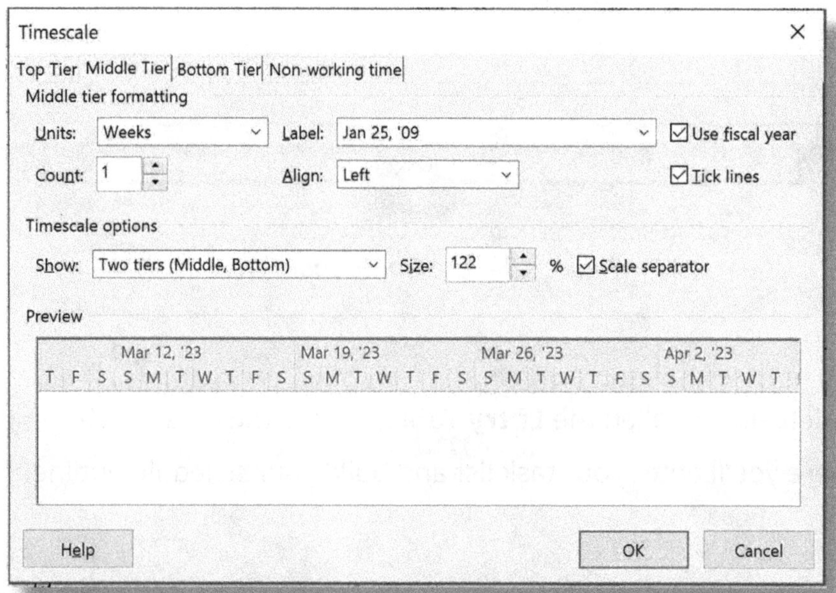

Figure 79 – Timescale Customization Options

You can specify things like the number of tiers you want to display, the format and time unit the tiers display, the frequency of unit labels on the timescale tiers and whether to base the timescale on fiscal or calendar years. You can also adjust the alignment, the spacing between units and whether to show tick lines. A preview of your adjustments is shown in the *Preview* field. Select the tab at the top representing the tier you want to display and make the adjustments you like.

Section 4

At the very bottom of the screen is the **Status Bar**. There are two parts to the Status bar. On the left, you'll find status indicators for the cell mode and the scheduling mode. *Ready* indicates the cell mode. The *New Tasks: Manual Scheduled* notification indicates the scheduling mode you're working in.

This means that all new tasks added to the schedule will be scheduled in the Manual scheduling mode. Project offers two scheduling modes, the **Manual** mode (the default mode) and the **Automatic** mode. The scheduling mode determines how Project behaves when scheduling tasks. We will further explain the two modes in Chapter 5.

On the right side of the Status bar, you'll find **Quick Access Shortcuts** for commonly used views. Use these shortcuts to quickly access the Gantt Chart, Task Usage, Team Planner and Resource Sheet views. As you get to know the usefulness of these common views, you'll find these shortcuts handy. The **Report** icon accesses your own customized report, which you'll learn to create in Chapter 17. Use the **Zoom slider** to zoom in and out of the Timescale. While the slider is a quick way to zoom, it can be a bit tricky to control. Another way to adjust the Timescale is the **Zoom** command on the View tab, located in the Zoom group. It performs the same zoom function, but allows you to chose precise or custom time units. You can also adjust the timescale view by updating the units using the **Timescale** command, which is located in the same group.

The Backstage View

To conclude our tour of the Project interface, we'll review the **Backstage** view. Select the **File** tab to access the Backstage menu of options, which are located on the far-left side of the screen (*Figure 80* below).

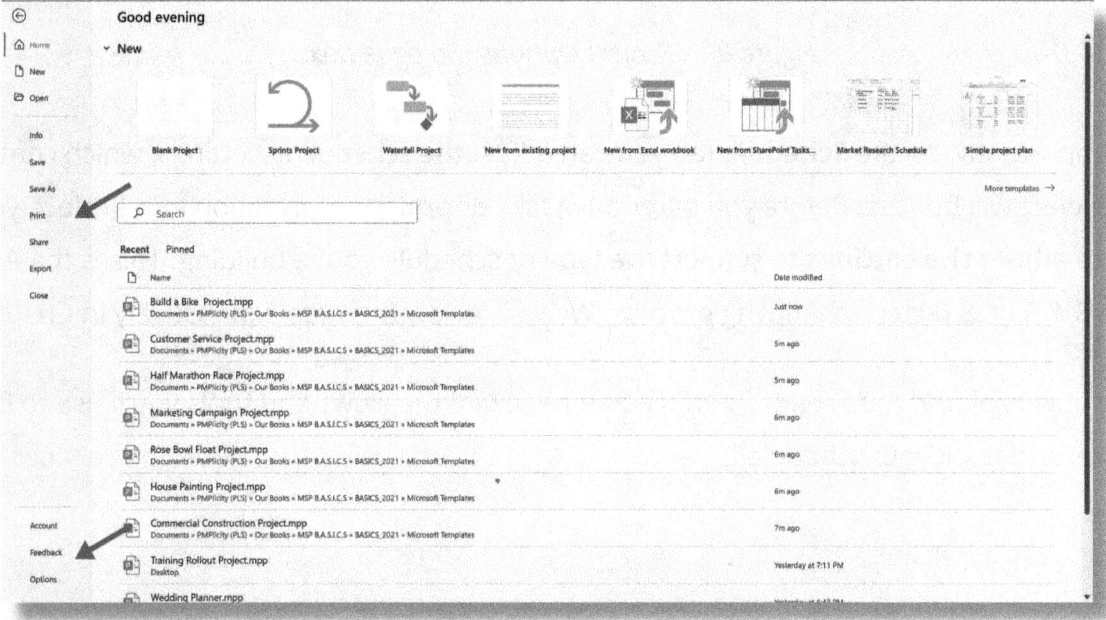

Figure 80 – Backstage Menu Options

The options on top are those common in most Microsoft Office applications. You can manage, save, print, share with SharePoint or export Project files. Use the **Account** area in the bottom-right to view and update information for your Microsoft Project account. **Feedback** lets you provide feedback to Microsoft. **Options** opens the *Project Options* dialogue box (*Figure 81* below) where you can customize various settings including, Display, Language, the Ribbon and much more.

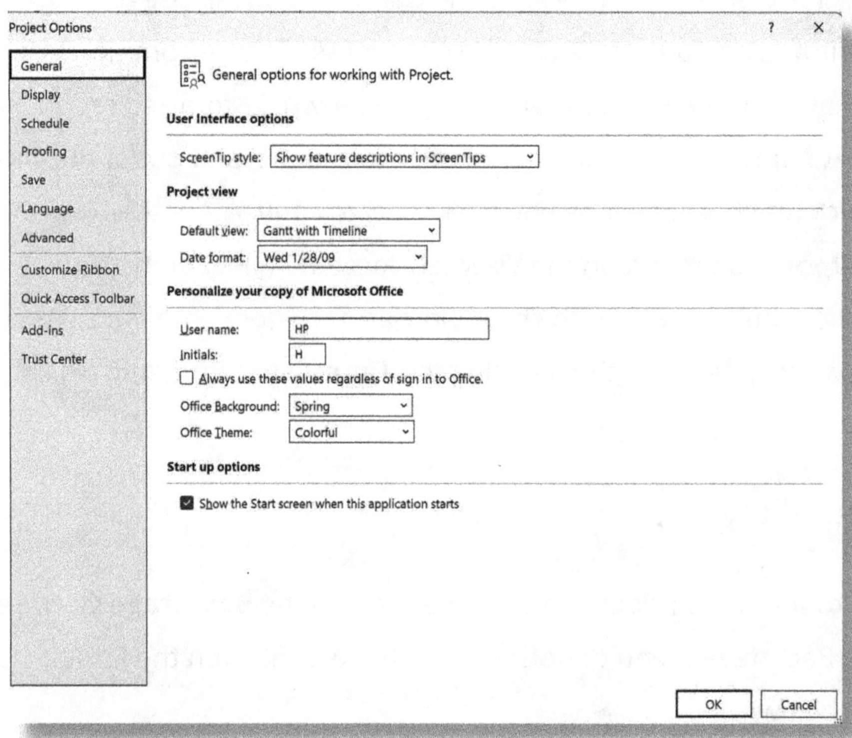

Figure 81 – Project Options Dialogue Box

Very Importantly, on the **Schedule** tab you can adjust the scheduling settings, which control how Project will behave. Before you enter any tasks or project information into Project, you'll want to **adjust the settings** to support the type of schedule you're building. This is the **A** step in the **B.A.S.I.C.S** 6-step scheduling process. We will review this step exhaustively in Chapter 5.

We've now explored the Project interface and reviewed the views and tools you'll use to build, analyze, and track your schedule.

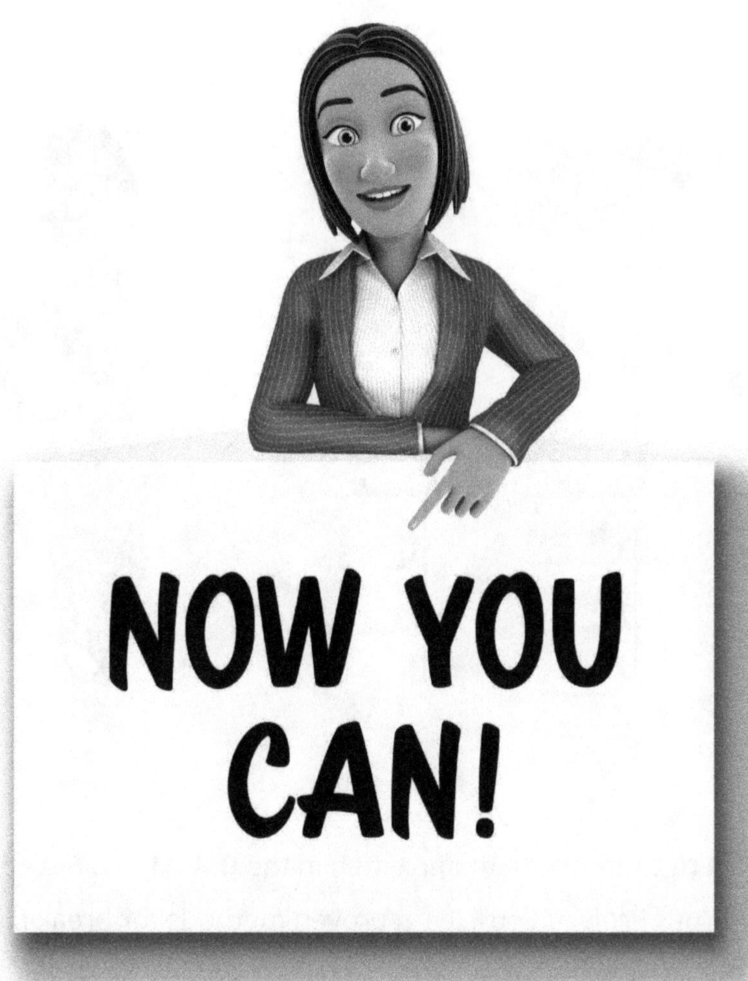

- ✓ Navigate the Project Interface
- ✓ Use the seven Tabs of the Ribbon
- ✓ Explain the Gantt Chart View
- ✓ Access the Different Views
- ✓ Access the Status Reports

Chapter 3 Breaking Down Your Project

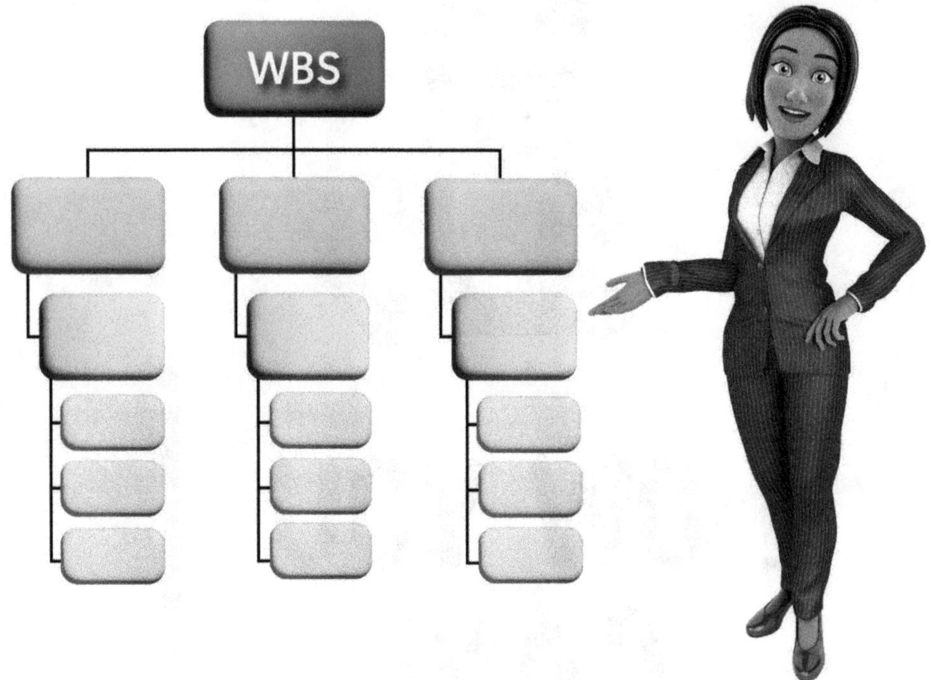

In this chapter, you'll learn to complete the first step in the **B.A.S.I.C.S.** 6-step scheduling process – Break Down Your Project. You'll learn proven methods for breaking down projects of any size and complexity into manageable parts.

When you're done, you'll be able to organize your project and give stakeholders the confidence that you'll deliver it successfully.

YOU'LL LEARN:

- Why You Should Break Down Your Project
- When You Should Break Down Your Project
- Who Should Break Down Your Project
- What a Broken-Down Project Is
- How to Break Down Your project

Microsoft Project is not an app you can use properly without some measure of pre-work. That pre-work is what the **B** in **B.A.S.I.C.S.** is all about. Breaking down your project is the necessary groundwork for successful schedule building and project execution.

Consider this project management scenario – You've been given your first major project, supporting one of your organization's important strategic goals. Because the project supports such a critical initiative, senior leaders have requested regular updates. Consequently, your boss is very nervous about this project and has expressed the need for successful delivery. You get the distinct impression that your career will be impacted positively or negatively, based on how well you manage this project. To make matters even more challenging, you don't have formal project management training. You're what is commonly called an "accidental" project manager. So, how can you guarantee success in this scenario? How can you gain credibility with your boss and senior leaders from the start – and increase their confidence in you as the project continues? The answer is, by giving them <u>a clear plan</u> of how you will deliver the product, service, or result that you've been tasked to deliver. This is what you'll learn to do in this chapter.

We'll start by considering a bit of ancient wisdom from Aristotle. This is his counsel on how to be successful in any challenging endeavor.

- "FIRST, have a definite, clear, practical ideal – a goal, an objective."
- "SECOND, have the necessary means to achieve your ends – wisdom, money, materials, and methods."
- "THIRD, adjust all your means to that end."

Aristotle provided a good blueprint for successfully organizing and delivering any project. Your first step is to develop a clear plan for delivering your project.

Projects begin as high-level objectives handed down from customers, leaders, stakeholders, or sponsors. For example, the project objective may be to "Plan the Olympics in Los Angeles", "Manage the build-out of a new headquarter facility", or "Manage the Pharmaceutical development process for a new drug". Whatever your project may be, your first step is to break down that high-level objective into something you can manage. In essence, you must convert a scope statement, like "Plan the Olympics" into a detailed set of deliverables that clearly show how the project will be delivered.

The project breakdown that you perform at the beginning of the project will not only make the effort manageable, but it will also become the framework for your schedule. This is an important step that every seasoned project manager knows *should* be done. Nonetheless, due to the pressure to get projects executed faster, it's often skipped.

As a result, many predictable and catastrophic outcomes occur. Many well-documented project failures, costing well into the billions of dollars, are attributable to projects never having been sufficiently broken down from the start.

Why Should You Break Down Your Project?

So, why should you breakdown your project? Here are 10 reasons you should complete this important step and 8 predictable consequences of not doing so.

10 Reasons to Break Down Your Project

1. To Show How the Project Objectives Will Be Achieved

When you break down your project, stakeholders can see the specific actions you plan to take to deliver the various components of the project - and ultimately the entire project scope. Many project professionals skip this step only to later encounter stakeholder and sponsor questions that can only be answered if the project were fully decomposed. Avoid this mistake and break down your project as quickly as possible after receiving your project scope statement.

2. To Define the Project in Terms of Specific Deliverables

In project management jargon, results are often referred to as deliverables - which are products, services, met objectives, attained goals or any other sought-after result. All project stakeholders understand results. This is why when you break down your project, it's important that your breakdown be **deliverable-oriented**. Each grouping of tasks should deliver some aspect or component of the project. Deliverable-oriented language is the language stakeholders understand best. It emphasizes outcomes and results over processes and procedures.

3. To Organize the Deliverables

When you organize your project deliverables into components, milestones, or phases, it allows stakeholders to see how the various components of the project fit into the larger objectives. This type of project organization enables each stakeholder to zoom in on the area that concerns them most and creates a basis for clear project communications.

4. To Organize the Project and the Project Team

Project organization is a direct byproduct of project decomposition. When you decompose a project, identify specific deliverables, and organize those deliverables into components, milestones, and phases, you will have ultimately created the framework required for an organized project and an organized project team.

5. To Show Which Organizations are Accountable for Which Deliverables

Project managers rarely perform the tasks they're accountable for delivering – they deliver the projects. Others perform the tasks associated with those projects. One of the benefits of breaking down your project is it allows you to quickly identify which teams and resources are accountable for which deliverables. This level of clarification is essential if you want to get an early start on your project. The earlier teams are made aware of their deliverables, the sooner they can plan their work.

6. To Increase Stakeholder Confidence that the Work Will Be Achieved

As mentioned earlier, a fully broken-down project will give stakeholders a clear idea how you intend to deliver the project. This level of clarity is rare in the early stages of a project, and it is the by-product of a fully decomposed project. The clearer stakeholders are about how you will deliver the project, the more confident they will become in your ability to deliver it successfully.

7. To Communicate Project Status in an Organized Way

This is where you can begin to see the trickle-down effects of a fully broken-down project. When projects are decomposed at the start, it facilitates effective project communication. For example, if you've identified five major phases or components of the project, these phases become familiar milestones to project stakeholders. Questions like *"In Which phase will we see a prototype?"* can be effectively answered by the project breakdown. It allows stakeholders to quickly discern in which phase of the project they can expect certain project deliverables.

As we'll discuss later in the chapter, work breakdown structures are often graphical, and provide a nice visual of how the objectives will be met.

8. To Make it Easier to Identify Schedule, Risk, and Budget Information

It's easier to identify a project risk or potential cost overrun if the project is organized into logical phases. The same holds true for scheduling and performance issues. For example, if your project breakdown plainly shows that clear requirements are a major component of the planning phase, it will be easier for stakeholders to make the connection between their need to provide clear requirements and your team's ability to develop designs to meet those requirements.

9. To Develop the Level of Detail Required to Manage and Control the Project

One of the chief sources of cost overruns and schedule delays is not having broken down project deliverables to a sufficient level of detail. It's easy to underestimate the cost of a phase if you haven't decomposed it enough to discover what each component truly costs. For example, suppose you're managing an entertainment event, and you're planning the security. If your project breakdown doesn't decompose the security work into both internal and external security, then down the line, you may discover that internal and external security are provided by two different vendors, with vastly different cost and schedule implications. Developing this level of detail in your breakdown can help mitigate issues like these.

10. To Help Determine Resource Requirements

Knowing which resources you'll need to complete the project deliverables up front is a huge advantage, especially if the resources are scarce, have unique skills or are in demand. Failing to determine resource requirements, such as technical skills, experience level, and knowledge requirements have led to many poorly staffed, and by extension, poorly executed projects. When you sufficiently break down your project, you get a better idea what level of expertise you will need to complete the project. A graphical depiction of your project's breakdown will show the work which must be done in logical groupings. These groupings can trigger team members to confirm that the right resources will be available when needed.

We've now looked at 10 compelling reasons you should break down your project. Despite these reasons, some may still be tempted to skip this step. Especially if there's pressure from senior leaders to get your project done faster.

To help strengthen your resolve, and to help you educate stakeholders on the importance of this work, we'll now look at 8 consequences of <u>not</u> breaking down your project. Some of these consequences may seem intuitive, as they are the reasons so many projects fail. What may not be so intuitive is the causal relationship between these consequences and insufficiently broken-down projects.

8 Consequences of Not Breaking Down Your Project

1. A Vague Project Scope

When projects are not broken down, the project stakeholders will have a limited understanding of the work required to deliver the project. Resource requirements, schedule impacts and costs will also be unclear. Conversely, when you break down your project into manageable parts (or phases), and ultimately into manageable tasks, those tasks can be assessed for cost and schedule impacts, assigned to the appropriate resources, and then monitored and controlled to keep the project on schedule.

2. Project Delays

Not breaking down your project into manageable phases and tasks increases the odds of project delays. This is because to realistically estimate the duration of a project phase, you must estimate the duration of each component of that phase. For example, to estimate the time required to complete the Design phase of any project, you must have some idea of how many elements will require a design. You would then estimate the time required to design each element and add those estimates together to provide a realistic overall estimate for the number of work hours required to complete the entire Design phase. Project delays are often more attributable to unrealistic time estimates than poor project execution. Break down your project to properly estimate durations and avoid delays.

3. Cost Overruns

Cost overruns are triggered by the same issues that cause schedule delays. It's easy to underestimate the cost of a phase if you haven't decomposed it enough to discover what each component truly costs. As with project delays, cost overruns are often more attributable to unrealistic cost estimates than to poor execution.

4. Unclear Work Assignments

Unclear work assignments can occur when tasks are assigned to resources at too high a level for them to decipher which aspects of the work are their responsibility and which aspects should be handled by others. The less you break down the project, the less clear your understanding will be about the work that must be done and the less realistic your expectations will be. As the project manager, clients and sponsors have assigned you the entire project scope statement. In turn, you will assign aspects of that project scope to the resources who will perform the work. In this sense, your job is to break down the project scope statement finely enough to create a task scope statement for every resource on your project. If you approach task assignments in this way, you will set better expectations, improve project communications, and deliver project outcomes more efficiently. If you don't, your resources may be unclear as to the specific work they must do to deliver their part of the project. This lack of clarity will ultimately result in inaction, push-back, and rework.

5. Failure to Deliver 100% of the Project

As simple as it may sound, the best way to ensure you deliver 100% of your project is to break down 100% of your project. This will allow you and your stakeholders to confirm that no deliverable is missing. One way to think about a fully broken-down project is as an exhaustive itemization of what will be included when you deliver the final product, service, or result - and what will <u>not</u> be included. This will naturally lead to conflict, as some stakeholders will expect things that may not be possible within the cost and schedule constraints. Don't shy away from this conflict. Rather, embrace it for its potential. Any conflicts you surface and resolve at this stage will result in clearer expectations as to what the finished product will include. Also, the best time to negotiate for more time or budget to satisfy expectations is at the beginning of your project.

6. Unclear Expectations

When you break down the project scope into clearly defined deliverables, stakeholders and sponsors can plainly see the impact of their expectations on the project schedule and budget. This helps to align their expectations with constraints related to scope, cost, schedule, risk, resources, or quality. It's not uncommon for stakeholders to adjust their expectations when they see these impacts. If an expectation or request is truly needed, then it can be accommodated through trade-offs between the scope, schedule, and cost.

Though it's never a pleasant process, resolving conflicting expectations is always easiest at the beginning of a project.

7. Unusable Products or Features

What makes a product or feature usable is the degree to which it satisfies the client's requirements. As mentioned earlier, these requirements (or expectations) are often refined as you break down your project scope statement into specific deliverables. The requirements for each deliverable become even more refined when resources are assigned to tasks. This is because resources will use their knowledge and experience to ask clarifying questions, which will result in further refinements. When an orderly decomposition process is not followed, there's a good chance that requirements will be missed, resulting in unusable products and features.

8. Scope Creep

There's a popular misconception that scope creep is what happens when stakeholders request things outside of the original scope of the project. But in fact, scope creep only happens when those requests have not been assessed for schedule and cost impacts, and when expectations have not been reset accordingly. These cost and schedule assessments can only be made if your project is broken down to the task level, which is the level where accurate cost and schedule estimations can be made. Scope creep is an undesirable outcome because it bypasses important cost and schedule impact assessments which leads to mismanaged expectations. If your stakeholders are holding you accountable for things that haven't been documented or vetted by your project team, this could be attributable to scope creep.
Of course, you can avoid this outcome by breaking down your project.

When Should You Break Down Your Project?

Before starting the process of breaking down your project, there are certain requirements that should be met that will help guarantee a successful project decomposition. You should only break down your project after the project scope has been clearly defined. This is a small concept, but it has BIG implications. Let's clarify what is meant by "clearly defined".
Four requirements should be met before you consider your project scope to be clearly defined. It's important to collaborate with your project stakeholders early in the process to ensure these four requirements are met.

Four Requirements of a Clearly Defined Project Scope

1. Clear Deliverables

Before your project scope is clearly defined, the project team must have a clear idea of the major deliverables of the project. Your client or project sponsor may not specify every single deliverable, but they should provide a detailed enough project scope statement that you and your project team can tease them out. Your objective is to define the project scope as granularly as possible at each stage in the project life cycle. The level of granularity required will vary based on the complexity of the project, but it should at least include a few of the major deliverables. This will help ensure everyone is on the same page about what you're delivering and what the schedule and cost implications might be.

2. Understanding the Business Need(s)

Many believe that only the project manager needs to understand the business needs and that the project resources only need to know how those business needs impact their specific area. However, the project team should also have a clear understanding of the business need(s) the project is meant to address. This gives the people who know the most about the technical aspects of the project the opportunity to cater their design solutions to the business needs they're meant to address. For example, a solutions architect may suggest one type of design if the business need is short-term in nature and a different design if they're addressing a long-term need. By making the team aware of the business needs, you're allowing the resources the widest possible view of the project.

3. Clear Requirements

Before you consider the project scope clearly defined, make sure your project team has a clear idea of the requirements of the project. This is an important step because the word "requirements" has huge implications within the project management profession. Requirements are the expressions of client expectations in clear, specific language. For this reason, project success is often equated to satisfied stakeholder requirements. To put it plainly, if your project team doesn't have a clear idea what the requirements are, your project is going to fail. Are we building a four-bedroom house or a three-bedroom house with a family room? Are we making red widgets or burgundy widgets? The success of your project requires that these distinctions be clearly spelled out at the beginning of your project.

4. Clear Expectations

Another consideration is that client expectations must be clear. What expectations must you satisfy before your stakeholders will consider the project a success? According to the PMBOK, the very definition of project success is "satisfied stakeholder expectations". Many otherwise well-managed projects fail because of unclear or conflicting client expectations. Sometimes project managers are reluctant to ask stakeholders the tough questions required for absolute clarity. Though they may sense that the client is expecting something that falls outside of schedule and budget constraints, they feel pressure to keep the client happy during the early stages of the project. Because of this, they avoid the "800-pound gorilla" and fail to ask the necessary questions. This is a grave and often unrecoverable mistake. Part of the Project Manager's role is to ask stakeholders targeted, specific questions and to facilitate meetings in which different stakeholders voice conflicting expectations. Unless these conflicts are fully resolved and each expectation is defined in terms of schedule and cost impact, it's impossible to prevent scope creep. If you find the idea of conflict resolution intimidating, consider taking a consultative, rather than a combative posture. Your job at this stage is simply to <u>define</u> each stakeholder expectation in terms of its potential impact to schedule, cost, risk, or quality, <u>facilitate</u> the conflict discussion and <u>document</u> final decisions. Despite the possibility of wildly conflicting expectations, remember that all stakeholders are governed by the same set of constraints. Setting clear stakeholder expectations is about using these constraints to facilitate the resolution of conflicting requests. Once you set clear expectations with your stakeholders, they can set clear expectations with their constituents, thereby significantly increasing your likelihood of project success.

We've now reviewed when you should break down your project – which is after the four requirements of a clearly defined project scope have been met.

Who Should Break Down Your Project?

Not that we've explained why and when you should break down your project, the next question is who should do this important work? The most popular response to this question is the **Project Manager**. After all, they should be knowledgeable about <u>all</u> technical aspects of the project. So, the PM should decompose the project...Right? While the project manager *should* be knowledgeable about the technical aspects of the project, they may not have the technical know-how to decompose the aspects of the project that are not related to project management.

How about the **Project Team**? They have the technical knowledge. Maybe they could have a team meeting to decompose the project scope statement into manageable parts. This is a logical choice. However, though the project team will have the technical expertise the project manager lacks, they can't speak to the aspects of the work that are project management-related, like securing adequate funding or setting the proper expectations with project sponsors and stakeholders. Now that we've brought **Sponsors** and **Stakeholders** into the mix, let's consider whether they should be the ones to break down the project. They could be good candidates since they'd have the best idea what the project outcome should be and may therefore be the best qualified to define their expectations in more specific terms. However, they lack both the project management and technical insights.

Given all these considerations, who should break down the project? Because each stakeholder possesses knowledge and a valuable perspective the others lack, the correct answer is **ALL THE ABOVE**. Therefore, the Project Manager should secure participation from stakeholders in each role. Some project professionals may consider this level of collaboration to be more than what's required. But consider the far-reaching impacts of an insufficiently broken-down project scope statement. As emphasized throughout this chapter, mistakes made at the beginning of a project often propagate through the project life cycle and result in project failure. The opposite is also true. Best practices established up front will also propagate through and manifest as clear expectations and a well-organized project.

6 Reasons to Include All Relevant Players

Once you're convinced that each player needs to be engaged in the process of breaking down your project, your next challenge will be to convince your stakeholders. Here are six reasons to include all relevant players when you break down your project into manageable parts.

1. **It Requires Expert Knowledge**. Subject Matter Experts must be engaged to explain the technical implications of one expectation versus another. This facilitates real-time feedback and allows high-level stakeholders to debate the downstream implications of their expectations. Such discussions often result in some requirements being scaled back or removed altogether from the project scope.

2. **To ensure 100% of the Supporting Details get Discussed, Assessed, and Factored In.** As mentioned earlier, schedule and cost overruns are often the result of project scope statements not being sufficiently broken down. Although you won't do a full project scope decomposition at this stage, the ability to interpret high-level expectations in terms of low-level impacts will prove invaluable at the start of any project.

3. **To Establish Accountability.** When you break down your project into manageable parts, you'll also be distributing accountability across the organization, from the department level down to the resources that will perform the work. Whenever escalations, clarifying questions, or praise for a job well done surface, your project breakdown will facilitate easy channeling to the appropriate parts of the business. Also, from an accounting standpoint, your project breakdown will allow you to quickly assign labor hours and capital purchases to appropriate departments.

4. **To Trigger Memory.** This is the most subtle reason to have the key players present – it triggers memory. As much as experts may be inclined to trust in their ability to recall things, the most thorough project decompositions are always the result of collaborative brainstorming sessions. One person suggests an activity, which causes another person to remember a related activity. This is how we avoid missing key pieces to the puzzle.

5. **To Establish Ownership.** The difference between accountability and ownership is like the difference between an engineer and her boss. The engineer has ownership of a task on your project. However, if something catastrophic happens on the project, then their boss (as well as the engineer) will be answerable (else, accountable) for the occurrence. Reason # 3 was to establish accountability at the boss level. Reason # 5 is to get even more specific and establish ownership at the resource level. Nothing builds project momentum faster than early notification that work is coming down the pipeline sooner rather than later. This allows task owners to shift work around, if necessary, to work on your deliverables. It also clarifies to project stakeholders who owns which portions of the work and which leadership towers may need to be engaged if issues arise.

6. It allows each party to **Validate the Project Scope Statement** by clarifying upfront how the scope of the project will impact their part of the business from a cost and scheduling perspective. This type of validation greatly improves the likelihood of project success by setting the right expectations at the start of the project. It clarifies to stakeholders why some expectations will turn into requirements, and why *some* will be removed from the scope of the project. It's not uncommon for such de-scoped items to turn into new project initiatives. Because those expectations will have the benefit of early analysis from the relevant subject matter experts, high-level stakeholders will benefit as much from the expectations that are removed from the project scope as the ones that remain in scope. As a result, if those requirements do become new projects, they will be initiated faster than they otherwise would have.

We've now explained who should break down your project and 6 reasons to engage all the key players who possess the expertise and valuable perspective to ensure clear expectations and a well-organized project.

What is a Broken-Down Project?

Now that we've established the Why, When, and Who, we can define What is a broken-down project? What end result are we looking for when we do this work? In project management jargon, a fully broken-down project is called a **Work Breakdown Structure** or **WBS**. A WBS is a breakdown of the work required to deliver a project into smaller, more manageable parts, which can then be broken down further into tasks that can be scheduled, priced, monitored and controlled. This work breakdown structure will become the framework of your project schedule.

To convert a work breakdown structure into a project schedule, you'll need to assign a resource to each task. You'll then collaborate with your resources to get each task forecasted, sequenced, priced, monitored and controlled – until you successfully deliver your project. This is what robust scheduling apps like Microsoft Project are designed to help you do. As mentioned earlier, the pre-work for using this robust tool, and the proper starting point, is to build a work breakdown structure. To demonstrate how your work breakdown structure can help you achieve project success, let's revisit the definition and break each part down to get a better understanding.

The first part of the definition, **"a breakdown of the work required to deliver a project"** describes the end game. What's not stated in the definition is what you're actually breaking down or decomposing, which is the project scope statement. Your goal is to break down your project scope statement as granularly as possible. The question is, how granular should that breakdown be? That's what the next part of the definition begins to answer – **"into smaller, more manageable parts".** The operative word here is manageable. The main reason to break a project down is that project scope statements are too high-level to be actionable, and by extension manageable. When you break down that project scope statement into a definitive number of distinct deliverables, your project will become more manageable. Both you and your stakeholders will have a better idea of how you will deliver it. However, at this stage, you won't be able to estimate things like time to completion, or total cost. This type of information will require a further level of breakdown. That's where the next part of the definition comes into play – **"which can then be broken down further into tasks"**. This is the actionable level – the task level where work gets done.

Unlike phases or major project deliverables, tasks have several important and distinct attributes, which makes them actionable. This brings us to the last part of the definition. The task level is where you can collaborate with the resources assigned to the tasks to get them **"forecasted, sequenced, priced, monitored and controlled"** – until you successfully deliver your project. In the next section, we'll examine each task attribute and clarify the role of each in successful project delivery.

Task Attributes

- Tasks can be **Assigned**. The pairing of a task and a resource is called an assignment.

- Tasks can be **Forecasted**. Every task has a start date, a finish date, and a duration. This is what is meant by forecasting a task – making an educated estimation of when it will be completed. Naturally, this forecast will depend on the task owner's schedule and proficiency level, among other things. One of the key features of Microsoft Project is this forecast can be used to track both time and cost.

- Tasks can be **Sequenced**. By sequencing, we mean that some tasks must be completed before other tasks can start. This is known as a Finish-to-Start task relationship. Other tasks can be worked in parallel, maybe sharing a Start-to-Start task relationship.

Microsoft Project lets you sequence tasks using all four task relationship types. If you're not familiar with the different task relationships, we'll explain them in Chapter 4, and provide examples of when you should use each type.

- Tasks can also be **Priced**. As mentioned, the pairing of a task and a resource is called an assignment. This pairing will trigger the first set of cost estimates. Project automatically calculates the cost of a task by multiplying the resource's pay rate by the hours they spend working on the task. You're probably starting to see how breaking your project down to the task level can give you a more accurate assessment of your project's cost.

- Tasks can also be **Monitored**. For example, when your resource says they can complete a task in 10 days, you can check in with the resource after 5 days (i.e., monitor their progress) to determine whether they're on schedule. As you'll see in later chapters, Project has several tracking tools to capture your progress data and re-forecast your schedule based upon these updates.

- Finally, tasks can be **Controlled**. In simple terms, controlling a task is the work you do to keep it on schedule. Using the prior example, if you monitor the resource working the task on the 5th day and determine that they need another 10 days to complete it (instead of another 5 days as they originally planned) you will need to intervene with actions to recover the project schedule. This is what is meant by "controlling" the task. Your intervening actions may include approving overtime or escalating the concern to senior leaders so they can reinforce the urgency and priority of your project. To perform all these actions, you must break your project down to the actionable task level.

Now that we've reviewed the definition of a fully broken-down project (or work breakdown structure), let's look at what this means practically. Suppose your project is to build your dream home. How do you break down such a lofty project into something you can manage? Your primary objective is to organize the project into levels of work, starting with the major deliverables.

Levels of Decomposition

Level One Deliverable

The first level of decomposition, **Level One**, would be the final deliverable – **Build Dream House**. This is what you plan to deliver at the end of the project. The level one deliverable comprises the full scope of the project. In practical terms, this is the expression of your project scope statement as a deliverable.

The WBS Coding Scheme

To keep things orderly as you decompose your project, you can incorporate the numerical system that the Project Management Institute refers to as the **WBS coding scheme**. Using this scheme, each component of the project is assigned a numerical code, corresponding with its position in the Work Breakdown Structure (WBS). For the Dream Home WBS, the level one, final deliverable "Build Dream Home" would be assigned numerical code **1** or **1.0**. In Microsoft Project, the task that describes your final deliverable is called the **Project Summary Task**. We'll delve into this feature and demonstrate its utility in an upcoming chapter. For now, just note that it's the top level in your WBS and it represents the final deliverable of your project. It's helpful to think of a WBS as an org chart. The org chart structure is what the "Structure" in Work Breakdown Structure is referring to. At the top of the org chart that will become our Dream House WBS is the "Build Dream Home" deliverable.

Level Two Deliverables

Now that we've identified the final deliverable of the project, we'll need to identify the components comprising the next level of deliverables - the **Level Two** deliverables. Since we're building a dream house, this level would include General Conditions (which covers areas like Architectural Drawings and Permits), Site Work, Foundation, Framing, Dry In, Exterior Finishes, Utility Rough-Ins, Interior Finishes, Landscaping and Groundwork, and Final Acceptance. By listing these ten major deliverables in your breakdown, you'll be demonstrating to your stakeholders exactly how you're going to deliver the project. Simply stated, once these ten deliverables are complete, you will have built your Dream Home. This is where you would begin to inspire confidence in your ability to manage the project.

Pop Quiz: How did we determine these ten major deliverables? As we learned earlier in explaining who should break down your project, such a robust and exhaustive set of deliverables could never come from the project manager alone. It's the output of a diverse team of key stakeholders and subject matter experts. You'll need this select team to remain engaged at some level until you have a fully decomposed project.

Let's take a closer look at the 10 Level Two deliverables, shown in *Figure 82* below.

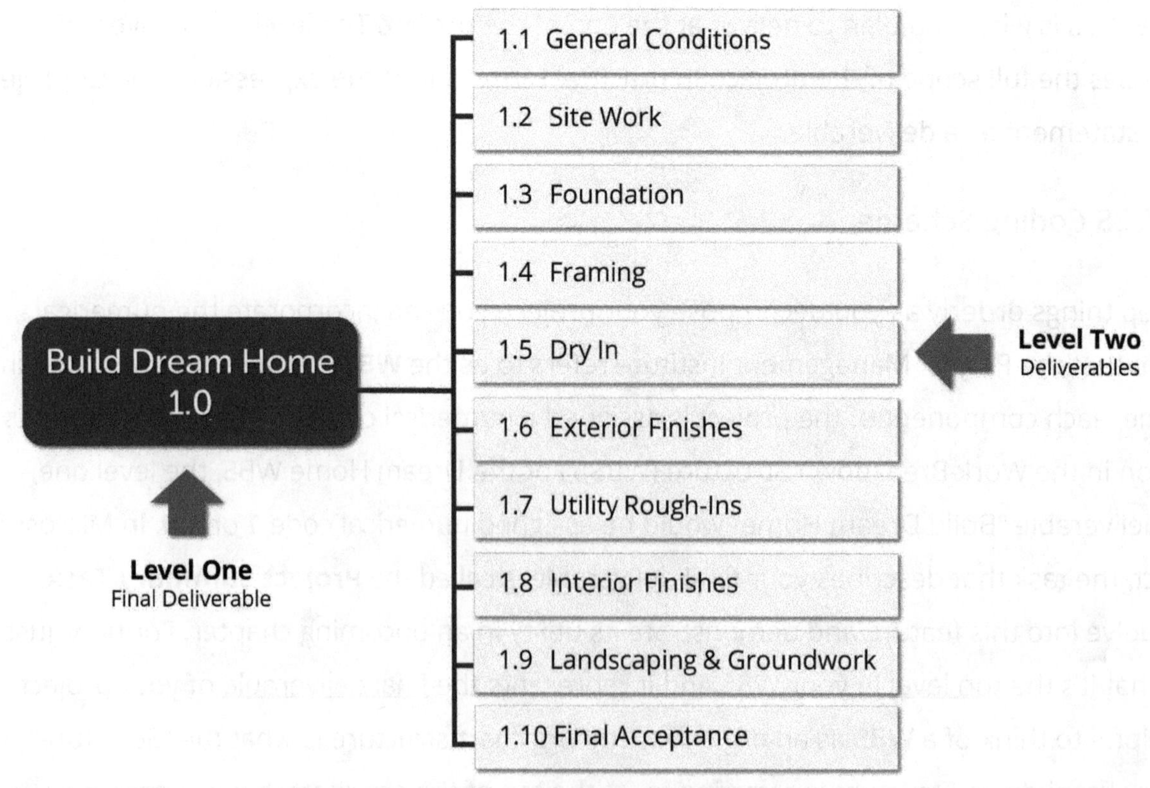

Figure 82 – Level Two Deliverables

Level two comprises all the work required to produce the level one deliverable. Since the level one deliverable required decomposition, it's considered a **parent-level** deliverable – which is any deliverable that gets further decomposed into sub-deliverables or **child** deliverables. In the WBS coding scheme, the level two deliverables would be coded **1.1** for General Conditions, **1.2** for Site Work, **1.3** for Foundation, and so forth.

The 100% Rule

One important rule to note when breaking down your project is the **100% Rule**. What this rule means is that 100% of the deliverables required to deliver your project must be included in your work breakdown structure. Equally important, your breakdown should not include more than 100% of the work required to deliver your project. For our Dream Home project, this means that when the ten level two deliverables are complete, the entire Dream Home project should be complete. This rule applies to each level of your Work Breakdown Structure. The formal definition of the 100% Rule is – **The sum of the work at the child level must equal 100% of the work represented by the parent level**. For example, when we break down the work required to complete the General Conditions work, we must be sure to capture 100% of the tasks comprising this deliverable. Only by ensuring the 100% rule is followed at each level of your project breakdown can you validate the integrity of your Work Breakdown Structure and, by extension, your project schedule. With this principle in mind, let's move on to the next level of decomposition – Level Three.

Level Three Deliverables

We must now determine what work is required to deliver each of the ten level two deliverables. Let's focus on deliverable 1.1 – General Conditions. We've learned from our subject matter experts that to complete the General Conditions deliverable, we'll need to secure architectural plans and all required permits. In keeping with the 100% rule, we've confirmed that these two **Level Three** deliverables comprise 100% of the work required to produce the General Conditions, parent level deliverable. The WBS codes for the Plans and Permits deliverables are 1.1.1 and 1.1.2, respectively (*Figure 83*).

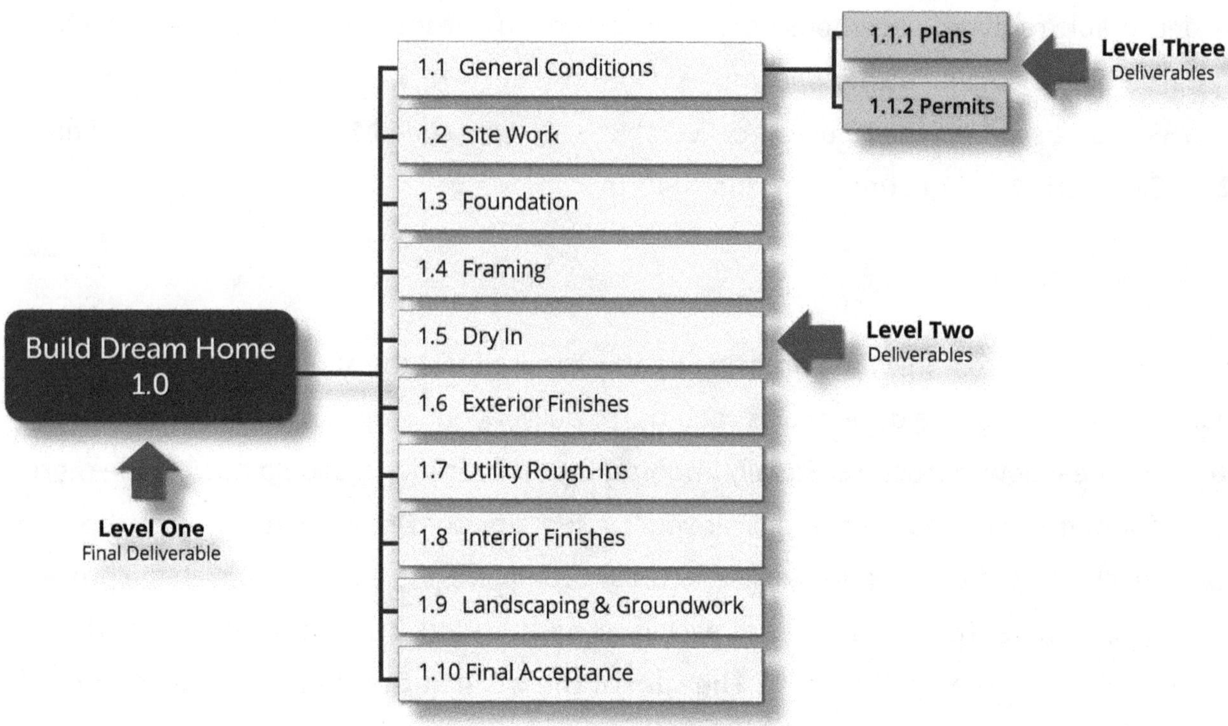

Figure 83 – Level Three Deliverables

The Exclusivity Rule

When organizing child deliverables like the level three deliverables, each child deliverable must belong to one and only one parent. For example, deliverable 1.1.2. Permits should only be included under the 1.1 General Conditions deliverable, and not repeated under another parent deliverable, such as 1.3 Foundation or 1.4 Framing. Though permits may also be required in other aspects of the work, we must capture this work in one and only one area. This exclusivity rule highlights that there are several correct ways to deconstruct any project. For instance, Permits can be included under General Conditions where it represents 100% of the permits for the Dream Home project, or trade-specific permits could be included under each respective deliverable as shown in *Figure 84*. By following this exclusivity rule, no deliverable will be listed under two different parent deliverables and your resources will be clear about where their unique deliverable is captured in your plan.

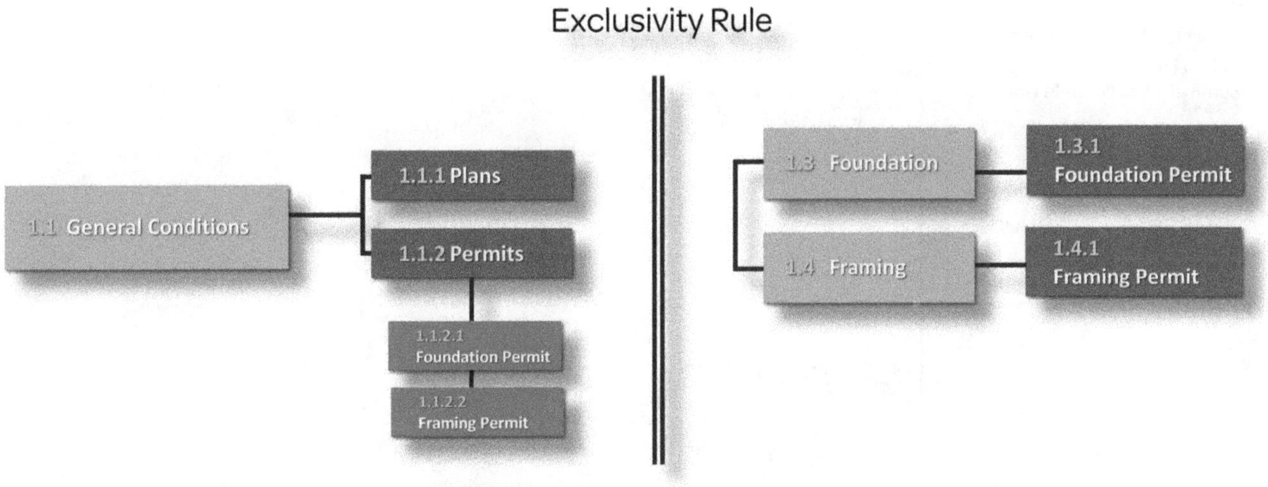

Exclusivity Rule

1.1 General Conditions
1.1.1 Plans
1.1.2 Permits
1.1.2.1 Foundation Permit
1.1.2.2 Framing Permit
1.3 Foundation
1.3.1 Foundation Permit
1.4 Framing
1.4.1 Framing Permit

Figure 84 – The Exclusivity Rule

Level Four Deliverables

Once we perform a similar breakdown for the remaining nine level two deliverables, we will have captured all the level three deliverables. While this represents significant progress, we still need another level of breakdown. Since we cannot perform a task called Plans or Permits, we must continue to decompose our project - down to the actionable level. Because Plans and Permits are not actionable, they are considered **Interim Deliverables** - which are sub-deliverables that summarize actionable work. This brings us to our final level of decomposition - **Level Four**.

The Actionable Level

For the 1.1 General Conditions deliverable, level four will represent the task level, where actionable work can be done. It will comprise 100% of the work required to produce parent level deliverables. We've learned from our subject matter experts that to satisfy the 1.1.1 Plans deliverable, we'll need to secure a set of final plans and sign the contract. In the WBS coding scheme, these two actionable deliverables, or tasks, would be coded **1.1.1.1** for Finalize Plans and **1.1.1.2** for Sign Contract. We've also been told by our SMEs that six tasks are required to produce the 1.1.2 Permits deliverable. *Figure 85* shows the level four decomposition of the 1.1 General Conditions deliverable.

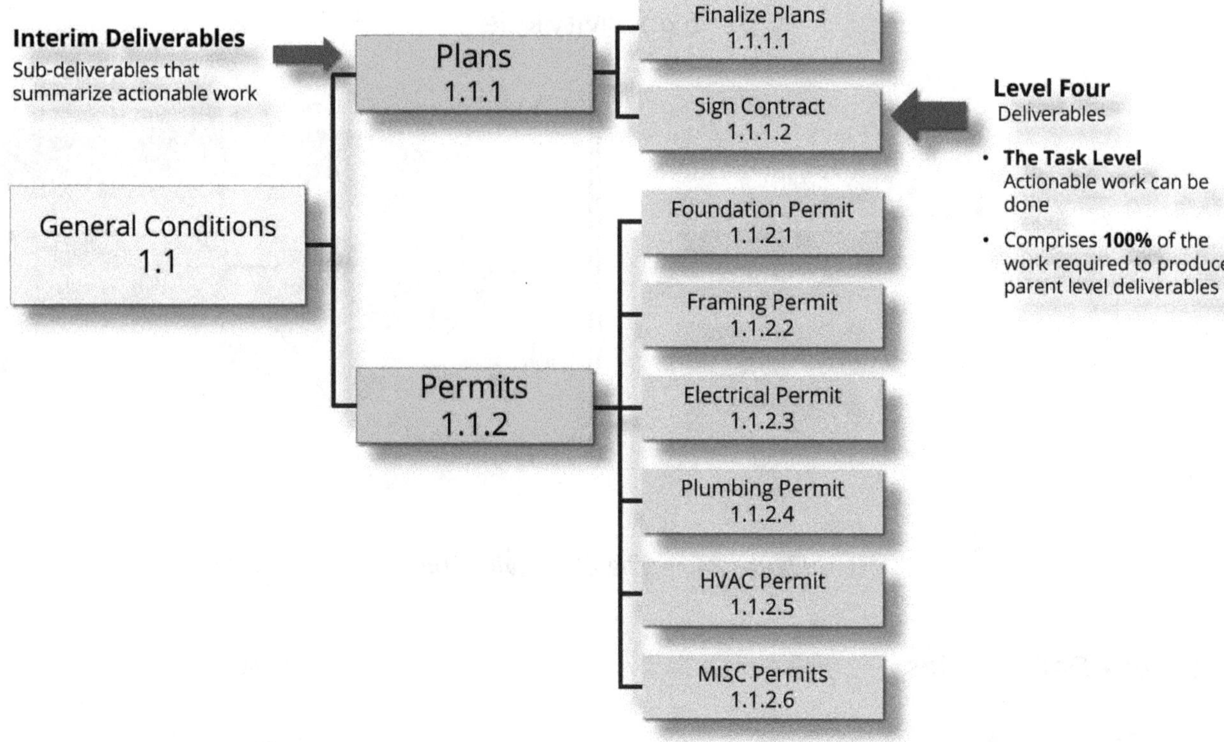

Figure 85 – The Actionable Task Level

To put this decomposition work into a practical context, the level two deliverable, called 1.1 General Conditions will be complete when the eight tasks under deliverables 1.1.1 Plans and 1.1.2 Permits are complete.

Now that we're at the task level, in this case level four, we can begin the work of assigning, scheduling, budgeting, monitoring, and controlling tasks. For example, we can assign the *Finalize Plans* task to the Architect. After speaking with the Architect, we learned that he estimates the task to be 80 hours of work and he's only available to work on the task 4 hours per day. So, the duration estimate for this task is 20 days (80 hrs. Work / 4 hrs. per day). With a Work estimate of 80 hours, and the Architect's hourly rate of $200 per hour, we can estimate a cost for this task of $16,000 ($200/hr. X 80 hrs.). This is where Microsoft Project's powerful scheduling engine goes to work. When you enter the work estimates and resource availability, Project will automatically calculate duration and cost. Moreover, once you have a similar breakdown for every task in your project, you can use Project to monitor these estimates to ensure they remain on schedule and on budget and to manage cost overruns and schedule delays when things don't go as planned.

Keep in mind, not every deliverable will require a level four breakdown to get to the task level. The breakdown level of each deliverable will be determined by the control needs of the deliverable. By breaking down your project according to the control needs of each deliverable, you will avoid being so high level that you're likely to miss things and so low level that you're likely to micromanage your resources. The same idea applies to projects in general. Not every project will require the same number of decomposition levels. Your level of decomposition should be determined by the control needs of your project. Every project will, however, need to be broken down to the task level, where actionable work can be assigned, scheduled, priced, monitored and controlled.

To summarize, a fully broken-down project (or work breakdown structure) contains 100% of the work required to deliver the project. At the top level (Level One) is the project's ultimate goal. The next level (Level Two) contains the major deliverables, often referred to as phases. The next level (Level Three and any additional levels) will contain Interim deliverables and the final level of your breakdown will contain the tasks or actionable work. *Figure 86* shows the completed Work Breakdown Structure for the Dream Home project. This is what you're after when you gather your project team, sponsors, and key stakeholders.

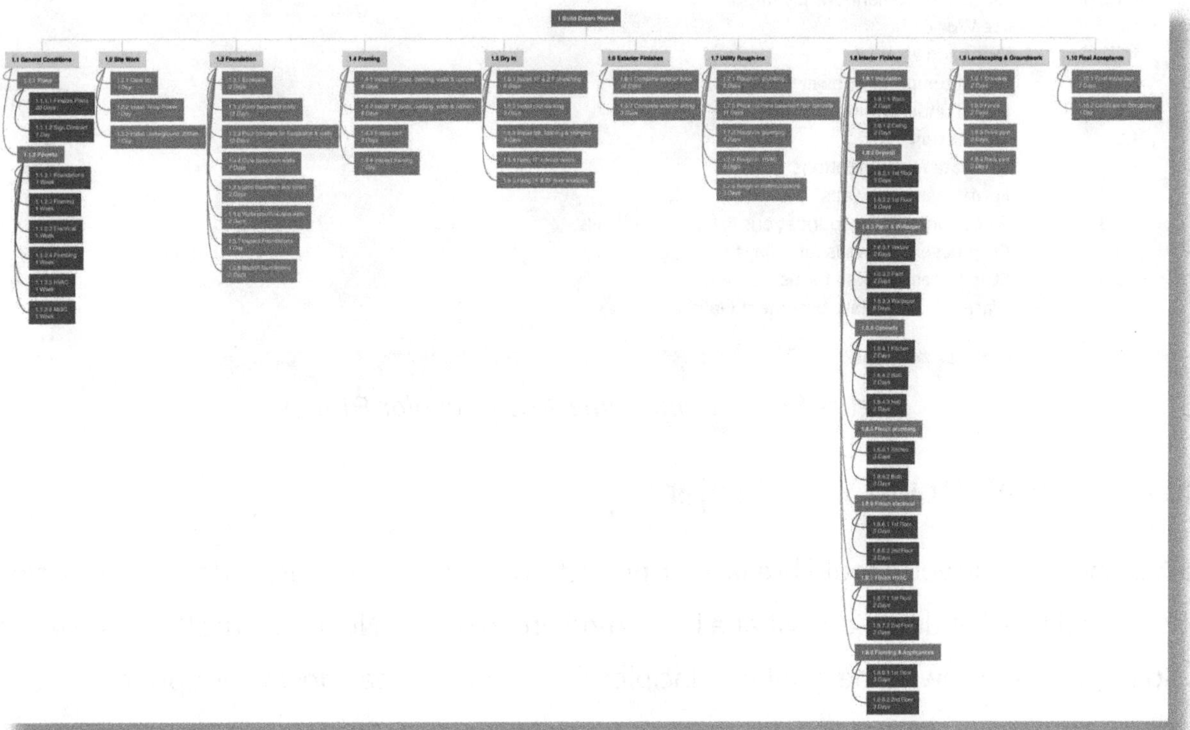

Figure 86 – Dream Home Complete WBS

High-level stakeholders may not be required when you get down to the lower decomposition levels, but they should certainly be involved through the level two breakdown. After you've worked with your experts to decompose the entire project, it's a good idea to re-engage your high-level stakeholders before constructing your schedule in Microsoft Project.

A graphical view of your work breakdown structure is an excellent communication tool. It allows your sponsors and stakeholders to quickly view your project at as high or low a level as they prefer and to refine their expectations around what your project will and will not be delivering. *Figure 87* below shows a portion of our graphical work breakdown structure in a tabular format. This is the way you will enter your WBS into scheduling software, like Microsoft Project.

1	**Build Dream Home**
1.1	**General Conditions**
1.1.1	**Plans**
1.1.1.1	Finalize plans and develop estimate with owner, architect
1.1.1.2	Sign contract and notice to proceed
1.1.2	**Permits**
1.1.2.1	Secure foundation permit
1.1.2.2	Secure framing permit
1.1.2.3	Secure electrical permit
1.1.2.4	Secure plumbing permit
1.1.2.5	Secure HVAC permit
1.1.2.6	Secure miscellaneous permits
1.2	**Site Work**
1.2.1	Clear and grub lot
1.2.2	Install temporary power service
1.2.3	Install underground utilities
1.3	**Foundation**
1.3.1	Excavate for foundations
1.3.2	Form basement walls
1.3.3	Place concrete for foundations & basement walls
1.3.4	Cure basement walls for 7 days
1.3.5	Strip basement wall forms
1.3.6	Waterproof/insulate basement walls

Figure 87 – Dream Home WBS - Tabular Format

How to Break Down Your Project

We've covered why you should break your project, when you should breakdown your project, who should break it down, and what a broken-down project is. Now the question is how to do it. So far, we've reviewed the guiding principles for breaking break down your project. We'll now put it all together and structure these principles into five concrete steps you can follow to produce a quality Work Breakdown Structure each time you approach a new or unfamiliar project.

5 Steps to Break Down Your Project

To break down your project, you'll need to:

1. Clarify the Project Scope
2. Gather the Project Stakeholders
3. Gather the Relevant Information
4. Develop your WBS
5. Check the Quality of your WBS

Let's take a closer look at each step.

Step 1 - Clarify the Project Scope

Most people have never heard of George Fuechsel, but nearly everyone has heard of the phrase he coined – *"Garbage in, Garbage out"*. Fuechsel was an early IBM programmer and instructor who used this phrase as a concise way to remind his students that computers can only process the input that they're given, and to therefore, write good code. The same is true for your work breakdown structure. If you use a vague project scope statement as your input, your output will be a vague WBS. To prevent this outcome, before you begin any breakdown work, you should get clear answers to questions like those listed below.

1. What is the project scope?
2. What requirements must be met to achieve business objectives?
3. What requirements must be met to satisfy <u>all</u> stakeholder expectations?
4. What assumptions are these requirements based on?
5. What distinct major deliverables are expected of this project?
6. What related deliverables are excluded from this project?
7. What are the constraints pertaining to budget, time, quality, risk, resources, and scope?

Clarifying these important details results in a clear project scope, clear requirements, and by extension, a clear breakdown of the work.

Step 2 – Gather the Stakeholders

A stakeholder is anyone who has an interest in your project, has influence on your project or is impacted by your project. Many projects have encountered challenges for ignoring stakeholders. A recent notable example is the Amazon HQ project, which was originally expected to be built in New York. Because key stakeholders were not properly notified and/or sufficiently engaged, the project was ultimately built in Washington DC, and not in New York, as planned. These stakeholders had more influence than was apparent in the early stages. To avoid challenges like this, identify as many stakeholders as you can before scheduling your project scope review meeting.

Here's a list of typical stakeholders:

- Project resources who will do the work
- End users of your project outcome
- Individuals and/or groups that are interested in your project outcome
- Individuals and/or groups that will be impacted by your project outcome
- Individuals and/or groups that can influence your project outcome
- Individuals and/or groups that become interested in your project as it progresses

Once you have as complete a list of stakeholders as possible, schedule your project scope review meeting. When in doubt as to whether someone is a stakeholder on your project, it's generally better to err on the side of having too many stakeholders than too few. Having a stakeholder opt out is always preferable to having a stakeholder derail your project because they were adversely impacted by your project outcome.

Step 3 – Gather the Relevant Information

Another thing you should do before having your project scope review meeting is gather any information that will save you time and result in a more efficient meeting. This will include things like org. charts (which can help you identify project resources, key stakeholders, and lines of accountability), the project charter (which may include a more exhaustive version of the project scope statement and business drivers) and any project management artifacts from similar projects, like WBS artifacts, project schedules, budget estimates, design documentation and any documented lessons learned.

Step 4 – Develop Your WBS

When it comes to breaking down your project and developing your WBS, you have two options:

- **Option 1:** Develop it using a preexisting WBS and/or schedule artifacts
- **Option 2:** Develop it from scratch

Using Preexisting Artifacts to Develop your WBS

If you're lucky enough to have preexisting artifacts to start with, your work will be dramatically reduced. For example, you can use schedule artifacts from similar projects to reverse engineer your WBS. These artifacts will often include many of the components you need to construct the WBS for your current project. Components might include your levels 1 through 4 deliverables and the tasks required to complete them. Consequently, you may be able to skip this step and move on to step 5, where you will check the quality of your WBS. To exploit this potential for increased efficiency, do a careful search using company records and internal resources. If no such records exist, try searching online for WBS artifacts from projects similar to yours. Also, this book's companion website – **mspbasics.com** includes samples of WBS templates across a range of industries and projects.

Developing your WBS from Scratch

If preexisting artifacts don't exist, and you must develop your WBS from scratch, you're not alone. Due to business drivers like digital transformation and post-COVID mergers and acquisitions, there's a dramatic increase in new and unfamiliar project types. Whatever the driver, if you must develop your work breakdown structure from scratch, you'll need to use a combination of **time-saving developmental tools** and **proven build methods**.

Using Time-Saving Developmental Tools

Typical Elements

A good list of **typical WBS elements** can trigger ideas for developing your WBS. The project management profession is mature enough that all projects - even ones that have never been done before - include some typical elements or deliverables that are common across a range of project categories. For example, if you're planning an event, be it a wedding or a marathon, you'll encounter typical elements like securing a venue, developing a list of participants, and hiring vendors. If you're implementing a new system of any type, your typical elements might include procuring the equipment, configuring it, and integrating it with existing systems. Project managers can usually shorten their work by identifying typical elements across a range of project types. *Figure 88* shows a list of 15 typical elements. You can use this list to kick-start your brainstorming efforts with your project team and stakeholders.

Typical Project Elements

Integration	Procurement	Supply Chain Management	Administration	Information/ Communication
Documentation	Training	Software Development	Testing	Planning
Analysis	Assembly	Configuration	Implementation	Registration

Figure 88 – Typical Project Elements

Using Typical Breakdown Logic Structures

Another time-saving developmental tool you can use is **typical breakdown logic structures**. There are several types to choose from. The one you choose should be based on the inherent structure of your project.

Component-based Logic Structures

If your project includes components that make up a system, consider this option to base your WBS on. *Figure 89* below shows a component-based logic structure for a project to build a bicycle.

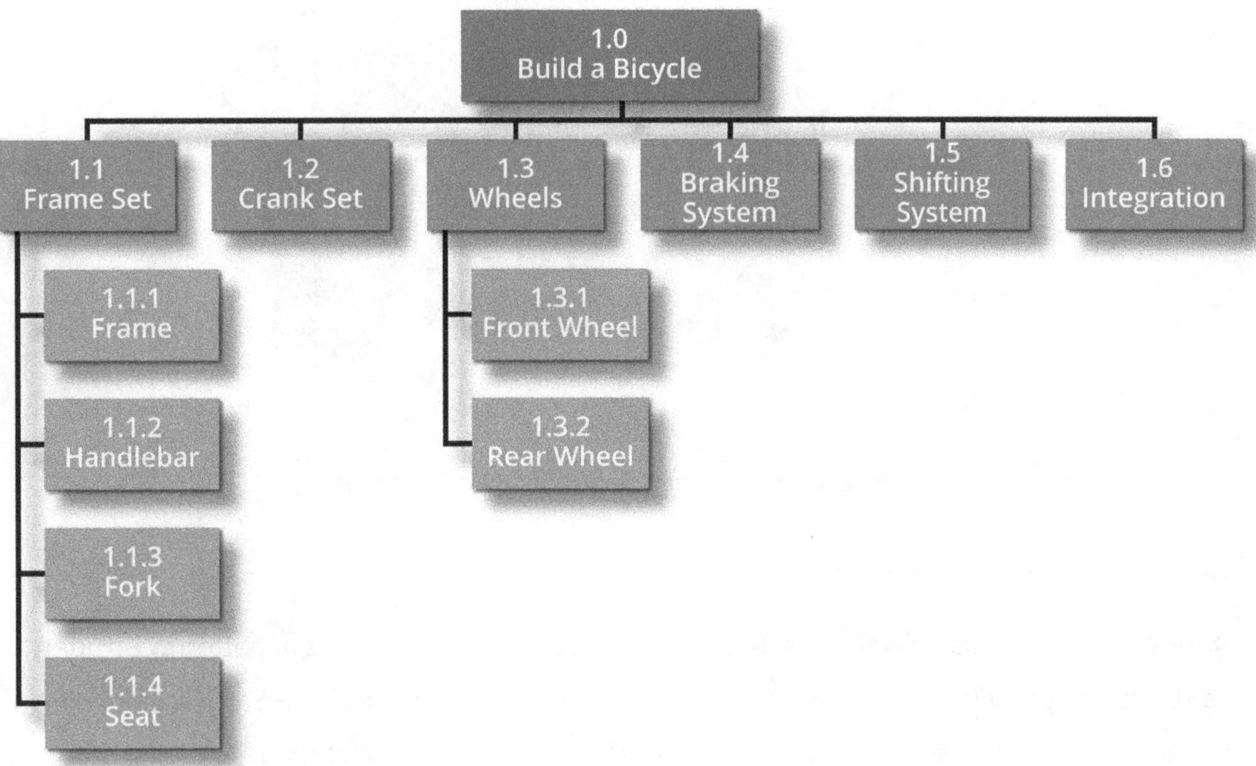

Figure 89 – Component-Based Logic Structure

Geography-based Logic Structure

If your project includes deliverables that must be deployed across geographies, consider this type of logic structure. *Figure 90* shows an example of a geography-based logic structure for a National Restaurant Chain.

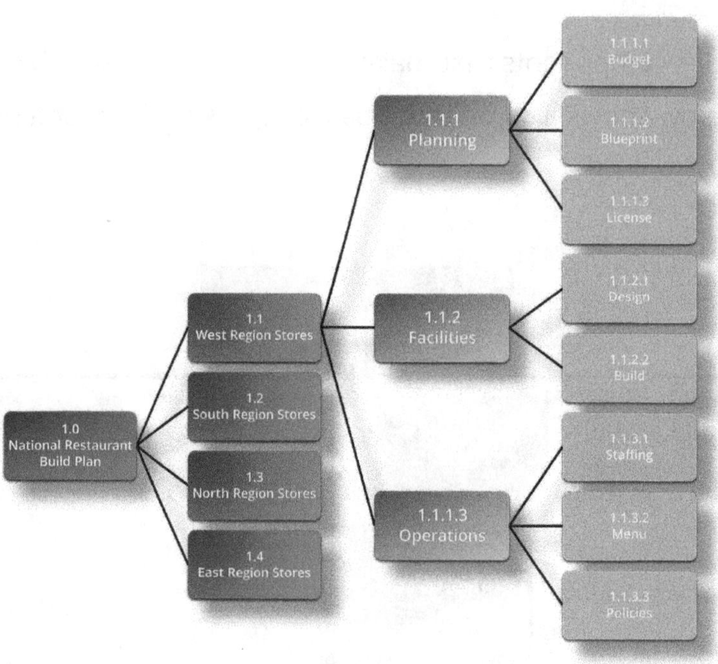

Figure 90 – Geography-Based Logic Structure

Sequence-Based Logic Structure

If your project includes deliverables that must be deployed in a sequential pattern, consider this structure type. *Figure 91* shows a sequence-based logic structure for a Software Build Plan that uses a traditional "waterfall" approach, which is very sequential and easy to follow.

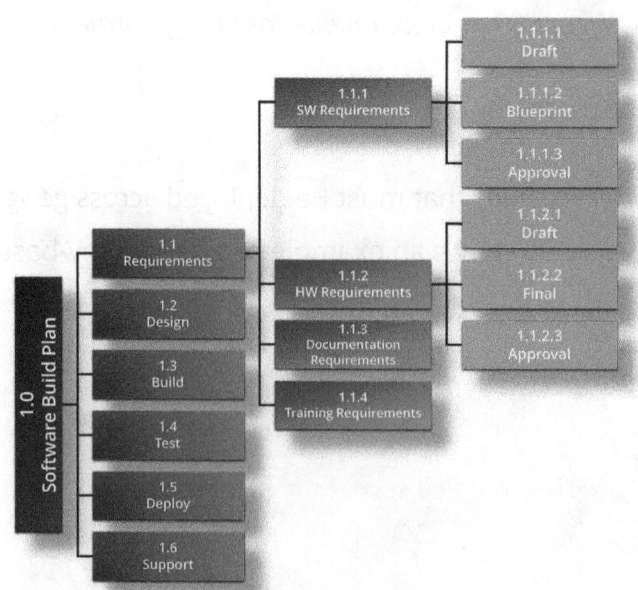

Figure 91 – Sequential-Based Logic Structure

Trade-based or Work Group-based Logic Structure

If your project includes deliverables that must be deployed by different trades or work groups, consider a trade-based or work group-based logic structure. *Figure 92* below shows this type of structure for a Construction Build Plan for a Modern Home or Office Facility.

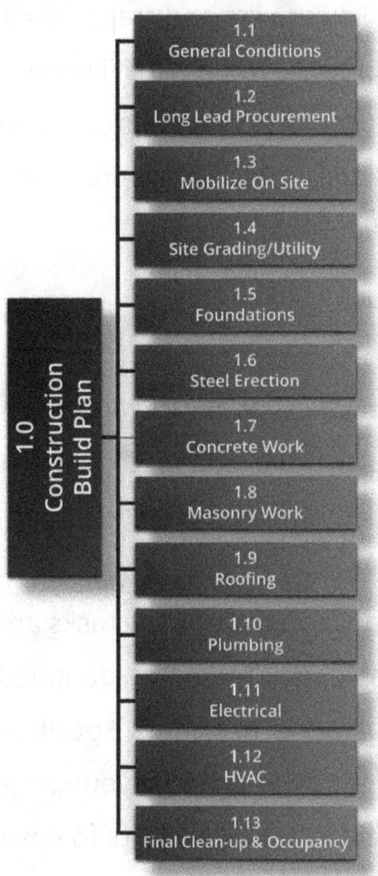

Figure 92 – Trade-Based or Work-Group Based Logic Structure

Not sure which Logic Structure works best for your project? As you peruse logic structures, consider things like how you will be asked to report on your project, and how your organization typically categorizes projects. For example, projects in your organization may typically be categorized by geography or by technological components, or maybe by trades or work areas. As you can see, there are many ways to organize your WBS. These examples may trigger you to develop your own logic structure, or you could use a hybrid structure, consisting of relevant aspects from the examples provided. As you develop your structure, bear in mind that this is also a communication tool. Therefore, when you're trying to decide upon a structure, lean toward simplicity. The more intuitive your WBS is to your project stakeholders, the more intuitive your project schedule will be.

Proven Build Methods

In addition to the time-saving developmental tools we've discussed, there are two proven build methods you can use to develop your WBS. The **Top-Down Planning** approach and the **Bottom-Up Planning** approach are the recognized build methods for constructing work breakdown structures. There are key drivers and steps for using either approach, and some drivers are common to either approach. While we will review each approach separately, in practice, both approaches are used in an intermittent and often overlapping fashion. By learning the drivers and steps related to both approaches, you'll be able to toggle between them with more deliberation and purpose.

Top-Down Planning

The Top-Down Planning approach is essentially the approach we've been reviewing thus far, which is to begin with the final deliverable, and break it down into smaller, more manageable parts. You should consider this method when your team has a clear idea which major deliverables constitute the overall scope of your project. This approach involves facilitating a structured brainstorming session to extract all the tasks and considerations that may contribute to each major deliverable your team has identified. It's important to ensure your team has enough experience to pass the 100% rule. Specifically, they must be qualified to identify 100% of the major deliverables comprising your project scope. If you have any doubts, cross check your work output against similar projects to ensure no major deliverables were missed. If you're confident your team has enough experience to pass the 100% rule, follow these **six steps** in your Top-down planning session for consistently strong results.

1. Assemble your project team and major stakeholders.

2. Define the final product.

3. Brainstorm to determine the major deliverables.

4. Brainstorm to break each major deliverable down to the task level.

5. Analyze to ensure 100% of the work is represented under each deliverable.

6. Refine the WBS until it's complete.

Bottom-Up Planning

If you're not sure your team has enough experience to identify 100% of the major deliverables of the project, you should consider using a Bottom-up Planning approach. Using the bottom-up method, you begin with brainstorming possible solutions to meet the final deliverable. Consider this approach when your team doesn't have a clear idea which major deliverables constitute the overall scope of your project. You know what the project objective is – you're just not quite sure how to get there. Even experienced project teams use this approach when they're managing a new or unfamiliar type of project. Bottom-Up Planning involves unstructured brainstorming to extract all the tasks, considerations and deliverables that may be required to deliver the full scope of the project. For maximum success, consider recording the session or assigning note takers ahead of time. Even two note takers are ideal, as the ideas can come out like popcorn – too many ideas to capture at the beginning and sparse ideas at the end.

Once you've made provisions to capture all the ideas, follow these **ten steps** for high-quality results from your Bottom-up planning session.

1. Assemble the project team and major stakeholders.

2. Brainstorm all tasks and deliverables required to deliver the project.

At this stage, try to avoid editing for redundancy or quality. The goal is to capture every idea as it comes out. Sometimes two ideas can sound similar, but by capturing both ideas at the ideation stage, and then later probing, you may uncover nuances between them which can lead to a more robust WBS.

3. Distinguish between tasks and deliverables.

4. In keeping with the *Exclusivity Rule*, associate each task to one and only one parent deliverable.

5. Analyze to ensure 100% of the work is represented under each deliverable.

6. Logically group deliverables together.

7. Logically group all deliverables to the next level up.

8. Analyze to ensure 100% of the work is represented at each level.

9. Continue grouping until you have identified the top-level major deliverables comprising the entire project.

10. Refine your WBS until it's complete.

Now that we've looked at both planning approaches, you can probably see how you might toggle intermittently between the two. We've now reviewed **Step #4** of how to break down your project – **Develop your WBS**. As we've discussed, there are many tools and processes you can use. You can use preexisting artifacts to get you going, or you can develop your WBS from scratch, using time-saving tools like typical elements and logic structures, or the proven build methods of Top-Down and Bottom-Up Planning.

Once you've developed your WBS, your confidence level in your ability to effectively manage your project will increase dramatically. You will have depicted how you will achieve your project objectives, defined those objectives in terms of specific deliverables all stakeholders can understand, organized those deliverables into logical phases and delineated clear areas of responsibility across your entire project team, thereby establishing a basis for accountability as your project moves from planning to execution.

Step 5 – Check the Quality of Your WBS

The last step to break down your project is to **check the quality of your WBS**. Considering the tangible benefits of building a robust work breakdown structure, it's a good idea to do a quality check before marking this important item complete on your task list. Below, is a checklist of **15 questions** you can ask to check the quality of your WBS. If you can answer each question with a resounding **YES!**, rest assured, you have built yourself a high-quality WBS!

WBS Quality Checklist

- ✓ Is your WBS organized into deliverable-oriented groupings?
- ✓ Does your WBS reflect the full scope of your project?
- ✓ Does your WBS clarify the work required to deliver the project?

- ✓ Does your WBS clearly communicate the scope of your project to all stakeholders?
- ✓ Does your WBS capture all the internal and external deliverables of your project?
- ✓ Does each phase or grouping include 100% of the work required to deliver it?
- ✓ Is your WBS depicted in a graphical or outline form that is easy to read?
- ✓ Are all major and minor deliverables organized in a hierarchical structure?
- ✓ Does your WBS coding scheme clearly identify each element in a way that clearly shows its place in the hierarchy?
- ✓ Does your WBS include input from those who will perform the work?
- ✓ Does your WBS include input or feedback from impacted stakeholders?
- ✓ Is your WBS logically organized?
- ✓ Does your WBS include enough detail to conceptualize the work?
- ✓ Does your WBS provide a clear way to identify lines of accountability?
- ✓ Does the level of decomposition adequately account for your project size, complexity, and control needs?

We have now covered the first step in the **B.A.S.I.C.S.** 6-step scheduling process – **Break Down Your Project**. We reviewed five definitive steps you can follow to produce a quality work breakdown structure, which is the chief prerequisite for building a schedule in Microsoft Project. Once you've developed your WBS, you'll use it to create your schedule outline.

- ✓ Explain Why you Should break down Your Project
- ✓ Explain When you Should Break Down Your Project
- ✓ Explain Who Should Break Down Your Project
- ✓ Explain What a Broken-Down Project Is
- ✓ Explain How to Break Down Your Project

Practice Exercise

Develop a Work Breakdown Structure (WBS)

For this practice exercise, you will **Develop a Work Breakdown Structure** for a Home Move project. You will start with a project task list and organize the project deliverables into levels of work, down to the actionable task level.

Go to **mspbasics.com** for "checkpoint" images to check your work as you go along.

INSTRUCTIONS: After a brainstorming session, you've created the following list of 35 categories and tasks for your **Home Move** project.

TASK LIST	
Utilities	Cleaners
Get Movers Quotes	Movers
Notifications & Transfers	Guide Movers
Hire Movers	Change of Address
Move Day	Get Labels
Packing	Labels Boxes
Get Boxes	Throw Away Items
Get Tape	Notify DMV
Transfer Internet Service	Hire Cleaners
Donate Items	Transfer Electricity Service
Get Padding	Notify Banks & Credit Cards
Vendors	Notify Post Office
Purging	Transfer Phone Service
Supplies	Greet Movers
Tape Boxes	Pay Movers
Transfer Gas Service	Do a Final Sweep
Get Cleaners Quotes	Celebrate!
Pack Boxes	

Organize the Deliverables

1. Organize the tasks into categories. There are six **Level One** deliverables.

CHECKPOINT: To check your results so far, go to **mspbasics.com**

- Select the **CheckPoint Images** tab.
- Select the version of the book you're using.
- Select **Chapter 3**. Then, go to **Checkpoint Image #1**

2. Of the remaining 28 tasks, 4 are "parent tasks" (interim deliverables). Organize these four tasks under the appropriate level one category.

CHECKPOINT: To check your results so far, go to **mspbasics.com**

- Select the **CheckPoint Images** tab.
- Select the version of the book you're using.
- Select **Chapter 3.** Then, go to **Checkpoint Image #2**

3. You are now at the actionable task level. Organize the remaining 24 tasks under the appropriate deliverables.

CHECKPOINT: To check your results so far, go to **mspbasics.com**

- Select the **CheckPoint Images** tab.
- Select the version of the book you're using.
- Select **Chapter 3.** Then, go to **Checkpoint Image #3**

Chapter 4 Understanding Tasks

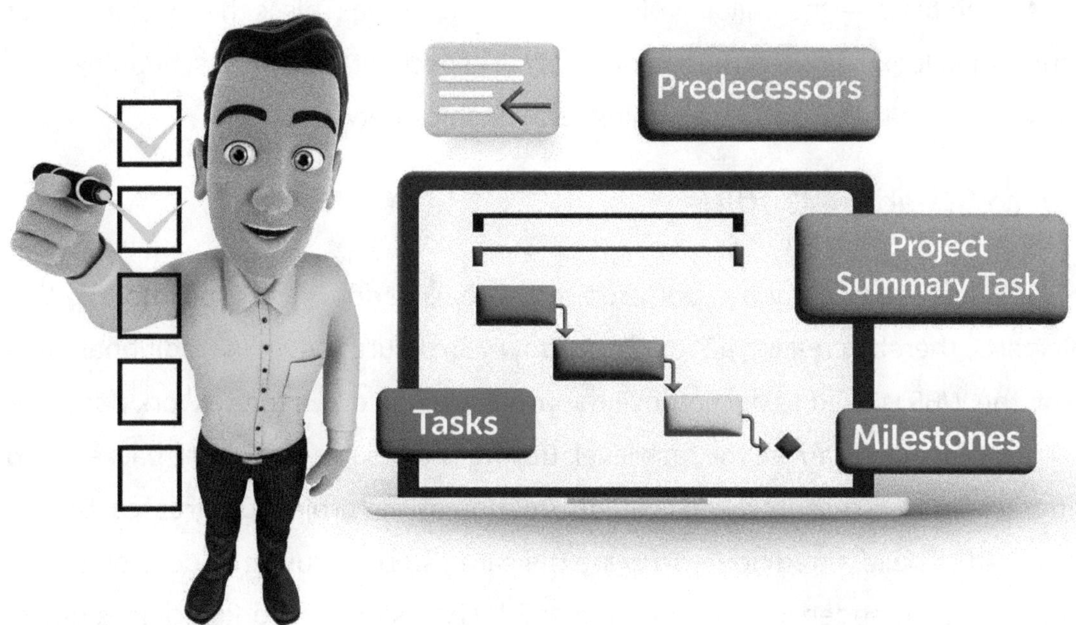

IN THIS CHAPTER you'll learn how to convert your WBS into your schedule outline. When you're done, you'll be able to create tasks, establish relationships between them and outline your project plan using summary tasks, subtasks, and milestones. You'll also be able to list important criteria your schedule must meet to function well as a project schedule.

YOU'LL LEARN:

- To Convert a WBS into a Schedule Outline
- To Explain the Parts of a Schedule
- To Explain the Project Summary Task
- To Explain Tasks, Summary Tasks, and Milestones
- To Explain Predecessors, Successors and Task Relationships
- To Explain and Use Leads and Lags
- What Makes a Schedule a Schedule?

The schedule outline is the framework of your project schedule. When built correctly, it can organize your tasks and make your schedule easier to read. When built incorrectly, it can trigger Project to calculate the project's duration incorrectly. To create a proper outline, you'll need to understand tasks — the building blocks of your schedule. This is the most important chapter in this book. It explains the most fundamental aspects of building a schedule — creating tasks, outlining them, and establishing relationships between them.

From WBS to Schedule Outline

In Chapter 3, you learned to organize your project by breaking down its scope into manageable parts, thereby creating a Work Breakdown Structure (WBS). In traditional project management, the WBS is used to decompose the project scope down to the work package level only, which is one level above the task level. Business units use WBS work packages to allocate and track budget, resource, and cost information as the project progresses. Because the steps required to build a traditional WBS are the same steps required to develop a schedule outline, we expanded its utility in Chapter 3 by breaking the work packages down a step further to get to the task level.

In this chapter, we will pick up where we left off and convert the WBS into the schedule outline in Microsoft Project. If you recall from Chapter 3, the tabular form of the WBS is the blueprint for the schedule outline. It contains the following important information, which you will enter directly into Project.

- The entire project task list, organized by phases
- The summary tasks
- The outline hierarchy of each task
- A WBS code for each task (so we can identify it's outline level in the schedule outline)

When you decompose your WBS a step beyond the work package level to get to the task level, building your schedule outline is simply a matter of transferring your WBS into Microsoft Project. In the next section, we'll lay the foundation for this work by identifying the parts of a schedule.

Components of the Schedule Outline

The schedule outline is created in the **Entry Table** of the **Gantt Chart view**. There are several components that make up the schedule outline. Using the *Software Development* project template shown in *Figure 93 below* , we'll identify each part. We'll further elaborate on each component throughout the chapter.

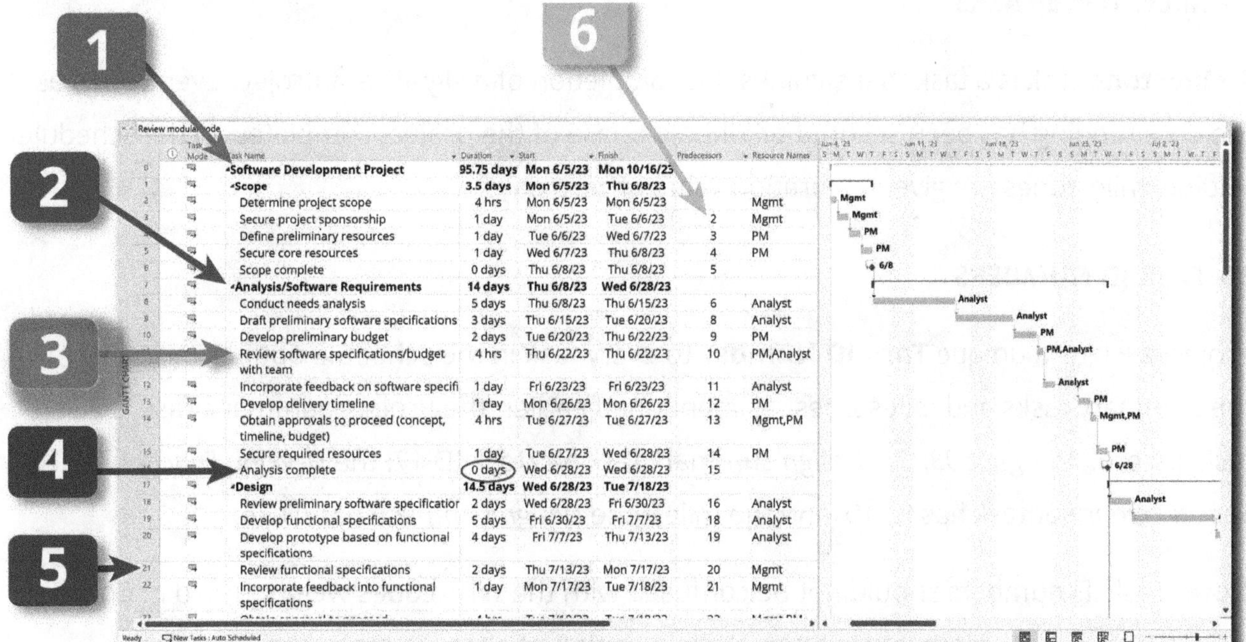

Figure 93 – Parts of a Schedule Outline

1 – THE PROJECT SUMMARY TASK

The **Project Summary Task** is the task that represents the highest level of the project outline and displays summarized information for the entire project. Its task ID number is zero. If you recall in Chapter 3, it is the project scope statement expressed as a deliverable.
It is the summary task (or parent task) for the entire project, and all the tasks in the project collapse beneath it.

2 – SUMMARY TASKS

In the schedule outline, a **Summary Task** (or parent task) is a task that has other tasks (children or subtasks) demoted beneath it. They generally represent the phases of the project. Project indicates summary tasks with bold typeface – their names, start and finish dates and their duration. In *Figure 93* above the *Scope*, *Analysis/Software Requirements*, and *Design* tasks are summary tasks.

3 - SUBTASKS

A **Subtask** (or child task) is a task that is demoted beneath a summary task(s). It represents an activity in the project, and has a start date, a finish date, and a duration value greater than zero.

4 - MILESTONE TASKS

A **Milestone** task is a task that signifies the completion of a significant project event, such as the date funding has been secured or when a phase of the project completes. In the schedule outline, milestones are given a duration value of zero days.

5 - TASK ID NUMBERS

Project assigns a unique **Task ID Number** to every task in the schedule outline, including the summary tasks and milestones. As mentioned earlier, the Project Summary Task is given task ID zero. In *Figure 93*, the *Design* summary task has task ID 17, the *Develop Functional Specifications* subtask has ID 19, and the milestone *Design Complete* has ID 24.

Note: Task ID numbers should not be confused with the WBS codes we discussed in Chapter 4. Task ID numbers represent the sequential position of a task in the schedule outline, whereas WBS codes (E.g., 4.2.1) represent the task's hierarchical position in the outline. Project automatically assigns both these numerical identifiers.

6 - PREDECESSORS & TASK RELATIONSHIPS

Task relationships and dependencies are created in the **Predecessors** column using the task ID numbers. Task relationships play a very important role in the schedule. They determine a task's start and finish dates, the project's critical path and its overall duration. We'll delve deeply into the different task relationship types and how to use them later in the chapter. As discussed in Chapter 2, the summary tasks, subtasks, milestones, and task relationships are depicted in the Gantt chart on the right, with task bars indicating the durations, and arrow connectors indicating the dependencies.

We've now reviewed the components that make up the schedule outline. Next, we will review the attributes of each component, their function in the schedule, and how Project handles them. We'll start with tasks — the building blocks of your schedule. As mentioned, to create a proper outline and to use Project effectively, you'll need to understand tasks.

What is a Task?

A **Task** is an activity required to complete a project. Tasks have a start date, a finish date, and a duration. They are given a unique ID that represents their sequence within the schedule outline. Project schedules consist of three types of tasks - Summary Tasks, Subtasks, and Milestones. Task durations and task relationships determine the project schedule.

Creating Tasks

In the Gantt Chart view, to create a task, simply type the task name into the **Task Name** column of the Entry table. You can also create a task using the **Insert Task** command, located on the **Task** tab, in the **Insert** group (*Figure 94* below).

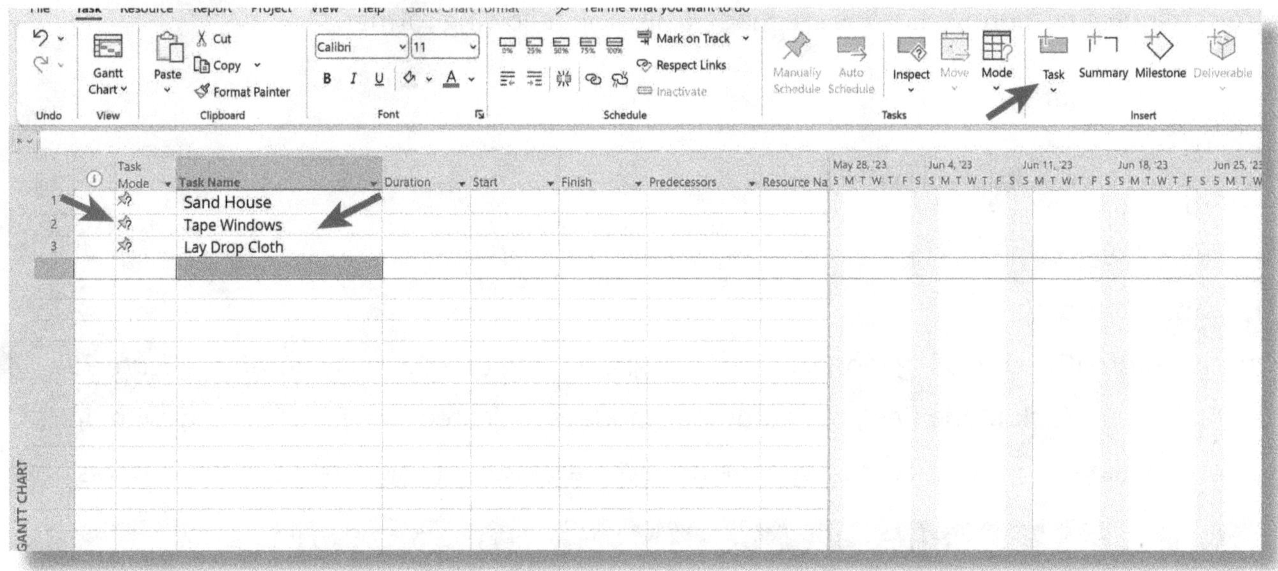

Figure 94 – Creating a New Task

Task Attributes

Naming Tasks

Task names should clearly describe the activities they represent. They should be as concise as possible and follow a noun-verb pattern, such as "Paint House" or "Tape Windows". Extra details about the task shouldn't be included in the task name. Task names should simply describe the work to those that are completing it.

Scheduling Mode

New tasks are also given a **Scheduling Mode**, which is indicated in the **Task Mode** field of the Entry table. There are two scheduling modes – the **Manual** mode and the **Automatic** mode. By default, Project schedules new tasks in the Manual scheduling mode, which is indicated with a pushpin icon. The scheduling mode you choose will determine the extent to which Project's scheduling engine is engaged. We'll explain the scheduling modes in more detail in Chapter 5.

Task Duration

Duration is the number of working days required to complete a task. It is entered and shown in the **Duration** field of the Entry table. Duration can be expressed in time increments ranging from minutes to months. Entries are made using the following format.

- 1m = 1 minute
- 1h = 1 hour
- 1d = 1 day
- 1w = 1 week
- 1mo = 1 month

In the Automatic scheduling mode, Project assigns all new tasks a 1-day duration (*Figure 95* below). In the **Task Mode** field, the Automatic mode is indicated by a task bar icon, with an arrow. By default, new tasks are given the project start date for their start and finish dates.

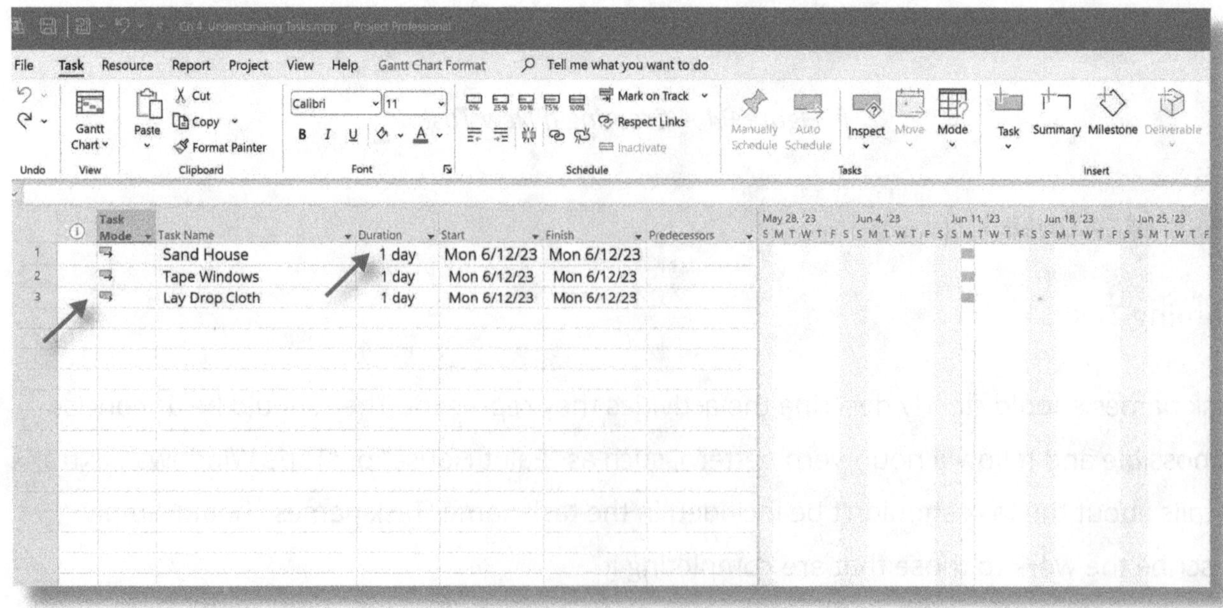

Figure 95 – Task Durations

Understanding Summary Tasks

A **Summary Task** (parent task) is a task with subtasks (children) demoted under it. They are used in a project plan to create hierarchy, and to group tasks into categories and sub-categories. Summary tasks generally represent the **phases** of a project. They are indicated in Project with **bold** typeface. *Figure 96* below shows a schedule for a House Painting project. The *Get Supplies*, *Prep House* and *Paint House* tasks are summary tasks. They represent the major phases in the project. The tasks beneath the summary tasks in each phase are subtasks (E.g., *List Supplies* and *Sand House*).

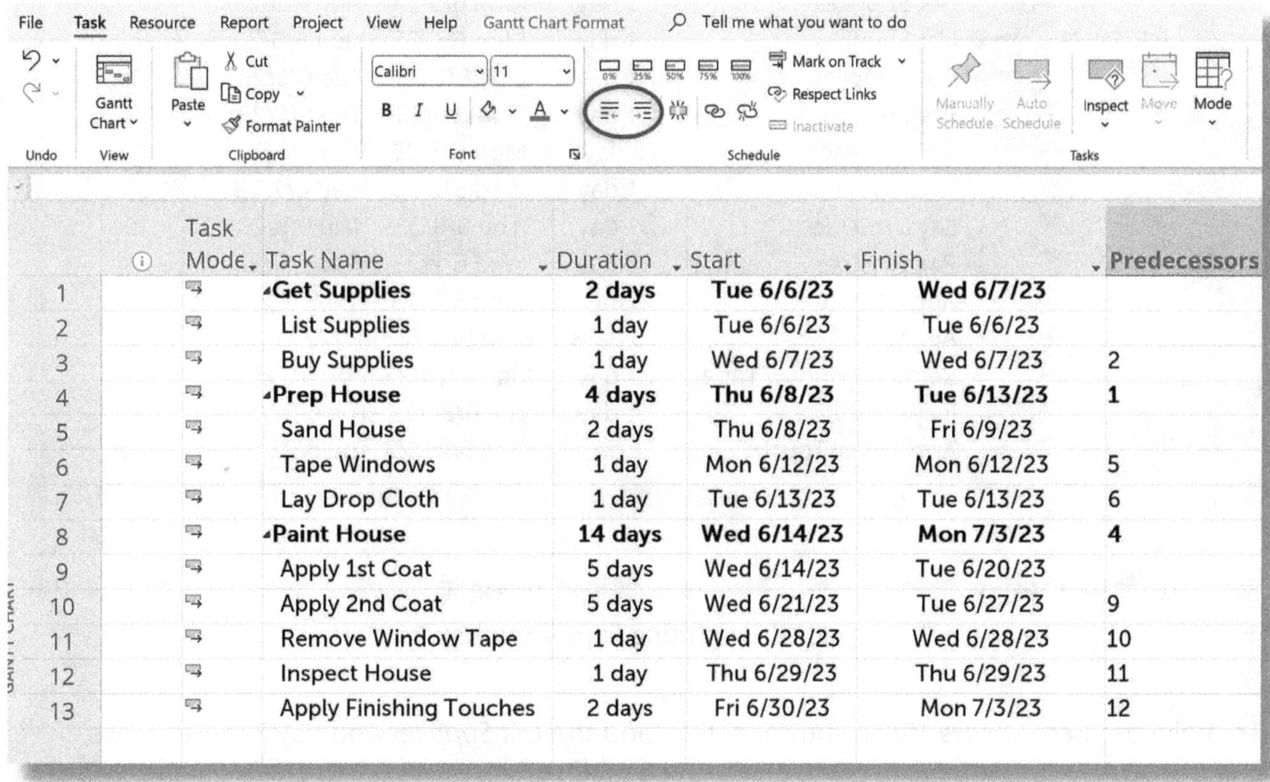

	Task Mode	Task Name	Duration	Start	Finish	Predecessors
1		**Get Supplies**	**2 days**	**Tue 6/6/23**	**Wed 6/7/23**	
2		List Supplies	1 day	Tue 6/6/23	Tue 6/6/23	
3		Buy Supplies	1 day	Wed 6/7/23	Wed 6/7/23	2
4		**Prep House**	**4 days**	**Thu 6/8/23**	**Tue 6/13/23**	**1**
5		Sand House	2 days	Thu 6/8/23	Fri 6/9/23	
6		Tape Windows	1 day	Mon 6/12/23	Mon 6/12/23	5
7		Lay Drop Cloth	1 day	Tue 6/13/23	Tue 6/13/23	6
8		**Paint House**	**14 days**	**Wed 6/14/23**	**Mon 7/3/23**	**4**
9		Apply 1st Coat	5 days	Wed 6/14/23	Tue 6/20/23	
10		Apply 2nd Coat	5 days	Wed 6/21/23	Tue 6/27/23	9
11		Remove Window Tape	1 day	Wed 6/28/23	Wed 6/28/23	10
12		Inspect House	1 day	Thu 6/29/23	Thu 6/29/23	11
13		Apply Finishing Touches	2 days	Fri 6/30/23	Mon 7/3/23	12

Figure 96 – Summary Tasks

Creating Summary Tasks

Creating Summary tasks performs the first **S** in the **B.A.S.I.C.S.** scheduling process – **Structure the Tasks,** which creates hierarchy in the schedule outline. We will review this step in more detail in Chapter 7. Summary tasks can be created using the **Indent Task** and **Outdent Task** commands on the **Task** tab, in the **Schedule** group (Circled in *Figure 96* above). Use the Indent Task command to demote a task(s) beneath the task above it.

Use the Outdent Task command to promote a task to a summary task above the task(s) beneath it. For example, *Figure 97* below shows the unstructured task list for the House Painting project.

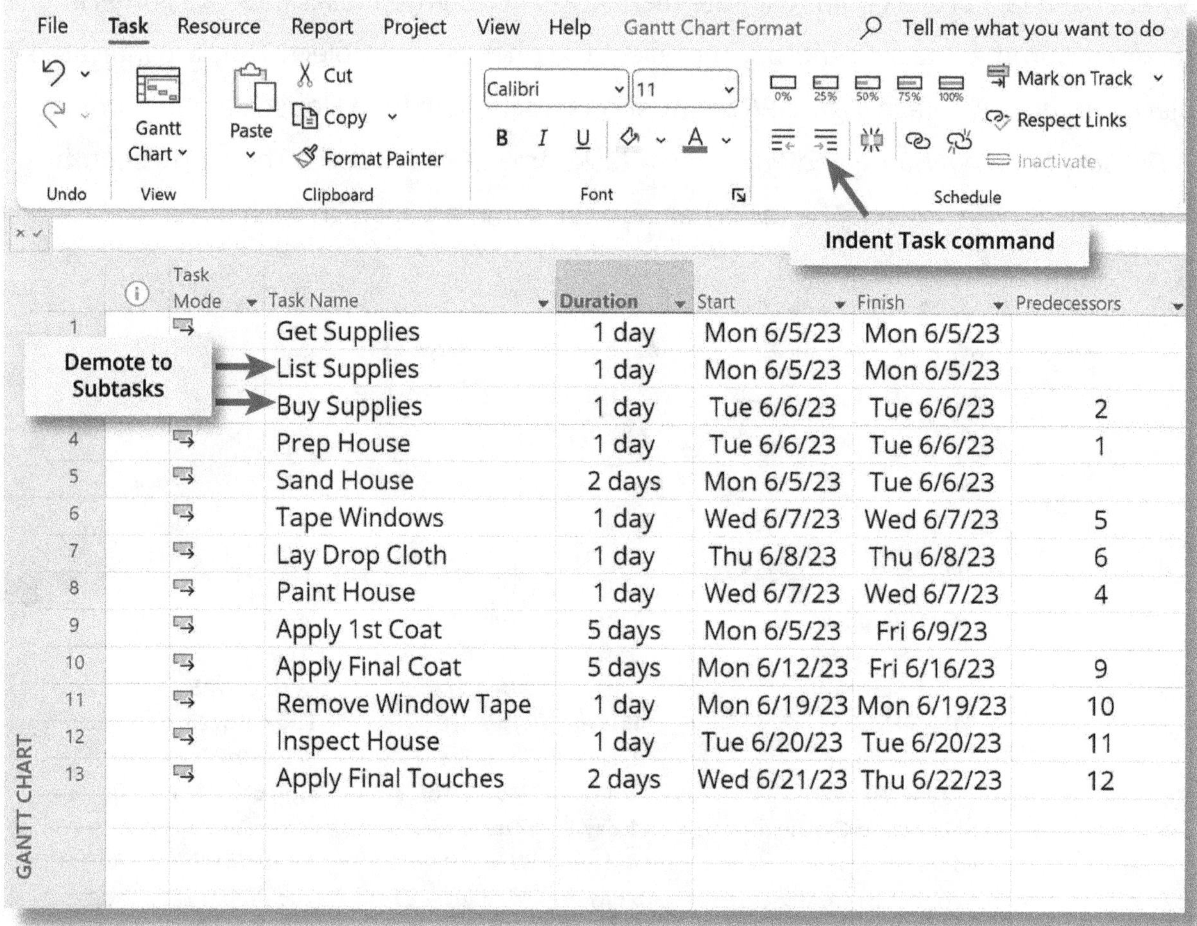

	Task Name	Duration	Start	Finish	Predecessors
1	Get Supplies	1 day	Mon 6/5/23	Mon 6/5/23	
2	List Supplies	1 day	Mon 6/5/23	Mon 6/5/23	
3	Buy Supplies	1 day	Tue 6/6/23	Tue 6/6/23	2
4	Prep House	1 day	Tue 6/6/23	Tue 6/6/23	1
5	Sand House	2 days	Mon 6/5/23	Tue 6/6/23	
6	Tape Windows	1 day	Wed 6/7/23	Wed 6/7/23	5
7	Lay Drop Cloth	1 day	Thu 6/8/23	Thu 6/8/23	6
8	Paint House	1 day	Wed 6/7/23	Wed 6/7/23	4
9	Apply 1st Coat	5 days	Mon 6/5/23	Fri 6/9/23	
10	Apply Final Coat	5 days	Mon 6/12/23	Fri 6/16/23	9
11	Remove Window Tape	1 day	Mon 6/19/23	Mon 6/19/23	10
12	Inspect House	1 day	Tue 6/20/23	Tue 6/20/23	11
13	Apply Final Touches	2 days	Wed 6/21/23	Thu 6/22/23	12

Figure 97 – Creating Summary Tasks

To make the *Get Supplies* task a summary task and the *List Supplies* and *Buy Supplies* tasks subtasks beneath it:

- Select the *List Supplies* and *Buy Supplies* tasks.
- Then, on the **Task** tab, in the **Schedule** group, select the **Indent Task** command to demote these two tasks to subtasks, and promote the *Get Supplies* task to a summary task.

Summary tasks can also be created using the **Insert Summary Task** command, located on the **Task** tab, in the **Insert** group (*Figure 98* below).

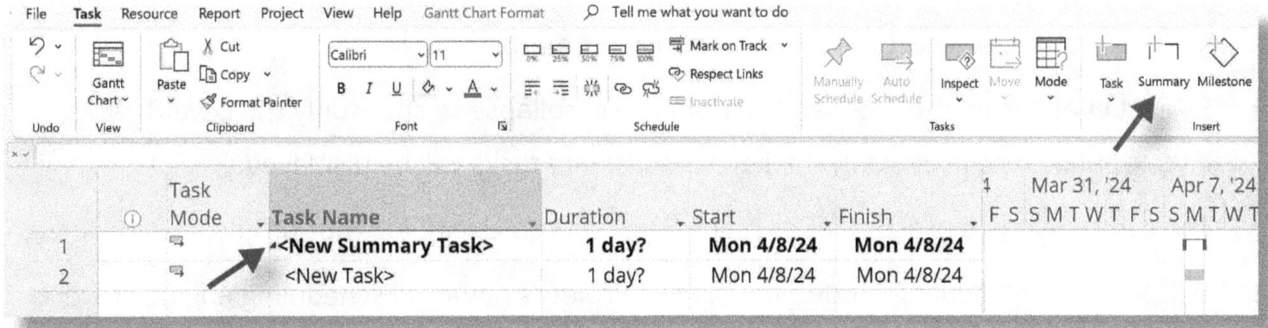

Figure 98 – Insert Summary Task Command

- Select the row in the Entry table where you would like to insert the summary task.
- Select the **Insert Summary Task** command.
- Rename the new summary task.

Project automatically creates a subtask beneath the summary task.

TIP: When creating your project outline, begin by entering your entire task list without structuring it (as shown in the previous *Figure 97*). Then, structure the tasks using the Indent Task icon to create summary tasks and subtasks. This will lead to less re-work.

After you've structured all the tasks in your project, you can check your outline using the **Show Outline** command (*Figure 99* below).

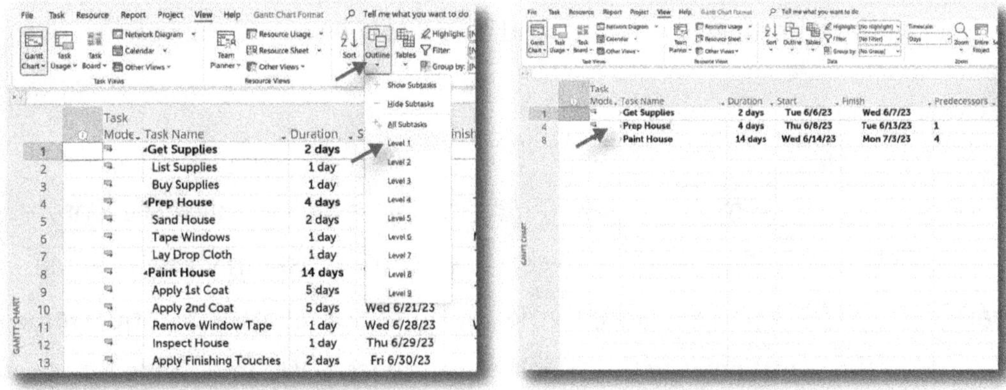

Figure 99 – Check Your Schedule Outline

To Check the Outline:

- Select the **View** tab.
- In the **Data** group, select the **Show Outline** command.
- Select **Level 1** from the pick-list. The outline will collapse to show only the Level 1 tasks. If your outline is correct, only the Level 1 summary tasks will be displayed.
- You can repeat this process for as many levels as you create for your project.

In the Automatic scheduling mode, you can see Project's powerful scheduling engine at work in the way it handles summary tasks. Here are some behaviors of summary tasks to keep in mind.

- When task dependencies have been established, a summary task's duration is automatically calculated from the durations, dependencies, and outline level of its subtasks.
- If a subtask is outdented, it will be promoted to the same level as its parent task.
- If a summary task is outdented, its subtasks will be outdented with it. Their parent-child relationship remains intact.
- If a summary task is deleted, its subtasks will also be deleted.

Note: Since summary task durations are automatically calculated from the durations, dependencies and outline level of their subtasks, their durations should not be manually entered. If the duration of a summary task is manually entered, Project will toggle the scheduling mode from Automatic to Manual and also apply a scheduling constraint to the task.

Using Milestones

Milestone tasks signify the completion of significant project deliverables or events. For this reason, they are often used as predecessors to other tasks in your schedule. They generally don't include project work, so they are often assigned a duration value of zero. They're indicated in the Gantt chart with a black diamond icon. When naming Milestones, best practice is to use a noun, past-tense verb naming scheme.

In *Figure 100* below, the *Supplies Gotten*, *House Prepped*, and *House Painted* tasks are milestone tasks, signifying the end of the respective phases.

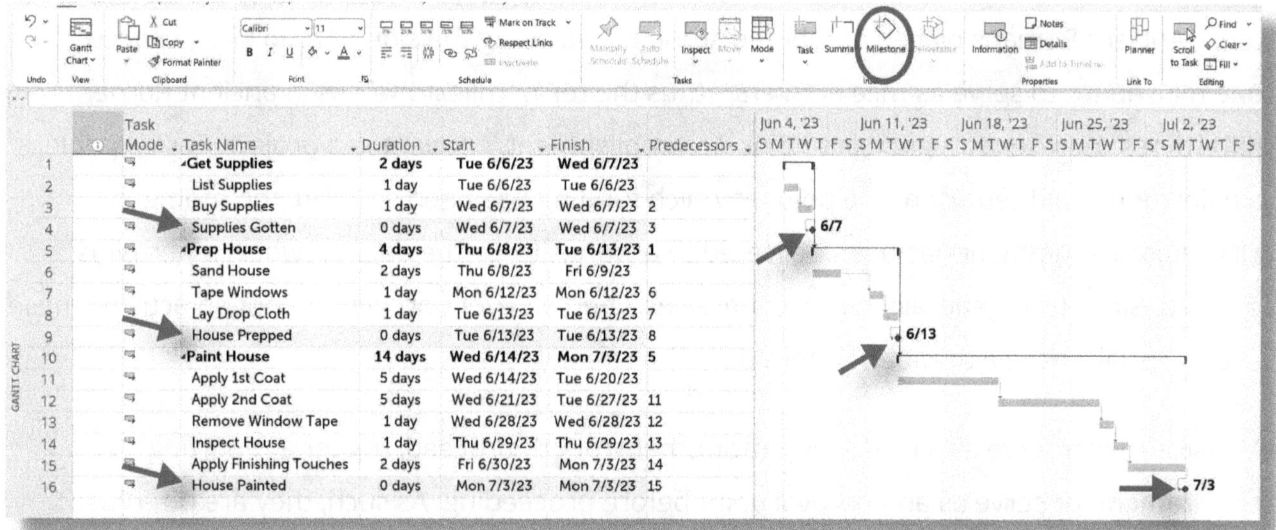

	Task Mode	Task Name	Duration	Start	Finish	Predecessors
1		**Get Supplies**	**2 days**	**Tue 6/6/23**	**Wed 6/7/23**	
2		List Supplies	1 day	Tue 6/6/23	Tue 6/6/23	
3		Buy Supplies	1 day	Wed 6/7/23	Wed 6/7/23	2
4		Supplies Gotten	0 days	Wed 6/7/23	Wed 6/7/23	3
5		**Prep House**	**4 days**	**Thu 6/8/23**	**Tue 6/13/23**	1
6		Sand House	2 days	Thu 6/8/23	Fri 6/9/23	
7		Tape Windows	1 day	Mon 6/12/23	Mon 6/12/23	6
8		Lay Drop Cloth	1 day	Tue 6/13/23	Tue 6/13/23	7
9		House Prepped	0 days	Tue 6/13/23	Tue 6/13/23	8
10		**Paint House**	**14 days**	**Wed 6/14/23**	**Mon 7/3/23**	5
11		Apply 1st Coat	5 days	Wed 6/14/23	Tue 6/20/23	
12		Apply 2nd Coat	5 days	Wed 6/21/23	Tue 6/27/23	11
13		Remove Window Tape	1 day	Wed 6/28/23	Wed 6/28/23	12
14		Inspect House	1 day	Thu 6/29/23	Thu 6/29/23	13
15		Apply Finishing Touches	2 days	Fri 6/30/23	Mon 7/3/23	14
16		House Painted	0 days	Mon 7/3/23	Mon 7/3/23	15

Figure 100 – Milestone Tasks

Using milestones in your schedule is optional, but they're useful because they can mark completed deliverables. These completed deliverables often drive other work and can therefore serve as predecessors to other tasks. The practice of using milestones as dependencies can also make your schedule easier to read, interpret and follow.

One common scheduling mistake when using milestones is to fail to link them to their appropriate dependencies. The consequence of not linking milestones to the schedule is that they will reflect inaccurate dates for significant scheduling events, like *Supplies Gotten* or *House Prepped*. This can lead to mismanaged expectations and unnecessary escalations. Avoid this mistake by making sure that each milestone has all the predecessors required for it to reflect accurately in the schedule.

Creating Milestones

There are two ways to create a Milestone:

1. Give a task a zero duration

2. Use the Insert Milestone command

- On the **Task** tab, in the **Insert** group, select the **Insert Milestone** command (circled in *Figure 100* above). Rename the milestone appropriately.

Milestone Use Cases

To fully grasp the concept of using milestone tasks, it's helpful to consider the history of the term. Ancient Romans placed numbered stone pillars along the side of roadways, spaced one mile apart, to serve as mile markers – thus the term "milestone". As in ancient Rome, milestones represent a significant point, accomplishment, or event in a project. For example, a milestone could represent the point at which funding has been secured, the moment all required equipment has been delivered to a work site, or the date on which a permit is granted. Since they generally represent a point when an event occurs and not an activity, these events usually have a duration of zero days.

Milestones can serve as a predecessor for other work to proceed, trigger a reporting requirement, or serve as an approval point before proceeding. As such, they are often used by project sponsors and initiators to communicate high-level expectations for when key outcomes should be delivered by the project manager. When milestones are used in this manner, they may be identified as **mandatory** (E.g., milestones that may be required by contract) or as **optional** (E.g., based on historical data only). Whichever use case, the important thing to keep in mind about milestones is that they must always be driven by their requisite predecessors. Failing to do so can result in unrealistic expectations as to when key events will occur.

Finally, it's a good idea to include a *finish* milestone at the end of each phase, and at the end of the entire project. Such milestones make your schedule easier to interpret and follow. Some schedulers also include a *start* milestone. How and where you decide to use milestones in your schedule will largely depend upon your personal style and preference. The key objective is to use them to make your schedule easier to build, interpret, follow, and manage.

The Project Summary Task

As mentioned earlier, the **Project Summary Task** is the task that represents the highest level of the project outline. It displays summarized information for the entire project. Its task ID should be zero. Because it summarizes the entire project, its duration is the entire project's duration, its cost is the entire project's cost, and its start and finish dates are the start and finish dates of the entire project (*Figure 101*). Without the project summary task, you would have to comb through reports and menus to determine this information.

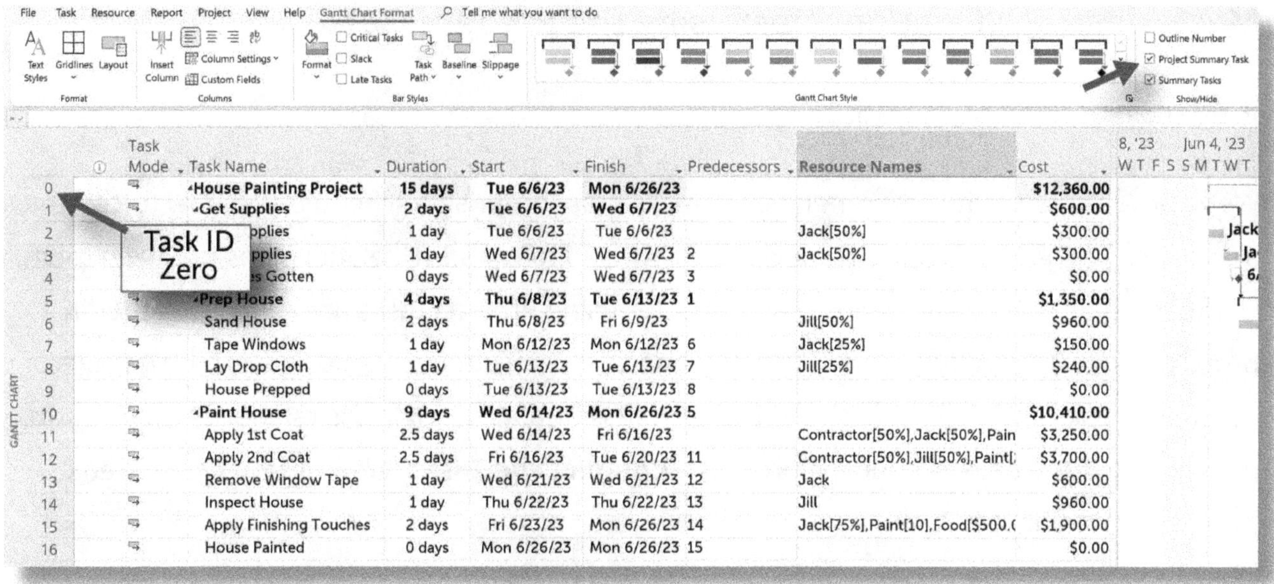

ID	Task Name	Duration	Start	Finish	Predecessors	Resource Names	Cost
0	**House Painting Project**	**15 days**	**Tue 6/6/23**	**Mon 6/26/23**			**$12,360.00**
1	**Get Supplies**	**2 days**	**Tue 6/6/23**	**Wed 6/7/23**			**$600.00**
2	pplies	1 day	Tue 6/6/23	Tue 6/6/23		Jack[50%]	$300.00
3	pplies	1 day	Wed 6/7/23	Wed 6/7/23	2	Jack[50%]	$300.00
4	s Gotten	0 days	Wed 6/7/23	Wed 6/7/23	3		$0.00
5	**Prep House**	**4 days**	**Thu 6/8/23**	**Tue 6/13/23**	**1**		**$1,350.00**
6	Sand House	2 days	Thu 6/8/23	Fri 6/9/23		Jill[50%]	$960.00
7	Tape Windows	1 day	Mon 6/12/23	Mon 6/12/23	6	Jack[25%]	$150.00
8	Lay Drop Cloth	1 day	Tue 6/13/23	Tue 6/13/23	7	Jill[25%]	$240.00
9	House Prepped	0 days	Tue 6/13/23	Tue 6/13/23	8		$0.00
10	**Paint House**	**9 days**	**Wed 6/14/23**	**Mon 6/26/23**	**5**		**$10,410.00**
11	Apply 1st Coat	2.5 days	Wed 6/14/23	Fri 6/16/23		Contractor[50%],Jack[50%],Pain	$3,250.00
12	Apply 2nd Coat	2.5 days	Fri 6/16/23	Tue 6/20/23	11	Contractor[50%],Jill[50%],Paint[	$3,700.00
13	Remove Window Tape	1 day	Wed 6/21/23	Wed 6/21/23	12	Jack	$600.00
14	Inspect House	1 day	Thu 6/22/23	Thu 6/22/23	13	Jill	$960.00
15	Apply Finishing Touches	2 days	Fri 6/23/23	Mon 6/26/23	14	Jack[75%],Paint[10],Food[$500.(	$1,900.00
16	House Painted	0 days	Mon 6/26/23	Mon 6/26/23	15		$0.00

Figure 101 – The Project Summary Task

In Figure 101 above, the Project Summary Task shows that the House Painting project has a 15-day duration, it starts on 6/6/23 and finishes on 6/26/23. Cumulative values will also be displayed for any fields that are added to the active table, such as the *Cost* field. In this case, the project's total cost is $12,360.

Displaying the Project Summary Task

The Project Summary Task should be displayed – and not manually entered as the first task in the schedule. When added to the schedule outline properly, its task ID will always be zero (and not ID 1). The Project Summary Task is the summary task for the entire project, and all summary tasks and subtasks collapse beneath it.

To properly display the Project Summary Task:

- Select the **Format** tab.
- In the **Show/Hide** group, check the **Project Summary Task** check-box.

Since the Project Summary Task is the project objective expressed as a deliverable, if your project file has been saved, it will be given the project's name by default. If your project file has not been saved, it will be given a generic name, E.g., *Project 1*.

Mastering Task Relationships: Using the Predecessors Field

Predecessors and Successors

We've now reviewed the different types of tasks that comprise a schedule and how to create and structure them in Project. Now, we'll review how to establish relationships between them. Understanding task relationships is essential for using Project. Tasks are linked together in a project plan by task relationships (or dependencies). These relationships govern how Project schedules tasks and determines your project's duration. Creating tasks relationships performs the C in the **B.A.S.I.C.S.** scheduling process – **Connect the Tasks**. We will review this step in more detail in Chapter 7.

Task relationships consist of Predecessor tasks and Successor tasks.

- A **Predecessor** is a task whose start date or finish date determines the start date or finish date of another task or tasks.
- A **Successor** is a task whose start date or finish date is determined by the start date or finish date of another task or tasks.

Task Relationship Types

There are four task relationship types in Project:

- Finish-to-Start (FS)
- Start-to-Start (SS)
- Finish-to-Finish (FF)
- Start-to-Finish (SF)

The following table includes a description of each task relationship type, how they're depicted in the Gantt chart and examples of how they can be used in practice.

Task Relationship Type	Description	Gantt Chart Appearance	Example
Finish-to-Start (FS) (default)	The finish date of the Predecessor task drives the start date of the Successor task		A book must be written (predecessor), before it can be edited (successor)
Start-to-Start (SS)	The start date of the Predecessor task drives the start date of the Successor task		When the event starts (predecessor), live streaming must start (successor)
Finish-to-Finish (FF)	The finish date of the Predecessor task drives the finish date of the Successor task		To serve a hot breakfast, the bacon must finish cooking (predecessor), when the eggs finish cooking (successor) Note: The FF task relationship determines when to start cooking each item, working backward from the serving time
Start-to-Finish (SF)	The start date of the Predecessor task drives the finish date of the Successor task		Once the new mail server is up and running (predecessor), the old server can be shut down (successor)

Creating Task Relationships

Task relationships are created using the **Predecessors** field of the Entry table. The default task relationship type is *Finish-to-Start*.

To create a *Finish-to-Start* dependency between tasks:

- Enter the task ID number of the predecessor task into the Predecessors field of the successor task. If a task has multiple predecessors, separate each task ID number with a comma.

A quick way to link tasks with the *Finish-to-Start* task relationship is with the **Link the Selected Tasks** command:

- Select the tasks you want to link.
- On the **Task** tab, in the **Schedule** group, select the **Link the Selected Tasks** command (*Figure 102* below).

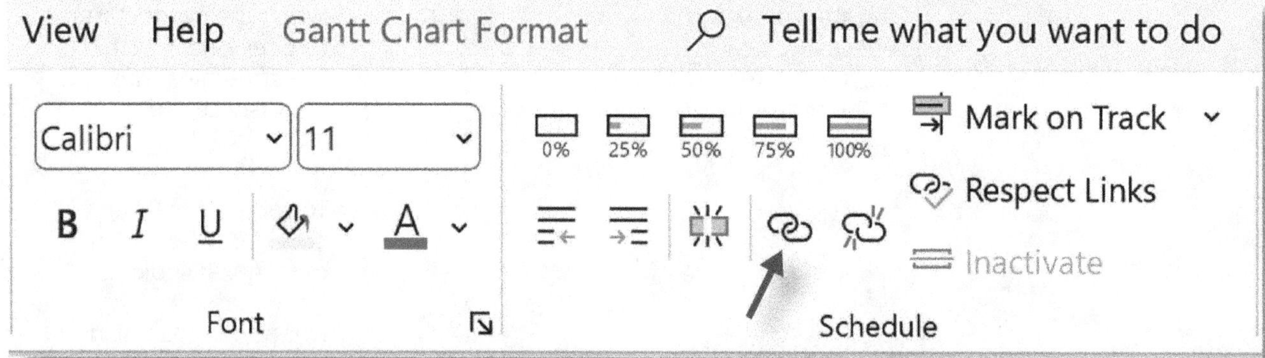

Figure 102 – Link the Selected Tasks Command

To create any of the other three task relationship types:

- Enter the task ID number of the predecessor task into the **Predecessors** field of the successor task, followed by the two-letter acronym for the task relationship type.

Figure 103 below shows an example of each task relationship type, and how they appear in the Predecessors field and in the Gantt Chart.

	Task Mode	Task Name	Duration	Start	Finish	Predecessors	Feb 11, '24 S M T W T F S
1		**Finish-to-Start Relationship**	**4 days**	**Tue 2/13/24**	**Fri 2/16/24**		
2		Write Book	2 days	Tue 2/13/24	Wed 2/14/24		
3		Edit Book	2 days	Thu 2/15/24	Fri 2/16/24	2	
4		**Start-to-Start**	**2 days**	**Tue 2/13/24**	**Wed 2/14/24**		
5		Start Event	2 days	Tue 2/13/24	Wed 2/14/24		
6		Start Live Streaming	2 days	Tue 2/13/24	Wed 2/14/24	5SS	
7		**Finish-to-Finish Relationship**	**4 days**	**Tue 2/13/24**	**Fri 2/16/24**		
8		Finish Cooking Bacon	4 days	Tue 2/13/24	Fri 2/16/24		
9		Finish Cooking Eggs	2 days	Thu 2/15/24	Fri 2/16/24	8FF	
10		**Start-to-Finish Relationship**	**2 days**	**Mon 2/12/24**	**Tue 2/13/24**		
11		Deploy New Email Server	1 day	Tue 2/13/24	Tue 2/13/24		
12		Shut Down Old Email Server	1 day	Mon 2/12/24	Tue 2/13/24	11SF	

Figure 103 – Task Relationship Types

Task Relationship Business Drivers

The business drivers or dependencies that dictate task relationships fall into four categories. They can be mandatory, discretionary, external, or internal. **Mandatory** drivers or dependencies may be legally or contractually required or inherent in the nature of the work. For example, issuance of a certificate of occupancy is legally required before an owner or tenant can occupy a newly constructed space. Another example of a mandatory dependency is that a sidewalk must be formed before concrete can be poured. Though this is not a legal requirement, the sequence of events is imposed by the inherent nature of the work. We can use these two examples to describe the next two categories of business dependencies. The example involving the issuance of a certificate of occupancy illustrates an **external** dependency. This is because the certificate of occupancy is issued by a party outside the project, thereby imposing a relationship between project activities and non-project activities. The example involving the sidewalk being poured and formed illustrates an **internal** dependency. These are dependencies fully within the project team's control. Another example of an internal dependency is that a project team cannot test a server until they have configured it. Before we describe the final category of business drivers or dependencies, it's important to note that the examples described thus far are mandatory dependencies and can be further classified as **mandatory-external** or **mandatory-internal** dependencies. Another way to refer to mandatory dependencies is hard dependencies or hard logic dependencies.

The alternative to mandatory dependencies represents the final category of business dependencies dictating task relationships, which is **discretionary** dependencies. Discretionary dependencies are also called preferred logic dependencies, soft logic dependencies, preferential logic dependencies or simply, soft dependencies. These business drivers dictate task relationships based on best practice, preference, or the need to get things done faster. What distinguishes them from mandatory dependencies is although there may be justifiable reasons to work certain tasks in succession, there are other acceptable or plausible sequences for getting the work done. For example, many construction projects start the electrical work after the plumbing work to reduce overall risk. However, when the schedule needs to be expedited, much of this work gets done in parallel. Further, since this dependency is fully within the project team's control it can also be classified as a **discretionary-internal** dependency.

An example of a **discretionary-external** dependency is that on a project requiring external vendors, the project manager may decide to issue RFPs (Request for Proposals) earlier in the project than normal to get vendors "on-boarded" faster and get an early start on future phases.

As you can see from these four categories, all task relationships should be driven by business needs. The better you understand these needs and the more accurately you can categorize them, the better informed you will be about which task relationships to use, and which business needs they're meant to satisfy.

Task Relationship Use Cases

As reviewed earlier, the four task relationship types are Finish-to-Start (FS), Start-to-Start (SS), Finish-to-Finish (FF) and Start-to-Finish (SF). Each task relationship type is distinctive and addresses a unique scheduling need. This section is meant to provide context for each task relationship type, and increase your understanding of the scheduling need each addresses. It will also help you make full use of the automation that full-featured scheduling apps like Microsoft Project provide. These fundamental concepts are your gateway to becoming a master scheduler. They will not only increase your confidence in your scheduling forecast, but also allow you to solve difficult business problems with skill and aplomb, thereby adding a consultative aspect to your role as a project management professional. We'll begin with the default task relationship type, Finish-to-Start (FS).

Finish-to-Start Use Cases

Because of its simplicity, the **Finish-to-Start (FS)** task relationship is the easiest to master. Many schedulers recommend using it exclusively if your schedule allows. This is sage advice. Finish-to-Start (FS) relationships make your schedule easy to interpret and follow because they clearly show which tasks other tasks depend on to complete. For this reason, many schedule builders ignore the most important words of this advice *"if your schedule allows"*. As a result, their schedules are unable to address common business problems, like determining the latest date a task can start to remain on schedule or determining when to start a task of shorter duration when it's being performed during the time-frame of a task with a longer duration or identifying ways to expedite a schedule.

Finish-to-Start (FS) task relationships can't solve these unique business problems. What they *can* do is help you identify the earliest date a task or milestone can start in your schedule, which is after all its predecessors are complete. They're also especially helpful at preventing your schedule from having *hanging* tasks or milestones - which are tasks or milestones without predecessors or successors. Hanging tasks and milestones cause scheduling errors. You can avoid such errors by ensuring every task or milestone has a predecessor, except for those that will inherently start on the proper date without the need of a predecessor. Examples would include the first task in your schedule, which will start on the project start date and thereby not require a driving task. There may also be other tasks in your schedule that can start on the project start date, that don't require predecessors. Another example would be the first subtask demoted under a summary task representing a phase. This task inherently starts when the phase starts. Aside from examples like these, every task in your schedule should have a predecessor. In most cases, that predecessor should have a Finish-to-Start relationship with its successor task.

The following chart lists five use cases for the **Finish-to-Start (FS)** task relationship, details of each use case and succinct task name descriptions for entry into Project.

	(FS) USE CASE	PREDECESSOR TASK	SUCCESSOR TASK
1	On a construction project, you must **finish** the task of submitting preliminary shop drawings, to **start** the task of ordering long lead time items such as electrical, plumbing or HVAC equipment.	Submit preliminary shop drawings	Order long lead items
2	On a marketing project, you must **finish** the task of launching a pretest campaign before you can **start** the task of determining the campaign's effectiveness.	Launch pretest campaign	Determine effectiveness

	(FS) USE CASE	PREDECESSOR TASK	SUCCESSOR TASK
3	On an event planning project, you must **finish** the task of finalizing your attendee list before you can **start** the task of reserving a block of hotel rooms.	Finalize attendee list	Reserve block of hotel rooms
4	On a clinical trial project, you must **finish** the task of enrolling subjects before you can **start** the task of administering initial dosing.	Enroll subjects	Administer initial dosing
5	On a cloud-computing project, you must **finish** the task of creating the virtual machine before you can **start** the task of configuring it.	Create virtual machine	Configure virtual machine

Start-to-Start Use Cases

The **Start-to-Start (SS)** task relationship allows a successor task to start at the same time as its predecessor. Although they will both start at the same time, one task is always the predecessor task. This is the task whose start date triggers the start date of the other task. The best way to determine which task is the predecessor is to imagine delaying one of the tasks. This will make it apparent that one task (the predecessor) can be delayed freely, while the inherent nature of the work will require the other task (the successor) to be delayed in accordance with its predecessor. This exercise also works in reverse. The inherent nature of the work would make it unreasonable to delay the successor task.

Example: Task 1 is to *Start a live event* and Task 2 is to *Live stream the event*. Although the tasks will begin together, Task 1 is the predecessor and Task 2 is the successor. We know this because if the start of the live event were delayed, then live streaming would need to be delayed accordingly. We can also confirm this in reverse. If the live event started on time and we began the live streaming at some later point, this would be unreasonable.

In Microsoft Project, if the proper task is identified as the predecessor, the start date of the successor task (*Live stream the event*) will always auto-update to remain in sync with the predecessor task (*Start a live event*). This is the type of business problem the Start-to-Start task relationship is meant to solve. When you apply this type of scheduling logic and automation, you can be confident that if your resources follow your schedule, the start of the live event will remain in sync with the start of the live streaming. Also, if the event is delayed for any reason, Project will automatically adjust the start of your live streaming task accordingly.

This Start-to-Start example would be properly categorized as a **mandatory dependency**. Nevertheless, Start-to-Start relationships have a higher occurrence of discretionary uses than any other task relationship type. This is because of their utility at expediting schedules. The first step most professionals will take to get work done faster is to work tasks in parallel. Project lets you model such "what-if" scenarios to not only see if working tasks in parallel will result in an expedited schedule, but also to see *which* tasks to work in parallel to achieve your desired result.

The following chart lists five use cases for the Start-to-Start (SS) task relationship, details of each use case and succinct task name descriptions for entry into Project.

	(SS) USE CASE	PREDECESSOR TASK	SUCCESSOR TASK
1	On a construction project, you may **start** the task of installing ceiling tile into the ceiling grid on the same day you **start** the task of hanging wallpaper.	Install ceiling tile	Hang wallpaper
2	On a training project, you may **start** the task of sending out registration confirmations on the same day you **start** the task of sending out prework requirements.	Send registration confirmations	Send pre-work requirements

	(SS) USE CASE	PREDECESSOR TASK	SUCCESSOR TASK
3	On a waterfall software development project, you may **start** the task of developing your unit test plans on the same day you **start** the task of developing your integration test plans.	Develop unit test plans	Develop integration test plans
4	On an SAP project, to stress test a new system, you must **start** the task of enabling system monitoring on the same day you **start** the task of load testing.	Enable system monitoring	Begin load testing
5	On a New Call Center project, you may **start** developing your phone support systems on the same day you **start** developing your online support systems.	Develop phone support systems	Develop online support systems

Finish-to-Finish Use Cases

A good way to conceptualize the business problem that the **Finish-to-Finish (FF)** task relationship addresses is to consider the problem one encounters when attempting to serve a hot meal that consists of more than one food item (E.g., bacon and eggs). The key to serving each food item hot is for their cooking times to finish together. This can be a challenge when each item has a different cooking time (or duration). Bacon may be cooked in about 9 minutes and eggs may cook in only 4 minutes. Therefore, if you begin cooking these items at the same time, you'll serve cold eggs. To serve both items hot, you would need to know precisely when to start cooking the item with the shortest cooking time, so it finishes together with the item with the longest cooking time. To solve this problem, the bacon and eggs will need a Finish-to-Finish task relationship. The task of cooking the bacon would be the predecessor and the task of cooking the eggs would be the successor task. There are two reasons to make the bacon the predecessor task. First, as soon as the last item is cooked, the meal can be served. Since the bacon has the longer duration, it would logically start first.

The second reason the bacon would be the predecessor is because to serve both items hot, the eggs (which have the shorter duration) must begin cooking at some point during the cooking cycle of the bacon, and not the other way around. The problem to solve is when do we start cooking the eggs, so that they finish cooking when the bacon finishes? This is the crux of the scheduling problem that the Finish-to-Finish task relationship is meant to address. It tells us the precise moment during the cooking cycle of the bacon, when we must start cooking the eggs, so that both finish at the same time. As this cooking dilemma illustrates, the purpose of the Finish-to-Finish relationship is not to tell you when a successor task must finish, it is to tell you the latest date by which a successor task must start.

A further illustration of the utility of the Finish-to-Finish relationship, is a problem I encountered managing projects to install and configure network elements into the AT&T network. These projects were multi-year projects, and it was challenging to get busy engineers to prioritize network elements that wouldn't be added to the network until the following year. They had a valid point. As project managers, we should have been able to inform the engineers of the latest date they could start working on these elements to deploy them into the network on time. Finish-to-Start task dependencies cannot solve this business problem. As mentioned earlier, Finish-to-Start relationships help you identify the earliest date a task or milestone can start in your schedule, which is after all its predecessors are complete. However, in this example, our engineers were asking us to provide the latest date by which they needed to start working on these elements to deploy them into the network on time. Moreover, if they configured a device too early, it could need another update before it went into service. To solve this problem, I created Finish-to-Finish task relationships between their task and another task that would be adversely impacted if their task were not finished. I could then make a credible case for a "drop dead date". As a result, I was one of the few technical project managers who could get engineers to prioritize my tasks. They knew that my request dates were credible. This is perhaps the best way to describe the business problem that the Finish-to-Finish task relationship solves. It takes all the slack out of the schedule and tells you "drop dead dates".

The following chart lists five additional use cases for Finish-to-Finish (FF) task relationships, details of each use case and succinct task name descriptions for entry into Project.

	(FF) USE CASE	PREDECESSOR TASK	SUCCESSOR TASK
1	On a construction project, you must **finish** the task of placing the rebars at the same time you **finish** the task of completing the wall forms.	Place rebars	Complete wall forms
2	On a software development, project during an agile sprint, you must **finish** the task of writing code at the same time you **finish** the task of testing that code to meet your Sprint goal.	Write code	Test code
3	On a film production project, you must **finish** editing scenes in a rented lab at the same time the lab rental period **finishes**.	End of rental period	Edit scenes
4	On a construction project, you must **finish** the task of putting in drywall at the same time you **finish** the task of putting in electrical installation.	Put in drywall	Put in electrical installation
5	On a Rose Bowl Float construction project, you must **finish** placing the roses on the float, as close as possible to the **finish** date of the allowed construction period, so the roses can be as fresh as possible, which is just before judging begins.	Judging begins	Place roses

Start-to-Finish Use Cases

There's a popular notion that the **Start-to-Finish (SF)** task relationship is rarely used and is thus rarely needed in business. While it is indeed rarely used, it is not because it is rarely needed in business. Its rare usage is more attributable to being rarely understood by practitioners. If you've ever had to shut down an old system and migrate to a new system, then you may have benefited from using the Start-to-Finish (SF) task relationship. This is the type of business problem it solves. It allows you to forecast when a new system would be operational, and thus when you could shut down the old system. Moreover, it tells you when a system targeted for replacement can be shut down without adversely affecting users who must rely on it to complete their work.

What makes this task relationship unique, is it's the only task relationship type where the predecessor occurs *after* the successor. It's also visually depicted this way in the Gantt chart in Project. To illustrate the utility of the Start-to-Finish dependency type, consider the business case of shutting down an active billing system and migrating to a new one. Since the current billing system is serving a critical business need, at no time can the business be without a billing system. Stated differently, at all times one system must be fully operational and the other system non-operational. To realize this objective, there must be a Start-to-Finish (SF) relationship between the task of shutting down the old system and the task of starting up the new system. To properly establish this dependency, we must first determine which of these tasks is the predecessor. Intuitively, it would appear to be the shut-down of the old system, since the new system goes live after the old system is shut down. Recall that a predecessor is a task whose start or finish date determines the start or finish date of another task.
Per this definition, although the task of starting up the new system appears to be determined by the old system shutting down, it is in fact, the opposite. Since at all times one system must be fully operational, the old system cannot be shut down until the new system comes online. Therefore, the start-up of the new system is the predecessor task and the shut-down of the old system is the successor task. At this point, many of our students ask, *"Why wouldn't you just use a Finish-to-Start relationship?"* They reason that once you finish using the old system, you can start using the new system. Therefore, the predecessor is the shut-down of the old system – right? Wrong. To see the error in this logic, consider what would happen if the start-up date of the new system were delayed a week. Would you still shut down the old system? No, you wouldn't, because at all times your business must have an operational billing system.

Thus, the true predecessor is the task of starting up the new system, even though it occurs after the successor task of shutting down the old system. As you can see, no other task relationship type can solve this sort of business dilemma. If used properly, the Start-to-Finish (SF) task relationship type can help you confidently forecast when an old system can be retired without adversely impacting users who rely on it to get work done.

The following chart lists five additional use cases for Start-to-Finish (SF) task relationships, details of each use case and succinct task name descriptions for entry into Project.

	(SF) USE CASE	PREDECESSOR TASK	SUCCESSOR TASK
1	On a construction project, you must **start** the task of receiving a heavy object, before you can **finish** the task of hoisting the object with a crane.	Receive heavy object	Hoist heavy object
2	On an IT project, you must **start** the task of operationalizing the new payroll system, before you **finish** the task of retiring the old payroll system.	Operationalize new payroll system	Retire old payroll system
3	On a hospital construction project in a developing country, you must **start** the task of connecting the hospital to the electrical grid before you can **finish** the task of powering down the generator.	Connect hospital to grid	Power down generator
4	On a gas pipeline upgrade project, you must **start** the task of implementing the new pipeline, before you **finish** the task of shutting down the old pipeline.	Implement new pipeline	Shut down old pipe-line

	(SF) USE CASE	PREDECESSOR TASK	SUCCESSOR TASK
5	For a supply chain project, you must **start** the task of signing in the security staff before you can **finish** the task of delivering high-value supplies.	Sign in security staff	Deliver high-value supplies

Understanding Lag and Lead Time

Once task relationships have been established, there may be scenarios where you will need to delay a successor task after its predecessor finishes or start a successor task before its predecessor finishes. In these cases, you can apply **Lag** or **Lead** time between tasks to delay or compress the schedule.

- **LAG** – Use lag time when the successor task should be delayed after its predecessor finishes.

Example – In the House Painting project schedule shown in *Figure 104* below, the *List Supplies* and *Buy Supplies* tasks have a Finish-to-Start task relationship. Accordingly, Project has scheduled the *Buy Supplies* task to begin on **6/4/24**, the next working day after the *List Supplies* task finishes.

	ⓘ	Task Mode	Task Name	Duration	Start	Finish	Predecessors
0			**House Painting Project**	**20 days**	**Mon 6/3/24**	**Fri 6/28/24**	
1			**Get Supplies**	**2 days**	**Mon 6/3/24**	**Tue 6/4/24**	
2			List Supplies	1 day	Mon 6/3/24	Mon 6/3/24	
3			Buy Supplies	1 day	Tue 6/4/24	Tue 6/4/24	2
4			Supplies Gotten	0 days	Mon 6/3/24	Mon 6/3/24	
5			**Prep House**	**4 days**	**Tue 6/4/24**	**Mon 6/10/24**	1
6			Sand House	2 days	Wed 6/5/24	Thu 6/6/24	
7			Tape Windows	1 day	Fri 6/7/24	Fri 6/7/24	6
8			Lay Drop Cloth	1 day	Mon 6/10/24	Mon 6/10/24	7
9			House Prepped	0 days	Tue 6/4/24	Tue 6/4/24	
10			**Paint House**	**14 days**	**Mon 6/10/24**	**Fri 6/28/24**	5
11			Apply First Coat	5 days	Tue 6/11/24	Mon 6/17/24	
12			Apply Final Coat	5 days	Tue 6/18/24	Mon 6/24/24	11
13			Remove Window Tape	1 day	Tue 6/25/24	Tue 6/25/24	12
14			Inspect House	1 day	Wed 6/26/24	Wed 6/26/24	13
15			Apply Finishing Touches	2 days	Thu 6/27/24	Fri 6/28/24	14
16			House Painted	0 days	Mon 6/10/24	Mon 6/10/24	

Figure 104 – House Painting Project Schedule

Let's suppose you experienced a two-day funding delay to buy the supplies. Funding will not be available until two days after the *List Supplies* task finishes. In this case, you could apply two days of **lag time** to the successor task *Buy Supplies* to prevent it from starting until the funds are available.

- **LEAD** – Use lead time when a successor task can start before its predecessor finishes.

Example – In the same House Painting schedule shown in *Figure 104*, the *Apply First Coat* and *Apply Final Coat* tasks have a Finish-to-Start task relationship. Accordingly, Project has scheduled the *Apply Final Coat* task to begin on **6/18/24**, five working days after the *Apply First Coat* task finishes.

To save time, the painter can start the *Apply Final Coat* task on the portions of the house that have dried, 2 days before the *Apply First Coat* task finishes (instead of waiting the entire 5 days). In this case, you could apply **lead** time to the successor task to accomplish this.

Creating Lag and Lead Time

Lag and Lead time are created in the **Predecessors** field of the Entry table, next to the successor task.

Lag time is expressed as a positive value (adding time to or delaying the start date of the successor task). Lag time values can be expressed as a number or a percentage. Using a percentage will delay the start of the successor task a percentage of time after the predecessor task is complete.

Enter Lag Time using the following syntax:

> Enter the **Predecessor task ID number**, followed by the **two-letter acronym for the task relationship type**, followed by a **plus sign**, followed by the **value of lag time**.
>
> **NOTE:** The lag value can also be expressed as a percentage of the predecessor's duration.
>
> Example: 15FS+2days or 15FS+50%

Lead time is expressed as a negative value (subtracting time from or overlapping the start date of the successor task). Lead time values can be expressed as a number or a percentage. Using a percentage will start the successor task after a percentage of the predecessor task is complete.

Enter Lead Time using the following syntax:

> The **Predecessor task ID number**, followed by the **two-letter acronym for the task relationship type**, followed by a **minus sign**, followed by the **value of lead time**.
>
> Example: 4FS-2days or 4FS-50%

> **NOTE:** Generally, because it is the default task relationship, the FS acronym for the Finish-to-Start task relationship does not appear in the Predecessors field — only the acronym for the other three relationship types appears. However, in the case of Lead and Lag entries, the FS acronym will appear in the syntax.

Figure 105 below shows the lag and lead entries for the funding delay and early start scenarios referenced earlier.

	Task Name	Duration	Start	Finish	Predecessors
0	**House Painting Project**	**20 days**	**Mon 6/3/24**	**Fri 6/28/24**	
1	**Get Supplies**	**4 days**	**Mon 6/3/24**	**Thu 6/6/24**	
2	List Supplies	1 day	Mon 6/3/24	Mon 6/3/24	
3	Buy Supplies	1 day	Thu 6/6/24	Thu 6/6/24	2FS+2 days
4	Supplies Gotten	0 days	Mon 6/3/24	Mon 6/3/24	
5	**Prep House**	**4 days**	**Thu 6/6/24**	**Wed 6/12/24**	
6	Sand House	2 days	Fri 6/7/24	Mon 6/10/24	
7	Tape Windows	1 day	Tue 6/11/24	Tue 6/11/24	6
8	Lay Drop Cloth	1 day	Wed 6/12/24	Wed 6/12/24	7
9	House Prepped	0 days	Thu 6/6/24	Thu 6/6/24	
10	**Paint House**	**12 days**	**Wed 6/12/24**	**Fri 6/28/24**	5
11	Apply First Coat	5 days	Thu 6/13/24	Wed 6/19/24	
12	Apply Final Coat	5 days	Tue 6/18/24	Mon 6/24/24	11FS-2 days
13	Remove Window Tape	1 day	Tue 6/25/24	Tue 6/25/24	12
14	Inspect House	1 day	Wed 6/26/24	Wed 6/26/24	
15	Apply Finishing Touches	2 days	Thu 6/27/24	Fri 6/28/24	
16	House Painted	0 days	Wed 6/12/24	Wed 6/12/24	

Lag Time

Lead Time

Figure 105 – Using Lag and Lead Time

When the 2-day Lag is applied to the *Buy Supplies* task, Project reschedules it to start on **6/6/24**, two business days after its predecessor *List Supplies* finishes. When the 2-day Lead is applied to the *Apply Final Coat* task, Project reschedules it to start on **6/18/24** two business days before its predecessor *Apply First Coat* finishes. In the Gantt chart, the task bars will also reflect the lead and lag time.

Here are more examples of Lead and Lag entries:

- **4FS–2days** (the successor task will start 2 days before predecessor task 4 finishes)
- **4FS+2 days** (the successor task will start 2 days after predecessor task 4 finishes)
- **4FS–50%** (the successor task will start after predecessor task 4 is 50% done)
- **4FS+50%** (the successor task will start "X" days after predecessor task 4 is done; where "X" = 50% of the duration of predecessor task 4)

Lead Use Cases

Lead time can be applied to any of the four task relationship types. Whichever dependency type is used, lead is always meant to cause work on a successor task to overlap work on its predecessor, causing it to start earlier than it normally would. For example, on a construction project, normally the successor task of *ordering long-lead items* (items that may need to be manufactured and will require an extended delivery time) would begin after *preliminary shop drawings* have been provided. However, if the completed sheets of the preliminary shop drawings could be provided 3 days before the entire set was provided, then some of the long-lead purchase items could be ordered three days earlier than they normally would have been ordered. The 3-day early start in this example is a 3-day lead. As you may well know, starting early is generally a good thing when it comes to scheduling. In fact, if the successor task in question were on the critical path of your schedule, then starting it 3 days earlier would result in your entire schedule finishing 3 days earlier. We will demonstrate this concept in Chapter 11.

Although lead time can be applied to each of the four task relationship types, it is most commonly applied to Finish-to-Start and Finish-to-Finish relationships. When lead time is applied to Finish-to-Finish task relationships, it is often to add in buffer time so that unforeseen challenges do not cause delays.

For example, when I managed network deployment projects at AT&T, many of my projects involved deploying new equipment into the AT&T network. Some of this equipment could take as long as 18 months to purchase, install and configure into the network. As such, as mentioned earlier, it was difficult to get busy engineers to prioritize this work. They would request that I involve them at the point where their work was truly needed. To accommodate their request, I would use Finish-to-Finish task relationships to tie their completion date to the completion date of a paired network element. However, in doing so, I would have to remove all the "wiggle room" (or slack) out of my schedule. To add some of that wiggle room back in, I would use lead time of up to 2 or 3 weeks. In effect, I was using lead time to add in buffer time so that unforeseen challenges would not cause delays. As you use your schedule to solve business challenges, think of lead time as a specialized tool in your tool kit. For example, you might solve a business problem by starting two tasks together and putting a small lead on the successor task so that it starts slightly ahead of its predecessor. Or you might use lead time in a Start-to-Finish scenario to add in a buffer for pre-work, to smoothly cut-over from an existing system to a new one. Whichever way you decide to apply lead time, the important thing to realize is that it serves a unique purpose in your scheduling toolkit. Like an Allen wrench, it may not be required in most applications, but when it is needed, nothing else will do.

Lag Use Cases

Lag time is the opposite of lead time. Rather than starting a task earlier than it normally would, it starts a task later than it normally would. For example, on a painting project, one would not apply the second coat of paint until the first coat of paint has dried. As such, there is a lag period between the application of the first coat and the application of the second coat. This is the business problem that lag time is meant to solve. It inserts time into the schedule to account for required periods in which no work occurs. Another use case would be a required soak testing period. Soak testing involves testing a system with a typical production load over a continuous time-frame to confirm it will perform as expected when it is introduced into the production environment. Some schedulers are tempted to use lag time when work is occurring, such as periods in which a document is being reviewed before approval is granted. Since this is an activity being performed by a resource, it should be represented on the schedule as a task, rather than a lag period. In the example of the soak testing, a resource will perform the activity of introducing a production load to the new system. This activity should be captured as a task.

However, if the soak period will run for 5 days, then the 5-day period could be represented as lag time. The practice of using lag time only to account for periods in the schedule in which no work occurs allows for better control of the project. It also establishes accountability by identifying an owner for each task in the schedule, including document review periods.

Although lag time can be applied to any task relationship type, it's typically applied to Finish-to-Start and Start-to-Start task relationships. When used in Start-to-Start task relationships, the intent is to start the successor task earlier. This may seem counter-intuitive since lag time generally starts tasks later. However, when lag time is used in a Start-to-Start relationship, it allows for the successor task to start as close *as possible* to the start date of the predecessor task. In this case, the lag time is used to account for the aspect of the predecessor task that must finish before the successor task can start. As with lead time, the important thing to realize about lag time is that it serves a unique purpose in your scheduling toolkit. It can help you start a task as close as possible to the start of another task, or account for intervals when no work occurs, but other work is prevented from starting until those intervals are fully exhausted.

What Makes a Schedule a Schedule?

You're now able to create tasks, structure them to create your schedule outline, and establish relationships between them. Once you've built your schedule, it's important to consider the criteria it should meet to function well as a project schedule. Despite the project management standardization efforts of organizations like the Project Management Institute, and the codification of project management methodologies like PRINCE2, in project management practice across the world there is still a wide range of acceptable artifacts meant to represent a project schedule.

In this section we've provided **eight criteria** that must be satisfied to rightly call a project management artifact a schedule. As you review each criterion, consider the business challenges one might encounter in the absence of it. Also, consider the competitive advantages that organizations that enforce these standards might enjoy, over ones that do not.

1. A true schedule distributes the work required to complete each task in your schedule across the business days and hours of your organization only – and never across non-business hours when resources do not work. This also applies to exceptions like vacation days. This helps to set realistic expectations.

2. A true schedule shows you when resources are truly needed, so you can efficiently use company resources. For example, on a project with 10 resources assigned, your schedule may show that in a given work week, only 1 or 2 resources have actionable tasks on your project. You may then decide to cancel your weekly project meeting and ask those resources to provide status instead of meeting.

3. A true schedule shows you dependencies between tasks and between projects so you can discern what drives each task and what may be causing a delay.

4. A true schedule allows you to quickly **detect** risks, and issues like over-allocated resources, cost overruns and schedule delays.

5. A true schedule allows you to model actions to **address** risks, and issues like over-allocated resources, cost overruns and schedule delays.

6. A true schedule allows you to model actions to expedite your schedule, reduce cost and mitigate risk.

7. A true schedule allows you to predict when your project will finish, based on current performance data, and predict how much your project will cost.

8. A true schedule allows you to quickly compare your planned results to your actual results, at any point during the life cycle of your project.

As you can see, a schedule is far more than a forecast. It's an active planning tool that is meant to function like a calculator. Because projects are so dynamic in nature, it's reasonable that the artifact we use to forecast the project's finish date and cost be dynamic as well. If your organization has too low a bar as to what it considers a schedule, you can use the lessons in the upcoming chapters to help raise that bar and begin overcoming the schedule challenges that plague organizations around the world.

We've now reviewed tasks – the building blocks of your schedule, the business drivers behind task relationships, and criteria you can use to determine whether a project management artifact can truly function as a schedule. In the next chapter, we'll begin putting these fundamentals into practice. We'll go behind the scenes and look at the settings in Project and the array of user-controlled scheduling options that determine the way Project schedules your tasks.

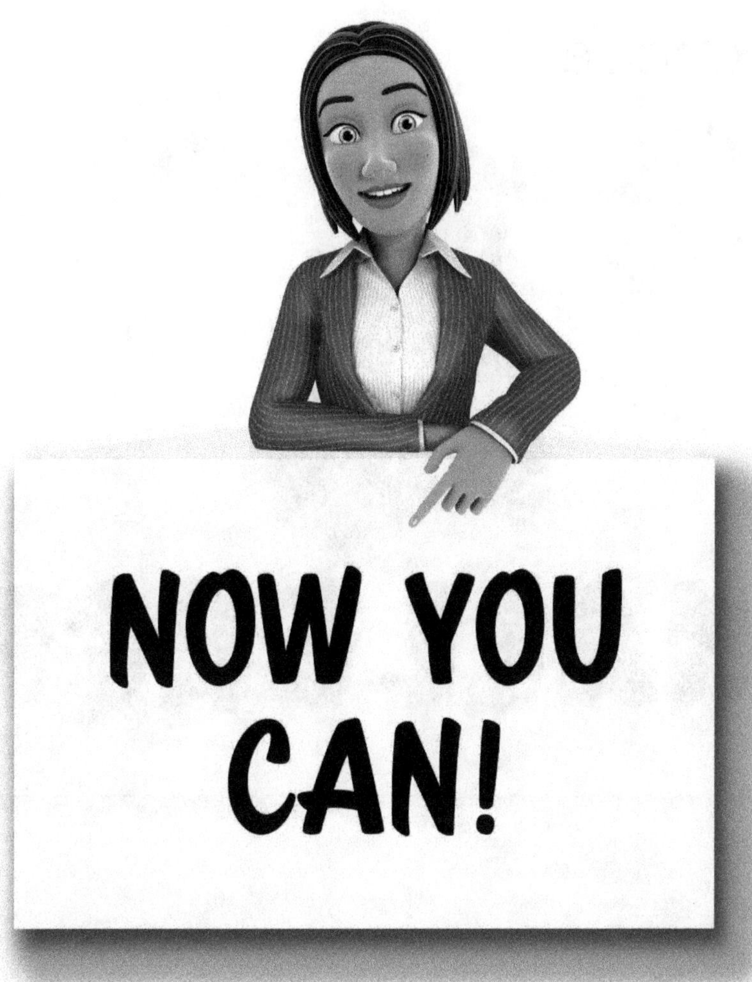

- ✓ Convert a WBS into a Schedule Outline
- ✓ Explain the Parts of a Schedule Outline
- ✓ Display the Project Summary Task
- ✓ Create Tasks, Summary Tasks, and Milestones
- ✓ Explain Task Relationships: Predecessors and Successors
- ✓ Use Leads and Lags
- ✓ Explain What Makes a Schedule a Schedule?

Practice Exercise

Develop a Schedule Outline: Create Tasks and Task Relationships

For this practice exercise, you will create a schedule for a House Painting project. You'll create summary tasks, subtasks, and milestones to develop the project outline, display the Project Summary task, create task relationships, and apply lag time.

Go to **mspbasics.com** for "checkpoint" images to check your work as you go along.

Follow the step-by-step instructions below to complete this Challenge practice exercise.

Start a New Project

From the opening view, select **Blank Project** to create a new project. You'll be taken to the Gantt Chart view.

Set the Project Start Date

We'll start by setting the project's start date. The start date is **6/3/24**.

1. Select the **Project** tab.
2. In the **Properties** group, select the **Project Information** command, to open the *Project Information* dialogue box.
3. In the **Start date** field, enter **6/3/24**.
4. Select **OK** to close the dialogue box.

Adjust the Settings

Next, we'll perform part of the **A** step in the **B.A.S.I.C.S.** scheduling process – **Adjust the Settings**. In the bottom left corner of the view is the **Status Bar**. Notice the *New Tasks: Manually Scheduled* notification. This means that all new tasks will be scheduled in the "Manual" scheduling mode. For this project, we would like Project to schedule tasks in the "Automatic" scheduling mode. To change the scheduling mode for all new tasks, we'll go to the **Backstage** view and adjust the settings:

1. Select the **File** tab to go **Backstage**. Then, select **Options** from the panel on the left, to open the *Project Options* dialog box.
2. In the *Project Options* dialogue box, select **Schedule** from the options on the left, to view the scheduling options.
3. Under the *Scheduling options for this project* section, select **Auto Scheduled** from the *New tasks created* pick-list.
4. Select **OK** to close the dialog box.

Notice the message in the Status Bar now reads *New Tasks: Auto Scheduled*. This means Project will schedule all new tasks in the Automatic scheduling mode.

CHECKPOINT: To check your results so far, go to **mspbasics.com**

- Select the **CheckPoint Images** tab.
- Select the version of the book you're using.
- Select **Chapter 4**. Then, go to **Checkpoint Image #1**

The **Tasks List** and the **Work Breakdown Structure** for the House Painting Project are shown in the graphic below.

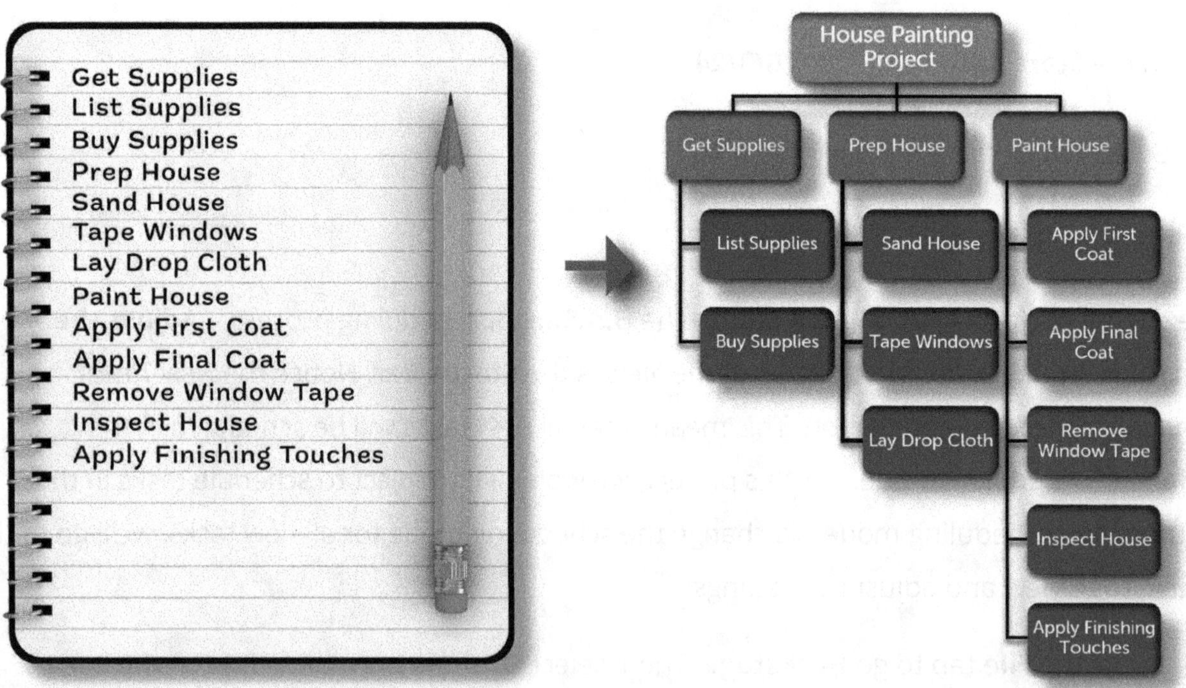

Enter the Task List into Project

Next, we will enter the task list into the Entry table, here in the Gantt Chart view.

1. Enter each of the task names (in the order they are shown on the task list) into the **Task Name** field of the **Entry table**. The *Get Supplies* task will have task ID 1, the *List Supplies* task will have task ID 2, and so forth. When you're done, you should have **13 tasks**.

By default, Project assigns a 1-day duration to each task and assigns the project start date as the Start and Finish dates. In the Gantt chart, a task bar is generated for each task, depicting its 1-day duration.

CHECKPOINT: To check your results so far, go to **mspbasics.com**

- Select the **CheckPoint Images** tab.
- Select the version of the book you're using.
- Select **Chapter 4**. Then, go to **Checkpoint Image #2**

Since we're not using the Timeline view for this exercise, we'll hide it to get more room in the current view.

1. Select the **View** tab.
2. In the **Split View** group, uncheck the **Timeline** check box to close the Timeline panel.

Structure the Tasks: Create the Schedule Outline

Next, we'll perform the first **S** step of the **B.A.S.I.C.S.** scheduling process – we'll **Structure the Task list** to create the schedule outline. We'll use the **Indent Task** command to create summary tasks and subtasks for the three phases of the project.

1. Select the *List Supplies* and *Buy Supplies* tasks.
2. Select the **Task** tab. In the **Schedule** group, select the **Indent Task** command. The *Get Supplies* task should now be promoted to a summary task, indicated with bold typeface. The *List Supplies* and *Buy Supplies* tasks should be demoted beneath it as subtasks. In the Gantt chart, the blue task bar for the *Get Supplies task* has been replaced with a black summary bar.
3. Next, select the *Sand House*, *Tape Windows,* and *Lay Drop Cloth* tasks. Select the **Indent Task** command to promote the *Prep House* task to a summary task and demote these three tasks beneath it as subtasks.

4. Now, select the *Apply First Coat*, *Apply Final Coat*, *Remove Window Tape*, *Inspect House* and *Apply Finishing Touches* tasks. Use the **Indent Task** command to promote the *Paint House* task to a summary task and demote these fives tasks beneath it as subtasks.

The three phases of the House Painting project should now be structured. Each task should have a 1-day duration and the project start date as its Start and Finish date.

CHECKPOINT: To check your results so far, go to **mspbasics.com**

- Select the **CheckPoint Images** tab.
- Select the version of the book you're using.
- Select **Chapter 4**. Then, go to **Checkpoint Image #3**

ESTIMATED DURATIONS: Notice the question marks next to the 1-day duration values. Project considers all task durations as estimated and indicates this with a question mark. If you don't like the question marks, you can remove them in the project settings:

1. Select the **File** tab to go **Backstage**. Then, select **Options** from the panel on the left, to open the *Project Options* dialog box.

2. In the *Project Options* dialogue box, select **Schedule** from the options on the left, to see the scheduling options.

3. Under the *Scheduling options for this project* section, uncheck the *Show that scheduled tasks have estimated durations* checkbox. This will remove the question marks from all tasks currently in the schedule.

4. Uncheck the *New scheduled tasks have estimated durations* checkbox to remove the question marks from all new tasks added to the schedule.

Create Milestones

Next, we'll create **Milestone** tasks to signify the completion of each phase. We'll start with Phase 1 – Get Supplies.

1. Select the *Prep House* summary task.

2. On the **Task** tab, in the **Insert** group, select the **Insert Milestone** command.
   A "New Milestone" task will be inserted as task ID 4 beneath the *Buy Supplies* task and will be given a duration value of zero. Also, a diamond icon will be added to the Gantt chart, indicating the milestone.

3. Type over the default name and rename the milestone **"Supplies Gotten"**.

4. To create the milestone for Phase 2 - Prep House, select the *Paint House* summary task.

5. Then, select the **Insert Milestone** command. A "New Milestone" task will be inserted as task ID 9 beneath the *Lay Drop Cloth* task.

6. Type over the default name and rename the milestone **"House Prepped"**.

7. We'll create the last milestone for Phase 3 - Paint House using a different method. In the **Task Name** field, in the cell beneath the *Apply Final Touches* task, enter the task name **"House Painted"**. The task ID for this task should be 16. It will be given a 1-day duration and a corresponding task bar in the Gantt chart.

8. In the **Duration** field for this task, enter **0** for the duration value. This task is now a milestone. Notice that the task bar in the Gantt chart has been replaced with a diamond icon.

CHECKPOINT: To check your results so far, go to **mspbasics.com**

- Select the **CheckPoint Images** tab.
- Select the version of the book you're using.
- Select **Chapter 4**. Then, go to **Checkpoint Image #4**

Enter Task Durations

Next, we'll perform the **I** step of the **B.A.S.I.C.S.** scheduling process – **Initialize the Durations**. To do this we'll give each task a Duration value. The duration values for each task are listed below.

1. In the **Duration** field of the Entry table, enter the respective duration for each subtask. For example, for the *List Supplies task*, enter 1d. **NOTE:** You won't enter a duration for the summary tasks. Project will automatically calculate the summary task durations, based on the durations of their subtasks and the task relationships.

TASK NAME	DURATION
List Supplies	1d
Buy Supplies	1d
Sand House	2d
Tape Windows	1d
Lay Drop Cloth	1d
Apply First Coat	5d
Apply Final Coat	5d
Remove Window Tape	1d
Inspect House	1d
Apply Finishing Touches	2d

After the duration values are entered, the task bars in the Gantt chart will be updated to reflect the new durations.

CHECKPOINT: To check your results so far, go to **mspbasics.com**

- Select the **CheckPoint Images** tab.
- Select the version of the book you're using.
- Select **Chapter 4**. Then, go to **Checkpoint Image #5**

Connect the Tasks: Create Task Relationships

Next, we'll perform the C step of the **B.A.S.I.C.S.** scheduling process –we'll **Connect the Tasks** and create the task relationships. The tasks in this schedule occur in sequence, so we'll give the tasks in each phase a *Finish-to-Start* task relationship. Each task is the predecessor of the following task.

The tasks and their predecessor's task ID numbers are listed in the following table.

1. In the **Predecessors** field of each task, **enter the task ID number** for its predecessor task.

TASK NAME	DURATION
Buy Supplies	2
Supplies Gotten	3
Sand House	4
Tape Windows	6
Lay Drop Cloth	7
House Prepped	8
Apply First Coat	9
Apply Final Coat	11
Remove Window Tape	12
Inspect House	13
Apply Finishing Touches	14
House Painted	15

CHECKPOINT: To check your results so far, go to **mspbasics.com**

- Select the **CheckPoint Images** tab.
- Select the version of the book you're using.
- Select **Chapter 4**. Then, go to **Checkpoint Image #6**

After the tasks relationships are created, notice that Project has updated the durations of the summary tasks based on the durations of their subtasks. Also, in the Gantt chart, the tasks bars are also connected, reflecting the task relationships.

Create a Start-to-Start Task Relationship

We've discovered that we already have the sanding supplies for the *Sand House* task. Consequently, this task doesn't have to wait for the *Buy Supplies* task to finish. It can start with the *List Supplies* task. To reflect this in the schedule, we'll give these tasks a *Start-to-Start* task relationship.

1. In the **Predecessors** field of the *Sand House* task, enter **2SS** to create a *Start-to-Start* relationship with the *List Supplies* task.

After this change is made, Project will update the Start and Finish dates of the *Sand House* task and all subsequent tasks. All the schedule updates will be highlighted in blue.

Use Lag Time

After the *Apply First Coat* task finishes, the paint must dry for 2 days before the *Apply Final Coat* task can begin. To account for this in the schedule, we will apply a 2-day Lag to the *Apply Final Coat* task. This will delay the start of this task 2 days after its predecessor finishes.

1. In the **Predecessors** field of the A*pply Final Coat* task, enter **11FS+2d** to create the lag time. After the lag time is added, Project will update the Start and Finish dates of the *Apply Final Coat task*, and all subsequent tasks.

Display the Project Summary Task

Last, we'll display the **Project Summary Task**, which is the highest level of the project outline (task ID zero). This will show us the overall project duration and the project finish date.

1. Select the **Format** tab. In the **Show/Hide** group, select the **Project Summary Task** checkbox.

2. Rename the project summary task **"House Painting Project"**.

After the Project Summary Task is displayed, it will show the overall project duration, which should be **20 days** and a project finish date of **6/28/24**.

You've now built a schedule for a House Painting project! You've created the project outline, created task relationships, applied lag time and displayed the Project Summary Task

CHECKPOINT: To check your results so far, go to **mspbasics.com**

- Select the **CheckPoint Images** tab.
- Select the version of the book you're using.
- Select **Chapter 4**. Then, go to **Checkpoint Image #7**

Chapter 5 Understanding Settings

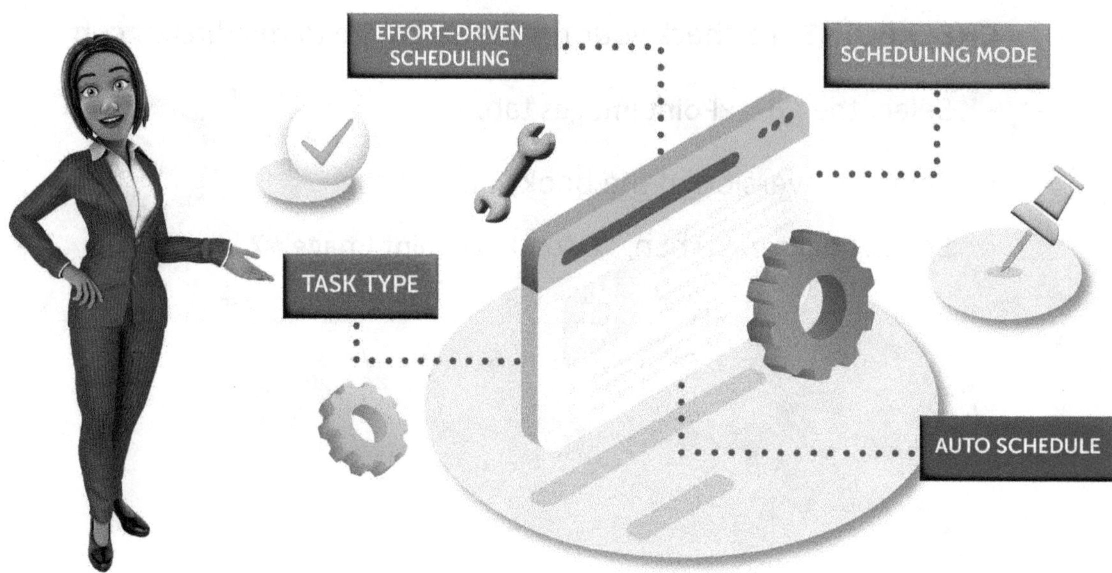

In the last chapter, we covered the most important aspects of building a schedule - creating tasks, outlining them, and establishing relationships between them. In this chapter, we'll review another fundamental topic - adjusting the settings in Microsoft Project. This is the **A** step in the **B.A.S.I.C.S.** scheduling process. A good understanding of settings can make the difference between a smooth and a frustrating experience using Project. We'll explore how Project's scheduling engine works and review important settings, such as the two Scheduling Modes, the Duration Equation, Effort-Driven Scheduling, and Task Type. When you're done, you'll be able to adjust the settings to control how Project behaves and build the type of schedule your project requires.

You'll Learn To:

- Use the Manual Schedule Mode
- Use the Automatic Scheduling Mode
- Explain the Duration Equation
- Explain Effort-Driven Scheduling
- Explain Task Type

Project is a robust scheduling tool with wide-ranging functionality. As such, it's important to understand the settings so that Project schedules tasks in a way that suits your Project.

Scheduling Modes

We'll begin with **Scheduling Modes**. There are two scheduling modes in Project, the **Automatic** scheduling mode and the **Manual** scheduling mode. The scheduling mode you choose determines the degree to which Project's scheduling engine is engaged and how it schedules tasks. By default, Project opens in the Manual scheduling mode. This is indicated in the *Status Bar* (located in the bottom left corner of the view) by the notification that reads *New Tasks: Manually Scheduled* (*Figure 106* below). Let's review the aspects of each scheduling mode.

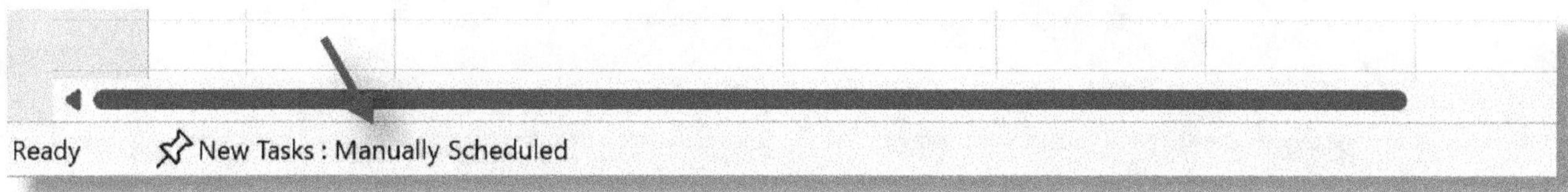

Figure 106 – Status Bar Scheduling Mode Notification

Using the Automatic Scheduling Mode

In the **Automatic** mode, Project's scheduling engine is fully engaged. Task start dates, finish dates, and duration values are calculated based on task relationships and factors like constraints and calendars. By default, Project starts each task as soon as possible. If schedule changes are made (like increasing the duration of a task), Project will automatically update any tasks that are impacted by the change. *Figure 107* shows tasks scheduled in the Automatic scheduling mode. In the **Task Mode** field, the Automatic scheduling mode is indicated by a task bar icon with an arrow. In the Gantt chart, it's indicated by blue task bars. The **Status Bar**, in the bottom left corner also shows the selected scheduling mode.

Automatic Mode Characteristics and Behaviors:

- Numeric fields require numeric entries
- Task relationships are respected
- New tasks are automatically given a 1-day duration and assigned the project start date for their start date (or the current date if the project start date has not been set).

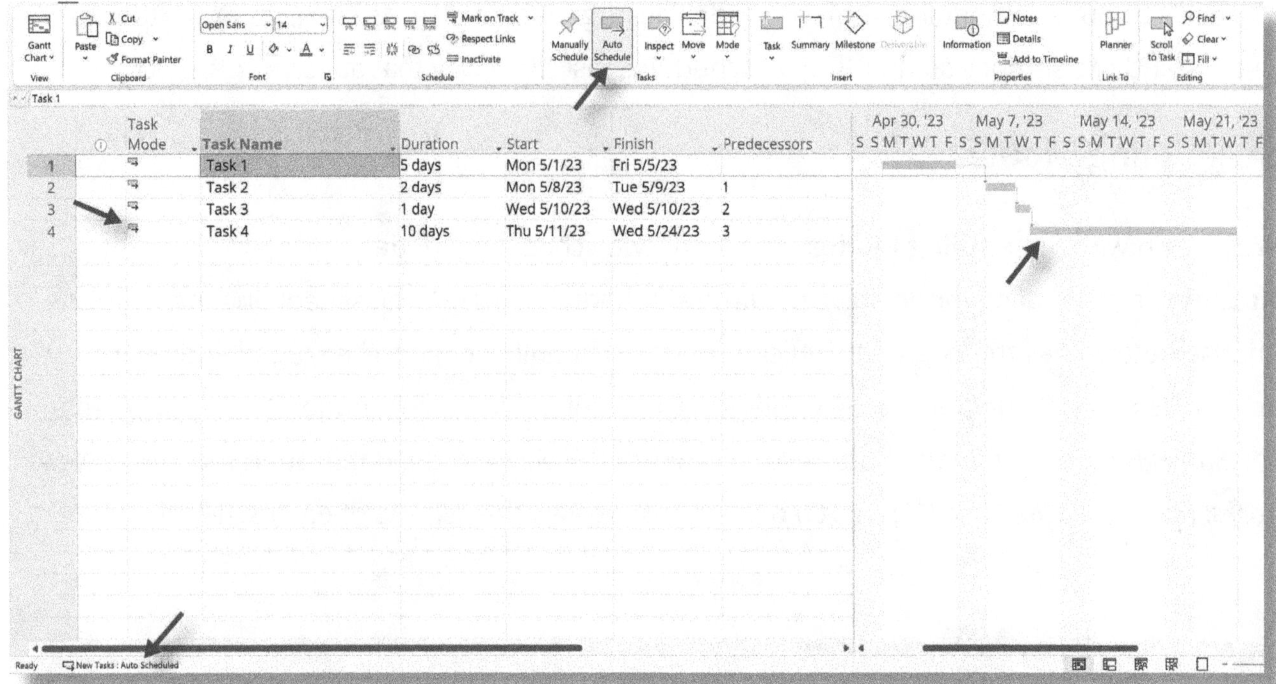

Figure 107 – Automatically Scheduled Tasks

Using the Manual Scheduling Mode

In the **Manual** mode, Project's scheduling engine is only partially engaged. The Manual scheduling mode was added to the 2010 version of Microsoft Project. It was incorporated to address the preferences of schedulers who use Excel to build schedules. These schedulers prefer the freedom to enter their ideal start and finish dates, without having to respect the scheduling rules imposed by Microsoft Project. In the Manual mode, users can schedule tasks manually and are less restricted by the rules of Project's scheduling engine. For example, text entries are allowed in numeric fields like the Duration field.

Manually scheduled tasks are not affected by:

- Changes in Duration
- Changes in Start Dates
- Changes in Finish Dates
- Changes in Task Relationships
- Occurrences that would normally cause Project to reschedule a task

To be clear, when these scheduling rules are disabled, Project will not calculate your schedule correctly. This is the most important thing to remember about building schedules in the Manual mode. Notwithstanding, some users find this mode helpful. It allows them to plot out their ideal scheduling scenarios. Whenever they wish to vet these scenarios against reality, they can toggle back to the automatic scheduling mode, in which the scheduling rules are fully enforced. Another benefit of the manual mode is that the more scheduling detail you add, the more the scheduling engine engages. For example, if you only provide a task name, Project will provide a task duration and a start date. Project will use this information to calculate the finish date. *Figure 108* below shows tasks scheduled in the Manual scheduling mode. In the *Task Mode* field, the Manual scheduling mode is indicated by a pushpin icon, and lighter blue task bars in the Gantt chart. As mentioned, the selected scheduling mode is also indicated in the *Status Bar*.

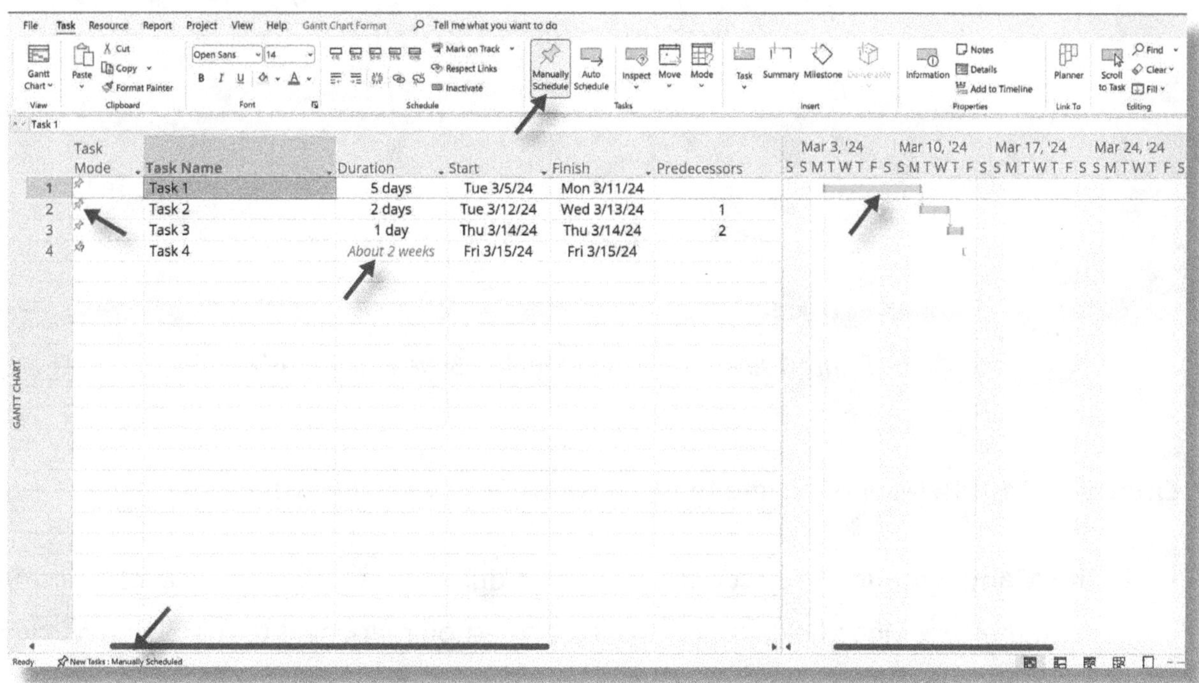

Figure 108 – Manually Scheduled Tasks

Comparing the Manual and the Automatic Scheduling Modes

Next, we'll take a closer look at how Project behaves in each scheduling mode. Using *Figure 109* below, we'll compare how Project responds to the same entries made in both scheduling modes.

Manual Mode Entries

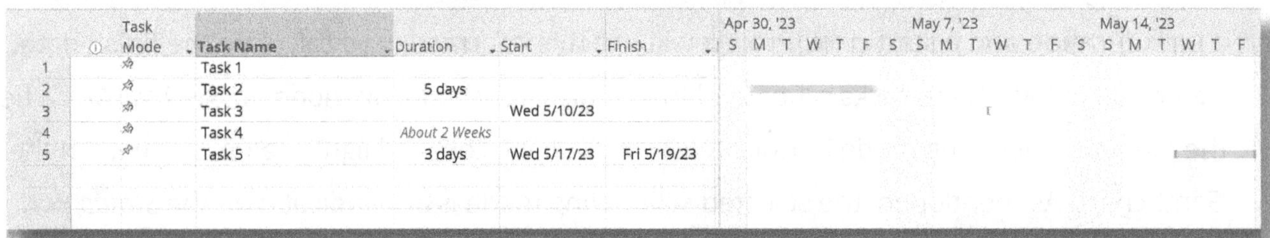

	Task Mode	Task Name	Duration	Start	Finish
1		Task 1			
2		Task 2	5 days		
3		Task 3		Wed 5/10/23	
4		Task 4	About 2 Weeks		
5		Task 5	3 days	Wed 5/17/23	Fri 5/19/23

Automatic Mode Entries

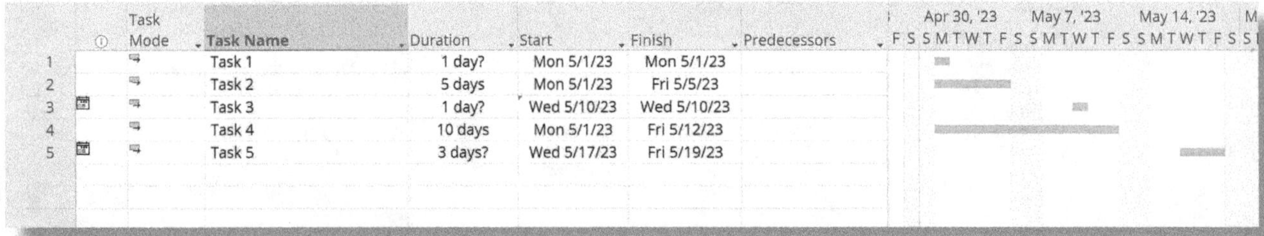

	Task Mode	Task Name	Duration	Start	Finish	Predecessors
1		Task 1	1 day?	Mon 5/1/23	Mon 5/1/23	
2		Task 2	5 days	Mon 5/1/23	Fri 5/5/23	
3		Task 3	1 day?	Wed 5/10/23	Wed 5/10/23	
4		Task 4	10 days	Mon 5/1/23	Fri 5/12/23	
5		Task 5	3 days?	Wed 5/17/23	Fri 5/19/23	

Figure 109 – Comparing the Two Scheduling Modes

Entry #1 – Task 1 was entered into the Task Name field of the Entry table.

- **In the Manual mode** – Project did not assign a duration, nor determine a start or finish date. In the Task Mode field, Project placed a question mark next to the pushpin icon to alert the user that more scheduling information is needed. In the Gantt chart, a task bar was not generated.

- **In the Automatic mode** – Project automatically assigned a 1-day duration to the task. Also, the project start date was assigned as the start date. Since the 1-day task will start at 8:00 AM and complete at 5:00 PM on the same day, Project uses the same date as the finish date. The question mark next to the 1-day duration entry represents that the duration was estimated by Project. In the Gantt Chart, a task bar was generated, representing the 1-day duration.

Entry #2 –Task 2 was entered into the Task Name field and a 5-day duration (5d) was entered into the Duration field.

- **In the Manual Mode** – Project did not determine a start or finish date for the task. In the Gantt Chart, a task bar was generated representing the 5-day duration.
- **In the Automatic Mode** – Project automatically determined the task's start and finish dates. The project start date was assigned as the start date and the finish date was calculated as 5 business days after the start date. In the Gantt Chart, a task bar was generated representing the 5-day duration. **NOTE:** Because we entered a 5-day duration, Project removed the question mark next to the duration value. The duration is no longer considered estimated.

Entry #3 –Task 3 was entered into the Task Name field and a 5/10/23 start date was entered into the Start field.

- **In the Manual Mode** – Project did not assign a duration to the task nor determine its finish date. In the Gantt chart, Project generated an end cap, corresponding with the 5/10/23 start date.
- **In the Automatic Mode** – Project assigned a 1-day duration to the task, the project start date as the task start date, and generated a task bar in the Gantt Chart. Because a manual entry was made in the Automatic mode, Project applied a *Start-No-Earlier-Than* scheduling constraint to the task (indicated by the calendar icon in the Indicators field). Project interpreted the manual entry as a command for the task to start no earlier than the entered date. Also, a scheduling notification was added to the Start field, alerting the user that the manual entry limits how Project can schedule tasks. The user has the choice to keep the constraint or remove it so Project can schedule the task to start earlier, if possible or later, if necessary. As a rule, start or finish dates should not be manually entered in the Automatic scheduling mode. It generates constraints, which limit scheduling flexibility. We'll discuss constraints further in Chapter 12.

Manual Mode Entries

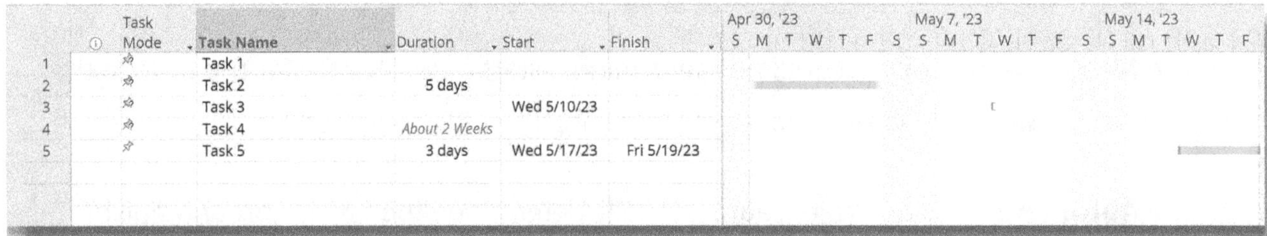

	Task Mode	Task Name	Duration	Start	Finish
1		Task 1			
2		Task 2	5 days		
3		Task 3		Wed 5/10/23	
4		Task 4	*About 2 Weeks*		
5		Task 5	3 days	Wed 5/17/23	Fri 5/19/23

Automatic Mode Entries

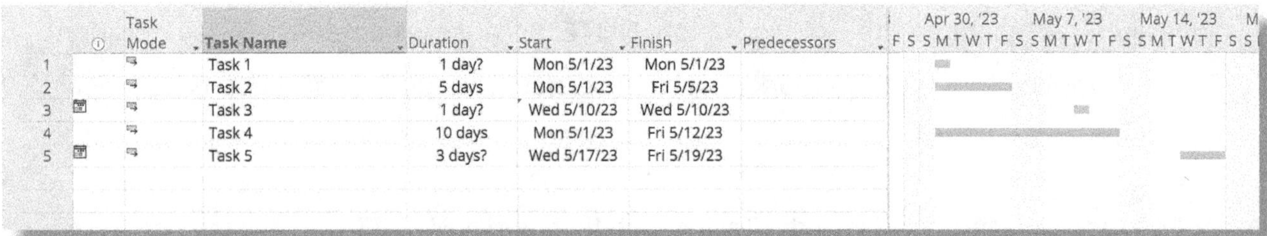

	Task Mode	Task Name	Duration	Start	Finish	Predecessors
1		Task 1	1 day?	Mon 5/1/23	Mon 5/1/23	
2		Task 2	5 days	Mon 5/1/23	Fri 5/5/23	
3		Task 3	1 day?	Wed 5/10/23	Wed 5/10/23	
4		Task 4	10 days	Mon 5/1/23	Fri 5/12/23	
5		Task 5	3 days?	Wed 5/17/23	Fri 5/19/23	

Figure 109 - Comparing the Scheduling Modes

Entry #4 – Task 4 was entered in the Task Name field and the text *"About 2 weeks"* was entered into the Duration field.

- **In the Manual Mode** – The text entry was allowed. Project did not determine a start or finish date nor generate a task bar in the Gantt chart.
- **In the Automatic Mode** –The text entry was not allowed. Project generated an alert that text is not supported in numeric fields in the Automatic mode. A numeric value (10d) is required to indicate the 2-week duration. When the 10-day duration was entered, Project assigned the project start date as the task start date and the finish date was calculated as 10 business days after the start date. A task bar indicating the 10-day duration was generated in the Gantt chart.

Entry #5 –Task 5 was entered into the Task Name field. 5/17/23 was entered into the Start field and 5/19/23 was entered into the Finish field.

- **In the Manual Mode** – Project calculated a 3-day duration from the start and finish dates. In the Gantt chart, a task bar was generated with end caps, representing the start and finish dates. Also, in the Task Mode field, Project removed the question mark.

- **In the Automatic Mode** – After the task name was entered, Project assigned a 1-day duration to the task and the start and finish dates. In the Gantt Chart, a task bar was generated, indicating the 1-day duration. After 5/17/23 was entered into Start field, Project applied a *Start No Earlier Than* scheduling constraint to the task. After 5/19/23 was entered into the Finish field, Project calculated a 3-day duration from the start and finish dates. In the Gantt Chart, the task bar was extended to match the 3-day duration. Also, after the finish date was entered, Project changed the scheduling constraint type from *Start No Earlier Than* to *Finish No Earlier Than*. As mentioned earlier, start and finish dates should not be manually entered when using the Automatic scheduling mode. Manually entering these dates will cause Project to constrain the schedule. It's best to let Project automatically determine start and finish dates using its scheduling engine. In upcoming chapters, we'll discuss how resources, constraints and other factors determine how Project schedules tasks in the Automatic scheduling mode.

Scheduling Modes and Task Relationships

Next, we'll review how task relationships are handled in the two scheduling modes. When tasks are linked in the Automatic scheduling mode, Project respects their task relationships. Also, summary task durations are calculated from the durations, dependencies, and outline levels of their subtasks. For example, in *Figure 110* below, the duration of *Summary Task 1* is 5 days, which is the sum of the durations of the three subtasks beneath it. The start date of each subtask was determined by the durations and finish dates of their predecessors.

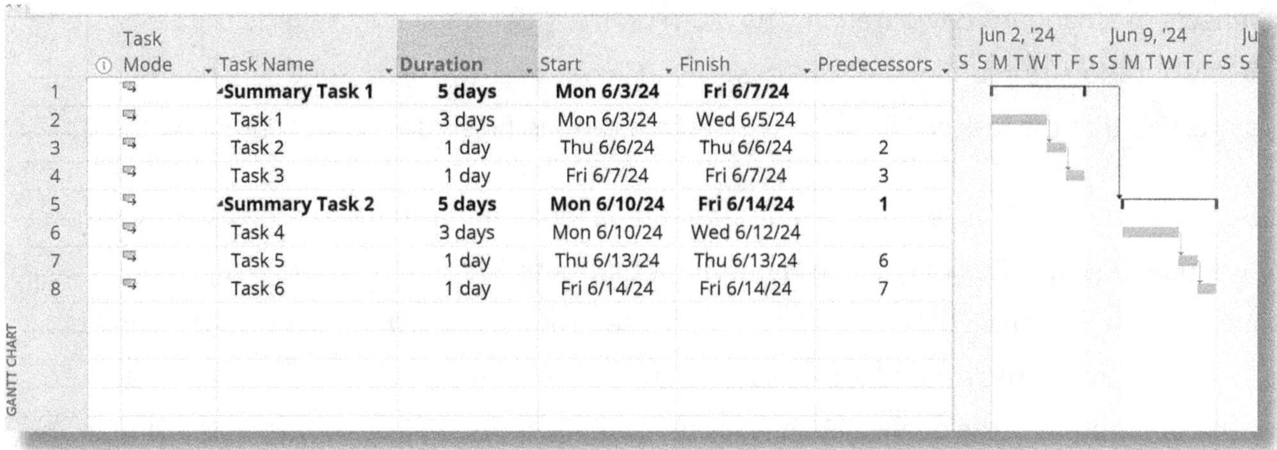

	Task Mode	Task Name	Duration	Start	Finish	Predecessors
1		**Summary Task 1**	**5 days**	**Mon 6/3/24**	**Fri 6/7/24**	
2		Task 1	3 days	Mon 6/3/24	Wed 6/5/24	
3		Task 2	1 day	Thu 6/6/24	Thu 6/6/24	2
4		Task 3	1 day	Fri 6/7/24	Fri 6/7/24	3
5		**Summary Task 2**	**5 days**	**Mon 6/10/24**	**Fri 6/14/24**	**1**
6		Task 4	3 days	Mon 6/10/24	Wed 6/12/24	
7		Task 5	1 day	Thu 6/13/24	Thu 6/13/24	6
8		Task 6	1 day	Fri 6/14/24	Fri 6/14/24	7

Figure 110 – Task Relationships in the Automatic Scheduling Mode

Figure 111 below shows task relationships in the Manual scheduling mode.

	Task Mode	Task Name	Duration	Start	Finish	Predecessors
1		**Summary Task 1**	**5 days**	**Mon 6/3/24**	**Fri 6/7/24**	
2		Task 1	3 days	Mon 6/3/24	Wed 6/5/24	
3		Task 2	1 day	Thu 6/6/24	Thu 6/6/24	2
4		Task 3	1 day	Fri 6/7/24	Fri 6/7/24	3
5		**Summary Task 2**	**8 days**	**Mon 6/3/24**	**Wed 6/12/24**	**1**
6		Task 4	3 days	Mon 6/3/24	Wed 6/5/24	
7		Task 5	1 day	Thu 6/6/24	Thu 6/6/24	6
8		Task 6	1 day	Fri 6/7/24	Fri 6/7/24	7

'24 Jun 2, '24 Jun 9, '24

T F S S M T W T F S S M T W T F S

GANTT CHART

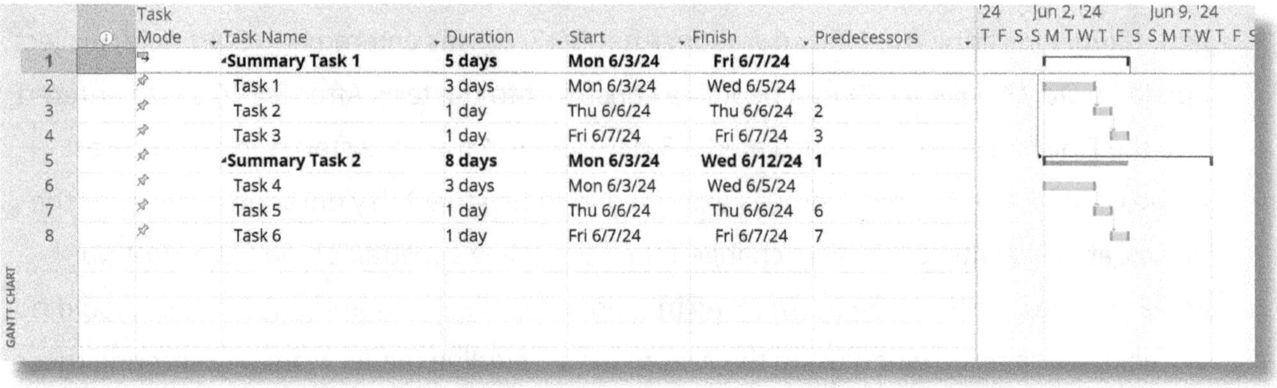

Figure 111 – Task Relationships in the Manual Scheduling Mode

Project also respects tasks relationships in the Manual mode, but manual overrides are allowed. Notice that the scheduling mode for *Summary Task 1* is the Automatic mode, even though the tasks are scheduled in the Manual mode. This is because the default mode for summary tasks in either scheduling mode is Automatic. As such, Project calculates their durations per their subtasks. However, in the Manual mode, summary task durations can be overridden with manual entries. When this occurs, Project will toggle the summary task to the Manual mode. For example, in *Figure 111* above, Project calculated a 5-day duration for *Summary Task 2* per its subtask durations. However, it allowed for an 8-day manual entry to override the calculation. After the manual entry was made, Project toggled the scheduling mode for this summary task to Manual. Also, this action created a scheduling inconsistency, which Project indicated in the Gantt chart with two summary bars. The black summary bar reflects the manual 8-day duration. The blue summary bar beneath it reflects the calculated 5-day duration (the sum of the subtasks). If you hover over the black summary bar, Project alerts you that the task will finish 3 days earlier than the finish date of the summary task.

Because Project allows for manual entries in the Manual mode, it doesn't consistently respect task relationships. This may cause **Scheduling Conflicts**. When this occurs, Project will indicate the potential scheduling conflict with a red squiggly underline beneath the conflicting date and dotted lines around the task bars in the Gantt chart. Hover over either indicator, to get a description of the conflict. Right-click for options to resolve the conflict. For example, in *Figure 112*, a start date of 6/4/24 was manually entered for *Task 5*. Since this start date occurs before its predecessor finishes, Project alerts of a potential scheduling conflict.

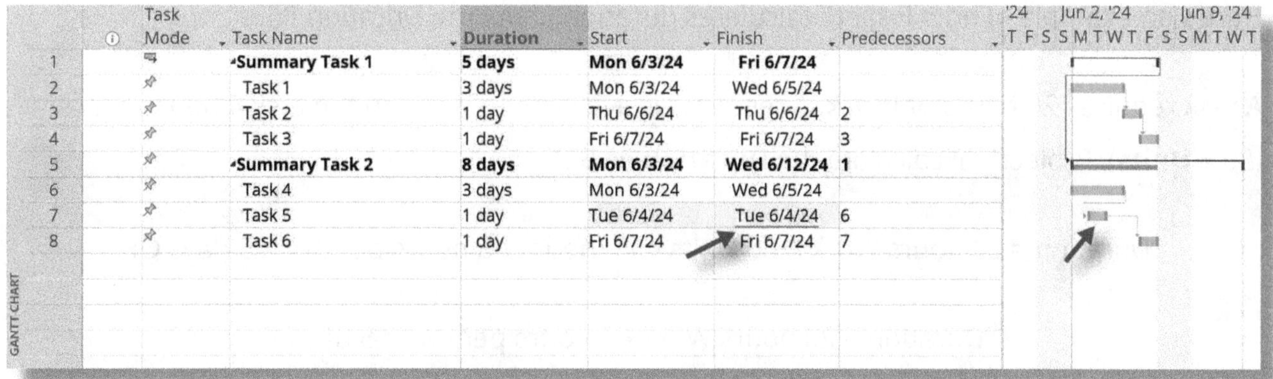

	Task Mode	Task Name	Duration	Start	Finish	Predecessors
1		Summary Task 1	5 days	Mon 6/3/24	Fri 6/7/24	
2		Task 1	3 days	Mon 6/3/24	Wed 6/5/24	
3		Task 2	1 day	Thu 6/6/24	Thu 6/6/24	2
4		Task 3	1 day	Fri 6/7/24	Fri 6/7/24	3
5		Summary Task 2	8 days	Mon 6/3/24	Wed 6/12/24	1
6		Task 4	3 days	Mon 6/3/24	Wed 6/5/24	
7		Task 5	1 day	Tue 6/4/24	Tue 6/4/24	6
8		Task 6	1 day	Fri 6/7/24	Fri 6/7/24	7

Figure 112 – Scheduling Conflicts

When working in the Manual mode, you can use the **Respect Links** feature to update tasks per their task relationships.

To use the Respect Links feature:

- Select the task(s) that you want Project to respect their links and reschedule.
- Select the **Task** tab. In the **Schedule** group, select the **Respect Links** command. Project will reschedule the tasks so that their dates are determined by their dependencies.

Understanding the Duration Equation

In the Automatic scheduling mode, Project uses the **Duration Equation** (also known as the Scheduling Formula) to calculate duration. The formula is expressed as:

DURATION = WORK/UNITS

Project makes scheduling calculations using the three variables in the Duration Equation. The variables are defined as follows:

- **DURATION** – The number of working days required to complete a task.
- **WORK** – The number of hours required to complete a task.
- **UNITS** – The percentage of an 8-hour workday a resource is assigned to work on a task. E.g., 2 hours per day = 25% Units (2 hours per day / 8-hour day = 25%).

Here's an example of how Project calculates duration using the Duration Equation:

A task requires 20 hours of **Work**. A resource is available to work on the task 4 hours per day (50% **Units**). Project will calculate the **Duration** as **5 days**.

Duration = 20 hours Work / .50 Units = 40 hours / 8 hours per day = 5 days OR

Duration = 20 hours Work / 4 hours per day = 5 days

Figure 113 below shows this example in Project.

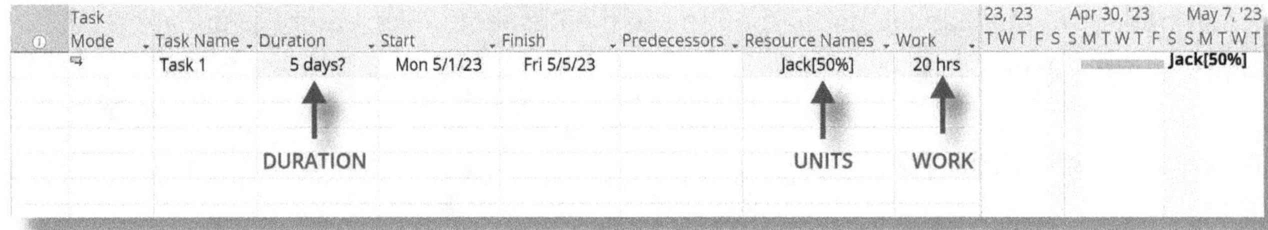

Figure 113 – The Duration Equation

In the next section, we'll review two of the most misunderstood (and under-appreciated) aspects of the software – **Effort-driven Scheduling** and **Task Type**. Understanding these settings will help you understand how the scheduling engine works and assist you when troubleshooting unexpected outcomes. We'll start with effort-driven scheduling.

Understanding Effort-Driven Scheduling

Effort-Driven Scheduling is a scheduling feature that keeps the work value constant (or fixed) and enables the duration value to increase or decrease as you assign resources to or remove resources from a task. Here's an example of how the feature works:

Task 1 has 40 hours of Work. One resource is assigned to work on the task at 100% Units (8 hours per day). Using the Duration Equation, Project will calculate the task duration as 5 days (40 hours/8 hours per day = 5 days). To expedite the schedule, a second resource is assigned to the task at 100% units. When the effort-driven feature is enabled, Project will keep the Work value constant at 40 hours and decrease the Duration per the collective resources' Units. Project will thus calculate the duration as 2.5 days (40 hours/16 hours per day = 2.5 days). If the second resource were to be removed, Project would automatically increase the duration back to 5 days.

Figure 114 below shows this scenario scheduled in Project with the effort-driven feature enabled.

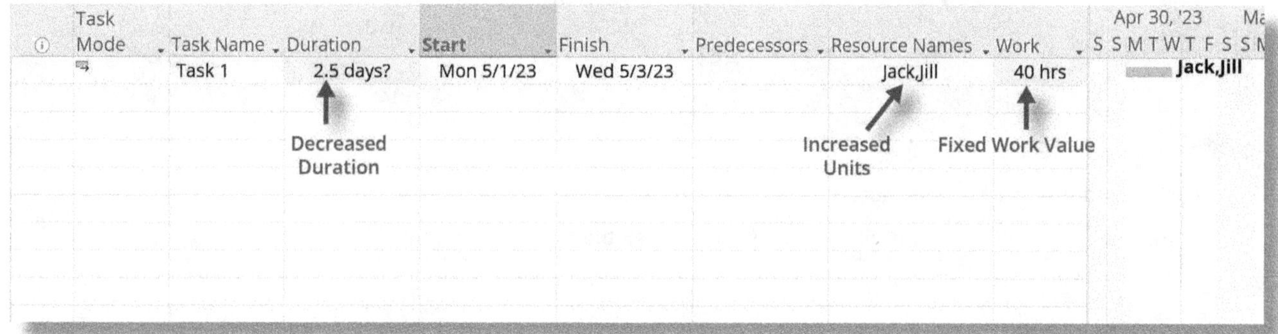

Figure 114 – Effort-Driven Scheduling

In simple terms, when the effort-driven feature is enabled, Project will fluctuate the duration up and down depending on how many resources are working on the task. When this feature is not enabled, Project will not fluctuate the duration based on the number of resources assigned. Therefore, you will want to disable this feature if your task durations are not meant to fluctuate based on the number of resources assigned to tasks. For example, when I managed infrastructure projects at AT&T, senior resources were often added to certain tasks to help troubleshoot an issue. These additional resources were not added to complete a task faster. They were added to ensure the task was completed per the original estimated time-frame. In these cases, I disabled the effort-driven scheduling feature so that Project would not factor the senior resources work hours into the duration of the task.

Action Indicators

When you add a second resource to a task that already has a resource assigned to it, Project will generate an **Action Indicator**, indicated by an alert icon in the left corner of the Task Name field. If you click the alert icon, you'll be given three options for rescheduling the task because of the new assignment (*Figure 115*). Each option adjusts one of the variables in the Duration Equation.

NOTE: If you've already adjusted the settings for your project, be sure to ignore this indicator. Selecting an option may override your settings.

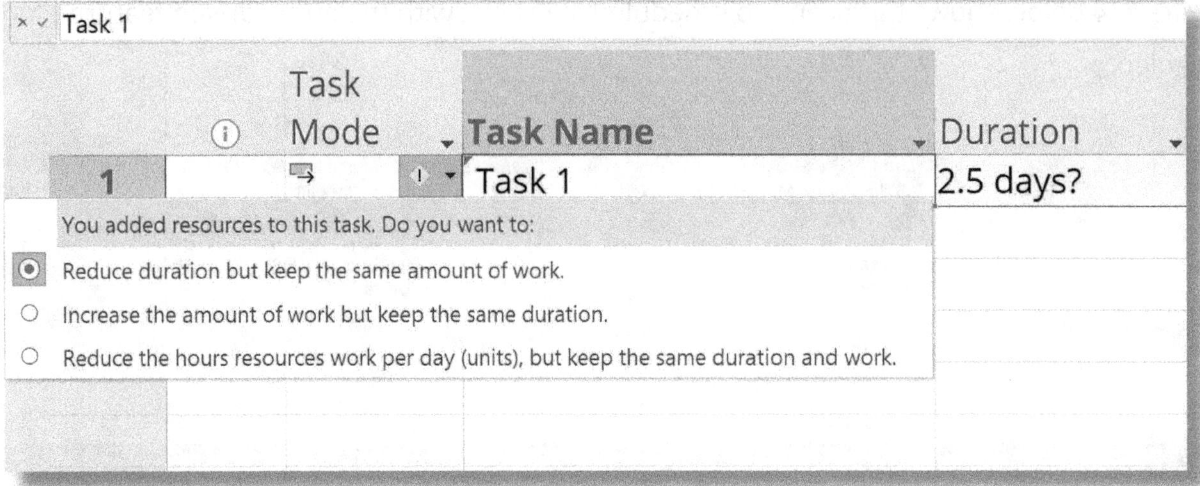

Figure 115 – Action Indicator

Enabling Effort-Driven Scheduling

You can enable the effort-driven scheduling feature for specific tasks or the entire project.

To enable effort-driven scheduling for a **specific task**:

- Double-click the task to open the *Task Information* dialogue box.
- Select the **Advanced** tab. Then, select the **Effort-driven** checkbox (*Figure 116* below).

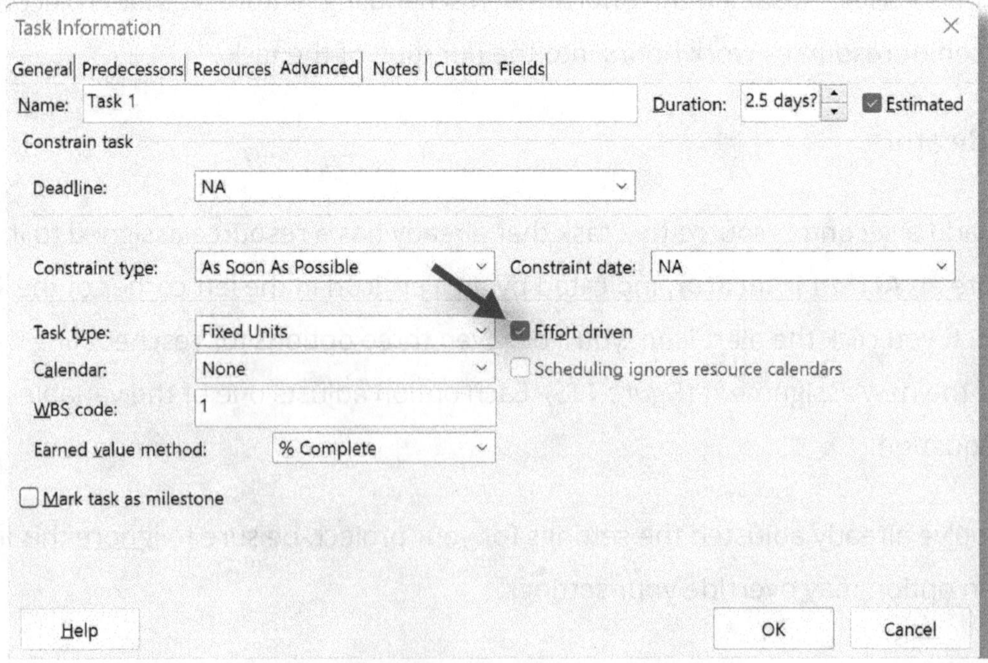

Figure 116 – Enable Effort-Driven Scheduling for a Specific Task

To enable effort-driven scheduling for the **entire project**:

- Select the **File** tab to go **Backstage**.
- Select **Options** from the options on the left, to open the *Project Options* dialogue box.
- In the *Project Options* dialogue box, select **Schedule** from the menu options on the left.
- Under the *Scheduling options for this project* section, select the **New tasks are effort-driven** checkbox (*Figure 117* below).

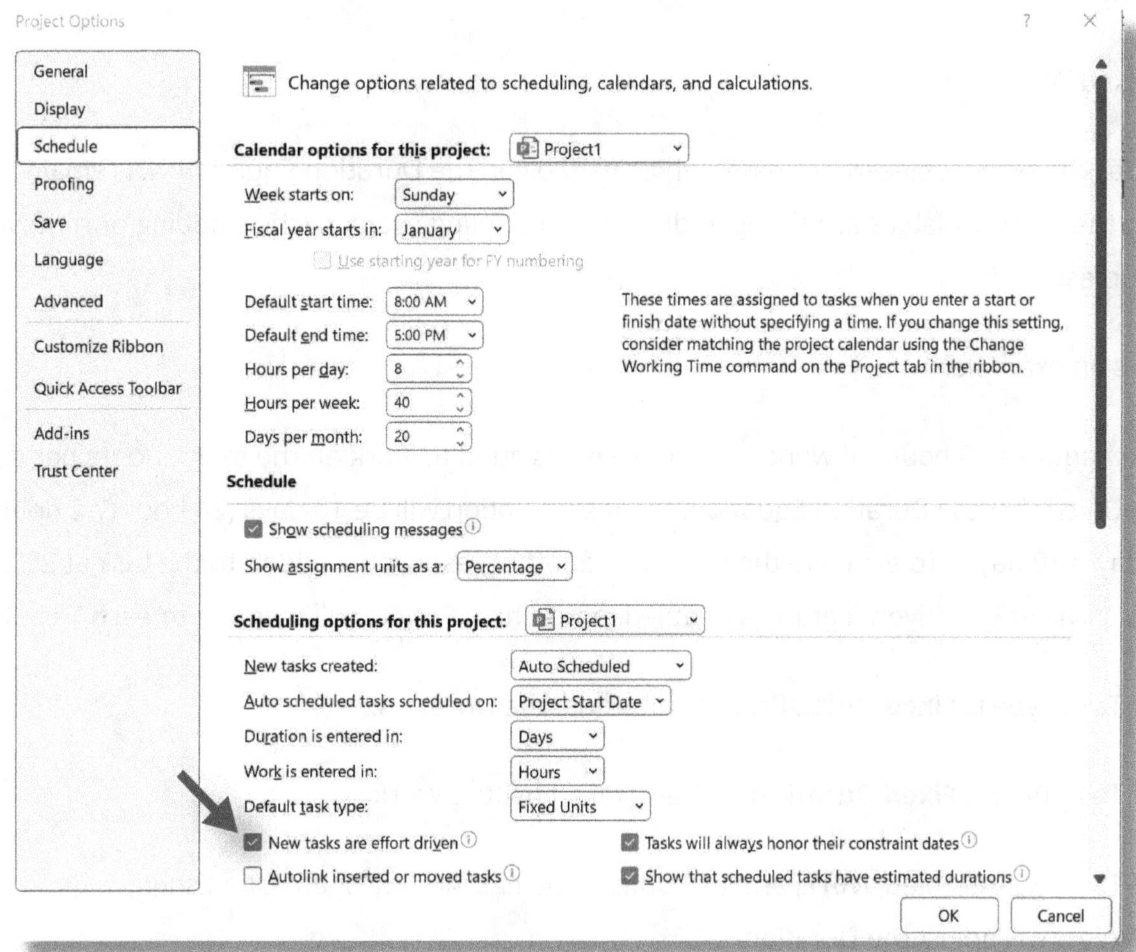

Figure 117 – Enable Effort-Driven Scheduling for the Entire Project

Understanding Task Type

Every task has a **Task Type** setting. Task Type works in conjunction with effort-driven scheduling to control how project schedules tasks. It fixes the Work, Units or Duration value, depending on the Task Type you choose.

There are three Task Types:

- Fixed Units (default)
- Fixed Duration
- Fixed Work

The Task Type you select determines which variable in the Duration Equation will remain fixed when the other variables are changed due to a scheduling event, such as adding or removing resources.

Here's an example.

A task requires 20 hours of work. A resource is assigned to work on the task 2 hours per day (25% Units). Per the Duration Equation, the task duration will be 10 days (20 hours / 2 hours per day = 10 days). To expedite the schedule, another resource is added to the task at 25% Units. If the effort-driven feature is enabled, here's how Project will respond to each Task Type.

- If Task Type is **Fixed Units**, Project will adjust the Duration.
- If Task Type is **Fixed Duration**, Project will adjust the Work.
- If Task Type is **Fixed Work**, and the Units value has already been established, Project will adjust the Duration.
- If Task Type is **Fixed Work**, and the Duration value has already been established, Project will adjust the Units.

Selecting the Task Type

Select the Task Type according to how you'd like Project to schedules tasks. You can select the Task Type for a specific task or for the entire project.

To select the Task Type for a **specific task**:

- Double-click the task to open the *Task Information* dialogue box.
- Select the **Advanced** tab. Under the *Task Type* section, select the Task Type you want from the pick-list (*Figure 118* below)

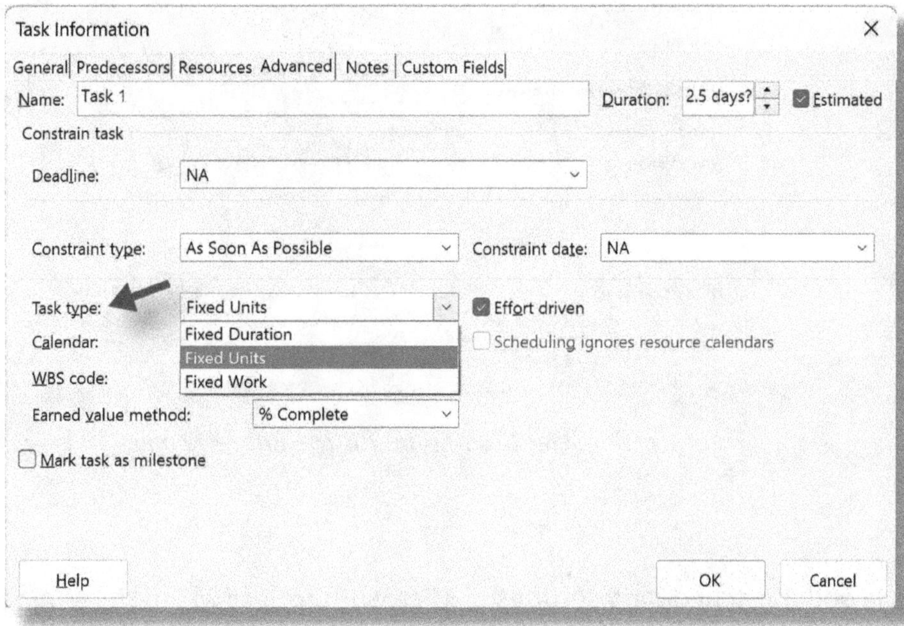

Figure 118 – Select Task Type for a Specific Task

To select the Task Type for the **entire project**:

- Select the **File** tab to go **Backstage**.
- Select **Options** from the options on the left to open the *Project Options* dialogue box.
- In the *Project Options* dialogue box, select the **Schedule** from the menu options on the left.
- Under the *Scheduling options for this project* section, select the Task Type you want from the *Default task* type pick-list (*Figure 119*).

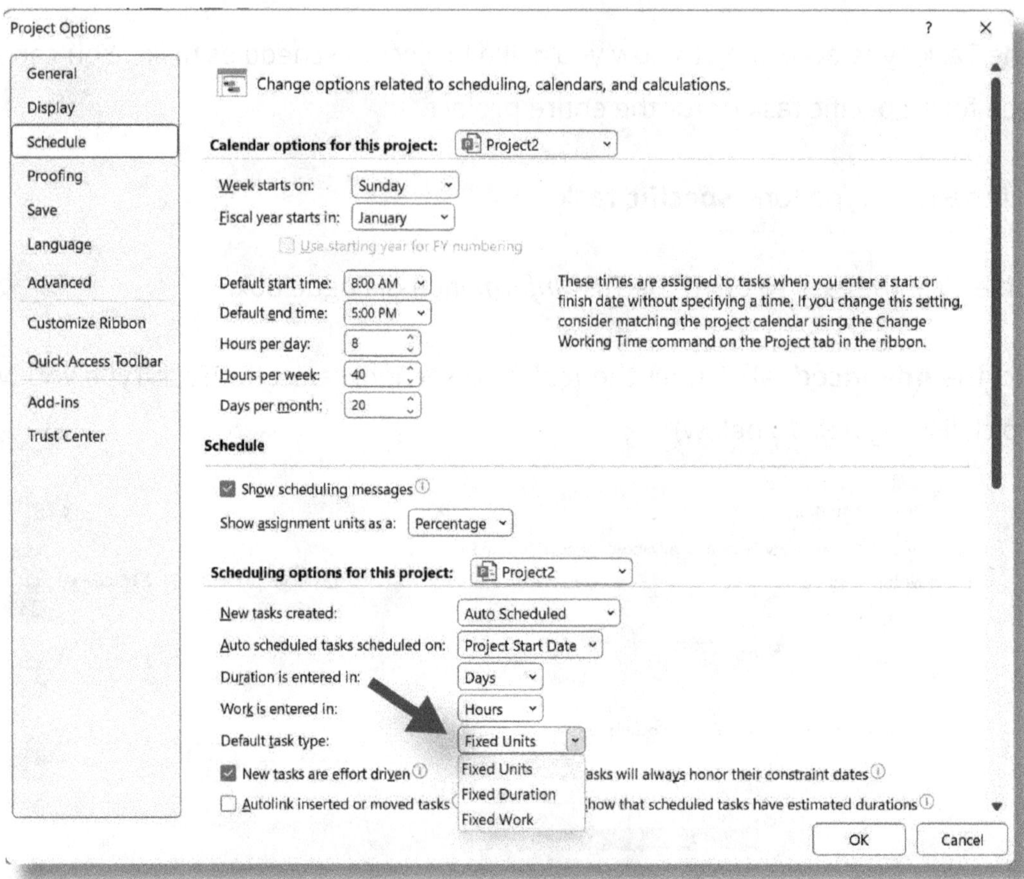

Figure 119 – Select Task Type for the Entire Project

We've now reviewed the scheduling settings in Microsoft Project which determine how Project schedule tasks. In the next two chapters, we'll put these fundamentals to use by applying them to the two scheduling approaches. If you had difficulty conceptualizing some of the settings, don't worry. The next two chapters will help by providing a practical context.

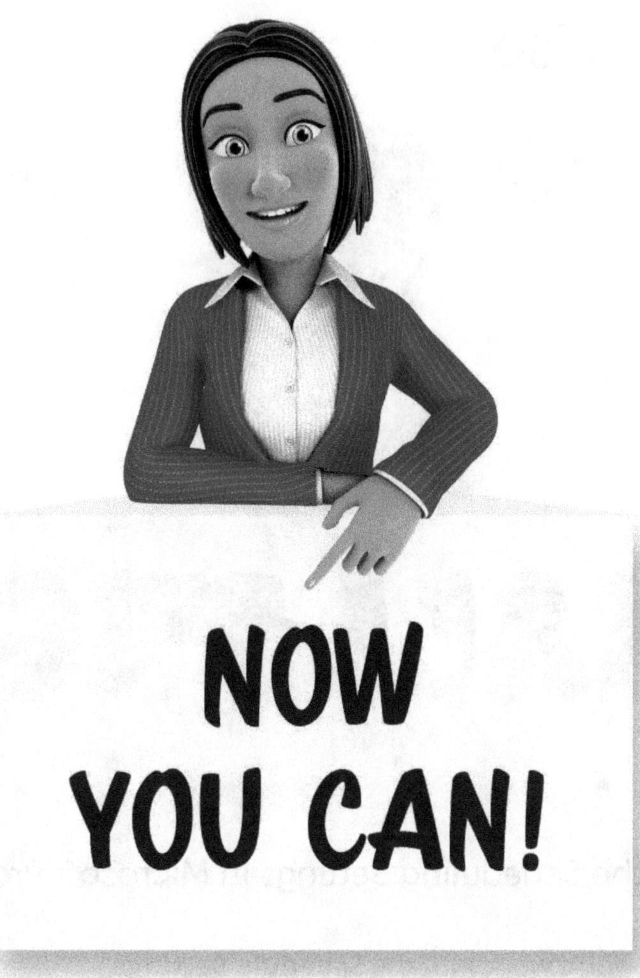

- ✓ Explain the Manual Scheduling Mode
- ✓ Explain the Automatic Scheduling Mode
- ✓ Explain the Duration Equation
- ✓ Explain Effort-Driven Scheduling
- ✓ Explain Task Type

To reinforce the concepts you learned in this chapter, be sure to complete the Practice Exercise on the next page.

Practice Exercise

Adjust the Scheduling Settings in Microsoft Project

For this practice exercise, you'll work with the **Schedule Settings**.
You'll build a Simple schedule for a Fence construction project and configure the settings using the features we reviewed throughout the chapter. You'll work with scheduling mode, task type, and effort-driven scheduling to observe how they function in a schedule.

Visit **mspbasics.com** for "checkpoint" images to check your work as you go along.

Follow the steps below to complete this Challenge practice exercise.

Start a New Project

We'll start by creating a new project for our **Build a Fence** project.

1. From the opening view, select **Blank Project** to create a new project plan. You'll be taken to the Gantt Chart view.

Adjust the Settings

Next, we'll perform the **A** step in the **B.A.S.I.C.S.** scheduling process – **Adjust the Settings**.

Select the Scheduling Mode

We'll start with the **Scheduling Mode**. We'll adjust the schedule settings so that all new tasks are scheduled in the **Automatic** scheduling mode.

1. Select the **File** tab to go **Backstage**.

2. Select **Options** from the menu options on the left to open the *Project Options* dialogue box. In the *Project Options* dialogue box, select **Schedule** from the menu options on the left.

3. Under the *Scheduling options for this project* section, select **Auto Scheduled** from the *New tasks created* pick-list. DO NOT CLOSE the *Project Options* dialog box.

Select the Task Type

Next, we'll adjust the settings to give all new tasks the **Fixed Duration** Task Type. This Task Type will cause Project to fix the duration values. The task durations will remain constant when scheduling changes are made.

1. In the *Project Options* dialogue box, under the *Scheduling options for this project* section, select **Fixed Duration** from the *Default task type* pick-list. DO NOT CLOSE the Project Options dialog box.

Disable Effort-Driven Scheduling

Next, we'll disable the effort-driven scheduling feature.

1. Under the *Scheduling options for this project* section, confirm that the **New tasks are effort-driven** feature is unchecked. This will disable the effort-driven feature. You can now close the *Project Options* dialog box.

CHECKPOINT: To check your results so far, go to **mspbasics.com**

- Select the **CheckPoint Images** tab.
- Select the version of the book you're using.
- Select **Chapter 5**. Then, go to **Checkpoint Image #1**

Enter the Project Start Date

Next, we'll set the **project start date**. The start date is **3/4/24**.

1. Select the **Project** tab. In the **Properties** group, select the **Project Information** command to open the *Project Information* dialogue box.

2. In the **Start** field, enter **3/4/24**. Then, select **OK** to close the dialogue box.

CHECKPOINT: To check your results so far, go to **mspbasics.com**

- Select the **CheckPoint Images** tab.
- Select the version of the book you're using.
- Select **Chapter 5**. Then, go to **Checkpoint Image #2**

Create the Project Outline

Next, we'll perform the step of the first **S** in the **B.A.S.I.C.S.** scheduling process – **Structure the Tasks** to create the project outline for our **Build a Fence** project.

The task list and WBS are shown below.

TASK ID	TASK NAME
1	Codes & Regulations
2	Check Building Codes
3	Check & Mark Property Lines
4	Measurement & Layout
5	Measure Fence
6	Determine Panel Quantity
7	Determine Post Quantity
8	Tools & Materials
9	Get Tools
10	Get Materials
11	Holes & Posts
12	Position Fence Posts
13	Dig Holes
14	Pour Gravel
15	Pour Concrete
16	Set Posts
17	Rails & Pickets
18	Attach Rails to Posts
19	Attach Pickets to Rails
20	Gate
21	Install Gate Posts
22	Install Hinges & Latch

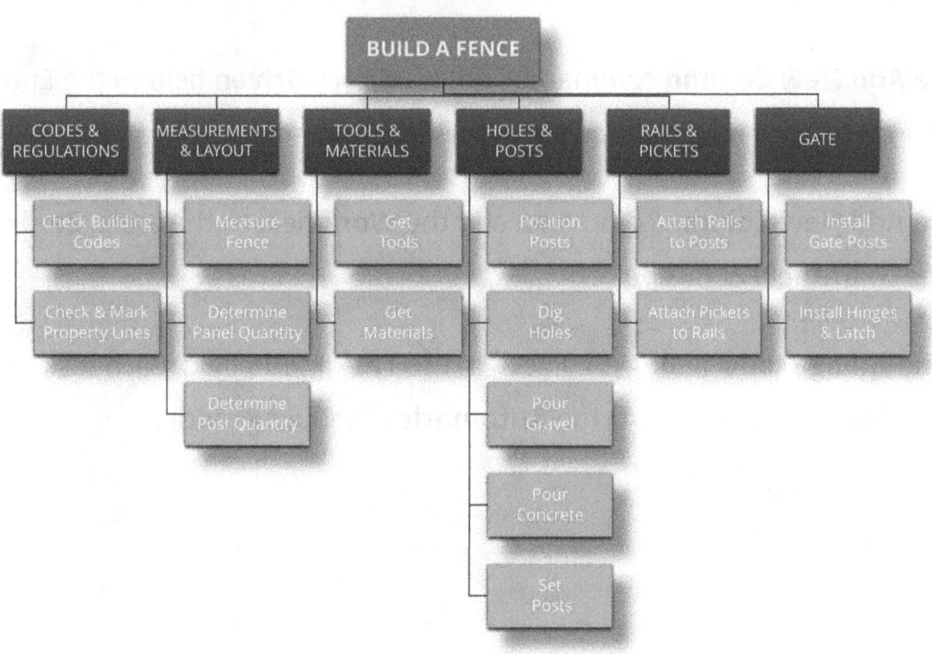

Enter the Task List

1. Enter the unstructured task list (in the order shown) into the **Task Name** field of the **Entry table**. When you're done, you should have **22 tasks**.

> **CHECKPOINT:** To check your results so far, go to **mspbasics.com**
>
> - Select the **CheckPoint Images** tab.
> - Select the version of the book you're using.
> - Select **Chapter 5**. Then, go to **Checkpoint Image #3**

Confirm the Schedule Settings

Before we structure the tasks, we'll confirm the settings we've selected by adding new columns to the Entry table. We'll do this using the **Add New Column** command. Next to the Resource Names column, you should see the Add New Column field. If you don't see the Add New Column field, drag the screen that divides the Entry table and the Gantt chart to the right until you see the Add New Column field.

1. Click on the **Add New Column** title to display the available fields you can add to the table. Enter the word "Type". Then, select **Type** to add the Task Type field to the table. If the settings are correct, you'll see **Fixed Duration** in this field for each task.

2. Using the **Add New Column** command, add the **Effort-Driven** field to the Entry table. If the settings are correct, you'll see **No** in the field for each task.

3. Using the **Add New Column** command, add the **Work** field to the table. Zero values will be populated to the field at this point.

4. If the **Scheduling Mode** setting is correct, in the **Task Mode** field, each task will have a task bar icon with an arrow indicating the **Automatic** scheduling mode.

CHECKPOINT: To check your results so far, go to **mspbasics.com**

- Select the **CheckPoint Images** tab.
- Select the version of the book you're using.
- Select **Chapter 5**. Then, go to **Checkpoint Image #4**

Structure the Tasks

Next, we'll structure the tasks to create the **summary tasks** and **subtasks** for each of the **6 phases** of our Build a Fence project.

To create Phase 1 – *Codes and Regulations*:

1. Select the *Check Building Codes* and *Check & Mark Property Lines* tasks.
2. Select the **Task** tab. In the **Schedule** group, select the **Indent Task** command to promote the *Codes and Regulations* task to a summary task and demote these two tasks beneath it as subtasks.

To create Phase 2 – *Measurements and Layout:*

1. Select the Measure Fence, *Determine Panel Quantity* and *Determine Post Quantity* tasks. Then, use the **Indent Task** command to promote the *Measurements and Layout* task to a summary task and demote these three tasks beneath it as subtasks.

To create Phase 3 – *Tools & Materials:*

1. Select the *Get Tools* and *Get Materials* tasks. Then, use the **Indent Task** command to promote the *Tools & Materials* task to a summary task and demote these two tasks beneath it as subtasks.

To create Phase 4 – *Holes & Posts*:

1. Select the *Position Fence Posts*, *Dig Holes*, *Pour Gravel*, *Pour Concrete* and *Set Posts* tasks. Then, use the **Indent Task** command to promote the *Holes & Posts* task to a summary task and demote these five tasks beneath it as subtasks.

To create Phase 5 – *Rails & Pickets*:

1. Select the *Attach Rails to Posts* and *Attach Pickets to Rails* tasks. Then, use the **Indent Task** command to promote the *Rails & Pickets* task to a summary task and demote these two tasks beneath it as subtasks.

To create Phase 6 – *Gate*:

1. Select the *Install Gate Posts* and *Install Hinges & Latch* tasks. Then, use the **Indent Task** command to promote the *Gate* task to a summary task and demote these two tasks beneath it as subtasks.

The 6 phases of the project should now be structured. Each task should have a 1-day duration and the project start date should be assigned as their start date. Because the tasks currently have a 1-day duration, the tasks will finish on the same day. In the Gantt chart, each task should have a task bar generated that represents its 1-day duration.

CHECKPOINT: To check your results so far, go to **mspbasics.com**

- Select the **CheckPoint Images** tab.
- Select the version of the book you're using.
- Select **Chapter 5**. Then, go to **Checkpoint Image #5**

Create Milestone Tasks

Next, we'll create a **Milestone** task as the last task in each phase, to signify the end of the phase. We'll start with Phase 1.

1. Select the *Measurements & Layout* summary task. Then, on the **Task** tab, in the **Insert** group, select the **Insert Milestone** command. Rename the New Milestone task "**Codes & Regulations Checked**".

2. To create the Phase 2 milestone, select the *Tools & Materials* summary task. Then, select the **Insert Milestone** command. Rename the milestone "**Measurements & Layout Completed"**.

3. To create the Phase 3 milestone, select the *Holes & Post* summary task. Then, select the **Insert Milestone** command. Rename the milestone **"Tools & Materials Gotten"**.

4. To create the Phase 4 milestone, select the *Rails & Pickets* summary task. Then, select the **Insert Milestone** command. Rename the milestone **"Holes & Posts Completed"**.

5. To create the Phase 5 milestone, select the *Gate* summary task. Then, select the **Insert Milestone** command. Rename the milestone "**Rails & Pickets Attached"**.

6. To create the Phase 6 milestone, in the **Task Name** field, select the cell beneath the *Install Hinges & Latch* task. Then, select the **Insert Milestone** command. Rename the milestone **"Gate Installed"**.

Each of the six milestones will be indicated in the Gantt Chart with a diamond icon.

Display the Project Summary Task.

Next, we'll display the **Project Summary Task**. This will show us the project's cumulative values.

1. Select the Gantt Chart **Format** tab, in the **Show/Hide** group, select the **Project Summary Task** checkbox.

2. Rename the Project Summary Task **"Build a Fence Project"**.

CHECKPOINT: To check your results so far, go to **mspbasics.com**

- Select the **CheckPoint Images** tab.
- Select the version of the book you're using.
- Select **Chapter 5**. Then, go to **Checkpoint Image #6**

Enter Task Durations

Next, we'll perform the **I** step in the **B.A.S.I.C.S.** scheduling process – **Initialize the Duration** values. The task durations for the subtasks in our Build a Fence project are listed in the table below.

1. Enter the duration value for each task into the **Duration** field of the Entry table as listed. We will not enter the duration values for the summary tasks because Project will calculate them for us.

TASK ID	TASK NAME	DURATION
2	Check Building Codes	**1d**
3	Check & Mark Property Lines	**2d**
6	Measure Fence	**1d**
7	Determine Panel Quantity	**2d**
8	Determine Post Quantity	**2d**
11	Get Tools	**5d**
12	Get Materials	**10d**
14	Position Fence Posts	**2d**
16	Dig Holes	**3d**
17	Pour Gravel	**2d**
18	Pour Concrete	**1d**
19	Set Posts	**1d**
22	Attach Rails to Posts	**1d**
23	Attach Pickets to Rails	**1d**
25	Install Gate Posts	**1d**
26	Install Hinges & Latch	**1d**

CHECKPOINT: To check your results so far, go to **mspbasics.com**

- Select the **CheckPoint Images** tab.
- Select the version of the book you're using.
- Select **Chapter 5**. Then, go to **Checkpoint Image #7**

After the duration values are entered, Project updates the summary task durations according to the sum of the durations of their subtasks. The task finish dates were updated according to their durations. In the Gantt Chart, the task bars were extended to reflect the new durations. Notice that the overall project duration (displayed in the Duration field of the Project Summary Task) was updated to **10 days**, which is not the collective sum of the summary task durations. The project finish date was updated to **3/15/24**, which is far too early for this project to finish. Because the tasks are not linked, Project has determined the project duration and finish date based on the longest task, which is the *Get Materials* task. This will change once the task relationships are established.

Create Task Relationships

Next, we'll perform the C step in the **B.A.S.I.C.S.** scheduling process – **Connect the Tasks**. We'll give all the tasks a *Finish-to-Start* task relationship. Since the tasks in this schedule follow one after another, they can be quickly linked with the *Finish-to-Start* relationship using a method we call "Lazy Linking".

NOTE: This method of linking the tasks should only be used if this sequencing truly reflects the dependencies in your schedule. In practice, each task should be considered individually when selecting its predecessor(s).

1. Select the entire project plan by selecting the empty gray cell above task ID 0.

2. Select the **Task** tab. In the **Schedule** group, select the **Link the Selected Tasks** command. The tasks will all be linked with the *Finish-to-Start* task relationship. In the Gantt Chart, the task bars will also be linked.

CHECKPOINT: To check your results so far, go to **mspbasics.com**

- Select the **CheckPoint Images** tab.
- Select the version of the book you're using.
- Select **Chapter 5**. Then, go to **Checkpoint Image #8**

Once the tasks are linked, you can see Project's scheduling engine at work in the Automatic scheduling mode. Each task was scheduled to start the next working day after its predecessor finished. Project adjusted the task start and finish dates respectively. The overall project duration was updated to **36 days**, which is the collective sum of the summary task durations. The project finish date was updated to **4/22/24**. Also, using the Change Highlighting feature, Project highlighted each update in the schedule in blue.

Apply Lag Time Between Tasks

Before the *Set Post* task can begin, the concrete must set for two days. To depict this in our schedule, we will add a 2-day lag to the *Pour Concrete* task. This will delay the start of the *Set Post* task 2 days, until the concrete has set. It's currently scheduled to begin on **4/16/24**, the next working day after the *Pour Concrete* task finishes.

1. In the **Predecessors** field for the *Pour Concrete* task, enter **17FS+2d**.

After the lag syntax is entered, Project updates the start for the *Set Post* task to start on **4/18/24**, two working days after the *Pour Concrete* task finishes. All other impacted tasks were updated and highlighted in blue, including the total project duration, which was updated to **38 days**. The lag is also shown in the Gantt chart.

CHECKPOINT: To check your results so far, go to **mspbasics.com**

- Select the **CheckPoint Images** tab.
- Select the version of the book you're using.
- Select **Chapter 5**. Then, go to **Checkpoint Image #9**

Assign Resources to Tasks

To demonstrate the effect of the Fixed Duration Task Type, we will assign resources to the *Check & Mark Property Lines* Task. We will review the different resource types and how they're handled in Project exhaustively in Ch. 8.

1. In the **Resource Names** field of the *Check & Mark Property Lines* task, enter **Jack** to assign this resource to the task. **NOTE:** Typing resource names directly into the Resource Names field quickly assigns resources to work on tasks 8 hours per day (100% Units). We'll review resource assignments in detail in Chapter 8.

After the resource is assigned, Project will populate **16 hours** of work into the Work field. Since this task has a 2-day duration and Jack will on the task for 8 hours each day, Project determined the Work for this task to be 16 hours.

CHECKPOINT: To check your results so far, go to **mspbasics.com**

- Select the **CheckPoint Images** tab.
- Select the version of the book you're using.
- Select **Chapter 5**. Then, go to **Checkpoint Image #10**

Next, you'll assign an additional resource to the *Check & Mark Property Lines* task.

1. In the **Resource Names** field. Enter **Jill** next to the Jack resource. Separate the two resource names with a comma. This entry will assign both Jack and Jill to this task.

After Jill is assigned to the task, Project generates an Action Indicator prompting us to select how the task is rescheduled as a result of the new assignment. It wants to know which variable to adjust in the Duration Equation. The options are to *Reduce the Duration, but keep the same amount of Work*, *Increase the amount of Work but keep the same Duration*, or *Reduce the number of hours resources work per day (Units) and keep the same Duration and Work*. Since we've already adjusted the settings for this project, and chose the Fixed Duration Task Type, we'll ignore this alert, and keep option two selected. Since the Fixed Duration Task Type fixes the duration value, Project kept the task duration at 2 days and adjusted the Work value from 16 hours to **32 hours**. Each resource is working on the task 8 hours per day for two days, which is 32 hours of work.

CHECKPOINT: To check your results so far, go to **mspbasics.com**

- Select the **CheckPoint Images** tab.
- Select the version of the book you're using.
- Select **Chapter 5**. Then, go to **Checkpoint Image #11**

Enable Effort-Driven Scheduling

The *Get Materials* task currently has a 10-day duration. To get this task done faster, we will assign two resources to the task. First, we'll enable the **Effort-Driven scheduling** feature for this task, to demonstrate its utility in expediting schedules. As mentioned earlier, when this feature is enabled, Project will fix the Work value and adjust the Duration value up or down when resources are added or removed from a task.

1. Double-click the *Get Materials* task to open the *Task Information* dialogue box.
2. Select the **Advanced** tab to see the scheduling options for this task.
3. Select the **Effort driven** checkbox to enable effort-driven scheduling for this task. DO NOT CLOSE the dialogue box.

This task currently has the Fixed Duration Task Type. Because we would like for Project to reduce the duration for this task when we assign the additional resource, we will change the Task Type to **Fixed Units**. This will cause Project to keep the Units (and Work) values constant and adjust the Duration value.

1. Select **Fixed Units** from the *Task Type* pick-list.
2. Select **OK** to close the *Task Information* dialogue box.

CHECKPOINT: To check your results so far, go to **mspbasics.com**

- Select the **CheckPoint Images** tab.
- Select the version of the book you're using.
- Select **Chapter 5**. Then, go to **Checkpoint Image #12**

Notice **Fixed Units** is now populated to the Type field and **Yes** is populated to the Effort-driven field. Next, we'll assign resources to the *Get Materials* task, to see the effect of the effort-driven feature.

1. In the **Resource Names** field of the *Get Materials* task, enter **Tom** to assign this resource to the task at 8 hours per day.

Project kept the Units value fixed (8 hours per day or 100% Units) and generated a work value of 80 hours (8 hours per day for 10 days). Also, the work value for the entire project (shown in the Work field for the Project Summary task) has been updated **112 hours**.

To expedite this task, we'll now assign an additional resource.

1. In the **Resource Names** field for the *Get Materials* task, enter **Jerry** next to the Tom resource. Separate each name with a comma. This will assign both Tom and Jerry to the task.

After the second resource is assigned, Project decreases the task's duration to **5 days**. Because the Task Type is Fixed Units, Project kept each resource's hours at 8 hours per day (16 hours collectively). Because the effort-driven feature is enabled, which fixes the work value, Project kept the work value at 80 hours and adjusted the unfixed variable, which is duration. Using the Duration Equation (D=W/U), the task duration was calculated at 5 days. Also, the overall project duration was reduced to **33 days**. The project finish date was updated to **4/17/24**.

CHECKPOINT: To check your results so far, go to **mspbasics.com**

- Select the **CheckPoint Images** tab.
- Select the version of the book you're using.
- Select **Chapter 5**. Then, go to **Checkpoint Image #13**

You've now worked with the scheduling mode, task type, and effort-driven scheduling features and observed how they function in a schedule.

Chapter 6 Selecting the Right Scheduling Method

In the last chapter, we reviewed the settings in Microsoft Project and how they affect the way tasks are scheduled. In addition to understanding settings, it's important to understand the two basic ways to build a schedule. In this chapter, we'll review the Simple scheduling method and the Detailed scheduling method. When you're done, you'll be able to select the right scheduling method for your project and adjust the settings to support that method.

You'll Learn To:

- Use the Simple Scheduling Method
- Use the Detailed Scheduling Method
- Compare the Two Scheduling Methods
- Select the Right Scheduling Method
- Adjust the Settings for Simple or Detailed Scheduling

Understanding the Two Scheduling Methods

The two scheduling methods are commonly referred to as Duration-based and Effort-based scheduling. We don't prefer these labels because both scheduling approaches use duration to calculate the schedule. One approach simply requires more scheduling detail than the other. Also, users often confuse the Effort-based scheduling approach with the Effort-driven scheduling feature. In this book, we'll refer to the two ways to build a schedule as **Simple Scheduling** (Duration-based scheduling) and **Detailed Scheduling** (Effort-based scheduling). Let's review both methods.

The Simple Scheduling Method

A **Simple Schedule** tracks time only (tasks durations and the project schedule). It's built by estimating the number of working days each task will take and entering those estimates directly into the Duration field of the Entry table in the Gantt Chart view. Once you've entered task durations and task dependencies, Project will calculate your finish date (*Figure 120* below). There are a few more steps, but this is the basic idea.

	Task Mode	Task Name	Duration	Start	Finish	Predecessors	Resources
1		**Get Supplies**	1 day	Tue 6/6/23	Tue 6/6/23		
2		List Supplies	1 day	Tue 6/6/23	Tue 6/6/23		
3		Buy Supplies	1 day	Tue 6/6/23	Tue 6/6/23		
4		Supplies Gotten	0 days	Tue 6/6/23	Tue 6/6/23		
5		**Prep House**	2 days	Tue 6/6/23	Wed 6/7/23		
6		Sand House	2 days	Tue 6/6/23	Wed 6/7/23		
7		Tape Windows	1 day	Tue 6/6/23	Tue 6/6/23		
8		Lay Drop Cloth	1 day	Tue 6/6/23	Tue 6/6/23		
9		House Prepped	0 days	Tue 6/6/23	Tue 6/6/23		
10		**Paint House**	5 days?	Tue 6/6/23	Mon 6/12/23		
11		Apply First Coat	5 days	Tue 6/6/23	Mon 6/12/23		
12		Apply Final Coat	5d	Tue 6/6/23	Mon 6/12/23		
13		Remove Window Tape	1 day?	Tue 6/6/23	Tue 6/6/23		
14		Inspect House	1 day?	Tue 6/6/23	Tue 6/6/23		
15		Apply Finishing Touches	1 day?	Tue 6/6/23	Tue 6/6/23		
16		House Painted	1 day?	Tue 6/6/23	Tue 6/6/23		

Figure 120 – Building a Simple Scheduling – Entering Task Duration

Using the Simple scheduling approach, resources can simply provide you with a time-frame in which they'll complete a task (E.g., 2 days), rather than the specific number of hours the task requires (E.g., 4 hours) or the number of hours they'll work on the task each day (E.g., 2 hours per day). Because of this flexibility, the Simple scheduling approach is used most often. The drawback, however, is this approach gives project stakeholders no visibility into the man-hours (Work), which are required to accurately generate project cost. Thus, the Simple scheduling approach is used to forecast and track **time** estimates only. It cannot be used to accurately forecast or track **cost** estimates.

Some aspects of the auto repair process depict the Simple scheduling approach. For example, you take your car in for repair and you're told your car will be repaired in 2 days. Only when you get the bill, do you discover that the repair required 4 hours of labor. Therefore, the labor hours were not used to determine the 2-day estimate. This is the chief characteristic of the Simple scheduling approach. It allows resources to estimate task durations without providing details like the number of hours the task requires. In the auto repair example, the 2-day estimate was a ballpark estimate and not a calculation based on man-hours or the mechanic's availability. Similarly, when using the Simple scheduling approach, the schedule is based on task durations and not on the details that make up task durations, namely man-hours (Work) and resource availability (Units).

Assigning Resources in a Simple Schedule

In a Simple schedule, resources are assigned for accountability only. Adding resources to tasks simply shows who's responsible for completing which tasks in the schedule. Resource assignments do not affect task durations in a Simple schedule. Resources can be assigned to tasks by entering their names directly into the **Resource Names** field of the Entry table (*Figure 121* below).

	Task Name	Duration	Start	Finish	Predecessors	Resource Names
1	**Get Supplies**	**2 days**	**Tue 6/6/23**	**Wed 6/7/23**		
2	List Supplies	1 day	Tue 6/6/23	Tue 6/6/23		Jill
3	Buy Supplies	1 day	Wed 6/7/23	Wed 6/7/23	2	Jack
4	**Prep House**	**4 days**	**Thu 6/8/23**	**Tue 6/13/23**	**1**	
5	Sand House	2 days	Thu 6/8/23	Fri 6/9/23		Jack
6	Tape Windows	1 day	Mon 6/12/23	Mon 6/12/23	5	
7	Lay Drop Cloth	1 day	Tue 6/13/23	Tue 6/13/23	6	
8	**Paint House**	**14 days**	**Wed 6/14/23**	**Mon 7/3/23**	**4**	
9	Apply 1st Coat	5 days	Wed 6/14/23	Tue 6/20/23		
10	Apply 2nd Coat	5 days	Wed 6/21/23	Tue 6/27/23	9	
11	Remove Window Tape	1 day	Wed 6/28/23	Wed 6/28/23	10	
12	Inspect House	1 day	Thu 6/29/23	Thu 6/29/23	11	
13	Apply Finishing Touches	2 days	Fri 6/30/23	Mon 7/3/23	12	

Figure 121 – Assigning Resources in a Simple Schedule

As mentioned in the previous chapter, this method results in resources being assigned to tasks at 100% Units (8 hour per day). Although resources will rarely work on tasks 8 hours per day, this exaggeration is acceptable in a Simple schedule. This is because resource Units do not affect task duration in a Simple schedule. As depicted in the auto repair example, the task duration is not derived from the units or work values. It's simply a ballpark estimate of how many days it will take to complete a task.

For this reason, resource pay rates should not be added to a Simple schedule. This is because Project calculates the cost of each task by multiplying the pay rate of the assigned resource by the work hours of the task. Since details like the specific work hours of the task are not known in a Simple schedule, Project will multiply the work hours associated with the entire task duration by the resource pay rate. This calculation would result in an exaggerated cost projection. For example, suppose a pay rate of $50 per hour is assigned to a resource in a Simple schedule. The resource is assigned to a 3-day task at 100% Units. The resource worked on the tasks for a total of 9 hours, spread evenly across the 3-day duration. In a Simple schedule, Project would calculate the cost of this task as $1,200 ($50 per hour x 24 hours of work, which is 3 days) instead of $450 ($50 per hour x 9 hours of work). This exaggerated cost calculation demonstrates that since the specific work hours are not known, **cost** should never be forecasted and tracked using a Simple schedule. Simple schedules are meant to track **time** only.

The Detailed Scheduling Method

If you only need to track time (task durations and the project schedule), the Simple scheduling method is the best option. It allows for simpler communication exchanges and produces schedules that are easier to read. If you need to track both **time** and **cost**, then you must build a **Detailed Schedule**. When you build a Detailed schedule, task durations should not be entered directly into the Duration field. Project will calculate task durations for you from the Work and Units values. Therefore, resources must provide you with the specific number of hours each task requires (Work) and the number of hours they'll work on the tasks each day (Units). For example, instead of estimating a 5-day duration for a task, they must provide the details that comprise their 5-day duration estimate – namely their Work and Units values. Thus, they might estimate 20 hours of Work for a task and may work on the task 4 hours per day (50% Units). Since they will work on the 20-hour task 4 hours per day, the task will require a 5-day duration (20 hours/4 hours per day = 5 days).

Establishing the Work Values

When you build a Detailed schedule, the resource's Work and Units values must be entered into Project, starting with the Work values. By Default, the Entry Table in the Gantt Chart view doesn't include a field for entering Work values. The "Work" field must be added to the Entry table using the **Add New Column** field. Work values are then entered directly into the "Work" field (*Figure 122*).

	Task Name	Duration	Start	Finish	Predecessors	Resource Names	Work	1, '23 W T F S Jan 7, '24 S M T W T F
0	**House Painting Project**	**1 day?**	**Mon 1/8/24**	**Mon 1/8/24**			**80 hrs**	
1	**Get Supplies**	**1 day?**	**Mon 1/8/24**	**Mon 1/8/24**			**8 hrs**	
2	List Supplies	1 day?	Mon 1/8/24	Mon 1/8/24			4 hrs	
3	Buy Supplies	1 day?	Mon 1/8/24	Mon 1/8/24			4 hrs	
4	Supplies Gotten	0 days	Mon 1/8/24	Mon 1/8/24			0 hrs	◆ 1/8
5	**Prep House**	**1 day?**	**Mon 1/8/24**	**Mon 1/8/24**			**16 hrs**	
6	Sand House	1 day?	Mon 1/8/24	Mon 1/8/24			12 hrs	
7	Tape Windows	1 day?	Mon 1/8/24	Mon 1/8/24			2 hrs	
8	Lay Drop Cloth	1 day?	Mon 1/8/24	Mon 1/8/24			2 hrs	
9	House Prepped	0 days	Mon 1/8/24	Mon 1/8/24			0 hrs	◆ 1/8
10	**Paint House**	**1 day?**	**Mon 1/8/24**	**Mon 1/8/24**			**56 hrs**	
11	Apply 1st Coat	1 day?	Mon 1/8/24	Mon 1/8/24			20 hrs	
12	Apply 2nd Coat	1 day?	Mon 1/8/24	Mon 1/8/24			20 hrs	
13	Remove Window Tape	1 day?	Mon 1/8/24	Mon 1/8/24			2 hrs	
14	Inspect House	1 day?	Mon 1/8/24	Mon 1/8/24			2 hrs	
15	Apply Finishing Touches	1 day?	Mon 1/8/24	Mon 1/8/24			12 hrs	
16	House Painted	0 days	Mon 1/8/24	Mon 1/8/24			0 hrs	◆ 1/8

Figure 122 – Building a Detailed Schedule – Entering Work Values

To add the Work column to the Entry table:

- Select the **Add New Column** field's title. This will display the available columns you can add to the table.
- Type **"Work"** or scroll down the list until you find the **Work** column, then select it.

Establishing the Units Values: Assigning Resources in a Detailed Schedule

Units values are established when resources are assigned to tasks. In a Detailed schedule, resources are assigned to tasks according to their precise availability. They are assigned with a Units value equal to the percentage of an 8-hour day they are available to work on the task. If more than one resource is assigned to a task, the Units value for the task will equal the collective Units of the resources assigned to it. For example, if Jack is assigned to a task at 25% Units, and Jill is assigned to the same task at 25% Units, the task will have a 50% Units value. Because resources are assigned with specific Units, they should not be assigned by entering their names directly into the Resource Names field. As mentioned, this approach results in resources being assigned at 100% Units. In a Detailed schedule, resources should be assigned using the *Assign Resources* dialogue box. We will explain this process in Chapter 8.

Once the Work and Units values are established, Project will calculate the task Durations using the Duration Equation (D=W/U). After the task dependencies are entered, Project will calculate the project finish date. There are a few more steps to this scheduling approach, but this is the basic idea.

The following table lists the corresponding Units value for the number of hours resources are available to work on tasks.

If the Resource is Available:	The Resource Units will be:
1 hour per day	**12.5%**
2 hours per day	**25%**
3 hours per day	**37.5%**
4 hours per day	**50%**
5 hours per day	**62.5%**
6 hours per day	**75%**
7 hours per day	**87.5%**
8 hours per day	**100%**

Comparing the Two Scheduling Methods

Using *Figure 123* below, we'll compare the two scheduling methods. The House Painting schedule on the top is a Simple schedule. The schedule on the bottom is a Detailed schedule.

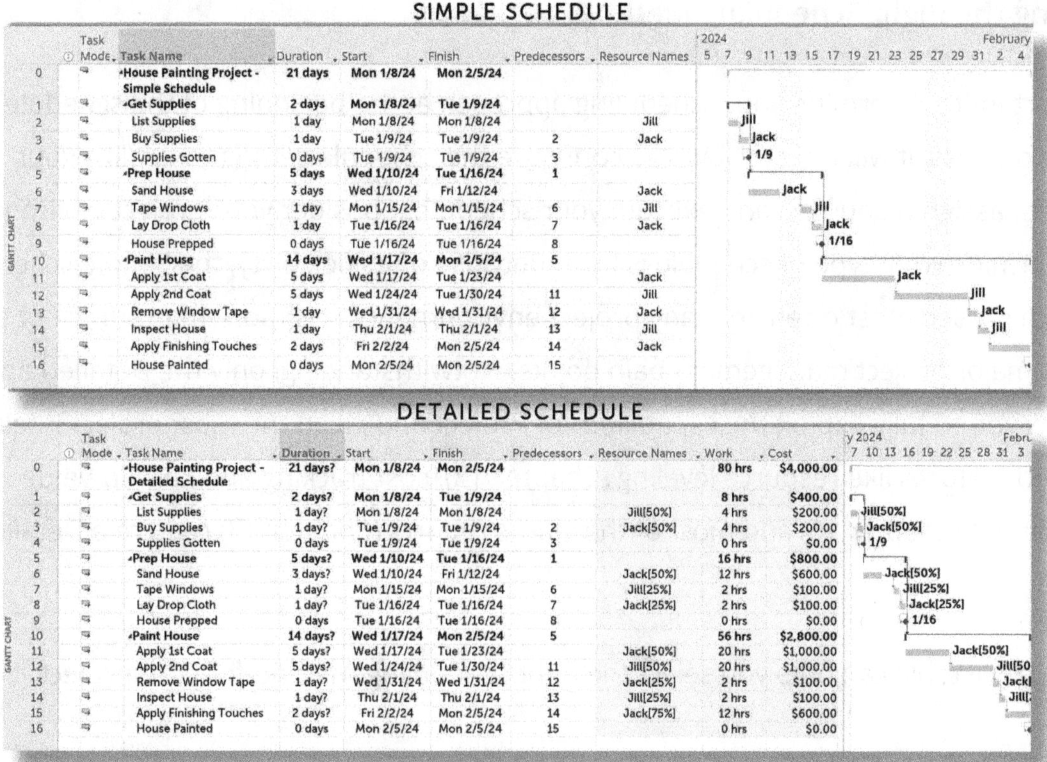

SIMPLE SCHEDULE

	Task Name	Duration	Start	Finish	Predecessors	Resource Names
0	House Painting Project - Simple Schedule	21 days	Mon 1/8/24	Mon 2/5/24		
1	Get Supplies	2 days	Mon 1/8/24	Tue 1/9/24		
2	List Supplies	1 day	Mon 1/8/24	Mon 1/8/24		Jill
3	Buy Supplies	1 day	Tue 1/9/24	Tue 1/9/24	2	Jack
4	Supplies Gotten	0 days	Tue 1/9/24	Tue 1/9/24	3	
5	Prep House	5 days	Wed 1/10/24	Tue 1/16/24	1	
6	Sand House	3 days	Wed 1/10/24	Fri 1/12/24		Jack
7	Tape Windows	1 day	Mon 1/15/24	Mon 1/15/24	6	Jill
8	Lay Drop Cloth	1 day	Tue 1/16/24	Tue 1/16/24	7	Jack
9	House Prepped	0 days	Tue 1/16/24	Tue 1/16/24	8	
10	Paint House	14 days	Wed 1/17/24	Mon 2/5/24	5	
11	Apply 1st Coat	5 days	Wed 1/17/24	Tue 1/23/24		Jack
12	Apply 2nd Coat	5 days	Wed 1/24/24	Tue 1/30/24	11	Jill
13	Remove Window Tape	1 day	Wed 1/31/24	Wed 1/31/24	12	Jack
14	Inspect House	1 day	Thu 2/1/24	Thu 2/1/24	13	Jill
15	Apply Finishing Touches	2 days	Fri 2/2/24	Mon 2/5/24	14	Jack
16	House Painted	0 days	Mon 2/5/24	Mon 2/5/24	15	

DETAILED SCHEDULE

	Task Name	Duration	Start	Finish	Predecessors	Resource Names	Work	Cost
0	House Painting Project - Detailed Schedule	21 days?	Mon 1/8/24	Mon 2/5/24			80 hrs	$4,000.00
1	Get Supplies	2 days?	Mon 1/8/24	Tue 1/9/24			8 hrs	$400.00
2	List Supplies	1 day?	Mon 1/8/24	Mon 1/8/24		Jill[50%]	4 hrs	$200.00
3	Buy Supplies	1 day?	Tue 1/9/24	Tue 1/9/24	2	Jack[50%]	4 hrs	$200.00
4	Supplies Gotten	0 days	Tue 1/9/24	Tue 1/9/24	3		0 hrs	$0.00
5	Prep House	5 days?	Wed 1/10/24	Tue 1/16/24	1		16 hrs	$800.00
6	Sand House	3 days?	Wed 1/10/24	Fri 1/12/24		Jack[50%]	12 hrs	$600.00
7	Tape Windows	1 day?	Mon 1/15/24	Mon 1/15/24	6	Jill[25%]	2 hrs	$100.00
8	Lay Drop Cloth	1 day?	Tue 1/16/24	Tue 1/16/24	7	Jack[25%]	2 hrs	$100.00
9	House Prepped	0 days	Tue 1/16/24	Tue 1/16/24	8		0 hrs	$0.00
10	Paint House	14 days?	Wed 1/17/24	Mon 2/5/24	5		56 hrs	$2,800.00
11	Apply 1st Coat	5 days?	Wed 1/17/24	Tue 1/23/24		Jack[50%]	20 hrs	$1,000.00
12	Apply 2nd Coat	5 days?	Wed 1/24/24	Tue 1/30/24	11	Jill[50%]	20 hrs	$1,000.00
13	Remove Window Tape	1 day?	Wed 1/31/24	Wed 1/31/24	12	Jack[25%]	2 hrs	$100.00
14	Inspect House	1 day?	Thu 2/1/24	Thu 2/1/24	13	Jill[25%]	2 hrs	$100.00
15	Apply Finishing Touches	2 days?	Fri 2/2/24	Mon 2/5/24	14	Jack[75%]	12 hrs	$600.00
16	House Painted	0 days	Mon 2/5/24	Mon 2/5/24	15		0 hrs	$0.00

Figure 123 – Comparing the Two Scheduling Methods

Both schedules have a 21-day project duration, beginning on 1/8/24 and ending on 2/5/24. Both schedules include tasks, durations, predecessors, and resources. These similarities demonstrate that scheduling calculations can be just as accurate in a Simple schedule as in a Detailed schedule. The key difference is the added detail provided in the Detailed schedule, namely cost and resource allocation information. For example, in the Simple schedule, we see that Jack is assigned to the *Sand House* task, which will take 3 days to complete. In the Detailed schedule, we're provided more information. We see that the task requires 12 hours of Work. We also see that Jack is assigned to the task at 50% Units, which means he will be working on the task 4 hours per day. In short, we see *why* the duration is 3 days. Since Jack's pay rate is $50 per hour, we also know that the task will cost $600.

Although the Detailed scheduling method involves more upfront planning, it delivers more project intelligence. Also, most of the reports included in Project contain data such as Work and Cost, which will only be accurate if you build a Detailed schedule. The extra details involved in the Detailed scheduling method allow you to exploit the full capability of the Microsoft Project scheduling engine. By contrast, the Simple scheduling method uses the scheduling engine primarily to calculate the schedule.

Selecting the Right Scheduling Method

It's important to determine your scheduling approach at the beginning of the schedule building process. It will impact how you configure the schedule settings, initialize your durations, assign resources, and execute your schedule. Consider your project environment and determine what type of schedule is best. Because of its flexibility, the Simple scheduling approach is used most often. In many project environments, it is more than sufficient to address major project management pain points. Notwithstanding, only the Detailed approach will allow you to fully exploit the capabilities of Project and glean the most project intelligence. Advanced features like resource leveling (Chapter 13), cost tracking and Earned Value Management (Chapter 16) and most of the status reports (Chapter 17) require a Detailed schedule.

The following table can help you select the right scheduling method for your project.

WORKPLACE REALITY	SIMPLE	DETAILED
My resources only provide duration estimates because they work on many other projects.	X	
My resource can provide Work and Availability estimates.		X
Work estimates are impossible to determine because this type of project has never been done before.	X	
If I asked for Work and Availability estimates, resources would feel micro-managed.	X	
My stakeholders expect me to provide Earned Value metrics		X
I would like Project to calculate the total cost of my project in addition to the project schedule.		X

Adjusting the Settings for Each Scheduling Method

After you determine which scheduling approach is best for your project, and before you build your schedule outline, you'll need to adjust the schedule settings to support that method. As reviewed in Chapter 5, settings are adjusted in the *Project Options* dialogue box.

Adjusting the Settings for a Simple Schedule

To configure Project for a **Simple Schedule**, adjust the settings as follows (*Figure 124*):

- Select the **File** tab to go **Backstage**. Select **Options** from the options on the left, to open the *Project Options* dialogue box.
- In the *Project Options* dialogue box, select **Schedule** from the menu options on the left to access the schedule settings.
- Under the *Scheduling options for this project* section, select **Auto Scheduled** from the *New tasks created* pick-list. This will enable Project to calculate the finish date from the task durations and task dependencies.

- Select **Fixed Duration** from the *Default task type* pick-list. This will fix your initial Duration estimate if Work or resource Units are adjusted.
- Uncheck the **New tasks are effort-driven** checkbox. This will disable the effort-driven scheduling feature.

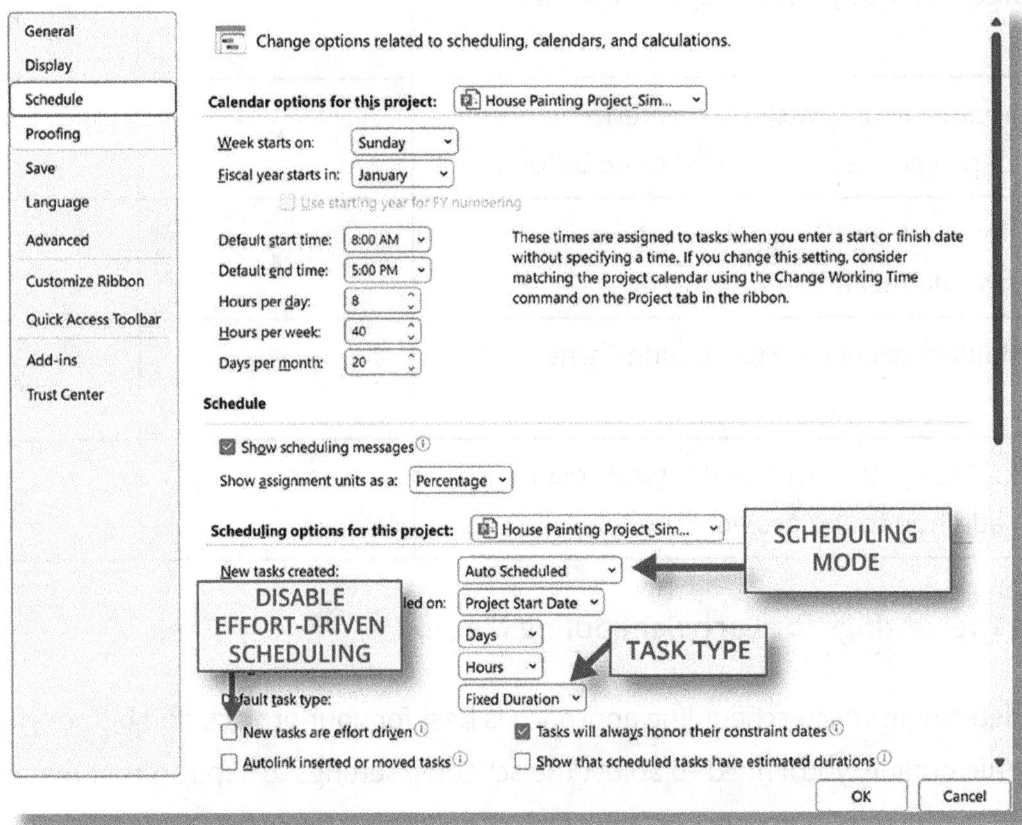

Figure 124 – Adjust the Settings for a Simple Schedule

Adjusting the Settings for a Detailed Schedule

To configure Project for a **Detailed Schedule**, adjust the settings as follows (*Figure 125*):

- Select the **File** tab to go **Backstage**.
- Select **Options** from the options on the left, to open the *Project Options* dialogue box.
- In the *Project Options* dialogue box, select **Schedule** from the menu options on the left to access the schedule settings.

- Under the *Scheduling options for this project* section, select **Auto Scheduled** from the *New tasks created* pick-list. This will enable Project to calculate the finish date from the task durations and task dependencies.

- Select **Fixed Units** from the *Default task type* pick-list. This will allow the resource Units to remain fixed if changes are made to the Work or Duration values.

- Check the **New tasks are effort-driven** checkbox. This will enable the effort-driven scheduling feature. The initial Work values will be fixed, and Project will increase or decrease task Duration as resources are added to or removed from tasks.

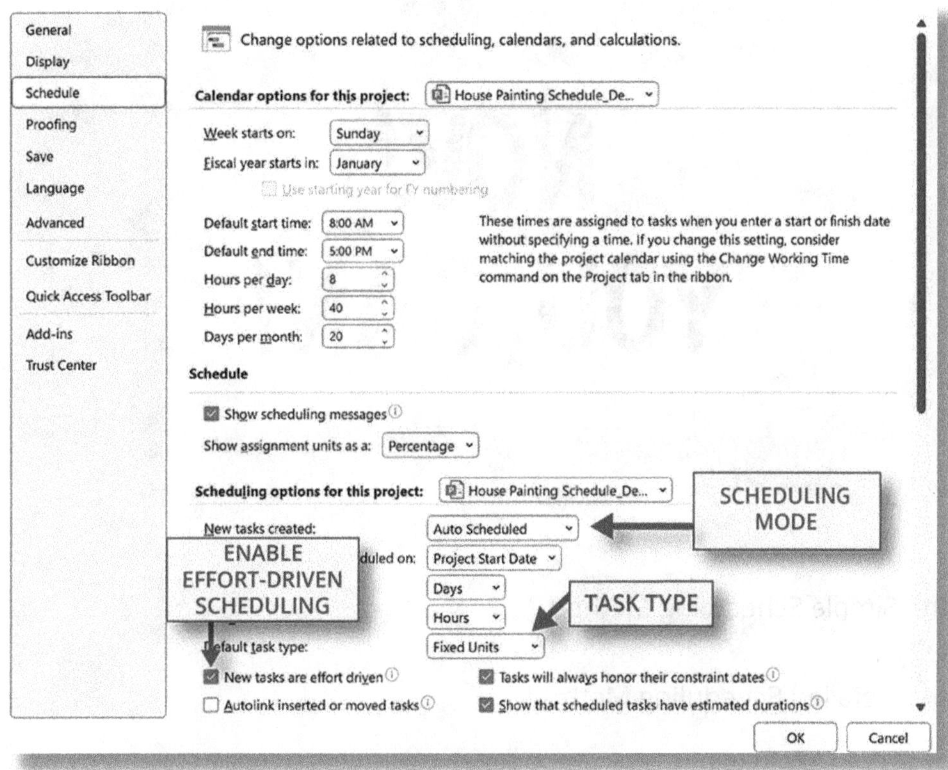

Figure 125 – Adjust the Settings for a Detailed Schedule

We've now reviewed the two ways to build a schedule, how to adjust project settings to support either method and use cases and benefits of using either approach.

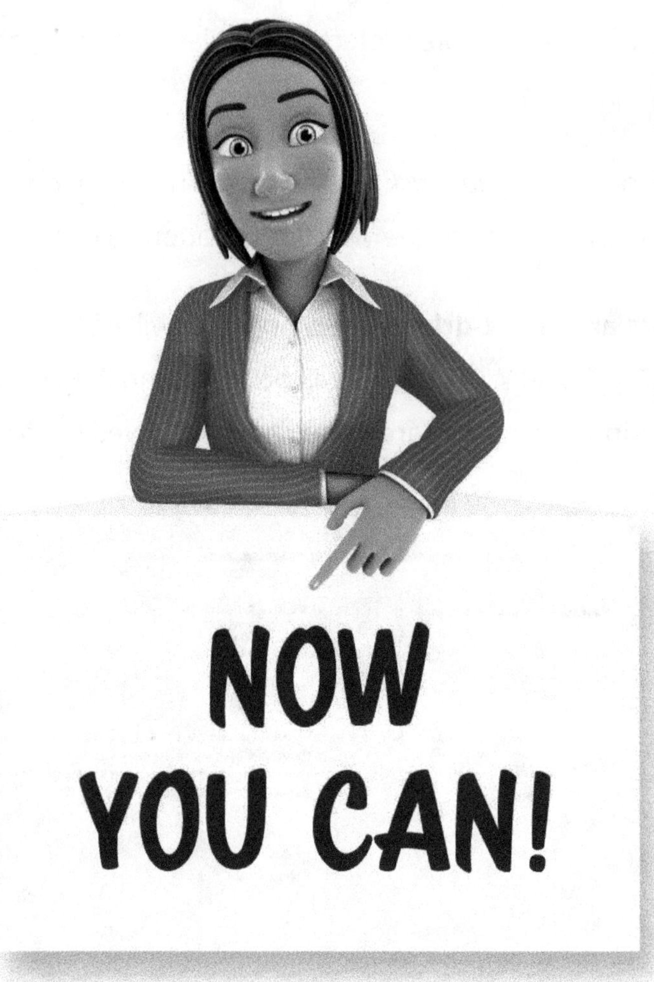

- ✓ Explain the Simple Scheduling Method
- ✓ Explain the Detailed Scheduling Method
- ✓ Select the Right Scheduling Method
- ✓ Adjust the Settings for Simple or Detailed Scheduling

Practice Exercise

Select the Scheduling Method

For this practice exercise, you'll answer questions concerning the two scheduling methods discussed in this chapter.

Go to **mspbasics.com** to check your answers

Part One: Select the Right Scheduling Method

Consider the following scenarios and select the most appropriate scheduling method.

Scenario #1

The resources assigned to your project are scarce. Because of the demand for their skills, they are often overbooked. As a result, they provide duration estimates within which they will complete their tasks. They do not provide work and availability estimates.

a. Simple Scheduling

b. Detailed Scheduling

Scenario #2

Senior leaders have asked you to provide a monthly cost overview report to the stakeholders funding your project. They would also like to view quarterly Earned Value metrics.

a. Simple Scheduling

b. Detailed Scheduling

CHECKPOINT: To check your results so far, go to **mspbasics.com**

- Select the **CheckPoint Images** tab.
- Select the version of the book you're using.
- Select **Chapter 6** to see the answers.

Part Two: Identify the Scheduling Method

What type of schedule is shown in **Image #1**?

a. Simple

b. Detailed

	Task Mode	Task Name	Duration	Start	Finish	Predecessors	Resource Names	Work	Cost
0		**House Painting Project - Detailed Schedule**	**21 days?**	**Mon 1/8/24**	**Mon 2/5/24**			**80 hrs**	**$4,000.00**
1		**Get Supplies**	**2 days?**	**Mon 1/8/24**	**Tue 1/9/24**			**8 hrs**	**$400.00**
2		List Supplies	1 day?	Mon 1/8/24	Mon 1/8/24		Jill[50%]	4 hrs	$200.00
3		Buy Supplies	1 day?	Tue 1/9/24	Tue 1/9/24	2	Jack[50%]	4 hrs	$200.00
4		Supplies Gotten	0 days	Tue 1/9/24	Tue 1/9/24	3		0 hrs	$0.00
5		**Prep House**	**5 days?**	**Wed 1/10/24**	**Tue 1/16/24**	1		**16 hrs**	**$800.00**
6		Sand House	3 days?	Wed 1/10/24	Fri 1/12/24		Jack[50%]	12 hrs	$600.00
7		Tape Windows	1 day?	Mon 1/15/24	Mon 1/15/24	6	Jill[25%]	2 hrs	$100.00
8		Lay Drop Cloth	1 day?	Tue 1/16/24	Tue 1/16/24	7	Jack[25%]	2 hrs	$100.00
9		House Prepped	0 days	Tue 1/16/24	Tue 1/16/24	8		0 hrs	$0.00
10		**Paint House**	**14 days?**	**Wed 1/17/24**	**Mon 2/5/24**	5		**56 hrs**	**$2,800.00**
11		Apply 1st Coat	5 days?	Wed 1/17/24	Tue 1/23/24		Jack[50%]	20 hrs	$1,000.00
12		Apply 2nd Coat	5 days?	Wed 1/24/24	Tue 1/30/24	11	Jill[50%]	20 hrs	$1,000.00
13		Remove Window Tape	1 day?	Wed 1/31/24	Wed 1/31/24	12	Jack[25%]	2 hrs	$100.00
14		Inspect House	1 day?	Thu 2/1/24	Thu 2/1/24	13	Jill[25%]	2 hrs	$100.00
15		Apply Finishing Touches	2 days?	Fri 2/2/24	Mon 2/5/24	14	Jack[75%]	12 hrs	$600.00
16		House Painted	0 days	Mon 2/5/24	Mon 2/5/24	15		0 hrs	$0.00

Image #1

What type of schedule is shown in **Image #2**?

a. Simple

b. Detailed

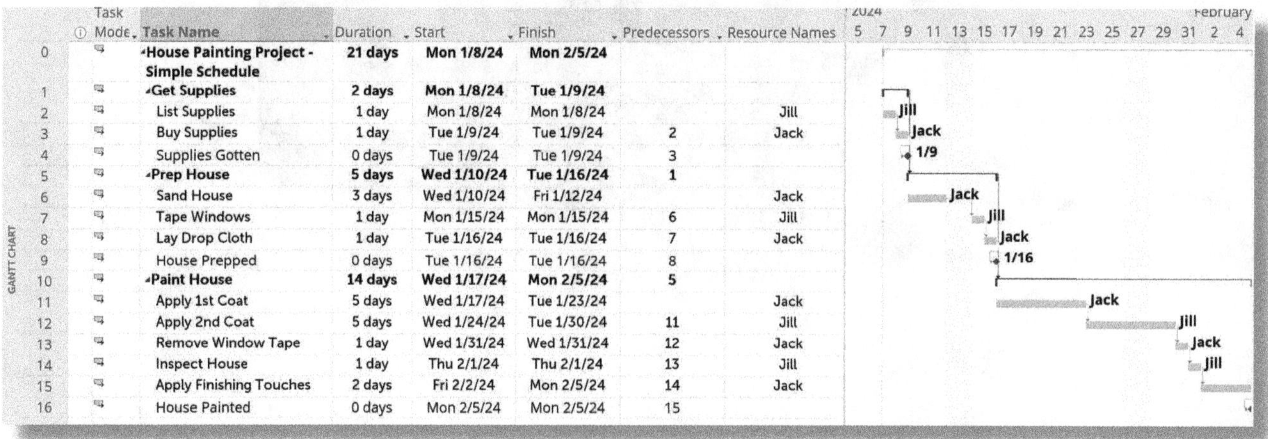

	Task Mode	Task Name	Duration	Start	Finish	Predecessors	Resource Names
0		**House Painting Project - Simple Schedule**	**21 days**	**Mon 1/8/24**	**Mon 2/5/24**		
1		**Get Supplies**	**2 days**	**Mon 1/8/24**	**Tue 1/9/24**		
2		List Supplies	1 day	Mon 1/8/24	Mon 1/8/24		Jill
3		Buy Supplies	1 day	Tue 1/9/24	Tue 1/9/24	2	Jack
4		Supplies Gotten	0 days	Tue 1/9/24	Tue 1/9/24	3	
5		**Prep House**	**5 days**	**Wed 1/10/24**	**Tue 1/16/24**	1	
6		Sand House	3 days	Wed 1/10/24	Fri 1/12/24		Jack
7		Tape Windows	1 day	Mon 1/15/24	Mon 1/15/24	6	Jill
8		Lay Drop Cloth	1 day	Tue 1/16/24	Tue 1/16/24	7	Jack
9		House Prepped	0 days	Tue 1/16/24	Tue 1/16/24	8	
10		**Paint House**	**14 days**	**Wed 1/17/24**	**Mon 2/5/24**	5	
11		Apply 1st Coat	5 days	Wed 1/17/24	Tue 1/23/24		Jack
12		Apply 2nd Coat	5 days	Wed 1/24/24	Tue 1/30/24	11	Jill
13		Remove Window Tape	1 day	Wed 1/31/24	Wed 1/31/24	12	Jack
14		Inspect House	1 day	Thu 2/1/24	Thu 2/1/24	13	Jill
15		Apply Finishing Touches	2 days	Fri 2/2/24	Mon 2/5/24	14	Jack
16		House Painted	0 days	Mon 2/5/24	Mon 2/5/24	15	

Image #2

A A
B B
C C

PART ONE Summary

This concludes Part One – Laying the Foundation. You've learned the advantages of scheduling with Microsoft Project over scheduling with Excel. You've learned important scheduling fundamentals, like building a Work Breakdown Structure, working with task relationships and the two ways to build a schedule. You've also learned to build your schedule outline using the key components of a schedule – tasks, summary tasks, project summary tasks, and milestones.

In Part Two – Building the Schedule, we'll put these fundamentals into practice.

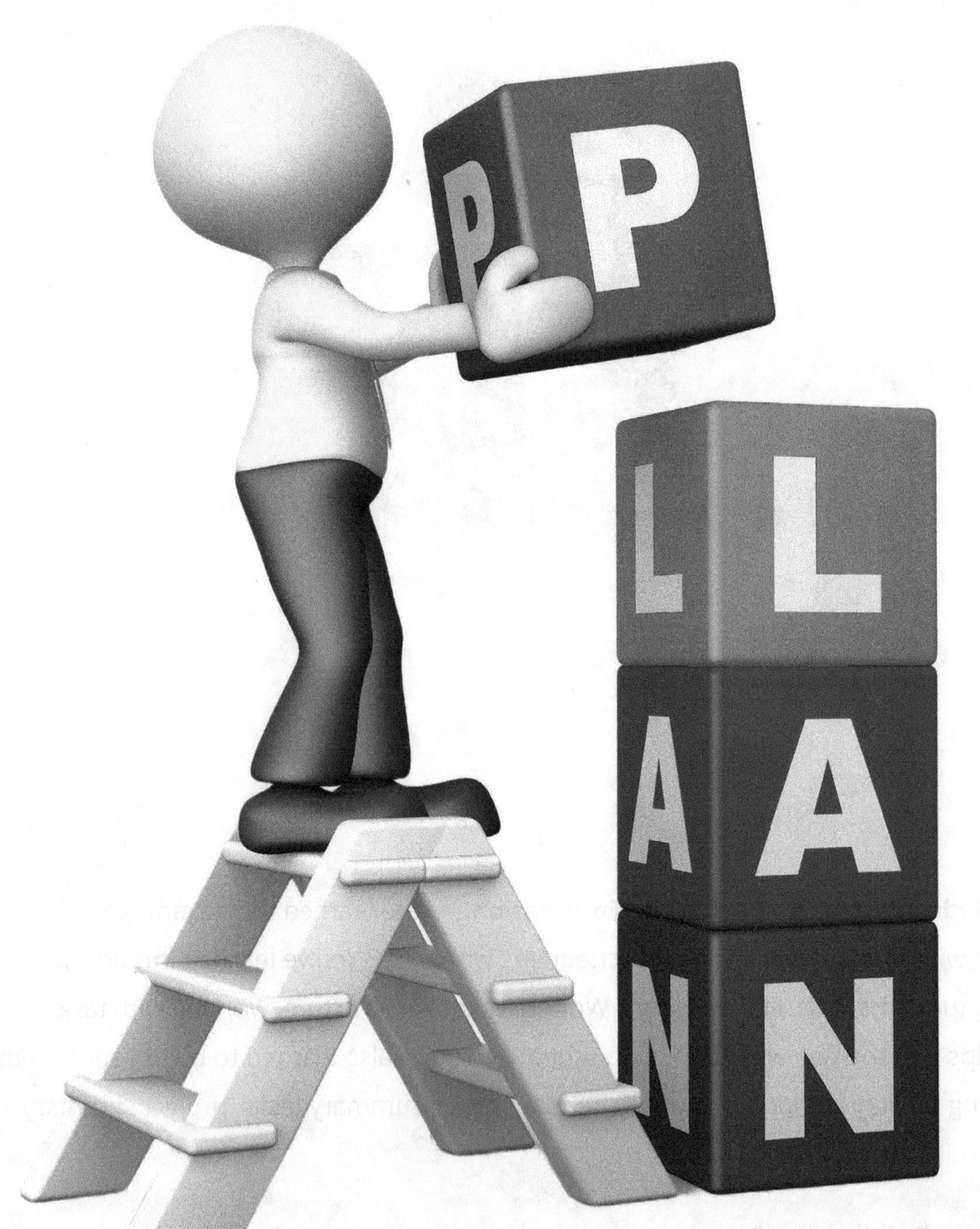
P
L
A
N

PART TWO: Building Your Schedule

IN PART TWO you'll learn to build schedules using the 6 steps in the B.A.S.I.C.S. scheduling approach. You'll learn to build Simple schedules™ when you need to track time only, and Detailed schedules™ when you need to track both time and cost. You'll also learn how to add, level, and manage resources, how to create calendars, how to document your schedule, how to compress it to meet critical deadlines and how to use constraints to reflect real business restrictions like delayed funding. Last, you'll learn to perform an in-depth inspection before beginning the execution phase.

Chapter 7 Building Your Schedule

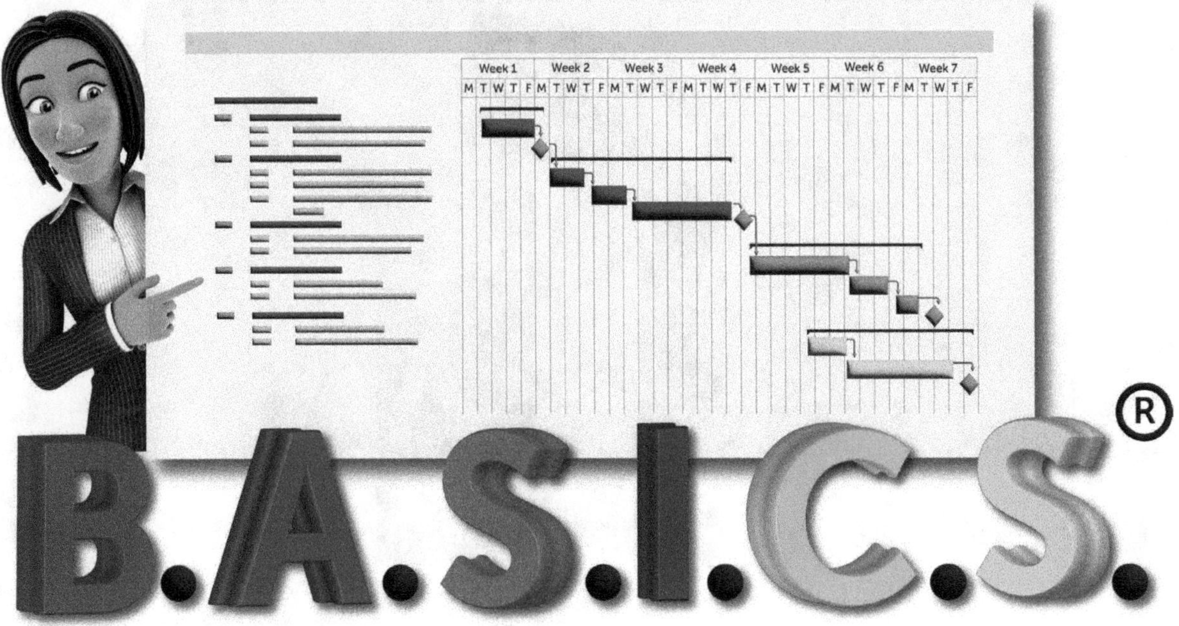

In the last chapter, we reviewed the two ways to build a schedule. In this chapter, we'll put those concepts into practice. We'll use the 6 steps in the **B.A.S.I.C.S.** scheduling process to build Simple and Detailed schedules™. Along the way, we'll apply many of the concepts we've covered in Part One and explore exciting software features.

You'll Learn To:

- Build a Simple Schedule
- Build a Detailed Schedule
- Use the B.A.S.I.C.S. 6-Step Scheduling Process
- Initialize Durations in a Simple Schedule
- Initialize Durations in a Detailed Schedule

Now that we've reviewed the fundamentals, we're ready to build a schedule!

To begin, you'll need to gather some initial scheduling information about your project.

Here's some information you'll need as you build your schedule:

- The Project Start Date
- A complete WBS, including all tasks and phases
- Vacation schedules and other Non-working days
- The Predecessor(s) of each phase, task, and milestone
- Duration estimates for each task (for Simple schedules)
- Work estimates for each task (for Detailed schedules)
- Units estimates for each task (for Detailed schedules)
- Resource pay rates (for Detailed schedules)

Using the B.A.S.I.C.S. Process to Build Schedules

The **B.A.S.I.**C.S. process includes the 6 steps you'll need to build and execute a schedule. By building your schedule in the order prescribed, your scheduling calculations will always be made after you configure Project for the type of schedule you're building. This will lead to less re-work and consistent results. In the next section, we'll review each step of the process to build a schedule using each scheduling method.

Step 1 - Break Down the Project

The first step is to **Break Down the Project**. As reviewed in Chapter 3, gather your team (or yourself!) and create a Work Breakdown Structure. Conduct a brainstorming session using the Top-down and Bottom-up planning methods. Be sure to follow the 100% Rule and the Exclusivity Rule. Also, be sure your WBS passes the quality check prescribed in Chapter 3. *Figure 126* shows a WBS for a House Painting project.

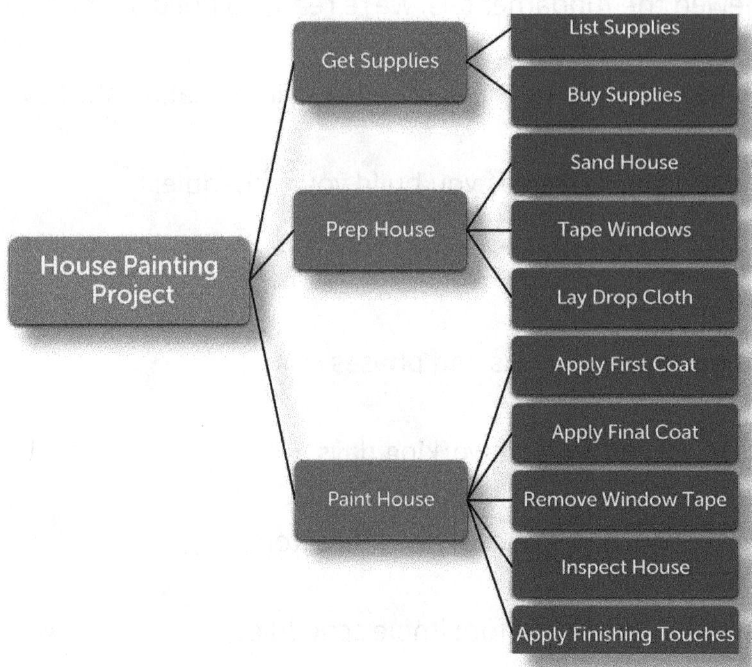

Figure 126 – House Painting Project - Work Breakdown Structure

Step 2 - Adjust the Settings

After you've broken down the project and created your WBS, you're ready to enter scheduling details into Microsoft Project and create your schedule outline. Before you enter tasks and other scheduling information, you must **Adjust the Settings** to support either a Simple or a Detailed schedule. Review Chapter 6 for an overview of the two scheduling methods.

From the opening view, select **Blank Project** to start a new project. The schedule settings are adjusted in the *Project Options* dialogue box.

To adjust the settings for a Simple schedule (*Figure 127*):

- Select the **File** tab to go **Backstage**.
- Select **Options** from the options on the left, to open the *Project Options* dialogue box.
- In the *Project Options* dialogue box, select **Schedule** from the menu options on the left to access the schedule settings.

- Under the *Scheduling options for this project* section, select **Auto Scheduled** from the *New tasks created* pick-list. This will enable Project to calculate the finish date from the task durations and task dependencies.
- Select **Fixed Duration** from the *Default task type* pick-list. This will fix your initial Duration estimate if Work or resource Units are adjusted.
- Uncheck the **New tasks are effort-driven** checkbox. This will disable the effort-driven scheduling feature.

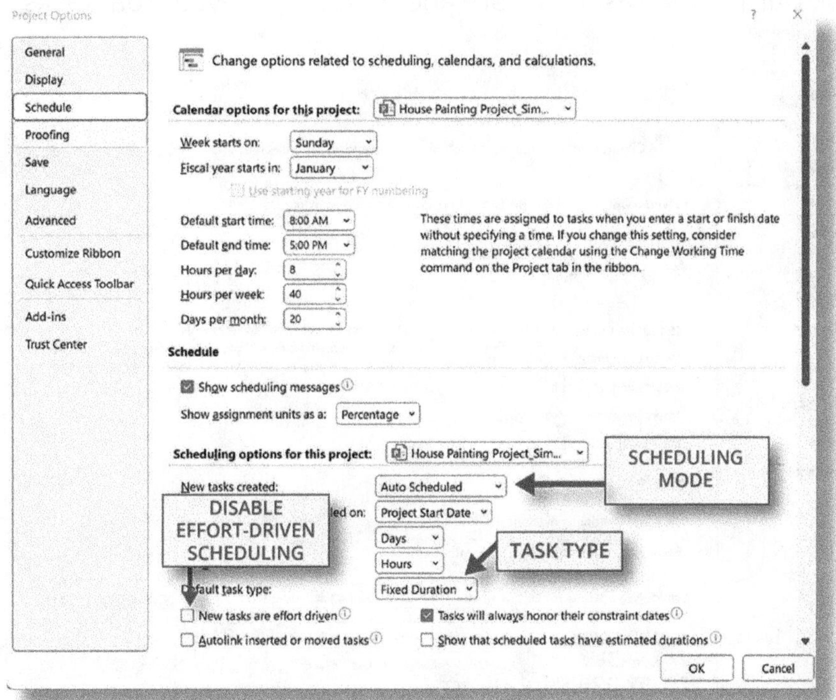

Figure 127 – Adjust the Settings for a Simple Schedule

To adjust the settings for a Detailed schedule (*Figure 128*):

- Select the **File** tab to go **Backstage**.
- Select **Options** from the options on the left, to open the *Project Options* dialogue box.
- In the *Project Options* dialogue box, select **Schedule** from the menu options on the left to access the schedule settings.

- Under the *Scheduling options for this project* section, select **Auto Scheduled** from the *New tasks created* pick-list. This will enable Project to calculate the finish date from the task durations and task dependencies.

- Select **Fixed Units** from the *Default task type* pick-list. This will allow the resource Units to remain fixed if changes are made to the Work or Duration values.

- Check the **New tasks are effort-driven** checkbox. This will enable the **effort-driven scheduling** feature. The initial Work values will be fixed, and Project will increase or decrease task Duration as resources are added to or removed from tasks.

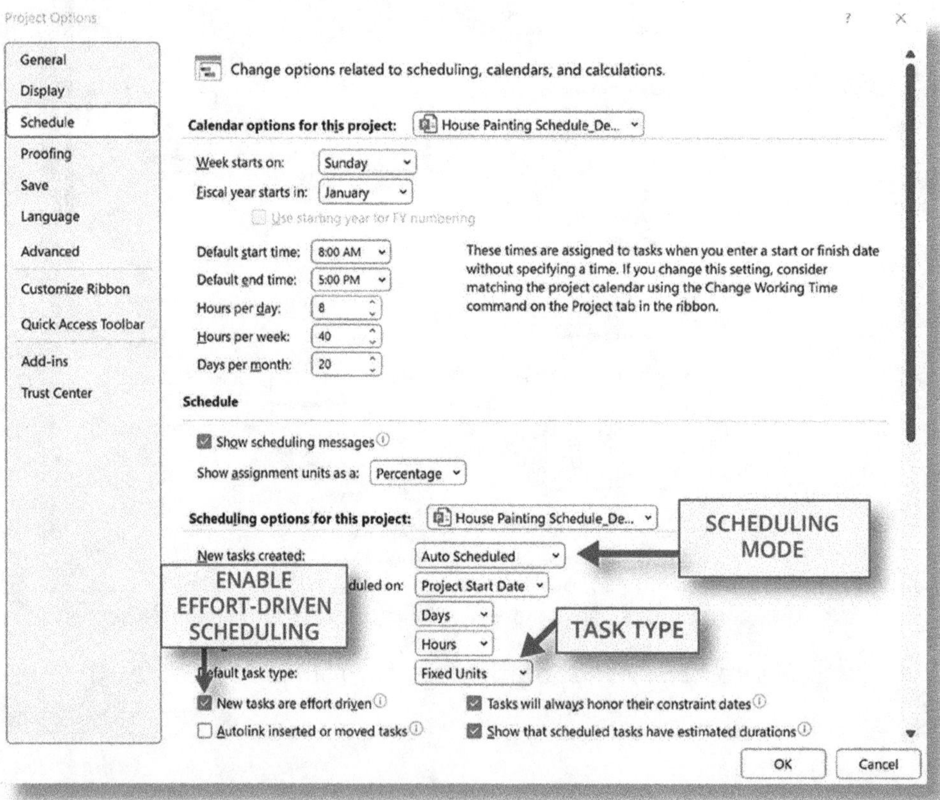

Figure 128 – Adjust the Settings for a Detailed Schedule

NOTE: The settings should always be adjusted before you assign resources, work, or durations to tasks. Performing this step out of sequence could result in scheduling calculations that are inconsistent with the scheduling method you've chosen. For more information about the schedule settings, review Chapter 5.

Setting the Project Start Date

It's important to use the proper method to set the **Project Start Date**. A common (and incorrect) approach is to enter the start date into the "Start" field of the first task in the schedule. As discussed in Chapter 5, this approach creates scheduling constraints that override Project's default scheduling behavior, which efficiently begins all tasks as soon as possible.

To set the Project Start Date:

- Select the **Project** tab. In the **Properties** group, select the **Project Information** command to open the *Project Information* dialogue box.
- Enter the date into the **Start date** field (*Figure 129* below).
- Select **OK** to close the dialogue box.

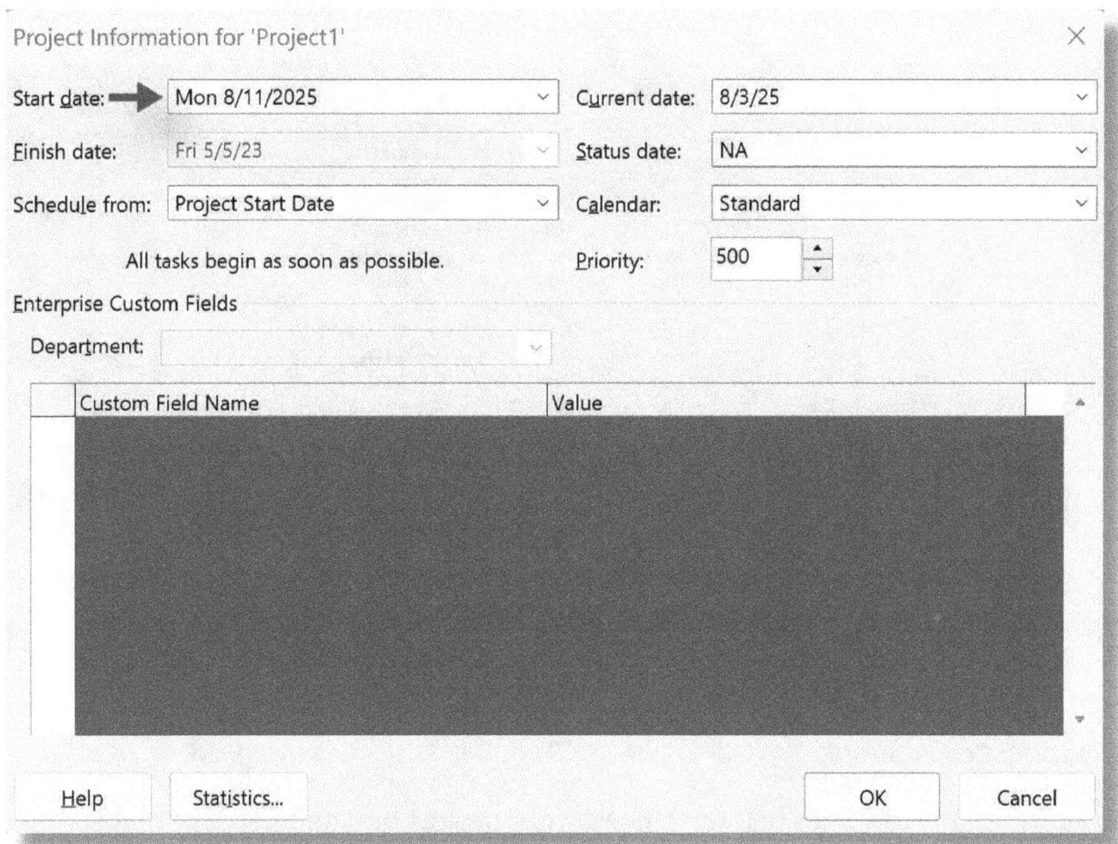

Figure 129 – Set the Project Start Date

Step 3 - Structure the Tasks

After you've adjusted the schedule settings and set the project start date, you're ready to **Structure the Tasks** to create the schedule outline. Begin by entering the unstructured tasks into the **Task Name** field of the Entry table in the Gantt Chart view. Begin with Task ID 1. For an efficient workflow, no task should be indented at this point. Once all the tasks are entered, use the **Indent Task** and **Outdent Task** commands on the Task tab in the Schedule group to structure the tasks (*Figure 130 below)*. Use the Indent Task command to demote tasks to subtasks. Use the Outdent Task command to promote tasks to summary tasks. Create as many levels of hierarchy as needed to create the phases and sub-phases for your project. Add Milestone tasks to signify important project events, such as the end of a phase. On the **Task** tab in the **Insert** group, use the **Insert Milestone** command or give any task a zero duration to create a milestone. For a refresher on summary task and subtask behaviors, review Chapter 4.

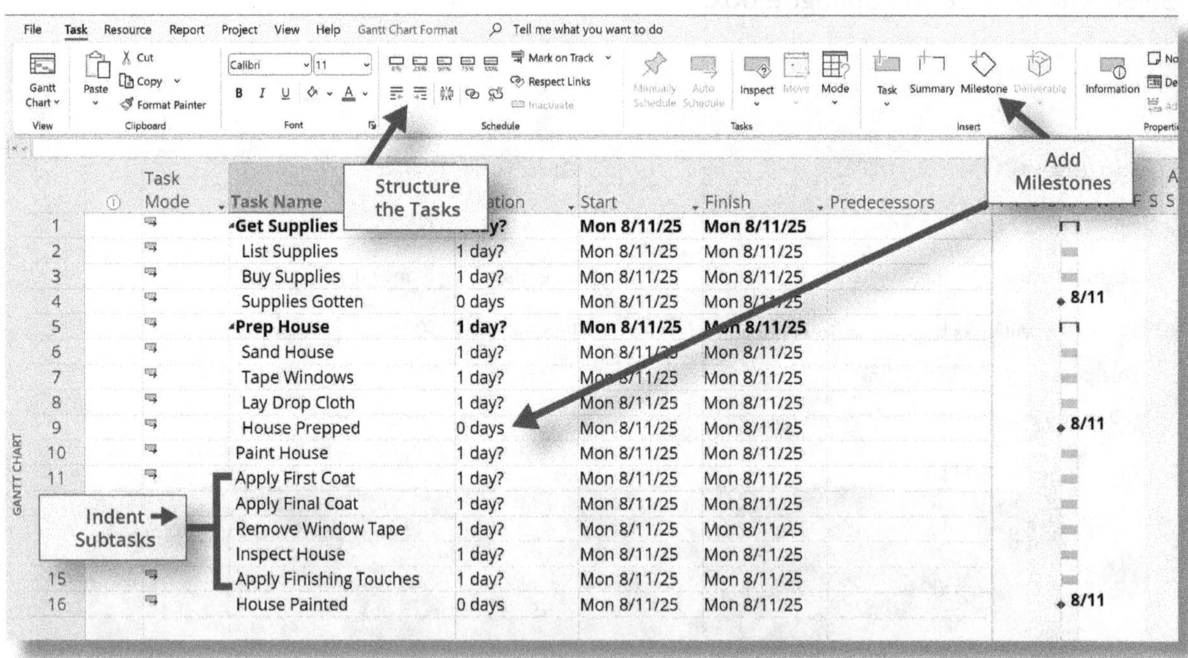

Figure 130 – Structure the Tasks

Show Outline Command

As you structure the tasks, it's helpful to check your project outline to ensure that summary tasks and subtasks are properly aligned. A handy way to check the outline is to use the **Show Outline** command. This feature lets you specify the outline level of the plan you want to view.

Also, with larger projects, you can collapse the outline to specific levels of the project and expand only the sections that you want to work with.

To use the Show Outline command:

- Select the **View** tab. In the **Data** group, select the outline level you want to view from the **Outline** command pick-list (*Figure 131* below)

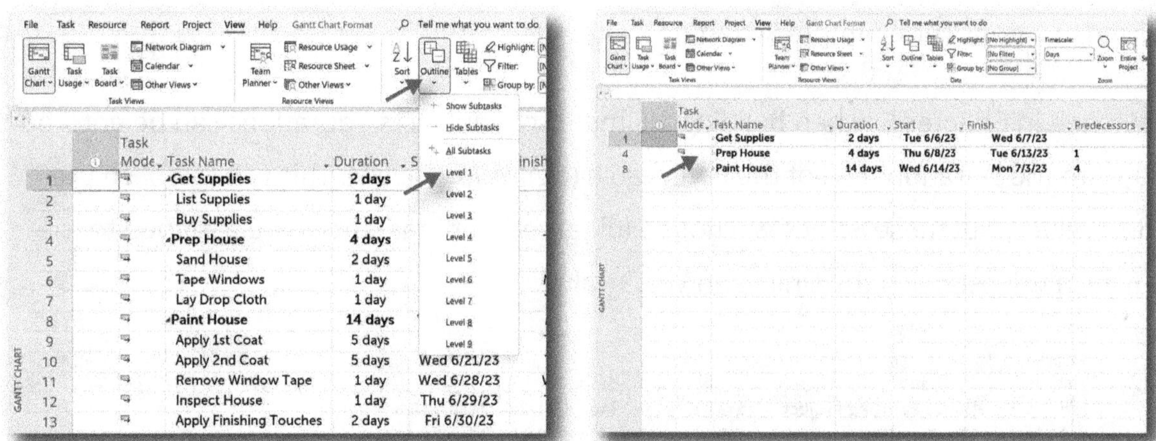

Figure 131 – Check the Schedule Outline

Display the Project Summary Task

Display the **Project Summary Task** to show the cumulative project information.
Once the schedule is completely built, this task will show summary items such as the project duration, the finish date, and the total cost.

To display the Project Summary Task:

- Select the Gantt Chart **Format** tab. In the **Show/Hide** group, select the **Project Summary Task** checkbox (*Figure 132* below).

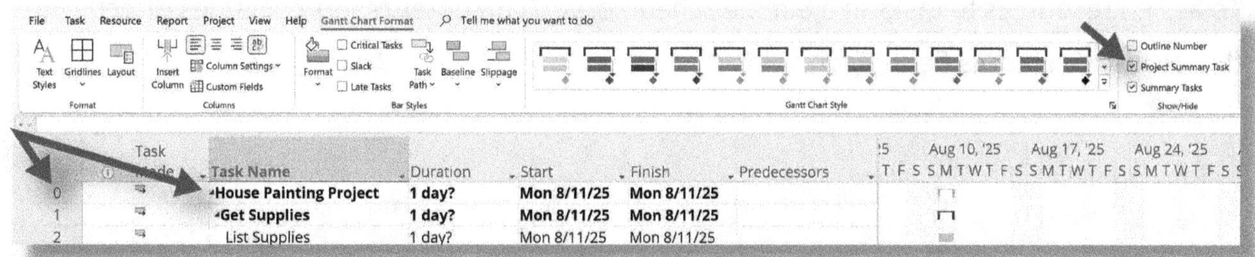

Figure 132 – Display the Project Summary Task

Step 4 - Initialize the Durations

After you've structured the tasks, you'll need to **Initialize the Task Durations**. Duration is the number of working days it takes to complete a task. Task duration is *Initialized* after each of the three variables in the Duration Equation (Work, Units and Duration) is assigned a value. How these values are assigned will depend on whether you're building a Simple or Detailed schedule.

Initialize Durations for a Simple Schedule

As explained in Chapter 6, when building a Simple schedule, task durations can be entered directly into the Duration field of the Entry table (*Figure 133 below*). This will establish the duration values, but these values will not be initialized until resources are assigned to the tasks (which will establish the Units and Work values).

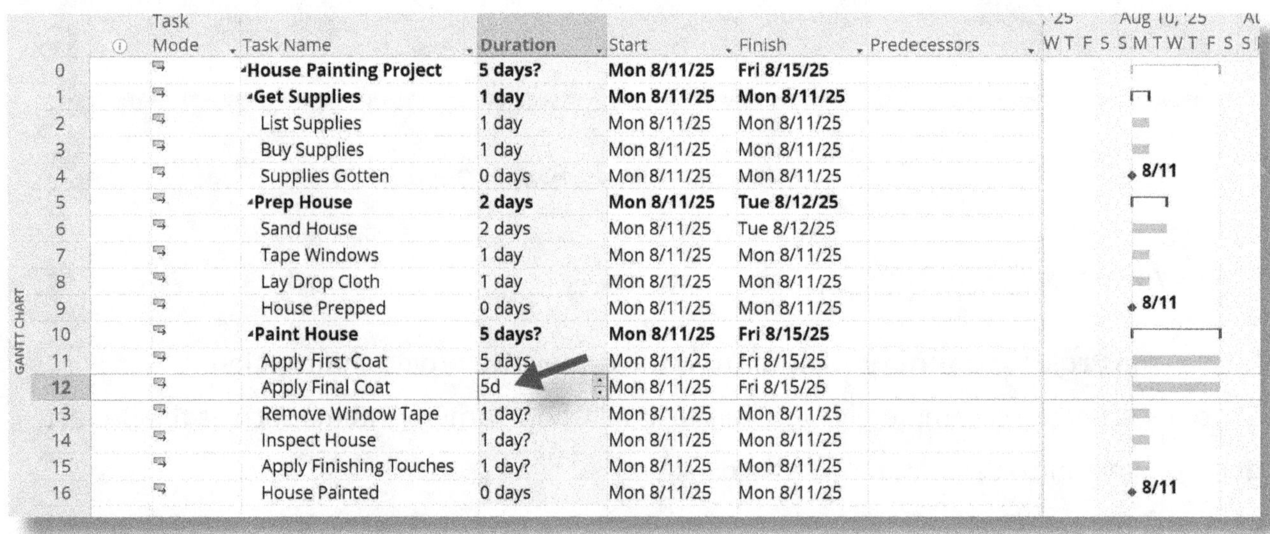

	Task Mode	Task Name	Duration	Start	Finish	Predecessors
0		**House Painting Project**	**5 days?**	**Mon 8/11/25**	**Fri 8/15/25**	
1		**Get Supplies**	**1 day**	**Mon 8/11/25**	**Mon 8/11/25**	
2		List Supplies	1 day	Mon 8/11/25	Mon 8/11/25	
3		Buy Supplies	1 day	Mon 8/11/25	Mon 8/11/25	
4		Supplies Gotten	0 days	Mon 8/11/25	Mon 8/11/25	
5		**Prep House**	**2 days**	**Mon 8/11/25**	**Tue 8/12/25**	
6		Sand House	2 days	Mon 8/11/25	Tue 8/12/25	
7		Tape Windows	1 day	Mon 8/11/25	Mon 8/11/25	
8		Lay Drop Cloth	1 day	Mon 8/11/25	Mon 8/11/25	
9		House Prepped	0 days	Mon 8/11/25	Mon 8/11/25	
10		**Paint House**	**5 days?**	**Mon 8/11/25**	**Fri 8/15/25**	
11		Apply First Coat	5 days	Mon 8/11/25	Fri 8/15/25	
12		Apply Final Coat	5d	Mon 8/11/25	Fri 8/15/25	
13		Remove Window Tape	1 day?	Mon 8/11/25	Mon 8/11/25	
14		Inspect House	1 day?	Mon 8/11/25	Mon 8/11/25	
15		Apply Finishing Touches	1 day?	Mon 8/11/25	Mon 8/11/25	
16		House Painted	0 days	Mon 8/11/25	Mon 8/11/25	

Figure 133 – Enter Task Durations in a Simple Schedule

Assign Resources to Tasks in a Simple Schedule

To assign resources to tasks in a Simple schedule, you can enter resource names directly into the **Resource Names** field (*Figure 134*).

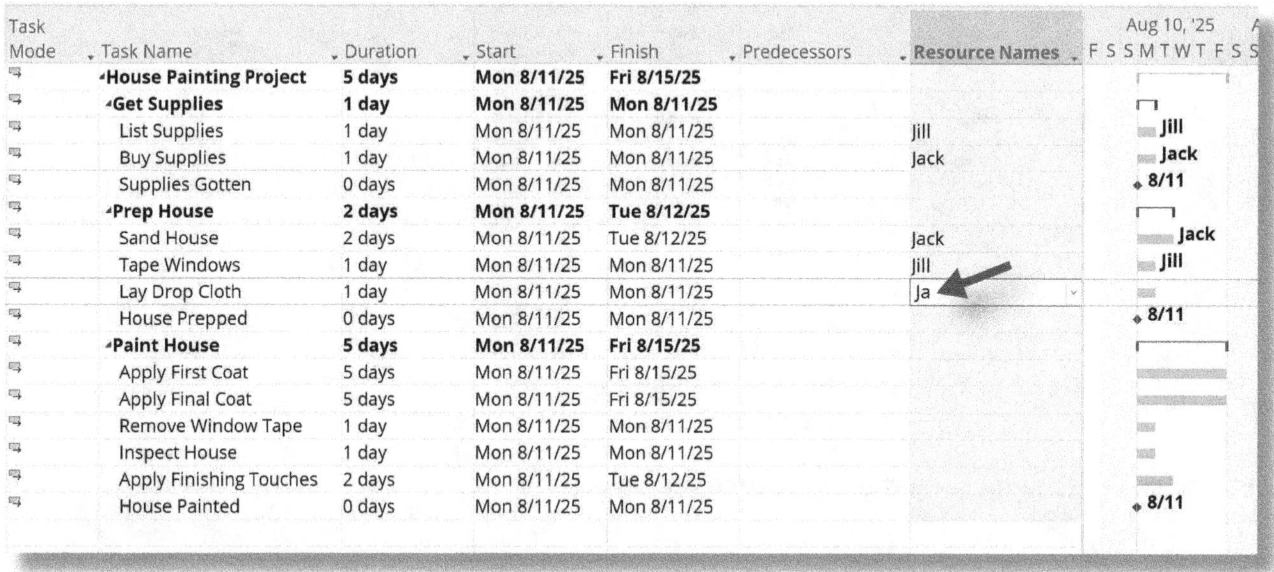

Task Mode	Task Name	Duration	Start	Finish	Predecessors	Resource Names
	House Painting Project	**5 days**	**Mon 8/11/25**	**Fri 8/15/25**		
	Get Supplies	**1 day**	**Mon 8/11/25**	**Mon 8/11/25**		
	List Supplies	1 day	Mon 8/11/25	Mon 8/11/25		Jill
	Buy Supplies	1 day	Mon 8/11/25	Mon 8/11/25		Jack
	Supplies Gotten	0 days	Mon 8/11/25	Mon 8/11/25		
	Prep House	**2 days**	**Mon 8/11/25**	**Tue 8/12/25**		
	Sand House	2 days	Mon 8/11/25	Tue 8/12/25		Jack
	Tape Windows	1 day	Mon 8/11/25	Mon 8/11/25		Jill
	Lay Drop Cloth	1 day	Mon 8/11/25	Mon 8/11/25		Ja
	House Prepped	0 days	Mon 8/11/25	Mon 8/11/25		
	Paint House	**5 days**	**Mon 8/11/25**	**Fri 8/15/25**		
	Apply First Coat	5 days	Mon 8/11/25	Fri 8/15/25		
	Apply Final Coat	5 days	Mon 8/11/25	Fri 8/15/25		
	Remove Window Tape	1 day	Mon 8/11/25	Mon 8/11/25		
	Inspect House	1 day	Mon 8/11/25	Mon 8/11/25		
	Apply Finishing Touches	2 days	Mon 8/11/25	Tue 8/12/25		
	House Painted	0 days	Mon 8/11/25	Mon 8/11/25		

Figure 134 – Assign Resources in a Simple Schedule

When you enter resource names into the Resource Names field, two events occur in the background:

1. Project establishes the resource assignment **Units** values at 100% (8 hours per day).

2. Project calculates the **Work** values from the **Duration** and **Units** values per the Duration Equation (D=W/U).

Once the Units and Work values have been established, the task durations will be initialized.

Initialize Durations for a Detailed Schedule

As discussed in Chapter 6, when building a Detailed schedule, task duration should not be entered directly into the Duration field. Project will calculate task durations from the Work and Units values.

Enter Work Values

The **Work** values are entered directly into the "Work" column of the Entry table *Figure 135*. This column must first be added to the table using the **Add New Column** command.

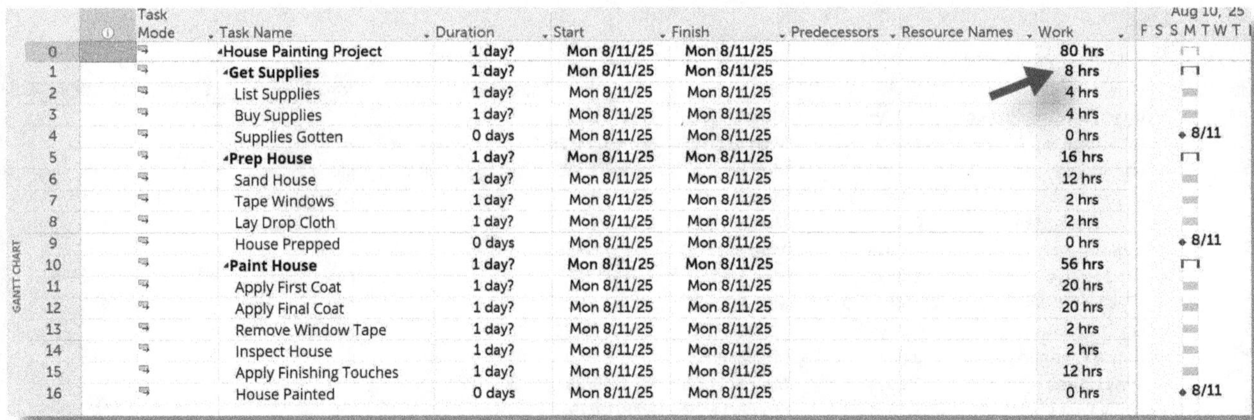

Figure 135 – Enter Work Values

Establish Units Values – Assign Resources to Tasks

Units values are established when resources are assigned to tasks. Resources are assigned with a Units value equal to the percentage of an 8-hour day they are available to work on tasks.

NOTE: In a Detailed schedule, before resources can be assigned to tasks, their information must be added to the schedule in the **Resource Sheet** view (*Figure 136* below). This is where information such as pay rates and groups is entered. Until resources are added, they will not be recognized in the schedule. We'll review this process in the next chapter, "Adding Resources to Your Schedule".

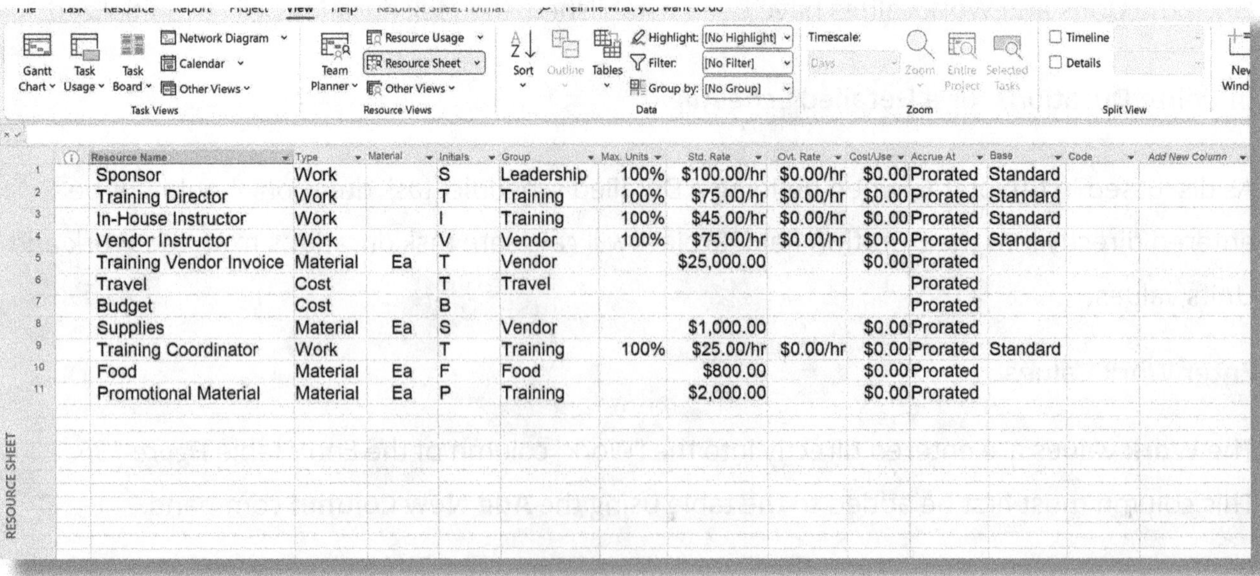

Figure 136 – The Resource Sheet View

Once their information has been added to the schedule, resources are assigned to tasks using the **Assign Resources** command:

To Assign Resources to Tasks using the Assign Resources command:

- In the **Entry table**, select the task name that you want to assign the resource(s) to.
- Select the **Resource** tab. In the **Assignments** group, select the **Assign Resources** command to open the *Assign Resources* dialogue box (*Figure 137* below).
- In the **Units** field for the resource you want to assign, type the Units value, then select **Assign** (or press Enter). To assign an additional resource to the same task, enter the Units values next to the resource you want to assign. Then, select **Assign**.
- Repeat these steps to assign resources to other tasks. Be sure to first select the task in the Entry table.
- Once all resources are assigned, select **Close** to close the *Assign Resources* dialogue box.

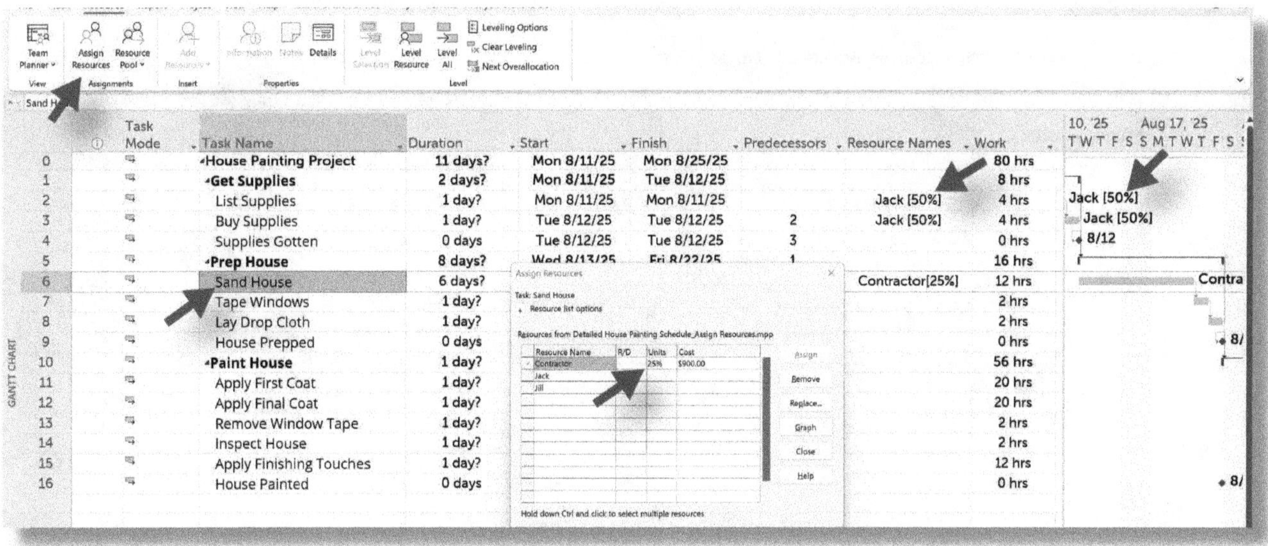

Figure 137 – Assign Resources to Tasks in a Detailed Schedule

When resources are assigned to a task, Project calculates the cost of the task by multiplying the resource(s) pay rate by the Work hours. The cost for each resource is shown in the Cost field of the *Assign Resources* dialogue box. Once the Work values have been entered and Units values have been established by assigning resources to tasks, the task Durations will be initialized.

Step 5 - Connect the Tasks

After you've initialized the task durations, **Connect the Tasks** using the task relationships discussed in Chapter 4. For each task (including Milestones) enter the predecessor's task ID numbers into the **Predecessors** field to create dependencies (*Figure 138* below). Apply lead and lag time as appropriate for your project.

	Task Mode	Task Name	Duration	Start	Finish	Predecessors	Resource Names	Jun 2, '24
0		House Painting Project	20 days	Mon 6/3/24	Fri 6/28/24			
1		Get Supplies	2 days	Mon 6/3/24	Tue 6/4/24			
2		List Supplies	1 day	Mon 6/3/24	Mon 6/3/24		Jill	Jill
3		Buy Supplies	1 day	Tue 6/4/24	Tue 6/4/24	2	Jack	Jack
4		Supplies Gotten	0 days	Tue 6/4/24	Tue 6/4/24	3		6/4
5		Prep House	4 days	Wed 6/5/24	Mon 6/10/24			
6		Sand House	2 days	Wed 6/5/24	Thu 6/6/24	4	Jack	Jack
7		Tape Windows	1 day	Fri 6/7/24	Fri 6/7/24	6	Jill	Jill

Figure 138 – Connect the Tasks

Task relationships can also be established using the *Task Information* dialogue box (*Figure 139* below).

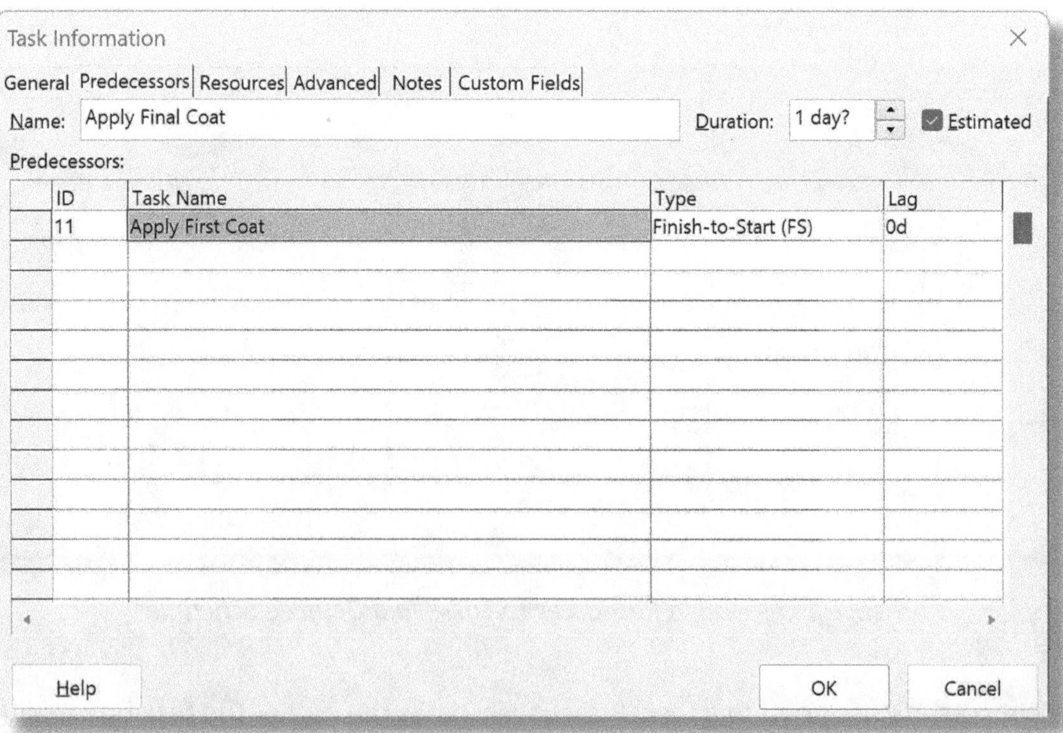

Figure 139 – Create Task Relationships in the Task Information Dialogue Box

To Establish Task Relationships in the *Task Information* dialogue box:

- Double-click the task to open the *Task Information* dialogue box.
- Select the **Predecessors** tab.
- In the **ID** field, enter the predecessor's task ID or select the predecessor's task name from the pick-list in the **Task Name** field.
- In the **Type** field, select the task relationship type you want.
- In the **Lag** field, apply lag or lead time (to enter lead time, enter a negative value).
- Select **OK** to close the *Task Information* dialogue box.

Step 6 - Start the Project

After completing the first 5 steps of the B.A.S.I.C.S. process, you're ready to **Start the Project**, and execute your schedule. We'll cover this step in Chapter 15. There are a lot of exciting things to learn before we get there, including adding resources, adding calendars, displaying the critical path, and compressing the schedule to meet a deadline!

We have now reviewed the B.A.S.I.C.S. scheduling process for building Simple or Detailed schedules. This approach will yield consistent and reliable scheduling results by ensuring that scheduling calculations occur after you've properly configured the software.

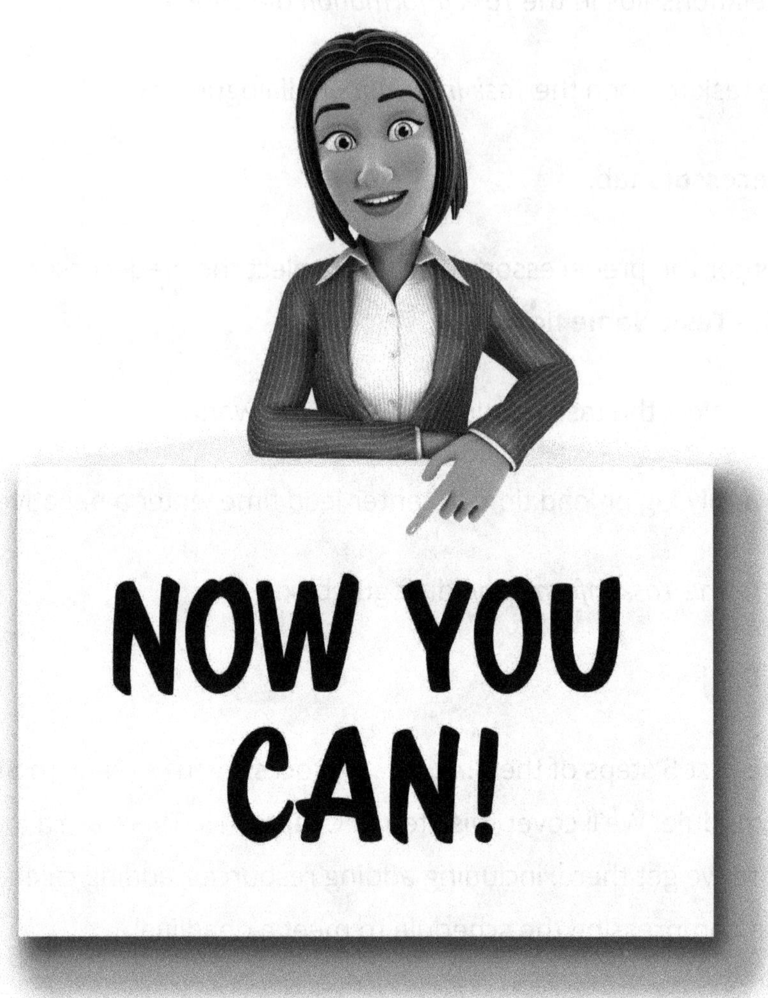

- ✓ Build a Simple Schedule
- ✓ Build a Detailed Schedule
- ✓ Use the B.A.S.I.C.S. Scheduling Process
- ✓ Initialize the Durations for a Simple Schedule
- ✓ Initialize the Durations for a Detailed Schedule

Build a Simple Schedule using the B.A.S.I.C.S. process

For this practice exercise, you'll build a Simple schedule for a House Painting project using the B.A.S.I.C.S. scheduling process.

Go to **mspbasics.com** for "checkpoint" images to check your work as you go along.

Follow these step-by-step instructions to complete this Challenge practice exercise.

NOTE: For consistent results, it's important to start this exercise with a blank project. Do not use a previously saved project file from a previous practice exercise.

Start a New Project

From the opening view, select **Blank Project** to create a new project. You'll be taken to the **Gantt Chart view**. Depending on how your version of Project is configured, the **Timeline View** panel may be displayed. Since we won't be using the panel for this exercise, we'll close it to see more of the Gantt Chart view.

To close the Timeline view panel:

1. Select the **View** tab. In the **Split View** group, uncheck the **Timeline** checkbox.

Breakdown the Project

Step 1, **Breakdown the Project** has already been done and is represented by the upcoming Working Breakdown Structure.

Adjust the Settings

Adjust the settings to support a Simple schedule:

1. Select the **File** tab to go **Backstage**.
2. Select **Options** from the options on the left, to open the *Project Options* dialogue box.
3. In the *Project Options* dialogue box, select **Schedule** from the menu options on the left to access the schedule settings.
4. Under the *Scheduling options for this project* section, select **Auto Scheduled** from the *New tasks created* pick-list. This will enable Project to calculate the finish date from the task durations and task dependencies.
5. Select **Fixed Duration** from the *Default task type* pick-list. This will fix your initial Duration estimate if Work or resource Units are adjusted.

6. Uncheck the **New tasks are effort-driven** checkbox. This will disable the effort-driven scheduling feature.

> **CHECKPOINT:** To check your results so far, go to **mspbasics.com**
> - Select the **CheckPoint Images** tab.
> - Select the version of the book you're using.
> - Select **Chapter 7**. Then, go to **Checkpoint Image #1**

Set the Project Start Date

Set the project start date as **6/3/24**.

1. Select the **Project** tab. In the **Properties** group, select the **Project Information** command to open the *Project Information* dialogue box.

2. In the **Start date** field, enter **6/3/24**. Click **OK** to close the *Project Information* dialogue box.

> **CHECKPOINT:** To check your results so far, go to **mspbasics.com**
> - Select the **CheckPoint Images** tab.
> - Select the version of the book you're using.
> - Select **Chapter 7**. Then, go to **Checkpoint Image #2**

The **Task List** and **Work Breakdown Structure** for the House Painting project are shown below.

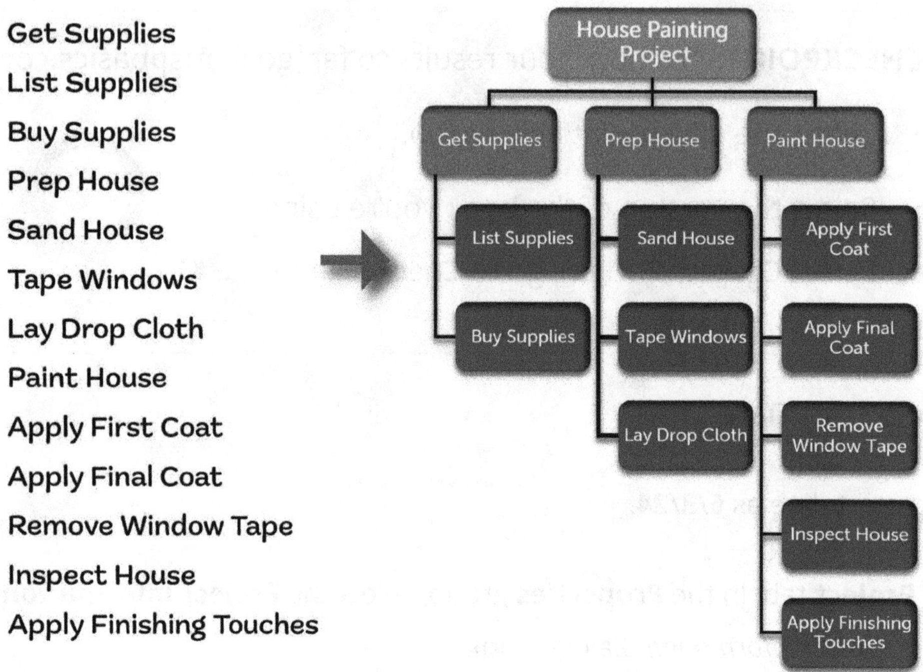

Enter the Task List

1. Enter the unstructured task list into the **Task Name** field of **Entry table.**

2. Enter each of the task names (in the order shown on the task list) . The *Get Supplies* task will have task ID 1, the *List Supplies* task will have task ID 2, and so forth.

Create Milestones

Create a **Milestone** task to signify the completion of each phase.

1. Select the *Prep House* summary task.

2. On the **Task** tab, in the **Insert** group, select the **Insert Milestone** command. A "New Milestone" task will be inserted as task ID 4 beneath the *Buy Supplies* task and will be given a duration value of zero. Also, a diamond icon will be added to the Gantt chart, indicating the milestone.

3. Type over the default name and rename the milestone **Supplies Gotten**.

4. To create the milestone for Phase 2, select the *Paint House* summary task. Then, select the **Insert Milestone** command. A "New Milestone" task will be inserted as task ID 9 beneath the *Lay Drop Cloth* task. Type over the default name and rename the milestone **House Prepped**.

5. To create the milestone for Phase 3, in the **Task Name** field, in the cell beneath the *Apply Final Touches* task, enter the task name **House Painted**. The task ID for this task should be 16. It will be given a 1-day duration and a corresponding task bar in the Gantt chart.

6. In the **Duration** field for this task, enter **0** for the duration value. This task will become a milestone. Notice that the task bar in the Gantt chart has been replaced with a diamond icon.

When you're done entering the tasks and milestones you should have **16 tasks**.

CHECKPOINT: To check your results so far, go to **mspbasics.com**

- Select the **CheckPoint Images** tab.
- Select the version of the book you're using.
- Select **Chapter 7**. Then, go to **Checkpoint Image #3**

Structure the Tasks to Create the Schedule Outline

Structure the Task list to create the schedule outline. Create summary tasks and subtasks for the three phases of the project.

1. Select the *List Supplies*, *Buy Supplies* and *Supplies Gotten* tasks.

2. Select the **Task** tab. In the **Schedule** group, select the **Indent Task** command.
   The *Get Supplies* task should now be promoted to a summary task, indicated with bold typeface. The *List Supplies, Buy Supplies* and *Supplies Gotten* tasks should be demoted beneath it as subtasks. In the Gantt chart, the blue task bar for the *Get Supplies* task, should be replaced with a black summary bar.

3. Next, select the *Sand House*, *Tape Windows*, *Lay Drop Cloth* and *House Prepped* tasks. Select the **Indent Task** command to promote the *Prep House* task to a summary task and demote these four tasks beneath it as subtasks.

4. Now, select the *Apply First Coat*, *Apply Final Coat*, *Remove Window Tape*, *Inspect House*, *Apply Finishing Touches* and *House Painted* tasks. Use the **Indent Task** command to promote the *Paint House* task to a summary task and demote these six tasks beneath it as subtasks.

The three phases of the House Painting project should now be structured.

CHECKPOINT: To check your results so far, go to **mspbasics.com**

- Select the **CheckPoint Images** tab.
- Select the version of the book you're using.
- Select **Chapter 7**. Then, go to **Checkpoint Image #4**

Initialize the Task Durations

The duration values for each task are listed in the table below.

TASK NAME	DURATION
List Supplies	1d
Buy Supplies	1d
Sand House	2d
Tape Windows	1d
Lay Drop Cloth	1d
Apply First Coat	5d
Apply Final Coat	5d
Remove Window Tape	1d
Inspect House	1d
Apply Finishing Touch	2d

1. In the **Duration** field of the Entry table, enter the respective duration for each subtask. For example, for the *List Supplies* task, enter **1d**.

Note: You won't enter a duration for the summary tasks. Project will automatically calculate the summary task durations, based on the durations of their subtasks and the task relationships.

After the task durations are entered, notice the task bars in the Gantt Chart have been extended to match the respective durations.

CHECKPOINT: To check your results so far, go to **mspbasics.com**

- Select the **CheckPoint Images** tab.
- Select the version of the book you're using.
- Select **Chapter 7**. Then, go to **Checkpoint Image #5**

Next, you'll **initialize the duration values** by assigning resources to the tasks to establish the **Units** values. The **Work** values for each task will be assigned in the background as 100% Units.

The resource assignments for each task are listed in the table below.

TASK NAME	RESOURCE
List Supplies	Jill
Buy Supplies	Jack
Sand House	Jack
Tape Windows	Jill
Lay Drop Cloth	Jack
Apply First Coat	Contractor, Jack
Apply Final Coat	Contractor, Jill
Remove Tape	Jack
Inspect House	Jill
Apply Finishing Touches	Jack

1. Enter the appropriate resource names into the **Resource Name** field of each task.

The resources will be assigned at 100% Units. For the tasks with two resources assigned to them, separate the resource names with a comma.

NOTE: As the resources are assigned to the tasks, they will become over-allocated (indicated by the red man icons in the **Indicators** field). This is because the tasks are not yet connected. Each task is currently starting on the same day. We'll cover resource over-allocation in Chapter 13, "Leveling Your Resources".

CHECKPOINT: To check your results so far, go to **mspbasics.com**

- Select the **CheckPoint Images** tab.
- Select the version of the book you're using.
- Select **Chapter 7**. Then, go to **Checkpoint Image #6**

Connect the Tasks: Create Task Relationships

The tasks in this schedule occur in sequence, so we'll give the tasks in each phase a **Finish-to-Start** task relationship. Each task is the predecessor of the following task.

The tasks and their predecessor task ID numbers are listed in the table below.

1. In the **Predecessors** field of each task, enter the **task ID** number for its predecessor task.

TASK NAME	PREDECESSOR TASK ID
Buy Supplies	2
Supplies Gotten Milestone	3
Sand House	4
Tape Windows	6
Lay Drop Cloth	7
House Prepped Milestone	8
Apply First Coat	9
Apply Final Coat	11
Remove Window Tape	12
Inspect House	13
Apply Finishing Touches	14
House Painted Milestone	15

Notice that the resources are no longer over-allocated. Project rescheduled the tasks according to their dependencies. Each task now starts after its predecessor finishes.
The summary task durations have been calculated per the durations of their subtasks. In the Gantt Chart, the task bars are also connected.

Display the Project Summary Task

To see the project duration and finish date, display the Project Summary Task:

1. Select the Gantt Chart **Format** tab. In the **Show/Hide** group, select the **Project Summary Task** checkbox. Rename the Project Summary Task **"House Painting Project"**.

2. The project duration should be **20 days** and the project finish date should be **6/28/24**.

CHECKPOINT: To check your results so far, go to **mspbasics.com**

- Select the **CheckPoint Images** tab.
- Select the version of the book you're using.
- Select **Chapter 7**. Then, go to **Checkpoint Image #7**

You have now built a Simple schedule using the first 5 steps of the B.A.S.I.C.S. scheduling approach. We'll review the last step, "Start the Project", in Chapter 15 "Executing your Schedule".

You will use this file to complete the Chapter 15 practice exercise.

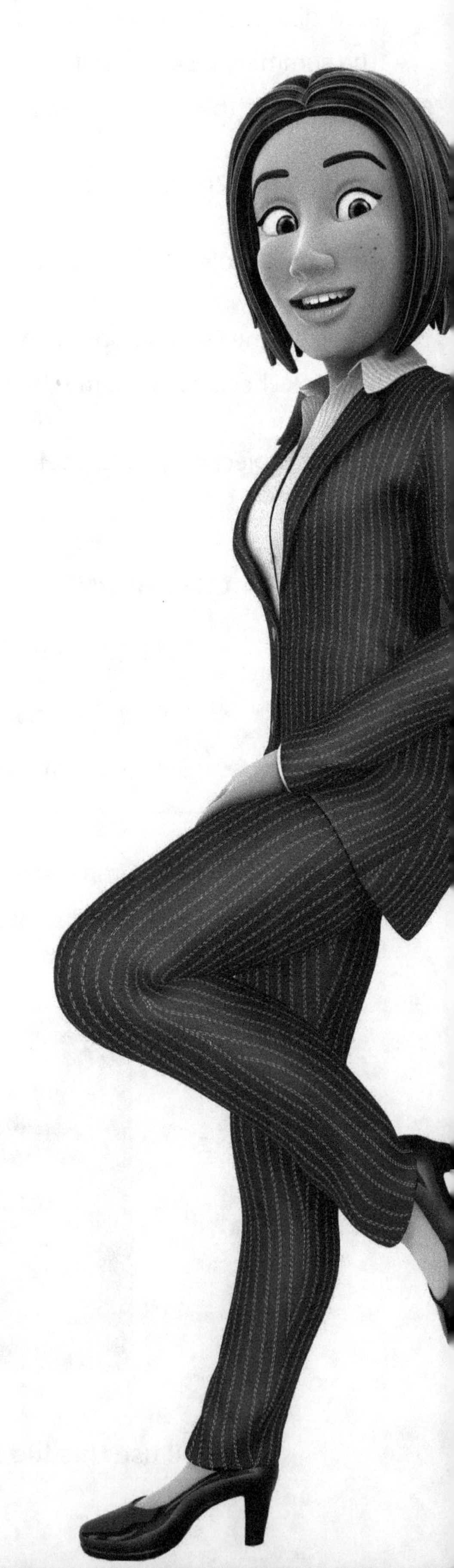

Chapter 8 Adding Resources to Your Schedule

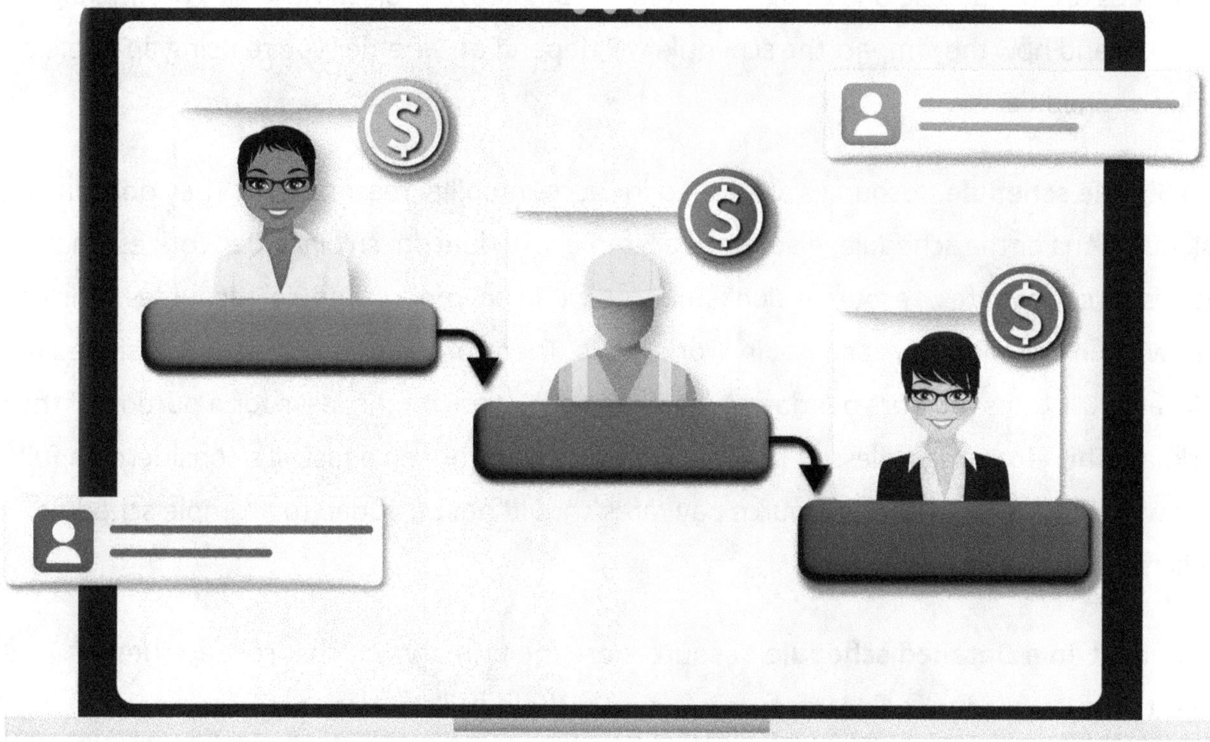

In the last chapter, you learned to build a Simple and a Detailed schedule using the 6-step B.A.S.I.C.S. scheduling process. In this chapter, we'll review **Resources** – the primary way that cost accrues in Project. When you're done, you'll be able to describe the three resource types you can work with in Project, create resources, add resource information to the schedule and assign resources to tasks.

You'll Learn to:

- Understand the Resource Types
- Create Resources
- Add Resource Information to the Schedule
- Assign Resources to Tasks

Understanding Resources and the Two Scheduling Methods

Resources are the people and things required to complete a project. How they are managed in Project and how they impact the schedule will depend on whether you're using a Simple or Detailed schedule.

In a Simple schedule, resources are added for accountability reasons only. They don't impact task durations or the schedule. Also, since a Simple schedule doesn't include Work estimates and resource pay rates, resources don't impact cost. In a Simple schedule, resources estimate their work in Duration days and not in Work hours. Therefore, they are generally assigned to tasks at 100% Units (8 hours per day), even if they only work on the tasks for a portion of their workday. Therefore, regardless of how many hours they work on a task, it's considered a full day's work. This is the reason resource pay rates should not be added to a Simple schedule. It will result in exaggerated costs.

By contrast, **in a Detailed schedule**, resources are the primary way that cost accrues in Project. In a Detailed schedule, resources estimate their work in Work hours and not in Duration days. When resource pay rates are added to the schedule, Project multiplies them by the Work hours and determines the cost for each task and ultimately, the entire project.

Understanding the Resource Types

In Microsoft Project, there are three types of resources – **Work**, **Material** and **Cost**. These three resource types represent the three ways cost can accrue in your project. Let's review the characteristics of each.

WORK RESOURCES are resources that have an hourly rate and a calendar. They can be people, equipment, or rentals, such as a conference room, a crane, or a lighting boom. They can also be generic, representing a trade or professional group, such as "Engineers" or "Architects".

MATERIAL RESOURCES are consumable supplies that are assigned a per unit rate and generate cost by the amount consumed. For example, if you're painting a house, the paint would be a material resource. Material resources can be assigned using a **Fixed Consumption Rate** or a **Variable Consumption Rate**. If the consumption rate is Fixed, Project calculates their cost by multiplying their cost per unit rate by the number of units assigned to a task.

For example, if paint has a rate of $50 per gallon, and 5 gallons are assigned to the task, the cost will be $250. If the consumption rate is Variable, Project calculates cost by multiplying the cost per unit rate by the number of gallons consumed within a specified time increment (E.g., 1 gallon per hour). For example, if paint has a rate of $50 per gallon and 2 gallons are consumed per hour, then after 5 hours, 5 gallons would be consumed, and the cost would be $500. The difference between the two consumption methods is, with a Fixed rate, the amount consumed is fixed, irrespective of task duration. With a Variable rate, the amount consumed varies with task duration. When assigning material resources to tasks, the consumption rate is entered in the Units field of the Assign Resources dialogue box. For a Fixed consumption rate, enter the quantity being assigned in the Units field (E.g., **5**). For a Variable consumption rate, enter the Unit per time increment (E.g., **1/h**).

COST RESOURCES are used to capture non-recurring cost items that don't accrue via an hourly rate and cannot be classified as consumable. There are two types of Cost resources – **Budget** and **Expense**. Budget cost resources are used as a placeholder for the Project Budget. We'll work with Budget cost resources in Chapter 18. Expense cost resources capture non-recurring expenses like food or travel. Since these expenses can vary from expenditure to expenditure, they must be assigned <u>after</u> the expenditure is made. For example, travel expenditure could be $1,000 for one business trip and $2,000 for another. After the expense has incurred, it can be assigned to the appropriate task in Project.

Creating Resources: Adding Resource Information to the Schedule

Resources and their information are added to the schedule and managed in the **Resource Sheet** view.

To access the Resource Sheet view:

- Select the **View** tab.
- In the **Resource Views** group, select **Resource Sheet** (*Figure 140*).

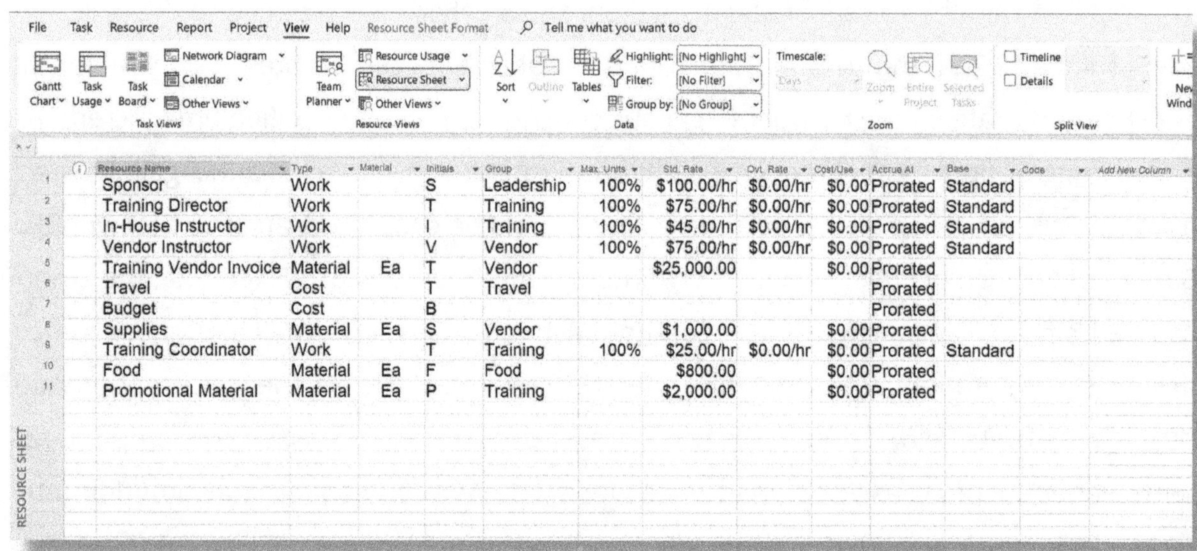

	Resource Name	Type	Material	Initials	Group	Max. Units	Std. Rate	Ovt. Rate	Cost/Use	Accrue At	Base	Code	Add New Column
1	Sponsor	Work		S	Leadership	100%	$100.00/hr	$0.00/hr	$0.00	Prorated	Standard		
2	Training Director	Work		T	Training	100%	$75.00/hr	$0.00/hr	$0.00	Prorated	Standard		
3	In-House Instructor	Work		I	Training	100%	$45.00/hr	$0.00/hr	$0.00	Prorated	Standard		
4	Vendor Instructor	Work		V	Vendor	100%	$75.00/hr	$0.00/hr	$0.00	Prorated	Standard		
5	Training Vendor Invoice	Material	Ea	T	Vendor		$25,000.00		$0.00	Prorated			
6	Travel	Cost		T	Travel					Prorated			
7	Budget	Cost		B						Prorated			
8	Supplies	Material	Ea	S	Vendor		$1,000.00		$0.00	Prorated			
9	Training Coordinator	Work		T	Training	100%	$25.00/hr	$0.00/hr	$0.00	Prorated	Standard		
10	Food	Material	Ea	F	Food		$800.00		$0.00	Prorated			
11	Promotional Material	Material	Ea	P	Training		$2,000.00		$0.00	Prorated			

Figure 140 – The Resource Sheet View

The **Resource Sheet view** displays resource information for the entire project. As we've reviewed, in a Simple schedule, resources can be assigned to tasks by entering their names into the Resource Names field of the Entry table. When this is done, those resources are populated to the Resource Sheet view as Work resources and are given some default information. In a Detailed schedule, resources and their information must be added to the Resource Sheet view *before* they can be assigned to tasks.

Fields in the Resource Sheet

Using *Figure 140* above, we'll review each field of the Resource Sheet.

- In the **Resource Name** field, enter the resource's name.
- In the **Type** field, select the resource type from the pick-list (Work, Material or Cost).
- In the **Material** field, enter the unit of measurement for a Material resource. E.g., gallons, boxes, or each).
- In the **Initials** field, enter an abbreviation for the resource name. By default, Project enters the first initial of the resource name.
- In the **Group** field, enter the name of the group that the resource belongs to. This field is handy for sorting and grouping resource data, which we'll cover in Chapter 14, "*Inspecting Your Schedule*".

- In the **Max.** (Max Units) field, enter the resource's Maximum Units. **Max Units** is the maximum capacity a resource is available to work on any given day. It is expressed as a percentage of an 8-hour day. By default, Project assigns 100% Max Units to new resources. This means that Project assumes that all resources are available to work on tasks the full eight-hour day. If the resource is only available 4 hours per day, their Max Units would be 50%.
- In the **Std. Rate** (Standard Rate) field, enter the pay rate for Work resources. For Material resources, if using a fixed consumption rate, enter the cost per unit (E.g., $50.00). If using a variable consumption rate, enter the unit per time increment (E.g., 1/h for 1 per hour). **NOTE:** The cost for Cost resources is not entered in the Std. Rate field. Cost values for Cost resources are entered in the "Units" field of the *Assign Resources* dialogue box after the amount is known.
- In the **Ovt.** (Overtime Rate) field, enter the resource's overtime pay rate.
- The **Cost/Use** (Cost Per Use) field pertains to Work and Material resources. For a Work resource, enter the set cost that accrues every time the resource is used. For example, some plumbers charge a fee for showing up, especially at odd hours. This fee must be paid whether they do work or not. For Material resources, enter any cost that's incurred once, regardless of the number of units. For example, storage fees.
- The **Accrue** (Accrue At) field is where you determine how cost should be dispensed throughout your project. The choices are Start, End or Prorated (default).
    - **Start** (pay up-front) – the entire cost of the task will accrue when the task starts.
    - **End** (pay at the end) – the entire cost of the task will accrue when the task finishes.
    - **Prorated** (pay as you go) – cost accrues evenly as task work is completed.
- In the **Base** (Base Calendar) field, select the base calendar you want Work resources to use. The base calendar options are Standard (default), 24 hours, and Nightshift. We'll review calendars in Chapter 9.
- In the **Code** field, enter any code, abbreviation, or number you want to associate with a resource. For example, you might use this field to designate the cost code for a resource.

Adding Additional Resource Information

In addition to the fields in the Resource Sheet, you can add more information about a resource in the *Resource Information* dialogue box.

- On the Resource Sheet, double-click a resource's name to access the *Resource Information* dialogue box (*Figure 141* below)

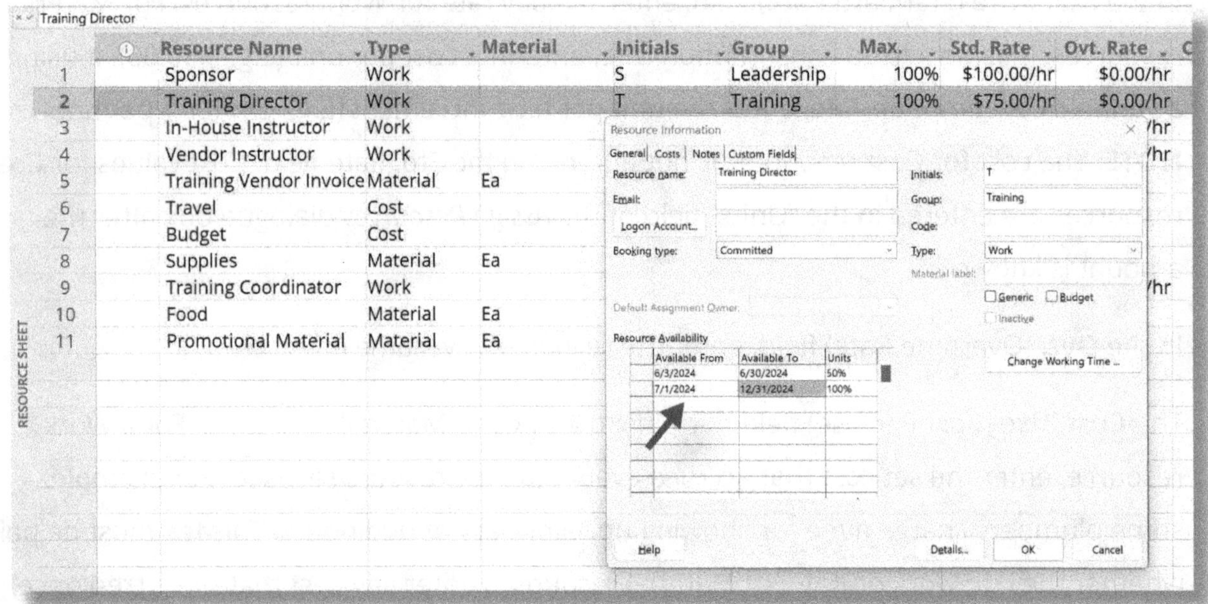

Figure 141 – The Resource Information Dialogue Box

The **General** tab is selected by default. On this tab, you can enter contact information for the resource such as an email address. You can also enter the resource's availability for different times of the year. *Figure 141* above shows that the *Training Director* resource is available at 50% Max Units from 06/01/2024 to 06/30/2024 but is available at 100% Max Units from 7/1/2024 to 12/31/2024.

On the **Costs** tab, you can add additional pay rates for a resource. For example, a resource might be paid one rate for one type of task and another rate for a different type of task. Enter the additional pay rates on tabs B, C, D & E, as needed. A resource's overtime rate can also be entered on this tab.

On the **Notes** tab, you can add any notes about the resource. We will review Resource Notes further in Chapter 10, *"Documenting Your Schedule"*.

The **Custom Fields** tab is where you can access custom fields. Custom fields can be created to store additional information about a resource.

Important Information about Max Units

Max Units vs. Assignment Units

It's important not to confuse **Max Units** with **Units**. *Max. Units* is the maximum capacity a resource is available to work on tasks on any given day. *Units* (or assignment Units) is the percentage of the day resources will work on specific tasks. For example, if a resource is available to work on tasks the entire 8-hour day, their Max Units would be 100%. However, they may work on a specific task for a portion of the day E.g., 2 hours. In this case, the resource's Max Units would be 100% and their Units (or assignment Units) would be 25%. Stated differently, you only need them 2 hours per day, though they're available to you 8 hours per day. Here's a rule of thumb to distinguish Max Units from resource Units. Max Units are entered in the "Max." Field of the Resource Sheet. It tells Project what percentage of an 8-hour day a resource is available to work on tasks. When assigning resources to tasks, resource Units are entered in the "Units" field in the *Assign Resources* dialogue box. It tells Project what percentage of an 8-hour day the assigned resource will work on a specific task.

Generic Resources and Max Units

As mentioned earlier, Work resources can be generic, representing a trade or professional group, such as "Engineers" or "Architects". If 4 engineers are assigned to the project and each is available to work on tasks 8 hours per day (100% Max Units each), then their collective Max Units would be 400%. This means that up to 32 engineering hours are available each day for task work.

Over-Allocated Resources

If a resource's Max Units are exceeded, meaning they're assigned to tasks beyond their capacity, then the resource becomes over-allocated. When this occurs, Project will create an alert of the overallocation with a red man icon in the Indicators field of the Gantt Chart view and with red typeface in resource views, like the Resource sheet view.

Assigning Resources to Tasks

There are several ways to assign resources to tasks. As discussed in Chapter 6, in a Simple schedule, resources can be assigned by entering the resource names directly into the Resource Names field of the Entry table. This will result in resources being assigned to tasks at 100% Units (8 hour per day).

In a Detailed schedule resources can be assigned using the **Assign Resources** command or the **Task Form**.

Assigning Resources using the Assign Resources Command

To assign resources using the Assign Resources command:

- In the Gantt Chart view, in the **Task Name** field of the Entry table, select the task you want to assign the resource(s) to.
- Select the **Resource** tab. In the **Assignments** group, select **Assign Resources** to open the *Assign Resources* dialogue box (*Figure 142*).
    - For a **Work** resource, enter the assignment Units value in the **Units** field, then select **Assign** (or press Enter).
    - For a **Material** resource, enter the quantity in the **Units** field, then select **Assign** (or press Enter).
    - For a **Cost** resource, enter the cost value in the **Cost** field, then press **Enter**.
- Repeat these steps to assign resources to each task. Be sure to first select the task in the Entry table.
- When all resources are assigned, select **CLOSE** to close the *Assign Resources* dialogue box.

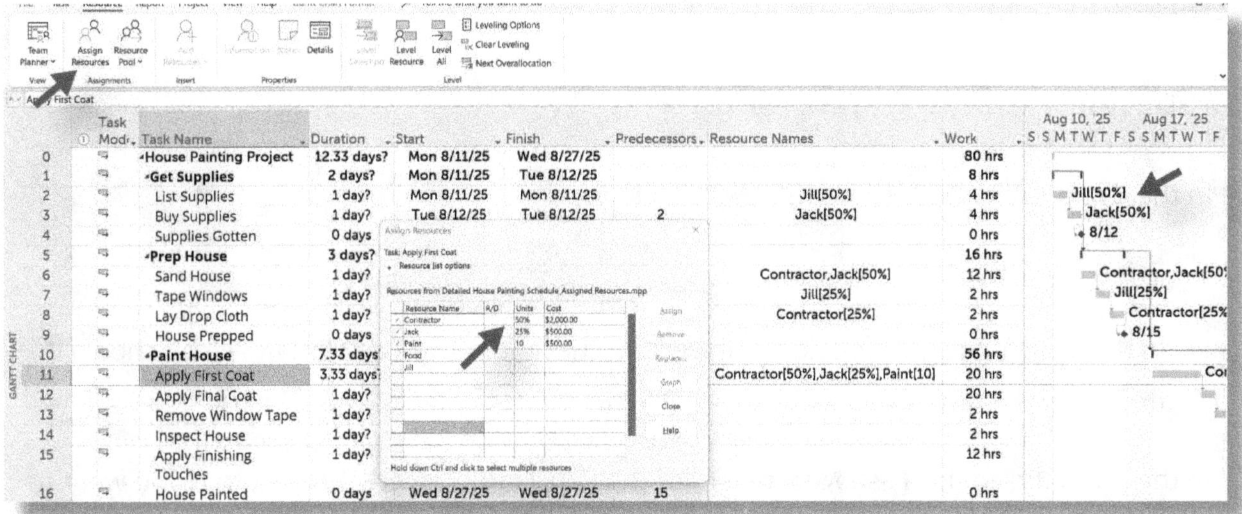

Figure 142 – Assign Resources Dialogue Box

When a resource is assigned to a task, the resource's name and units will populate to the **Resource Names** field of the Entry table. In the Gantt chart, resource names and Units are shown with the task bars. As mentioned earlier, resources are the primary way that cost accrues on a project. When resource pay rates have been added to the Resource Sheet, Project will automatically calculate the task cost as resources are assigned to tasks. The cost for each resource will appear in the *Cost* field of the *Assign Resources* dialogue box. To see the cost for each task in the schedule, the **Cost** field must be added to the table of the current view, using the **Add New Column** field (*Figure 143* below).

	Task Name	Duration	Start	Finish	Predecessors	Resource Names	Work	Cost
0	**House Painting Project**	13.5 days?	Mon 8/11/25	Thu 8/28/25			80 hrs	$11,150.00
1	**Get Supplies**	2 days?	Mon 8/11/25	Tue 8/12/25			8 hrs	$600.00
2	List Supplies	1 day?	Mon 8/11/25	Mon 8/11/25		Jill[50%]	4 hrs	$300.00
3	Buy Supplies	1 day?	Tue 8/12/25	Tue 8/12/25	2	Jack[50%]	4 hrs	$300.00
4	Supplies Gotten	0 days	Tue 8/12/25	Tue 8/12/25	3		0 hrs	$0.00
5	**Prep House**	3 days?	Wed 8/13/25	Fri 8/15/25	1		16 hrs	$1,950.00
6	Sand House	1 day?	Wed 8/13/25	Wed 8/13/25		Contractor,Jack[50%]	12 hrs	$1,500.00
7	Tape Windows	1 day?	Thu 8/14/25	Thu 8/14/25	6	Jill[25%]	2 hrs	$150.00
8	Lay Drop Cloth	1 day?	Fri 8/15/25	Fri 8/15/25	7	Contractor[25%]	2 hrs	$300.00
9	House Prepped	0 days	Fri 8/15/25	Fri 8/15/25	8		0 hrs	$0.00
10	**Paint House**	8.5 days?	Mon 8/18/25	Thu 8/28/25	5		56 hrs	$8,600.00
11	Apply First Coat	2.5 days?	Mon 8/18/25	Wed 8/20/25		Contractor[50%],Jack[50%],Paint[20]	20 hrs	$3,250.00
12	Apply Final Coat	2.5 days?	Wed 8/20/25	Fri 8/22/25	11	Contractor[50%],Jill[50%],Paint[20]	20 hrs	$3,250.00
13	Remove Window Tape	1 day?	Mon 8/25/25	Mon 8/25/25	12	Jack[25%]	2 hrs	$150.00
14	Inspect House	1 day?	Tue 8/26/25	Tue 8/26/25	13	Jack[25%]	2 hrs	$150.00
15	Apply Finishing Touches	1.5 days?	Wed 8/27/25	Thu 8/28/25	14	Contractor	12 hrs	$1,800.00
16	House Painted	0 days	Thu 8/28/25	Thu 8/28/25	15		0 hrs	$0.00

Figure 143 – View Project Cost – Add the Cost Field

Assign Resources using the Task Form

To assign resources using the **Task Form**:

- In the Gantt Chart view, split the view as follows:
    - Select the **View** tab.
    - In the **Split View** group, select the **Details** checkbox. The **Task Form** will be shown in the bottom pane.
- In the top pane, in the **Task Name** field of the Entry table, select the task that you want to assign the resource(s) to.
- In the bottom pane in the **Task Form**, in the **Resource Name** field, select the resource you want to assign from the pick-list (*Figure 144* below).

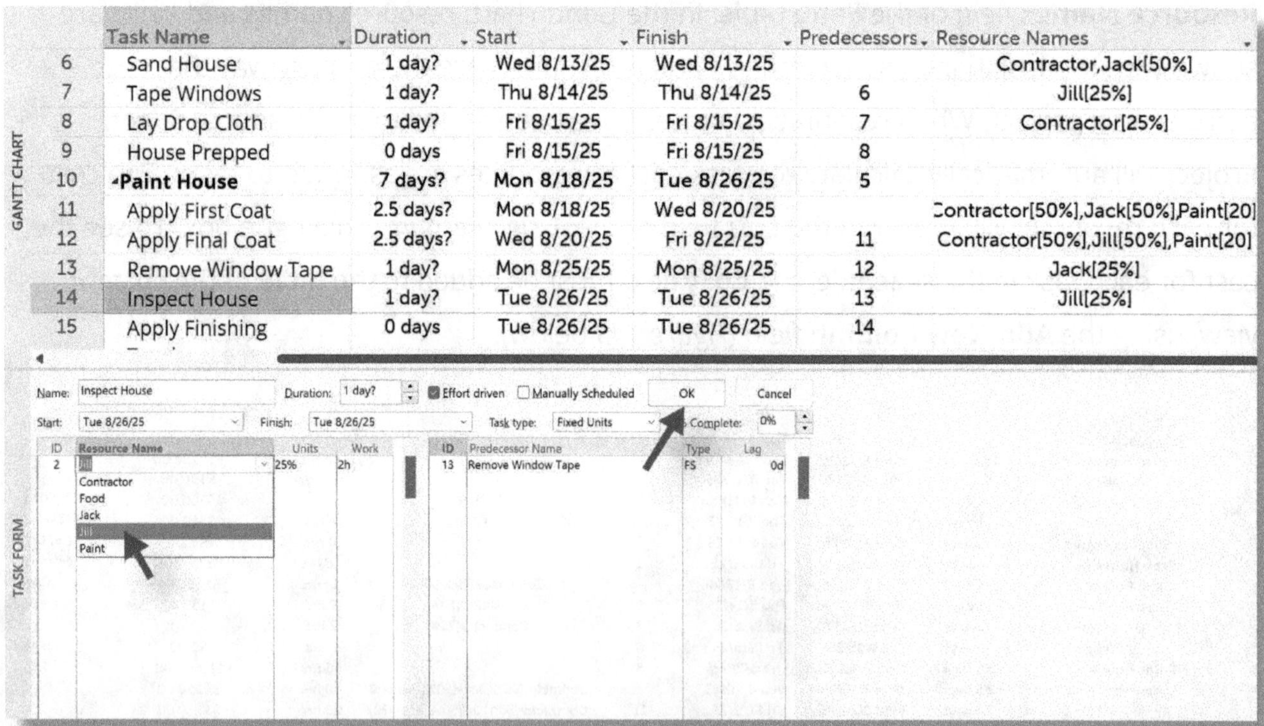

Figure 144 – Assign Resources Using the Task Form

- For a **Work** resource, enter the Units in the **Units** field.
- For a **Material** resource, enter the Units quantity in the **Units** field.
- Select **OK** to assign the resources.

- Repeat these steps to assign resources to each task. Be sure to first select the task in the Entry table in the top pane.
- After all resources are assigned, on the **View** tab, in the **Split View** group, uncheck the **Details** checkbox to unsplit the view and hide the Task Form.

NOTE: Cost resources cannot be assigned using the Task Form. Cost resources must be assigned using the *Assign Resources* dialogue box, where the Cost field is available.

One advantage of assigning resources in the Task Form is that the "Work" field is provided, which means you don't have to add a Work column to the Entry table in the Gantt chart view to enter the work values. You can enter Work directly in the Task Form.

Creating a Combination View

Any active view can be split to create a **combination view** - one view in the top pane and another view in the bottom pane. For example, you can display task information in the top pane and resource information in the bottom pane. When the view is split, the default forms for that view will be shown in the bottom pane. Right-click anywhere in the bottom pane to select any of the built in forms to view additional information for a task or resource.

We have now reviewed resources – the primary way that cost accrues on a project. We've explained the three resource types, how to create resources and add their information to the schedule, and how to assign resources to tasks.

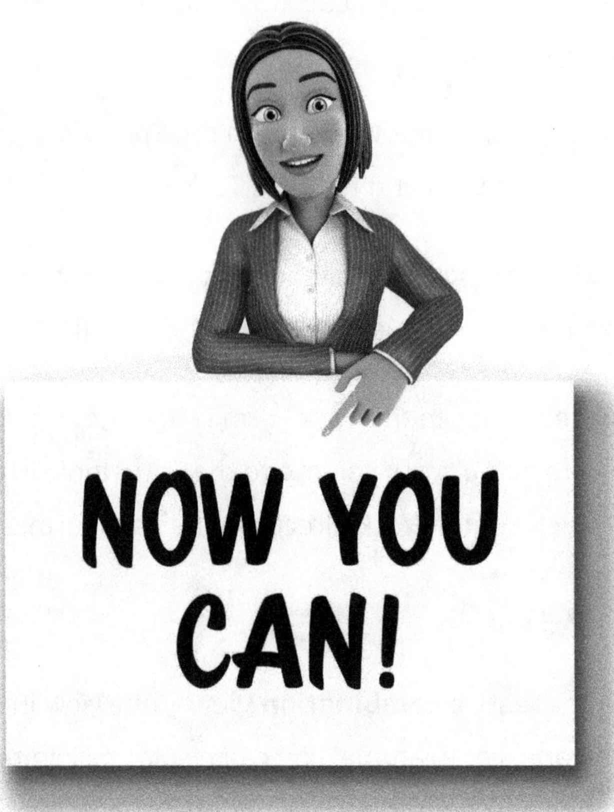

- ✓ Understand the Resource Types
- ✓ Create Resources
- ✓ Add Resource Information to the Schedule
- ✓ Assign Resources to Tasks

Practice Exercise

Build a Detailed Schedule Using the B.A.S.I.C.S.

For this practice exercise, you will build a **Detailed** schedule for the House Painting project using the B.A.S.I.C.S. scheduling process.

Go to **mspbasics.com** for "checkpoint" images to check your work as you go along.

Follow the step-by-step instructions below to complete this Challenge practice exercise.

NOTE: It's important to start this exercise with a blank project. Do not use a saved project file from a previous practice exercise.

Start a New Project

From the opening view, select **Blank Project** to create a new project. You'll be taken to the **Gantt Chart** view.

Breakdown the Project

Step 1, **Breakdown the Project** has already been done and is represented by the upcoming Work Breakdown Structure.

Adjust the Settings and Set the Project Start Date

Adjust the settings to support a **Detailed** schedule:

1. Select the **File** tab to go **Backstage**.
2. Select **Options** from the options on the left, to open the *Project Options* dialogue box.
3. In the *Project Options* dialogue box, select **Schedule** from the menu options on the left to access the schedule settings.
4. Under the *Scheduling options for this project* section, select **Auto Scheduled** from the *New tasks created* pick-list. This will enable Project to calculate the finish date from the task durations and task dependencies.
5. Select **Fixed Units** from the *Default task type* pick-list. This will allow the resource Units to remain fixed if changes are made to the Work or Duration values.
6. <u>Check</u> the **New tasks are effort-driven** checkbox. This will enable the effort-driven scheduling feature. The initial Work values will be fixed, and Project will increase or decrease task Duration as resources are added to or removed from tasks.

CHECKPOINT: To check your results so far, go to **mspbasics.com**

- Select the **CheckPoint Images** tab.
- Select the version of the book you're using.
- Select **Chapter 8**. Then, go to **Checkpoint Image #1**

Set the Project Start Date

Set the project start date as **6/3/24**.

1. Select the **Project** tab. In the **Properties** group, select the **Project Information** command to open the *Project Information* dialogue box.
2. In the **Start date** field, enter **6/3/24**. Click **OK** to close the *Project Information* dialogue box.

CHECKPOINT: To check your results so far, go to **mspbasics.com**

- Select the **CheckPoint Images** tab.
- Select the version of the book you're using.
- Select **Chapter 8**. Then, go to **Checkpoint Image #2**

The **Task List** and **Work Breakdown** Structure for the House Painting project are shown in the following graphic.

Enter the Task List

1. Enter the unstructured task list into the **Task Name** field of the **Entry table**.
2. Enter each of the task names (in the order shown on the task list). The *Get Supplies* task will have task ID 1, the *List Supplies* task will have task ID 2, and so forth.

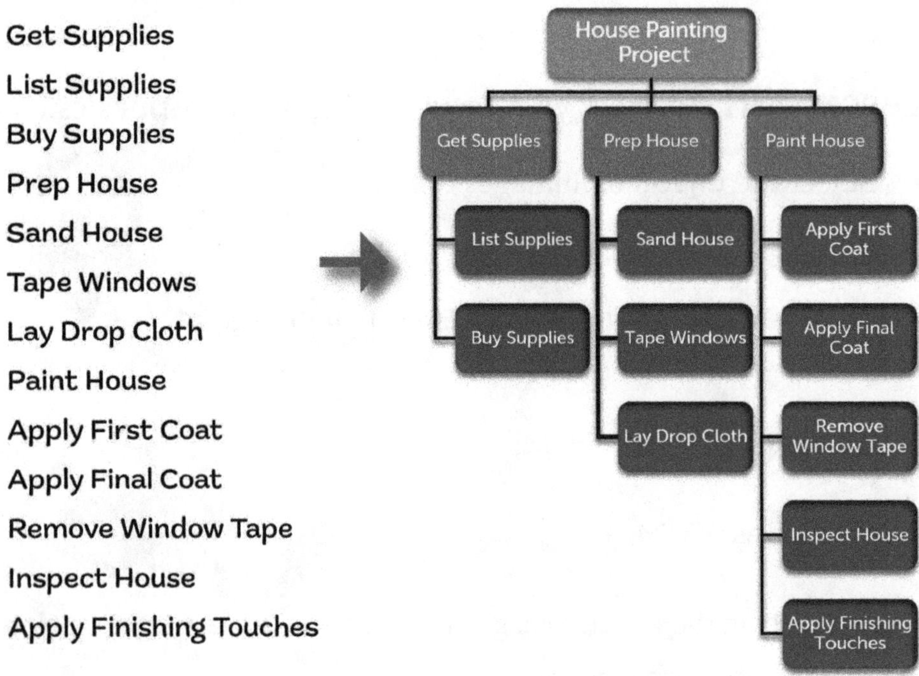

Create Milestones

Create a **Milestone** task to signify the completion of each phase.

1. Select the *Prep House* summary task.

2. On the **Task** tab, in the **Insert** group, select the **Insert Milestone** command. A "New Milestone" task will be inserted as task ID 4 beneath the *Buy Supplies* task and will be given a duration value of zero. Also, a diamond icon will be added to the Gantt chart, indicating the milestone.

3. Type over the default name and rename the milestone **"Supplies Gotten"**.

4. To create the milestone for Phase 2 – Prep House, select the *Paint House* summary task. Then, select the **Insert Milestone** command. A "New Milestone" task will be inserted as task ID 9 beneath the *Lay Drop Cloth* task. Type over the default name and rename the milestone **"House Prepped"**.

5. To create the milestone for Phase 3 – Paint House, in the **Task Name** field, in the cell beneath the *Apply Final Touches* task, enter the task name "**House Painted"**.
The task ID for this task should be 16. It will be given a 1-day duration and a corresponding task bar in the Gantt chart.

6. In the **Duration** field for this task, enter **0** for the duration value. This task will become a milestone. Notice that the task bar in the Gantt chart has been replaced with a diamond icon.

When you're done entering the tasks and milestones you should have **16 tasks**.

CHECKPOINT: To check your results so far, go to **mspbasics.com**

- Select the **CheckPoint Images** tab.
- Select the version of the book you're using.
- Select **Chapter 8**. Then, go to **Checkpoint Image #3**

Structure the Tasks to Create the Schedule Outline

Structure the task list to create the schedule outline. Create summary tasks and subtasks for the three phases of the project.

1. Select the *List Supplies*, *Buy Supplies* and *Supplies Gotten* tasks.

2. Select the **Task** tab. In the **Schedule** group, select the **Indent Task** command. The *Get Supplies* task should now be promoted to a summary task, indicated with bold typeface. The *List Supplies*, *Buy Supplies* and *Supplies Gotten* tasks should be demoted beneath it as subtasks. In the Gantt chart, the blue task bar for the *Get Supplies* task, should be replaced with a black summary bar.

3. Next, select the *Sand House*, *Tape Windows*, *Lay Drop Cloth* and *House Prepped* tasks. Select the **Indent Task** command to promote the *Prep House* task to a summary task and demote these four tasks beneath it as subtasks.

4. Now, select the *Apply First Coat*, *Apply Final Coat*, *Remove Window Tape*, *Inspect House*, *Apply Finishing Touches* and *House Painted* tasks. Use the **Indent Task** command to promote the *Paint House* task to a summary task and demote these six tasks beneath it as subtasks.

The three phases of the House Painting project should now be structured.

CHECKPOINT: To check your results so far, go to **mspbasics.com**

- Select the **CheckPoint Images** tab.
- Select the version of the book you're using.
- Select **Chapter 8.** Then, go to **Checkpoint Image #4**

Display the Project Summary Task

To see the summary values for the project as you build the schedule, display the Project Summary Task.

1. Select the Gantt Chart **Format** tab. In the **Show/Hide** group, select the **Project Summary Task** checkbox.

2. Rename the Project Summary Task **"House Painting Project"**.

Initialize the Task Durations - Enter Work and Assign Resources

Next, you'll **initialize the duration** values by establishing the **Work** and **Units** values. Project will calculate (and initialize) the Durations from the Work and Units values.

Enter the Work Values

To enter the **Work** values, the "Work" column must be added to the Entry table using the **Add New Column** field. If you don't see the "Add New Column" field, you'll need to drag the line that divides the Entry table from the Gantt Chart to the right until you see the "Add New Column" field.

1. Click on the title of the **Add New Column** field. This will display the columns you can add to the table.

2. Enter the word **"Work"** to display the Work column, or scroll down until you see "Work", then select it.

3. In the **Work** column for each task, enter the work values listed in the following table.

4. Do not enter work values for summary tasks. Project will calculate the work values for the summary tasks per their subtasks.

TASK NAME	WORK HOURS
List Supplies	4h
Buy Supplies	4h
Sand House	12h
Tape Windows	2h
Lay Drop Cloth	2h
Apply First Coat	20h
Apply Final Coat	20h
Remove Window Tape	2h
Inspect House	2h
Apply Finishing Touches	12h

After the Work hours are entered for each task, the total work hours for the project (shown for the Project Summary Task) should be **80 hours**.

CHECKPOINT: To check your results so far, go to **mspbasics.com**

- Select the **CheckPoint Images** tab.
- Select the version of the book you're using.
- Select **Chapter 8.** Then, go to **Checkpoint Image #5**

Create Resources

Next, you'll create **Work**, **Material** and **Cost** resources and add their resource information to the schedule. To create the resources, switch to the **Resource Sheet View**.

1. Select the **View** tab. In the **Resource Views** group, select **Resource Sheet**.

2. Enter the resource information listed in the following table into the appropriate fields of the Resource Sheet. Leave the default selections for categories that are not listed.

Resource Name	Type	Material Label	Group	Max. Units	Std. Rate
Jack	Work		Painters	100%	$75
Jill	Work		Painters	100%	$75
Contractor	Work		Contractors	100%	$150
Paint	Material	Gallon	Supplies		$50
Food	Cost		Food		

CHECKPOINT: To check your results so far, go to **mspbasics.com**

- Select the **CheckPoint Images** tab.
- Select the version of the book you're using.
- Select **Chapter 8.** Then, go to **Checkpoint Image #6**

Display the Project Cost

Since resource pay rates have been added to the schedule, when resources are assigned to tasks, Project will automatically calculate the cost for each task and ultimately, the entire schedule.

To view the cost, you'll use the **Add New Column** command to add the "Cost" column to the Entry table.

1. Return to the Gantt Chart view by selecting the **Gantt Chart view** quick access icon, located in the top left corner of the ribbon.

2. In the Entry table, click on the title of the **Add New Column** field. This will display the columns you can add to the table.

3. Enter the word **"Cost"** to display the **Cost** column, or scroll down until you see "Cost", then select it.

Since resources have not been assigned to the tasks, the cost for each task will currently be **$0.00.**

Assign Resources to Tasks

Next, you'll assign resources to the tasks using the **Assign Resources** command. This will establish the **Units** values.

The tasks and resource assignments are listed in the table below.

TASK NAME	RESOURCE(S)	UNITS (Work Resources)	UNITS (Material Resources)	COST
List Supplies	Jill	50%		
Buy Supplies	Jack	50%		
Sand House	Jack	50%		
Tape Windows	Jill	25%		
Lay Drop Cloth	Jack	25%		
Apply First Coat	Contractor Jack Paint	50% 50%	10	
Apply Final Coat	Contractor Jill Paint	50% 50%	10	
Remove Window Tape	Jack	25%		
Inspect House	Jill	25%		
Apply Finishing Touches	Jack Paint Food	75%	2	$500

1. In the **Task Name** field of the **Entry table**, select the task you want to assign the resource(s) to.

2. Select the **Resource** tab. In the **Assignments** group, select **Assign Resources** to open the *Assign Resources* dialogue box.

3. In the *Assign Resources* dialogue box:

   - For a **Work** resource, enter their Units value in the **Units** field of the resource you're assigning, then click **Assign** (or press enter).
   - For a **Material** resource, enter the Units value in the **Units** field of the resource you're assigning, then click **Assign** (or press enter).
   - For a **Cost** resource, enter the cost value in the **Cost** field of the resource you're assigning.

4. Repeat these steps for each task. Be sure to first select the task name in the Entry table, before assigning the resources.

5. When all the resources have been assigned to the tasks, select **Close** to close the *Assign Resources* dialogue box.

After the resources are assigned, their names and Units will populate in the **Resource Names** field. They will also be shown with the respective task bars in the Gantt chart. In the **Cost** field, the cost for each task will be displayed. The total project cost of **$9,100** will be shown in the Cost field for the Project Summary task. Also, the resources will all be over-allocated (indicated by the red man icons in the **Indicators** field). This is because the tasks are not yet connected. The tasks are all being worked on the same day. We'll cover resource over-allocation in Chapter 13, *"Leveling Your Resources"*.

CHECKPOINT: To check your results so far, go to **mspbasics.com**

- Select the **CheckPoint Images** tab.
- Select the version of the book you're using.
- Select **Chapter 8**. Then, go to **Checkpoint Image #7**

The **Work** and **Units** values have now been established, and the task **Durations** are now *Initialized*. Using the Duration Equation, Project calculated the task durations per the Work and Units values.

Notice the tasks with more than one resource assigned. Since the effort-driven feature is enabled, Project left the Work value constant and calculated the Duration by dividing the Work between the collective resources' Units values.

Connect the Tasks: Create Task Relationships

Next, you'll **connect the tasks** and establish dependencies. The tasks in this schedule occur in sequence, so you'll give the tasks in each phase a **Finish-to-Start** task relationship. Each task is the predecessor of the following task.

The tasks and their predecessor task ID numbers are listed in the table below.

1. In the **Predecessors** field of each task, enter the **task ID** number for its predecessor task.

TASK NAME	PREDECESSOR TASK ID
Buy Supplies	2
Supplies Gotten Milestone	3
Sand House	4
Tape Windows	6
Lay Drop Cloth	7
House Prepped Milestone	8
Apply First Coat	9
Apply Final Coat	11
Remove Window Tape	12
Inspect House	13
Apply Finishing Touches	14
House Painted Milestone	15

Apply Lag Time Between Tasks

After the *Apply First Coat* task and the *Apply Final Coat* tasks are finished, the paint must dry for two days. Their respective successor tasks, *Apply Final Cost* and *Remove Window Tape* cannot begin until the paint has dried. To depict this in the schedule, you will add a **2-day lag** to each of these tasks. These tasks are currently scheduled to begin on **6/14/24** and **6/19/24** respectively. The project duration is currently **16 days**.

To add the Lag Time:

1. In the **Predecessors** field for the *Apply Final Coat* task, enter **11FS+2d**.

2. In the **Predecessors** field for the *Remove Window Tape* task, enter **12FS+2d**.

After the lag time is entered, Project will update the start date for the *Apply Final Coat* task to **4/18/24** and the *Remove Window Tape* task to **6/25/24**. All other impacted tasks will be updated and highlighted in blue. The total project duration will be updated to **20 days**. The lag will also be shown in the Gantt chart. Since the task relationships have been established, the resources should no longer over-allocated. Project rescheduled the tasks according to their task relationships. Each task now starts after its predecessor finishes. Project also calculated the project finish date as **6/28/24**.

CHECKPOINT: To check your results so far, go to **mspbasics.com**

- Select the **CheckPoint Images** tab.
- Select the version of the book you're using.
- Select **Chapter 8**. Then, go to **Checkpoint Image #8**

You have now built a **Detailed** schedule using the first 5 steps of the B.A.S.I.C.S. scheduling process. We'll review the last step, "Start the Project", in Chapter 15 *"Executing your Schedule"*.

You will use this file to complete the **Chapter 16** practice exercise.

"I'm on
Vacation
New Week"

Chapter 9 Adding Calendars To Your Schedule

In the last chapter, you learned to add resources to the schedule. In this chapter, you'll learn to add **Calendars** to the schedule and observe how they affect the scheduling of tasks.
You'll learn about the Project Calendar and how to tailor it to suit your project. You'll learn to use Resource and Task calendars to create schedule exceptions for things like vacation days and special work hours. You'll also learn how Project handles competing calendars, and how to use the Elapsed Duration designation.

You'll Learn To:

- Explain the Microsoft Project Work Week
- Use Base Calendars
- Use The Project Calendar
- Apply Resource Calendars
- Apply Task Calendars
- Explain Calendar Precedence
- Use Elapsed Duration or Work

Understanding the Microsoft Project Work Week

By default, Project only schedules work during business days. Business days are referred to as "working times" in Project. Non-business days are referred to as "non-working times". The default work week in Project is Monday through Friday, from 8:00 am to 5:00 pm, with a 1-hour lunch break from 12:00 pm to 1:00 pm. A "week" in Project is 5 business days. For example, if you enter a 1-week task duration (1w), this equates to 5 business days (and not 7 business days). Entering a 5-day duration (5d) will yield the same result as entering 1w. A "month" in Project equates to 4 weeks, or 20 business days.

Since Project only schedules work during business hours, it's important to distinguish between calendar days and business days. Calendar days include weekends, whereas business days do not. In Project, task duration always refers to business days. For example, if a task with a 5-day duration begins on Thursday, its duration will span 7 calendar days, but task work will only be scheduled across 5 business days (Thursday, Friday, Monday, Tuesday, and Wednesday).

Understanding Calendars

In Microsoft Project, **Calendars** are used to define working and non-working times for tasks and resources. There are four calendar types n Microsoft Project – Base calendars, Project calendars, Task calendars and Resource calendars.

Base Calendars

Base Calendars specify the work hours for each day, the workdays for each week, and any exceptions, such as holidays. They serve as a "base" for the other three calendar types. They can be used as templates that can be modified to reflect the appropriate working times for projects, resources, and tasks. Base calendars are like base models of cars. They include the basic features that will meet the minimum needs of most drivers. Similarly, Project includes Base calendars that will likely meet the needs of most schedulers. The purpose of base calendars is to provide schedulers a "turn-key" experience, in which they will not need to create a custom calendar to reflect the operating hours of their business.

There are three Base calendar options in Project:

- **Standard** (default) – Monday thru Friday; 8:00 am – 5:00 pm (1-hour lunch break from 12:00 pm to 1:00 pm)
- **Night Shift** – Monday night thru Saturday morning; 11:00 pm – 8:00 am (1-hour lunch break from 3:00 am to 4:00 am)
- **24-Hours** – No defined working times; Runs continuously

The Project Calendar

The **Project Calendar** defines the working and non-working times for the entire project. When you build your schedule, you'll need to select one of the three Base calendars as your Project calendar. Tasks will then be scheduled per the days and hours of your Project calendar. Microsoft Project uses the *Standard* Base calendar by default. It was created to work for most projects. However, if none of the Base calendar options work for your operating hours, you can create a custom calendar. We'll demonstrate how to do this later in the chapter.

To select a Base Calendar for the Project Calendar:

- Select the **Project** tab. In the **Properties** group, select **Project Information** to open the *Project Information* dialogue box (*Figure145* below).
- From the **Calendar** pick-list, select the Base calendar you want as the Project calendar.
- Select **OK** to close the *Project Information* dialogue box.

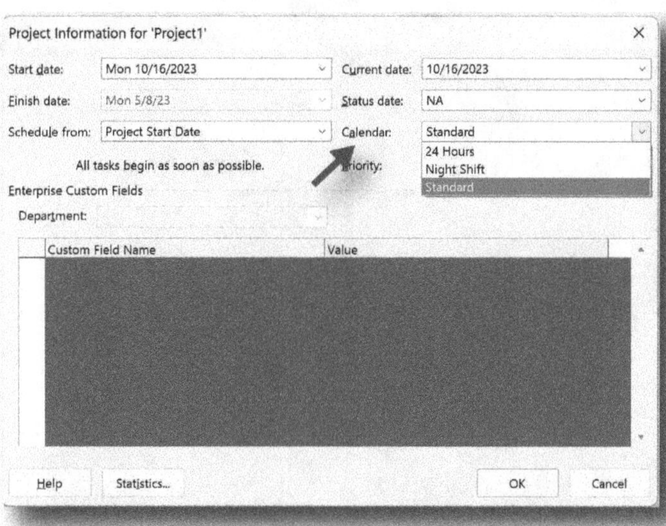

Figure 145 – Set the Project Calendar

Creating Exceptions to the Project Calendar

As your project progresses, you will invariably need to account for times when work will not occur. For example, work may not occur during a company-wide event or during a national holiday. Such times are considered exceptions to the Project calendar or non-working times in Project. You can create such exceptions using the **Change Working Time** command.

To create an exception to the Project calendar for non-working time:

- Select the **Project** tab. In the **Properties** group, select **Change Working Time** to open the *Change Working Time* dialogue box (*Figure 146* below).
- In the **For calendar** field, confirm **Standard** (**Project calendar)** is selected. This will ensure the scheduling exception(s) apply to the entire project.
- Select the **Exceptions** tab.
- In the **Name** field, enter the title for the exception (E.g., "Training" or "Holiday").
- In the **Start** field, enter the start date of the non-working time.
- In the **Finish** field, enter the finish date of the non-working time.
- Select **OK** to close the *Change Working Time* dialogue box.

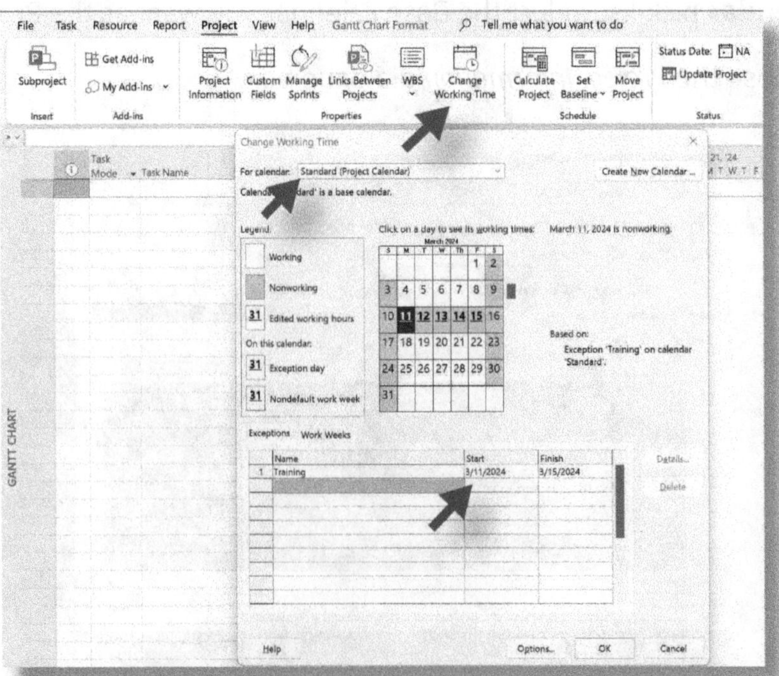

Figure 146 – Set Exceptions for the Project Calendar

Resource Calendars

Resource Calendars create exceptions for Work resources. They can be used to schedule non-working days for a resource, such as vacation time or to create special work schedules. If the resource assigned to a task is on vacation and a Resource calendar has been created for the vacation time, Project will automatically schedule their work around their vacation time.

To create a Resource calendar for non-working times:

- Select the **Project** tab. In the **Properties** group, select **Change Working Time** to open the *Change Working Time* dialog box (*Figure 147* below).
- In the **For calendar** field, select the resource from the pick-list. The scheduling exception(s) will apply only to the selected resource and not the entire project.
- Select the **Exceptions** tab.
- In the **Name** field, enter the title for the exception (E.g., "Vacation").
- In the **Start** field, enter the start date of the non-working time.
- In the **Finish** field, enter the finish date of the non-working time.
- Select **OK** to close the *Change Working Time* dialogue box.

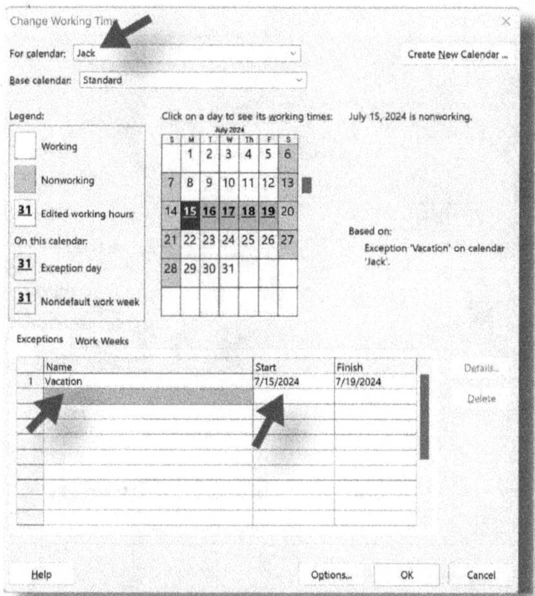

Figure 147 – Create a Resource Calendar for Non-Working Days

Resource calendars can also be used to create a special work schedule for a resource. For example, a resource may work a "4/10" work schedule, where they work four 10-hour days from Monday through Thursday and never work on Fridays.

To create a Resource calendar for a special work schedule:

- Select the **Project** tab. In the **Properties** group, select **Change Working Time** to open the *Change Working Time* dialog box (*Figure 148* below).
- In the **For calendar** field, select the resource from the pick-list. The scheduling exception(s) will apply only to the selected resource and not the entire project.
- Select the **Work Weeks** tab.
- In the **Name** field, select the **[Default]** cell. Then select **Details** to open the *Details dialogue box.*
- In the *Details* dialogue box, under the **Select day(s)** section, press and hold the Ctrl key while selecting the resource's non-working day(s).
- Then, select the **Set day(s) to nonworking times** option.
- Select **OK** to close the *Details* dialog box.
- Select **OK** again to close the *Change Working Time* dialog box.

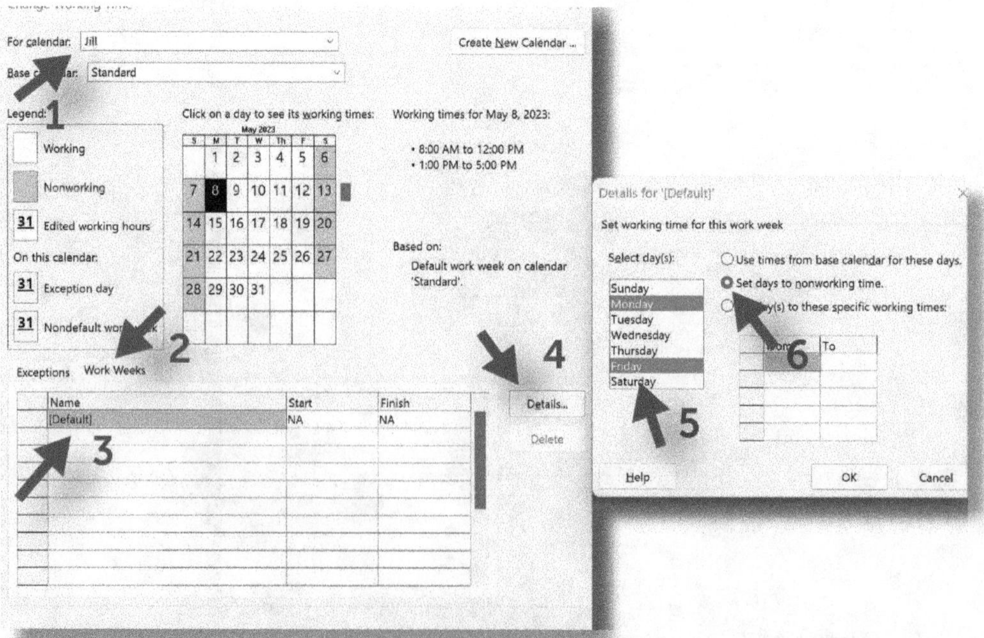

Figure 148 – Create a Resource Calendar for Special Work Weeks

NOTE: If a resource is working a 4/10 schedule and you are building a Detailed schedule, be sure to set their Max. Units to 120% (10 hours per day max) instead of 100% (8 hours per day max). This is done in the Resource Sheet view. This will increase their maximum working limit so that they do not become over-allocated after 8 hours. We will cover the Max. Units feature and resource leveling in Chapter 13.

Task Calendars

Task Calendars set exceptions for tasks. If work on a task needs to occur outside of normal business hours, you can use a Task calendar to create the exception. For example, if your Project calendar is the *Standard* calendar and work needs to occur on the weekend, you can use a Task calendar to schedule the weekend work. Any resources assigned to the task will be scheduled to work through the weekend. Task calendars are created by applying a Base calendar to a task. You can choose one of the three Base calendars in Project (Standard, 24-Hours, Nightshift) or you can create a custom Base calendar.

To create a Task calendar:

STEP 1 – Create a custom Base calendar *(Figure 149)*:

- Select the **Project** tab.
- In the **Properties** group, select **Change Working Time** to open the *Change Working Time* dialog box.
- Select **Create New Calendar** to open the *Create New Base Calendar* dialogue box.
- In the *Create New Base Calendar* dialogue box, in the **Name** field, enter a name for the new Base calendar.
- If you want to create the Base calendar from scratch, select the **Create new base calendar** option. If the working times you want are similar to those in an existing Base calendar, select the **Make a copy of** option, then select the Base calendar you want to copy from the pick-list in the **calendar** field.
- Select **OK** to close the *Create New Base Calendar* dialogue box. DO NOT CLOSE the *Change Working Time* dialogue box.

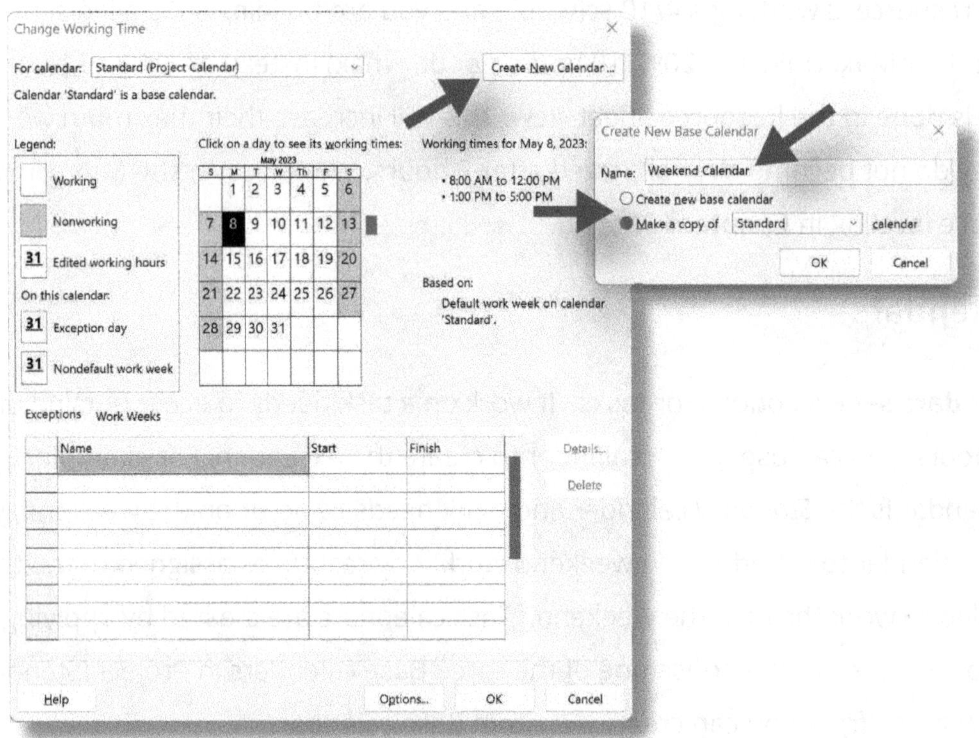

Figure 149 – Create a New Base Calendar

STEP 2 – **Enter the working times for the new Base calendar** (*Figure 150*):

- In the *Change Working Time* dialogue box, select the **Work Weeks** tab.
- In the **Name** field, select the **[Default]** cell and then select **Details** to open the *Details* dialogue box.
- In the **Select day(s)** field, press and hold the Ctrl key while selecting the working days for the new Base calendar.
- Select the **Set days to these specific working times** option.
- Then Select **OK** to close the *Details* dialogue box.
- Select **OK** again to close the *Change Working Time* dialogue box. The new Base Calendar will now appear in the **Calendar** pick-list among the Base Calendar options.

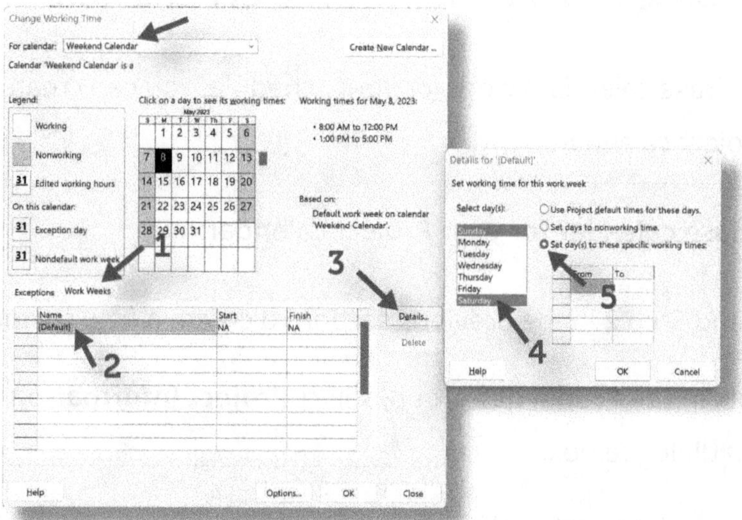

Figure 150 – Enter Working Times for a New Base Calendar

STEP 3 – **Apply the custom Base calendar to the task as a Task Calendar:**

- In the Gantt Chart view, double-click the task you want to add the Task calendar to, to open the *Task Information* dialogue box.
- Select the **Advanced** tab.
- From the **Calendar** pick-list, select the new Base calendar (*Figure 151* below).
- Select **OK** to close the *Task Information* dialogue box. In the **Indicators** field, Project will generate an indicator denoting that the task has a Task calendar. Hover over the icon to see the name of the Task calendar.

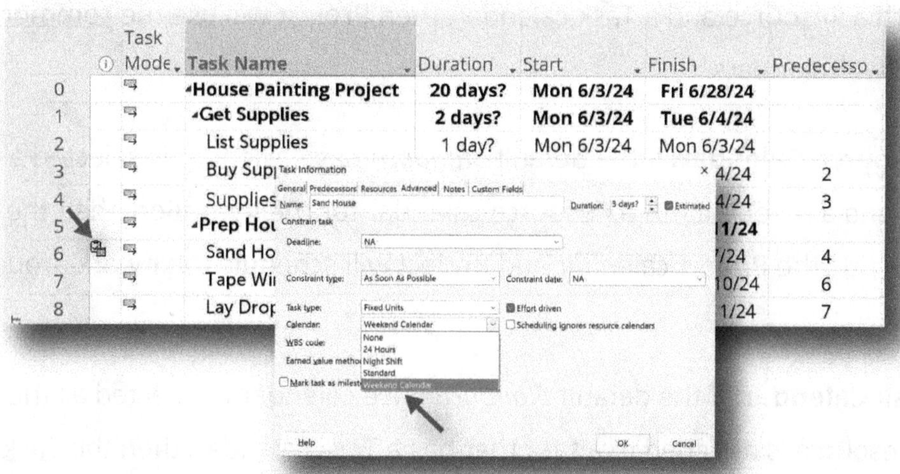

Figure 151 – Add a Task Calendar to a Task

Create a Custom Base Calendar for the Project Calendar

If none of the existing Base calendars work for your schedule, you can create a **custom Base calendar** for your Project calendar.

To create a custom Base calendar for your Project calendar:

- Complete Step 1 and Step 2 in the previous section to create a new custom Base calendar.
- On the **Project** tab, in the **Properties** group, select **Project Information** to open the *Project Information* dialogue box.
- From the **Calendar** pick-list, select the new custom Base calendar as the Project calendar.
- Select **OK** to close the *Project Information* dialogue box.

Calendar Precedence

Since a project schedule can contain several calendars, there are rules of precedence that govern how Project schedules tasks.

Here's the pecking order:

- If there is no Task or Resource calendar, then the Project calendar rules the day.
- If there is either a Resource or a Task calendar, then it is the boss.
- If there is both a Resource and a Task calendar, then Project will use the common hours between the two calendars.

Example 1 – Resource Calendar: If the default *Standard* base calendar is selected as the Project calendar and a resource has a Resource calendar for their vacation, then the Resource Calendar will override the Project calendar and Project will schedule their work around their vacation.

Example 2 – Task Calendar: If the default *Standard* Base calendar is selected as the Project calendar and a resource is assigned to a task that has a Task calendar, then the Task Calendar will override the Project calendar and Project will schedule the resource to work according to the Task calendar.

Example 3 - Task Calendar and Resource Calendar: If a resource has a Resource calendar and they are assigned to a task which has a Task calendar, Project will schedule the resource to work during the hours that are common to both the Task and Resource calendars. For example, the Task calendar hours are 8am to 5pm and the Resource Calendar hours are 6am to 2pm. In this case, the common hours are 8am to 2pm. Project will schedule the resource to work during those common hours only.

Elapsed Duration/Work

If you're using the *Standard* Project calendar and you need Project to schedule a task through the weekend, you can use the **Elapsed Duration** or **Elapsed Work** designation. Elapsed duration and work designations cause Project to schedule work during the non-working times specified in the Project calendar. For example, if a 4-hour task begins on Friday at 4:00 pm, Project will schedule the task for 1 hour on Friday (4:00 pm - 5:00 pm) and 3 hours on the next working day (Monday, 8:00 am - 11:00 am). By contrast, if you used the elapsed duration designation by entering the duration as **4eh** instead of **4h**, then Project will schedule the task for 1 hour on Friday and 3 hours on the following day (Saturday, 8:00 am - 11:00 am). You can use the elapsed designation in either the **Duration** or **Work** fields.

The elapsed entries allowed in Project include:

- 1emo (1 elapsed month)
- 1ew (1 elapsed week)
- 1ed (1 elapsed day)
- 1eh (1 elapsed hour)
- 1emin (1 elapsed minute)

We've now reviewed calendars and how they affect the way Project schedules tasks. We've explained Base calendars, the Project calendar, Task and Resource calendars and the Elapsed Duration/Work designation.

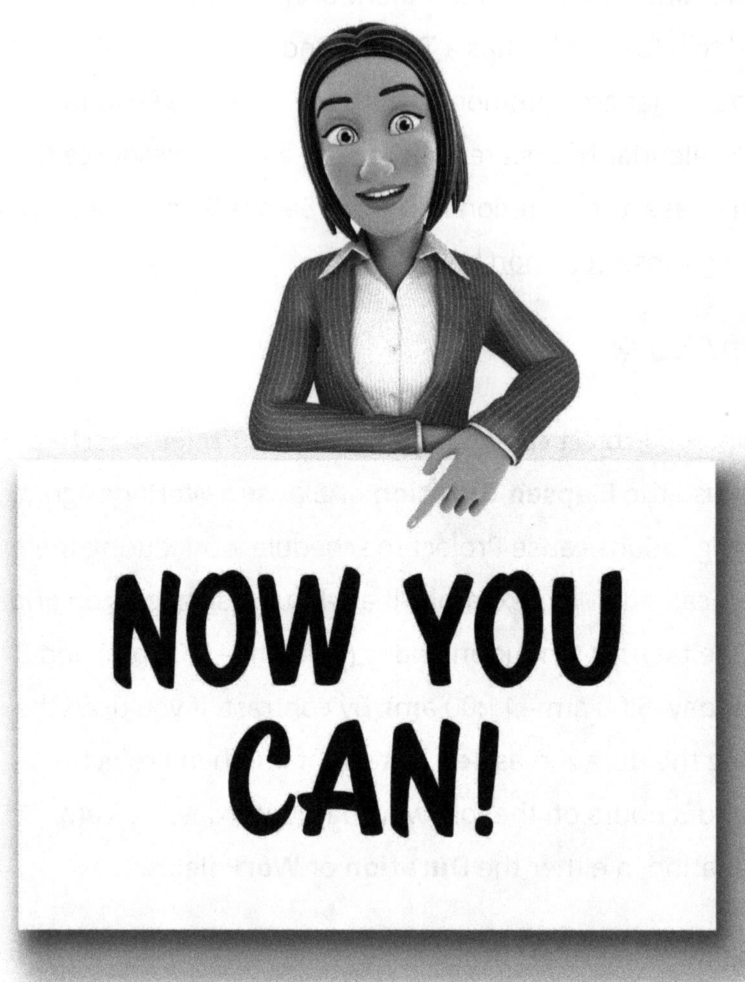

- ✓ Explain the Microsoft Project Work Week
- ✓ Explain Base Calendars
- ✓ Explain the Project Calendar
- ✓ Create a Resource Calendar
- ✓ Create a Task Calendar
- ✓ Explain Calendar Precedence
- ✓ Use Elapsed Duration

Practice Exercise

Work with Calendars

For this practice exercise, you'll work with **calendars**. You'll work with the Project calendar, a Resource calendar and a Task calendar to observe how they function in a schedule. You'll also become familiar with the built-in project templates included with Project.

Go to **mspbasics.com** for "checkpoint" images to check your work as you go along.

Follow the steps below to complete this practice exercise.

Start a Project from a Template

You will use the *Software Development Plan* project template to complete this exercise.

NOTE: The templates are hosted on a companion website. You'll need to be connected to the Internet to access them.

1. From the opening view, select the **New** tab, from the options on the left.
2. Double-click the *Software Development Plan* project template. If you don't see this template among the options, select **Show more** to see more templates. You can also use the search box.

When the project plan opens, the view will be split. A custom report will be in the top pane and the Gantt Chart view will be in the bottom pane.

1. **Unsplit the view** by selecting the **View** tab. Then, in the **Split View** group, uncheck the **Details** checkbox. The custom report will become the current view.
2. **Switch to the Gantt Chart view** by selecting the **Gantt Chart** quick access command in the left corner of the ribbon.

In the Entry table, the project plan will be collapsed, displaying only the Level 1 tasks in the outline. Expand the outline using the **Show Outline** feature as follows:

1. On the **View** tab, in the **Data** group, select the **Outline** command. Then, select **All Subtasks** from the pick-list.

Set the Project Start Date and the Project Calendar

Next, you'll set the project start date as **January 6, 2025**.

1. Select the **Project** tab. In the **Properties** group, select the **Project Information** command to open the *Project Information* dialogue box.
2. Enter **1/6/25** into the **Start date** field. DO NOT CLOSE the *Project Information* dialogue box.

3. In the **Calendar** field, confirm that *Standard* is selected. This sets the *Standard* Base calendar as the Project calendar. As such, the working days for this project will be Monday through Friday, from 8:00 am to 5:00 pm (with a 1-hour lunch break from 12:00 pm to 1:00 pm).

4. Select **OK** to close the *Project Information* dialogue box.

CHECKPOINT: To check your results so far, go to **mspbasics.com**

- Select the **CheckPoint Images** tab.
- Select the version of the book you're using.
- Select **Chapter 9**. Then, go to **Checkpoint Image #1**

Create Exceptions for the Project Calendar: Establish Non-Working Days

Your company is conducting a training event from 2/10/25 to 2/14/25. You'll establish these days as non-working days on the Project calendar and observe their impact on the schedule. Notice in the *Finish* field of the Project Summary Task, that the project is currently scheduled to finish on **5/19/25**.

To establish the non-working days:

1. Select the **Project** tab. In the **Properties** group, select the **Change Working Time** command to open the *Change Working Time* dialogue box.

2. In the **For calendar** field, confirm that *Standard (Project Calendar)* is selected. This will establish the non-working days for the Project Calendar and the entire project.

3. Confirm the **Exceptions** tab is selected.

4. In the **Name** field, enter **Training** for the title of the event.

5. In the **Start** field, enter **2/10/25**.

6. In the **Finish** field, enter **2/14/25**.

7. Select **OK** to close the *Change Working Time* dialogue box.

After the non-working days have been established, Project will update the schedule to reflect these days as non-working days. Project will reschedule the tasks that were scheduled during the training week. The new start and finish dates for the impacted tasks will be highlighted in blue. The project finish date will also be updated to **5/26/25**. In the Gantt Chart, the non-working days will be shaded with vertical gray bars, along with the weekend days.

CHECKPOINT: To check your results so far, go to **mspbasics.com**

- Select the **CheckPoint Images** tab.
- Select the version of the book you're using.
- Select **Chapter 9** Then, go to **Checkpoint Image #2**

Create Exceptions for Resources: Create a Resource Calendar for Non-Working Days

The *Analyst* resource will be on vacation from 1/13/25 to 1/17/25. Currently, this resource is scheduled to work on Task 8 *Conduct Needs Analysis* and Task 9 *Draft preliminary software specifications* during this time-frame. **NOTE:** To see the resource assignments, you may need to slide the right side of the screen to the right to see the **Resource Names** field.

To incorporate the vacation time into the schedule, you'll create a **Resource calendar** for the *Analyst* resource.

To create a Resource Calendar for Non-Working Days:

1. On the **Project** tab, in the **Properties** group, select the **Change Working Time** command to re-open the *Change Working Time* dialogue box.

2. In the **For calendar** field, select **Analyst** from the pick-list. This will establish the exceptions for the Analyst resource's calendar and not the Project calendar.

   NOTE: It's important to select the right calendar because if another resource is assigned to do the work while the Analyst resource is on vacation, Project will schedule the work during this period. If the Project calendar is selected, no work would be scheduled, even if another resource is assigned to the task.

3. Confirm the **Exceptions** tab is selected.

4. In the **Name** field, enter **"Vacation"** as the title for the event.

5. In the **Start** field, enter **1/13/25**.

6. In the **Finish** field, enter **1/17/25**.

7. Select **OK** to close the *Change Working Time* dialogue box.

CHECKPOINT: To check your results so far, go to **mspbasics.com**

- Select the **CheckPoint Images** tab.
- Select the version of the book you're using.
- Select **Chapter 9** Then, go to **Checkpoint Image #3**

After the non-working days are established, Project will update the schedule accordingly. The work for the tasks that the *Analyst* is assigned to will be rescheduled around the vacation time. For example, the *Analyst* will start task 8 *Conduct needs analysis* on 1/9/25. Since this task has a 5-day duration, it was originally scheduled to finish 5 working days later, on 1/16/25. After the Resource calendar was created, Project updated the finish date to 1/23/25. The *Analyst* will work on the task on Thursday, 1/9/25 and Friday, 1/10/25. Since the next working day is Monday, 1/13/25, when the resource starts their vacation, Project rescheduled day 3 of the work to resume after the resource returns to work on 1/20/25. Project also updated the project finish date to **6/2/25** and rescheduled all other impacted tasks, which are highlighted in blue.

Create Exceptions for a Resource: Create a Resource Calendar for a Special Work Schedule

The *Developer* resource works a Monday through Thursday schedule. She doesn't work on Fridays. To reflect this in the schedule, you'll create a **Resource Calendar** for this resource to incorporate the special work schedule.

1. On the **Project** tab, in the **Properties** group, select the **Change Working Time** command to re-open the *Change Working Time* dialogue box.

2. In the **For calendar** field, select the **Developer** resource from the pick-list.

3. Select the **Work Weeks** tab.

4. In the **Name** field, select the **[Default]** cell. Then, select **Details** to open the *Details* dialogue box.

5. In the **Select day(s)** field, select **Friday**. Then, **select the set days to non-working time** option.

6. Select **OK** to close the *Details* dialog box. Notice in the *Change Working Time* dialog box that Fridays are now grayed out in the *Developer's* Resource calendar.

7. Select **OK** again, to close the *Change Working Time* dialog box.

CHECKPOINT: To check your results so far, go to **mspbasics.com**

- Select the **CheckPoint Images** tab.
- Select the version of the book you're using.
- Select **Chapter 9** Then, go to **Checkpoint Image #4**

As indicated by the fields highlighted in blue, Project rescheduled all tasks affected by the *Developer's* special work schedule – namely tasks previously scheduled on Fridays. The schedule updates begin with task 28 *Assign Development Staff*. This task was originally scheduled to begin on Friday 3/7/25, the next working day after its predecessor task 27 finishes. Because the *Developer* doesn't work on Fridays, Project rescheduled the task to start on Monday, 3/10/25. The project finish date has also been updated to 6/12/25.

Create a Task Calendar

Recall that the *Standard* Base calendar is set as the Project calendar. The work week for this project is Monday through Friday, from 8:00 am to 5:00 pm. To expedite the schedule, work for task 43 *Test module integration* needs to occur on the weekends, around the clock. To create this exception in the schedule, you'll create a **Task calendar** for task 43 by applying the *24 Hours* Base calendar to the task.

To create a Task Calendar:

1. Double-click the task name of task 43 *Test module integration* to open the *Task Information* dialogue box.

2. Select the **Advanced** tab.

3. Select **24 Hours** from the **Calendar** pick-list. This will select the *24 Hours* Base calendar as the calendar.

4. Check the **Scheduling ignores resource calendars** checkbox. This will cause Project to ignore any Resource calendars and use the Task calendar when scheduling.

5. Before you save the selections, notice in the Entry table that this task is scheduled to start on Thursday, **5/6/25** and finish on the following Tuesday, **5/13/25**.

6. Select **OK** to close the *Task Information* dialogue box.

In the **Indicators** field for task 43 *Test module integration*, Project added an icon indicating the Task calendar. The finish date for this task should be updated to **5/8/25**. This task is scheduled to be worked continuously for its 5-day duration, from 5/6/25 through 5/8/25. The project finish date was updated from 6/12/25 to **6/9/25**.

CHECKPOINT: To check your results so far, go to **mspbasics.com**

- Select the **CheckPoint Images** tab.
- Select the version of the book you're using.
- Select **Chapter 9** Then, go to **Checkpoint Image #5**

View Scheduled Work in the Task Usage View

Next, you'll switch to the **Task Usage View** to see the how Project scheduled the work for task 43, as a result of the Task calendar.

1. Select the **View** tab.

2. In the **Task Views** group, select the **Task Usage** icon to switch to the *Task Usage* view.

In the *Task Usage* view, tasks, their start and finish dates, total work hours and the resources assigned to them are shown in the *Usage* table on the left. The scheduled work hours for each task are shown on the right.

1. Scroll down to task 43 *Test module integration*. In the *Usage* table on the left, in the Work field, you can see that this task has 40 hours of work.

To see how Project scheduled the work for this task, you'll use the **Scroll to Task** command to bring the work values for this task into the view on the right.

1. In the *Usage* table on the left, select the *Test Module Integration* task name.

2. Select the **Task** tab. In the **Editing** group, select the **Scroll to Task** command.
   On the right, you can see how Project scheduled the 40 hours of work for this task. 9 hours of work were scheduled on Tuesday, 5/6/25, 24 hours of work on Wednesday, 5/7/25, and 7 hours of work on Thursday, 5/8/25.

3. Return to the Gantt Chart view by selecting the **Gantt Chart View** quick access icon in the top left corner of the ribbon.

CHECKPOINT: To check your results so far, go to **mspbasics.com**

- Select the **CheckPoint Images** tab.
- Select the version of the book you're using.
- Select **Chapter 9** Then, go to **Checkpoint Image #6**

You've now worked with calendars and observed how they affect the way tasks are scheduled. You've worked with the Project calendar, Resource and Tasks calendars.

SAVE THIS PROJECT FILE.

You will use this file to complete the Chapter 10 practice exercise.

Chapter 10 Documenting Your Schedule

In the last chapter, you learned to add calendars to the schedule. In this chapter, you'll learn to **document your schedule**. When you're done, you'll be able to use notes, hyperlinks and files to embed useful information about tasks and resources directly into your schedule.

You'll Learn:

- Reasons to Document the Schedule
- To Enter Document Properties
- To Add Notes to Tasks and Resources
- To Add Hyperlinks to Tasks and Resources
- To Add Files to Tasks and Resources

Why Document Your Schedule?

Project includes many useful features that allow you to add important notes and reference material to your schedule. These features will come in handy during the execution and closing phases of your project.

Here are some reasons to document your schedule:

- To establish authorship
- To document project issues
- To document agreements
- To document resource commitments
- To document risks
- To explain delays and cost overruns
- To document initial assumptions
- To capture lessons learned

Entering Document Properties

When you create a schedule, you may want to include useful information about the project within the file. Such information can be added to the **Document Properties**. Document Properties (also known as document meta-data) are details about a file that describe or identify it. For example, authorship can be established and then displayed in headers and footers. Document properties are entered Backstage using the *Advanced Properties* dialogue box.

To enter document properties:

- Select the **File** tab to go **Backstage**. Then, select **Info** from the tabs on the left (*Figure 152*). On the right side of the view, you'll find links to copy the file's path and local path, Manage Project Web App accounts and manage items between the project file and the Global Template. Under the *Project Information* section, you'll find project data that Project automatically records, such as the project start and finish dates, and the selected Project calendar.

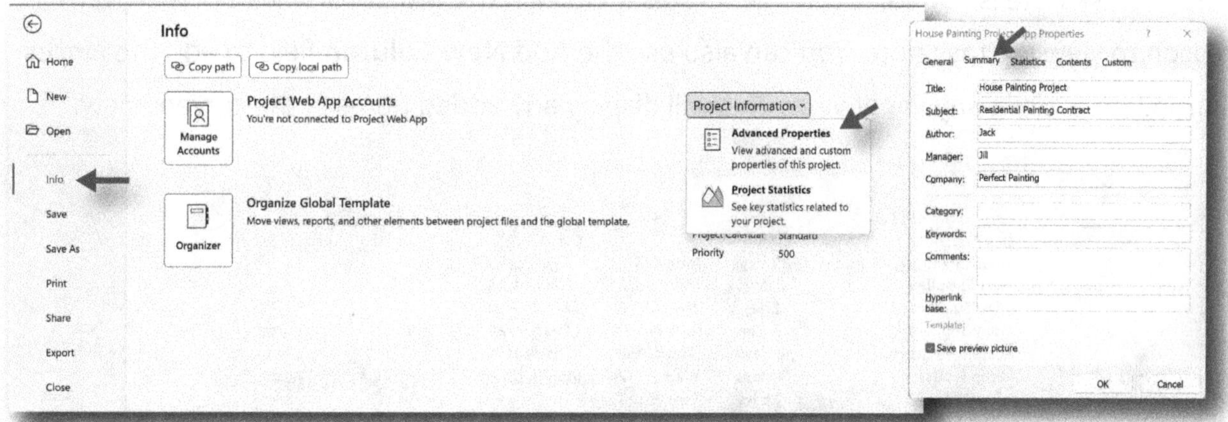

Figure 152 – Enter Document Properties

- Using the **Project Information** pick-list, select **Advanced Properties** to open the *Advanced Properties* dialogue box.

- Confirm the **Summary** tab is selected.

- Enter the project information you want to record into the appropriate fields.
  The *Author* field is where you establish ownership of the file. You can also record other information about the project, like the subject, company and any keywords or comments you'd like to include. Check the "save a preview of file" checkbox to save a thumbnail image of the file. When the file is saved, you'll have the option to add the document properties in the header and footer of documents, such as reports.

- Select **OK** to close the *Advance Properties* dialogue box.

Adding Task Notes

Task Notes are an excellent way to document additional information about the tasks in your project. Task notes are created in the *Task Information* dialogue box.

To create a Task Note:

- Double-click the task name to open the *Task Information* dialogue box (*Figure 153*).

- Select the **Notes** tab. Type the note into the Notes field.

- Select **OK** to close the *Task Information* dialogue box.

After the task note is added, Project generates an icon in the **Indicators** field. Hover over the icon to view the task note. You can also use the **Add New Column** field to add the **Notes** column to a table in any sheet view. This will display any added notes in the current view.

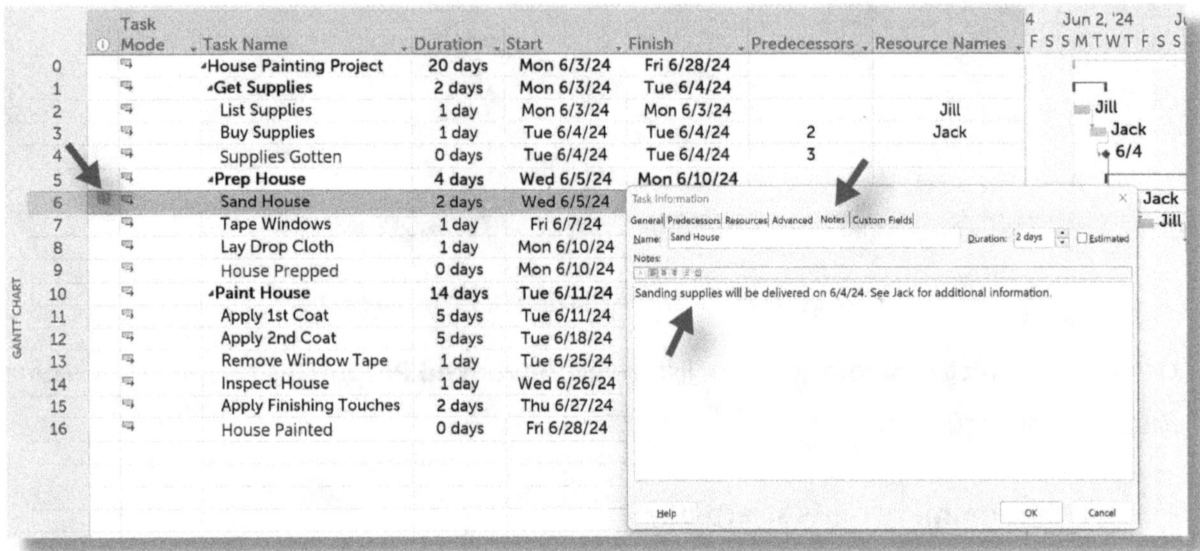

Figure 153 – Adding Task Notes

Adding Hyperlinks to Tasks

Hyperlinks can be added to tasks to access a website or a file directly from a task. This is a handy way to link relevant information about a task to the schedule. For example, a resource assigned to the task may post important information on a *SharePoint* site. Using a hyperlink, you can link the task to the site and access it directly from within your project file. You can also link a task to a file stored on your computer, such as a Job Aid explaining a process related to the task. The advantage of creating a hyperlink to a file over embedding the file, is that the link will always access the latest version of the file. Also, embedding files into your schedule increases the file size.

To add a Hyperlink to a task:

- Right-click the task you want to add the hyperlink to. From the shortcut menu select **Link** to open the *Insert Hyperlink* dialogue box (*Figure 154*).

To link to a website:

- In the **Text to display** field, type the text you want to display, when you hover over the target.
- In the **Address** field, type the website address.

To link to a file:

- In the **Text to display** field, type the text you want to display when you hover over the target.
- In the **Look in** field, browse for the file on your computer. Then, select the file you want and click **OK**.
- Select **OK** to close the *Insert Hyperlink* dialogue box.

After you add a hyperlink to a task, Project will create a hyperlink target in the **Indicators** field next to the task. Hover over the target to view the text you entered for the website or file. Click the hyperlink to access the website or file.

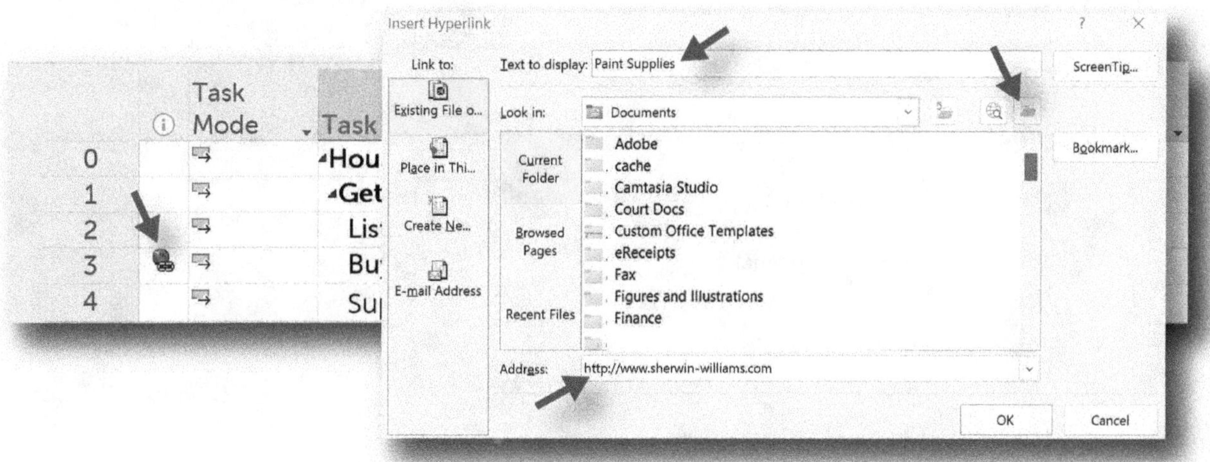

Figure 154 – Adding Hyperlinks to Tasks

Adding Resource Notes

In Chapter 8, we discussed adding resource information to your project plan using the *Resource Information* dialogue box. **Resource Notes** are another handy way to add resource information to the schedule. For example, you can add a note when a resource is on vacation.

To add a note to a Resource:

- Go to the **Resource Sheet view** by selecting the **View** tab. Then, in the **Resource Views** group, select **Resource Sheet**.
- Double-click the resource you want to add a note to. The *Resource Information* dialogue box will open (*Figure 155* below).
- Select the **Notes** tab.
- Type the note in the **Notes** field.
- Select **OK** to close the *Resource Information* dialogue box.

After you add a Resource note, Project will create an icon in the **Indicators** field, next to the resource's name in the *Resource Sheet* view. Hover over the icon to view the note.
As mentioned earlier, you can also use the **Add New Column** field to add the "Notes" column to the *Resource sheet* view.

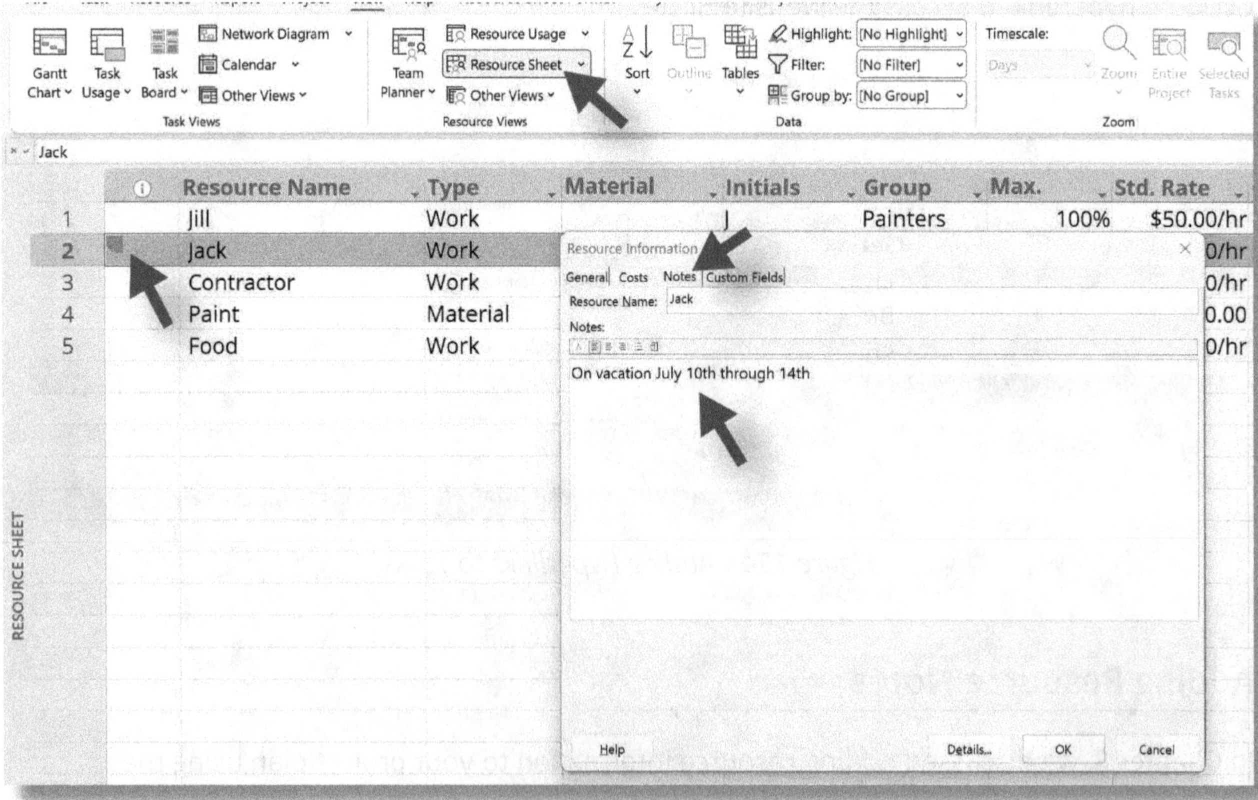

Figure 155 – Adding Resource Notes

Adding Hyperlinks to Resources

Like tasks, hyperlinks can be added to resources to access a website or file directly from the *Resource Sheet* view. You may be asking, "Why would I need to do this?". Many teams use websites to allow others to request resources from their team, or to post expected turn-around times for work requests. In such cases, adding a hyperlink to the resource would keep you from having to exit Project to access this information.

To add a Hyperlink to a resource:

- In the *Resource Sheet* view, right-click the name of the resource you want to add the hyperlink to.
- From the shortcut menu, select **Link** to open the *Insert Hyperlink* dialogue box (*Figure 156*).

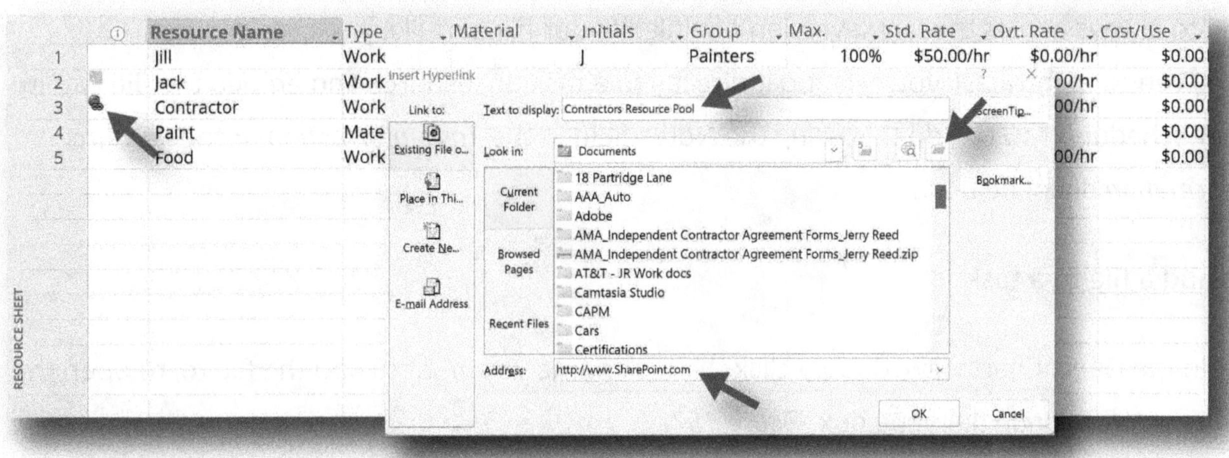

Figure 156 – Adding Hyperlinks to Resources

To link to a website:

- In the **Text to display** field, type the text you want to display when you hover over the target.
- In the **Address** field, type the website address.

To link to a file:

- In the **Text to display** field, type the text you want to display when you hover over the target.
- In the **Look in** field, browse for the file on your computer. Then, select the file you want and click **OK**.
- Select **OK** to close the *Insert Hyperlink* dialogue box.

After you add a hyperlink to a resource, Project will create a hyperlink target in the **Indicators** field, next to the resource's name.

Adding Files to Task and Resources

So far, we've added files to tasks and resources using hyperlinks. As mentioned, this allows you to always access the latest version of a file. If your file isn't likely to change often (E.g., vendor contracts), you can add it directly to a task or resource and embed the file within your schedule. You can do this using the Notes field in the *Task Information* or the *Resource Information* dialogue boxes.

To add a file to a task:

- In the Gantt Chart view, double-click the task name you want to add the file to, to open the *Task Information* dialogue box (*Figure 157*).
- Select the **Notes** tab.
- In the **Notes** field, click the **Insert Object** icon to open the *Insert Object* dialogue box.
- Select **Create from File**, then select **Browse** to locate the file.
- Select **Insert** to add the file.
- Select the **Display As Icon** checkbox if you want the file displayed as an icon that links to the document. Otherwise, the document will be displayed directly in the Notes field.

- Select **OK** to insert the file into the Notes field (there may be a brief lag as the file loads). This will also close the *Insert Object* dialogue box.

- Select **OK** again to close the *Task Information* dialogue box.

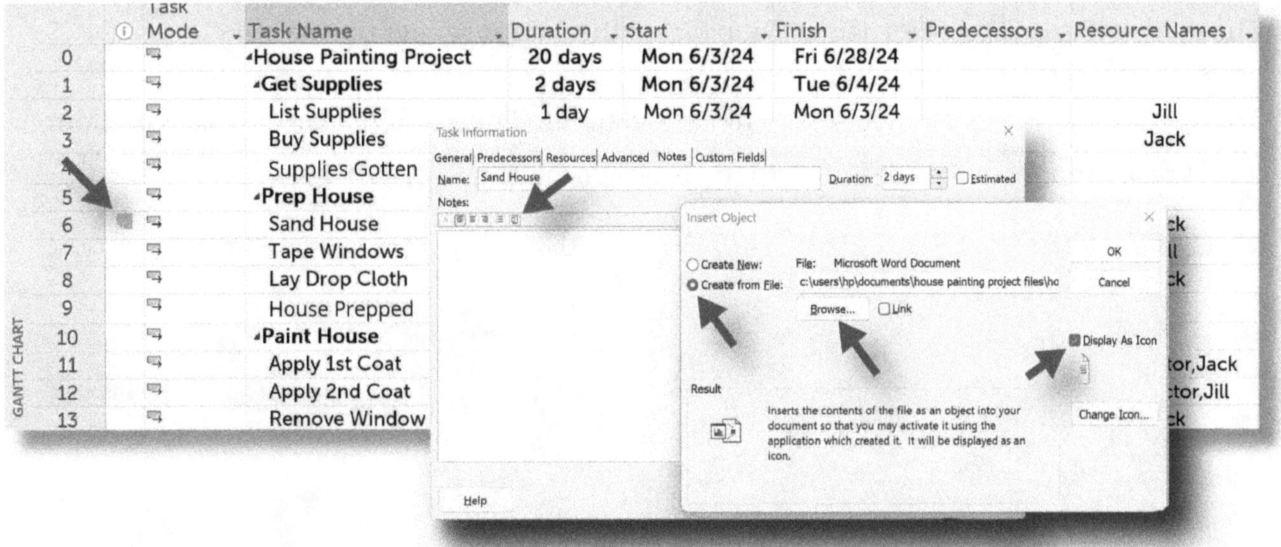

Figure 157 – Adding Files to Tasks

After you add the file, Project will create an icon in the **Indicators** field of the Entry table next to the task. Double-click the icon to access the file.

To add a file to a resource:

- In the Resource Sheet, double-click the resource you want to add the file to. The *Resource Information* dialogue box will open.

- Select the **Notes** tab.

- In the Notes field, click the **Insert Object** icon to open the *Insert Object* dialogue box.

- Select **Create from File**, then select **Browse** to locate the file.

- Select **Insert** to add the file.

- Select the **Display As Icon** checkbox if you want the file displayed as an icon that links to the document. Otherwise, the document will be displayed directly in the Notes field.

- Select **OK** to insert the file into the Notes field and to close the *Insert Object* dialogue box.
- Select **OK** again to close the *Resource Information* dialogue box.

After you add the file, Project will create a Notes icon in the **Indicators** field of the Resource Sheet, next to the resource's name. Double-click the icon to access the file.

You've now learned to use notes, hyperlinks and files to link and embed useful information about tasks and resources directly into the project schedule.

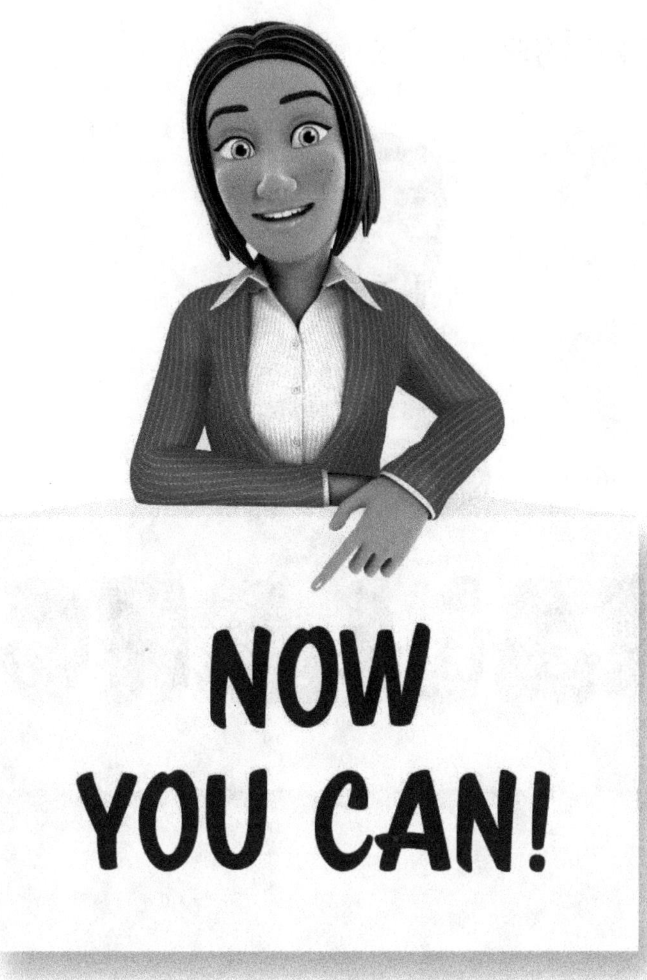

- ✓ Explain Reasons to Document the Schedule
- ✓ Enter Document Properties
- ✓ Add Notes to Tasks and Resources
- ✓ Add Hyperlinks to Tasks and Resources
- ✓ Add Files to Tasks and Resources

Practice Exercise

Document the Schedule

For this practice exercise, you will document the schedule. You'll work with Task Notes, Resource Notes and Hyperlinks to add task and resource information to the schedule.

Go to **mspbasics.com** for "Checkpoint Images" to check your work as you go along.

Follow the steps below to complete this practice exercise.

Open a Saved Project File

Open the *Software Development* project plan you saved from the Chapter 9 practice exercise. **NOTE:** The file should contain all the completed steps from the exercise.

Create a Resource Note

In the Chapter 9 practice exercise, you created a Resource calendar for the *Analyst* resource to incorporate vacation days into the schedule. Now, you'll create a **Resource Note** for the *Analyst* to document the schedule regarding the vacation.

1. Switch to the Resource Sheet view by selecting the **View** tab. Then, in the **Resource Views** group, select **Resource Sheet**.

2. Double-click the *Analyst's* name to open the *Resource Information* dialogue box.

3. Confirm the **Notes** tab is selected. In the Notes field, type **"On Vacation 1/13/25 to 1/17/25"**.

4. Select **OK** to close the *Resource Information* dialogue box.

After the Resource Note is created, Project will generate an icon in the **Indicators** field of the Resource Sheet, next to the *Analyst* resource's name. Hover over the icon to read the note.

CHECKPOINT: To check your results so far, go to **mspbasics.com**

- Select the **CheckPoint Images** tab.
- Select the version of the book you're using.
- Select **Chapter 10.** Then, go to **Checkpoint Image #1**

Create a Task Note

Next, you'll create a **Task Note** to document additional information about a task. Return to the Gantt Chart view by selecting the **Gantt Chart** icon in the top left corner of the ribbon.

1. Double-click task 14 *Obtain approvals to proceed (concept, timeline, budget)* to open the *Task Information* dialogue box.

2. Confirm the **Notes** tab is selected. In the Notes field, type **"Meet with management to confirm budget approval"**.

3. Select **OK** to close the *Task Information* dialogue box.

After the task note is created, Project will generate an icon in the **Indicators** field of the Entry table, next to task 14. Hover over the icon to read the note.

CHECKPOINT: To check your results so far, go to **mspbasics.com**

- Select the **CheckPoint Images** tab.
- Select the version of the book you're using.
- Select **Chapter 10**. Then, go to **Checkpoint Image #2**

Add a Hyperlink to a Task

Last, you'll add a hyperlink to a task. You'll add a link to the hardware vendor's website.

1. Right-click task 70 *Install/deploy software*. From the shortcut menu, select **Link** to open the *Insert Hyperlink* dialogue box.

2. In the **Text to display** field, type **"Hardware Vendor"**.

3. In the **Address** field, type **www.dell.com**.

4. Select **OK** to close the *Insert Hyperlink* dialogue box.

After the link is added to the task, Project will generate a target in the **Indicators** field. Hover over the link to view the text you entered. Double-click the link to access the website directly from the project plan (you'll need to first click away from the link).

CHECKPOINT: To check your results so far, go to **mspbasics.com**

- Select the **CheckPoint Images** tab.
- Select the version of the book you're using.
- Select **Chapter 10.** Then, go to **Checkpoint Image #3**

You've now documented the schedule. You've worked with notes and hyperlinks to add task and resource information to the schedule.

Chapter 11 Compressing Your Schedule

In the last chapter, you learned to document the schedule. In this chapter, you'll learn to **Compress the Schedule** to get work done faster. When you're done, you'll be able to view your project's Critical Path and see how it affects the project's duration. You'll also be able to explain slack, use lead time, add deadlines to tasks, and use the Task Path feature.

You'll Learn To:

- Compress the Schedule
- View the Critical Path
- Understand Slack
- Use Lead Time Effectively
- Use the Task Path Feature
- Add Deadlines to Tasks

Why Compress Your Schedule?

No justification is needed as to why you'd want to speed up your schedule, but here are some things to consider:

- **Release Resources Quicker** – The faster you deliver your project, the faster you can release resources to work on other projects.
- **Exploit Business Opportunities** – Delivering projects faster can enable your business to compete in the marketplace sooner.
- **Speed is Contagious!** – Delivering milestones quicker fosters a results-oriented culture.
- **Easier Politics** – No one will fault you for being ahead of schedule!
- **Better use of Company Resources** – Compressed schedules allow you to deliver more projects per year.

Key Terms

Before we review ways to compress your schedule, you should be familiar with a few key terms.

- **Slack (or Float)** – The number of days a task can be delayed before it will delay another task(s) or the project schedule.
- **Lead Time** – The number of days a successor task can start before its predecessor finishes.
- **Change Highlighting** – The Microsoft Project feature that highlights updates after a change is made to the schedule.

Understanding the Critical Path

The **Critical Path** is the series of tasks that stretch from the start date to the finish date of a schedule and determine its duration.

Tasks on the Critical Path have the following characteristics:

✓ Each task has no slack.

✓ Each task is a driving predecessor to the next task in the series.

✓ If any critical path task is compressed or delayed, the overall schedule will be compressed or delayed accordingly.

✓ Their collective sum equals the total project duration.

Because of these characteristics, the critical path tells you which task(s) to compress to speed up your schedule. The tasks on the critical path are considered *critical* because their scheduling determines the project finish date. Since they have no slack, they cannot be delayed without delaying the schedule. Conversely, a schedule can only be compressed if a task(s) on the critical path is compressed.

To grasp the concept of critical path, it's helpful to know how the critical path got its name. The first scheduling app (Microsoft Project) was released in 1984. So, how did the world manage schedules before then? The answer is PDM – Precedence Diagram Methods. Using PDM, every task in a schedule is plotted sequentially on a network diagram (like the Network Diagram view shown in Chapter 2). Using this visualization, one can determine which sequence of tasks comprises the longest network path from start to finish. Since this network path represents the total duration of the project, it is called the Critical Path.

Understanding Slack

As reviewed in the previous section, tasks on the critical path share certain characteristics – most notably, they have no wiggle room, or **Slack**.

There are two kinds of Slack:

- **Free Slack** – The number of days a task can be delayed before it will delay another task(s).
- **Total Slack** – The number of days a task can be delayed before it will delay the project schedule.

The following examples show how Free Slack and Total Slack impact the schedule:

- **Example 1** – A task has 10 days of *Total Slack*, which means it can be delayed 10 days without delaying the overall schedule. If the task is delayed 10 days, it becomes a critical path task because it no longer has slack. If it is delayed 11 days, the overall schedule will be delayed 1day.
- **Example 2** – A task has 4 days of *Free Slack*, which means it can be delayed 4 days without delaying the start date of its successor task. If it is delayed 5 days, the successor task will be delayed 1day. Although this will not delay the overall schedule, it will delay the impacted task owner's start date. Therefore, it would be a good idea to check with the task owner before exceeding the 4 days of Free Slack.
- **Example 3** – A task has 0 days of *Total Slack*, which means it is on the critical path. If this task is delayed one day, the entire project will be delayed one day. If this task is completed one day early, the entire project will be completed one day early.

Displaying the Critical Path in the Schedule

Being aware of your project's critical path allows you to manage the project with better intelligence. Microsoft Project automatically calculates the critical path in the background, and automatically updates it if it changes. You can display the critical path in your schedule so you're always mindful of it. You can highlight the critical path tasks in the Entry table and in the Gantt chart. In the Gantt chart, their task bars will be highlighted in red (*Figure 158 below*).

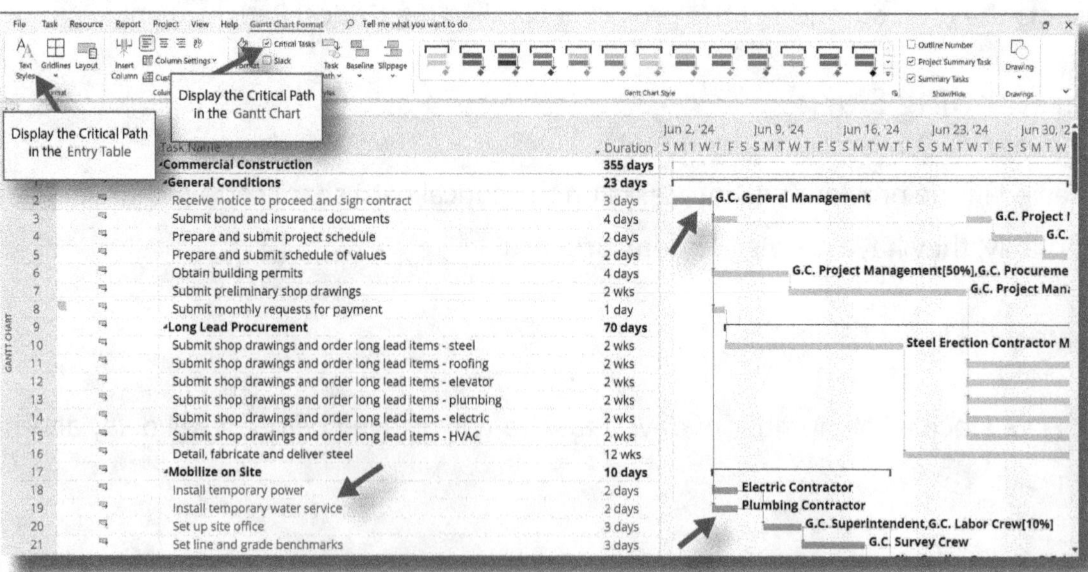

Figure 158 – Display the Critical Path in the Schedule

In the Entry table, their task names can be highlighted with red typeface (or any color you choose). Highlighting the critical path allows you to quickly identify which tasks can be compressed to speed up the schedule. For example, if the schedule in *Figure 158* needed to be compressed 1 day, you'd know that only the tasks highlighted in red should be considered. Compressing the tasks that are NOT highlighted will NOT speed up the schedule. Keeping the critical path visible enables you to anticipate project delays before they occur.

To highlight the Critical Path tasks in the Gantt chart:

- Select the **Format** tab. In the **Bar Styles** group, select the **Critical Tasks** checkbox. The critical path tasks will be highlighted with red task bars in the Gantt Chart.

To highlight the Critical Path tasks in the Entry table:

- Select the **Format** tab. In the **Format** group, select the **Text Styles** command to open the *Text Styles* dialogue box (*Figure 159* below)
- Select **Critical Tasks** from the **Item to Change** pick list.
- In the **Color** field, select the color you want to highlight the critical path task names with.

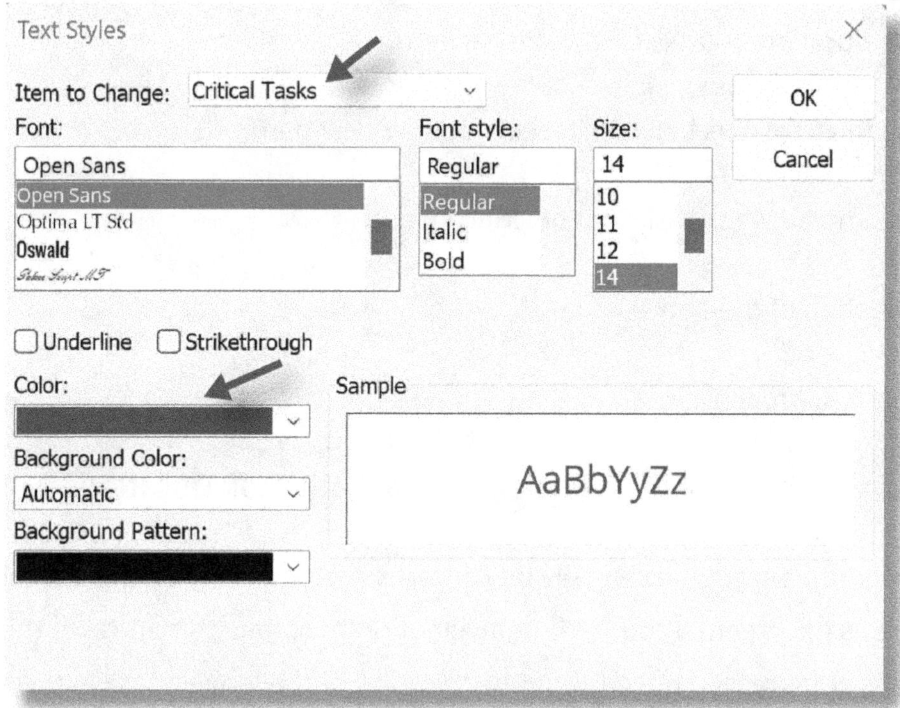

Figure 159 – Display the Critical Path in the Entry Table

How to Compress a Schedule

Before we review ways to compress a schedule, it's important to note that the critical path is dynamic. It changes as you enter progress data and update your schedule. This is a natural consequence of tasks starting earlier or later than expected or completing in a shorter or longer time-frame than initially estimated. Although Project will automatically recalculate your critical path after every schedule update, it's important to convey its dynamic nature to project stakeholders. Otherwise, they may develop expectations based upon tasks that may have been on the critical path at one point but may not be on the current critical path. Bearing this point in mind, let's review ways to compress a schedule.

According to the PMBOK, there are two ways to compress a schedule. You can **Crash** a schedule (add more resources to complete tasks faster), or you can **Fast-Track** a schedule (use lead time between tasks to perform work in parallel rather than in series). While these methods work in *certain* instances, they don't in *all* instances. These approaches only work when they are applied to tasks on the critical path. The opposite is also true. These approaches will *never* work when they are applied to tasks that are not on the critical path.

There are four ways to compress a schedule in Project:

1. Reduce the duration of tasks on the critical path.

2. Adjust task relationships between tasks on the critical path.

3. Apply lead time between tasks on the critical path.

4. Any combination of the above.

Let's look at each approach.

Compressing the Schedule by Reducing Critical Path Task Durations

As explained earlier, a schedule can only be compressed if a task(s) on the critical path is compressed. This may seem a counter-intuitive notion to some. It's natural to think that a schedule can be compressed by reducing the duration of the longest task in the schedule.

For example, in *Figure 160*, the *Commercial Construction* project has a duration of 344 days.

	Task Name	Duration	Start	Finish	Predecessors	Gantt chart label
0	**Commercial Construction**	**344 days**	**Mon 6/3/24**	**Thu 9/25/25**		
1	**General Conditions**	**17 days**	**Mon 6/3/24**	**Tue 6/25/24**		
2	Receive notice to proceed and sign contract	3 days	Mon 6/3/24	Wed 6/5/24		G.C. General Management
3	Submit bond and insurance documents	2 days	Thu 6/6/24	Fri 6/7/24	2	G.C. Project Management,G.C. General Management[25%]
4	Prepare and submit project schedule	2 days	Mon 6/10/24	Tue 6/11/24	3	G.C. Project Management[25%],G.C. Scheduler
5	Prepare and submit schedule of values	2 days	Wed 6/12/24	Thu 6/13/24	4	G.C. General Management[10%],G.C. Project Management
6	Obtain building permits	4 days	Thu 6/6/24	Tue 6/11/24	2	G.C. Project Management[50%],G.C. Procurement[50%]
7	Submit preliminary shop drawings	2 wks	Wed 6/12/24	Tue 6/25/24	6	G.C. Project Management[50%],G.C. Procurement[50
8	Submit monthly requests for payment	1 day	Thu 6/6/24	Thu 6/6/24	2	
9	**Long Lead Procurement**	**70 days**	**Fri 6/7/24**	**Thu 9/12/24**		
10	Submit shop drawings and order long lead items - steel	2 wks	Fri 6/7/24	Thu 6/20/24	8	Steel Erection Contractor Management
11	Submit shop drawings and order long lead items - roofing	2 wks	Wed 6/26/24	Tue 7/9/24	7	Roofing Contractor Management
12	Submit shop drawings and order long lead items - elevator	2 wks	Wed 6/26/24	Tue 7/9/24	7	Elevator Contractor Management
13	Submit shop drawings and order long lead items - plumbing	2 wks	Wed 6/26/24	Tue 7/9/24	7	Plumbing Contractor Management
14	Submit shop drawings and order long lead items - electric	2 wks	Wed 6/26/24	Tue 7/9/24	7	Electric Contractor Management
15	Submit shop drawings and order long lead items - HVAC	2 wks	Wed 6/26/24	Tue 7/9/24	7	HVAC Contractor Management
16	Detail, fabricate and deliver steel	12 wks	Fri 6/21/24	Thu 9/12/24	10	Steel Erect
17	**Mobilize on Site**	**10 days**	**Thu 6/6/24**	**Wed 6/19/24**		
18	Install temporary power	2 days	Thu 6/6/24	Fri 6/7/24	2	Electric Contractor
19	Install temporary water service	2 days	Thu 6/6/24	Fri 6/7/24	2	Plumbing Contractor
20	Set up site office	3 days	Mon 6/10/24	Wed 6/12/24	18,19	G.C. Superintendent,G.C. Labor Crew[10%]
21	Set line and grade benchmarks	3 days	Thu 6/13/24	Mon 6/17/24	20	G.C. Survey Crew
22	Prepare site - lay down yard and temporary fencing	2 days	Tue 6/18/24	Wed 6/19/24	21	Site Grading Contractor,G.C. Labor Crew[10%]
23	**Site Grading and Utilities**	**35 days**	**Thu 6/20/24**	**Wed 8/7/24**		
24	Clear and grub site	3 days	Thu 6/20/24	Mon 6/24/24	20,22	Site Grading Contractor
25	Stone site access and temporary parking area	2 days	Tue 6/25/24	Wed 6/26/24	24,22	Site Grading Contractor
26	Rough grade site (cut and fill)	1 wk	Thu 6/27/24	Wed 7/3/24	25	Site Grading Contractor
27	Install storm drainage	2 wks	Thu 7/4/24	Wed 7/17/24	26	Site Grading Contractor
28	Install exterior fire line and building fire riser	2 wks	Thu 7/4/24	Wed 7/17/24	26	Plumbing Contractor

Figure 160 – Compressing the Schedule – Working with Critical Path Tasks

The longest task in this schedule is a 12-week task – task 16 *Detail, fabricate and deliver steel*. This task is not on the critical path. Even if the duration of this task is reduced from 12 weeks to 1 day, the project duration will still be 344 days! Conversely, if the duration of any of the critical path tasks highlighted in red is reduced, the project duration will be reduced accordingly.

Compressing the Schedule by Adjusting Task Relationships

Another way to compress the schedule is to adjust task relationships between the tasks on the critical path. For example, in *Figure 161*, the *Commercial Construction* schedule shown on the top has a 342-day duration. Task 20, *Set up site office* and Task 21, *Set line and grade benchmarks* are critical path tasks, with a Finish-to-Start task relationship. To compress the schedule on the bottom, these tasks were given a Start-to-Start task relationship instead. Adjusting the task relationship compressed the schedule by 3 days. The start date of successor task 21 *Set line and grade benchmarks* was rescheduled from 6/13/24 to 6/10/24. The project duration was reduced to 339 days.

GANTT CHART

	Task Mode	Task Name	Duration	Start	Finish	Predecessors
0		**Commercial Construction**	**342 days**	**Mon 6/3/24**	**Tue 9/23/25**	
1		**General Conditions**	**17 days**	**Mon 6/3/24**	**Tue 6/25/24**	
9		**Long Lead Procurement**	**70 days**	**Fri 6/7/24**	**Thu 9/12/24**	
17		**Mobilize on Site**	**8 days**	**Thu 6/6/24**	**Mon 6/17/24**	
18		Install temporary power	2 days	Thu 6/6/24	Fri 6/7/24	2
19		Install temporary water service	2 days	Thu 6/6/24	Fri 6/7/24	2
20		Set up site office	3 days	Mon 6/10/24	Wed 6/12/24	18,19
21		Set line and grade benchmarks	3 days	Thu 6/13/24	Mon 6/17/24	20
22		Prepare site - lay down yard and temporary fencing	2 days	Fri 6/14/24	Mon 6/17/24	21FS-2 days
23		**Site Grading and Utilities**	**35 days**	**Tue 6/18/24**	**Mon 8/5/24**	
24		Clear and grub site	3 days	Tue 6/18/24	Thu 6/20/24	20,22
25		Stone site access and temporary parking area	2 days	Fri 6/21/24	Mon 6/24/24	24,22
26		Rough grade site (cut and fill)	1 wk	Tue 6/25/24	Mon 7/1/24	25
27		Install storm drainage	2 wks	Tue 7/2/24	Mon 7/15/24	26
28		Install exterior fire line and building fire riser	2 wks	Tue 7/2/24	Mon 7/15/24	26
29		Perform final site grading	2 wks	Tue 7/16/24	Mon 7/29/24	27FF+1 day,28
30		Erect building batter boards and layout building	1 wk	Tue 7/30/24	Mon 8/5/24	29

GANTT CHART

	Task Mode	Task Name	Duration	Start	Finish	Predecessors
0		**Commercial Construction**	**339 days**	**Mon 6/3/24**	**Thu 9/18/25**	
1		**General Conditions**	**17 days**	**Mon 6/3/24**	**Tue 6/25/24**	
9		**Long Lead Procurement**	**70 days**	**Fri 6/7/24**	**Thu 9/12/24**	
17		**Mobilize on Site**	**5 days**	**Thu 6/6/24**	**Wed 6/12/24**	
18		Install temporary power	2 days	Thu 6/6/24	Fri 6/7/24	2
19		Install temporary water service	2 days	Thu 6/6/24	Fri 6/7/24	2
20		Set up site office	3 days	Mon 6/10/24	Wed 6/12/24	18,19
21		Set line and grade benchmarks	3 days	Mon 6/10/24	Wed 6/12/24	20SS
22		Prepare site - lay down yard and temporary fencing	2 days	Tue 6/11/24	Wed 6/12/24	21FS-2 days
23		**Site Grading and Utilities**	**35 days**	**Thu 6/13/24**	**Wed 7/31/24**	
24		Clear and grub site	3 days	Thu 6/13/24	Mon 6/17/24	20,22
25		Stone site access and temporary parking area	2 days	Tue 6/18/24	Wed 6/19/24	24,22
26		Rough grade site (cut and fill)	1 wk	Thu 6/20/24	Wed 6/26/24	25
27		Install storm drainage	2 wks	Thu 6/27/24	Wed 7/10/24	26
28		Install exterior fire line and building fire riser	2 wks	Thu 6/27/24	Wed 7/10/24	26
29		Perform final site grading	2 wks	Thu 7/11/24	Wed 7/24/24	27FF+1 day,28
30		Erect building batter boards and layout building	1 wk	Thu 7/25/24	Wed 7/31/24	29

Figure 161 – Adjusting Task Relationships to Compress the Schedule

Compressing the Schedule by Applying Lead Time

As discussed in Chapter 4, **Lead** time is the number of days a successor task can start before its predecessor finishes. To use Lead time to compress the schedule, you must know which tasks are on the critical path. Your schedule will only compress if you apply Lead time between tasks on the critical path. In *Figure 162*, the *Commercial Construction* schedule shown on the top has a 344-day duration. Task 21 *Set line and grade benchmarks* and task 22 *Prepare site - lay down yard and temporary fencing* are critical path tasks that have a Finish-to-Start task relationship. To compress the schedule, a 2-day lead was applied to successor task 22 *Prepare site - lay down yard and temporary fencing*.

The results of the applied lead time are shown in the schedule on the bottom. The start date of task 22 was rescheduled from 6/18/24 to 614/24. The project duration was reduced from 344 days to 342 days.

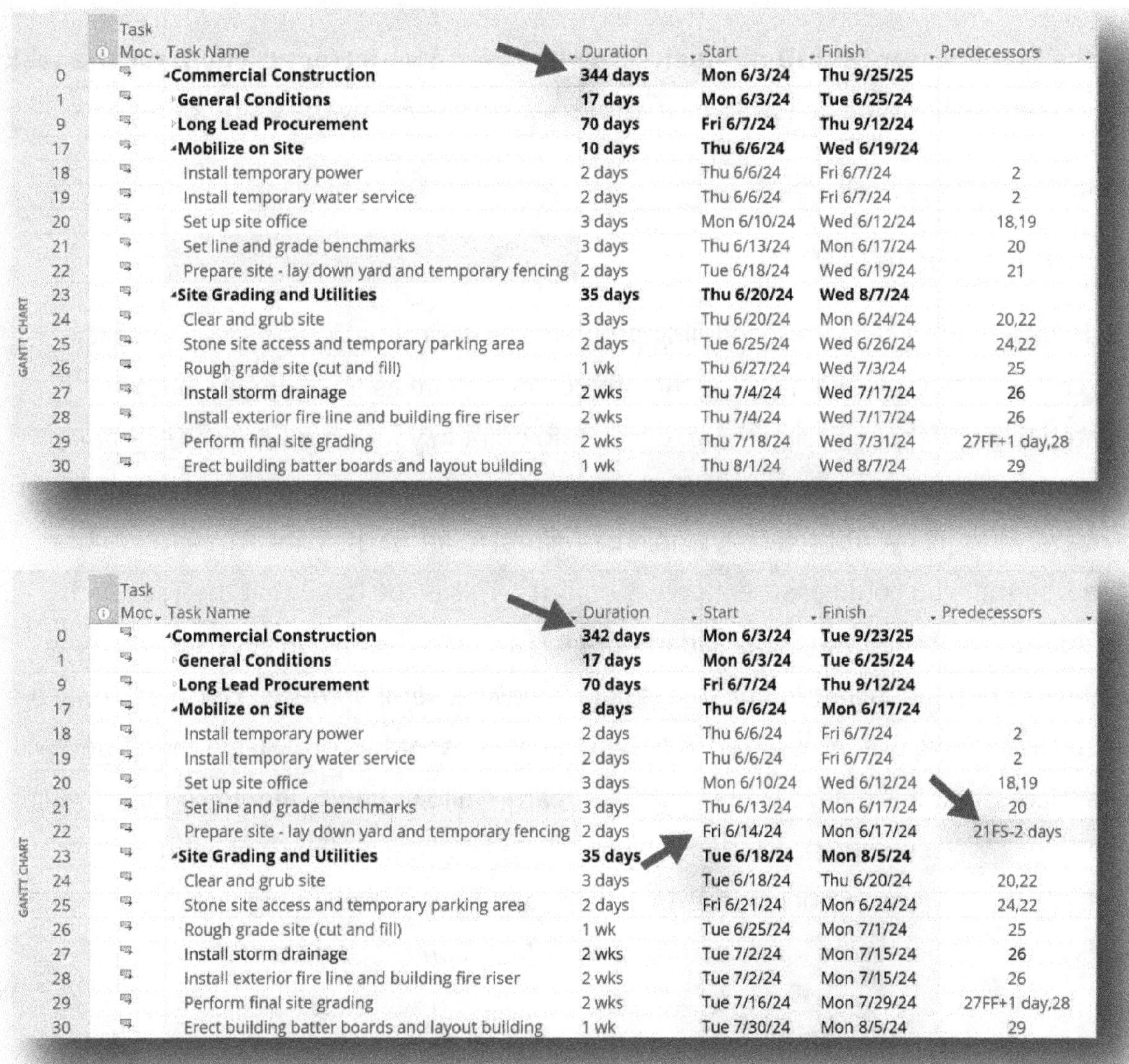

	Task Mode	Task Name	Duration	Start	Finish	Predecessors
0		**Commercial Construction**	**344 days**	**Mon 6/3/24**	**Thu 9/25/25**	
1		**General Conditions**	**17 days**	**Mon 6/3/24**	**Tue 6/25/24**	
9		**Long Lead Procurement**	**70 days**	**Fri 6/7/24**	**Thu 9/12/24**	
17		**Mobilize on Site**	**10 days**	**Thu 6/6/24**	**Wed 6/19/24**	
18		Install temporary power	2 days	Thu 6/6/24	Fri 6/7/24	2
19		Install temporary water service	2 days	Thu 6/6/24	Fri 6/7/24	2
20		Set up site office	3 days	Mon 6/10/24	Wed 6/12/24	18,19
21		Set line and grade benchmarks	3 days	Thu 6/13/24	Mon 6/17/24	20
22		Prepare site - lay down yard and temporary fencing	2 days	Tue 6/18/24	Wed 6/19/24	21
23		**Site Grading and Utilities**	**35 days**	**Thu 6/20/24**	**Wed 8/7/24**	
24		Clear and grub site	3 days	Thu 6/20/24	Mon 6/24/24	20,22
25		Stone site access and temporary parking area	2 days	Tue 6/25/24	Wed 6/26/24	24,22
26		Rough grade site (cut and fill)	1 wk	Thu 6/27/24	Wed 7/3/24	25
27		Install storm drainage	2 wks	Thu 7/4/24	Wed 7/17/24	26
28		Install exterior fire line and building fire riser	2 wks	Thu 7/4/24	Wed 7/17/24	26
29		Perform final site grading	2 wks	Thu 7/18/24	Wed 7/31/24	27FF+1 day,28
30		Erect building batter boards and layout building	1 wk	Thu 8/1/24	Wed 8/7/24	29

	Task Mode	Task Name	Duration	Start	Finish	Predecessors
0		**Commercial Construction**	**342 days**	**Mon 6/3/24**	**Tue 9/23/25**	
1		**General Conditions**	**17 days**	**Mon 6/3/24**	**Tue 6/25/24**	
9		**Long Lead Procurement**	**70 days**	**Fri 6/7/24**	**Thu 9/12/24**	
17		**Mobilize on Site**	**8 days**	**Thu 6/6/24**	**Mon 6/17/24**	
18		Install temporary power	2 days	Thu 6/6/24	Fri 6/7/24	2
19		Install temporary water service	2 days	Thu 6/6/24	Fri 6/7/24	2
20		Set up site office	3 days	Mon 6/10/24	Wed 6/12/24	18,19
21		Set line and grade benchmarks	3 days	Thu 6/13/24	Mon 6/17/24	20
22		Prepare site - lay down yard and temporary fencing	2 days	Fri 6/14/24	Mon 6/17/24	21FS-2 days
23		**Site Grading and Utilities**	**35 days**	**Tue 6/18/24**	**Mon 8/5/24**	
24		Clear and grub site	3 days	Tue 6/18/24	Thu 6/20/24	20,22
25		Stone site access and temporary parking area	2 days	Fri 6/21/24	Mon 6/24/24	24,22
26		Rough grade site (cut and fill)	1 wk	Tue 6/25/24	Mon 7/1/24	25
27		Install storm drainage	2 wks	Tue 7/2/24	Mon 7/15/24	26
28		Install exterior fire line and building fire riser	2 wks	Tue 7/2/24	Mon 7/15/24	26
29		Perform final site grading	2 wks	Tue 7/16/24	Mon 7/29/24	27FF+1 day,28
30		Erect building batter boards and layout building	1 wk	Tue 7/30/24	Mon 8/5/24	29

Figure 162 – Using Lead Time to Compress the Schedule

As discussed in Chapter 4, lead time is expressed as a negative value (subtracting time from or overlapping the start date of the successor task). Lead time values can be expressed as a number or a percentage. Using a percentage will start the successor task after a percentage of the predecessor task is complete.

To apply Lead Time:

- In the **Predecessors** field of the Entry table, Lead time is applied to the successor task using the following syntax:

Enter the **Predecessor task ID number**, followed by the **two-letter acronym for the task relationship type**, followed by a **minus sign**, followed by the **value of lead.**

Example: 4FS-2days or 4FS-50%

Using the Task Path Feature

The **Task Path** feature solves a scheduling problem the critical path can't solve. Recall that the critical path is calculated using the project finish date as an endpoint. But what if you wanted to know the critical path up to a certain point in your schedule? For example, suppose your stakeholders are contractually bound to meet a milestone date that occurs at the halfway mark in your project. It would be helpful to know the critical path up to that milestone, so that you could ensure it occurs on time. This is the issue that the Task Path feature addresses. It shows the critical path for any task or milestone in your schedule by highlighting its dependencies. Although a task may have several predecessors, it can only be delayed by its "driving predecessor(s)". A **Driving Predecessor** has no "wiggle room" and will delay its successor if it is delayed. The Task Path feature allows you to identify a task's driving predecessor(s), predecessor(s), driven successor(s), and successor(s) by highlighting their Gantt task bars. In *Figure 163* below, the Task Path feature was used to highlight the Driving Predecessors and Successors for milestone task 31 *Development Complete*.

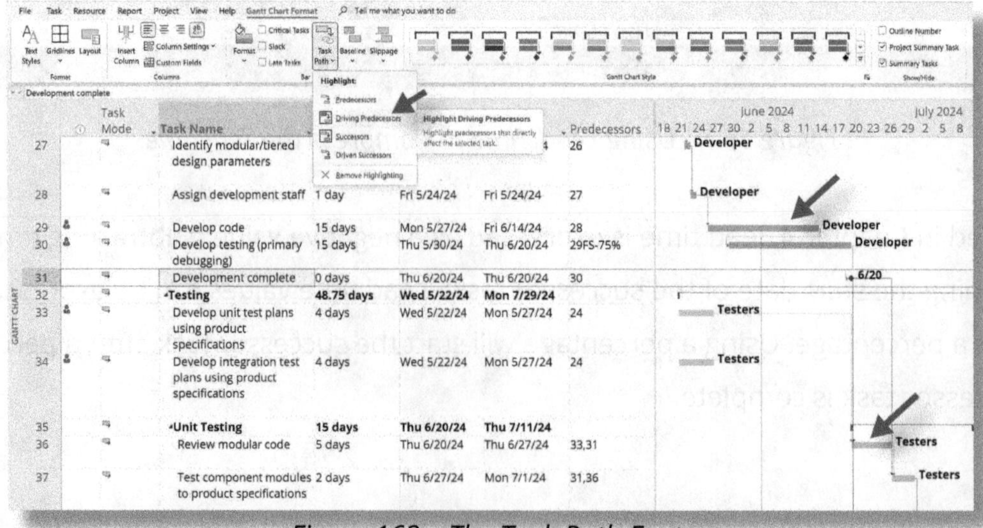

Figure 163 – The Task Path Feature

To view the Task Path for a task:

- Select the task for which you want to view the Task Path.
- On the **Format** tab, in the **Bar Styles** group, select the **Task Path** command.
- From the **Highlight** pick-list, select the option you want.

Adding Deadlines to Tasks

When managing your schedule, you may need to be alerted if a task finishes beyond a certain date. The **Deadline** feature allows you to flag a task with the latest date you'd like it to finish. When a deadline is applied to a task, Project generates a green arrow icon in the Gantt chart as a visual reminder of the date (*Figure 164* below). If the task exceeds its deadline, Project will generate an alert icon in the **Indicators** field.

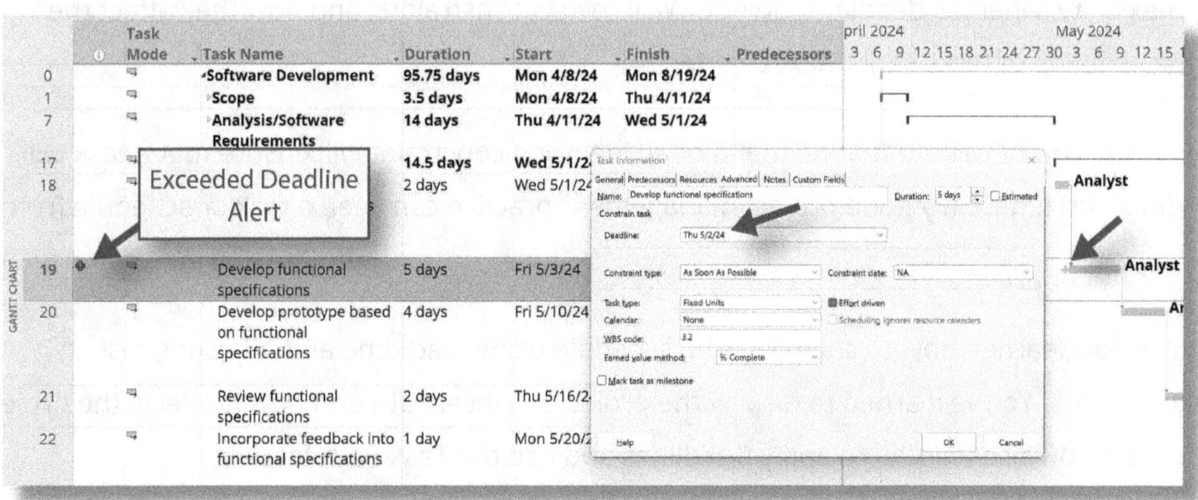

Figure 164 – Adding Deadlines to Tasks

To add a Deadline to a task:

- Double-click the task name to open the *Task Information* dialogue box.
- Select the **Advanced** tab.
- In the **Deadline** field, enter the date or select it from the drop-down calendar (*Figure 164* above).

Important Notes about Deadlines

- While deadlines are useful indicators, they can cause Project to introduce negative slack into the schedule, which alters the critical path. Negative slack indicates that there is not enough time scheduled for the task. If you enter a deadline date that is before the end of the task's total slack, Project will recalculate total slack by using the deadline date rather than the task's late finish date. Therefore, if you're using deadlines, be sure to remove them before displaying the critical path. To remove a deadline, in the *Task Information* dialogue box, simply delete the date shown in the Deadline field. You can always reapply a deadline after viewing the critical path.

- A common mistake that project managers make is to use a *Constraint* when the scheduling situation calls for a *Deadline*. If you want a visual reminder of a targeted completion date, use a deadline and not a constraint. Constraints impact the schedule and limit scheduling flexibility, whereas deadlines do not. We'll review constraints, and how they affect the scheduling of tasks in the next chapter.

- It's important to note that neither a deadline nor a constraint will ensure that a task will finish on time. Only good project management practice can keep a task or schedule from slipping.

You've now learned how to compress the schedule using lead time and adjusting task relationships. You've learned to display the project's Critical Path and how it affects the project duration. You also learned to apply Deadlines and use the Task Path feature.

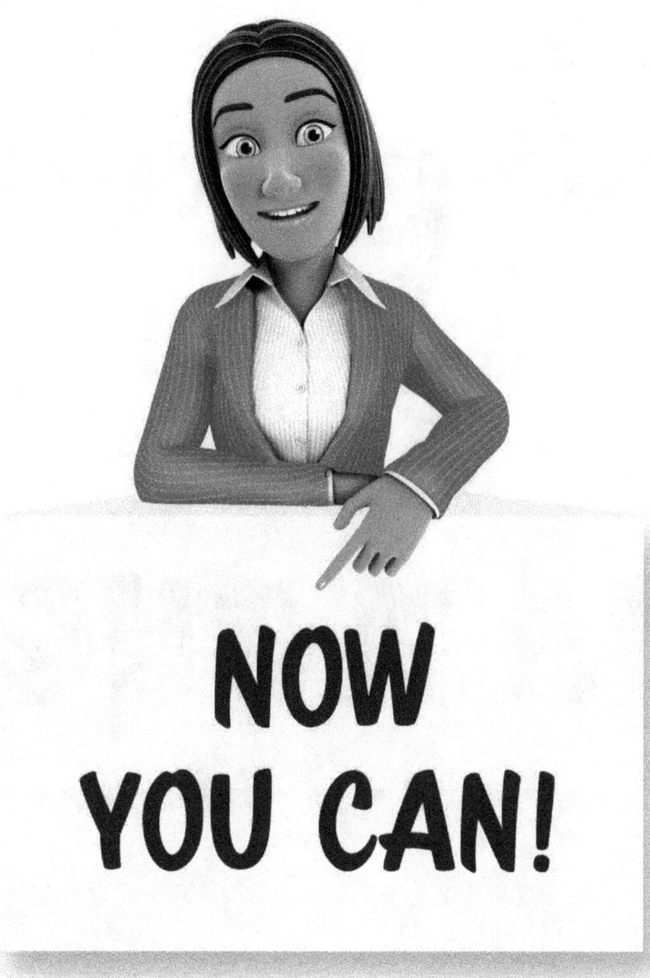

- ✓ Compress the Schedule
- ✓ View the Critical Path
- ✓ Understand Slack
- ✓ Use Lead Time Effectively
- ✓ Use the Task Path Feature
- ✓ Add Deadlines to Tasks

Practice Exercise

Compress a Schedule

For this practice exercise, you'll work with Slack, the Critical Path and Lead time to compress a project schedule.

Go to **mspbasics.com** for "checkpoint" images to check your work as you go along.

Follow the steps below to complete this practice exercise.

Start a Project from a Template

You'll use the *Commercial Construction* project template to complete this exercise.

NOTE: The templates are hosted on a companion website. You'll need to be connected to the Internet to access them.

1. From the opening view, select the **New** tab, from the options on the left.

2. Double-click the *Commercial Construction* project template. If you don't see this template among the options, select **Show more** to see more templates. You can also use the search box.

Close the Timeline View Panel

When the project template opens, the **Timeline View** panel will be displayed beneath the ribbon. It provides a summary of the project timeline and shows the major phases of the project and their scheduled start and finish dates. Since you won't be using the Timeline View panel for this exercise, you'll hide it to see more of the view.

1. Select the **View** tab. In the **Split View** group, uncheck the **Timeline** checkbox.

2. To further adjust the view, slide the right half of the screen to the right, until you can see the **Add New Column** field in the Entry table.

Set the Project Start Date

For this *Commercial Construction* project you're managing, your construction site is in Southern California. You've hired "all-season" construction crews to do the work.

Set the project start date to **5/5/25** as follows:

1. Select the **Project** tab.

2. In the **Properties** group, select the **Project Information** command to open the *Project Information* dialogue box.

3. Enter **5/5/25** in the **Start date** field.

4. Select **OK** to close the *Project Information* dialogue box.

CHECKPOINT: To check your results so far, go to **mspbasics.com**

- Select the **CheckPoint Images** tab.
- Select the version of the book you're using.
- Select **Chapter 11**. Then, go to **Checkpoint Image #1**

Highlight the Critical Path

The building you're constructing will obtain the certificate of occupancy on **8/26/26**. This is indicated in the schedule by task #142. Your client has requested that you expedite the schedule and obtain the certificate of occupancy by **8/5/26**. To accommodate this request, you will need to compress the schedule by 3 weeks. To see which tasks can be compressed to expedite the schedule, you'll highlight the Critical Path in the Gantt chart and in the Entry table.

To display the Critical Path in the Gantt Chart:

1. Select the Gantt Chart **Format** tab.

2. In the **Bar Styles** group, select the **Critical Tasks** checkbox. The critical path tasks will be highlighted with red task bars in the Gantt chart.

To display the Critical Path tasks in the Entry table:

1. On the Gantt Chart **Format** tab, in the **Format** group, select the **Text Styles** command to open the *Text Styles* dialogue box.

2. In the I**tem to Change** field, select **Critical Tasks** from the pick-list.

3. In the **Color** field, select red for the color.

4. Select **OK** to close the *Text Styles* dialogue box. The critical path tasks will be highlighted in the Entry table with red typeface.

CHECKPOINT: To check your results so far, go to **mspbasics.com**

- Select the **CheckPoint Images** tab.
- Select the version of the book you're using.
- Select **Chapter 11**. Then, go to **Checkpoint Image #2**

Display Total Slack, Free Slack, and Successor Tasks

To get more information about the impact of compressing or delaying tasks, you'll use the **Add New Column** command to add the **Total Slack**, **Free Slack** and **Successors** columns to the Entry table.

To add these fields to the Entry table:

1. Select the **Add New Column** title to display the columns you can add to the table.
2. Type **Total Slack**, then select it when it appears.
3. Select the **Add New Column** title. Then, type **Free Slack** and select it when it appears.
4. Select the **Add New Column** title. Then, type **Successors** and select it when it appears.

CHECKPOINT: To check your results so far, go to **mspbasics.com**

- Select the **CheckPoint Images** tab.
- Select the version of the book you're using.
- Select **Chapter 11**. Then, go to **Checkpoint Image #3**

Before you begin to compress the schedule, let's review what these added fields tell us about the schedule. Scroll down to task 58 *Strip forms from 2nd floor slab*. Because this task is not highlighted in red, we know it is not on the critical path. In the *Total Slack* field, you can see that this task has 99 days of Total Slack. This means it can be delayed 99 days without delaying the schedule. It is currently scheduled to finish on 11/20/25, which is long before the project is scheduled to finish.

Because of this, it may be tempting to let this task slip. However, in the *Free Slack* field, we can see that this task has zero Free Slack. This means it can be delayed zero days before it will delay another task. To put this into context, if you delay this task, it will not delay the schedule, but it will delay the start date of its successor task. Therefore, you should check with the task owner to ensure that they are available to work this task on the new start date. In the *Successors* field, we see that this task has several successors – tasks 69, 70, 71 & 72. Therefore, delaying task 58 would also delay these four tasks. In the *Resource Names* field, we can see that these tasks are being worked on by 4 different resource groups. In the event task 58 should need to be delayed, it would be a good idea to check with these resources and confirm they are still available. As you can see these fields provide useful schedule information. Notice, the critical path tasks (which are highlighted in red) have zero Total Slack. As such, they directly impact the project finish date and can be compressed to meet your client's request to speed up the certificate of occupancy date (the finish date of task 142).

Apply a Deadline to a Task

Next, you'll add a **Deadline** to task 142 *Obtain certificate of occupancy* as a visual reminder of the **8/5/26** date your client has requested.

To add the deadline to the task:

1. Double-click the task name of task 142 to open the *Task Information* dialogue box.
2. Select the **Advanced** tab.
3. In the **Deadline** field, type or select **8/5/26**.
4. Select **OK** to close the *Task Information* dialogue box.

CHECKPOINT: To check your results so far, go to **mspbasics.com**

- Select the **CheckPoint Images** tab.
- Select the version of the book you're using.
- Select **Chapter 11**. Then, go to **Checkpoint Image #4**

A few things occurred when the deadline was applied. Project generated a green arrow icon in the Gantt chart to indicate that the task has a deadline. The arrow corresponds with the deadline date on the timescale. Because this task is currently scheduled to finish on 8/26/26, which exceeds its 8/5/26 deadline, its task bar extends past the deadline marker. **NOTE:** If you can't see the Gantt chart task bar for task 142, bring it into the view using the **Scroll to Task** feature as follows:

1. Select task 142.

2. Select the **Task** tab.

3. In the **Editing** group, select the **Scroll to Task** command.

Because the task exceeded its deadline, Project generated an alert in the **Indicators** field. Hover over the icon to see the notification. In the Total Slack field, notice that many tasks, including task 142, now have negative slack values. As mentioned earlier, when you add deadlines, Project will add negative slack, which distorts the critical path calculations. Since you'll be using the critical path to compress the schedule, you'll remove the deadline for now and add it back later.

To remove the Deadline:

1. Double-click the task name for task 142 to open the *Task Information* dialogue box.

2. Delete the date from the **Deadline** field.

3. Select **OK** to close the *Task Information* dialogue box. The deadline will be removed, and the Total Slack will be recalculated throughout the schedule.

Apply Lead Time

Next, you'll use **Lead** time to compress the schedule. You'll start by adding lead time between two critical path tasks. Scroll up to tasks 93 *Install window wall aluminum and glass* and 94 *Install interior stud walls and drywall*. These tasks have a Finish-to-Start relationship. You've spoken to the Window and Drywall contractors, and they've agreed that the Drywall contractor can begin task 94 one week before task 93 finishes. You'll represent this in the schedule by applying a 1-week lead between these tasks.

Apply the Lead time as follows:

1. In the **Predecessors** field of the successor task 94 I*nstall interior stud walls and drywall*, enter **93FS-1w**.

CHECKPOINT: To check your results so far, go to **mspbasics.com**

- Select the **CheckPoint Images** tab.
- Select the version of the book you're using.
- Select **Chapter 11**. Then, go to **Checkpoint Image #5**

After the lead time was applied, Project highlighted all schedule updates in blue. Task 94 *Install interior stud walls and drywall* was rescheduled to start on **3/31/26**. In the Gantt chart, the lead time is indicated by the overlapping task bars. If you scroll up to the Project Summary task, you can see that the project duration was reduced from 344 days to **339** days. Scroll down to task 142 *Obtain certificate of occupancy* to see how the 1-week lead affected this task. The finish date for this task was updated to **8/19/26**. You're closer to the 8/5/26 deadline, but not quite there. You'll need to compress the schedule further to make your client's date. To do this, you'll apply more lead time between critical path tasks.

Scroll up to critical path tasks 98 *Install millwork and wood trim* and 99 *Paint walls and woodwork*. These tasks have a Finish-to-Start relationship. They also each have other predecessors (tasks 94 & 95 respectively). You can see by the blue highlighting that these tasks were rescheduled because of the 1-week lead you just applied. You've spoken to the G.C. Finish Carpenter Crew and the Painting Contractor and they've agreed that task 99 can begin one week before task 98 finishes. You'll represent this in the schedule by applying a 1-week lead between these tasks as follows:

2. In the **Predecessors** field of successor task 99 *Paint walls and woodwork*, enter **98FS-1w**.

NOTE: Be sure not to remove the other predecessor's task ID (task 95). The lead entry should be separated from the other predecessor with a comma. See Checkpoint image #6 for clarification.

CHECKPOINT: To check your results so far, go to **mspbasics.com**

- Select the **CheckPoint Images** tab.
- Select the version of the book you're using.
- Select **Chapter 11**. Then, go to **Checkpoint Image #6**

After the lead time was applied, Project rescheduled task 99 *Paint walls and woodwork* to start on **5/19/26.** In the Gantt chart, the lead time is indicated by the overlapping task bars. If you scroll up to the Project Summary task, you can see that the project duration was reduced from 339 days to **334 days**. Scroll down to task 142 to see how this 1-week lead time compressed the schedule toward your 8/5/26 deadline. The finish date for this task has been compressed to **8/12/26.** You'll still need to compress the schedule another week to make the deadline.

Update the Duration for a Critical Path Task

This time, you'll reduce the duration for a critical path task to reduce the project's duration. Scroll up to critical path task 105 *Install building carpet*. This task currently has a 4-week duration. You can see by the blue highlighting that it has been rescheduled to start on 6/16/26 and finish on 7/13/26. You've negotiated with the Carpet Contractor to bring in additional resources and complete the task in 3 weeks. Before you enter the new duration, take note that the next task, which is task 106 *Install hardware and accessories* is currently not on the critical path.

Reduce the duration for task 105 as follows:

1. In the **Duration** field of task 105 *Install building carpet*, enter **3w**.

After the duration value was changed, Project updated the task's finish date to **7/6/26.** Notice that task 106 is now on the critical path. This is what was referenced earlier in the chapter regarding the dynamic nature of the critical path. Scroll down to task 142 *Obtain certificate of occupancy* to see how the duration change affected this task.

The task should now meet your client's 8/5/26 deadline!

As a final step, you'll re-add the deadline to task 142 *Obtain certificate of occupancy* to see the effects in the schedule.

Re-add the deadline to the task as follows:

1. Double-click the task name of task 142, to open the *Task Information* dialogue box.

2. Select the **Advanced** tab.

3. In the **Deadline** field, type or select **8/5/26**.

4. Select **OK** to close the *Task Information* dialogue box.

In the *Indicators* field of the Entry table, notice that Project did not generate an alert. This is because task 142 no longer exceeds its deadline. In the Gantt chart, notice that the end of the task bar now corresponds with the green arrow deadline indicator. If you can't see the indicator in the Gantt chart, slide the zoom slider in the bottom right corner, to the right, to zoom in. Then, use the scroll bar to scroll to the deadline indicator in the timeline.

You've now worked with Slack, the Critical Path and Lead time to compress a schedule.

SAVE THIS PROJECT FILE.

You will use this file to complete the **Chapter 12** practice exercise.

Chapter 12 Constraining Your Schedule

In the last chapter, you learned to compress the schedule. You learned to use the Critical Path, Lead time and task relationships to reduce the project duration. In this chapter, you'll learn to **Constrain the Schedule**. Constraints are one of the most misused features of Microsoft Project. In this chapter, we'll discuss the proper way to use them. When you're done, you'll be able to explain the eight constraint types, apply constraints to tasks, identify when a task has been constrained and use the Planning Wizard feature to resolve scheduling conflicts.

You'll Learn:

- To Explain the Eight Constraint Types
- To Schedule from the Start or Finish Date
- To Apply Constraints to Tasks
- When to Use and Not Use Constraints
- To Use the Planning Wizard to Resolve Scheduling Conflicts

By default, Project's scheduling engine starts each task as soon as possible. While this is generally advantageous, it may not always fit your business reality. In such cases, you may need to constrain your schedule. Constraints allow you to tailor the scheduling behavior of Project to fit your business realities.

Here are some practical use cases for constraining your schedule:

- A funding delay is preventing a task from starting after its predecessor completes.
- A task is temporarily unworkable, despite its predecessor being complete.
- Although a task's predecessor is complete, it can't be worked until a resource finishes working on a higher priority project.

What do these use cases have in common? Each scenario requires tasks to start sometime after their predecessors complete. These scheduling requirements run counter to Project's default behavior, which is to begin all tasks as soon as possible - *immediately* after their predecessors complete. To address such business needs, Project's default scheduling behavior would need to be constrained. This is the focus of this chapter.

Constraint Types

A **Constraint** is a restriction applied to a task that impacts its start or finish date. There are eight constraint types available in Project. Each addresses a unique scheduling problem. Following is a description of each constraint type, along with a use case.

- **As Soon As Possible** (default) – The task will **start** as soon as possible.

Use Case: A 2-day task starts on a Monday and has three days of Total Slack. This means the task can start as late as Thursday without delaying the project schedule. Due to the high priority of the project and the risky nature of the task, the project manager insists the task be performed as soon as possible to account for any unforeseen delays. Therefore, they use the default **As Soon As Possible** constraint. Project will schedule the task to start on Monday.

NOTE: Since this is the default constraint type, it is already applied to each new task.

- **As Late As Possible** – The task will **start** as late as possible.

Use Case: A reliable contractor has requested to start their 2-day task on your project as late as possible so they can address a pressing matter. Their task has three days of Total Slack and is scheduled to start on a Monday. Since this contractor has consistently delivered in the past, you would like to honor their request. You apply the **As Late As Possible** constraint to their task. Project will then use the three days of slack and reschedule the start date from Monday to Thursday. If the task is completed in 2 days as agreed, your schedule will not be delayed.

- **Finish No Earlier Than** – The task will **finish** on the specified date or later.

Use Case: Alex is managing a project to deploy Virtual Server A. Bryce is managing a project to deploy Virtual Server B. These projects must finish together because Virtual Server A must be able to fail over to Virtual Server B. Alex's project (Virtual Server A) is running one month ahead of Bryce's project (Virtual Server B). Since these projects must finish together, Alex applies a **Finish No Earlier Than** constraint to the milestone task representing the project finish date, using the estimated finish date of Bryce's project as the Constraint date. Project will reschedule the finish date milestone task so that it does not finish before Bryce's project is expected to finish.

- **Finish No Later Than** – The task will **finish** on the specified date or sooner.

Use Case: A project manager is managing a 2-year project. Owing to the long project duration, the engineer assigned to the project has requested to start their work as late as possible. The project manager confirms that their task has 90 days of Total Slack. To honor their request, she identifies a task in the schedule that would not be able to start unless the engineer's task was complete. She then applies a **Finish No Later Than** constraint to the engineer's task, using the start date of the identified task as the **Constraint date**. Project will reschedule the engineer's task so that it finishes on or before the start date of the identified task. The project manager communicates the new start date of the engineer's task and advises them that they must start their task on or before this date to ensure the project finishes on time.

- **Must Finish On** – The task will **finish** on the specified date.

Use Case: A project manager is shipping vaccine to a buyer. The vaccine must be used within 10 days of arrival before it expires. The buyer's contract specifies that the vaccine must be delivered to the buyer's address on day 1 of the 10-day expiry period. To satisfy the contract terms, the project manager applies a **Must Finish On** constraint to the task that represents the vaccine delivery, using day 1 of the 10-day expiry period as the **Constraint date**. Project will schedule the task to finish on the specified date. Project will also notify you if this constraint causes a scheduling conflict and provide options for resolving the conflict.

- **Must Start On** – The task will **start** on the specified date.

Use Case: A project manager is managing a pharmaceutical project to introduce a new vaccine. The vaccine must be shipped from the supplier and used within 10 days of arrival before it expires. To maximize administration of the vaccine, the project manager applies a **Must Start On** constraint to the task representing the clinical trial dosing, using day 1 of the 10-day expiry period as the **Constraint date**. Project will schedule the task to start on the specified date. Project will notify you if this constraint causes a scheduling conflict and provide options for resolving the conflict.

- **Start No Earlier Than** – The task will start on the specified date or later.

Use Case: An IT project manager must hire a cabling contractor for a project to downsize commercial office space. Their preferred vendor is fast, familiar with their standards, does excellent work and has the most competitive quote. However, they are not available until the first day of Spring. To accommodate their preferred vendor's schedule, the project manager applies a **Start No Earlier Than** constraint to the preferred vendor's first task, using the first day of Spring as the **Constraint date**. Project will schedule the task to start on the specified date or later, depending on its predecessors.

- **Start No Later Than** – The task will start on the specified date or sooner.

Use Case: A construction project manager is managing a street improvement project. Since asphalt paving efforts can be adversely impacted by cold weather, the project manager applies a **Start No Later Than** constraint to the start milestone task of the project, using the first day of August as the **Constraint date**. Project will schedule the task to start on the specified date or earlier.

Applying Constraints to Tasks

To apply a constraint to a task:

- Double-click the task name of the task you want to apply the constraint to. The *Task Information* dialogue box will open (*Figure 165 below*).
- Select the **Advanced** tab.
- Select the constraint type you want from the **Constraint type** pick-list.
- Enter the date into the **Constraint date** field.
- Select **OK** to close the *Task Information* dialogue box.

After the constraint is applied, Project will generate an icon in the **Indicators** field of the Entry table.

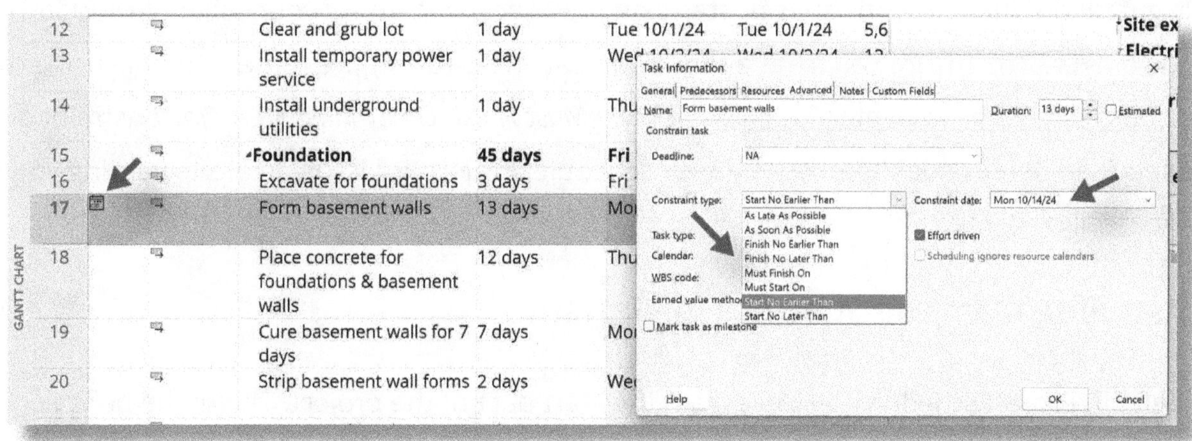

Figure 165 – Apply Constraints to Tasks

Manual Start or Finish Date Entries and Constraints

Constraints are one of the most misused features of Microsoft Project. This is because users are inclined to enter dates into the Start and Finish fields, instead of letting Project calculate those dates. This action unknowingly creates constraints in the schedule. As explained in Chapter 5, when using the Automatic scheduling mode, start and finish dates should not be manually entered. Doing so causes Project to constrain the schedule. For example, if you enter a start date for any task, Project will add a *Start-No-Earlier Than* constraint to that task.

Project interprets the manual entry as a command for the task to start no earlier than the entered date. This may seem harmless, but it's not. This constraint limits scheduling flexibility, which could cause unintended delays. This is because it prevents the task from starting earlier than the constraint date, even if its predecessors are complete. If task finish dates are entered, Project will apply a *Finish-No-Earlier Than* constraint to the task, and also constrain the schedule. It's best to avoid entering start and finish dates and let Project automatically determine them using its scheduling engine.

When to Use and Not Use Constraints

USE constraints when you must override the normal scheduling behavior of Project due to a business driver such as delayed funding, delayed resource availability, or any of the drivers described earlier in the use cases.

AVOID constraints when your goal is to get your project done faster. The *Must Finish On* and the *Must Start On* constraints are commonly misapplied for this reason. These constraints can only guarantee that a task finishes or starts on the specified date – *if* your schedule supports it. The only way to ensure you meet a required deadline is to compress the schedule using the methods discussed in Chapter 11. If you apply a *Must Finish On* or *Must Start On* constraint and the specified date is not supported by your schedule, Project will issue an alert, warning you of the scheduling conflict.

Scheduling from the Start or Finish Date

By default, Project schedules all tasks from the start date of the project. This is the behavior most schedulers require. When tasks are scheduled from the start date, Project forces all tasks to start as soon as possible by applying the default *As Soon as Possible* constraint to all new tasks. The *As Soon as Possible* constraint will have no effect on tasks on the Critical Path because they have zero Total Slack and are therefore already starting as soon as possible. This constraint type will however, impact tasks that are not on the critical path and therefore have Total Slack values greater than zero. It will cause them to start as soon as possible *within* the Total Slack period. For example, a 2-day task that has three days of Total Slack will be forced to start on a Monday, even though it could have started as late as Thursday of that same week without delaying the schedule. In most cases, this is the behavior schedulers require, as it will result in the project finishing as early as possible.

There are cases however, when schedulers will require the opposite behavior. They will need to model a scenario in which the project finishes as late as possible. For example, your stakeholders may want to start a high-priority, long-term project as late as possible so they can complete some smaller, short-term projects before the high-priority project begins. In such a case, it would be helpful to know the latest date by which they must start the high-priority project, so they can complete as many small, short-term projects as possible before it starts. To determine the latest date by which to start the high-priority project, tasks must be scheduled from the project finish date. When you schedule tasks from the project finish date, Project will begin all tasks as late as possible. For example, when this setting is applied, a 2-day task that has three days of Total Slack will be forced to start on a Thursday, when it could have started as early as Monday of that same week.

If your project requires tasks to be scheduled from the finish date, you must adjust the project settings as follows:

- Select the **Project** tab. In the **Properties** group, select the **Information** command to open the *Project Information* dialogue box.
- Select **Project Finish Date** from the **Schedule from** pick-list (*Figure 166* below).
- Select **OK** to close the *Project Information* dialogue box.

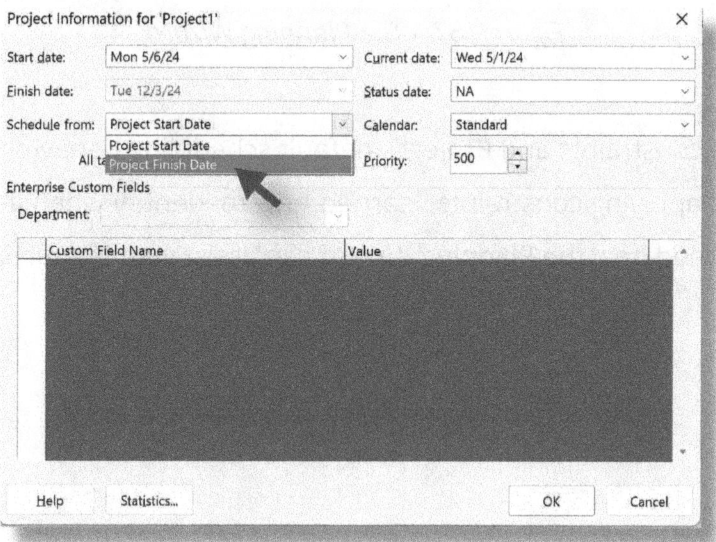

Figure 166 – Schedule Tasks from the Project Finish Date

If you want Project to schedule tasks from the project start date, leave the default **Project Start Date** in the **Schedule from** field.

Scheduling Conflicts and the Planning Wizard

Constraints must be used appropriately to avoid **Scheduling Conflicts**. Scheduling conflicts occur when conflicting requirements are imposed on a task. If you apply a constraint to a task that causes a scheduling conflict, Project will alert you of the conflict and offer options to resolve the issue using the **Planning Wizard** (*Figure 167 below*).

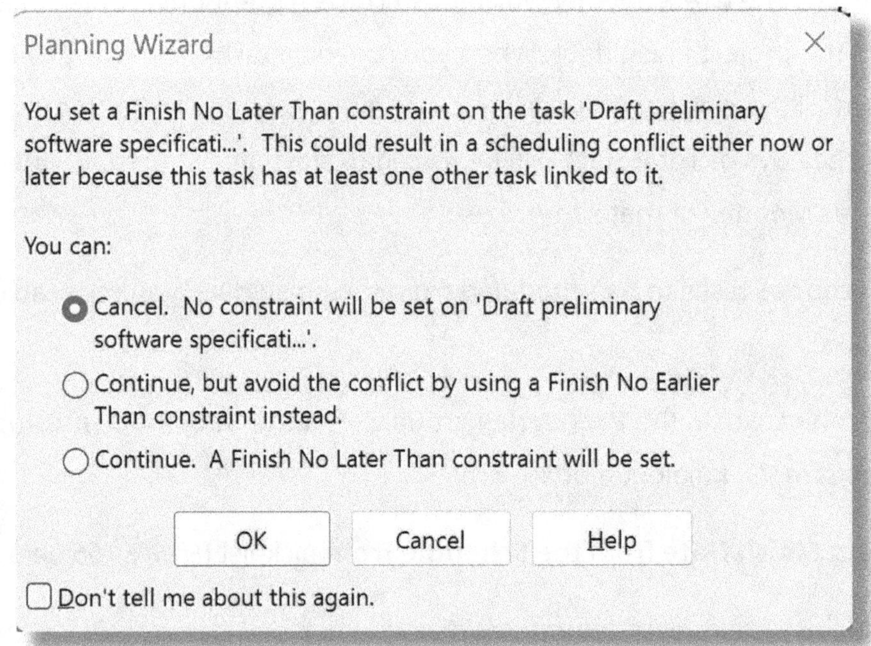

Figure 167 – The Planning Wizard

We've now reviewed constraints and Project's default scheduling behaviors. We've reviewed proper use cases for applying constraints, learned how to identify when a task has been constrained and learned how the Planning Wizard can assist with identifying and resolving scheduling conflicts.

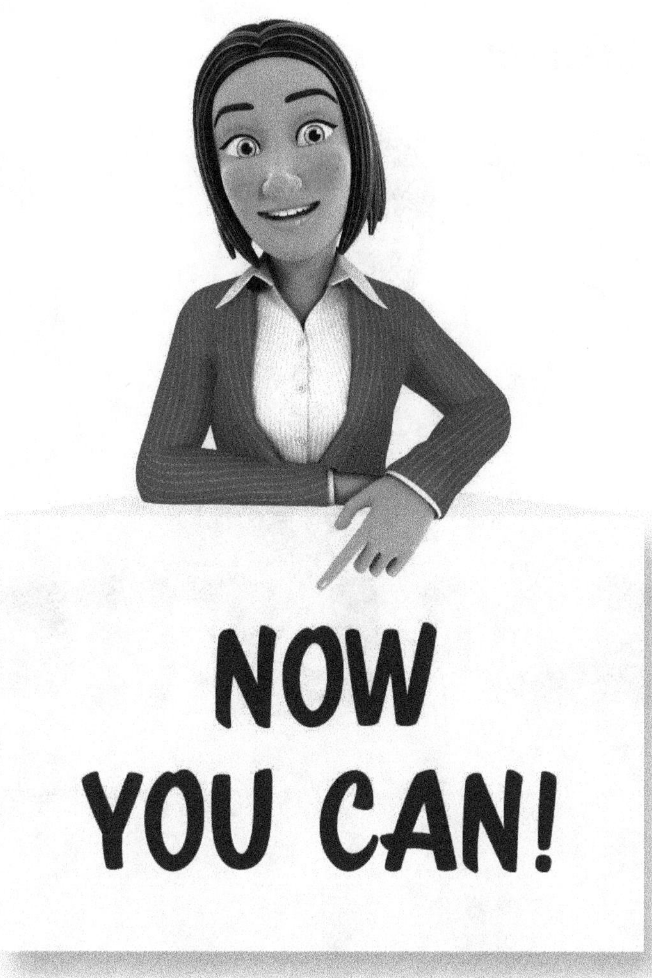

- ✓ Explain the Eight Constraint Types
- ✓ Schedule Tasks from the Start or Finish Date
- ✓ Apply Constraints to Tasks
- ✓ Explain When to Use and Not Use Constraints
- ✓ Use the Planning Wizard to Resolve Scheduling Conflicts

Practice Exercise

Constrain a Schedule

For this practice exercise, you will **constrain a schedule**. You'll work with the different constraint types to create exceptions to override Project's default scheduling behavior.

Go to **mspbasics.com** for "Checkpoint" images to check your work as you go along.

Follow the steps below to complete this practice exercise.

Open an Existing Project Plan

Open the *Commercial Construction* project plan that you saved from the Chapter 11 practice exercise. **NOTE:** The file should contain all the completed steps from the Chapter 11 exercise.

Apply Constraints to Tasks

Take note of the current project finish date of **8/6/26**. You'll reference this date later in the exercise. Scroll to task 6 *Obtain building permits*. This task is scheduled to start on 5/8/25. You've been notified that no building permits will be approved before 6/2/25. Therefore, this task cannot begin on its scheduled start date. To account for this delay, you'll apply a *Start No Earlier Than* constraint to the task as follows:

Double-click the task name of task 6 *Obtain building permits* to open the *Task Information* dialogue box.

1. Select the **Advanced** tab.
2. In the **Constraint type** field, select **Start No Earlier Than** from the pick-list.
3. In the **Constraint date** field, enter or select **6/2/25**.
4. Select **OK** to close the *Task Information* dialogue box.

After the constraint is applied, Project will reschedule the task to start on **6/2/20**. An icon will be added to the **Indicators** field to indicate the applied constraint. Hover over the icon for details about the constraint. In the Gantt chart, the task bars will also depict the delayed start date.

CHECKPOINT: To check your results so far, go to **mspbasics.com**

- Select the **CheckPoint Images** tab.
- Select the version of the book you're using.
- Select **Chapter 12.** Then, go to **Checkpoint Image #1**

Scroll to task 15 *Submit shop drawings and order long lead items – HVAC*. This task is currently scheduled to start on 6/20/25 and finish on 7/3/25. The HVAC Contractor assigned to the task has correctly observed that his shop drawings will not be used until 10/28/25, when the successor task 54 begins. As a favor, he has asked you to delay his task as late as possible, so he can devote resources to more critical projects. Since this task isn't on the critical path and has 16.4 weeks of Total and Free slack, you agree to accommodate his request. But, to allow room for potential delays, you'll need him to start the task on 9/1/25. To incorporate this stipulation into the schedule, you'll apply a *Must Start On* constraint to this task as follows:

1. Double-click the task name of task 15 *Submit shop drawings and order long lead items – HVAC* to open the *Task Information* dialogue box.

2. Select the **Advanced** tab.

3. In the **Constraint type** field, select **Must Start On**.

4. In the **Constraint date** field, enter or select **9/1/25**.

5. Select **OK** to close the *Task Information* dialogue box. **After you select OK**, Project opens the **Planning Wizard** to notify you that you set a *Must Start On* constraint on the task and this could result in a scheduling conflict because the task is linked to other tasks. **Select option 3**, *Continue. A Must Start On constraint will be set.*

6. Select **OK** to close the Planning Wizard.

After the constraint is applied, Project will reschedule the task to start on **9/1/25** and an icon will be generated in the **Indicators** field. Notice that this task is now on the critical path (indicated by the red highlighting). This is because delaying the start date removed the Total Slack.

CHECKPOINT: To check your results so far, go to **mspbasics.com**

- Select the **CheckPoint Images** tab.
- Select the version of the book you're using.
- Select **Chapter 12**. Then, go to **Checkpoint Image #2**

Scroll to task 104 *Hang Wallpaper*. This task is currently scheduled to start on 6/9/26 and finish on 6/22/26. The Painting Contractor has called in a favor and has asked you to delay his task as late as possible because he has a competing project with a more urgent completion target. You've checked your schedule and observed that his task isn't on the critical path and has 2 weeks of Total Slack. So, you agree to grant his request. To reflect this delay in the schedule, you'll apply an *As Late As Possible* constraint to this task as follows:

1. Double-click the task name of task 104 *Hang Wallpaper* to open the *Task Information* dialogue box.
2. Select the **Advanced** tab.
3. In the **Constraint type** field, select **As Late As Possible**.
4. Because the task will start as late as possible, do not type a date in the **Constraint date** field. Project will calculate this date.
5. Select **OK** to close the *Task Information* dialogue box.

After the constraint is applied, Project will reschedule the task to begin on **6/23/26**, which is the latest date the task can start without delaying the schedule. As such, the task is now on the critical path and its Total and Free slack are now zero. Like the default *As Soon As Possible* constraint type, Project doesn't generate a constraint indicator for the *As Late As Possible* constraint type.

CHECKPOINT: To check your results so far, go to **mspbasics.com**

- Select the **CheckPoint Images** tab.
- Select the version of the book you're using.
- Select **Chapter 12**. Then, go to **Checkpoint Image #3**

Scroll to the top of the plan to view the project finish date. Notice that the finish date is still **8/6/26**. Applying the constraints didn't affect the project duration. This is because no constraints were applied to the critical path tasks. All constraints were applied to tasks with available slack. You've now worked with constraints to create exceptions to override Project's default scheduling behavior.

MAX. UNITS

Chapter 13 Leveling Your Resources

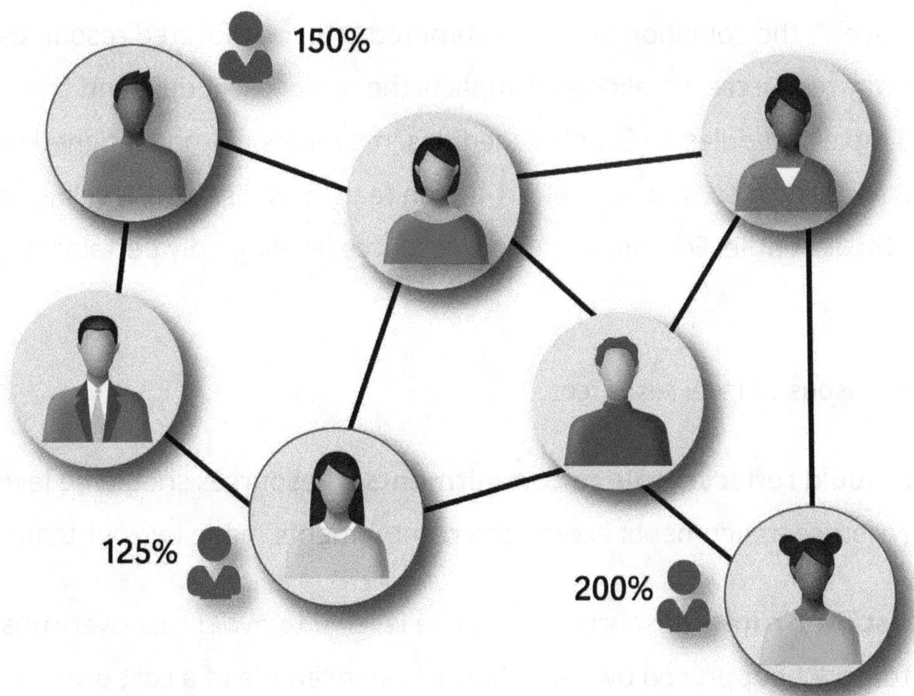

In the last chapter you learned to constrain the schedule. You learned the eight constraint types you can use in Project and use cases for applying each. In this chapter, we'll review **Resource Leveling**. You'll learn what those *red men* are and how to get rid of them! When you're done, you'll be able to offload over-committed resources using automatic and manual leveling methods. You'll also be able to use the Resource Usage, Leveling Gantt and Team Planner views to inspect and level over-committed resources.

You'll Learn To:

- Explain Max. Units
- Use Automatic Resource Leveling
- Level Resources Manually
- Use the Leveling Gantt View
- Use the Resource Usage View
- Use the Team Planner View
- Split Tasks

Understanding Resource Leveling

Resource Leveling is the re-distribution of work to level it across the project team. It resolves (or "levels") the condition of over-committed or over-allocated resources. In Detailed schedules, the way resources are allocated impacts the project schedule and cost. This is not the case with Simple schedules. In Simple schedules, resources are not assigned to tasks per their specific availability. Also, since the effort-driven feature is disabled, leveling resources will not impact the schedule. For these reasons, resource leveling only pertains to Detailed scheduling.

Here are some reasons to level resources:

- **Schedules should reflect resource commitments** - Resources should be leveled whenever resource assignments exceed the commitments made by your team.
- **To avoid cost over-runs** - Resources should be leveled to avoid cost over-runs. Causing resources to work unapproved overtime hours is an example of a cost over-run that could have been avoided by resource leveling.
- **To avoid unrealistic scheduling expectations** - Because resource leveling will almost certainly delay your schedule, it should always be done before schedules are presented to stakeholders.

Max. Units

As discussed in Chapter 8, **Max. Units** represents a resource's maximum capacity to work on tasks in any given day. It is expressed as a percentage of an 8-hour day. By default, Project assigns 100% Max Units to all new resources. This means the default assumption that Project makes is that resources are available to work on their assigned tasks an entire 8-hour workday. If this is not the case for the resources assigned to your project, you will need to adjust their Max Units accordingly. For example, if a resource is only available to work on assigned tasks for 4 hours per day, their Max. Units should be adjusted to 50%.

Over-Allocated Resources

When a resource is scheduled to work beyond their Max Units value, the resource becomes **over-allocated**. For example, a resource with 50% Max. Units can work on tasks for up to 4 hours per day without becoming over-allocated. If their collective task assignments on any given day total 5 hours or more, they will become over-allocated. When this occurs, Project will generate a red man icon in the Indicators field of the Entry table, next to each task the resource is assigned to (*Figure 168* below). In other views, such as the Resource Usage view and the Team Planner view, over-allocated resources are highlighted with red typeface.

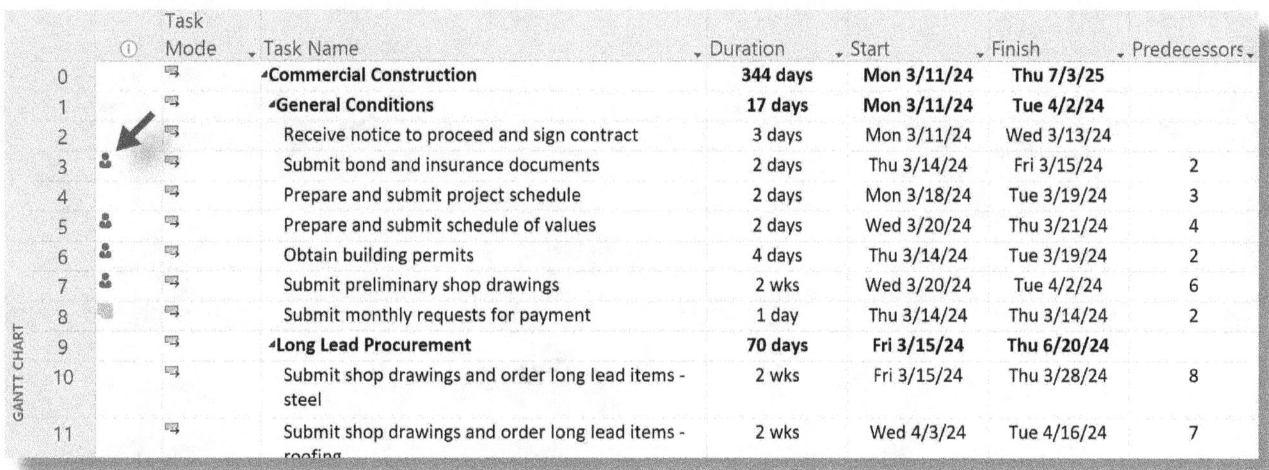

	ⓘ	Task Mode	Task Name	Duration	Start	Finish	Predecessors
0			**Commercial Construction**	**344 days**	**Mon 3/11/24**	**Thu 7/3/25**	
1			**General Conditions**	**17 days**	**Mon 3/11/24**	**Tue 4/2/24**	
2			Receive notice to proceed and sign contract	3 days	Mon 3/11/24	Wed 3/13/24	
3			Submit bond and insurance documents	2 days	Thu 3/14/24	Fri 3/15/24	2
4			Prepare and submit project schedule	2 days	Mon 3/18/24	Tue 3/19/24	3
5			Prepare and submit schedule of values	2 days	Wed 3/20/24	Thu 3/21/24	4
6			Obtain building permits	4 days	Thu 3/14/24	Tue 3/19/24	2
7			Submit preliminary shop drawings	2 wks	Wed 3/20/24	Tue 4/2/24	6
8			Submit monthly requests for payment	1 day	Thu 3/14/24	Thu 3/14/24	2
9			**Long Lead Procurement**	**70 days**	**Fri 3/15/24**	**Thu 6/20/24**	
10			Submit shop drawings and order long lead items - steel	2 wks	Fri 3/15/24	Thu 3/28/24	8
11			Submit shop drawings and order long lead items - roofing	2 wks	Wed 4/3/24	Tue 4/16/24	7

Figure 168 – Over-Allocated Resource Indicator

Removing the Red Men from Simple Schedules

Although resource leveling will not impact a Simple schedule, many schedulers prefer to remove the red man icons that appear in the Indicators field. This is because they can alarm stakeholders and appear to be errors. To quickly remove the over-allocations (and the red men) in a Simple schedule, you can increase the Max. Units value of the over-allocated resources until the red men disappear. You can do this in the Resource Sheet view, in the Max. Units field. These icons will disappear when every resource is assigned within their Max. Units capacity.

IMPORTANT NOTE: This cosmetic exercise should never be performed in Detailed schedules. Doing so would be like disabling the "Check Engine" indicator in your car. The over-allocation red man indicator is meant to alert you that you have assigned your resources beyond capacity within the time-frame of their task assignment(s).

Analyzing Over-Allocations – Using the Resource Usage View

Before you level over-allocated resources, you must identify the task assignments that caused the over-allocation. You can get this information in the **Resource Usage view**.
This view shows resources and their task assignment details. The *Usage* table on the left shows resources, their task assignments, and cumulative work hours (*Figure 169 below*).

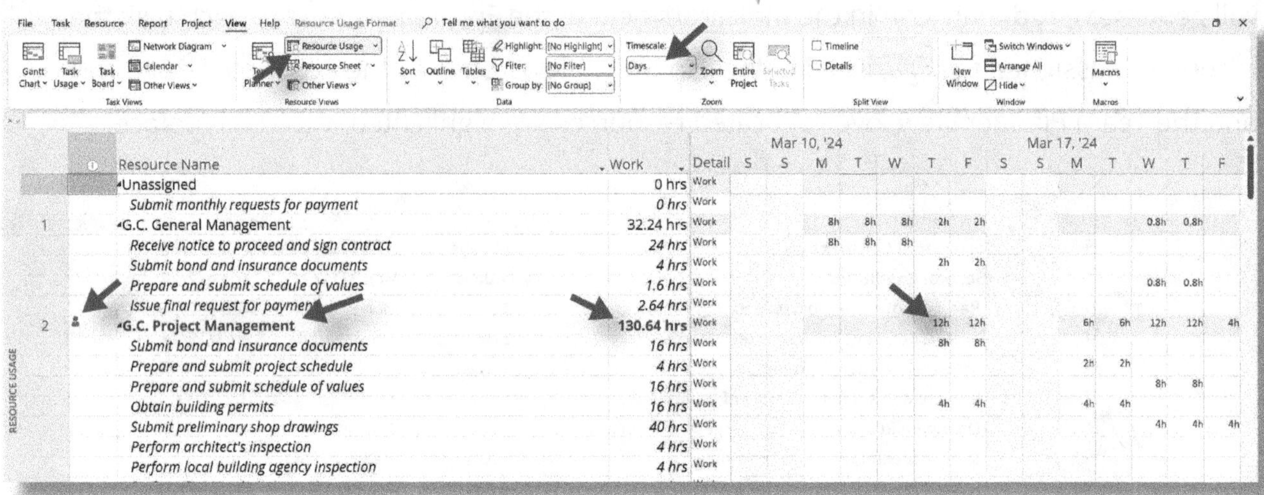

Figure 169 – The Resource Usage View

On the right, the work hours are displayed across the timescale increment that you choose. As mentioned, the over-allocated resources and the assignments causing the over-allocations are highlighted in red typeface. In *Figure 169* above, the G.C. Project Management resource is over-allocated on May 14th, May 15th, May 20th and May 21st. He's scheduled to work 12 hours on these dates, which exceeds his 100% Max. Units capacity of up to 8 hours per day. For example, on May 14th, he's scheduled to work 8 hours on the *Submit bond and insurance documents* task and 4 hours on the *Obtain building permits* task.

To view and edit additional information about an assignment, you can double-click the task name to open the *Assignment Information* dialog box (*Figure 170*). For example, you can select the Work contour option that Project uses to distribute work hours. *Flat* is chosen by default. With this option, Project distributes work evenly across the duration of the task. Using the pick-list, you can change the work contour to any of the eight options, including *Front Loaded*, and *Back Loaded*. As you can see, the Resource Usage view is very useful for analyzing resource over-allocations.

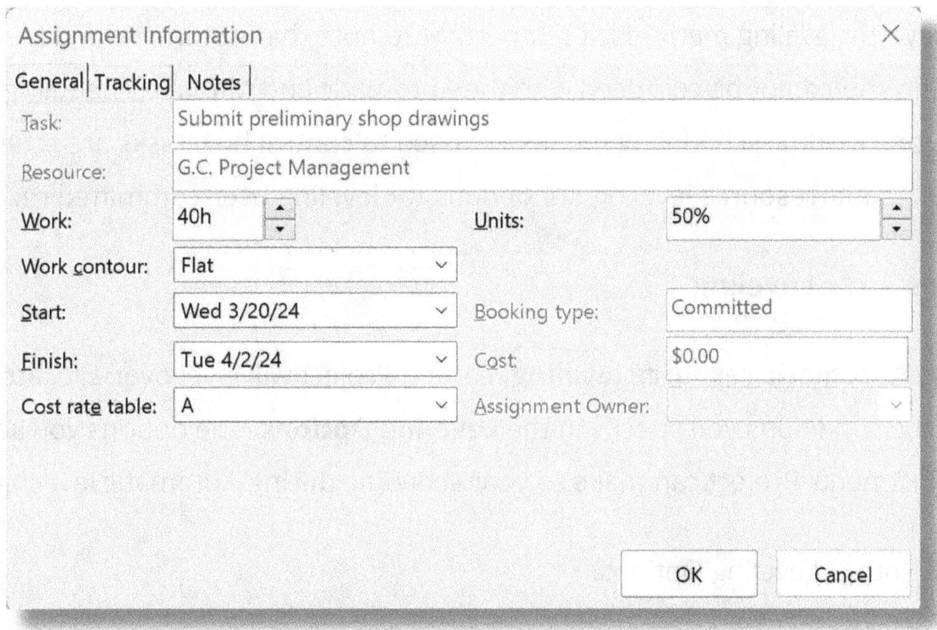

Figure 170 – The Assignment Information Dialogue Box

To access the Resource Usage view:

- Select the **View** tab.
- In the **Resource Views** group, select **Resource Usage**.

Resource Leveling Methods

Resource leveling can be done **Automatically** or **Manually**. Automatic leveling is done by Project, using the Automatic leveling feature. Manual leveling is done by you, using a variety of methods. Whether you level resources automatically or manually, it will always result in delayed tasks and in many cases a delayed project schedule as well. This is because leveling causes resources to work less time on tasks by respecting their maximum capacity to work. For this reason, resource leveling should always be performed before you present your schedule to stakeholders. This will ensure your projections are realistic and will therefore set the right expectations. When you use the Automatic Leveling feature, Project will resolve over-allocated resources by making adjustments that least delay the schedule. As you'll discover in this chapter, you can do everything Project can do to level resources – such as delaying start dates, splitting tasks and adjusting resource assignment units. The difference is, you understand the business realities of your project, and can therefore make more realistic adjustments to the schedule.

Before we review the leveling methods, it's important to note that Automatic and Manual resource leveling should not be confused with the Automatic and Manual scheduling modes. The Automatic and Manual scheduling modes are used to control how tasks are scheduled. Automatic and Manual resource leveling are options for leveling over-committed resources.

Automatic Resource Leveling

When using the **Automatic resource leveling** feature, Project will level over-allocated resources per the conditions you specify in the **Leveling Options**. The options you select control the adjustments Project can make to your schedule during Automatic leveling.

To select the Resource Leveling Options:

- Select the **Resource** tab.
- In the **Level** group, select **Leveling Options** to open the *Resource Leveling* dialogue box.

We'll review the Automatic Resource Leveling options using *Figure 171* below.

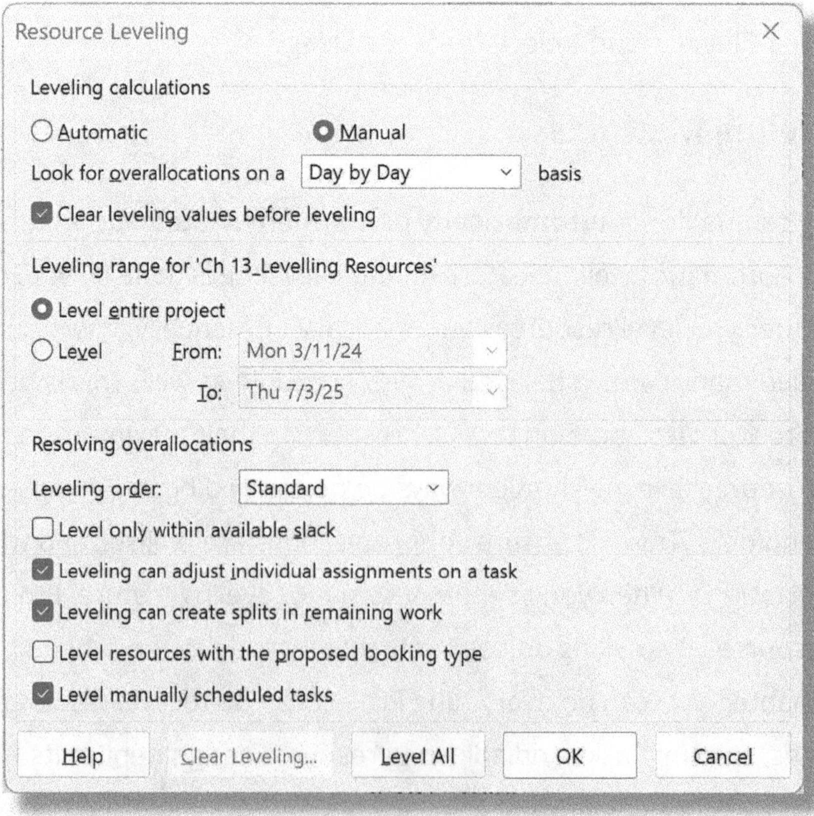

Figure 171 – Automatic Resource Leveling Options

Leveling calculations – There are two options for this setting – **Automatic** and **Manual**. Manual is selected by default. If you select the Automatic option, Project will automatically level resources as soon as they become over-allocated. If you select the Manual option, Project will level resources only when you tell it to, by using the resource leveling features. General practice is to use the Manual option, as it allows you to control when resource adjustments are made in your schedule.

Look for overallocations on a ...basis – This option lets you choose how granularly Project will look for over-allocations. The choices are Minute by Minute, Hour by Hour, Day by Day, Week by Week and Month by Month. General practice is to use Day by Day, which is selected by default.

Clear leveling values before leveling – This option will clear values from a previous leveling attempt and level **all** tasks. If this box is unchecked, Project will only level **new** and unleveled tasks from the previous leveling attempt.

Leveling range – This option allows you to choose whether Project will level resources across the entire project or only within a specified date range.

Leveling order – This option lets you choose the order in which Project will delay tasks to level resources. There are 3 choices:

- **ID only** – Project will delay tasks with higher Task ID values first.
- **Standard** (default) – Project considers the following conditions (in respective order) to determine which tasks to delay: Predecessor relationships, Slack, Dates, Priorities and Constraints.
- **Priority, Standard** – Project considers the same conditions as the Standard option, except it looks for task priority first.

NOTE: You can set task priority by double-clicking a task name to open the *Task Information* dialogue box. On the **General** tab, set the priority in the **Priority** field. Set a value between 1 and 1000. The higher you set the task priority number, the less likely the task will be adjusted during resource leveling. By default, tasks are given a priority value of 500.

Level only within available slack – This option allows you to choose whether you wish to perform **Resource Smoothing** or **Resource Leveling**. When this option is selected, you'll be performing Resource Smoothing. Project will assess the slack value of tasks and delay them within their available slack. When this option is deselected, you'll be performing Resource Leveling. Project will extend the project finish date to resolve over-allocations. Although Resource Smoothing will prevent Project from extending the finish date, it may result in some resources remaining over-allocated. Conversely, Resource Leveling will always resolve all over-allocated resources.

Leveling can adjust individual assignments on a task – This option allows Project to adjust individual assignments on a task until the over-allocation condition clears up. For example, a resource that is assigned at 50% Units may be reduced to 25% Units – if that will resolve the over-allocation condition.

Leveling can create splits in remaining work – When this option is selected, Project will split the remaining work on a task (delaying the task) to resolve an over-allocation.

Level resources with the proposed booking type – This option relates to **Project Server** only. Project will consider the *Booking Type* (proposed or committed) when leveling resources. If selected, Project will make changes to committed resources before making changes to proposed resources. If left unchecked, Project will only impact committed resources.

Level manually scheduled tasks – When this option is selected, Project will include tasks scheduled in the Manual scheduling mode when leveling.

How to use Automatic Resource Leveling

Once you've set your leveling options, complete the following steps to Automatically level resources:

- Select the **Resource** tab.
- In the **Level group**, select **Level All** to level the entire project OR select **Level Resource** to level a specific resource.

Viewing the Effects of Automatic Leveling in the Leveling Gantt View

After using the Automatic leveling features, Project will highlight the updates to all impacted tasks using the Change Highlighting feature. You can also view the adjustments Project made to resolve over-allocations in the **Leveling Gantt view** (*Figure 172* below).

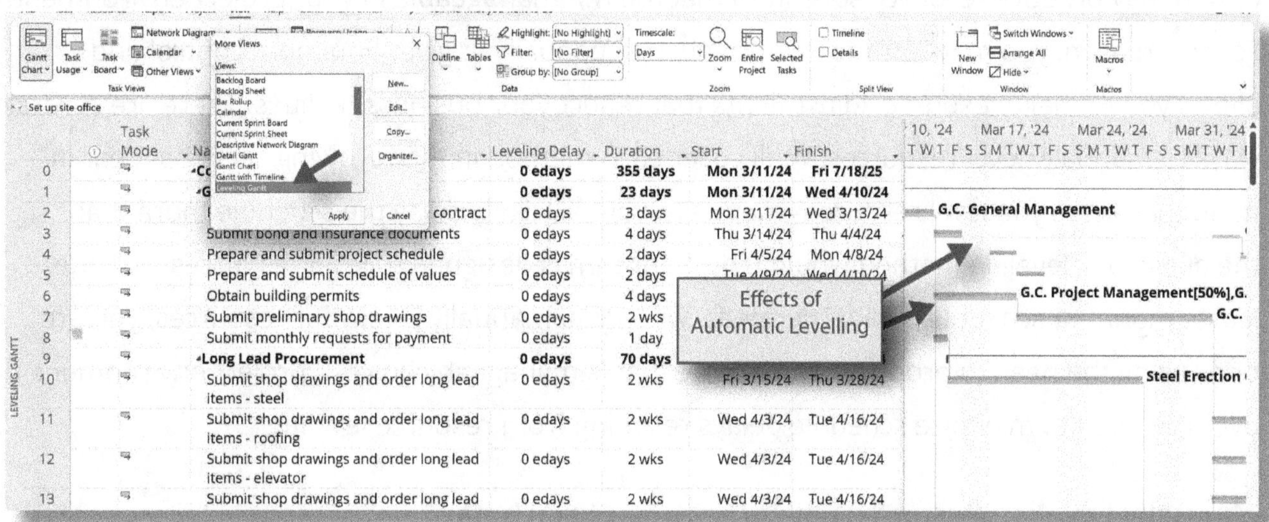

Figure 172 – The Leveling Gantt View

To access the Leveling Gantt view:

- Select the **View** tab.
- In the **Resource Views** group, select **Other Views**, then select **More Views**.
- In the *More Views* dialogue box, select **Leveling Gantt**, then select **Apply**.

This view shows the before-and-after effects of Automatic resource leveling. The *Delay* table on the left shows the tasks, their start and finish dates and the amount of leveling delay caused by Automatic resource leveling. In the Gantt chart, the task bars depict how Project resolved the over-allocations. The tasks that have been leveled have two sets of task bars. The gold task bars on the top represent the tasks <u>before</u> they were leveled. The blue task bars on the bottom represent the tasks <u>after</u> they were leveled. For example, in *Figure172*, to resolve the over-allocation for task 3 *Submit bond and insurance documents*, Project split the remaining work. As you can see, this action delayed the task quite a bit. The task was originally scheduled to finish on 3/15/24. After the leveling, it was rescheduled to finish on 4/4/24. Hover over the tasks bars to view leveled and pre-leveled start and finish dates.

Manual Resource Leveling

As mentioned earlier, using the Automatic leveling method allows Project to automatically level resources by making adjustments that least delay the schedule. Though efficient, this option may produce resource schedules that are not manageable in your project environment. For this reason, you may want to level resources manually. It gives you more control and allows you to make resource adjustments that reflect your business realities. There are several ways to manually level resources. We'll cover each method in the following sections. Bear in mind that when you level resources manually, you will likely delay the schedule more than the automatic leveling method would. The algorithm is designed to level resources with the least amount of schedule delay. Therefore, when you manually level your resources, you are prioritizing the need to produce an outcome that is manageable in your project environment over the need to minimize schedule delays resulting from resource leveling.

Manually Leveling Resources by Increasing Max. Units

The fastest way to manually level resources is to **increase a resource's Max. Units** value. For example, in *Figure 173* below, the G.C. Project Management resource is over-allocated on March 14th, March 15th, March 20th and March 21st. This resource is scheduled to work 12 hours on these dates, which exceeds their 100% Max. Units capacity of 8 hours per day.

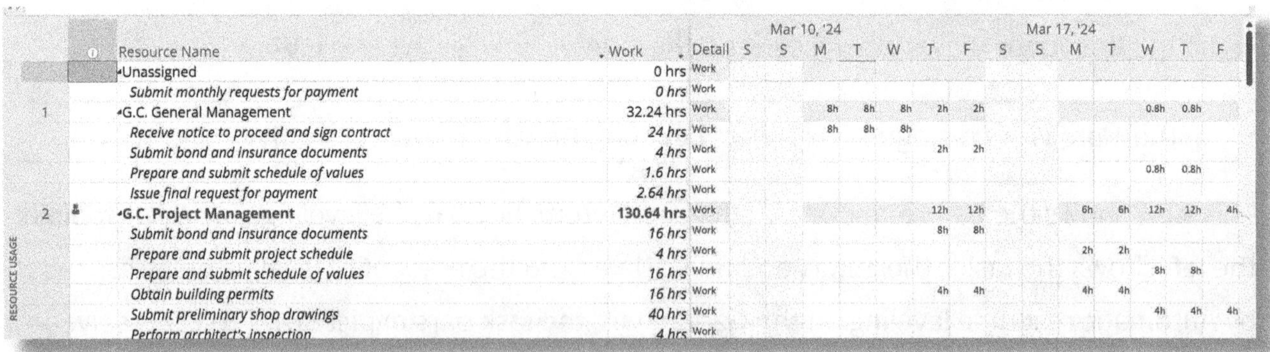

Figure 173 – Working with Over-Allocated Resources

Increasing this resource's Max. Units to 150% (12 hours per day) would resolve the over-allocations. Bear in mind, working 12 hours per day may not be practical. Also, increasing Max. Units can also increase cost, so it may not always be the best solution.

To adjust a resources Max. Units:

- Select the **View** tab.
- In the **Resource Views** group, select **Resource Sheet** to access the *Resource Sheet* view.
- Adjust the resource's Max Units value in the **Max. Units** field.

Manually Leveling Resources by Redistributing Task Work

Another way to manually level resources is to **redistribute task work**. The Resource Usage view is not only handy for identifying over-allocations, but it's also a good place to resolve them. For example, in *Figure 173*, to resolve the G.C. Project Management resource's over-allocations on March 14th and March 15th, the work hours for the *Submit bond and insurance documents* task could be manually reduced from 8 hours to 4 hours. The remaining 4 hours could be redistributed to another day(s), when the resource can work on the task within their Max. Units capacity. The same adjustment can be made for the *Prepare and submit schedule of values* task on March 20th and March 21st.

Manually Leveling Resources by Splitting a Task

Resources can also be manually leveled by **Splitting a Task**. Splitting a task interrupts the work and resumes it on a later date. There are a couple of ways to split a task. One way is to manually adjust the work hours in the Resource Usage view. For example, in *Figure 174*, in the schedule on the top, the G.C Project Management resource is over-allocated on Friday, March 15th. To resolve the over-allocation, you could interrupt the work on task 6 *Obtain building permits* so that no work occurs on Friday, March 15th and resume the work on Monday, March 18th. The schedule on the bottom reflects this update. Task 6 has been split from March 15th to March 18th. To interrupt the work on March 15th the 4h entry was replaced with 0h.

NOTE: There is no need to make 0h entries on Saturdays and Sundays because these are non-working days. Also, after an entry is made, Project will add a notification icon in the Indicators field notifying you that the assignment has been edited.

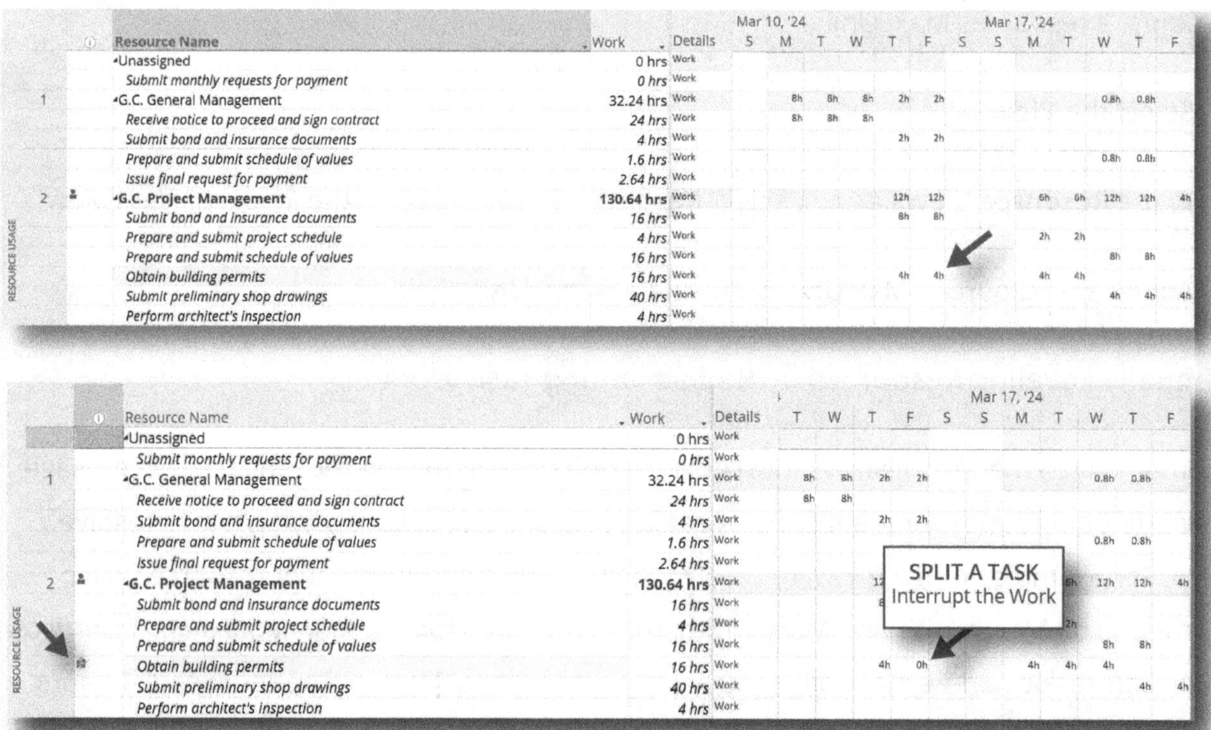

Figure 174 – Split Tasks to Level Resources in the Resource Usage View

In the Gantt Chart view, when a task is split, Project indicates the split with a dotted line in the task bar where the work is interrupted (*Figure 175* below). Project will also delay the task's finish date to reflect the split.

	Task Name	Duration	Start	Finish
0	**Commercial Construction**	**344 days**	**Mon 3/11/24**	**Thu 7/3/25**
1	**General Conditions**	**18 days**	**Mon 3/11/24**	**Wed 4/3/24**
2	Receive notice to proceed and sign contract	3 days	Mon 3/11/24	Wed 3/13/24
3	Submit bond and insurance documents	2 days	Thu 3/14/24	Fri 3/15/24
4	Prepare and submit project schedule	2 days	Mon 3/18/24	Tue 3/19/24
5	Prepare and submit schedule of values	2 days	Wed 3/20/24	Thu 3/21/24
6	Obtain building permits	4 days	Thu 3/14/24	Wed 3/20/24
7	Submit preliminary shop drawings	2 wks	Thu 3/21/24	Wed 4/3/24
8	Submit monthly requests for payment	1 day	Thu 3/14/24	Thu 3/14/24
9	**Long Lead Procurement**	**70 days**	**Fri 3/15/24**	**Thu 6/20/24**
10	Submit shop drawings and order long lead items - steel	2 wks	Fri 3/15/24	Thu 3/28/24
11	Submit shop drawings and order long lead	2 wks	Thu 4/4/24	Wed 4/17/24

Figure 175 – Split Tasks Depicted in the Gantt Chart

Tasks can also be split directly in the Gantt Chart view, using the **Split Task** command.

To split a task in the Gantt Chart view:

- In the Entry table of the Gantt Chart view, select the task you want to split. You may need to adjust the view to zoom in on the task bar in the Gantt chart.

Adjust the view as follows:

- Select the **Task** tab. In the **Editing** group, select the **Scroll to Task** command to bring the task bar forward.
- To zoom in on the task bar, select the **View** tab. In the **Zoom** group, select **Days** from the **Timescale** pick list. You could also use the zoom slider in the lower right corner to zoom in on the task bar.
- Last, you may also need to use the scroll bar to bring the Gantt chart into view.

To split the task:

- On the **Task** tab, in the **Schedule** group, select the **Split Task** command (the mouse cursor will change to the split task arrow).
- Hover (don't click) over the task bar until the date you want to interrupt the task work appears (*Figure 176* below).
- Then, click and drag to the right until the date you want to resume the task work appears, then release the click.
- Project will split the task and update the finish date accordingly.

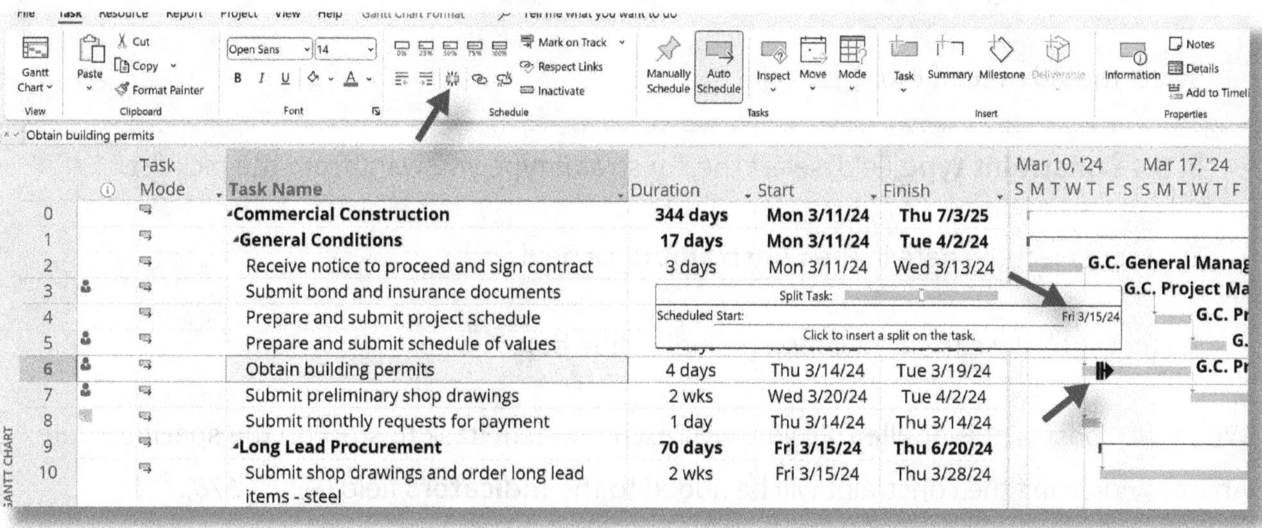

Figure 176 – Using the Split Task Command

Manually Leveling Resources by Using Constraints

Another way to manually level resources is to use a **constraint** to delay a task. For example, in *Figure 177* below, the G.C. Project Management resource is over-allocated on Wednesday, March 20th and Thursday, March 21st. He's scheduled to work 12 hours on both days. To resolve the over-allocation on March 21st, the 4 hours of work scheduled for the *Submit preliminary shop drawings* task can be delayed to Friday, March 22nd by applying a *Start No Earlier Than* 3/22/24 constraint. As reviewed in Chapter 12, this constraint type causes Project to delay a task until the specified date, even if its predecessor has already finished.

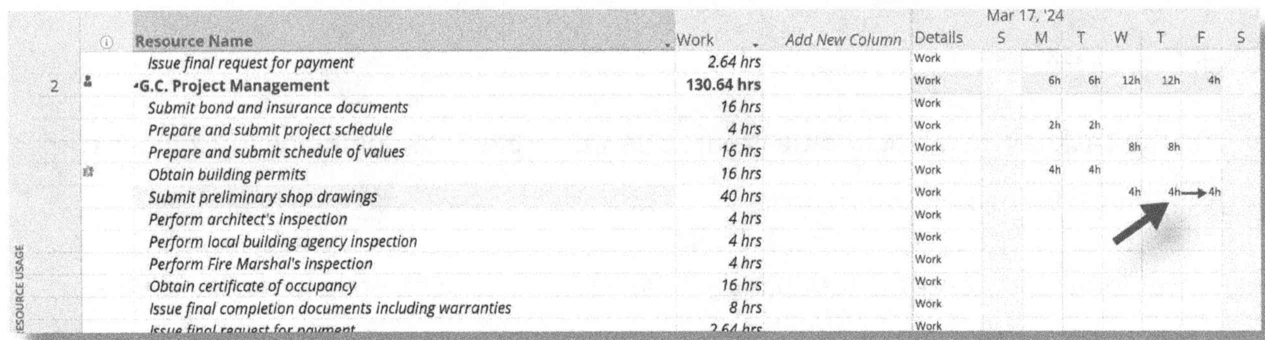

Figure 177 – Working with Over-Allocated Resources

To apply a constraint to a task:

- In the Gantt Chart view, double-click the task name of the task to open the *Task Information* dialogue box (*Figure 178*).
- Select the **Advanced** tab.
- In the **Constraint type** field, select the constraint type you want from the pick-list.
- Enter or select the date in the **Constraint date** field.
- Select **OK** to close the *Task Information* dialogue box.

When the constraint is applied, Project will reschedule the task to start on the specified date. An icon indicating the constraint will be added to the **Indicators** field (*Figure 178*).

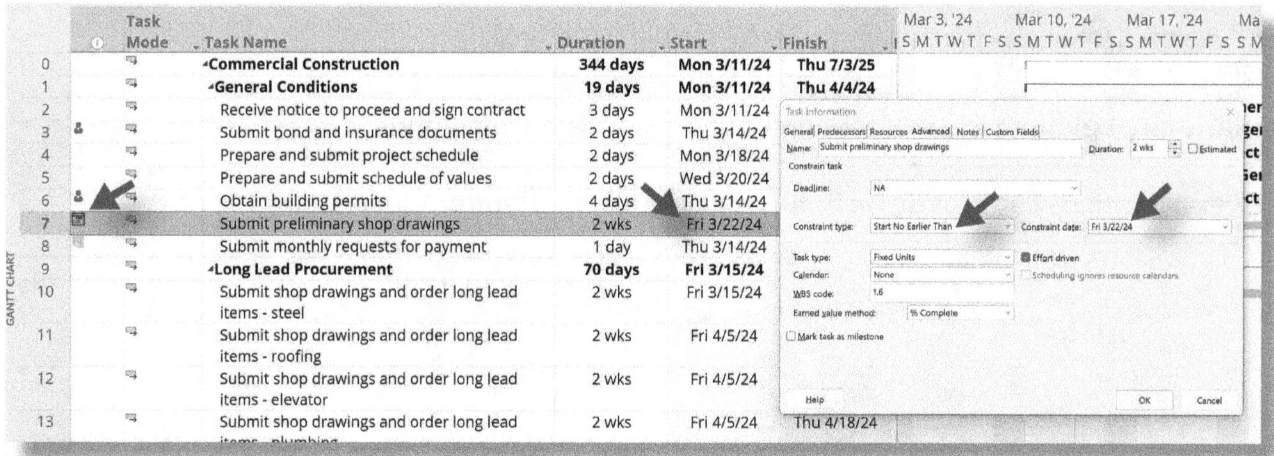

Figure 178 – Using Constraints to Level Resources

Manually Leveling Resources by Reassigning Work

Another way to manually level resources is to **reassign** their **work** to another resource. This can be done using the **Assign Resources** command, and the **Replace** option.

To reassign work:

- In the Gantt Chart view, in the Entry table, select the task that you want to reassign the work on.
- Select the **Resource** tab.
- In the **Assignments** group, select **Assign Resources** to open the *Assign Resources* dialogue box (*Figure 179* below).
- Select the current resource, then click **Replace** to open the *Replace Resource* dialogue box.

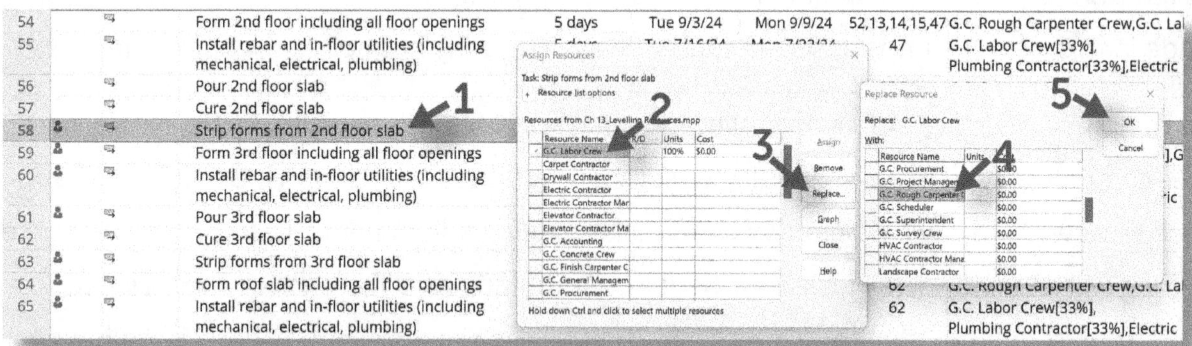

Figure 179 – Reassign Task Work to Level Resources

- Select the new resource, then select **OK** to close the *Replace Resource* dialogue box.
- Select **Close** to close the *Assign Resources* dialogue box.

Manually Leveling Resources using the Team Planner View

Over-allocations can also be resolved using the **Team Planner View** (*Figure 180* below).

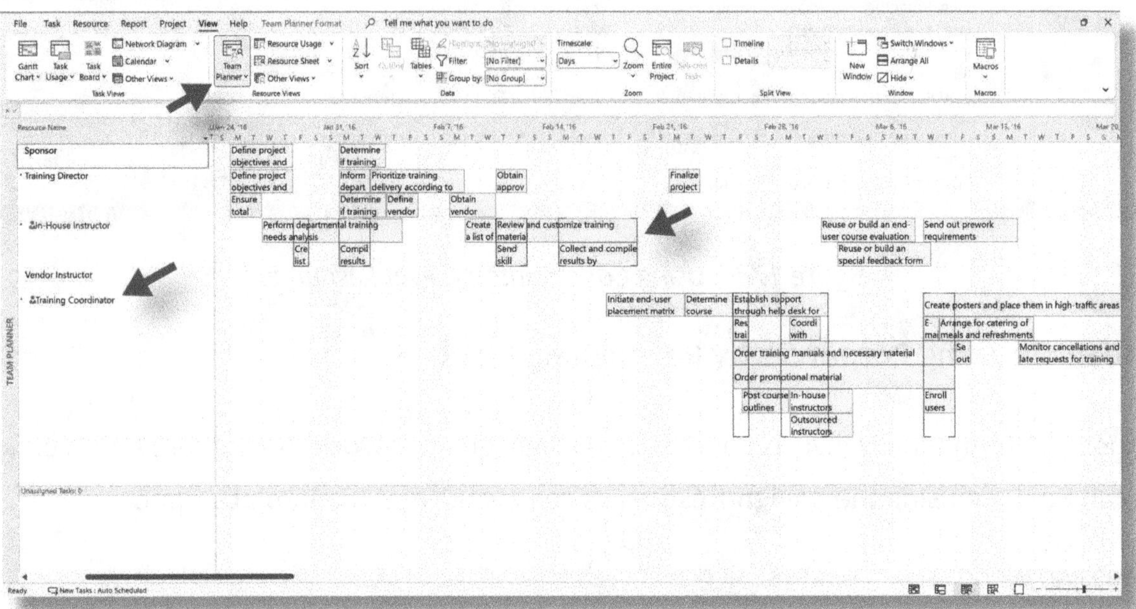

Figure 180 – Use the Team Planner View to Level Resources

This view is only available in the Microsoft Project Professional version. Like the Resource Usage view, the Team Planner view shows resources and their task assignments. Over-allocated resources are highlighted with red typeface .The blue bars on the right, represent the tasks they're assigned to. The red outlining reflects the task assignments causing the over-allocation(s). What this view offers that the Resource Usage View doesn't, is a drag and drop feature that allows you to make assignment adjustments directly in the view. While it's tempting to use this method of leveling for its simplicity, bear in mind that any adjustments made in this view can impact the schedule in ways that may not be readily apparent.

We've now reviewed resource over-allocation and ways to automatically and manually level over-committed resources. We've also reviewed how to use the Resource Usage and Team Planner views to inspect assignments and make leveling adjustments. In summary, resource leveling will generally delay tasks or schedules. Automatic leveling resolves over-allocations with the least amount of schedule delay. Manual leveling requires more work, but allows you to balance scheduling efficiency with business realities.

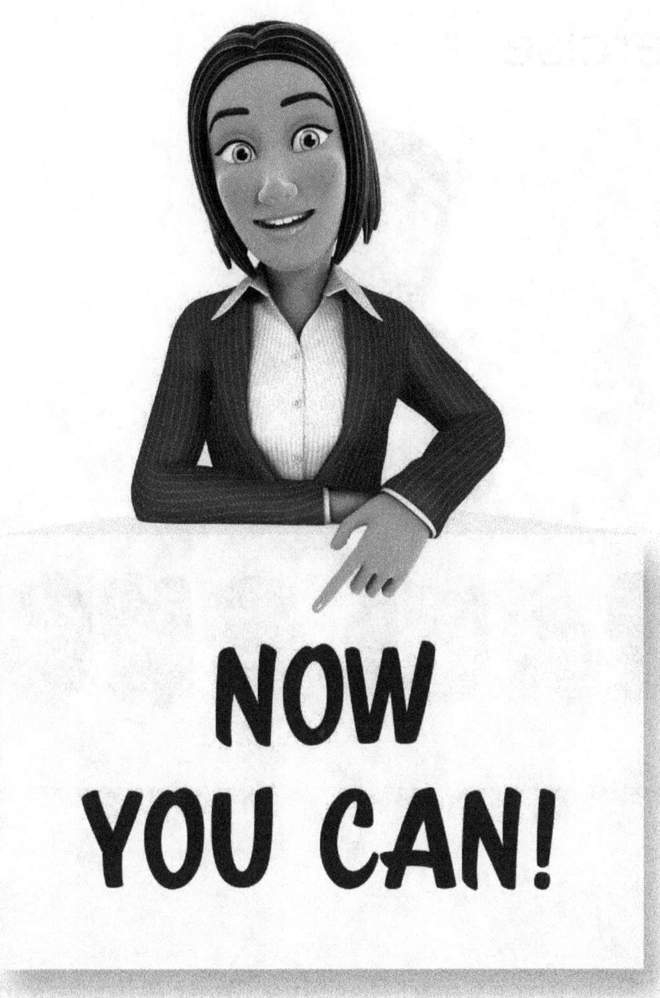

- ✓ Explain Max. Units
- ✓ Use Automatic Resource Leveling
- ✓ Level Resources Manually
- ✓ Use the Leveling Gantt View
- ✓ Use the Resource Usage View
- ✓ Use the Team Planner View
- ✓ Split Tasks

Practice Exercise

Level Resources and Resolve Over-Allocations

For this practice exercise, you will **level over-allocated resources**. You will resolve over-allocations using **Manual** and **Automatic** resource leveling methods.

Go to **mspbasics.com** for "Checkpoint" images to check your work as you go along.

Follow the steps below to complete this practice exercise.

PART ONE –LEVEL RESOURCES MANUALLY

Start a Project from a Template

You'll use the *Marketing Campaign Plan* project template to complete this exercise.

Note: The templates are hosted on a companion website. You'll need to be connected to the Internet to access them.

1. From the opening view, select the **New** tab, from the options on the left.
2. Double-click the *Marketing Campaign Plan* project template. If you don't see this template among the options, select **Show more** to see more templates. You can also use the search box.

Hide the Timeline Panel

Since we won't be using the Timeline panel for this exercise, you'll close it to see more of the Gantt Chart view.

To close the Timeline view panel:

1. Select the **View** tab.
2. In the **Split View** group, uncheck the **Timeline** checkbox.

Set the Project Start Date and the Current Date

Set the project start date to **6/3/24** as follows:

1. Select the **Project** tab.
2. In the **Properties** group, select the **Project Information** command to open the *Project Information* dialogue box.
3. Enter **6/3/24** in the **Start date** field. DO NOT Click OK. Remain in the *Project Information* dialogue box.

4. In the **Current date** field, enter or select **6/3/24**. Since the current date varies, this will cause your results to be consistent with the checkpoint images.

5. Select **OK** to close the *Project Information* dialogue box.

6. Take note of the project finish date of **3/14/25**. You'll reference it later in the exercise.

CHECKPOINT: To check your results so far, go to **mspbasics.com**

- Select the **CheckPoint Images** tab.
- Select the version of the book you're using.
- Select **Chapter 13**. Then, go to **Checkpoint Image #1**

Identify Over-Allocations

If you scroll down the project plan, you'll notice several tasks with over-allocated resources assigned to them (indicated by the red men icon in the **Indicators** column). To identify which task assignments caused the over-allocations, you'll switch to the **Resource Usage View** as follows:

1. Select the **View** tab.

2. In the **Resource Views** group, select **Resource Usage**.

In this view, resources, their task assignments, and cumulative work hours are listed on the left. Their work hours across the timeline are displayed on the right. Over-allocations are highlighted in red typeface. For example, scroll down until you see the Marketing Research resource on the left. Using the scroll bar on the bottom right, scroll to the right until you can see the over-allocations for the Marketing Research resource on October 16th, 17th, and 18th. The work hours on these dates will be highlighted in red typeface. This resource is scheduled to work 16 hours on each of these days, which exceeds their 100% Max. Units of 8 hours per day.

Next, you will manually resolve the over-allocations for each resource using various leveling methods.

Manually Level Resources by Increasing Max. Units

You'll resolve some of the over-allocations by increasing Max. Units. As reviewed earlier in the chapter, resources become over-allocated when their Max. Units value is exceeded.

Switch to the **Resource Sheet View** as follows:

1. Select the **View** tab.
2. In the **Resource Views** group, select **Resource Sheet**.

The following resources are over-allocated (as indicated by red typeface):

- Marketing Lead
- Marketing Research
- Marketing Staff
- Marketing Rep
- Internal PR
- PR Company

With the exception of the Marketing Lead, these are *Generic* resource groups and not individual resources. The over-allocations can be resolved by increasing the Max. Units of these resource groups to reflect the number of resources available in the group. You've spoken with your stakeholders, and each group has allocated up to 5 resources to the project. Each resource in the group is available at 100% Max. Units. Therefore, the collective Max. Units for each resource group is 500%. Increase the Max. Units for each resource group listed above (excluding the Marketing Lead) to 500% as follows:

1. In the **Max.** field for each resource, enter **500**.

After the Max. Units are adjusted, the over-allocations for the Marketing Research, Marketing Staff, Marketing Rep, Internal PR and PR Company resources should be resolved.

CHECKPOINT: To check your results so far, go to **mspbasics.com**

- Select the **CheckPoint Images** tab.
- Select the version of the book you're using.
- Select **Chapter 13.** Then, go to **Checkpoint Image #2**

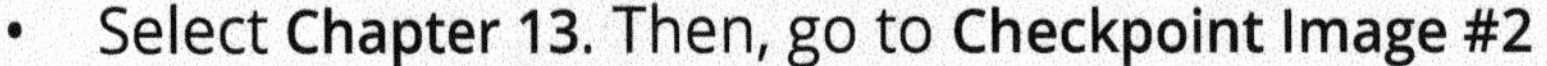

You'll resolve the over-allocations for the Marketing Lead resource using other methods.

Manually Level Resources by Applying Constraints

Return to the Gantt Chart view by selecting the **Gantt Chart** quick access icon in the top left corner of the ribbon. The Marketing Lead is over-allocated on tasks 30, 31, 32, 113, 114 & 115. Scroll down to tasks 30, 31 & 32.

Use the **Scroll to Task** feature to bring the task bar for task 30 into the view as follows:

1. Select task 30 *Determine organization regional campaigns.*
2. Select the **Task** tab.
3. In the **Editing** group, select the **Scroll to Task** command.

In the Gantt chart, notice that the task bars for tasks 30, 31 & 32 are stacked. These tasks are scheduled concurrently, rather than in series. This is causing the over-allocation for the Marketing Lead. She's scheduled to work on all three tasks at the same time. Each task has a 5-day duration and is scheduled to start on 9/3/24, when their common predecessor (task 26) finishes. You'll resolve the over-allocations for tasks 31 *Determine organization global campaigns* and 32 *Determine organization country campaigns* by applying **Start No Earlier Than** constraints to delay their start dates.

To apply the Start No Earlier Than constraint to task 31:

1. Double-click the task name for task 31 to open the *Task Information* dialogue box.
2. Select the **Advanced** tab.

3. In the **Constraint type** field, select **Start No Earlier Than.**

4. In the **Constraint date** field, type or select **9/10/24.**

5. Select **OK** to close the *Task Information* dialogue box.

After the constraint is applied, the over-allocation for task 31 should be resolved. This task should be rescheduled to start on **9/10/24**, which is the next working day after the preceding task (task 30) finishes.

CHECKPOINT: To check your results so far, go to **mspbasics.com**

- Select the **CheckPoint Images** tab.
- Select the version of the book you're using.
- Select **Chapter 13**. Then, go to **Checkpoint Image #3**

To apply a Start No Earlier Than constraint to task 32:

1. Double-click the task name for task 32 to open the *Task Information dialogue* box.

2. Select the **Advanced** tab.

3. In the **Constraint type** field, select **Start No Earlier Than.**

4. In the **Constraint date** field, type or select **9/17/24.**

5. Select **OK** to close the *Task Information* dialogue box.

After the constraint is applied, the overallocation for task 32 should be resolved. This task should be rescheduled to start on **9/17/24**, the next working day after the preceding task (task 31) finishes. This should have also resolved the over-allocation for task 30, because these tasks are no longer being worked on the same date. In the Gantt chart, notice the task bars for tasks 30, 31 & 32 are now positioned in sequence.

CHECKPOINT: To check your results so far, go to **mspbasics.com**

- Select the **CheckPoint Images** tab.
- Select the version of the book you're using.
- Select **Chapter 13**. Then, go to **Checkpoint Image #4**

Manually Level Resources by Reassigning Work

Scroll down to tasks 113, 114 & 115. Use the **Scroll to Task** feature to bring the task bar for task 113 into the view as follows:

1. Select task 113 *Evaluate campaign effectiveness*.
2. Select the **Task** tab.
3. In the **Editing** group, select the **Scroll to Task** command.

The Marketing Lead should be still over-allocated on tasks 113, 114 & 115 because their dates overlap. Task 113 and task 114 are both scheduled to start on 3/5/25. Also, task 115 is scheduled to start on 3/6/25, which overlaps with task 113. First, you'll resolve the over-allocation for task 114 *Review regional sales* by reassigning the work to another resource. You've been told that a resource from the Marketing Staff group can replace the Marketing Lead on this task.

To replace the resource:

1. Select task 114 *Review Regional Sales*.
2. Select the **Resource** tab.
3. In the **Assignments** group, select **Assign Resources** to open the *Assign Resources* dialogue box.
4. In the **Resource Name** field of the *Assign Resources* dialogue box, select the **Marketing Lead** resource, then select **Replace**.

5. In the *Replace Resource* dialogue box, scroll down and select the **Marketing Staff** resource, then select **OK**.

6. Select **Close** to close the *Assign Resources* dialogue box.

After the resource is replaced, the over-allocation for task 114 *Review Regional Sales* should be resolved. In the Resource Names field of the Entry table, the Marketing Staff resource should now be assigned, along with the Sales resource.

CHECKPOINT: To check your results so far, go to **mspbasics.com**

- Select the **CheckPoint Images** tab.
- Select the version of the book you're using.
- Select **Chapter 13**. Then, go to **Checkpoint Image #5**

Manually Level Resources by Splitting a Task (Interrupting Task Work)

Next, you will resolve the over-allocations for task 113 *Evaluate campaign effectiveness* and task 115 *Review global sales* by splitting task 113. As reviewed earlier in the chapter, splitting a task interrupts the work and resumes it on a later date. Task 113 *Evaluate campaign effectiveness* is a 3-day task. Work is scheduled to occur on 3/5/25, 3/6/25, and 3/7/25. This overlaps with task 115 *Review global sales*, which is a 1-day task, scheduled on 3/6/25. You will split task 113 so that no work occurs on **3/6/25** and resumes on **3/7/25**.

You'll split the task using its task bar. Zoom in on the task bar as follows:

1. Select the **View** tab.

2. In the **Zoom** group, select **Days** from the **Timescale** pick-list.

3. Use the **Zoom slider** in the bottom right corner of the view to zoom in further if you'd like.

To Split the task:

1. Select task 113 *Evaluate campaign effectiveness*.

2. Select the **Task** tab. In the **Schedule** group, select the **Split Task** command (the mouse cursor will change to the Split Task arrow).

3. Hover (don't click) the mouse pointer over the task 113 task bar until the **Scheduled start date** of **Thursday 3/6/25** appears.

4. Now, click and drag (don't release) to the right until the **Task Start** of **Friday 3/7/25** appears, then release.

After the task is split, the overallocation for tasks 113 and 115 should be resolved. The finish date for task 113 should be updated to 3/10/25. In the Gantt chart, the split task will be depicted with a dotted line on the task bar, where the work is interrupted.

You've now manually leveled resources by increasing Max. Units, applying constraints, reassigning task work, and splitting a task. All the project resources should be leveled. There should be no more red men! Note the new project finish date of **3/28/25**. The manual resource leveling efforts delayed the schedule 2 weeks from 3/14/25.

CHECKPOINT: To check your results so far, go to **mspbasics.com**

- Select the **CheckPoint Images** tab.
- Select the version of the book you're using.
- Select **Chapter 13.** Then, go to **Checkpoint Image #6**

Next, you'll level the same resources using the Automatic resource leveling method.

PART TWO – USE AUTOMATIC LEVELING

Start a New Project from a Template

Open a new *Marketing Campaign Plan* project template to complete Part Two of this exercise, as follows:

1. From the opening view, select the **New** tab, from the options on the left.

2. Double-click the *Marketing Campaign Plan* project template. If you don't see this template among the options, select **Show more** to see more templates. You can also use the search box.

Hide the Timeline Panel

Since we won't be using the **Timeline** panel for this exercise, you'll close it to see more of the Gantt Chart view.

To close the Timeline view panel:

1. Select the **View** tab.
2. In the **Split View** group, uncheck the **Timeline** checkbox.

Set the Project Start Date and the Current Date

Set the project start date to **6/3/24** as follows:

1. Select the **Project** tab.
2. In the **Properties** group, select the **Project Information** command to open the *Project Information* dialogue box.
3. Enter **6/3/24** in the **Start date** field. DO NOT Click OK. Remain in the *Project Information* dialogue box.
4. In the **Current date** field, enter or select **6/3/24.**
5. Click **OK** to close the *Project Information* dialogue box.
6. Take note of the project finish date of **3/14/25**. You'll reference it shortly.

Next, you'll level all the over-allocated resources using the **Automatic leveling** feature.

To Level Resources using Automatic Resource Leveling:

1. Select the **Resource** tab.
2. In the **Level** group, select **Level All** to level over-allocated resources for the entire project.

After Automatic leveling is performed, the updated project finish date should be **5/14/25**. Automatically leveling the resources delayed the schedule 2 months, from 3/14/25.

CHECKPOINT: To check your results so far, go to **mspbasics.com**

- Select the **CheckPoint Images** tab.
- Select the version of the book you're using.
- Select **Chapter 13**. Then, go to **Checkpoint Image #7**

To see the before and after effects of the Automatic resource leveling and how Project delayed the tasks, switch to the Leveling Gantt view, as follows:

1. Select the **View** tab.

2. In the **Resource Views** group, select **Other Views**, then select **More Views**.

3. In the *More Views* dialogue box, select **Leveling Gantt**, then select **Apply**.

NOTE: Automatic resource leveling allows Project to automatically level resources by making adjustments that least delay the schedule. Generally, Automatic leveling results in less delay than Manual leveling. In this case, since we adjusted resource's Max. Units to account for multiple resources in a group (which doesn't occur with Automatic leveling), the Manual method resulted in less schedule delay.

You've now leveled resources using Manual and Automatic resource leveling.

Chapter 14 Inspecting Your Schedule

In the last chapter, you learned to level over-allocated resources using Manual and Automatic resource leveling methods. In this chapter, you'll learn to view, organize, and **inspect project data** before publishing a project schedule. When you're done, you'll be able to sort, group and filter task and resource data, use the Task Inspector and create custom groups and filters.

You'll Learn:

- What to Inspect
- To Sort, Group and Filter Project Data
- To Use the Auto Filter
- To Create Custom Groups and Filters
- To Use the Task Inspector

Why Inspect Your Schedule?

After you've built your schedule, it's a good idea to inspect it.

Here are eight reasons:

1. To confirm your schedule is accurate
2. To confirm your schedule is aggressive, but realistic
3. To confirm dollars are being spent wisely
4. To avoid embarrassment
5. To correct mistakes
6. To avoid over-commitment
7. To prepare alternatives
8. Because others will!

Things to Inspect

20 THINGS TO CHECK BEFORE PUBLISHING YOUR SCHEDULE	
1. Project Start Date	11. Task Type Settings
2. Project Calendar	12. Effort-Driven Settings
3. Resource Calendars	13. Constraints
4. Resource Allocation	14. Work Estimates
5. Task Calendars	15. Duration Estimates
6. Non-Working Days	16. Task Notes
7. Work Restriction Periods	17. Resource Notes
8. Project Outline	18. Costs
9. Critical Path	19. Spelling
10. Task Relationships	20. Style (E.g., font, spacing, structure)

KEY TERMS

When inspecting your schedule, it's helpful to examine your project data in various views that show different subsets of information. The following features allow you extract, re-sequence and summarize task and resource data using the criteria you specify.

- **Sorting** – The re-sequencing of task or resource data per user-defined criteria.
- **Grouping** – The re-sequencing and grouping of task or resource data into summarized user-defined criteria.
- **Filtering** – The extraction of task or resource data per user-defined criteria.

Sorting Project Data

Using the Auto Filter to Sort Data

There are several ways to sort project data. One way is to use the **Auto Filter**. In task and resource views, you'll find the Auto filter arrows next to the column headers. This feature can be used to sort, group or filter columns of data. You can sort project data in ascending or descending order, or by any of the built-in options.

NOTE: If you don't see the Auto Filter arrows next to the column headers, you'll need to enable them as follows:

- Select the **View** tab.
- In the **Data** group, select **Display Auto Filter** from the **Filter** pick-list.

To sort the data in any field using the Auto Filter:

- In the field you want to sort, select the **Auto Filter** arrow to view the pick-list of sorting options (*Figure 181*). For example, you can sort the Task Name field in alphabetical order. You could also sort resource pay rates in ascending or descending order.
- Select the option you want from the pick-list. Project will sort the information in the field accordingly.

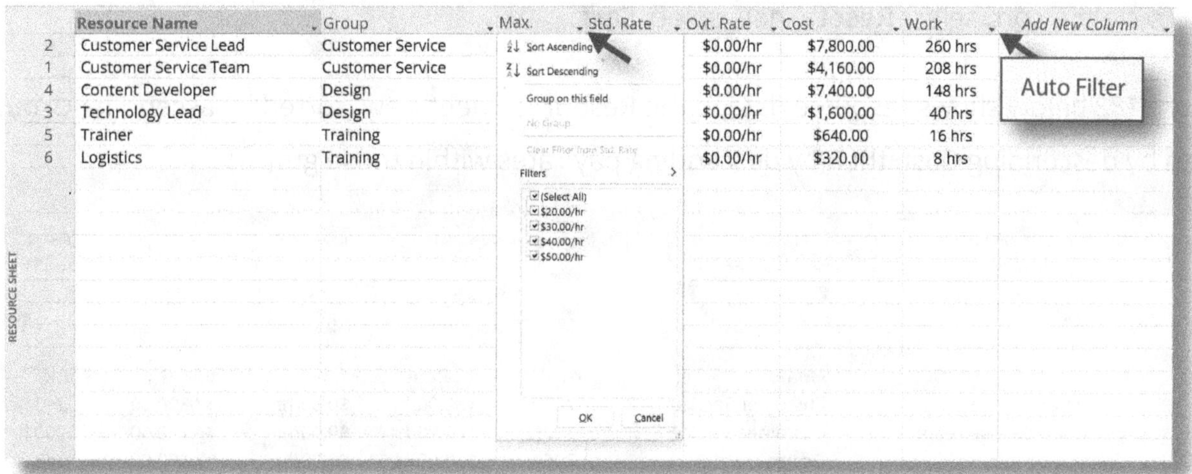

Figure 181 – Using the Auto Filter

Using the Sort Command to Sort Data

The **Sort** command allows you to arrange the data in a view using up to three levels of sorting criteria. For example, in a task view, you could sort tasks by the resources assigned to them. In a resource view, you could sort resource data by Group, Cost and Pay Rates.

NOTE: Some criteria must first be added to the schedule, such as resource groups.

To use the Sort command in a task or resource view:

- Select the **View** tab. In the **Data** group, select the **Sort** command, then select **Sort by** to open the *Sort* dialogue box (*Figure 182*).
- From the **Sort by** pick-list, select the first criterion you want to sort by.
- From the **Then by** pick-lists, select the next two levels of criteria (if applicable).
- Select an **Ascending** or **Descending** option for each level.
- Once you've selected the sorting criteria and sorting orders, select **Sort**.
- Select the **Permanently renumber tasks** or **Permanently renumber resources** check-boxes to permanently renumber the tasks and resources per the sorting outcomes.
- In a task view, select the **Keep outline structure** checkbox to ensure you can restore your project to its original structure after you sort the data.

- To clear a sort, select **Reset**. Then, select **Sort**.

Figure 182 below shows resource data in the Resource Sheet view, sorted by ascending Group, then by descending Cost, then by descending pay rates within those groups.

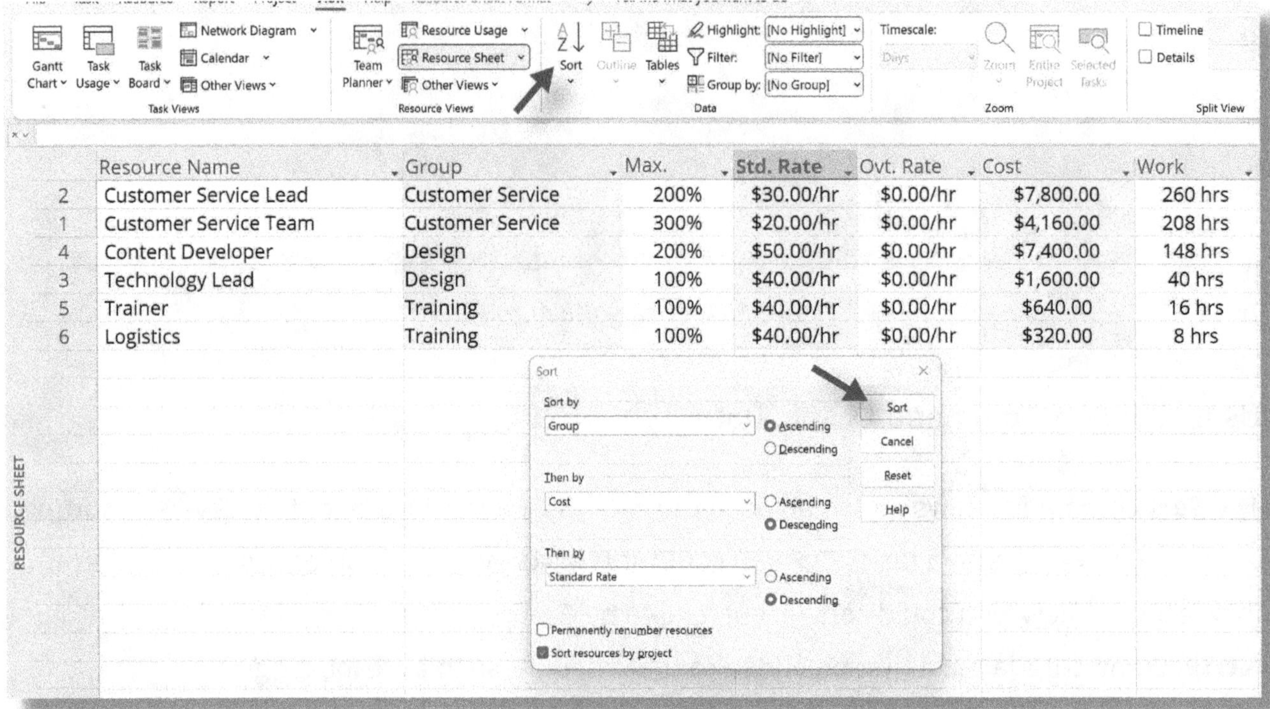

	Resource Name	Group	Max.	Std. Rate	Ovt. Rate	Cost	Work
2	Customer Service Lead	Customer Service	200%	$30.00/hr	$0.00/hr	$7,800.00	260 hrs
1	Customer Service Team	Customer Service	300%	$20.00/hr	$0.00/hr	$4,160.00	208 hrs
4	Content Developer	Design	200%	$50.00/hr	$0.00/hr	$7,400.00	148 hrs
3	Technology Lead	Design	100%	$40.00/hr	$0.00/hr	$1,600.00	40 hrs
5	Trainer	Training	100%	$40.00/hr	$0.00/hr	$640.00	16 hrs
6	Logistics	Training	100%	$40.00/hr	$0.00/hr	$320.00	8 hrs

Figure 182 – Using the Sort Command

Grouping Project Data

Grouping organizes data into criteria similarly to sorting. One advantage of grouping is that Project automatically summarizes and highlights the grouped information, including cost values. This makes the grouping features handy for reporting high level project information. There are several ways to group task and resource data.

Using the Group on this Field Command

In resource views that contain groupable data, the **Auto Filter** includes the **Group on this Field** command (*Figure 183*). This option allows you to group data by a certain field.

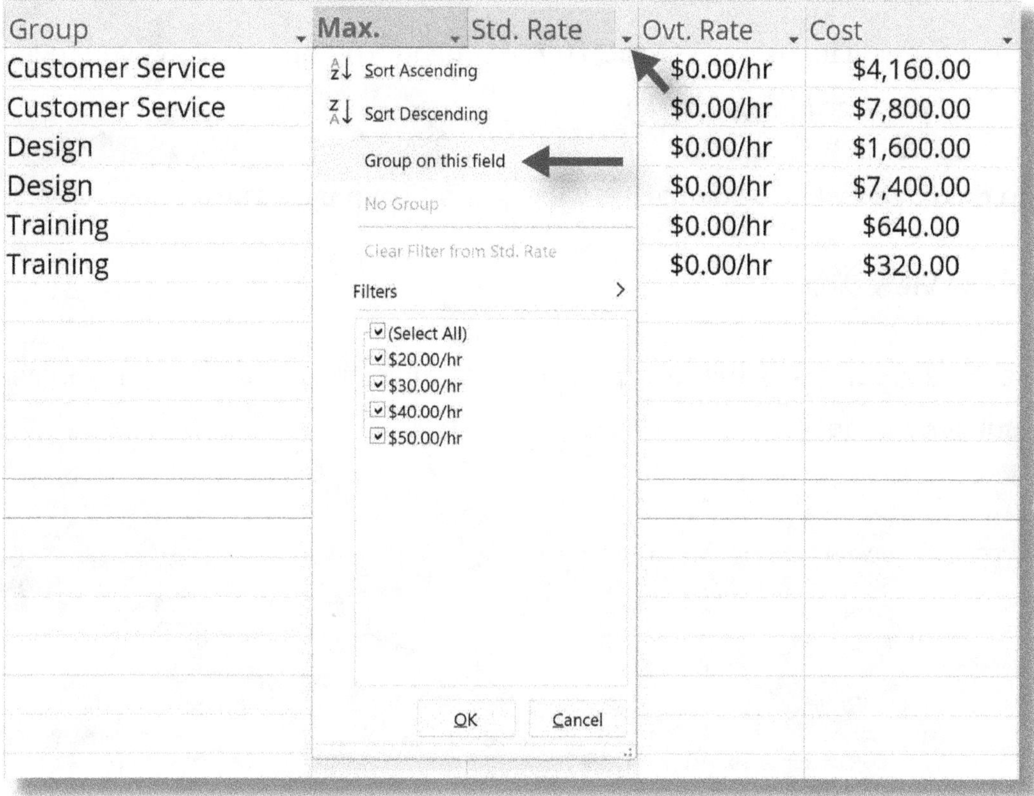

Figure 183 – Using the Group on this field Command

For example, in *Figure 184* below, resource information in the Resource Sheet view was grouped by the Std. Rate field. Project automatically highlighted summarized values for each rate grouping. For example, three resources are in the $40 per hour grouping. Their summarized Max. Units is 300%. The summarized cost for these resources is $2,560.

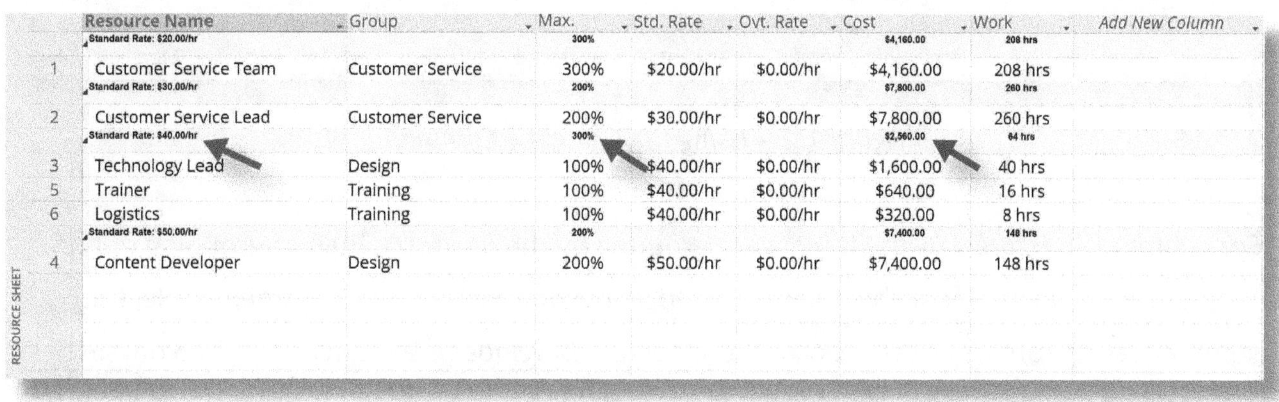

Figure 184 – Using the Group on this Field command to Group Resource Information

Using the Group by Command to Group Data

You can also group data using the **Group by** command. This option allows you to group tasks or resources by one grouping criterion.

To group data in a task or resource view using the Group by feature:

- Select the **View** tab.
- In the **Data** group, using the **Group by** pick-list, select the group criterion you want from the **Built-In** options (*Figure 185* below).

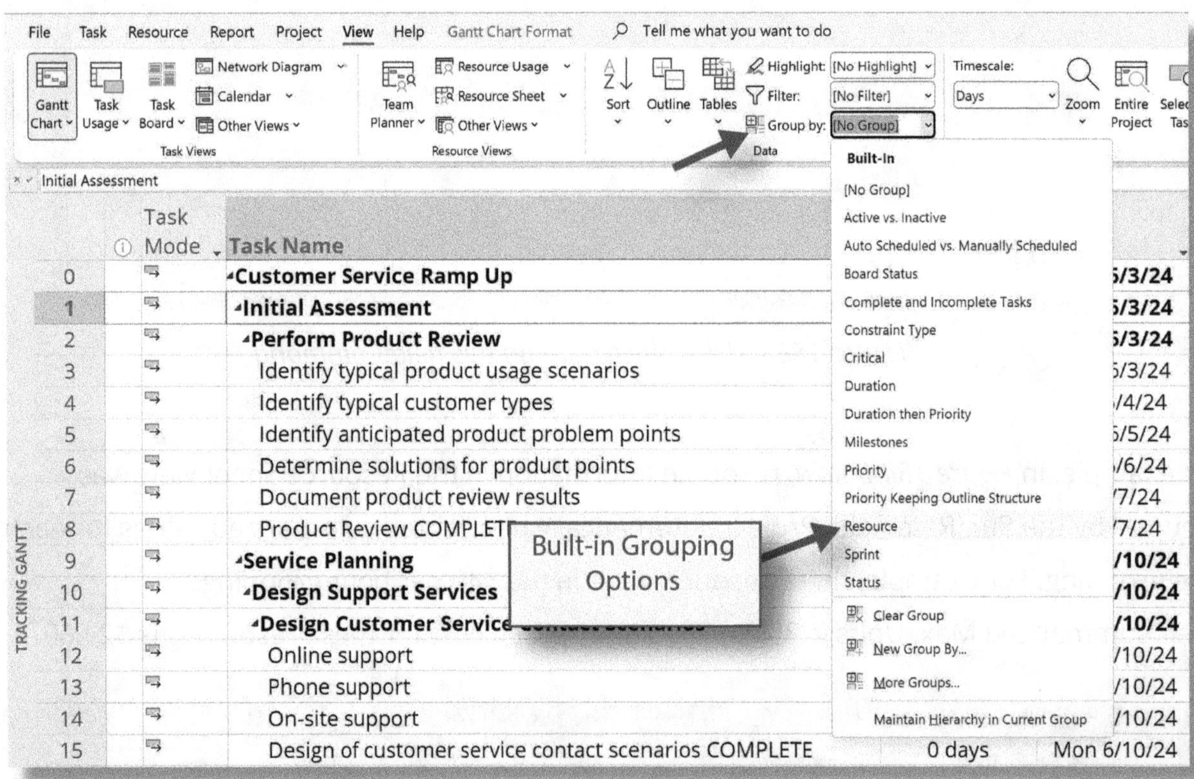

Figure 185 – Using the Group by Command

For example, in *Figure 186*, the tasks were grouped by the Resource Built-In grouping option. Project automatically highlighted summarized values for each grouping. For example, the summarized durations of the tasks that the *Content Developer* is assigned to is 63.5 days. These tasks will be worked from 6/10/24 to 9/5/24.

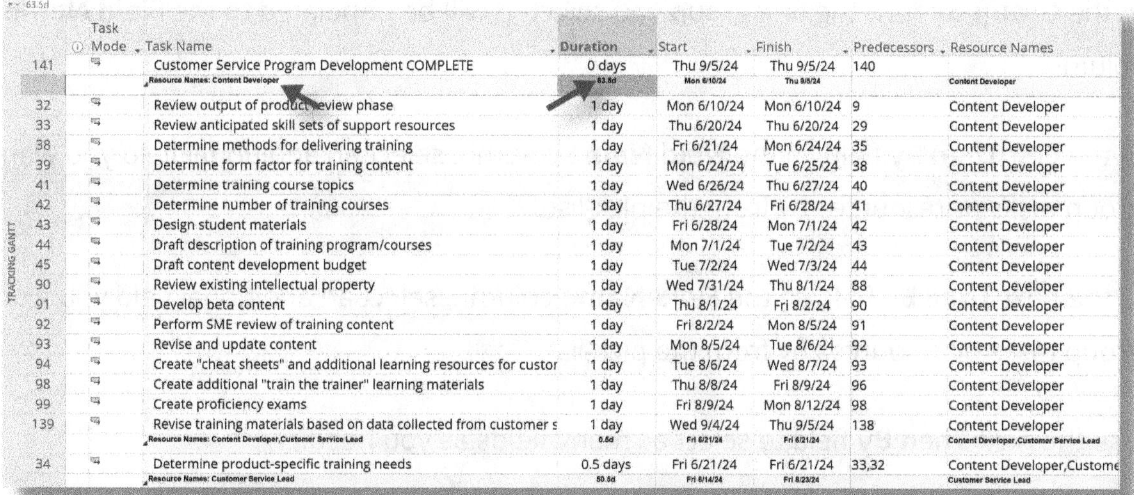

Figure 186 – Using the Group by Feature to Group Tasks

Group Data by Multiple Criteria

You can also group data by more than one criterion, as follows:

- Select the **View** tab.
- In the **Data** group, select **More Groups** from the **Group by** pick-list to open the *More Groups* dialog box. If you're in a task view, you'll see the grouping options for tasks (*Figure 187* below – left side). If you're in a resource view, you'll see the options for resources.
- Select the first grouping criterion you want from the list of options. Then select **Edit** to open the *Group Definition* dialog box (*Figure 187* below – right side).

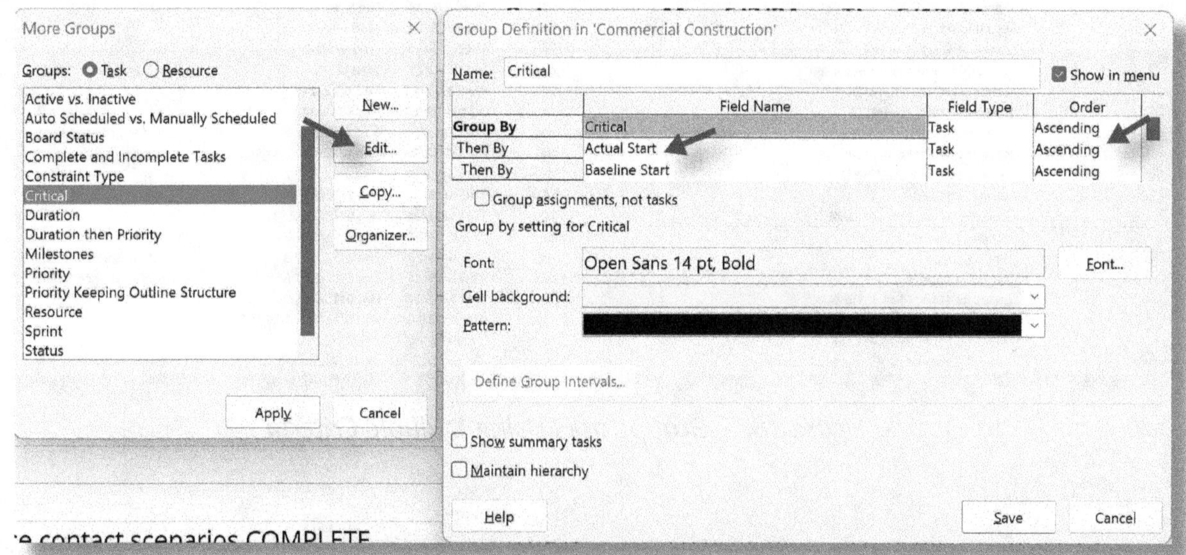

Figure 187 – Group Data by Multiple Criteria

- In the **Group By** row, the first group you selected will be populated to the **Field Name** column.
- In the first **Then By** field, in the **Field Name** column, select an additional field you want to group tasks or resources by from the pick-list.
- In the next **Then By** field, in the **Field Name** column, select an additional field you want to group tasks or resources by from the pick-list.
- Use the next **Then By** field to select as many fields as you need.
- In the **Order** field, select **Ascending** or **Descending** for each field.
- To select formatting options for each field, select the **Field Name** in the **Group By** or **Then By** field. Then, under the **Group by setting for** section, choose the options you want in the Font, Cell background, and Pattern fields.
- Once you've selected the options you want, select **Save** to close the *Group Definition* dialog box. Then, select **Apply** to apply the grouping and to close the *More Groups* dialog box.
- In *Figure 188* below, the tasks are grouped by Critical tasks, then by Actual start date and then by Baseline start date, each in ascending order.

	Task Mode	Task Name	Duration	Start	Finish	Predecessors	Resource Names
122		Resource Readiness Training COMPLETE	0 days	Tue 8/27/24	Tue 8/27/24	121	
		Critical: Yes	**69.5d**	**Wed 6/5/24**	**Tue 9/10/24**		
		Actual Start: Wed 6/5/24	**1d**	**Wed 6/5/24**	**Wed 6/5/24**		
		Baseline Start: Tue 6/4/24	**1d**	**Wed 6/5/24**	**Wed 6/5/24**		
4		Identify typical customer types	1 day	Wed 6/5/24	Wed 6/5/24	3	Customer Service Team
		Actual Start: Wed 6/12/24	**1d**	**Wed 6/12/24**	**Wed 6/12/24**		
		Baseline Start: Fri 6/7/24	**1d**	**Wed 6/12/24**	**Wed 6/12/24**		
7		Document product review results	1 day	Wed 6/12/24	Wed 6/12/24	6	Customer Service Team
		Baseline Start: Fri 6/7/24	**1d**	**Wed 6/12/24**	**Wed 6/12/24**		
8		Product Review COMPLETE	1 day	Wed 6/12/24	Wed 6/12/24	7	
		Actual Start: NA	**63.5d**	**Thu 6/13/24**	**Tue 9/10/24**		
		Baseline Start: Mon 6/10/24	**1d**	**Thu 6/13/24**	**Thu 6/13/24**		
12		Online support	1 day	Thu 6/13/24	Thu 6/13/24	8	Customer Service Team
13		Phone support	1 day	Thu 6/13/24	Thu 6/13/24	8	Customer Service Team
14		On-site support	1 day	Thu 6/13/24	Thu 6/13/24	8	Customer Service Team
		Baseline Start: Mon 6/10/24	**0d**	**Thu 6/13/24**	**Thu 6/13/24**		
15		Design of customer service contact scenarios COMPLETE	0 days	Thu 6/13/24	Thu 6/13/24	14,12,13	
		Baseline Start: Tue 6/11/24	**1d**	**Fri 6/14/24**	**Fri 6/14/24**		
17		Identify types of problems to be solved	1 day	Fri 6/14/24	Fri 6/14/24	15	Customer Service Team

TRACKING GANTT

Figure 188 – Group Tasks Using Multiple Criteria

Creating Custom Groups

If the grouping criteria you want is not available in the Built-in options, you can create a **Custom Group**. Moreover, if the custom group you want to create is similar to a Built-in group (E.g., Resource Group or Milestones), you can save time by using the **Copy** option to create the custom group.

To create a custom group using the Copy option:

- Select the **View** tab.
- In the **Data** group, select **More Groups** from the **Group by** pick-list to open the *More Groups* dialog box. If you're in a task view, you'll see the grouping options for tasks. If you're in a resource view, you'll see the options for resources.
- Select the **Built-in** group you want to copy. Then, select **Copy** to open the *Group Definition* dialogue box (*Figure 189* below).

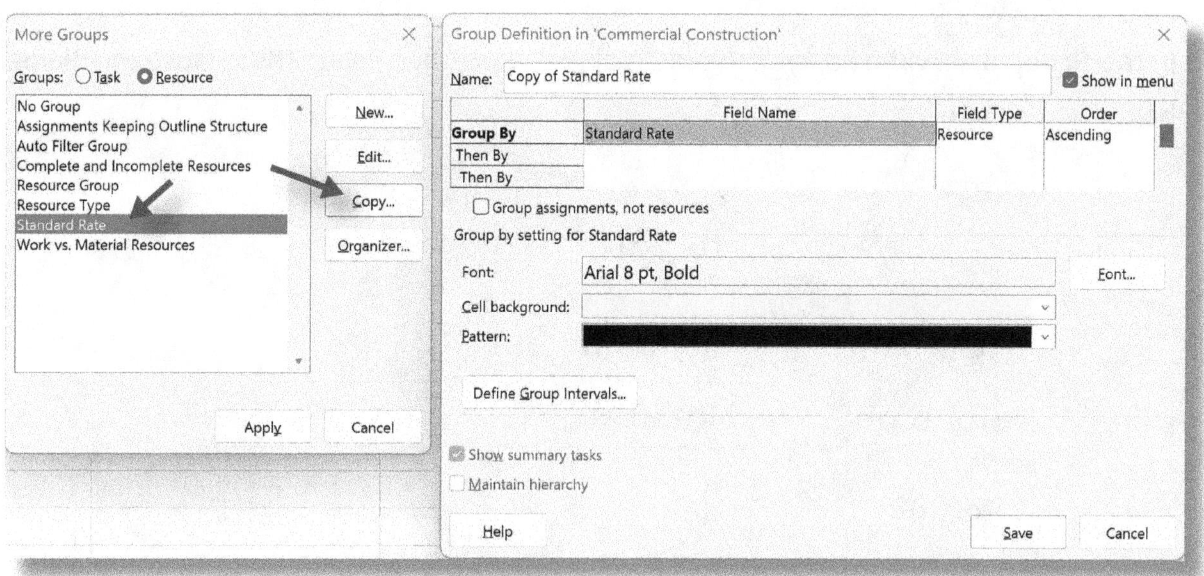

Figure 189 – Create a Custom Group

- In the **Name** field, enter a name for the new custom group.
- In the **Group By** row, in the **Field Name** column, the group that you're copying will be populated into the cell.

- In the first **Then By** field, enter or select the name of the next grouping criterion you want.
- In the next **Then By** field, in the **Field Name** column, select an additional field you want to group tasks or resources by from the pick-list. Repeat this step for as many fields as you need.
- In the **Order** field, select **Ascending** or **Descending** for each field.
- To select formatting options for each field, select the **Field Name** in the **Group By** or **Then By** field. Then, under the **Group by setting for** section, choose the options you want in the Font, Cell background, and Pattern fields.
- To define the intervals that Project uses to group the fields, select the **Define Group Intervals** command to open the *Define Group Interval* dialogue box (*Figure 190* below).
- In the **Group on** field, select **Interval**.
- In the **Start at** field, select the start number.
- In the **Group interval** field, type the interval you want, then select **OK** to close the dialogue box.

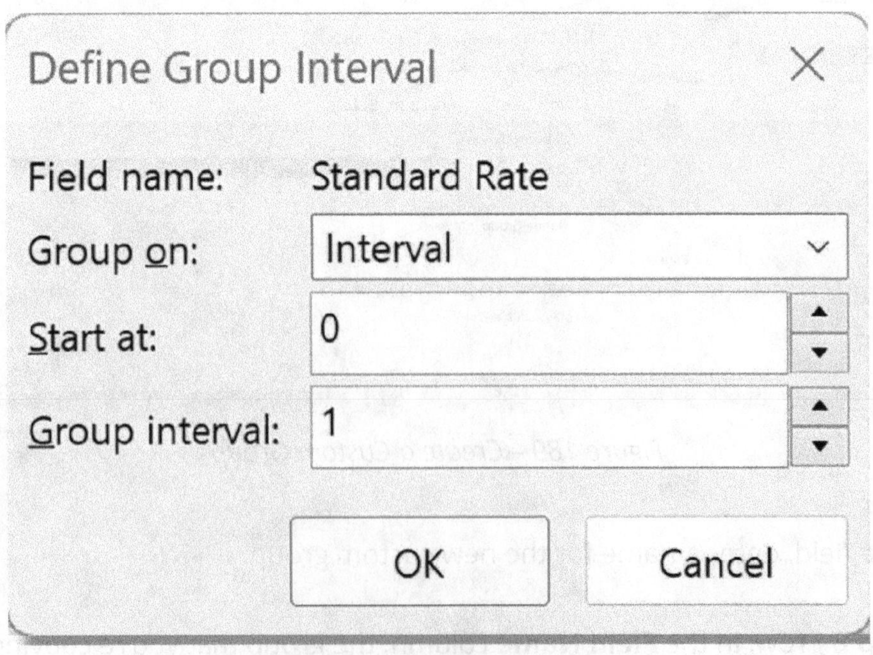

Figure 190 – Define Group Intervals

- Once you've selected the options you want, select **Save** to close the *Group Definition* dialog box. Then select **Apply** to apply the new group and to close the *More Groups* dialog box. The custom group will appear in the **More Groups** Built-in options.

To apply a custom group to a task or resource view:

- Select the **View** tab.
- In the **Data** group, select **More Groups** from the **Group by** pick-list.
- Then, select the new custom group from the Built-in options in the Task or Resource groups.
- Select **Apply** to apply the custom group to the view you're in.

Clearing Grouping Results

Before sharing your schedule, you may want to clear any grouping results you've applied.

To clear grouping results:

- Select the **View** tab.
- In the **Data** group, select **Clear Group** from the **Group by** pick-list. You can also select **No Group**.

Filtering Project Data

Filtering allows you to extract task or resource data to view only data that meets the criteria you specify. There are several ways to filter project data.

Using the Auto Filter to filter data

Project includes many **Pre-Set Filters** that can be applied using the **Auto Filter** in most task and resource views. This feature can be used to filter columns of data.

To apply a Pre-Set filter:

- In a task or resource view, select the **Auto Filter** arrow in any field.
- Select **Filters**. Then, select the Pre-set filter you want (*Figure 191*).

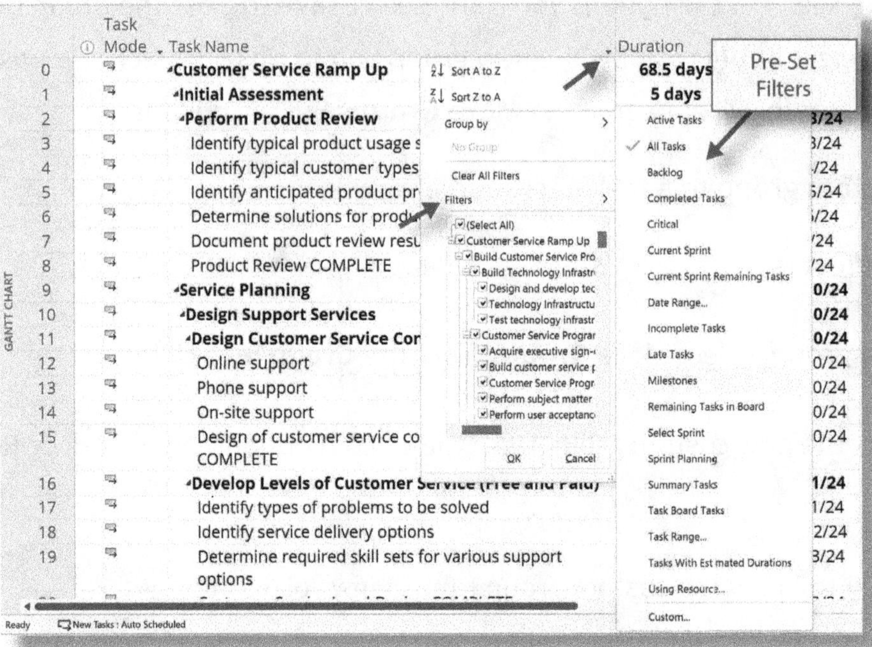

Figure 191 – Using the Pre-Set Filters

In *Figure 192* below, using the Auto Filter in the Task Name field, the *Milestones* Pre-set filter was applied to the Gantt Chart view. The tasks were filtered to display only the milestone tasks. The summary tasks will also be shown in the filter results. **NOTE**: When a filter is applied in a view, the *Filter Applied* notification will appear in the Status Bar in the bottom left corner of the view. On the **View** tab, in the **Data** group, the chosen filter will also be displayed in the **Filter** field.

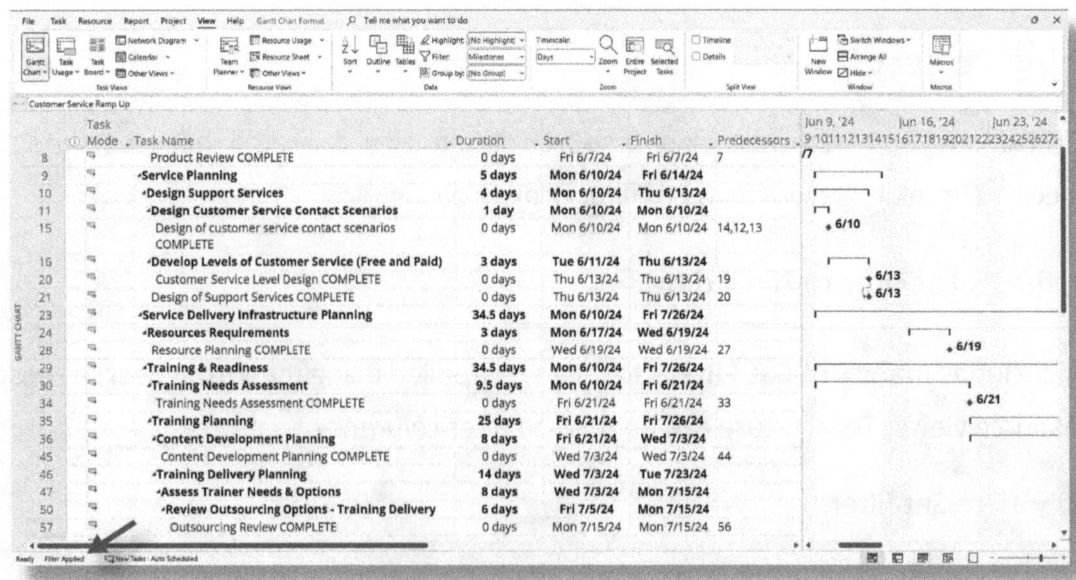

Figure 192 – Using the Milestones Pre-Set Filter

Applying a Custom Auto Filter

You can also apply a **Custom Auto Filter** to extract project data associated with a certain criterion you specify. For example, you may want to view only the tasks that are associated with a certain project group (E.g., "Customer Service"). In this case, you could apply a custom Auto Filter to display only the tasks that contain the words "Customer Service".

To apply a Custom Auto Filter:

- In a task or resource view, select the **Auto Filter** arrow in any column.
- Select **Filters**. Then, select **Custom** from the bottom of the Pre-set filters list to open the *Custom AutoFilter* dialogue box (*Figure 193* below).

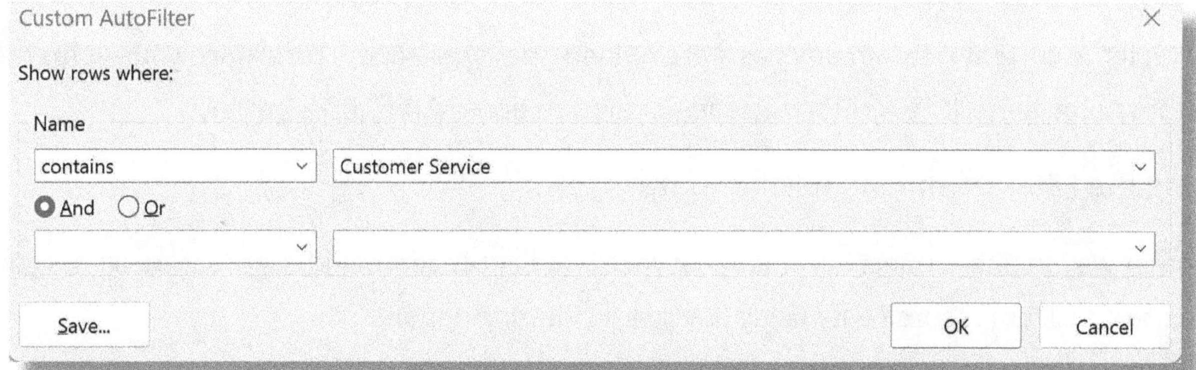

Figure 193 – Custom AutoFilter dialogue box

- In the **Name** field, enter or select the condition you want for the filter from the pick-list of options. In the adjacent field, type or select the filtering criterion you want from the pick-list.
- If you want to apply an additional condition to the filter, in the second **Name** field, select the condition you want for the filter from the pick-list of options. In the adjacent field, type or select the filtering criterion you want from the pick-list.
- Select **And** to meet both conditions in the filter.
- Select **Or** to meet one condition or the other.
- Select **OK** to apply the custom Auto Filter to the current view. OR
- Select **Save** to save your AutoFilter settings. When you save the AutoFilter settings, the filter is saved in your file and will be available using the *More Filters* dialog box.

Figure 194 below shows the results of a custom Auto Filter with the condition to show tasks that contain the words "Customer Service".

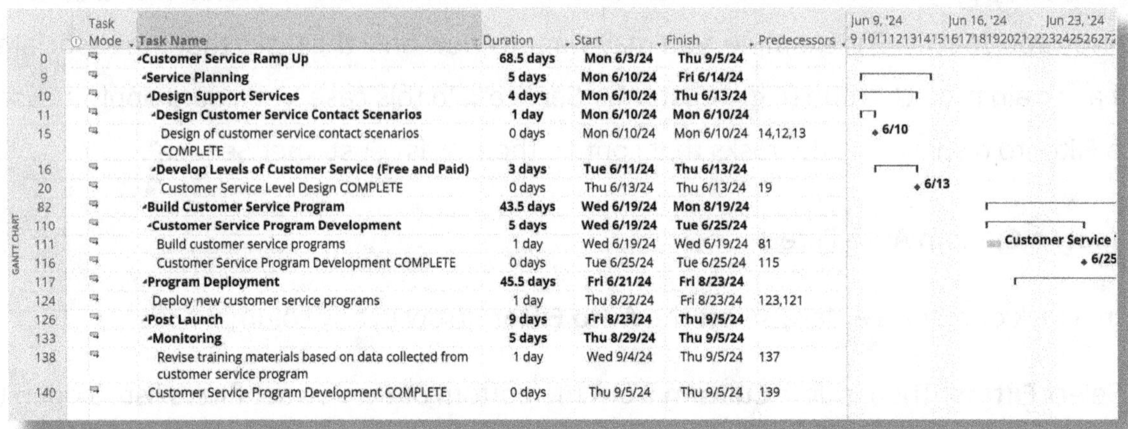

Figure 194 – Using a Custom AutoFilter to Filter Tasks

NOTE: If the current view already has a predefined filter applied, the conditions you set for the custom AutoFilter will be included as additional conditions to the current filter.

Using the Filter Command to Filter Data

Another way to filter project information is to use the **Filter** command. This feature allows you to extract task or resource data using the Built-in filtering options.

To filter data in a task or resource view using the Filter feature:

- Select the **View** tab. In the **Data** group, in the **Filter** field, select the criterion you want from the Built-in pick-list (*Figure 195*).

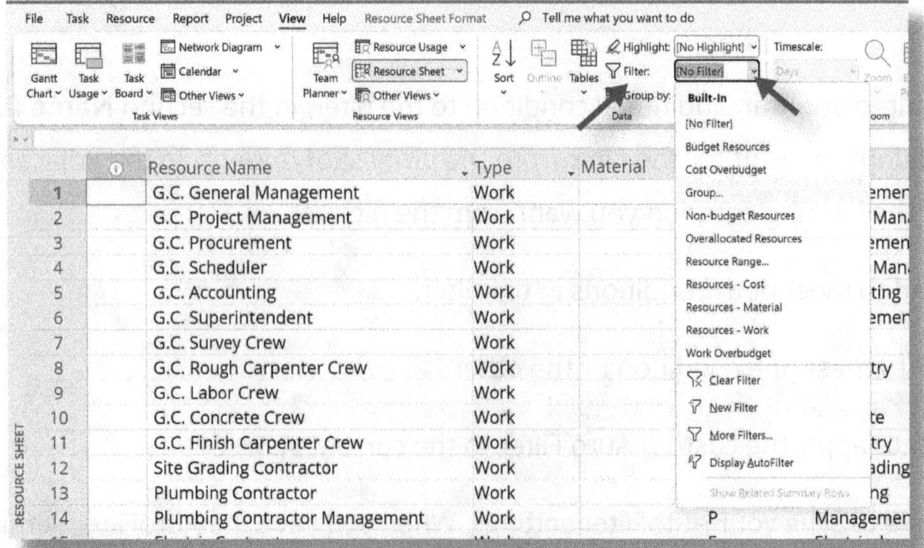

Figure 195 – Using the Filter Command

In *Figure 196* below, the Resource Sheet view was filtered to show only the over-allocated resources.

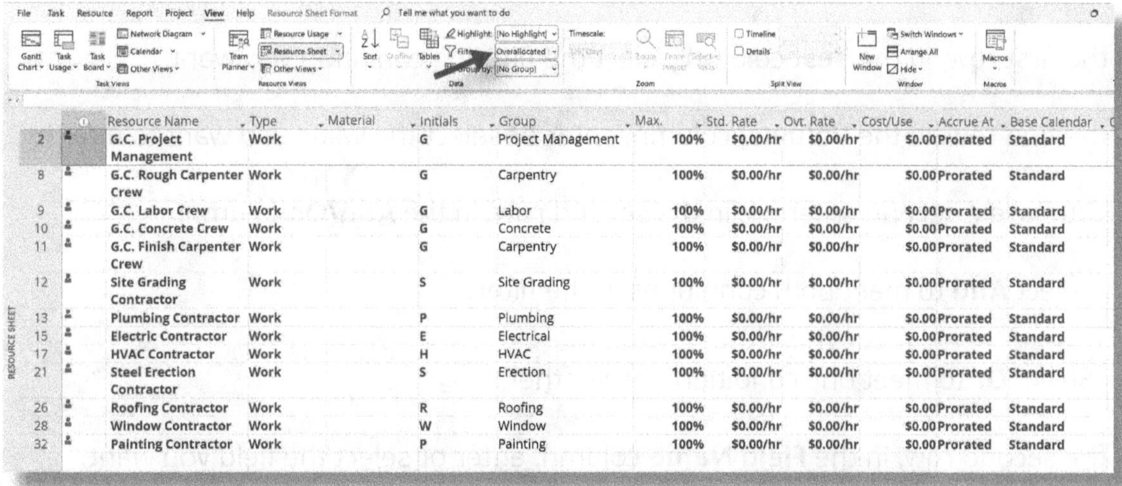

Figure 196 – Using the Filter Command to Filter Resource Data

Creating a Custom Filter

If the filter criteria you want isn't included in the Pre-set or Built-in filters, you can create a **Custom Filter**.

To create a custom filter:

- Select the **View** tab. In the **Data** group, select **More Filters** from the **Filters** pick-list to open the *More Filters* dialog box. If you're in a task view, the Pre-set filters for tasks are shown (*Figure 197* – left). If you're in a resource view, the Pre-set filters for resources are shown.
- Select **New** to open the *Filter Definition* dialog box (*Figure 197* – right).

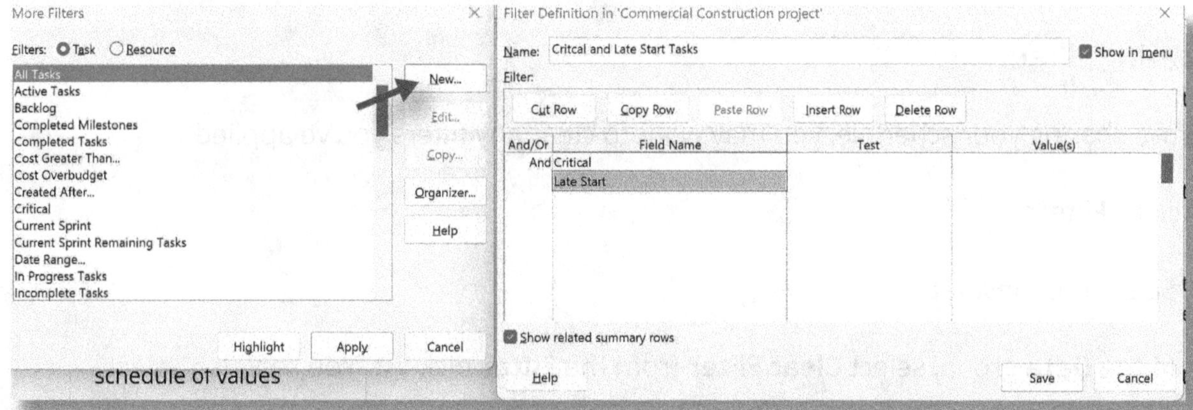

Figure 197 – Create a Custom Filter

- In the **Name** field, enter a name for the new custom filter.
- In the first row, in the **Field Name** column, enter or select the field you want.
- In the first row, in the **Test** column, select the filtering condition you want.
- In the first row, in the **Value(s)** column, enter or select the value you want to filter by.
- If you have a second criterion, in the second row, in the **And/Or** column:
    - Select **And** to meet both conditions in the filter.
    - Select **Or** to meet one condition or the other.
- In the second row, in the **Field Name** column, enter or select the field you want.
- In the second row, in the **Test** column, select the filtering condition you want.
- In the second row, in the **Value(s)** column, enter or select the value you want to filter by.
- Select **Save** to save the new custom filter and to close the *Filter Definition* dialog box. The new filter will appear in the **More Filters** Task or Resource Built-in options.

To apply a custom filter to a task or resource view:

- Select the **View** tab.
- In the **Data** group, from the **Filter** pick-list, select **More Filters**.
- Select the custom group from the Built-in options in the Task or Resource filters.
- Click **Apply** to apply the custom filter to the view you're in.

Clearing Filters

Before sharing your schedule, you may want to clear any filters you've applied.

To clear Filters:

- Select the **View** tab.
- In the **Data** group, select **Clear Filter** from the **Filter** pick-list. You can also select **No Filter**.

Using the Task Inspector

Before you share your schedule, you may also want to inspect the tasks to ensure that their scheduling information is correct. The **Task Inspector** is an efficient way to inspect your schedule. This feature allows you to view detailed scheduling information for a specific task. It shows you the factors affecting a task's start date, including Scheduling Mode, Predecessor information, Calendars, and Constraints (if applied). In *Figure 198* below, the Task Inspector has been displayed to inspect task 16 *Detail, fabricate and deliver steel*. In the panel on the left, Project shows the predecessors, the scheduling mode, and the Resource calendar applied to the resource.

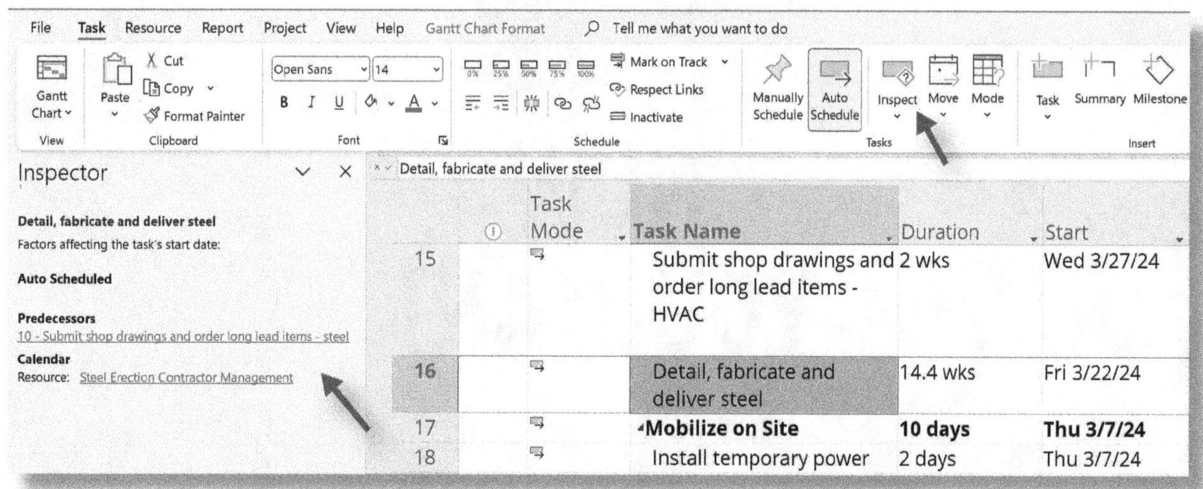

Figure 198 – Using the Task Inspector

To use the Task Inspector:

- In a task view (like the Gantt Chart view) select the task you want to inspect.
- On the **Task** tab, in the **Tasks** group, select the **Inspect** command. Project will display scheduling information for the selected task in a panel on the left.

We've now reviewed ways to view, organize and inspect project data before publishing a project schedule.

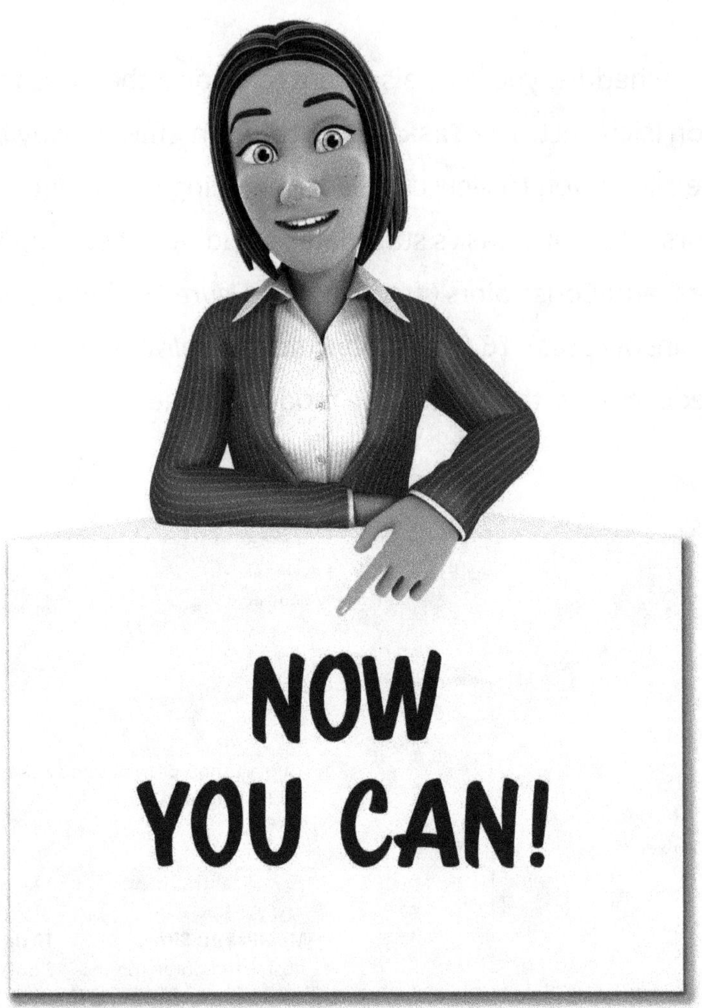

- ✓ Sort Project Data
- ✓ Group Project Data
- ✓ Filter Project Data
- ✓ Create Custom Groups and Filters
- ✓ Use the Task Inspector

This chapter includes a **BONUS VIDEO** from the "Microsoft Project B.A.S.I.C.S." video course. The videos include tutorials of the information covered in the chapters, software demonstrations and other useful information.

To Watch this Chapter's Video:

- ✓ Visit mspbasics.com.
- ✓ Select **CheckPoint Images** from the menu.
- ✓ Select your version of the book.
- ✓ Select **Chapter 14**.
- ✓ Enjoy the video!

P
L
A
N

Part Two Summary

This concludes Part Two - Building the Schedule. You've learned to build schedules using the steps in the B.A.S.I.C.S. scheduling process and the key fundamentals supporting each step. You've learned to build Simple schedules™ when you need to track time only, and Detailed schedules™ when you need to track both time and cost. You've learned how to create, level, and manage resources, how to compress your schedule to meet critical deadlines, how to use constraints to reflect real business restrictions like delayed funding and you've learned to perform an in-depth inspection before beginning the execution phase.

In Part Three - Executing the Schedule, you'll learn to perform the final step in the B.A.S.I.C.S. scheduling process - **Start the Project**. You'll learn to take a schedule through the execution and closing phases of the project life cycle.

S
S
T
T
A
A
R
R
T
T

PART THREE Executing Your Schedule

IN PART THREE you'll learn to execute your schedule and track it to completion. You'll learn key execution practices, such as capturing your initial scheduling forecast in a baseline, inputting actual performance data, and tracking costs. You'll also learn to create dynamic status reports, customize the Project interface, and use advanced features, such Earned Value tables and to create Master schedules to manage projects, programs and portfolios.

Chapter 15 Executing Your Schedule

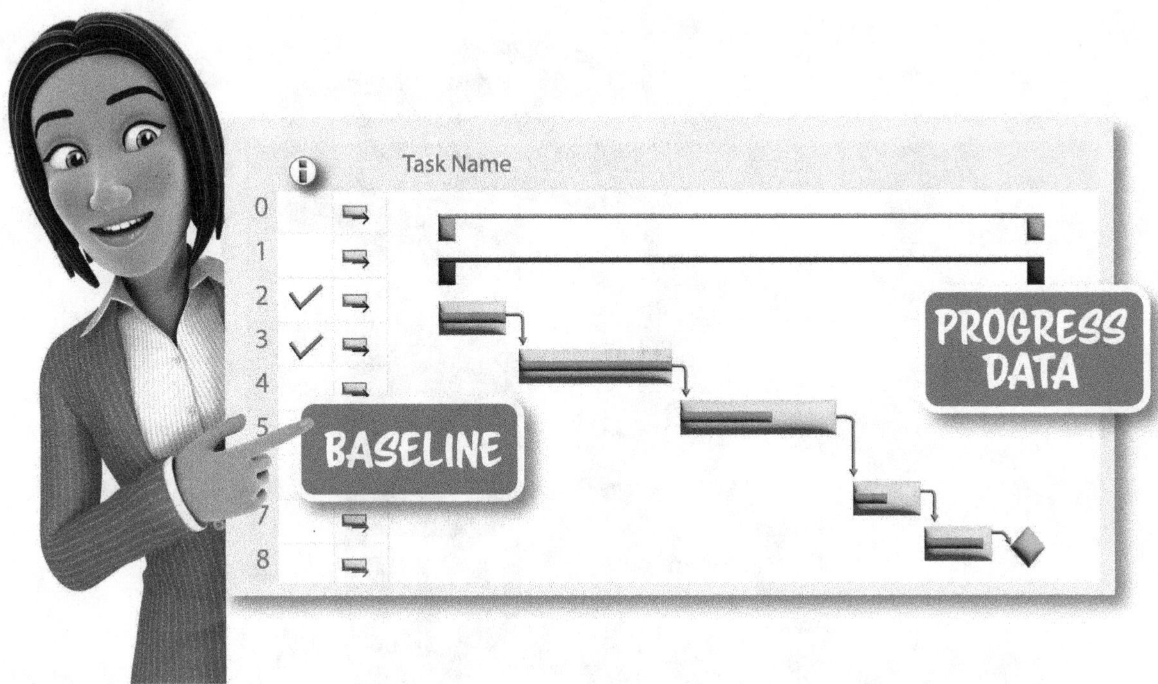

In the last chapter, you learned to inspect your schedule. You learned to use the sorting, grouping, and filtering features to analyze task and resource data. In this chapter, you'll learn to **execute your schedule**. You'll learn to perform the last step in the B.A.S.I.C.S. scheduling process – **Start the Project**. When you're done, you'll be able to baseline your schedule, view expected progress, use the tracking fields to enter progress data, update your schedule and inactivate tasks.

You'll Learn To:

- Save a Baseline
- Move the Project
- Track a Schedule
- Enter Progress Data (Actuals)
- Update the Schedule
- Use the Tracking Gantt View
- Inactivate Tasks

The Execution Phase - Starting the Project!

So far, you've learned to build a Simple and a Detailed schedule. You've added resources, calendars, and documentation to the schedule, you've compressed and constrained the schedule and you've leveled resources. In PMBOK® jargon, you've completed the **Planning phase**. Now, you're ready to begin the **Execution phase**. The execution phase is about starting the project work and monitoring and controlling the work, so that all deliverables are completed according to plan. Before we begin to execute the schedule, let's look at a list of job qualifications that an ideal candidate must have for an open position. Try to guess the profession.

- ✓ Well organized
- ✓ Assertive
- ✓ Firm decision maker
- ✓ Composed under pressure
- ✓ High in situational awareness
- ✓ Able to analyze risk in real time
- ✓ Highly flexible
- ✓ Excellent communicator

You may have concluded that the profession is a Project Manager. However, these are the qualifications for an Air-Traffic Controller. Project Managers and Air-Traffic Controllers have similar traits. For example, the average commercial flight time from Los Angeles to Chicago is just over 4 hours. However, a military jet could travel this distance in about 1 hour. There are several reasons for this time difference. One reason is commercial airlines don't use direct travel routes. Consequently, much of the flight time is spent off course. The air-traffic controller's job is to make real-time course corrections and sequence the aircraft for an on-time landing. Similarly, typical projects spend much of their life cycle off schedule. The project manager's job is to monitor and control in-flight projects by making real-time adjustments to ensure an on-time delivery. Microsoft Project includes useful features for tracking progress and making real-time updates while your project is in the execution phase. We'll begin with Baselines.

Baselines

Before task work begins on your project, it's important to record key information from the planning phase, so you can later compare your planned results to your actual results. To capture your planned results, you must **Baseline** your schedule. A Baseline is a copy of your original project plan before it's executed. It includes your original Start and Finish dates and your original Duration, Work, and Cost estimates. Since a baseline is a copy of your original plan, when a project is behind schedule, it is really behind the baseline schedule forecast. Similarly, when it is over budget, it is really over the baseline cost forecast.

Project not only captures your original forecast, but it also captures a **time-phased distribution** of your original resource allocation and work, duration, and cost estimate for every task in your schedule. Here's an example to clarify what is meant by "time-phased distribution". If a resource commits to completing 10 hours of work across a 5-day period at 25% Units, Project will distribute the estimate evenly across those 5 days. Therefore, it will assign 2 hours of work to the resource across 5 days. This is what is meant by a time-phased distribution. You can use this time-phased distribution to get as granular as you'd like when determining why a task has fallen behind schedule and what may be done to recover the schedule.

Setting a Baseline

When you save a baseline, Project takes a snapshot of the original plan and saves it within your project file. You can save up to 11 baselines. The first one is labeled *Baseline* (which is considered *Baseline 0*). Additional baselines are labeled *Baseline 1* through *Baseline 10*. Although up to 11 baselines are allowed, best practice is to only re-baseline in justifiable cases (like major scope changes). The reason for this is, when you re-baseline your schedule, you are no longer comparing current results to the original plan. This could result in communication challenges and mismanaged expectations. For example, senior-level stakeholders who may have been more engaged at the beginning of your project and less engaged after you've re-baselined, may be inclined to assess your progress per the original baseline and not per the new baseline.

To save a Baseline:

- Select the **Project** tab.
- In the **Schedule** group, select the **Set Baseline** command, then select **Set Baseline** again to open the *Set Baseline* dialogue box (*Figure 199* below).

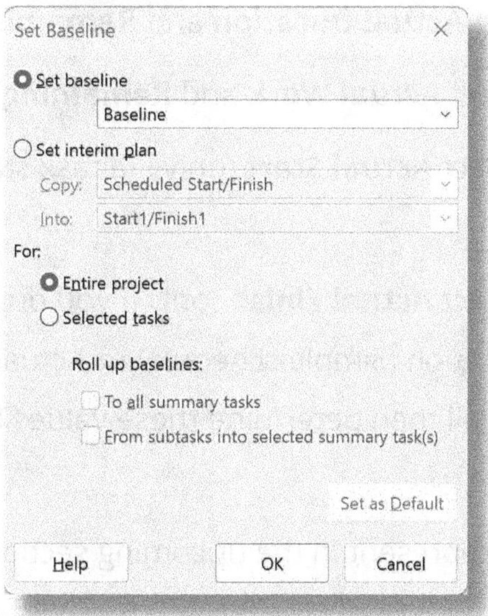

Figure 199 – Set a Baseline

- Ensure the **Set Baseline** option is selected. Then, select the baseline you're saving (0 through 10) from the **Set Baseline** pick list. *Baseline* (*Baseline 0*) will already be populated to the field for the initial baseline.
- In the **For** section, select **Entire project** to baseline the entire project or select **Selected tasks** to baseline selected tasks only.
- If you're only setting a baseline for selected tasks (and not the entire project), in the **Roll up baselines** section, you can select how you want Project to roll up the baseline data. There are two options. Select **To all summary tasks** if you want updated baseline data for the selected tasks to be rolled up to the corresponding summary tasks. This ensures that baseline data for summary tasks accurately reflects their subtask baseline data. Select **From subtasks into selected summary task(s)** if you want baseline data for selected summary tasks to be updated to reflect both deletions of subtasks and added tasks for which you previously saved baseline values.
- Select **OK** to close the *Set Baseline* dialogue box.

Collecting Progress Data (Actuals)

Once you've baselined your schedule, and work has started on your project, you can begin to collect **Progress Data** (also called Actuals) to track progress against the plan. The type of schedule you've built (Simple or Detailed) should determine the progress data you collect.

- For a Simple schedule, collect **Actual Duration** and **Remaining Duration**.
- For a Detailed schedule, collect **Actual Work** and **Remaining Work**.
- For both schedule types, collect **Actual Start** (only if a task starts earlier or later than planned).
- For both schedule types, collect **Actual Finish** (only if you don't have access to Actual Duration and Remaining Duration (Simple schedule) or Actual Work, and Remaining Work (Detailed schedule). Project will then determine these values based on the actual finish date).

We'll review what these actuals represent in the upcoming section.

Status Date

When you collect progress data from your team, you'll need to note the date through which the work was performed. This date is called the **Status Date**. You'll need to set the status date when you enter progress data. Project references this date when rescheduling uncompleted task work and for Earned Value calculations. If the status date is not set, Project will use the current date as the status date. We'll review how to set the status date shortly.

Understanding Progress Data (Actuals)

By definition, **Duration** is the sum of *Actual* Duration and *Remaining* Duration. Up to now, whenever we've entered a value into the Duration field, that value has represented the amount of Remaining Duration only. Actual Duration in the Planning phase is always zero, because no work has occurred. The same is true for the Work values. Work is the sum of *Actual* Work and *Remaining* Work. For example, if a task in the Planning phase has a 10-day duration, this means that Actual duration is 0 days and Remaining duration is 10 days. The same applies to Work. If a task in the Planning phase has a 40-hour work estimate, this means that Actual Work is 0 hours and Remaining Work is 40 hours.

As mentioned earlier, Actual and Remaining Duration or Actual and Remaining Work values are the progress data ("Actuals") you will collect and enter in the Execution phase. The balance of the uncompleted work on your project will always be captured in the Remaining Duration and Remaining Work fields.

Viewing Expected Outcomes

Before you meet with your project team to collect progress data, you should have an idea which tasks should have progressed since the last status date. This will give you the option of meeting only with the resources expected to have progress data. You won't likely need to get status from every resource assigned to your project; only those who should have done work since the last status date. A handy way to get this information is to apply the **Late Tasks** filter. Applying the Late Tasks filter will display the tasks that should have progressed as of the current date.

To Filter for Late Tasks:

- In the Gantt Chart view, select the **Auto-filter** arrow in the **Task Name** field.
- Select **Filters**, then select **Late Tasks**. Project will display only the tasks that should have work progress as of the current date (*Figure 200* below).

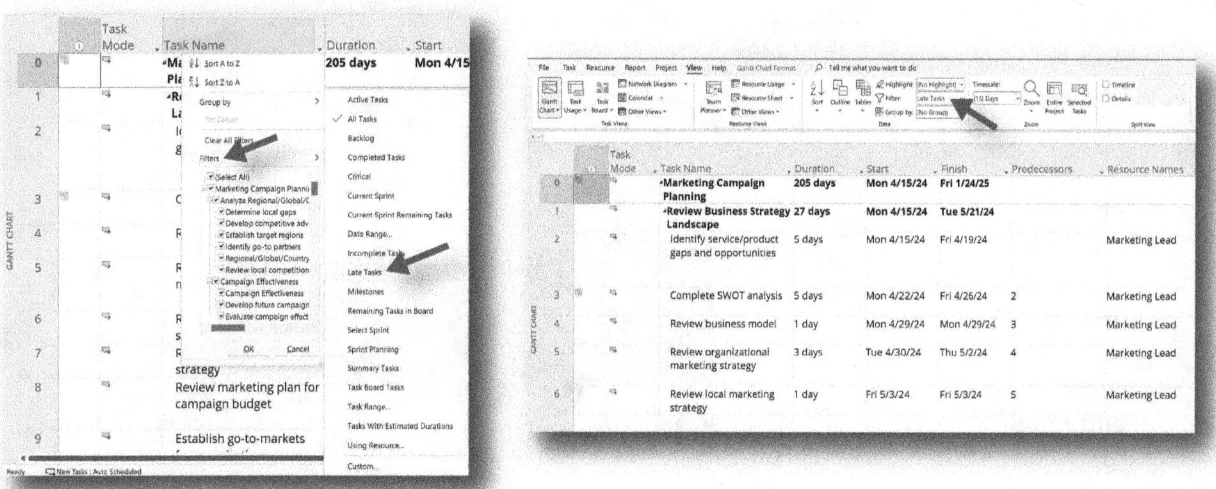

Figure 200 – Filter for Late Tasks

Setting the Status Date

As mentioned earlier, when you enter progress data into Project, you'll need to set the **status date** – the date through which work was performed. This should be done before you enter the actuals.

To set the Status Date:

- Select the **Project** tab.
- In the **Properties** group, select the **Project Information** command to open the *Project Information* dialogue box.
- In the **Status date** field, enter the status date (*Figure 201* below).
- Select **OK** to close the *Project Information* dialogue box. The status date will be shown on the ribbon, in the **Status** group, on the **Project** tab.

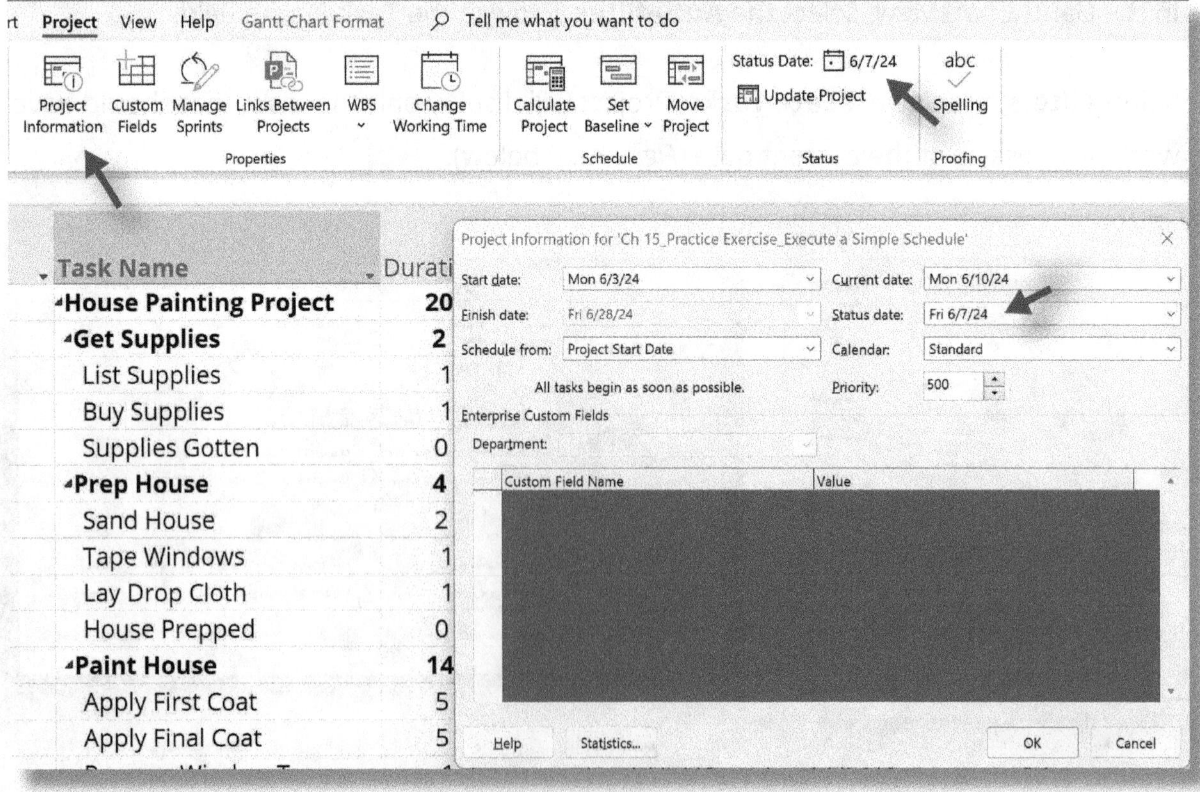

Figure 201 – Set the Status Date

Entering Progress Data (Actuals)

After you've entered the status date and collected actuals from your team, you'll need to enter these updates into Project. As mentioned earlier, the type of schedule you've built (Simple or Detailed) should determine the progress data you collect. It should also determine the fields and views you use to enter the progress data.

Entering Progress Data (Actuals) in a Simple schedule

To enter actuals for a Simple schedule, you can add the relevant tracking fields to the Entry table in the Gantt Chart view. Use the **Add New Column** command to add the **Actual Start**, **Actual Duration**, and **Remaining Duration** fields to the view. Enter the corresponding actuals directly into these fields. When you enter the progress data, Project will update the duration values in real-time. After you enter a value for Actual Duration, Project will populate the Remaining Duration field per the initial duration estimate. For example, if the initial duration estimate for a task was 10 days, and you enter 7 days in the Actual Duration field, Project will populate the Remaining Duration field with 3 days. If the actual Remaining Duration value exceeds the value Project populated, simply type over the populated value with the correct Remaining Duration value. Project will then update the task's duration in the Duration field accordingly. In *Figure 202* below, progress data has been entered for tasks 2 through 5 in a Simple schedule. Task 5 *Review organizational marketing strategy* has a Baseline Duration of 10 days. Since the value showing in the Duration field is 12 days, this means the task is behind schedule (behind baseline) by 2 days. The Actual Duration entry of 7 days shows the number of days the task has been worked on. To have remained on schedule, the Remaining Duration entry needed to be 3 days. Since the Remaining Duration entry is 5 days, the task is 2 days behind schedule.

		Task Mode	Task Name	Duration	Start	Finish	Predecessors	Resource Names	Actual Start	Actual Duration	Remaining Duration	Baseline Duration
0			**Marketing Campaign Planning**	**214 days**	**Mon 3/4/24**	**Thu 12/26/24**			**Mon 3/4/24**	**13.01 days**	**200.99 days**	**212 days**
1			**Review Business Strategy Landscape**	**36 days**	**Mon 3/4/24**	**Mon 4/22/24**			**Mon 3/4/24**	**18 days**	**18 days**	**34 days**
2	✓		Identify service/product gaps and opportunities	5 days	Mon 3/4/24	Fri 3/8/24		Marketing Lead	Mon 3/4/24	5 days	0 days	5 days
3	✓		Complete SWOT analysis	5 days	Mon 3/11/24	Fri 3/15/24	2	Marketing Lead	Mon 3/11/24	5 days	0 days	5 days
4	✓		Review business model	1 day	Mon 3/18/24	Mon 3/18/24	3	Marketing Lead	Mon 3/18/24	1 day	0 days	1 day
5			Review organizational marketing strategy	12 days	Tue 3/19/24	Wed 4/3/24	4	Marketing Lead	Tue 3/19/24	7 days	5 days	10 days
6			Review local marketing strategy	1 day	Thu 4/4/24	Thu 4/4/24	5	Marketing Lead	NA	0 days	1 day	1 day
7			Review global marketing strategy	1 day	Fri 4/5/24	Fri 4/5/24	6	Marketing Rep	NA	0 days	1 day	1 day

GANTT CHART

Figure 202 – Entering Progress Data in a Simple Schedule

This example shows the purpose of the Actual Duration and Remaining Duration fields. The purpose of the Actual Duration field is to capture the work that occurred. It should always be a cumulative value, reflective of the total number of days the task has been worked on. The purpose of the Remaining Duration field is to capture the resource's best estimate of the remaining days required to complete the task. Because the Duration field is the sum of Actual and Remaining Duration, it is a forecast field. It forecasts the total number of days required to complete a task at any given point. It's meant to be a dynamic field, as the forecast to task completion can vary from status date to status date. Owing to the dynamic nature of this forecast field, it must always be compared to the baseline duration value to determine the status of a task. The entries in *Figure 202* show how the Actual and Remaining Duration fields are meant to work. Currently, the Actual Duration value is 7 days and the Remaining Duration value is 5 days. If the resource reports in the next status check that they completed the remaining 5 days, you would enter the cumulative Actual Duration value of 12 days and not the incremental value of 5 days. Project does not keep a record of the prior Actual Duration entries. When the task is complete, enter a value of zero in the Remaining Duration field and Project will mark the task as complete.

Entering Progress Data in a Detailed schedule

For a Detailed schedule, you can also enter values directly into the relevant tracking fields. Use the **Add New Column** command to add the **Actual Start**, **Actual Work**, and **Remaining Work** fields to the view. When you enter the actuals, Project will update the Work values in real time. As with the duration fields, after you enter a value for Actual Work, Project will populate the Remaining Work field per the initial work estimate. If the actual Remaining Work value exceeds the value Project populated, simply type over the populated value with the correct Remaining Work value. In *Figure 203*, progress data has been entered for tasks 2 through 5 in a Detailed schedule. Task 5 *Review organizational marketing strategy* has a Baseline Work value of 20 hours. However, the Actual Work value is 18 hours and the Remaining Work value is 6 hours. Since Work is the sum of Actual Work and Remaining Work, Project updated the Work field to 24 hours. This shows that the task is delayed. It exceeds the Baseline Work value by 4 hours. Since the *Marketing Lead* resource assigned to this task is assigned at 25% Units (2 hours per day), the additional 4 hours of work resulted in a 2-day delay. For this reason, the task duration (shown in the Duration field) exceeds the Baseline Duration by 2 days.

As with Simple schedules, when you enter progress data into Project for Detailed schedules, always use cumulative values for Actual Work entries. For example, in *Figure 203*, the Actual Work value is 18 hours. If the resource reports in the next status check that they completed the remaining 6 hours of work, you would enter the cumulative Actual Work value of 24 hours and not the incremental value of 6 hours. When the task is complete, enter a value of zero in the Remaining Work field and Project will mark the task as complete.

	Task Mode	Task Name	Duration	Start	Finish	Predecessors	Resource Names	Work	Actual Start	Actual Work	Remaining Work	Baseline Duration	Baseline Work
0		**Marketing Campaign Planning**	**213.25 days**	**Tue 3/5/24**	**Fri 12/27/24**			**2,656 hrs**	**Tue 3/5/24**	**72 hrs**	**2,584 hrs**	**212 days**	**2,652 hrs**
1		**Review Business Strategy Landscape**	**35.25 days**	**Tue 3/5/24**	**Tue 4/23/24**			**216 hrs**	**Tue 3/5/24**	**72 hrs**	**144 hrs**	**34 days**	**212 hrs**
2	✓	Identify service/product gaps and opportunities	5 days	Tue 3/5/24	Mon 3/11/24		Marketing Lead[50%]	20 hrs	Tue 3/5/24	20 hrs	0 hrs	5 days	20 hrs
3	✓	Complete SWOT analysis	5 days	Tue 3/12/24	Mon 3/18/24	2	Marketing Lead[50%	20 hrs	Tue 3/12/24	20 hrs	0 hrs	5 days	20 hrs
4	✓	Review business model	1 day	Tue 3/19/24	Tue 3/19/24	3	Marketing Lead	8 hrs	Tue 3/19/24	8 hrs	0 hrs	1 day	8 hrs
5		Review organizational marketing strategy	12 days	Wed 3/20/24	Thu 4/4/24	4	Marketing Lead[25%]	24 hrs	Wed 3/20/24	18 hrs	6 hrs	10 days	20 hrs
6		Review local marketing strategy	1 day	Wed 4/3/24	Fri 4/5/24	5	Marketing Lead	8 hrs	Wed 4/3/24	6 hrs	2 hrs	1 day	8 hrs
7		Review global marketing	1 day	Fri 4/5/24	Mon 4/8/24	6	Marketing Rep	8 hrs	NA	0 hrs	8 hrs	1 day	8 hrs

Figure 203 – Entering Progress Data in a Detailed Schedule

Entering Progress Data when Multiple Resources are Assigned to a Task

When multiple resources are assigned to a task, you'll need to enter progress data for each resource individually. This can be done by creating a combination view and entering the progress data into the *Work* table of the *Task Form* (*Figure 204* below).

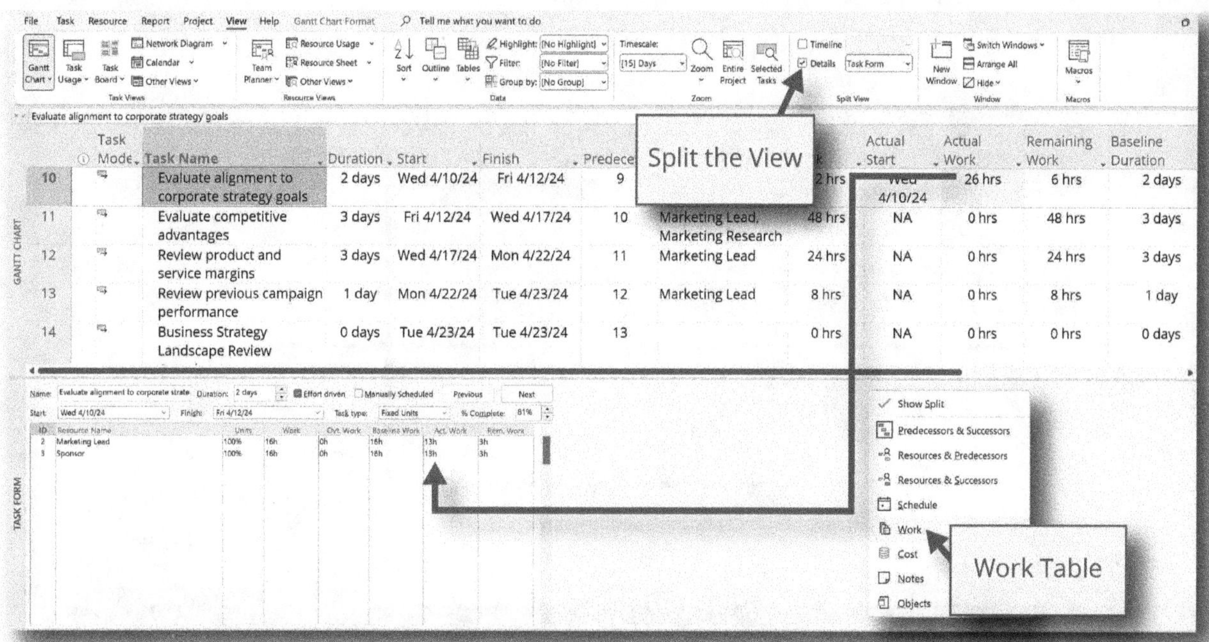

Figure 204 – Entering Progress Data Using a Combination View

To create a combination view with the Work table:

- In the Gantt Chart view, select the **View** tab.
- In the **Split View** group, select the **Details** checkbox to split the view. By default, in the bottom pane, the *Task Form* will be displayed with the *Predecessor and Successors table.*
- To display the *Work* table in the *Task Form*, right-click anywhere in the bottom pane to display the *Task Form* table pick list. Then, select **Work**.

This combination view allows you to enter progress data at the **Task Level** or the **Assignment Level**. The top pane represents the Task level. The bottom pane represents the Assignment level. A task level entry "rolls down" to the assignment level. This means that the values entered at the task level will be distributed among the resources assigned to the task.
For example, in *Figure 204*, in the top pane, 26 hours of Actual Work was entered at the task level for task 10 *Evaluate alignment to corporate strategy goals*. In the bottom pane, in the Task Form, Project rolled the down the work and divided the 26 hours of Actual Work evenly between the two resources (Marketing Lead and Sponsor) at the assignment level. However, this even distribution of the work may not reflect the actual progress of either resource.

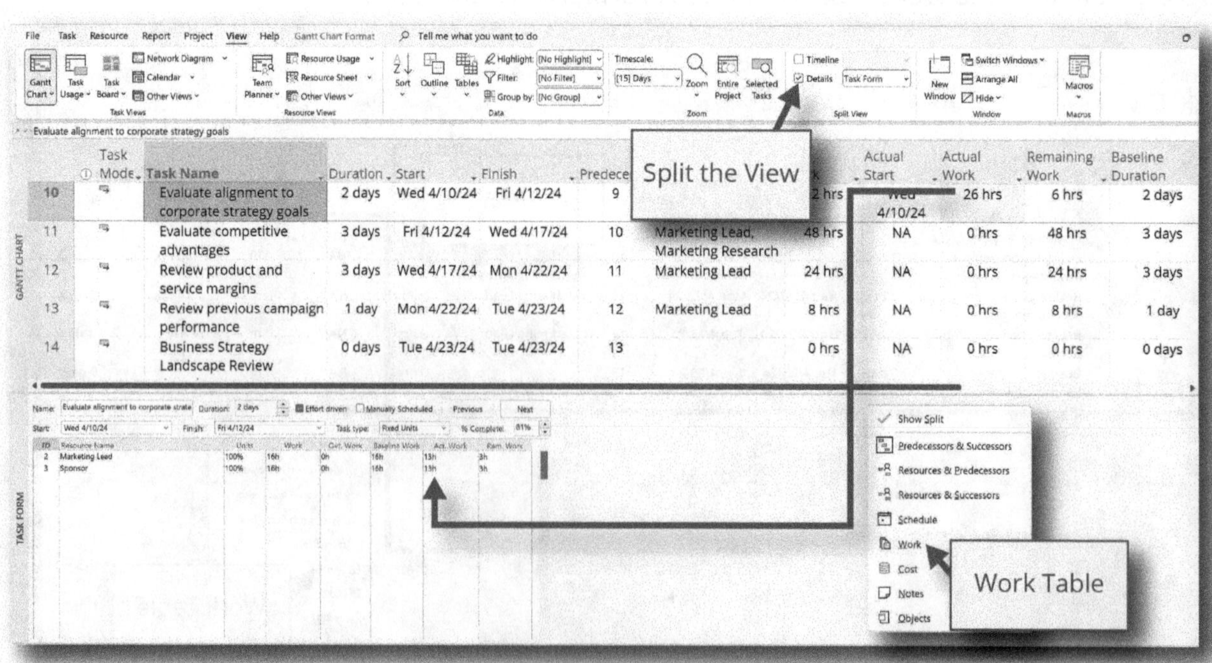

Figure 205 - Entering Progress Data at the Assignment Level

Conversely, an assignment level entry rolls *up* to the task level. If progress data is entered for each resource assigned to the task at the assignment level, the collective sum will be reflected at the task level. This allows you to enter specific progress data for each resource.
For example, in *Figure 205*, the 26 hours of Actual Work for task 10 were entered at the assignment level as 16 hours of Actual Work for the Marketing Lead resource and 10 hours of Actual Work for the Sponsor resource. Project rolled the collective sum of 26 hours up to the task level, which is reflected in the top pane in the Actual Work field.

Entering progress data at the task level versus the assignment level yields dramatically different results in terms of duration and cost. This is because resources may have varying pay rates and may be assigned to the task at varying Units. For this reason, when multiple resources are assigned to a single task, it is advisable to enter progress data at the assignment level. This will help ensure that cost and duration values are accurate. The same guideline applies when entering other tracking data, such as Actual Start and Actual Finish dates. If the resources' Actual Start and Actual Finish dates are not the same, you'll need to enter those values at the assignment level, using a combination view. In this case, you'll enter the progress data in the Resource Usage view, instead of the Gantt Chart view.

To create a combination view in the Resource Usage view:

- In the Gantt Chart view, select the **View** tab.
- In the **Split View** group, select the **Details** checkbox to split the view.
- Display the Resource Usage view in the top or bottom pane, as follows:
    - Click anywhere in the top or bottom pane to select it. On the **View** tab, in the **Resource Views group**, select **Resource Usage**.
- Use the **Add New Column** command to add the **Actual Start** and **Actual Finish** fields to the *Resource Usage* table.
- To enter the actuals, locate the tasks under each resource's name and enter the Actual Start and Actual Finish dates into the respective fields (*Figure 206*).

	Task Mode	Task Name	Duration	Start	Finish	Predecess	Resource Names	Work	Actual Start	Actual Work	Remaining Work	Baseline Duration
10		Evaluate alignment to corporate strategy goals	2 days	Wed 4/10/24	Fri 4/12/24	9	Marketing Lead, Sponsor	32 hrs	Wed 4/10/24	26 hrs	6 hrs	2 days
11		Evaluate competitive advantages	3 days	Fri 4/12/24	Wed 4/17/24	10	Marketing Lead, Marketing Research	48 hrs	NA	0 hrs	48 hrs	3 days
12		Review product and service margins	3 days	Wed 4/17/24	Mon 4/22/24	11	Marketing Lead	24 hrs	NA	0 hrs	24 hrs	3 days
13		Review previous campaign performance	1 day	Mon 4/22/24	Tue 4/23/24	12	Marketing Lead	8 hrs	NA	0 hrs	8 hrs	1 day
14		Business Strategy Landscape Review	0 days	Tue 4/23/24	Tue 4/23/24	13		0 hrs	NA	0 hrs	0 hrs	0 days

	Resource Name	Work	Actual Start	Actual Finish	Add New Column
2	**Marketing Lead**	**824 hrs**	**NA**	**NA**	
	Identify service/product gaps and opportunities	*20 hrs*	*Tue 3/5/24*	*Mon 3/11/24*	
	Complete SWOT analysis	*20 hrs*	*Tue 3/12/24*	*Mon 3/18/24*	
	Review business model	*8 hrs*	*Tue 3/19/24*	*Tue 3/19/24*	
	Review organizational marketing strategy	*24 hrs*	*Wed 3/20/24*	*NA*	
	Review local marketing strategy	*8 hrs*	*Wed 4/3/24*	*NA*	
	Establish go-to-markets for organization	*8 hrs*	*NA*	*NA*	
	Evaluate alignment to corporate strategy goals	*16 hrs*	*Wed 4/10/24*	*Fri 4/12/24*	
	Evaluate competitive advantages	*24 hrs*	*NA*	*NA*	
	Review product and service margins	*24 hrs*	*NA*	*NA*	

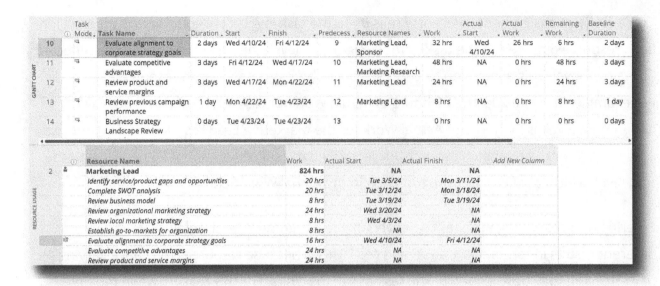

Figure 206 – Enter Progress Data in the Resource Usage View

Entering Progress Data – Using % Complete

When updating the progress of a task, it may be tempting to use the **% Complete** commands on the **Task** tab, in the **Schedule** group (*Figure 207* below) to record progress.

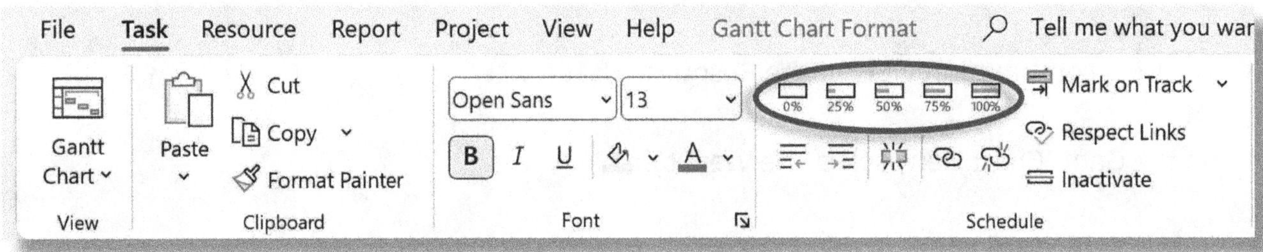

Figure 207 – Using the % Complete Commands

Unless the progress is **0%** or **100%**, this method should be avoided. It's best to track and record Actual and Remaining Duration or Actual and Remaining Work. This is because completion percentages can be subjective. Optimistic resources may overestimate completion percentages and pessimistic resources may underestimate them. Also, it's difficult to accurately distinguish between the different completion percentages. This can lead to schedule delays. For example, on a 10-day critical path task, entering the progress status as 30% complete when it is actually 40% complete will delay the schedule by 1 day. Since entering inaccurate progress data creates inaccurate schedules, "ballpark" estimates should be strictly avoided. Progress data should be entered using the methods we described in the prior section.

Viewing the % Complete fields

When you enter progress data, Project updates the completion percentage of duration and work for each task in the following fields.

- **% Complete** – Percentage of Duration Complete
- **% Work Complete** – Percentage of Work Complete

For the reasons mentioned earlier, these values should not be entered as progress data. They should be treated as view-only fields. They are meant to provide a quantitative status to measure the completion percentage of your project. Since they are calculated from your actual progress, they should never be overridden.

Updating the Schedule

Once you've entered your actuals, your schedule may need to be updated. Although most updates will occur automatically after entering progress data, some will require you to manually **update the schedule**. For example, if a resource doesn't work on a task they were assigned in any given week, then their work would need to be rescheduled to the following week. Further, all uncompleted work that was supposed to occur before the status date will need to be rescheduled.

Each time you enter your team's progress data, follow these steps to update the schedule:

- Select the **Project** tab.
- In the **Status** group, select **Update Project** to open the *Update Project* dialogue box (*Figure 208* below).

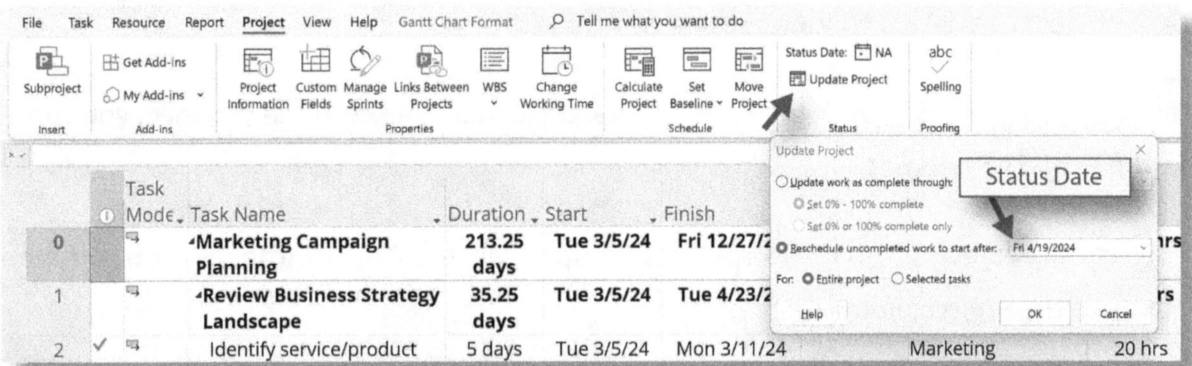

Figure 208 – Update the Schedule

- Select the **Reschedule uncompleted work to start after** option. Then, enter the status date in the **Date** field.

  NOTE: The Status Date is the date on which you are entering the actuals.

- In the **For** section, select **Entire Project**. Then, select **OK** to close the *Update Project* dialogue box. If necessary, Project will then reschedule any uncompleted tasks and highlight the updates.

The **Update Project** command can also be used to quickly update the schedule if all tasks were performed as scheduled. You can automatically update the schedule per the date you enter.

To update the project if all tasks were performed as scheduled:

- In the **Status** group, select **Update Project** to open the *Update Project* dialogue box.
- Select the **Update work as complete through** option.
- In the **Date** field, enter or select the date you want to update work as complete through. If you don't specify the date, Project will use the current date.

Comparing Baseline Information with the Current Plan

You can display baseline values in different views, tables, and in the built-in reports that include baseline data. Following are ways to compare baseline information against the current plan.

Using Project Statistics to view Baseline Information

To compare baseline data with the current data, the actual data, and the variance, you can view the **Project Statistics**.

- Select the **Project** tab, in the **Properties** group, select the **Project Information** command to open the *Project Information* dialog box.
- Select **Statistics** to open the *Project Statistics* dialog box (*Figure 209*).

Here, you can compare important baseline statistics, such as the Current Finish date against the Baseline Finish date and the Current Cost against the Baseline Cost.

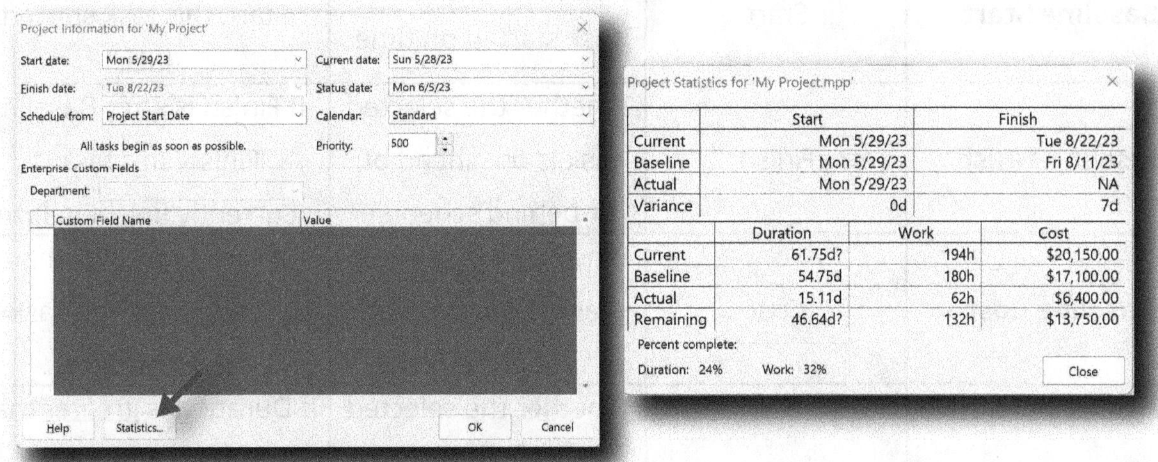

Figure 209 – View Baseline Information using Project Statistics

Adding Baseline Fields to the Current View

The **Add New Column** command can be used to add baseline fields to the current view. This will allow you to quickly compare your project's performance against the plan. There are several Baseline fields you can display. For example, you can add the *Baseline Start* or *Baseline Finish* fields to the Entry table in the Gantt Chart view. This will allow you to compare the original start and finish dates of the project to the current start and finish dates. The current start and finish dates are always the dates shown in the *Start* and *Finish* fields. If you add the *Baseline Cost* field, you can compare the original cost projections to the current costs, which are shown in the *Cost* field.

The following table shows key baseline fields you can add to a view to assess how your project is currently performing against the plan.

COMPARE THIS	TO THIS	TO DETERMINE THIS	INTERPRETATION
Baseline Start	Start	Whether the selected task started on time	If Start is after Baseline Start, this task started **late**
Baseline Finish	Finish	Whether the selected task is on, ahead of, or behind schedule	If Finish is after Baseline Finish, this task is currently finishing **late**
Baseline Cost	Cost	Whether the selected task is on, over, or under budget	If Cost is greater than Baseline Cost, this task is **over budget**.
Baseline Duration	Duration	Whether the selected task is taking less or more time than originally planned	If Duration is greater than Baseline Duration, this task is taking **longer** than originally planned.
Baseline Work	Work	Whether the selected task is requiring less or more Work than originally planned	If Work is greater than Baseline Work, this task requires **more work** than originally planned. Also, since Work gets multiplied by resource pay rate, this task will also be **over budget**.

Using the Variance Table to View Baseline Information

You can also view baseline data in the **Variance table**. This table displays the current Start and Finish dates and the Baseline Start and Finish dates (*Figure 210*). It allows you to compare current project results against baseline values.

To switch to the Variance table:

- Select the **View** tab.
- In the **Data** group, select the **Tables** command. Then, select **Variance** from the pick-list.

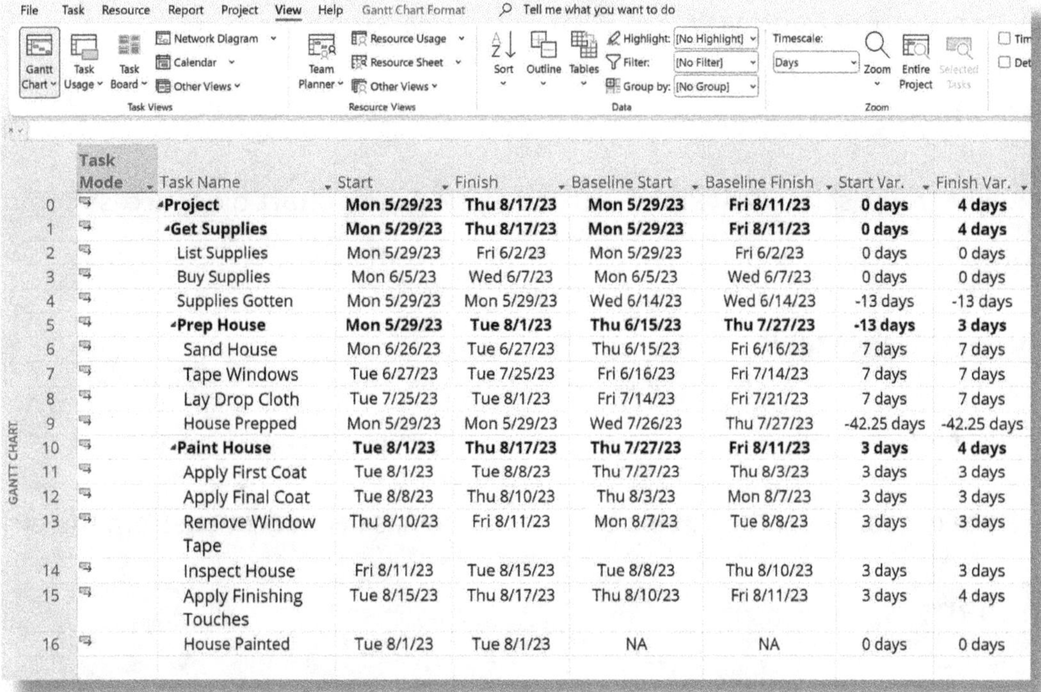

	Task Mode	Task Name	Start	Finish	Baseline Start	Baseline Finish	Start Var.	Finish Var.
0		**Project**	**Mon 5/29/23**	**Thu 8/17/23**	**Mon 5/29/23**	**Fri 8/11/23**	**0 days**	**4 days**
1		**Get Supplies**	**Mon 5/29/23**	**Thu 8/17/23**	**Mon 5/29/23**	**Fri 8/11/23**	**0 days**	**4 days**
2		List Supplies	Mon 5/29/23	Fri 6/2/23	Mon 5/29/23	Fri 6/2/23	0 days	0 days
3		Buy Supplies	Mon 6/5/23	Wed 6/7/23	Mon 6/5/23	Wed 6/7/23	0 days	0 days
4		Supplies Gotten	Mon 5/29/23	Mon 5/29/23	Wed 6/14/23	Wed 6/14/23	-13 days	-13 days
5		**Prep House**	**Mon 5/29/23**	**Tue 8/1/23**	**Thu 6/15/23**	**Thu 7/27/23**	**-13 days**	**3 days**
6		Sand House	Mon 6/26/23	Tue 6/27/23	Thu 6/15/23	Fri 6/16/23	7 days	7 days
7		Tape Windows	Tue 6/27/23	Tue 7/25/23	Fri 6/16/23	Fri 7/14/23	7 days	7 days
8		Lay Drop Cloth	Tue 7/25/23	Tue 8/1/23	Fri 7/14/23	Fri 7/21/23	7 days	7 days
9		House Prepped	Mon 5/29/23	Mon 5/29/23	Wed 7/26/23	Thu 7/27/23	-42.25 days	-42.25 days
10		**Paint House**	**Tue 8/1/23**	**Thu 8/17/23**	**Thu 7/27/23**	**Fri 8/11/23**	**3 days**	**4 days**
11		Apply First Coat	Tue 8/1/23	Tue 8/8/23	Thu 7/27/23	Thu 8/3/23	3 days	3 days
12		Apply Final Coat	Tue 8/8/23	Thu 8/10/23	Thu 8/3/23	Mon 8/7/23	3 days	3 days
13		Remove Window Tape	Thu 8/10/23	Fri 8/11/23	Mon 8/7/23	Tue 8/8/23	3 days	3 days
14		Inspect House	Fri 8/11/23	Tue 8/15/23	Tue 8/8/23	Thu 8/10/23	3 days	3 days
15		Apply Finishing Touches	Tue 8/15/23	Thu 8/17/23	Thu 8/10/23	Fri 8/11/23	3 days	4 days
16		House Painted	Tue 8/1/23	Tue 8/1/23	NA	NA	0 days	0 days

Figure 210 – View Baseline Data in the Variance Table

Using the Tracking Gantt View to View Baseline Information

The **Tracking Gantt** view is another way to compare the current schedule with the baselined schedule. This view provides a visual comparison of the baseline start and finish dates and the actual start and finish dates (*Figure 211* below). In the Gantt chart, you'll find two sets of task bars. The top, blue task bars represent tasks as they are currently scheduled (Critical Path tasks are highlighted with red task bars). The bottom, gray task bars represent the original, baseline schedule. It's also helpful to change the table in this view to the *Variance* table, which shows the actual and baseline start and finish dates, and any variance between them.

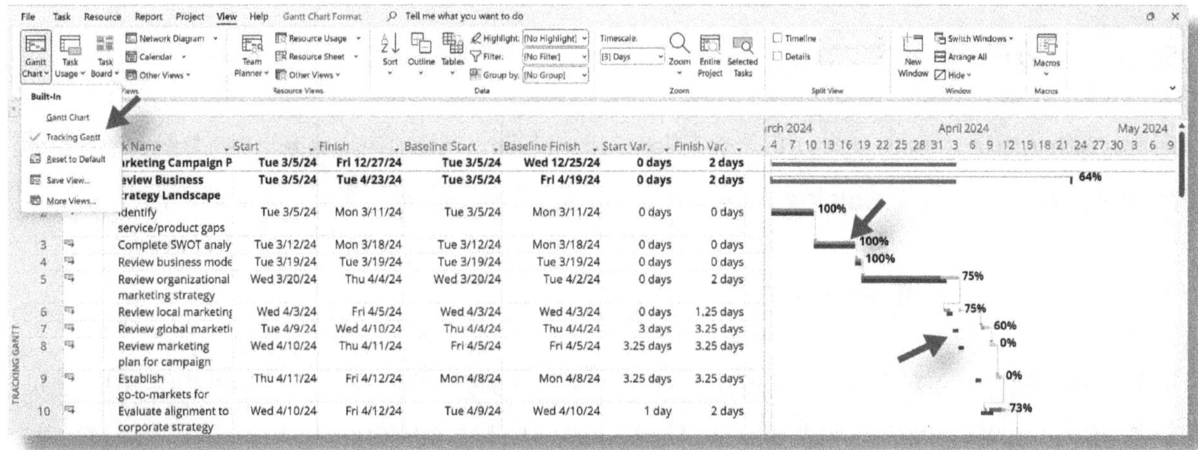

Figure 211 – The Tracking Gantt View

To display the Tracking Gantt view:

- Select the **Task** tab.
- In the **View** group, select **Tracking Gantt** from the **Gantt Chart** quick access command pick-list.

To display the Variance table:

- Select the **View** tab.
- In the **Data** group, select the **Tables** command. Then, select **Variance** from the pick-list.

Interim Plans

As you update your schedule, you may want to keep a history of weekly performance against the baseline. An **Interim Plan** is useful for this purpose. An Interim Plan (also called an Interim Baseline) is another way to record project data to assess your project's performance.
The difference between a baseline and an interim plan is when they're set and the amount of data they record. Baselines are set *before* a project starts. Interim plans are saved *after* the project starts. An Interim Plan is a partial copy of the original schedule. It saves only two values – the **Current Start** and **Current Finish** dates for all tasks. No resource allocation or time-phased values are saved. You can save up to 10 Interim Plans. The first Interim plan is saved as *Start1/Finish1*. Additional Interim plans are saved as *Start2/Finish2* through *Start10/Finish10*.

To save an Interim Plan:

- Select the **Project** tab.
- In the **Schedule** group, select the **Set Baseline** command, then select **Set Baseline** again to open the *Set Baseline* dialogue box.
- Select the **Set Interim plan** option (*Figure 212*).
- In the **Copy** field, *Scheduled Start/Finish* is selected by default for the initial Interim plan. This option will copy the start and finish dates from the current plan.

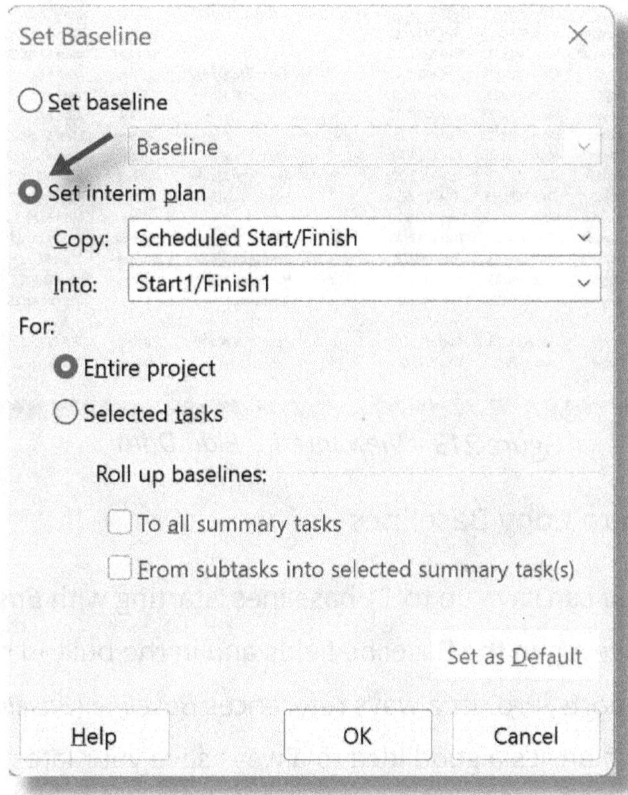

Figure 212 – Set an Interim Plan

- In the **Into** field, select the Interim plan that you want to copy the values into. *Start1/Finish1* will be selected by default for the initial Interim plan. For subsequent Interim plans select *Start2/Finish2* through *Start10/Finish 10*.

- In the **For** section, select **Entire project** to save an Interim Plan for the entire project or select **Selected tasks** to save an Interim plan for selected tasks.

- Select **OK** to close the *Set Baseline* dialogue box.

Interim plan data is saved in various Interim plan *Start* and *Finish* fields. To view Interim plan data, use the **Add New Column** command to add the relevant *Start* and *Finish* fields to the view. Add the fields that correspond to the Interim plan you selected in the **Into** field of the *Set Baseline* dialogue box. For example, if you selected *Start1/Finish1*, add the *Start 1* and *Finish 1* fields to the view to see the Interim plan data (*Figure 213*).

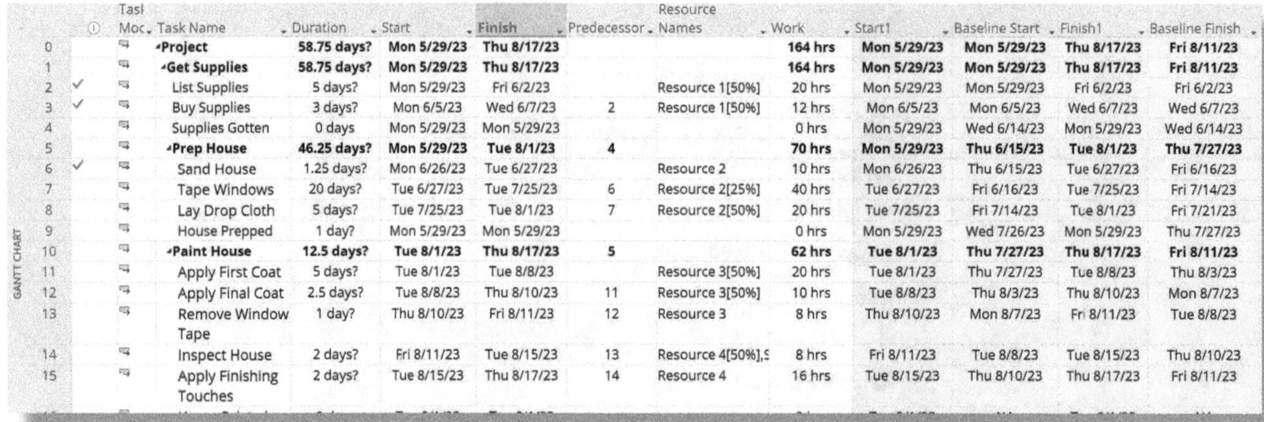

		Task Mode	Task Name	Duration	Start	Finish	Predecessors	Resource Names	Work	Start1	Baseline Start	Finish1	Baseline Finish
0			**Project**	**58.75 days?**	**Mon 5/29/23**	**Thu 8/17/23**			**164 hrs**	**Mon 5/29/23**	**Mon 5/29/23**	**Thu 8/17/23**	**Fri 8/11/23**
1			**Get Supplies**	**58.75 days?**	**Mon 5/29/23**	**Thu 8/17/23**			**164 hrs**	**Mon 5/29/23**	**Mon 5/29/23**	**Thu 8/17/23**	**Fri 8/11/23**
2	✓		List Supplies	5 days?	Mon 5/29/23	Fri 6/2/23		Resource 1[50%]	20 hrs	Mon 5/29/23	Mon 5/29/23	Fri 6/2/23	Fri 6/2/23
3	✓		Buy Supplies	3 days?	Mon 6/5/23	Wed 6/7/23	2	Resource 1[50%]	12 hrs	Mon 6/5/23	Mon 6/5/23	Wed 6/7/23	Wed 6/7/23
4			Supplies Gotten	0 days	Mon 5/29/23	Mon 5/29/23			0 hrs	Mon 5/29/23	Wed 6/14/23	Mon 5/29/23	Wed 6/14/23
5			**Prep House**	**46.25 days?**	**Mon 5/29/23**	**Tue 8/1/23**	**4**		**70 hrs**	**Mon 5/29/23**	**Thu 6/15/23**	**Tue 8/1/23**	**Thu 7/27/23**
6	✓		Sand House	1.25 days?	Mon 6/26/23	Tue 6/27/23		Resource 2	10 hrs	Mon 6/26/23	Thu 6/15/23	Tue 6/27/23	Fri 6/16/23
7			Tape Windows	20 days?	Tue 6/27/23	Tue 7/25/23	6	Resource 2[25%]	40 hrs	Tue 6/27/23	Fri 6/16/23	Tue 7/25/23	Fri 7/14/23
8			Lay Drop Cloth	5 days?	Tue 7/25/23	Tue 8/1/23	7	Resource 2[50%]	20 hrs	Tue 7/25/23	Fri 7/14/23	Tue 8/1/23	Fri 7/21/23
9			House Prepped	1 day?	Mon 5/29/23	Mon 5/29/23			0 hrs	Mon 5/29/23	Wed 7/26/23	Mon 5/29/23	Thu 7/27/23
10			**Paint House**	**12.5 days?**	**Tue 8/1/23**	**Thu 8/17/23**	**5**		**62 hrs**	**Tue 8/1/23**	**Thu 7/27/23**	**Thu 8/17/23**	**Fri 8/11/23**
11			Apply First Coat	5 days?	Tue 8/1/23	Tue 8/8/23		Resource 3[50%]	20 hrs	Tue 8/1/23	Thu 7/27/23	Tue 8/8/23	Thu 8/3/23
12			Apply Final Coat	2.5 days?	Tue 8/8/23	Thu 8/10/23	11	Resource 3[50%]	10 hrs	Tue 8/8/23	Thu 8/3/23	Thu 8/10/23	Mon 8/7/23
13			Remove Window Tape	1 day?	Thu 8/10/23	Fri 8/11/23	12	Resource 3	8 hrs	Thu 8/10/23	Mon 8/7/23	Fri 8/11/23	Tue 8/8/23
14			Inspect House	2 days?	Fri 8/11/23	Tue 8/15/23	13	Resource 4[50%],S	8 hrs	Fri 8/11/23	Tue 8/8/23	Tue 8/15/23	Thu 8/10/23
15			Apply Finishing Touches	2 days?	Tue 8/15/23	Thu 8/17/23	14	Resource 4	16 hrs	Tue 8/15/23	Thu 8/10/23	Thu 8/17/23	Fri 8/11/23

Figure 213 – View Interim Plan Data

Using an Interim Plan to Copy Baselines

As mentioned earlier, you can save up to 11 baselines, starting with *Baseline* (*Baseline 0*) through *Baseline 10*. However, in the Baseline fields and in the built-in reports, such as the Earned Value metrics reports, Project always references *Baseline* (*Baseline 0*). Therefore, if you re-baseline your project plan, it's a good idea to always save your latest baseline as *Baseline 0*, so Project will always reference the current data. To do this, you can use an Interim Plan to copy baseline information. This will allow you to save current data as Baseline 0, without overriding your original baseline data.

Here's how it works.

STEP 1: As reviewed earlier, save your original baseline as *Baseline* (*Baseline 0*).

STEP 2: Copy baseline data using an Interim Plan:

- Select the **Project** tab.
- In the **Schedule** group, select the **Set Baseline** command, then select **Set Baseline** again to open the *Set Baseline* dialogue box.
- Select the **Set Interim plan** option.
- In the **Copy** field, select *Baseline* (*Baseline 0*) from the pick-list.
- In the **Into** field, select the next baseline you're saving. E.g., *Baseline 1* from the pick-list (*Figure 214*). This will copy the data from *Baseline* (*Baseline 0*) into *Baseline 1*.

- In the **For** section, select **Entire project** to save an Interim plan for the entire project.
- Select **OK** to close the *Set Baseline* dialogue box.

Although you're saving an Interim plan, when you populate the **Copy** and **Into** fields with baselines, the baseline data for the entire project will be copied, and not just the start and finish dates.

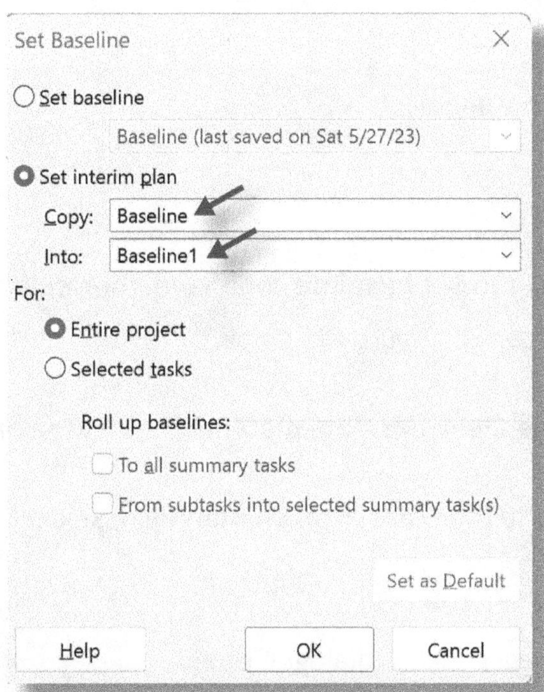

Figure 214 – Copy Baseline Data Using an Interim Plan

STEP 3: Save New Baselines as *Baseline* (*Baseline 0*):

- When you re-baseline your project plan, save it as *Baseline* (*Baseline 0*) by leaving *Baseline (last saved as....)* in the **Set Baseline field** of the *Set Baseline* dialogue box.

NOTE: When you re-save *Baseline 0*, Project will alert you that you've already used *Baseline 0* and will ask if you're sure you want to override the data. If you've completed step 2 and have already saved a copy of the original baseline as *Baseline 1*, select **Yes**. If you should need to re-baseline again, save a copy of the next baseline as *Baseline 2*, and so-forth.

The idea is – every time you re-baseline, over-ride *Baseline 0* for reporting <u>and</u> save a copy as the next sequential baseline for history.

Clearing Baselines and Interim Plans

If something changes in your original plan after you've baselined your project, you can also **Clear a Baseline or Interim plan**. Suppose an additional phase was added to your project. You would of course want this phase included in the baseline. If no progress data was entered before the phase was added, you could clear the Baseline or Interim plan and set a new one that includes the new phase.

To Clear a Baseline or Interim Plan:

- Select the **Project** tab.
- In the **Data** group, select the **Set baseline** command, then select **Clear Baseline** to open the *Clear Baseline* dialogue box (*Figure 215* below)
- To clear a Baseline, in the **Clear baseline plan** field, select the baseline you want to clear.
- To clear an Interim plan, in the **Clear interim plan** field, select the Interim plan you want to clear.
- Select **OK** to close the *Clear Baseline* dialogue box.

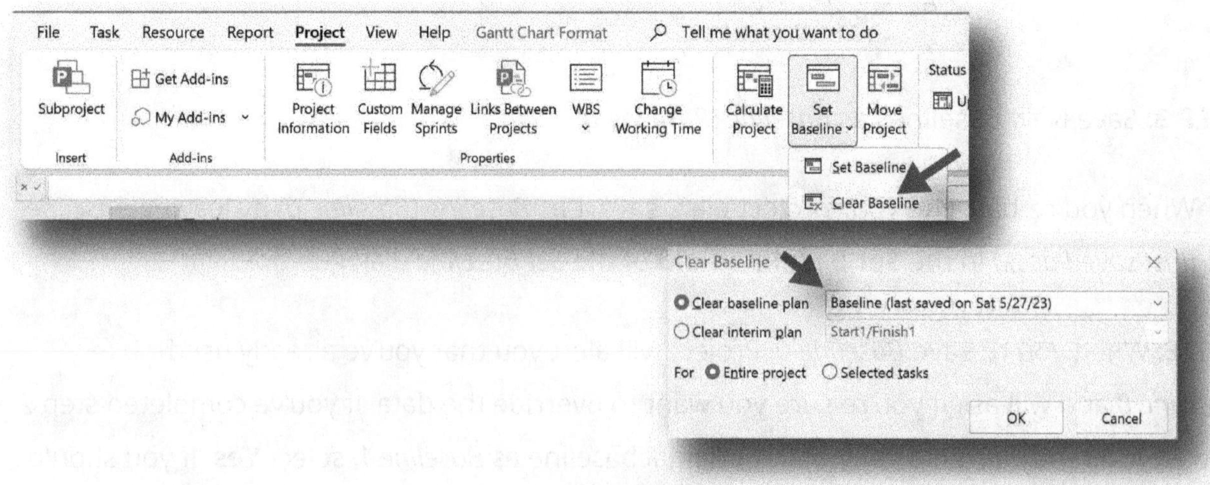

Figure 215 - Clear a Baseline or Interim Plan

Moving the Project

There may be times when a project cannot begin on the scheduled start date. Delayed funding and unavailable resources are common reasons. In such cases, consider **Moving the Project**, rather than changing the project start date (in the *Project Information* dialogue box). This will move the entire project forward, whereas changing the start date will only move the tasks impacted by a revised project start date.

To move the project:

- Select the **Project** tab.
- In the **Schedule** group, select the **Move Project** command to open the *Move Project* dialogue box (*Figure 216* below).
- Enter or select the new start date in the **New project start date** field.
- Select **OK** to close the *Move Project* dialogue box.

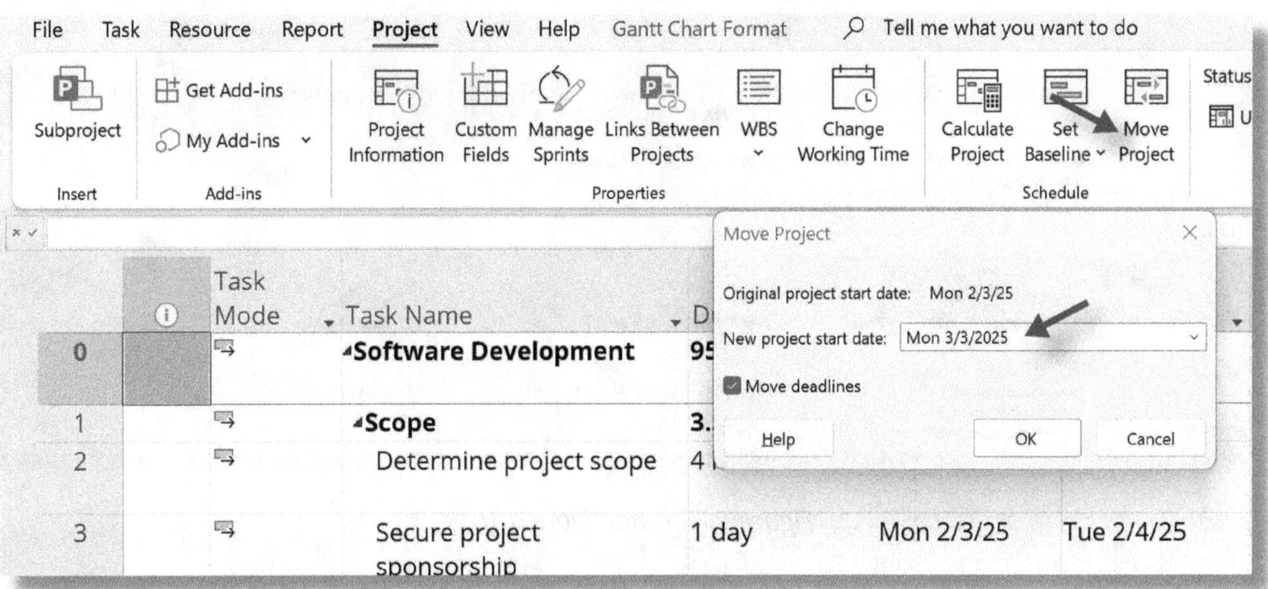

Figure 216 – Move the Project

Inactivating Tasks

As your project progresses, certain tasks may become unnecessary. For example, some tasks may be outsourced. You may not want to delete these task(s) from the schedule, as to keep the task information in your plan. In such cases, you can **Inactive a task**. Inactivating a task will keep the task details in the plan, but the task will not affect the schedule. This feature is only available in the Project Professional version of the software.

To Inactivate a task:

- Select the task(s) you want to inactivate.
- Select the **Task** tab. In the **Schedule** group, select the **Inactivate** command.

Inactive tasks are grayed out in the schedule and their task names and scheduling information are lined through (*Figure 217* below). In the Gantt chart, the task bars are white.

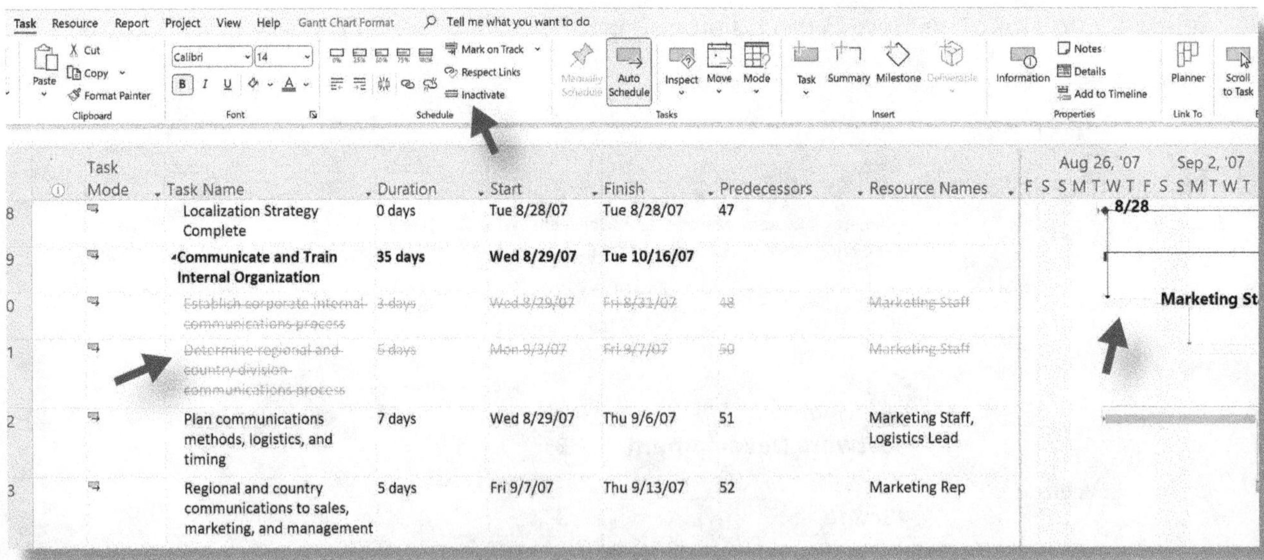

Figure 217 – Inactivate a Task

You've now learned to perform the last step in the B.A.S.I.C.S. scheduling process – **Start the Project** and execute a schedule! You've learned to set a baseline, view expected outcomes before collecting progress data, enter progress data, use the tracking fields, move the start date, inactivate a task, and update the schedule based on newly entered progress data.

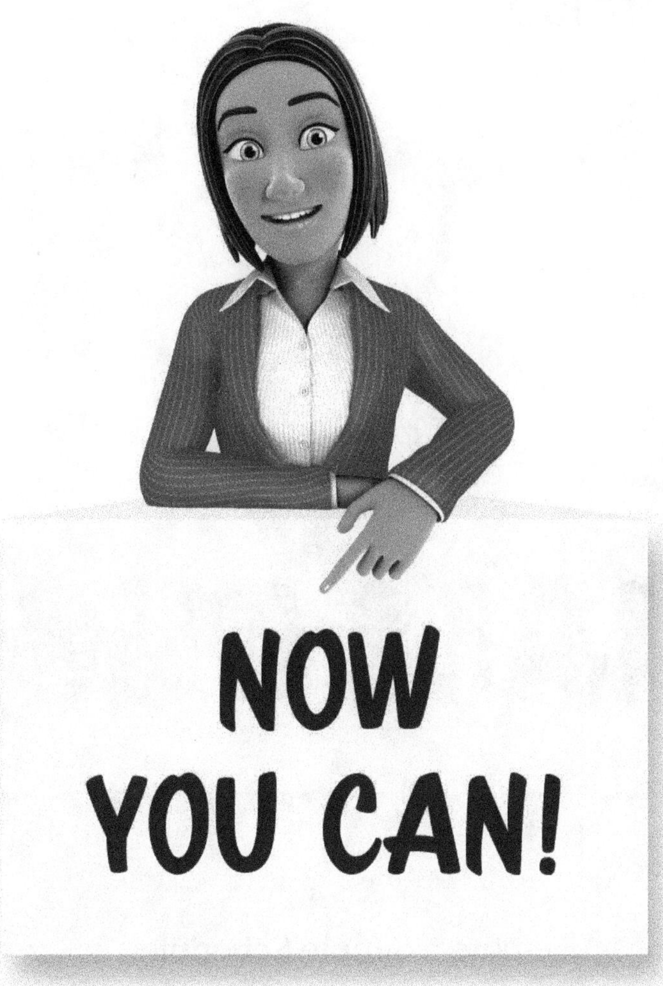

- ✓ Save a Baseline
- ✓ Move the Project
- ✓ Track a Schedule
- ✓ Enter Progress Data (Actuals)
- ✓ Update the Schedule
- ✓ Use the Tracking Gantt View
- ✓ Inactivate Tasks

Practice Exercise

Execute a Simple Schedule

For this practice exercise, you'll perform the final step in the B.A.S.I.C.S. scheduling approach – **Start the Project**. You will execute the Simple schedule you built for the Chapter 7 practice exercise.

Go to **mspbasics.com** for "Checkpoint" images to check your work as you go along.

Follow the steps below to complete this exercise:

Open an Existing Project Plan

1. Open the Simple "House Painting" project plan that you saved from the Chapter 7 practice exercise. **NOTE:** The file should contain all the completed steps from the exercise.

CHECKPOINT: To confirm that you're starting with the right file, go to **mspbasics.com**

- Select the **CheckPoint Images** tab.
- Select the version of the book you're using.
- Select **Chapter 15**. Then, go to **Checkpoint Image #1**

Set a Deadline for the Project Finish Date

Set a deadline for the project finish date by applying a deadline to the task 16 milestone task, *House Painted*.

Set the Deadline as follows:

1. Double-click the task name of task 16, *House Painted*, to open the *Task Information* dialogue box.
2. Select the **Advanced** tab.
3. In the **Deadline** field, enter **6/28/24**.
4. Select **OK** to close the *Task Information* dialogue box.

CHECKPOINT: To check your results so far, go to **mspbasics.com**

- Select the **CheckPoint Images** tab.
- Select the version of the book you're using.
- Select **Chapter 15**. Then, go to **Checkpoint Image #2**

Set the Current Date

Assume the current date is 6/3/24. Set this date as the "Current Date" in Project, as follows:

1. Select the **Project** tab.
2. In the **Properties** group, select the **Project Information** command to open the *Project Information* dialogue box.
3. In the **Current Date** field, enter or select **6/3/24**.
4. Select **OK** to close the *Project Information* dialogue box.

NOTE: You should see a vertical green line in the Gantt chart indicating the current date (the indicator will correspond with 6/3/24 on the timescale). If you don't see the vertical green line, use the Zoom slider in the bottom right corner to zoom in on the timeline.

CHECKPOINT: To check your results so far, go to **mspbasics.com**

- Select the **CheckPoint Images** tab.
- Select the version of the book you're using.
- Select **Chapter 15**. Then, go to **Checkpoint Image #3**

Baseline the Schedule

Set a Baseline as follows:

1. On the **Project** tab, in the **Schedule** group, select the **Set Baseline command**. Then, select **Set Baseline** again to open the *Set Baseline dialogue* box.
2. Be sure that the **Set Baseline** option is selected. Since this is the initial baseline, *Baseline* should already be selected in the baseline field.
3. Select **OK** to close the *Set Baseline* dialogue box.

Confirm the baseline was set as follows:

1. In the **Schedule** group, select the **Set Baseline** command. Then, select **Set Baseline** again to re-open the *Set Baseline* dialogue box.
2. The baseline field should now display *Baseline (last saved on... the current date).*
3. Select **Cancel** to close the *Set Baseline* dialogue box.

CHECKPOINT: To check your results so far, go to **mspbasics.com**

- Select the **CheckPoint Images** tab.
- Select the version of the book you're using.
- Select **Chapter 15**. Then, go to **Checkpoint Image #4**

UPDATE 1

Update the Current Date and Set the Status Date

Assume that 1 week has passed and the current date is now Monday, 6/10/24. You met with your team last Friday, 6/7/24 to collect progress data.

Set **6/10/24** as the new **Current date** and **6/7/24** as the **Status date** as follows:

1. On the **Project** tab, in the Properties group, select the **Project Information** command to open the *Project Information* dialogue box.
2. In the **Current date** field, enter or select **6/10/24**.
3. In the **Status date** field, enter or select **6/7/24**.
4. Select **OK** to close the *Project Information* dialogue box. The 6/7/24 status date should now be displayed on the ribbon, in the **Status** group.

CHECKPOINT: To check your results so far, go to **mspbasics.com**

- Select the **CheckPoint Images** tab.
- Select the version of the book you're using.
- Select **Chapter 15**. Then, go to **Checkpoint Image #5**

Apply the Late Tasks Filter

You're ready to enter the actuals you received from your team on 6/7/24. To make this task easier, you'll apply the **Late Task filter** to see which tasks should have work done as of the current date, 6/10/24.

Apply the Filter for Late Tasks as follows:

1. In the **Task Name** field of the Entry table, select the **Auto-filter** arrow.
2. Select **Filters** from the pick-list, then select **Late Tasks**.

When the Later Tasks filter is applied, tasks 1 through 6 should be displayed. These are the tasks that should have had work done as of 6/7/24.

CHECKPOINT: To check your results so far, go to **mspbasics.com**

- Select the **CheckPoint Images** tab.
- Select the version of the book you're using.
- Select **Chapter 15**. Then, go to **Checkpoint Image #6**

Add the Tracking Fields to the View

Next, you'll add the tracking fields for a Simple schedule to the Entry table. Use the **Add New Column** field to add the **Actual Start**, **Actual Duration** and **Remaining Duration** fields to the view. If you don't see the Add New Column field, slide the right half of the screen to the right, until you can see it.

To add each Tracking Field:

1. Select the header of the **Add New Column** field to display the pick-list of columns you can add to the table.
2. Type **Actual Start**. When it appears, select it.
3. Repeat these steps to add the **Actual Duration** and **Remaining Duration** fields to the table.

Enter the Progress Data (Update 1)

The progress data (actuals) that the project team gave you are listed in the table below.

1. Enter the **Actual Start, Actual Duration** and **Remaining Duration** values into the respective tracking fields for the listed tasks.

RESOURCE NAME	TASK ID	TASK NAME	ACTUAL START	ACTUAL DURATION	REMAINING DURATION
Jill	2	List Supplies	06/03/24	0.5 day (0.5d)	0
Jack	3	Buy Supplies	06/04/24	1 day (1d)	0
Jack	6	Sand House	06/05/24	3 days (3d)	1 day (1d)

After the progress data is entered, Project will add check-marks in the **Indicators** field of tasks 2 and 3, to indicate that these tasks are 100% complete. They have a Remaining Duration value of zero. In the Gantt chart, the task bars for tasks 2, 3 & 6 will now have a progress bar inside their task bars, indicating their completion progress. Since tasks 2 and 3 are now complete, Phase 1 of the project, *Get Supplies* is complete. Also, since its predecessors are complete, the task 4 milestone, *Supplies Gotten* can be updated as 100% complete.

Mark the Supplies Gotten milestone task 100% complete as follows:

1. Select the **Task** tab.
2. Select task 4, *Supplies Gotten*.
3. In the **Schedule** group, select the **100% Complete** command. Project will place a check mark next to this task and add its progress bar to the Gantt chart.

CHECKPOINT: To check your results so far, go to **mspbasics.com**

- Select the **CheckPoint Images** tab.
- Select the version of the book you're using.
- Select **Chapter 15**. Then, go to **Checkpoint Image #7**

Clear the Late Tasks Filter

Now, you'll clear the Late Task filter to display the entire project outline.

Clear the filter as follows:

1. Select the **View** tab.
2. In the **Data** group, select **Clear Filter** from the **Filter** pick-list.

Schedule Tracking Questions for Update 1:

1. Is the project on schedule, ahead of schedule or behind schedule?
2. If the project is not on schedule, by how many days is it ahead or behind schedule?
3. Why?

CHECKPOINT: To check your answers, go to **mspbasics.com**

- Select the **CheckPoint Images** tab.
- Select the version of the book you're using.
- Select **Chapter 15**. Then, go to **Checkpoint Image #8**

UPDATE 2

Update the Current Date and Set the Status Date

Assume another week has passed and the current date is Monday, 6/17/24. You will meet with your team today to collect progress data.

Set **6/17/24** as the new **Current date** and **6/17/24** as the **Status Date** as follows:

1. On the **Project** tab, in the **Properties** group, select the **Project Information** command to open the *Project Information* dialogue box.
2. In the **Current date** field, enter or select **6/17/24.**
3. In the **Status da**te field, enter or select **6/17/24**.
4. Select **OK** to close the *Project Information* dialogue box. The new status date of 6/17/24 should now be displayed on the ribbon, in the **Status** group.

CHECKPOINT: To check your results so far, go to **mspbasics.com**

- Select the **CheckPoint Images** tab.
- Select the version of the book you're using.
- Select **Chapter 15.** Then, go to **Checkpoint Image #9**

Apply the Late Tasks Filter

You're ready to check with the project team to get another status on the current work. Before you meet, you'll apply the **Late Task filter** to see which tasks should have work done as of the current date (6/17/24).

Apply the Late Tasks filter, as follows:

1. In the **Task Name** field of the Entry table, select the **Auto-filter** arrow.
2. Select **Filters** from the pick-list, then select **Late Tasks**.

When the Later Tasks filter is applied, tasks 5 through 11 should be displayed.

These are the tasks that should have had work done as of 6/17/24.

CHECKPOINT: To check your results so far, go to **mspbasics.com**

- Select the **CheckPoint Images** tab.
- Select the version of the book you're using.
- Select **Chapter 15**. Then, go to **Checkpoint Image #10**

Enter the Progress Data (Update 2)

The project team has given you the progress data (actuals) listed in the following table.

1. Enter the **Actual Start**, **Actual Duration** and **Remaining Duration** values into the respective tracking fields for the listed tasks.

RESOURCE NAME	TASK ID	TASK NAME	ACTUAL START	ACTUAL DURATION	REMAINING DURATION
Jack	6	Sand House	06/05/24	4 days (4d)	0
Jill	7	Tape Windows	06/11/24	1 day (1d)	0
Jack	8	Lay Drop Cloth	06/12/24	1 day (1d)	0
Contractor, Jack	11	Apply First Coat	6/13/24	1 day (1d)	1 day (1d)

After the progress data is entered, Project will add check-marks in the **Indicators** field of tasks 6, 7 and 8, to indicate that these tasks are 100% complete. They have a Remaining Duration value of zero. In the Gantt chart, the task bars for tasks 6, 7 & 8 will now have a progress bar inside their task bars, indicating their completion progress. Since tasks 6, 7 and 8 are now complete, Phase 2 of the project, *Prep House* is complete. Also, since its predecessors are complete, the task 9 milestone, *House Prepped* can be updated as 100% complete.

Mark the House Prepped milestone task 100% complete as follows:

1. Select the **Task** tab.

2. Select task 9, *House Prepped*.

3. In the **Schedule** group, select the **100% Complete** command. Project will place a check mark next to this task and add its progress bar to the Gantt chart.

> **CHECKPOINT:** To check your results so far, go to **mspbasics.com**
>
> - Select the **CheckPoint Images** tab.
> - Select the version of the book you're using.
> - Select **Chapter 15**. Then, go to **Checkpoint Image #11**
>
> 

Clear the Late Tasks Filter

Clear the Late Tasks filter to display the entire schedule, as follows:

1. Select the **View** tab.

2. In the **Data** group, select **Clear Filter** from the Filter pick-list.

Schedule Tracking Questions for Update 2:

1. Is the project on schedule, ahead of schedule or behind schedule?

2. If the project is not on schedule, by how many days is it ahead or behind schedule?

3. Why?

> **CHECKPOINT:** To check your answers, go to **mspbasics.com**
>
> - Select the **CheckPoint Images** tab.
> - Select the version of the book you're using.
> - Select **Chapter 15**. Then, go to **Checkpoint Image #12**
>
> 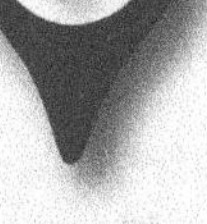

UPDATE 3

Update the Current Date and Set the Status Date

Assume two weeks have passed and the current date is Monday, 7/1/24. You met with your team last Friday 6/28/24 to collect progress data.

Set **7/1/24** as the new **Current date** and **6/28/24** as the new **Status date** as follows:

1. On the **Project** tab, in the **Properties** group, select the **Project Information** command to open the *Project Information* dialogue box.

2. In the **Current date** field, enter or select **7/1/24.**

3. In the **Status date** field, enter or select **6/28/24.**

4. Select **OK** to close the *Project Information* dialogue box. The new status date of 6/28/24 should now be displayed on the ribbon, in the **Status** group.

CHECKPOINT: To check your results so far, go to **mspbasics.com**

- Select the **CheckPoint Images** tab.
- Select the version of the book you're using.
- Select **Chapter 15.** Then, go to **Checkpoint Image #13**

Apply the Late Tasks Filter

You're ready to check with the project team to get another status on the current work. Before you meet, you'll apply the **Late Tasks filter** to see which tasks should have work done as of the current date (6/28/24).

Apply the Late Tasks filter, as follows:

1. In the Task **Name** field of the Entry table, select the **Auto-filter** arrow.

2. Select **Filters** from the pick-list, then select **Late Tasks.**

When the Late Tasks filter is applied, tasks 10 through 16 should be displayed. These are the tasks that should have had work done as of 6/28/24.

CHECKPOINT: To check your results so far, go to **mspbasics.com**

- Select the **CheckPoint Images** tab.
- Select the version of the book you're using.
- Select **Chapter 15.** Then, go to **Checkpoint Image #14**

Enter the Progress Data (Update 3)

The project team has told you that they have completed all their remaining work, as scheduled. Instead of entering the Actual Start, Actual Duration and Remaining Duration values, you'll update the schedule using the **Update Project** command.

Update the schedule as follows:

1. Select the **Project** tab.
2. In the **Status** group, select the **Update Project** command to open the *Update Project* dialogue box.
3. Be sure the **Update work as completed through** option is selected.
4. In the **Date** field, enter the **6/28/24** Status date.
5. Select the **Set 0% or 100% complete only** option.
6. In the **For** section, be sure **Entire project** is selected.
7. Select **OK** to update the schedule. Project will mark tasks 10 through 16 complete, indicated by a check-mark in the **Indicators** field.

Clear the Late Tasks Filter

Clear the Late Tasks filter to display the entire schedule, as follows:

1. Select the **View** tab.
2. In the **Data** group, select **Clear Filter** from the **Filter** pick-list.

CHECKPOINT: To check your results so far, go to **mspbasics.com**

- Select the **CheckPoint Images** tab.
- Select the version of the book you're using.
- Select **Chapter 15**. Then, go to **Checkpoint Image #15**

Schedule Tracking Questions for Update 3:

1. Is the project on schedule, ahead of schedule or behind schedule?
2. If the project is not on schedule, by how many days is it ahead or behind schedule?
3. Why?

CHECKPOINT: To check your answers, go to **mspbasics.com**

- Select the **CheckPoint Images** tab.
- Select the version of the book you're using.
- Select **Chapter 15**. Then, go to **Checkpoint Image #16**

Congratulations! You've now executed a Simple schedule! You've now performed the last step in the B.A.S.I.C.S. scheduling approach – **Start the Project**.

Chapter 16 Tracking Costs and Earned Value

In the last chapter, you learned to execute the schedule. You learned to baseline the schedule, enter progress data, update the schedule, and inactivate tasks. In this chapter, you'll learn to **track project costs**. When you're done, you'll be able to assign a project budget, explain cost variance, use the Cost table, explain Earned Value Management, use the Earned Value table, and use the Earned Value reports.

You'll Learn To:

- Assign a Project Budget
- Understand Cost Variance
- Use the Cost Table
- Simplify Earned Value Management
- Use the Earned Value Table
- Use the Earned Value Reports

Cost Variance Metrics

In any of the Microsoft Project desktop versions, you can track project costs using **Cost Variance** and **Earned Value Management (EVM) metrics**. Cost Variance metrics answer simple variance questions like *"How are we doing against the baselined schedule and cost forecast?"* EVM metrics answer this question and several more, like the following:

"Based on current performance results, for every dollar we spend in the future, how much value will we realize?"

"Based on current performance results, on any day in the future, how far will we be behind or ahead of schedule?"

"Based on current performance results, how much will we spend by the time this project is finished?"

As you can see by the nature of these questions, the project intelligence we can gather from EVM metrics is much more comprehensive than that we can glean from analyzing simple cost variance. This is because EVM allows us to not only see project status and progress data, but also forecast what our project status will be at any point in the future. It achieves this by monetizing your schedule performance and measuring both your schedule and cost efficiency. Based on this performance efficiency, it can forecast your project performance at any point in the future. The Project Management Institute defines Earned Value Management as ***a methodology that combines scope, schedule, and resource measurements to assess project performance and progress***.

Assigning a Project Budget

To track project costs and make the best use of the variance metrics in Project, it's helpful to assign a **project budget**. This can be done by creating a **Budget Cost Resource** and assigning it to your project. Once you enter progress data, you can use the Budget Cost Resource to compare the planned project budget to actual cost. It's important not to confuse your baseline cost with your project budget. Ideally, when you baseline your schedule, it will be under budget. This is because projects generally include a certain amount of overage to account for things that may not go as planned. To distinguish between these concepts, think of your baseline cost as the approved version of your cost projection. At the beginning of your project, this cost projection should be well under your spending limit. Think of your project budget as your spending limit. This is the value you will be assigning to your Budget Cost Resource.

Creating a Budget Cost Resource

As mentioned earlier, a **Budget Cost Resource** can be used to assign a project budget. Budget Cost Resources are assigned to the Project Summary Task and cannot be assigned to individual tasks. They must first be created in the *Resource Sheet* view.

To create a Budget Cost Resource:

- Select the **View** tab. In the **Resource Views** group, select **Resource Sheet** to get to the *Resource Sheet* view.
- In the **Resource Name** field, name the resource **Budget** (*Figure 218* below)
- In the **Type** field, select **Cost** to create a *Cost* resource.
- Double-click the **Budget** resource name to open the *Resource Information* dialogue box.
- Select the **General** tab.
- Be sure that the **Budget** checkbox is checked. This will designate the resource as a "Budget" resource.
- Select **OK** to close the *Resource Information* dialogue box.

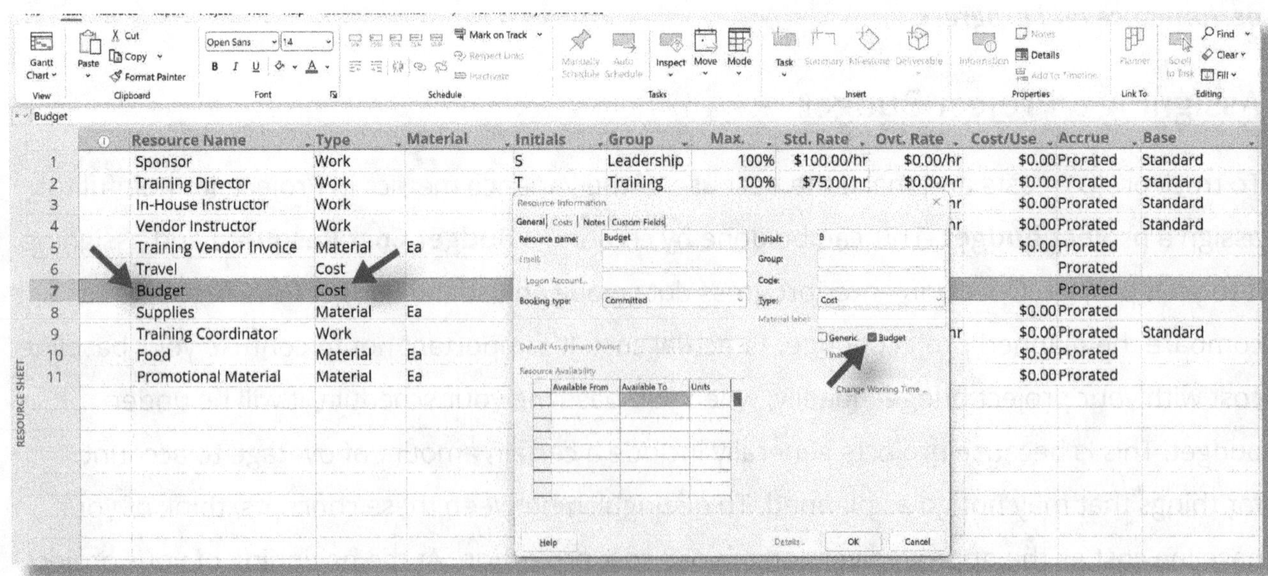

Figure 218 – Create a Budget Cost Resource

Once you've created the Budget Cost resource, you'll need to assign it to the Project Summary Task.

To assign the Budget Cost Resource to the Project Summary Task:

- Switch to the Gantt Chart view. Select the **Format** tab. In the **Show/Hide** group, select the **Project Summary Task** checkbox to display the Project Summary Task.
- Select the **Resources** tab. In the **Assignments** group, select the **Assign Resources** command to open the *Assign Resources* dialogue box (*Figure 219* below).
- In the **Resource Name** field, select the **Budget** resource, then select **Assign**.
- Select **Close** to close the *Assign Resources* dialogue box. The Budget Cost resource will be assigned to the Project Summary task.

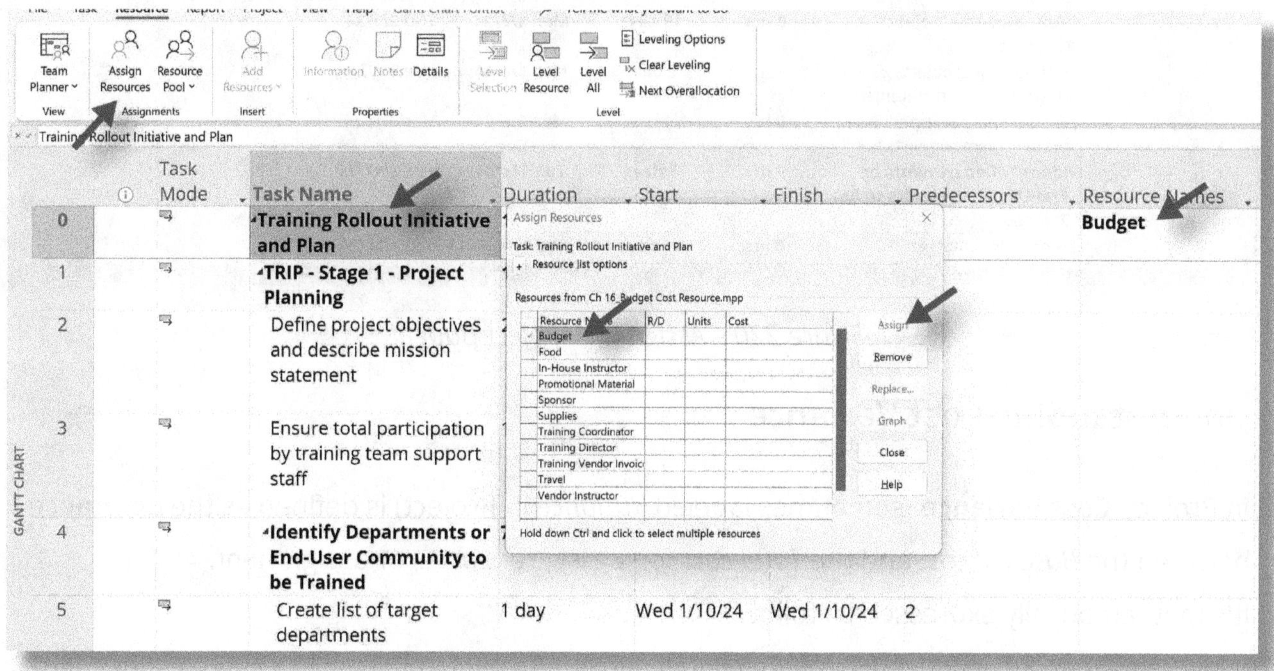

Figure 219 – Assign the Budget Cost Resource to the Project Summary Task

After you've assigned the Budget Cost Resource to Project Summary Task, you can then assign the project budget.

To assign the Project Budget:

- Switch to the **Task Usage view** by selecting the **View** tab. Then, in the **Task Views** group, select the **Task Usage** quick access command.
- Use the **Add New Column** field to add the **Budget Cost** field to the table. If you don't see the Add New Column field, slide the right side of the view to the right, until you see it.
- In the **Budget Cost** field, in the row of the Budget resource, enter the value for the project budget. *Figure 220* below shows an assigned project budget of $100,000.00.

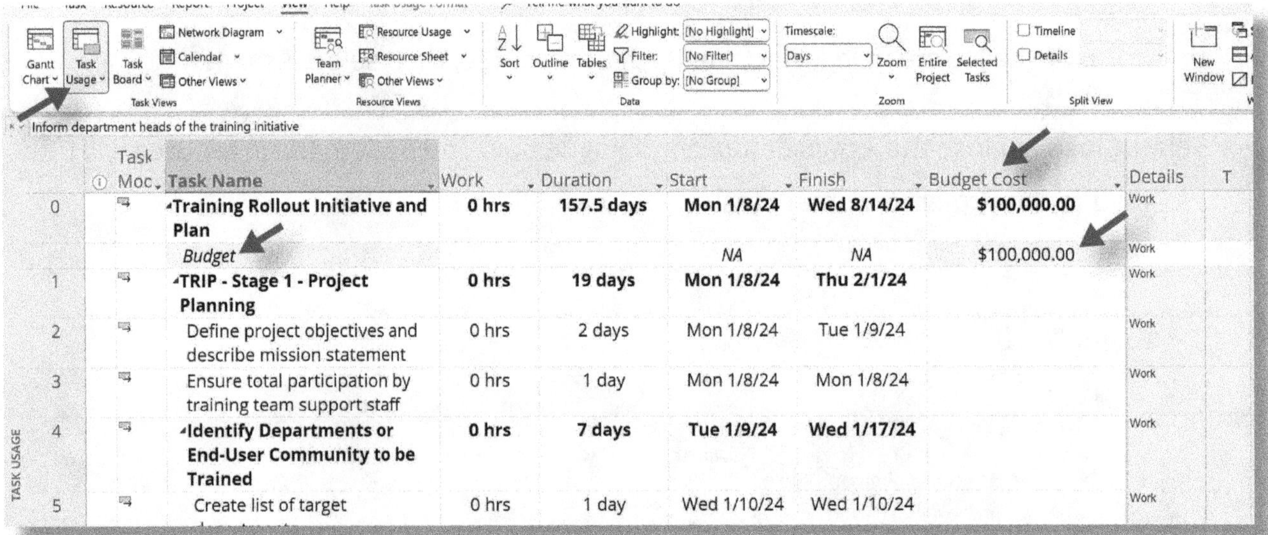

Figure 220 – Assign the Project Budget

Understanding Cost Variance

In Project, **Cost Variance** (sometimes labeled *Variance* in Project) is defined as the difference between the *Baseline cost* and the *Total cost* for a task, resource, or assignment.
It's mathematically expressed as follows:

COST VARIANCE = Cost – Baseline Cost

Based on this mathematical expression, it's apparent that a positive Cost Variance is not preferable, as it would indicate an **over-budget** condition. This would mean that the current cost projection is greater than the baseline cost. Moreover, a negative cost variance would indicate an **under-budget** condition and a Cost Variance of zero would indicate an **on-budget** condition.

The term **Cost** (sometimes labeled *Total Cost* in Project) in the Cost Variance equation is like the terms Work and Duration, defined in the prior chapter. It's the sum of actual and remaining values. Its mathematical expression is as follows:

COST = Actual Cost + Remaining Cost

Combining these concepts, we can express Cost Variance in simple terms. It's a reflection of what you've spent (Actuals Cost) and still must spend (Remaining Cost) minus what you said you would spend (Baseline Values). Cost Variance can thus be expressed more broadly as follows:

VARIANCE = Actual Cost + Remaining Cost – Baseline Cost.

Finally, in practical terms there are two types of Variances. These will not appear as fields you can add in Project, but you must understand them to effectively monitor and control project budgets. The first is **Actual Variance**. This is Variance without the remaining estimate. The second is **Estimated Variance**. This is Variance with the remaining estimate. To clarify the difference, let's consider an example. Suppose your project's baseline cost was $100K and at the halfway mark you'd spent $75K. Suppose further that your baseline projection was to have spent $50K to that point. What is your Variance? It is clearly $25K since you are $25K over budget at this point. Also, there is nothing you can do about it. This is because it is a measure of costs that have already been spent. Therefore, this is *Actual* Variance. Now, let's suppose Your team has not only spent $75K of your budget, but are projecting to spend another $50K before they finish the work. What is your Variance now? At a minimum, it would include the $25K we already know about. But since they are estimating to spend another $50K, the Variance would also include this estimate. Therefore, the Variance is now $75K. This is what is meant by *Estimated* Variance. It includes the $25K of sunk cost and the $50K of estimated cost. Why is this important? Because since the $50K has not yet been spent, you can intervene and make decisions that may result in a lower estimate.

Now that we have reviewed how Project calculates Cost Variance, let's review the Cost table, which is the table that prominently features the Cost Variance metric. In the next section, we'll view Cost Variance by using the Cost table.

Viewing Cost Variance using the Cost Table

If resource pay rates have been added to the Resource Sheet view, Project will accrue cost in the background as you enter progress data. As your project progresses, you can compare your current cost projection to your Baseline cost. If you created a Budget Cost Resource, you could also compare your current cost projection to your Project budget. The simplest way to access these fields is to switch to the **Cost table** in the Gantt Chart view and add the **Budget Cost** field.

To add the Budget Cost field to the Cost Table in the Gantt Chart view:

- Select the **View** tab.
- In the **Data** group, select **Cost** from the **Tables** pick-list.
- Use the **Add New Column** command to add the **Budget Cost** field to the table (*Figure 221* below).

	Task Name	Actual	Total Cost	Fixed Cost	Fixed Cost Accrual	Baseline	Variance	Remaining	Budget Cost
0	**Training Rollout Initiative and Plan**	**$12,800.00**	**$88,290.00**	**$0.00**	**Prorated**	**$85,490.00**	**$2,800.00**	**$75,490.00**	**$100,000.00**
1	**TRIP - Stage 1 - Project Planning**	**$12,800.00**	**$65,020.00**	**$0.00**	**Prorated**	**$62,220.00**	**$2,800.00**	**$52,220.00**	
2	Define project objectives and describe mission statement	$12,800.00	$15,600.00	$0.00	Prorated	$12,800.00	$2,800.00	$2,800.00	
3	Ensure total participation by training team support staff	$0.00	$300.00	$0.00	Prorated	$300.00	$0.00	$300.00	
4	**Identify Departments or End-User Community to be Trained**	**$0.00**	**$5,550.00**	**$0.00**	**Prorated**	**$5,550.00**	**$0.00**	**$5,550.00**	
5	Create list of target departments	$0.00	$360.00	$0.00	Prorated	$360.00	$0.00	$360.00	
6	Perform departmental training needs analysis	$0.00	$2,520.00	$0.00	Prorated	$2,520.00	$0.00	$2,520.00	
7	Compile results and present findings to training coordinator	$0.00	$720.00	$0.00	Prorated	$720.00	$0.00	$720.00	
8	Prioritize training delivery according to critical need	$0.00	$600.00	$0.00	Prorated	$600.00	$0.00	$600.00	
9	Inform department heads of the training initiative	$0.00	$300.00	$0.00	Prorated	$300.00	$0.00	$300.00	
10	Determine if training can be done in-house or outsourced	$0.00	$1,050.00	$0.00	Prorated	$1,050.00	$0.00	$1,050.00	

Figure 221 – View Cost Variance Using the Cost Table

The Cost Table displays the following cost fields:

- The **Actual (Actual Cost)** field shows costs incurred for work already performed by resources on their tasks, along with any other recorded costs associated with the task.
- The **Total Cost** field shows the total or projected cost for a task, resource, or assignment, based on costs already incurred by work performed by resources assigned to the task, in addition to the costs planned for the remaining work.

- The **Fixed Cost** field shows any non-resource task expense.
- The **Fixed Cost Accrual** field provides choices for how and when fixed costs are to be charged to the cost of a task. The options are Start, Prorated and End. Use the pick-list to select an option.
- The **Baseline (Baseline Cost)** field shows the planned costs at the time the project is baselined.
- The **Variance** field shows the difference between the Baseline cost and Total cost for a task, resource, or assignment.
- The **Remaining (Remaining Cost)** field shows the remaining scheduled expense that will be incurred in completing the remaining scheduled work. When you first create a task, the Remaining Cost field is the same as the Cost field. Once resources begin to work on the task and report actual work, Project calculates Remaining Cost as Remaining Work X Standard Rate + Remaining Overtime Cost.

Understanding Earned Value Management (EVM)

As mentioned earlier, **Earned Value Management** allows you to not only see project status and progress data, but also forecast what your project status will be at any point in the future. The following simple use case can enable you to grasp what is often viewed as the most complex topic in project management. We'll use it to explain each earned value metric.

A Simple Use Case – The Fenwick Fencing Fiasco

What you envisioned to be a simple, low-cost project, turned out to be a difficult, expensive one in the end. Your project scope was to **build a square fence** around a plot of land you recently inherited. You decided to use a contractor recommended by a family member. Your contract negotiation with the Fenwick Fencing company began smoothly. They estimated to build your fence for $100 per side, for a grand total cost of $400. They also agreed to build one side per day. They would start the work on a Monday and complete the project by Thursday. At the end of the day on a Tuesday, you decided to check in on the fencing contractor after work, to see if things were running according to plan. Your timing was perfect. The contractor was shutting down operations for the day and was still at the work site.

You discovered to your dismay, that they had only completed one side. To make matters worse, they had already spent the entire $400 budget. This was clearly not the status you were hoping for, but at least some good can come from this fiasco. We can use it to better understand each Earned Value metric. We'll begin with the easiest metric and work our way to the most complex ones. We'll start with Actual Cost.

Actual Cost (AC)

Actual Cost (AC) is the actual cost incurred to complete actual work, up to the status date. In our fence project, the status date is the end of day on Tuesday. And the actual cost incurred to complete one side is $400. Therefore, Actual Cost = $400.

Budget at Completion (BAC)

The **Budget at Completion (BAC)** is the total planned or baselined cost. This is how much you budgeted for the project. In our fence project, the budget was $400. Therefore, Budget at Completion = $400.

Estimate at Completion (EAC)

The **Estimate at Completion (EAC)** is the expected total cost based on performance, up to the status date. This is how much your project will cost at the end if you continue to use the Fenwick Fencing company. In our project, the numbers are so round and simple that we can calculate EAC without using a calculator. Since Fenwick used $400 to complete one side, how much will they use to complete four sides? If you're thinking $1600, you're thinking correctly (4 sides x $400 per side = $1600). Therefore, **Estimate at Completion = $1600**.

If you were able to follow this example, you just figured out one of the most complex EVM metrics without using a calculator! What you just figured out in your head is what EVM figures out by dividing the Budget at Completion by the contractor's cost efficiency. Let's review how we would arrive at both of these metrics. The first one is easy for us because earlier, we determined the Budget at Completion to be $400. To determine the contractor's cost efficiency, we must consider their cost performance to date. Based on their track record, this contractor will complete **one** fence per $400 investment, whereas our baseline agreement requires them to complete **four** fences per $400 investment.

Therefore, their cost efficiency is **one** divided by **four**, or 25%. We will later identify this cost efficiency metric as their CPI or Cost Performance Index. The important thing to note at this point is that most situations you encounter in the field will not involve such clean, round numbers. Therefore, you will need to determine the EAC value by using the equation for EAC, which is: **EAC = BAC/CPI**.

Estimate to Completion (ETC)

The **Estimate to Completion (ETC)** is how much more money you will need to come up with if you continue using Fenwick Fencing. Earlier, we calculated Estimate at Completion to be $1600. Also, recall that we've already spent $400. Therefore, we will need to come up with an additional $1200 if we decide to continue using Fenwick Fencing. Therefore, **Estimate to Completion (ETC) = $1200**.

If you were able to follow this example, then you've once again figured out one of the more complex EVM metrics without using a calculator. It may not surprise you to know that EVM figures out ETC the same way you did, by subtracting Actual Cost ($400) from the Estimate at Completion ($1600). The EVM equation for ETC is: **ETC = EAC - AC**

Planned Value (PV)

The **Planned Value (PV)** is the value of the work that was scheduled to be completed as of the status date. In our simple example, the status date is the end of the day on Tuesday. By this time, we planned for two sides to be completed. Also, per our baseline agreement, each side was to cost $100. Therefore, our **Planned Value (PV)** by the end of the day on Tuesday is **$200**.

As with almost every EVM metric, there is an equation we can use when we don't have such clean round numbers. The equation for PV is: **PV = Planned % Complete x BAC**. To arrive at **PV** using this equation, you would need to first determine your **Planned % Complete** as of the end of the day on Tuesday. Recall that, we planned for two sides to be complete. Since there are a total of 4 sides, our Planned % Complete was 50%. When you multiply this completion percentage by the **BAC**, which again is $400, then you would arrive at the $200 calculation for Planned Value.

Earned Value (EV)

The **Earned Value (EV)** is the value of the work that has been completed as of the status date. In our simple example, only one side of the fencing is complete as of the status date, which is the end of the day on Tuesday. As we have established, the value of one side of fencing is $100. Therefore, **Earned Value = $100**.

The EVM equation for calculating Earned Value is: **EV = Actual % Complete x BAC**.

To arrive at **EV** using this equation, you would need to first determine your **Actual % Complete** as of the end of the day on Tuesday. Since only 1 of the 4 sides is complete, the **Actual % Complete** is 25%. When you multiply this completion percentage by the **BAC**, which again is $400, then you would arrive at the $100 calculation for Earned Value.

Schedule Performance Index (SPI)

Now that we have determined Planned Value and Earned Value, we can exploit the advantages of tracking project costs using Earned Value Management over simple variance assessment techniques, such as determining if we are over or under-budget. Those advantages include the ability to forecast where the budget and schedule will be at any point in the future, based on current performance. This is accomplished by using EV and PV to calculate the schedule and cost efficiency. In this section, we'll calculate the schedule efficiency.

Because our simple use case involves clean, round numbers, we can deduce the schedule efficiency without using the equation. For example, we know that by our status date, which is the end of the day on Tuesday, the contractor should have completed two sides of fencing. We also know that they have only completed one side of fencing. Therefore, their schedule efficiency is 50%. Since past performance is a strong predictor of future performance, we can safely deduce that at any point in the future, this contractor will be 50% behind schedule. When they should have completed 6 months of work, they will have completed 3 months of work. When they should have completed 2 years of work, they will have completed 1 year of work. As you can imagine, this is valuable information on any project. It allows for early detection and intervention before schedule and costs proceed down a predictably bad path.

When you don't have clean, round numbers, you can calculate SPI using the appropriate EVM equation, which is: **SPI = EV/PV**. In our case, since EV is $100 and PV is $200, SPI calculates to **50%**.

As you can imagine, the ideal SPI is 100%, or 1.0. This would mean that whenever the contractor or project team *should* have completed 6 months of work, they *will* have completed 6 months of work. An SPI of greater than 1.0 is even more favorable. This would mean that when the team should have completed 6 months of work, they will have completed **more** than 6 months of work. Conversely, a SPI of less than 1.0 would mean that when the team should have completed 6 months of work, they will have completed **less** than 6 months of work.

Now, let's turn our attention to cost efficiency.

Cost Performance Index (CPI)

As with schedule efficiency, because our simple use case involves clean, round numbers, we can also deduce the cost efficiency without using the EVM equation for CPI. For example, we know that by our status date, which is the end of the day on Tuesday, the contractor had used our entire $400 budget to complete 1 side of fencing. We also know that per our baseline agreement, the value of 1 side of fencing is only $100. Therefore, this contractor spent $400 to deliver $100 worth of value. This means their cost efficiency is 25%. As bad as this contractor's schedule efficiency was, their cost efficiency is much worse! In practical terms, when this contractor has spent $10K of our money, they will have only delivered $2,500 of real value. When they've spent $100K of our money, they will only have delivered $25K in value. When they've spent $1M, they will only have delivered $250K of value. Therefore, when deciding whether to cut ties with a vendor and pay a contract cancellation fee, it would be a good idea to first calculate their CPI. In some cases, it may be more cost effective to pay the contract cancellation fee and use a vendor with a higher cost efficiency.

When you don't have clean, round numbers, you can calculate CPI using the appropriate EVM equation, which is: **CPI = EV/AC**. In our case, since EV is $100 and Actual Cost (AC) is $400, CPI calculates to **25%**.

Like SPI, the ideal CPI is 100%, or 1.0. This would mean that whenever the contractor or project team *should* have delivered $100K of value, they *will* have delivered $100K of value. And when they *should* have delivered $1M of value, they *will* have delivered $1M of value, and so on.

Like SPI, CPI of greater than 1.0 is even more favorable. This would mean that when the team should have delivered $1M of value, they will have delivered **more** than $1M of value. Conversely, a CPI of less than 1.0 would mean that when the team should have delivered $1M of value, they will have delivered **less** than $1M of value.

Schedule Variance (SV)

In addition to enabling forecasting capabilities, Earned Value Management assigns a monetary value to schedule delays. How can a schedule delay be monetized? By considering the value that should have been realized by the status date. In our simple use case, by the end of the day on Tuesday, we should have realized $200 in value. This is because two sides of our fence should have been constructed and each side is worth $100, per our baseline agreement. Therefore, our Planned Value was $200.

If we were to now compare this with the value we have earned, then we can monetize our schedule delay. Specifically, as of our status date, only one side has been completed. Although this is less than ideal, this one side does have value. We have already established that each side is worth $100 in value per our baseline agreement. Therefore, our Earned Value is $100. If we were to therefore subtract the $200 in Planned Value from the $100 in Earned Value, we could assign a monetary value of **-$100** to the schedule delay. The EVM equation for Schedule Variance is: **SV = EV – PV.**

Because the Planned Value is always subtracted from the Earned Value, a negative Schedule Variance represents a status of **behind schedule**. A Schedule Variance of zero represents a status of **on schedule**. Finally, a positive Schedule Variance represents a status of **ahead of schedule**.

Cost Variance (CV)

EVM calculates **Cost Variance (CV)** as you might expect it would. For example, Fenwick Fencing has spent $400 and delivered $100 in value. Are they on budget, over budget or under budget? They are clearly over budget. By how much are they over budget? They are clearly over budget by $300.

The EVM equation for Cost Variance (CV) follows the same logic. It subtracts the Actual Cost ($400) from the Earned Value ($100) and arrives at a Cost Variance of **- $300.**
The equation is: **CV = EV – AC.**

Because the Actual Cost is always subtracted from the Earned Value, a negative Cost Variance represents a status of **over budget**. A Cost Variance of zero represents a status of **on budget**. Finally, a positive Cost Variance represents a status of **under budget**.

Conclusion

As you can see, the project intelligence we can gather from EVM metrics is much more comprehensive than the insights we can glean from analyzing simple cost variance. EVM allows us to not only see project status and progress data, but also forecast what our project status will be at any point in the future. It accomplishes this by monetizing your schedule performance and measuring both your schedule and cost efficiency. Based on this performance efficiency, it can forecast your project performance at any point in the future.

Each of the desktop versions of Microsoft Project will automatically calculate the Earned Value Metrics for you in the background. Your only task will be to access the Earned Value table so you can view and report status. In the next section, we'll summarize each EVM term and review the steps for using the Earned Value table. We'll also review the settings you will need to adjust for your Earned Value metrics to calculate correctly.

Using the Earned Value Table

To view accurate Earned Value Metrics, you'll need to have baselined your Detailed schedule, added resource pay rates in the Resource Sheet view and entered progress data through your status date. If you need a refresher on these topics, reference the respective chapters. Any mistakes you make in any of these prerequisites will result in miscalculated EVM metrics.

Adjusting the EVM Settings

Next, you will need to adjust the way Project calculates Earned Value metrics. By default, Project calculates Earned Value Metrics based on **% Complete**. As we emphasized in Chapter 15, best practice is to track your schedule with more and not less precision. When you get progress data from your resources based on completion percentages, your schedule will become less precise because optimistic resources will provide overly optimistic completion percentages and cautious resources will provide overly cautious ones. Best practice is to secure precise estimates, such as the number of actual hours worked and the number of hours remaining until task completion. In keeping with this practice, you will need to change the default EVM calculation method from **% Complete** to **Physical % Complete**. This will allow you to enter a completion percentage that is reflective of your true project status.

To change the EVM calculation method to % Physical Complete:

- Select the **File** tab to go Backstage.
- Select **Options** from the options on the left, to option the *Project Options* dialogue box.
- Select **Advanced** from the options on the left.
- Scroll down to the **Earned Value options for this project:** section. Then, in the **Default task Earned Value method:** field, select **Physical % Complete** (*Figure 222* below).
- Select **OK**, to close the *Project Options* dialog box.

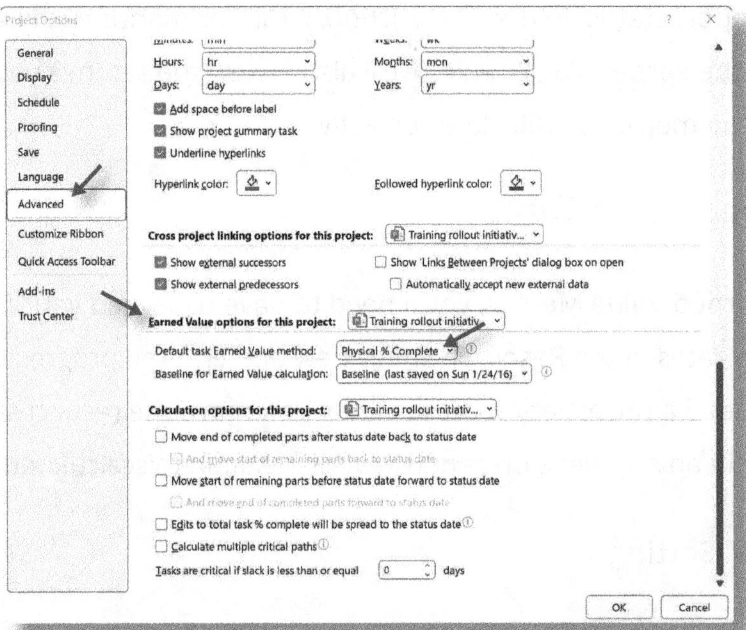

Figure 222 – Adjust the EVM Settings

After you adjust the EVM settings, use the **Add New Column** command to add the **Physical % Complete** column to the Entry table in the Gantt chart view *(Figure 223)*. Then, be sure to enter your project's completion percentages next to the appropriate tasks. For example, if we were to build our Fenwick Fencing schedule in Project, it would consist of four tasks. Each task would represent one side of the fence. After adding costs and baselining the schedule, we would then need to enter a Physical Completion percentage of 100% for task 1, *Build side 1*.

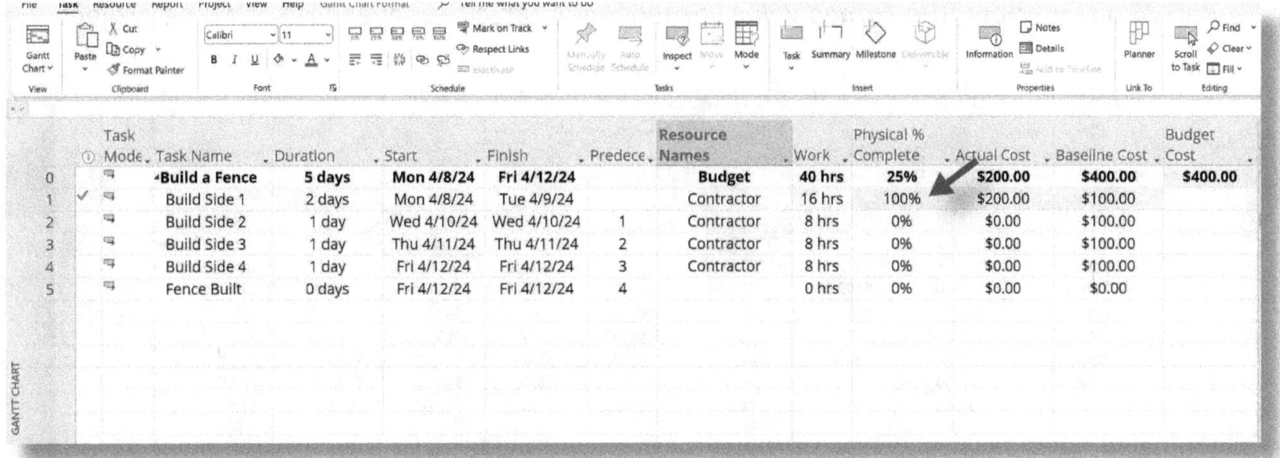

		Task Mode	Task Name	Duration	Start	Finish	Predecessors	Resource Names	Work	Physical % Complete	Actual Cost	Baseline Cost	Budget Cost
0			**Build a Fence**	**5 days**	**Mon 4/8/24**	**Fri 4/12/24**		**Budget**	**40 hrs**	**25%**	**$200.00**	**$400.00**	**$400.00**
1	✓		Build Side 1	2 days	Mon 4/8/24	Tue 4/9/24		Contractor	16 hrs	100%	$200.00	$100.00	
2			Build Side 2	1 day	Wed 4/10/24	Wed 4/10/24	1	Contractor	8 hrs	0%	$0.00	$100.00	
3			Build Side 3	1 day	Thu 4/11/24	Thu 4/11/24	2	Contractor	8 hrs	0%	$0.00	$100.00	
4			Build Side 4	1 day	Fri 4/12/24	Fri 4/12/24	3	Contractor	8 hrs	0%	$0.00	$100.00	
5			Fence Built	0 days	Fri 4/12/24	Fri 4/12/24	4		0 hrs	0%	$0.00	$0.00	

Figure 223 – Enter Physical % Complete

VIDEO: Want to see a demo of the Earned Value metrics being calculated in Microsoft Project for the Fenwick Fencing Fiasco?

Check out our YouTube page at https://youtu.be/pigrCPzKWsA

Using the Earned Value Tables

Finally, to view Earned Value metrics, you'll need to display an **Earned Value table**. Project includes three Earned Value tables – "Earned Value" (for tasks and resources), "Earned Value Cost Indicators" and "Earned Value Schedule Indicators".

To display an Earned Value table:

- Select the **View** tab.
- In the **Data** group, from the **Tables** command pick-list, select **More Tables** to open the *More Tables* dialogue box.
- Select the **Earned Value table** you want, then select **Apply**.

Figure 224 below shows the *Earned Value* Earned Value table displayed for the fence project.

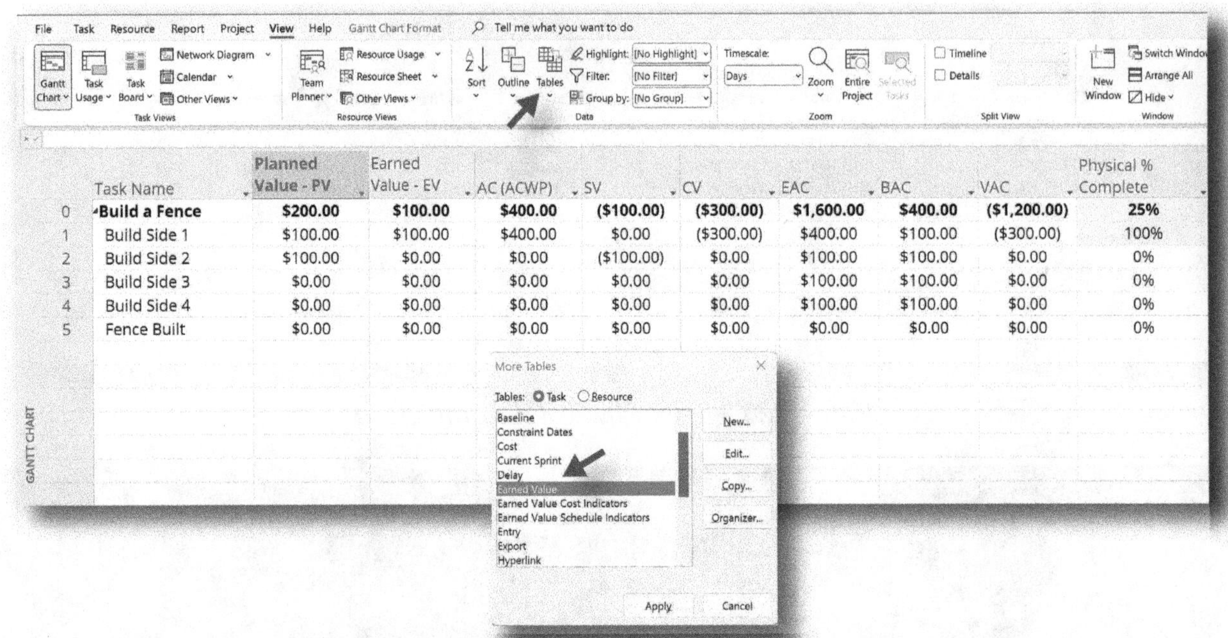

	Task Name	Planned Value - PV	Earned Value - EV	AC (ACWP)	SV	CV	EAC	BAC	VAC	Physical % Complete
0	**Build a Fence**	**$200.00**	**$100.00**	**$400.00**	**($100.00)**	**($300.00)**	**$1,600.00**	**$400.00**	**($1,200.00)**	**25%**
1	Build Side 1	$100.00	$100.00	$400.00	$0.00	($300.00)	$400.00	$100.00	($300.00)	100%
2	Build Side 2	$100.00	$0.00	$0.00	($100.00)	$0.00	$100.00	$100.00	$0.00	0%
3	Build Side 3	$0.00	$0.00	$0.00	$0.00	$0.00	$100.00	$100.00	$0.00	0%
4	Build Side 4	$0.00	$0.00	$0.00	$0.00	$0.00	$100.00	$100.00	$0.00	0%
5	Fence Built	$0.00	$0.00	$0.00	$0.00	$0.00	$0.00	$0.00	$0.00	0%

Figure 224 – Display the Earned Value Tables

Here is a summary of the Earned Value metrics available in Project:

- **EV or BCWP (Earned Value)** – the portion of the budgeted cost that should have been spent to complete each task's actual work, up to the status date
- **CPI (Cost Performance Index)** – the ratio of budgeted to actual cost, up to the status date (EV/AC)
- **SPI (Schedule Performance Index)** – the ratio of performed work to scheduled work, up to the status date (EV/PV)
- **PV or BCWS (Planned Value)** – the value of the work scheduled to be completed, as of the status date
- **AC (ACWP)** – the actual cost incurred to complete each task's actual work, up to the status date
- **SV (Schedule Variance)** – the difference between the budgeted cost of work performed and the budgeted cost of work scheduled, up to the status date (EV - PV)

- **CV (Cost Variance)** – the difference between the budgeted and actual cost of work performed, up to the status date (EV - AC)
- **EAC (Estimate At Completion)** – the expected total cost of a task based on performance, up to the status date (BAC/ CPI)
- **BAC (Budget At Completion)** – the total planned or baselined cost (this value equals the Cost field value when the baseline is saved)
- **VAC (Variance At Completion)** – the difference between the BAC (Budget At Completion) and the EAC (Estimate At Completion); (BAC - EAC)

Using Earned Value Reports

From the 2013 version of Project forward, the reporting features were greatly enhanced. The new reports are customizable and now include dynamic graphs, charts, and tables to view and share project data. There are several Cost and Dashboard reports that can be used to view and track project costs, including Earned Value metrics. You can access all the reports from the **Reports** tab.

To view Earned Value metrics using the Built-In Reports:

- Select the **Reports** tab.
- In the **View Reports** group, select the **Costs** reports command, then select the **Earned Value Report** from the pick-list. Project will display the Earned Value report for your project (Figure 225).

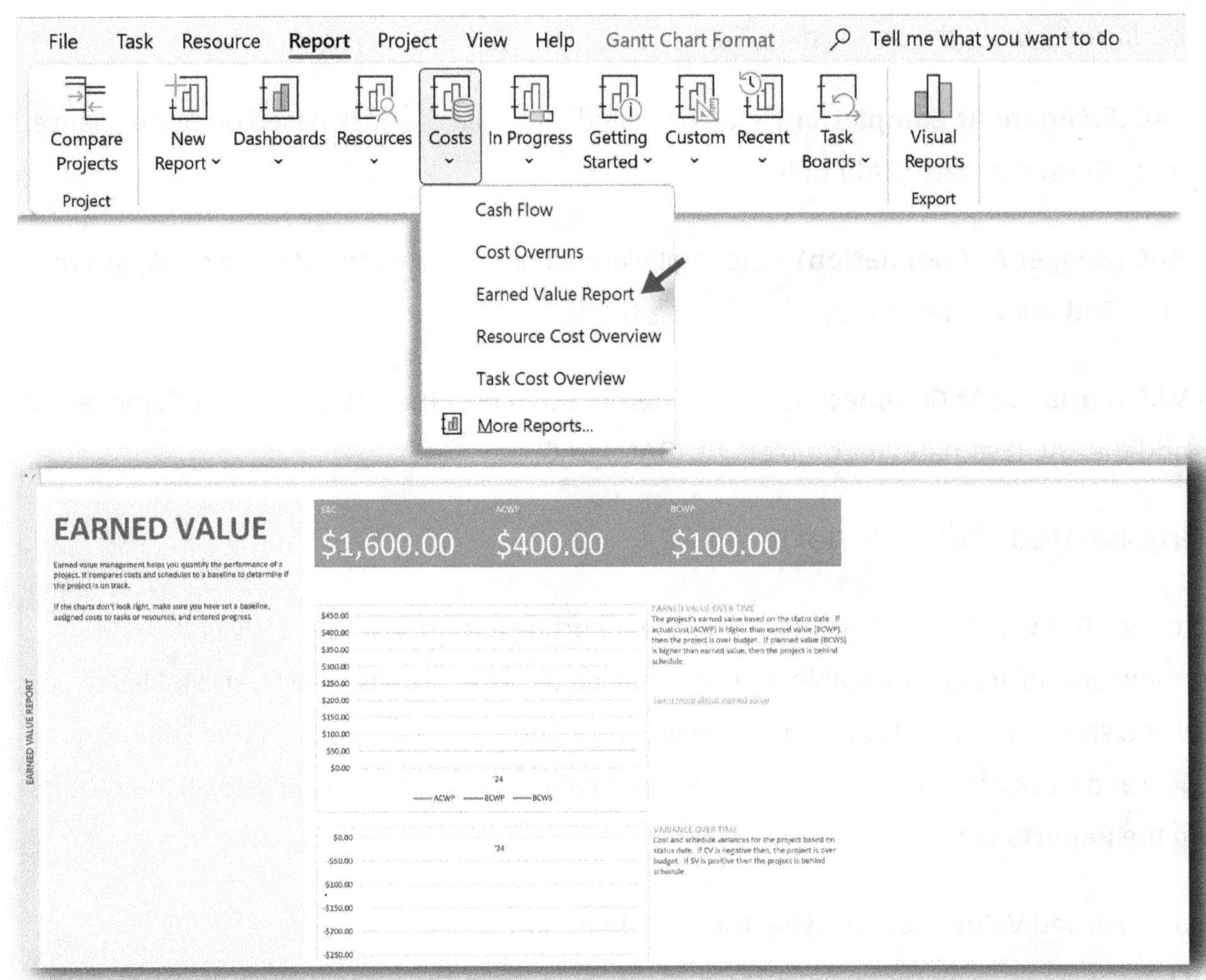

Figure 225 – The Earned Value Report

You've now learned to assign a project budget, explain cost variance, use the Cost table, explain Earned Value Management, use the Earned Value table, and use the Earned Value reports. In the next chapter, we'll learn to use all the dynamic status reports Project creates in the background as you build and execute your schedule.

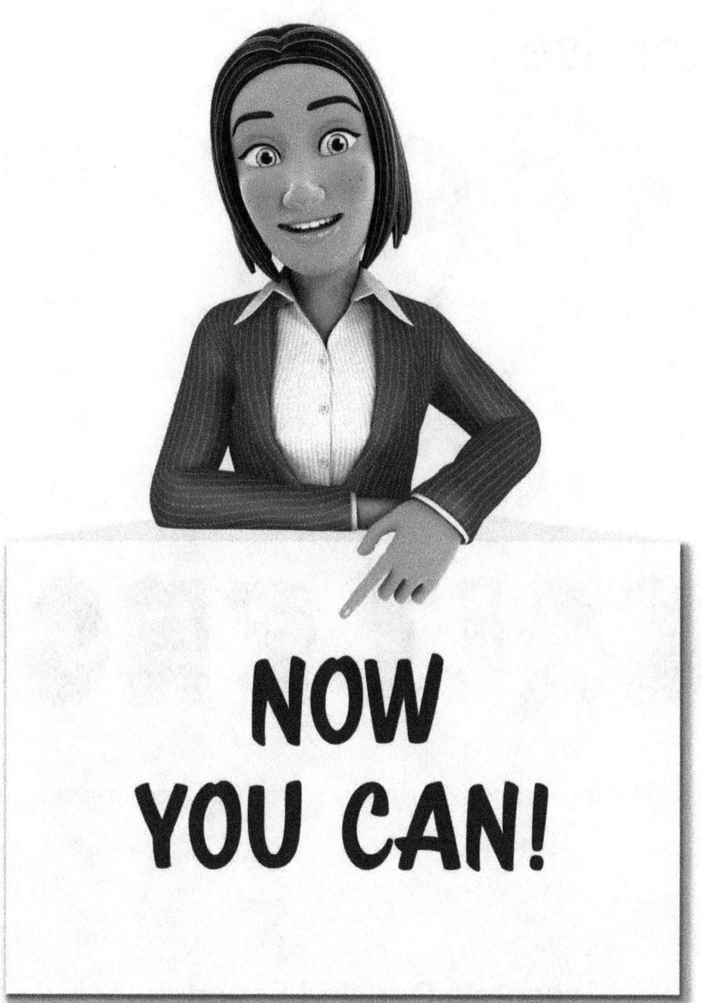

- ✓ Assign a Project Budget
- ✓ Explain Cost Variance
- ✓ Use the Cost Table
- ✓ Explain Earned Value
- ✓ Use the Earned Value Table
- ✓ Use the Earned Value Reports

Practice Exercise

Execute a Detailed Schedule

For this practice exercise, you'll complete the final step in the B.A.S.I.C.S. scheduling approach – **Start the Project**. You will execute the Detailed schedule you built in the Chapter 8 practice exercise.

Go to **mspbasics.com** for "Checkpoint" images to check your work as you go along.

Follow the steps below to complete this Practice exercise:

Open an Existing Project Plan

1. Open the Detailed "House Painting" project plan that you saved from the Chapter 8 practice exercise. **NOTE:** The file should contain all the completed steps from the exercise.

> **CHECKPOINT:** To confirm you're starting with the right file, go to **mspbasics.com**
>
> - Select the **CheckPoint Images** tab.
> - Select the version of the book you're using.
> - Select **Chapter 16**. Then, go to **Checkpoint Image #1**

Set a Deadline for the Project Finish Date

Set a deadline for the project finish date by applying a deadline to the task 16 milestone task, *House Painted*.

Set the Deadline as follows:

1. Double-click the task name of task 16, *House Painted* to open the *Task Information* dialogue box.
2. Select the **Advanced** tab.
3. In the **Deadline** field, enter **6/28/24.**
4. Select **OK** to close the *Task Information* dialogue box.

> **CHECKPOINT:** To check your results so far, go to **mspbasics.com**
>
> - Select the **CheckPoint Images** tab.
> - Select the version of the book you're using.
> - Select **Chapter 16**. Then, go to **Checkpoint Image #2**

Set the Current Date

Assume the current date is 6/3/24. Set this date as the "Current Date" in Project, as follows:

1. Select the **Project** tab.

2. In the **Properties** group, select the **Project Information** command to open the *Project Information* dialogue box.

3. In the **Current date** field, enter or select **6/3/24**.

4. Select **OK** to close the *Project Information* dialogue box.

NOTE: You should see a vertical green line in the Gantt chart indicating the current date (the indicator will correspond with 6/3/24 on the timescale). If you don't see the vertical green line, use the Zoom slider in the bottom right corner to zoom in on the timeline.

CHECKPOINT: To check your results so far, go to **mspbasics.com**

- Select the **CheckPoint Images** tab.
- Select the version of the book you're using.
- Select **Chapter 16**. Then, go to **Checkpoint Image #3**

Baseline the Schedule

Set a Baseline as follows:

1. On the **Project** tab, in the **Schedule** group, select the **Set Baseline** command. Then, select **Set Baseline** again to open the *Set Baseline* dialogue box.

2. Be sure that the **Set Baseline** option is selected. Since this is the initial baseline, *Baseline* should already be selected in the baseline field.

3. Select **OK** to close the *Set Baseline* dialogue box.

Confirm the baseline was set as follows:

1. In the **Schedule** group, select the **Set Baseline** command. Then, select **Set Baseline** again to re-open the *Set Baseline* dialogue box.

2. The baseline field should now display *Baseline (last saved on... the current date).*

3. Select **Cancel** to close the *Set Baseline* dialogue box.

CHECKPOINT: To check your results so far, go to **mspbasics.com**

- Select the **CheckPoint Images** tab.
- Select the version of the book you're using.
- Select **Chapter 16**. Then, go to **Checkpoint Image #4**

UPDATE 1

Update the Current Date and Set the Status Date

Assume that 1 week has passed and the current date is now Monday, 6/10/24. You met with your team last Friday, 6/7/24 to collect progress data.

Set **6/10/24** as the new **Current date** and **6/7/24** as the **Status date** as follows:

1. On the **Project** tab, in the **Properties** group, select the **Project Information** command to open the *Project Information* dialogue box.

2. In the **Current date** field, enter or select **6/10/24**.

3. In the **Status date** field, enter or select **6/7/24**.

4. Select **OK** to close the *Project Information* dialogue box. The 6/7/24 Status date should now be displayed on the ribbon, in the **Status** group.

CHECKPOINT: To check your results so far, go to **mspbasics.com**

- Select the **CheckPoint Images** tab.
- Select the version of the book you're using.
- Select **Chapter 16**. Then, go to **Checkpoint Image #5**

Apply the Late Tasks Filter

You're ready to enter the actuals you received from your team on 6/7/24. To make this task easier, you'll apply the **Late Tasks filter** to see which tasks should have work done as of the current date, 6/10/24.

Apply the Late Tasks filter as follows:

1. In the **Task Name** field of the Entry table, select the **Auto-filter** arrow.
2. Select **Filters** from the pick-list, then select **Late Tasks**.

When the Late Tasks filter is applied, tasks 1 through 6 should be displayed. These are the tasks that should have had work done as of 6/7/24.

CHECKPOINT: To check your results so far, go to **mspbasics.com**

- Select the **CheckPoint Images** tab.
- Select the version of the book you're using.
- Select **Chapter 16**. Then, go to **Checkpoint Image #6**

Add the Tracking Fields to the View

Next, you'll add the tracking fields for a Detailed schedule to the Entry table. Use the **Add New Column** field to add the **Actual Start**, **Actual Work** and **Remaining Work** fields to the view. If you don't see the Add New Column field, slide the right half of the screen to the right, until you can see it.

To add each Tracking Field:

1. Select the header of the **Add New Column** field to display the pick-list of columns you can add to the table.

2. Type **Actual Start**. When it appears, select it.

3. Repeat these steps to add the **Actual Work** and **Remaining Work** fields to the table.

Enter the Progress Data (Update 1)

The progress data (actuals) that the project team gave you are listed in the table below.

1. Enter the **Actual Start**, **Actual Work** and **Remaining Work** values into the respective tracking fields for the listed tasks.

RESOURCE NAME	TASK ID	TASK NAME	ACTUAL START	ACTUAL WORK	REMAINING WORK
Jill	2	List Supplies	06/03/24	4 hours (4h)	0
Jack	3	Buy Supplies	06/04/24	4 hours (4h)	0
Jack	6	Sand House	06/05/24	8 hours (8h)	8 hours (8h)

After the progress data is entered, Project will add check-marks in the **Indicators** field of tasks 2 and 3, to indicate that these tasks are 100% complete. They have a Remaining Work value of zero. In the Gantt chart, the task bars for tasks 2, 3 & 6 should now have a progress bar inside their task bars, indicating their completion progress. Since tasks 2 and 3 are now complete, Phase 1 of the project, *Get Supplies* is complete. Also, since its predecessors are complete, the task 4 milestone, *Supplies Gotten* can be updated as 100% complete.

Mark the *Supplies Gotten* milestone task 100% complete as follows:

1. Select the **Task** tab.

2. Select task 4 *Supplies Gotten*.

3. In the **Schedule** group, select the **100% Complete** command. Project will place a check mark next to this task and add its progress bar to the Gantt chart.

CHECKPOINT: To check your results so far, go to **mspbasics.com**

- Select the **CheckPoint Images** tab.
- Select the version of the book you're using.
- Select **Chapter 16**. Then, go to **Checkpoint Image #7**

Clear the Late Tasks Filter

Clear the Late Tasks filter to display the entire project outline as follows:

1. Select the **View** tab.
2. In the **Data** group, select **Clear Filter** from the **Filter** pick-list.

Notice that after the actuals were entered, the project finish date was updated to 7/1/24. Because this is after the 6/28/24 project deadline applied to the *House Painted* milestone, Project has added a "deadline exceeded" alert icon in the Indicators field of task 16.

Display the Cost Table

Next, you'll change the table to the **Cost Table**. This view will allow you to compare the baselined costs to the current costs.

To display the Cost table:

1. Select the **View** tab.
2. In the **Data** group, select **Cost** from the **Tables** command pick-list.

CHECKPOINT: To check your results so far, go to **mspbasics.com**

- Select the **CheckPoint Images** tab.
- Select the version of the book you're using.
- Select **Chapter 16**. Then, go to **Checkpoint Image #8**

Cost Tracking Questions:

1. Is the project over or under the Baseline cost?
2. By what amount is it over or under the Baseline cost?
3. Which task(s) is over or under the Baseline cost?

CHECKPOINT: To check your answers, go to **mspbasics.com**

- Select the **CheckPoint Images** tab.
- Select the version of the book you're using.
- Select **Chapter 16**. Then, go to **Checkpoint Image #9**

Switch Back to the Entry Table

1. On the **View** tab, in the **Data** group, select **Entry** from the **Tables** command pick-list.

UPDATE 2

Update the Current Date and Set the Status Date

Assume another week has passed and the current date is Monday, 6/17/24. You will meet with your team today to collect progress data.

Set **6/17/24** as the new **Current date** and **6/17/24** as the **Status date** as follows:

1. On the **Project** tab, in the **Properties** group, select the **Project Information** command to open the *Project Information* dialogue box.
2. In the **Current date** field, enter or select **6/17/24**.
3. In the **Status date** field, enter or select **6/17/24**.
4. Select **OK** to close the *Project Information* dialogue box. The new Status date of 6/17/24 should now be displayed on the ribbon, in the **Status** group.

CHECKPOINT: To check your results so far, go to **mspbasics.com**

- Select the **CheckPoint Images** tab.
- Select the version of the book you're using.
- Select **Chapter 16**. Then, go to **Checkpoint Image #10**

Apply the Late Tasks Filter

You're ready to check with the project team to get another status on the current work. Before you meet, you'll apply the **Late Tasks filter** to see which tasks should have work done as of the current date (6/17/24).

Apply the Late Tasks filter, as follows:

1. In the **Task Name** field of the Entry table, select the **Auto-filter** arrow.
2. Select **Filters** from the pick-list, then select **Late Tasks.**

When the Late Tasks filter is applied, tasks 5 through 11 should be displayed. These are the tasks that should have had work done as of 6/17/24.

CHECKPOINT: To check your results so far, go to **mspbasics.com**

- Select the **CheckPoint Images** tab.
- Select the version of the book you're using.
- Select **Chapter 16.** Then, go to **Checkpoint Image #11**

Enter the Progress Data (Update 2)

The project team has given you the progress data (actuals) listed in the following table.

1. Enter the **Actual Start**, **Actual Work** and **Remaining Work** values into the respective tracking fields for the listed tasks.

RESOURCE NAME	TASK ID	TASK NAME	ACTUAL START	ACTUAL WORK	REMAINING WORK
Jack	6	Sand House	06/05/24	16 hours (16h)	0
Jill	7	Tape Windows	06/11/24	2 hours (2h)	0
Jack	8	Lay Drop Cloth	06/12/24	4 hours (4h)	0

After the progress data is entered, Project will add check-marks in the Indicators field of tasks 6, 7 and 8, to indicate that these tasks are 100% complete. They have a Remaining Work value of zero. In the Gantt chart, the task bars for tasks 6, 7 & 8 should now have a progress bar inside their task bars, indicating their completion progress. Since tasks 6, 7 and 8 are now complete, Phase 2 of the project, *Prep House* is complete. Also, since its predecessors are complete, the task 9 milestone, *House Prepped* can be updated as 100% complete.

Mark the House Prepped milestone task 100% complete as follows:

1. Select the **Task** tab.
2. Select task 9 *House Prepped*.
3. In the **Schedule** group, select the **100% Complete** command. Project will place a check mark next to this task and add its progress bar to the Gantt chart.

Clear the Late Tasks Filter

Clear the Late Tasks filter to display the entire schedule, as follows:

1. Select the **View** tab.
2. In the **Data** group, select **Clear Filter** from the **Filter** pick-list.

CHECKPOINT: To check your results so far, go to **mspbasics.com**

- Select the **CheckPoint Images** tab.
- Select the version of the book you're using.
- Select **Chapter 16.** Then, go to **Checkpoint Image #12**

Switch back to the Cost table:

1. Select the **View** tab.
2. In the **Data** group, select **Cost** from the **Tables** command pick-list.

Cost Tracking Questions:

CHECKPOINT: To check your results so far, go to **mspbasics.com**

- Select the **CheckPoint Images** tab.
- Select the version of the book you're using.
- Select **Chapter 16.** Then, go to **Checkpoint Image #13**

1. Is the project over or under the Baseline cost?
2. By what amount is it over or under the Baseline cost?
3. Which task(s) is over or under Baseline cost?

Congratulations! You've now performed the last step in the B.A.S.I.C.S. scheduling approach – **Start the Project**, and executed a Detailed schedule!

CHECKPOINT: To check your answers, go to **mspbasics.com**

- Select the **CheckPoint Images** tab.
- Select the version of the book you're using.
- Select **Chapter 16**. Then, go to **Checkpoint Image #14**

SAVE THIS FILE. You will use it in the Chapter 17 Practice Exercise.

Chapter 17 Creating Status Reports

In the last chapter, you learned to track project costs. You learned to assign a project budget, compare budgeted cost to actual cost, and review Cost Variance and Earned Value metrics.

In this chapter, you'll learn to **create status reports**. When you're done, you'll be able to share Gantt chart reports, customize and share Timeline reports, use the dynamic built-in reports to share project information and use the Copy Picture feature to capture project data and export it to other applications like PowerPoint.

You'll Learn To:

- Share Gantt Chart Reports
- Use the Copy Picture Feature
- Use the Timeline View
- Use the Built-In Reports

A key function of the project manager's role is to effectively communicate project status. Microsoft Project contains many features to help you create accurate, professional status reports.

Sharing Gantt Chart Reports

The **Gantt Chart view** is the most commonly used view in Microsoft Project. It contains an at-a-glance view of your project schedule, including tasks, resources, costs, and a graphical depiction of the timeline. Because of the useful information contained in this view, many users provide status updates by simply forwarding a copy of their Microsoft Project plan. This is not always the best approach because some stakeholders may not have access to Microsoft Project, which is required to open and view the project plan. Even if the recipient has a Microsoft Project license, the level of detail included in the entire project file can be overwhelming. Moreover, if you send stakeholders your source file, you are no longer the sole owner of it. Others could update the file inadvertently (or not so inadvertently) and this could lead to mismanaged expectations. For these reasons, if you do decide to share your project file, consider storing it on a file sharing platform like SharePoint. This would allow you to send a link to the source file and create read-only access where appropriate. If you're wary of sharing your source file, Project offers many alternatives for sharing project information. We'll start with the Copy Picture feature.

Using the Copy Picture Feature

The **Copy Picture** feature is a handy way to share a snapshot of your project details. It captures an image of the current view or selected content and copies it to the clipboard. You can then render the image for screen (suitable for use in applications like PowerPoint, Word, or Outlook), for printing, or you can save the image as a GIF file.

To use the Copy Picture feature:

- Select the **Task** tab.

- In the **Clipboard** group, select **Copy Picture** from the **Copy** command pick-list to open the *Copy Picture* dialogue box (*Figure 226*).

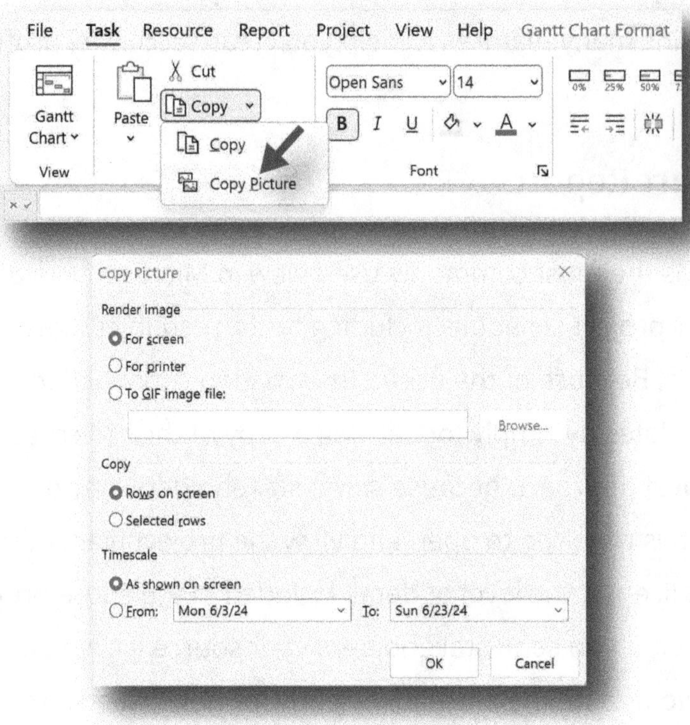

Figure 226 – Using the Copy Picture Feature

- In the **Render image** section, the **For screen** option captures an image with a resolution that's suited for viewing on a monitor. The **For printer** option captures an image that is suited for printing. The **To GIF image file** option saves the image as a GIF file. Use the **Browse** command to select a location to save the file.

- In the **Copy** section, select the **Rows on screen** option to copy the current view. Select the **Selected rows** option to copy specific rows you've selected.

- In the **Timescale** section, select the **As shown on screen** option to copy the timeline from the current view, or choose specific dates using the **From** option.

- Select **OK** to copy the image to the clipboard and close the *Copy Picture* dialogue box.

After the image is copied to the clipboard, you can share the content by printing, pasting, or exporting the image to other applications, like PowerPoint or Word.

Using the Timeline View to Share Project Information

Another way to communicate project status is to share an image of the **Timeline View**. The Timeline view is a customizable summary of the project timeline. It includes only the tasks and milestones you choose to display. Depending on how you've configured Project, when you open a new project or a project template, the Timeline view panel will be displayed beneath the ribbon (*Figure 227* below). For new projects, the Timeline view will be empty.

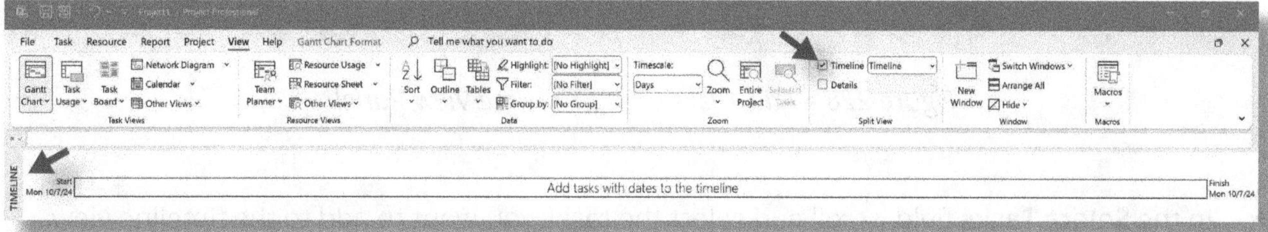

Figure 227 – The Timeline View Panel

If the Timeline view panel is not displayed, display it as follows:

- Select the **View** tab.
- In the **Split View** group, select the **Timeline** checkbox.

Before you capture an image of the Timeline view, you'll need to add the tasks you want to share.

To add tasks to the Timeline View:

- Click anywhere in the Timeline panel to select it. When the Timeline panel is selected, the contextual Format tab will be labeled **Timeline Format**, and the Timeline Tools will be displayed on the ribbon. These are the commands you will use to customize the Timeline view panel.
- In the **Insert** group, select the **Existing Tasks** command to open the *Add Tasks to Timeline* dialogue box (*Figure 228*).

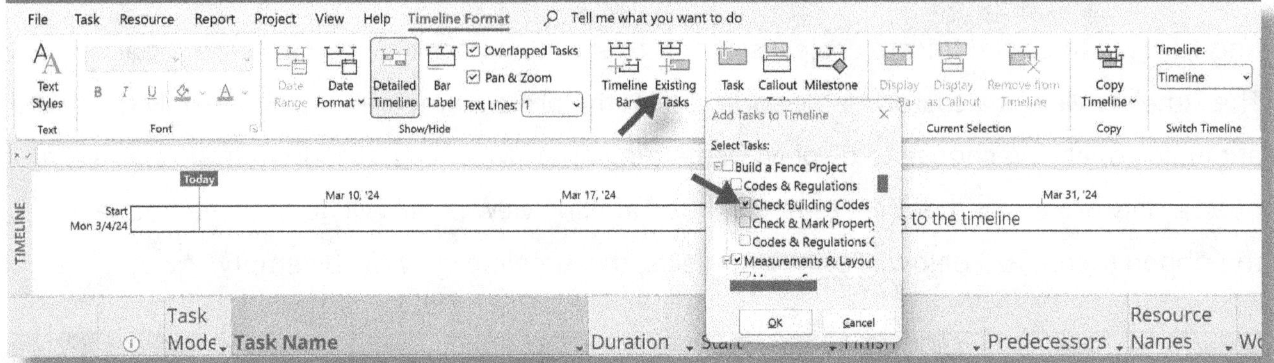

Figure 228 – Add Tasks to the Timeline View Panel

- In the **Select Tasks** field, scroll and select the tasks you want to add to the timeline view. For example, for a high-level status report, you might want to select only the summary tasks representing the major phases of the project.

- Once you've selected the tasks, select **OK** to close the *Add Tasks to Timeline* dialogue box. The selected tasks will appear as timeline bars in the Timeline view panel.

Customize the Timeline View Panel:

After you add tasks to the timeline panel, you can customize the view to create a more dynamic status report. You can use the **Timeline Tools** on the ribbon to change the font or the color of the timeline bars, you can display call-out tasks and make other customizations. Using *Figure 229* below, we'll review the formatting commands available in the Timeline Tools.

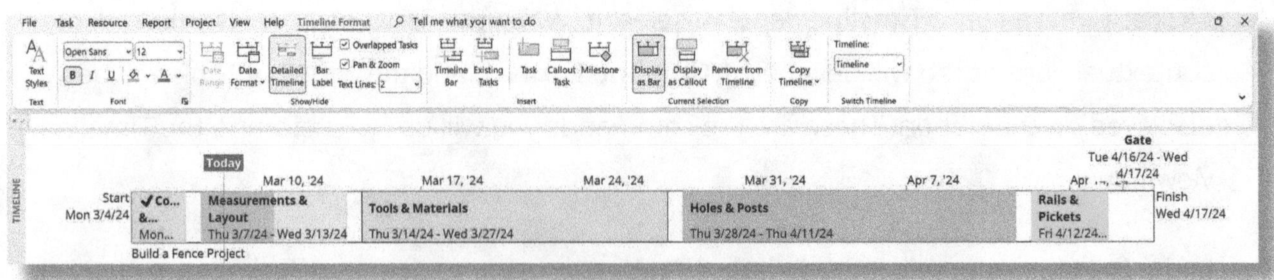

Figure 229 – Customize the Timeline View Panel

- In the **Text** group, use the **Text Styles** command to change the way that text appears on certain items in the view.
- Use the commands in the **Font** group to color the timeline bars or change the styling of the font.
- In the **Show/Hide** group, the **Date Range** command let you customize a selected timeline bar to show a specific date range.
- The **Date Format** command lets you format how the dates appear in the view. You can also use this command to show or hide dates.
- The **Detailed Timeline** command lets you determine how much detail you'd like to display, such as task names and dates.
- The **Bar Label** command lets you specify names for the timeline.
- The **Overlapped Tasks** command lets you display overlapping tasks on multiple rows to improve the readability of task names.
- The **Pan and Zoom** command displays the pan and zoom control, which allows you to use the Timeline view to navigate the main view.
- The **Text Lines** command lets you specify how many lines are used to display the task name. This also improves readability.
- In the **Insert** group, the **Timeline Bar** command lets you add additional timelines to the view. This is a newer feature added to Project. It also allows you to group similar tasks.
- Use the **Existing Task** command to add tasks that are currently in the project to the timeline view.
- The **Task** command lets you add a new task to the project plan. The new task will be added to the Timeline view and the project plan.
- The **Callout Task** command lets you add a new task to project plan. The new task will be added to the Timeline view as a *Callout* task and to the project plan.

- The **Milestone** command lets you add a new milestone to the project plan. The new milestone will be added to the Timeline view and to the project plan.

- In the **Current Selection** group, the **Display as Bar** and **Display as Callout** commands let you display a selected task as a Timeline Bar or as a Callout Task. For example, in *Figure 229*, the *Gate* task has been added to the timeline as a Callout task.

- Use the **Remove from Timeline** command to remove tasks from the Timeline view. This command will not remove the task from the project plan, only the timeline panel.

- In the **Switch Timeline** group, if you've added multiple timelines to the view, you can use the **Timeline** command to toggle between them.

After you customize the Timeline view, like the Copy Picture feature, you can copy it to the clipboard to paste it as a report into other applications. Once you save your project file, the tasks and customizations you add to the timeline view panel will be saved. You can toggle the timeline panel on or off and your customizations will remain in the panel.

To Copy the Timeline View:

- Click anywhere in the timeline panel to select it and access the Timeline Tools.

- In the **Copy** group, select the **Copy Timeline** command.

- From the **Copy Timeline** command pick list, select the option you want. You can copy the image for email, presentation, or full size. When you select an option, an image of the Timeline view will be copied to the Clipboard. You can then paste the image into an application, such as Outlook or PowerPoint.

To Export the Timeline view to a PDF or XPS file:

- Click the Timeline panel to select it.

- Select the **File** tab. Then, select **Export**.

- Select **Create PDF/XPS Document**. Then, select the **Create PDF/XPS** icon.

- In the **File name** field, choose the location where you'd like to save the file and name the file.

- In the **Save as type** field, select **PDF Files** or **XPS Files** from the pick-list.
- Select **OK** to open the *Document Export Options* dialogue box.
- In the **Publish range** section, select **All** to export all dates or select **From** to select a date range.
- In the **Include Non-Printing information** section, you can choose to add document properties and show markup.
- In the **PDF options** section, you can format the file to the PDA/A format. This format will prohibit features ill-suited for long-term archiving and encryption.
- Select **OK** to save the file and close the *Document Export Options* dialogue box.

Display the Timeline as a View

You can also display the timeline as its own view (instead of just a panel in the current view), as shown in *Figure 230 below*. This is a good option for sharing complex or multiple timelines.

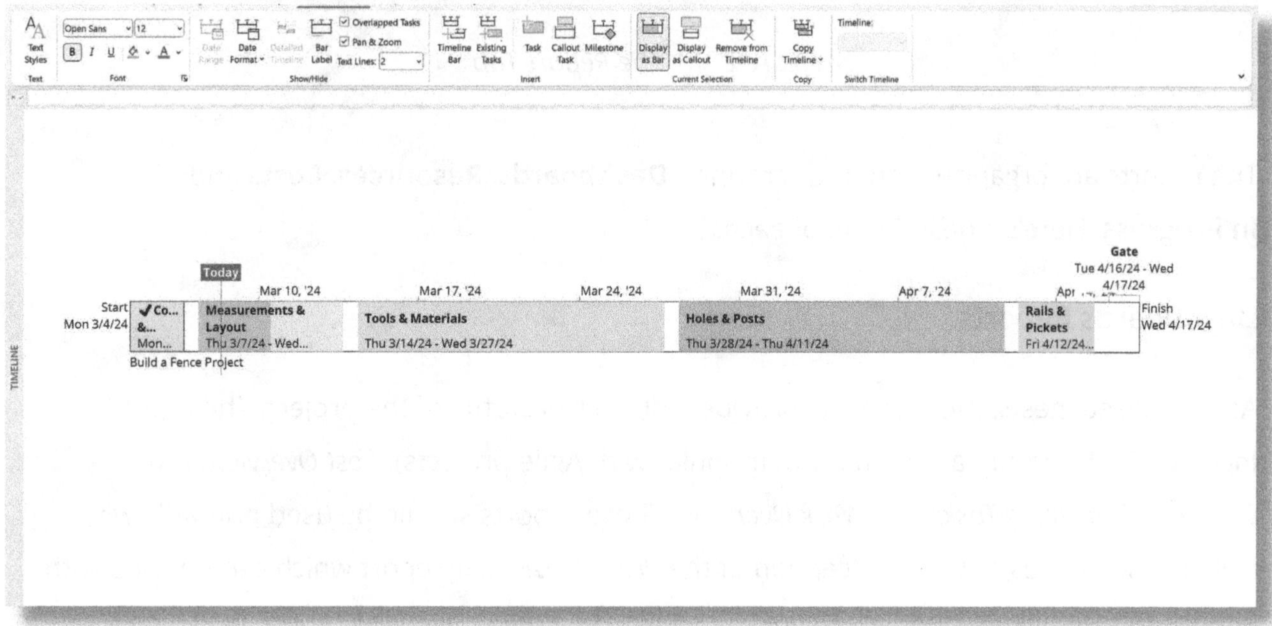

Figure 230 – Display the Timeline as a View

To display the Timeline as its own view:

- Select the **View** tab.
- In the **Resource Views** group, from the **Other Views** pick-list, select **More Views** to open the *More Views* dialogue box.
- Select **Timeline** from the list. Then, select **Apply**.

Using the Built-in Reports to Share Project Status

Microsoft Project includes several built-in Task, Resource and Cost reports. These reports are a dynamic and effective way to communicate project status. They are customizable and include charts, graphs and tables that can be used to share project data. All the reports can be accessed from the Report tab *(Figure 231* below).

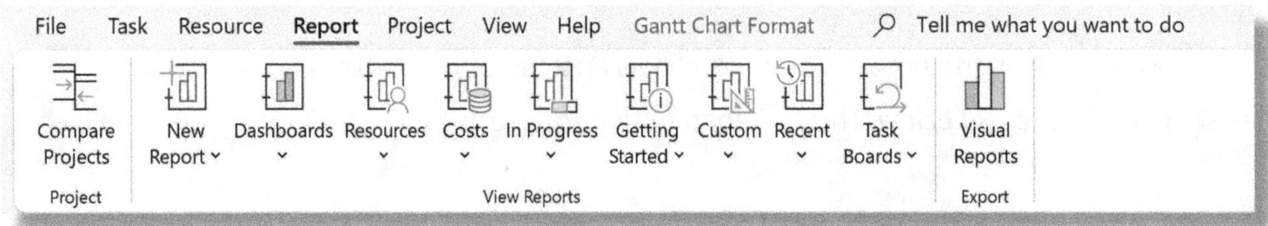

Figure 231 – The Report Tab

The reports are organized into four groups – **Dashboards**, **Resources**, **Costs** and **In Progress**. Here's a description of each.

Dashboards Reports

As the title suggests, these reports provide a high-level status of the project. The reports included in this group are *Burn-Down* (popular with Agile projects), *Cost Overview*, *Project Overview*, *Upcoming Tasks* and *Work Overview*. These reports should be used primarily with Detailed schedules, with the exception of the *Project Overview* report which can be used with Simple and Detailed schedules. *Figure 232* shows the *Project Overview* report, which provides a summary of the overall project status. This report combines graphs and tables to show status for each phase of the project.

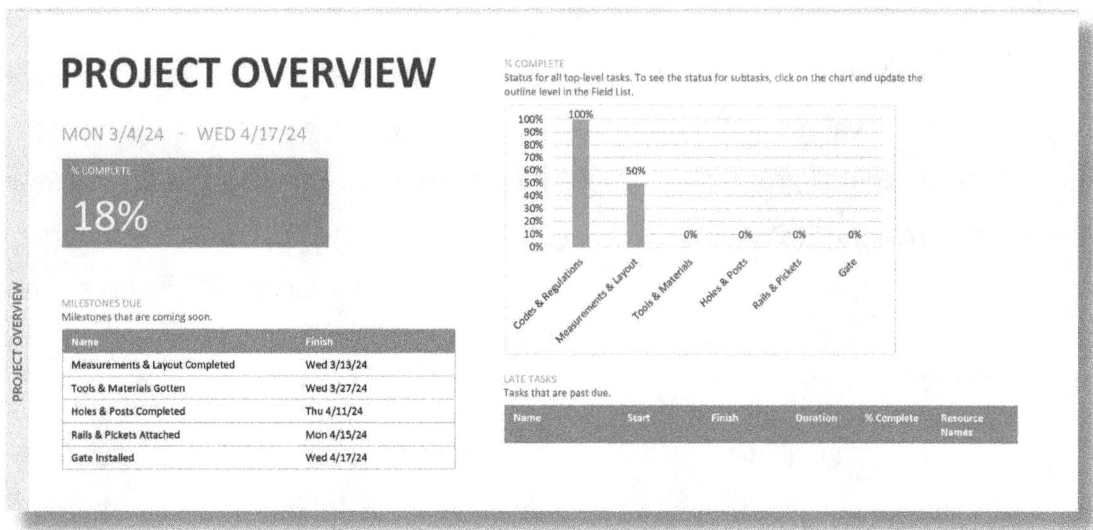

Figure 232 – The Project Overview Report

Resources Reports

These reports provide resource allocation metrics and should be used exclusively with Detailed schedules, where resources are assigned with specificity. The reports included in this group are *Over-allocated Resources* and *Resource Overview*. *Figure 233* shows the *Resource Overview* report. This report combines graphs and tables to show a status for each resource assigned to the project.

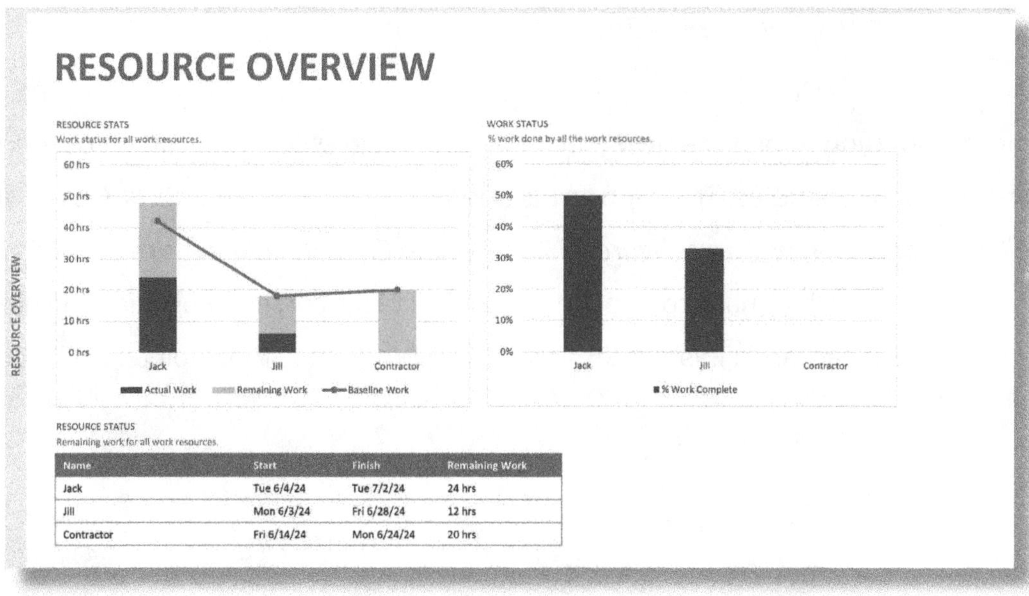

Figure 233 – The Resource Overview Report

Costs Reports

These reports provide insightful cost metrics and should be used exclusively with Detailed schedules, where work values and pay rates are included, which generate project cost. The reports included in this group are *Cash Flow, Cost Overruns, Earned Value Report, Resource Cost Overview* and *Task Cost Overview. Figure 234* below shows the *Cost Overruns* report. This report includes graphs, charts and tables that show cost variance for resources and tasks

In Progress Reports

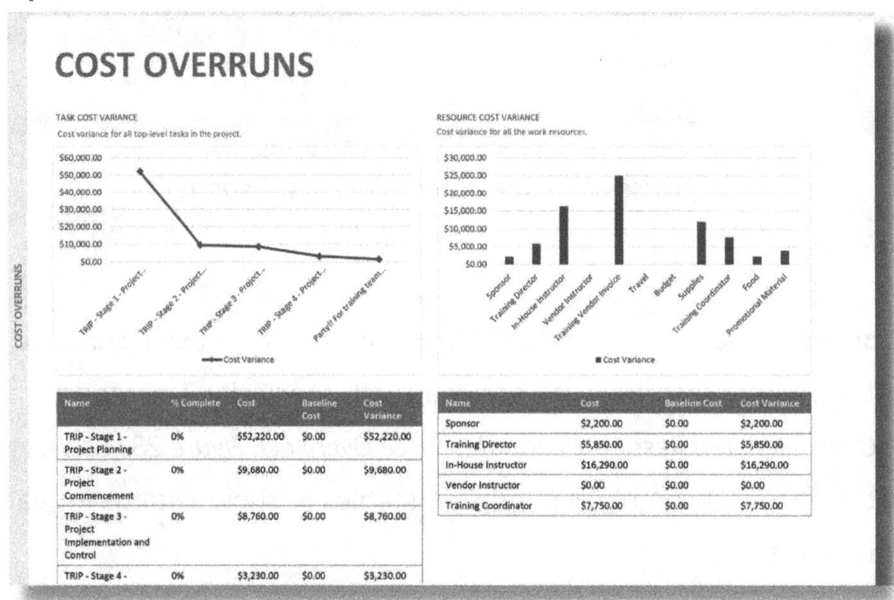

Name	% Complete	Cost	Baseline Cost	Cost Variance
TRIP - Stage 1 - Project Planning	0%	$52,220.00	$0.00	$52,220.00
TRIP - Stage 2 - Project Commencement	0%	$9,680.00	$0.00	$9,680.00
TRIP - Stage 3 - Project Implementation and Control	0%	$8,760.00	$0.00	$8,760.00
TRIP - Stage 4 -	0%	$3,230.00	$0.00	$3,230.00

Name	Cost	Baseline Cost	Cost Variance
Sponsor	$2,200.00	$0.00	$2,200.00
Training Director	$5,850.00	$0.00	$5,850.00
In-House Instructor	$16,290.00	$0.00	$16,290.00
Vendor Instructor	$0.00	$0.00	$0.00
Training Coordinator	$7,750.00	$0.00	$7,750.00

Figure 234 – The Cost Overruns Report

These reports allow you to analyze how your project is progressing and can be used for Simple and Detailed schedules. The reports included in this group are *Critical Tasks, Late Tasks, Milestone Report* and *Slipping Tasks. Figure 235* shows the *Critical Tasks* report. This report includes a chart and a table that provide a status of the tasks currently on the Critical Path. Assigned resources, Start and Finish dates, Remaining Work and % Complete are listed.

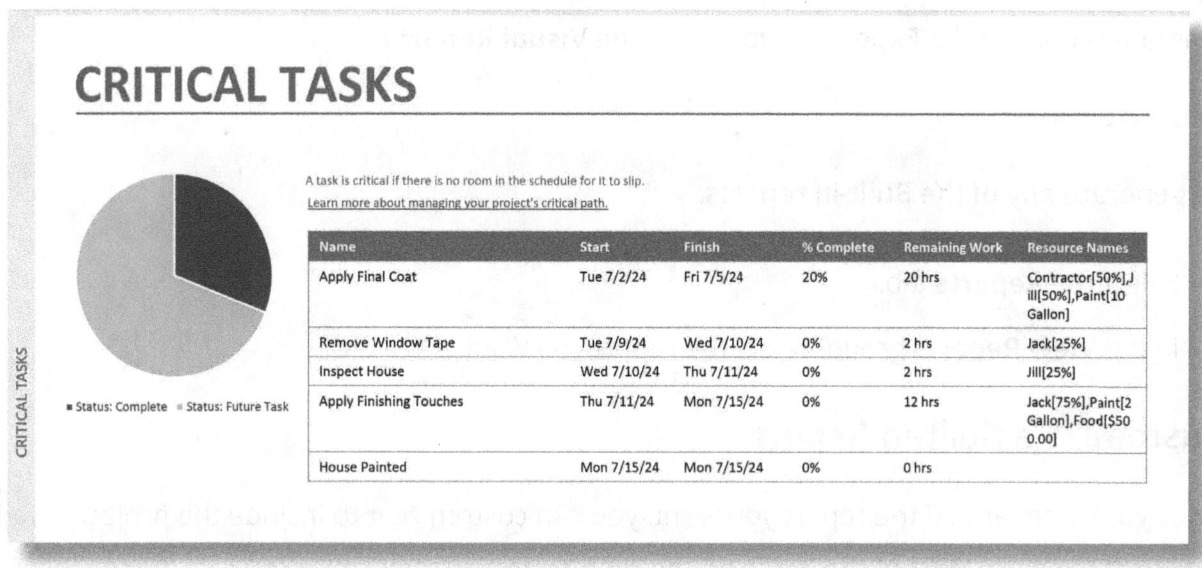

CRITICAL TASKS

A task is critical if there is no room in the schedule for it to slip.
Learn more about managing your project's critical path.

Name	Start	Finish	% Complete	Remaining Work	Resource Names
Apply Final Coat	Tue 7/2/24	Fri 7/5/24	20%	20 hrs	Contractor[50%],Jill[50%],Paint[10 Gallon]
Remove Window Tape	Tue 7/9/24	Wed 7/10/24	0%	2 hrs	Jack[25%]
Inspect House	Wed 7/10/24	Thu 7/11/24	0%	2 hrs	Jill[25%]
Apply Finishing Touches	Thu 7/11/24	Mon 7/15/24	0%	12 hrs	Jack[75%],Paint[2 Gallon],Food[$50 0.00]
House Painted	Mon 7/15/24	Mon 7/15/24	0%	0 hrs	

Figure 235 – The Critical Tasks Report

Task Boards Reports

If you're using the Online Desktop Client version of Project, you'll find the Task Boards reports. These reports allow you to view information from the Task Board views used for the Agile features, including current Sprint information. The reports included in this group are *Boards – Task Status*, *Boards – Work Status*, *Current Sprint – Task Status*, *Current Sprint – Work Status* and *Sprint Status*. *Figure 236* below shows the *Task Boards – Task Status* report. This report includes charts and tables that show the Task Board status of each task in various categories.

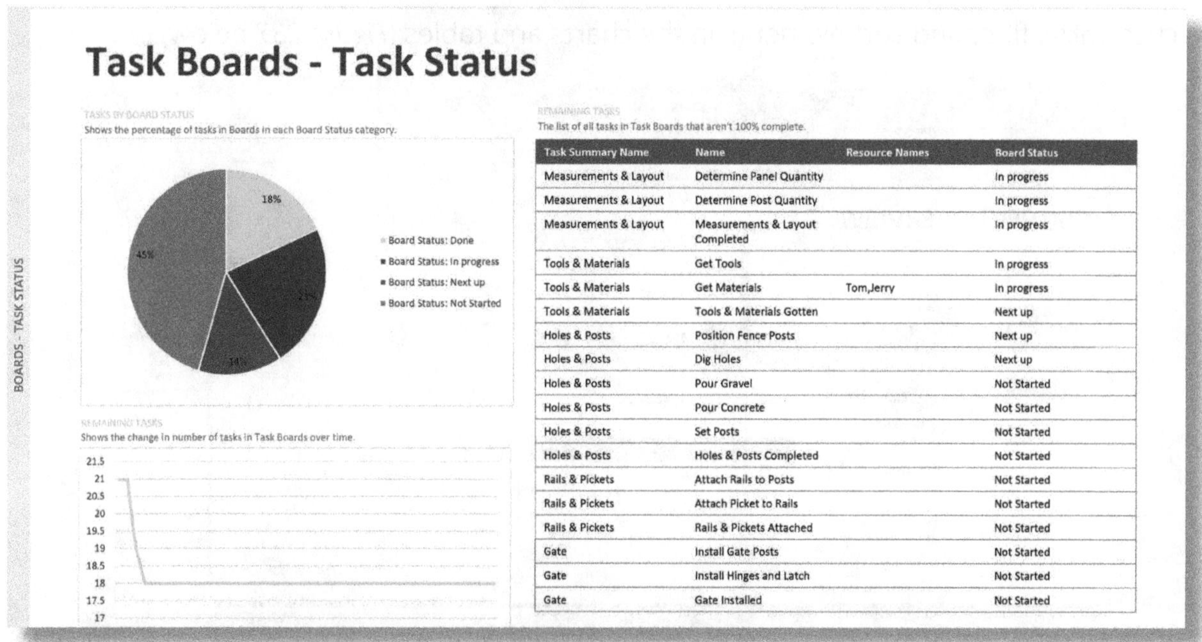

Task Boards - Task Status

The list of all tasks in Task Boards that aren't 100% complete.

Task Summary Name	Name	Resource Names	Board Status
Measurements & Layout	Determine Panel Quantity		In progress
Measurements & Layout	Determine Post Quantity		In progress
Measurements & Layout	Measurements & Layout Completed		In progress
Tools & Materials	Get Tools		In progress
Tools & Materials	Get Materials	Tom,Jerry	In progress
Tools & Materials	Tools & Materials Gotten		Next up
Holes & Posts	Position Fence Posts		Next up
Holes & Posts	Dig Holes		Next up
Holes & Posts	Pour Gravel		Not Started
Holes & Posts	Pour Concrete		Not Started
Holes & Posts	Set Posts		Not Started
Holes & Posts	Holes & Posts Completed		Not Started
Rails & Pickets	Attach Rails to Posts		Not Started
Rails & Pickets	Attach Picket to Rails		Not Started
Rails & Pickets	Rails & Pickets Attached		Not Started
Gate	Install Gate Posts		Not Started
Gate	Install Hinges and Latch		Not Started
Gate	Gate Installed		Not Started

Figure 236 – The Task Boards - Task Status Report

If you prefer Excel or Visio reports, you'll find ten pre-built, customizable PivotTable and Pivot Diagram reports in the **Export** group, under the **Visual Reports**.

Generate a Report

To generate any of the Built-in reports:

- Select the **Reports** tab.
- In the **View Reports** group, select the report you want.

Customize a Built-In Report

Once you've generated the report you want, you can customize it to include the project details you want to share. Most of the items on the reports are customizable. You can change the design, the theme and customize the elements in the report, such as the graphs, charts, and tables. There are many tools on the contextual *Report Design* Format tab that you can use to tailor a report.

To Customize a Report:

- Select an item in the report to display the contextual commands on the ribbon in the **Report Design**, **Label Design**, **Report Tools**, **Chart Tools**, and **Table Tools** options.
- Use the **Field List** panel on the right to change the data shown in a report and to customize, filter and sort elements in the charts and tables (*Figure 237* below).

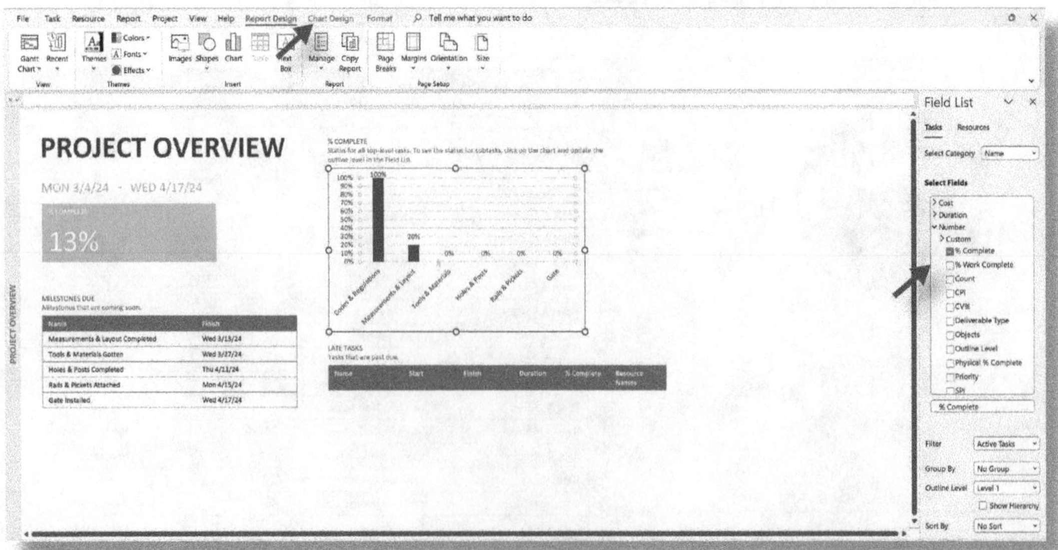

Figure 237 – Customize a Built-In Report

Create a Custom New Report

If you don't find a report you want in the Built-in reports, you can also create your own **custom new report**.

To create a custom new report:

- On the **Report** tab, in the **View Reports** group, select the **New Report** command *(Figure 238 below)*.

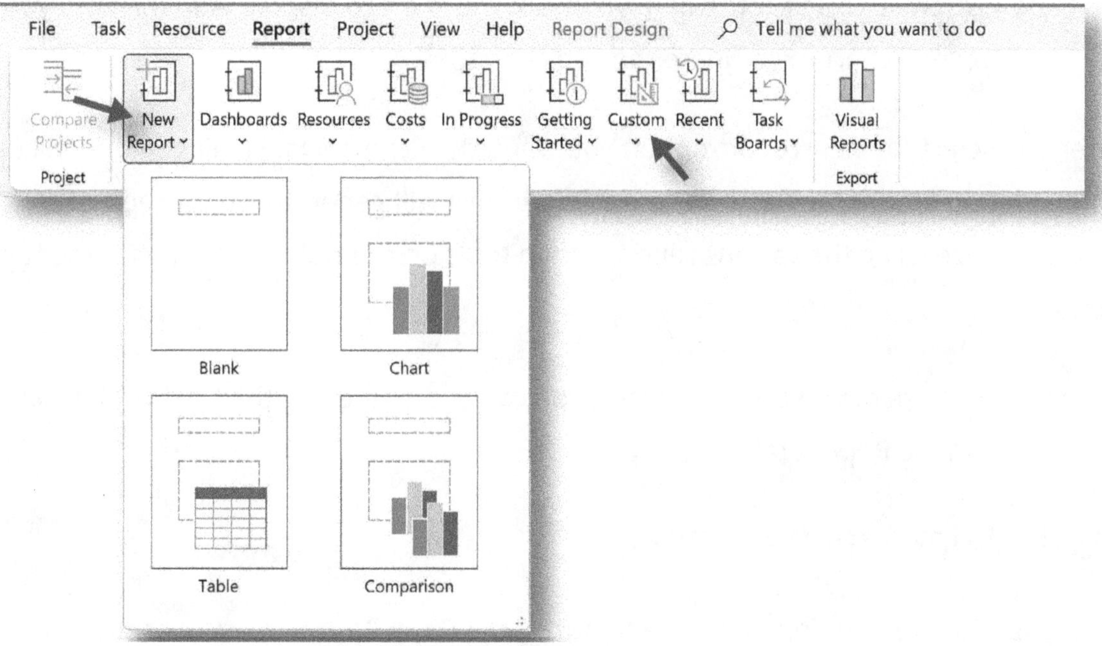

Figure 238 – Create a New Custom Report

- Select one of the four options for creating a new report:
  - Select **Blank** to create a new report completely from scratch. Use the tools on the *Report Tools Design* Format tab to add charts, tables, text, and images to the report.
  - Select **Chart** to add a chart comparing Actual Work, Remaining Work, and Work as a base for the new report. Use the **Field List** panel to add different fields and to format the chart elements.

- Select **Table** to add a table to the report as a base. Use the **Field List** panel to select the fields you want to display in the table. *Name*, *Start*, *Finish*, and *% Complete* are added by default. Use the **Outline level** box to select the number of levels in the project outline that you want the table to show. Use the *Table Tools* and *Table Tools Layout* tools to customize the look of the table.

- Select **Comparison** to place two charts side-by-side in the new report to compare their data. The charts will contain the same data at first. Select one of the charts and use the **Field List** panel to select the data you want the chart to display. Add the data you want to the second chart to compare the two charts.

- After you select the new report option you want, the *Report Name* dialogue box will open. Enter a name for the report, then select **OK**. Project will generate a base report that you can customize using the various report design tools on the ribbon and the Field List panel options.

- After your custom new report is created, you can access it using the **Custom Reports** command on the **Report** tab.

Using the Copy Report Feature

Like the Copy Picture and Copy Timeline features, the **Copy Report** feature captures an image of a report and saves it to the clipboard. You can paste the image into applications, such as Word or PowerPoint.

To Copy a Report:

- Click anywhere in the report to access the *Report Design* tools on the ribbon.

- Select the contextual **Report Design** tab on the ribbon.

- In the **Report** group, select the **Copy Report** command (*Figure 239*). Project will copy an image of the report to the clipboard.

- Paste the report to the application you want, such as PowerPoint or Word.

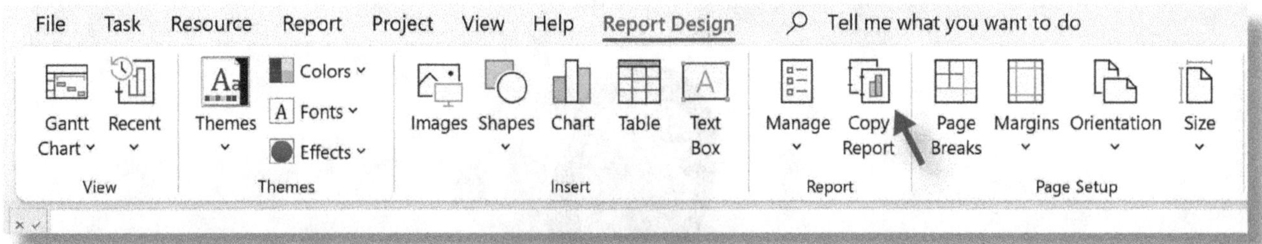

Figure 239 – Use the Copy Report Command

You can also export reports to a file, as follows:

- Select the **File** tab. Then, select **Export**.
- Select **Create PDF/XPS Document**. Then, select the **Create PDF/XPS** icon.
- In the **File name** field, choose the location where you'd like to save the file. Then, name the file.
- In the **Save as type** field, select **PDF Files** or **XPS Files** from the pick-list.
- Select **OK** to open the *Document Export Options* dialogue box.
- Select the options you want for the file (for a description of each, see the *To Export the Timeline View to a PDF or XPS File* previous section).
- Select **OK** to save the file and close the *Document Export Options* dialogue box.

You've now learned to create status reports. You've learned to create Gantt chart reports, customize the Timeline view panel, use and customize the built-in reports, create a custom report and use the Copy features to copy and export project information into other apps.

Want to watch a demonstration of these features and other customizations? Check out the Chapter 20 video in the **Microsoft Project B.A.S.I.C.S.** companion video course.

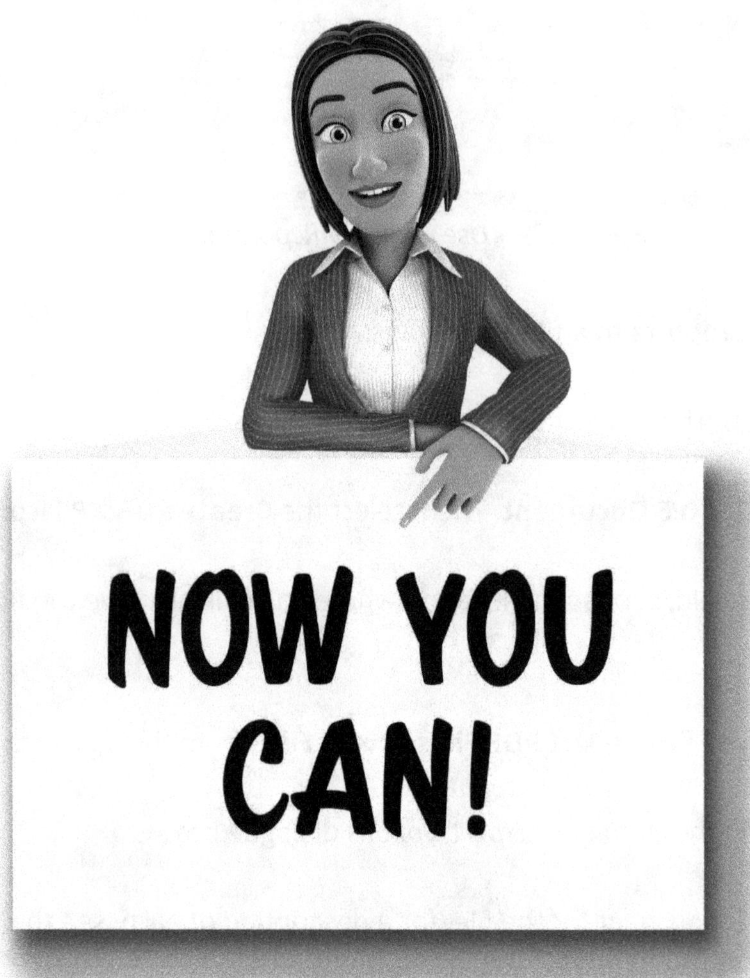

- ✓ Share Gantt Chart Reports
- ✓ Use the Copy Picture Feature
- ✓ Use the Timeline View
- ✓ Use and Customize the Built-In Reports
- ✓ Create a New Custom Report
- ✓ Use the Copy Report Feature

Practice Exercise

Create Status Reports

For this practice exercise, you'll create status reports. You'll use the Copy features and the Built-in reports to share project information.

NOTE: You'll also use Microsoft PowerPoint for this exercise.

Go to **mspbasics.com** for "Checkpoint" images to check your work as you go along.

Follow the steps below to complete this practice exercise:

Open an Existing Project Plan

1. Open the Detailed "House Painting" project plan that you saved from the Chapter 16 practice exercise. **NOTE:** The file should contain all the completed steps from the exercise.

CHECKPOINT: To confirm you're starting with the right file, go to **mspbasics.com**

- Select the **CheckPoint Images** tab.
- Select the version of the book you're using.
- Select **Chapter 17**. Then, go to **Checkpoint Image #1**

Adjust the view

You'll start by adjusting the **Gantt Chart view** for a cleaner presentation of the status report.

Switch to the **Entry** table in the Gantt Chart view:

1. Select the **View** tab.
2. In the **Data** group, select **Entry** from the **Tables** command pick-list.

Next, you'll hide the columns in the Entry table that you don't want included in your status report. Hide the **Resource Names** and **Work** columns, as follows:

1. Right-click the **Resource Names** column header.
2. Select **Hide Column** from the pick-list.
3. Repeat these steps to hide the **Work** column.

To further adjust the view, slide the screen to the left until it aligns with the right edge of the **"Cost"** column.

Next, use the **Entire Project** command to zoom in to see the entire Gantt chart:

1. Select the **View** tab.

2. In the **Zoom** group, select the **Entire Project** command.

CHECKPOINT: To check your results so far, go to **mspbasics.com**

- Select the **CheckPoint Images** tab.
- Select the version of the book you're using.
- Select **Chapter 17.** Then, go to **Checkpoint Image #2**

Use the Copy Picture feature to Create a Status Report

Now that you've cleaned up the Gantt Chart view, you're ready to a create status report.

You'll use the **Copy Picture** feature to capture an image of the Gantt Chart view to paste into a PowerPoint presentation.

To capture an image of the Gantt Chart view using the Copy Picture feature:

1. Select the **Task** tab.

2. In the **Clipboard** group, from the **Copy** command pick-list, select **Copy Picture** to open the *Copy Picture* dialogue box.

3. In the **Render Image** section, be sure **For Screen** is selected. This will copy an image of the current view to the clipboard that is optimized for screen, for use in applications like PowerPoint.

4. Select **OK** to close the *Copy Picture* dialogue box. The image will be captured to the clipboard.

To paste the image into a PowerPoint slide:

1. Open a blank presentation in PowerPoint and select the **Home** tab.

2. On the ribbon, in the **Slides** group, select the **Layout** command. Then, select the **Title and Content** layout style from the pick-list.

3. In the PowerPoint slide, click inside the content box. Using your keyboard, paste the image into the slide by pressing **Ctrl-V** (Windows) or **Cmd-V** (Mac).

4. In the *title* text frame, title the slide **"House Painting Project Status"**. If you have PowerPoint 2019 or later, you can use the *Designer* feature to enhance the slide for a more dynamic report.

CHECKPOINT: To check your results so far, go to **mspbasics.com**

- Select the **CheckPoint Images** tab.
- Select the version of the book you're using.
- Select **Chapter 17**. Then, go to **Checkpoint Image #3**

Customize the Timeline View to Share Project Status

The shareholders have asked for a high-level status of your House Painting project. They're particularly interested in the start date of the *Apply First Coat* task, which begins Phase 3 of the project. You'll customize the Timeline View panel to create a status report.

To display the Timeline View panel:

1. Select the **View** tab.

2. In the **Split View** group, select the **Timeline** checkbox.

Add tasks the timeline view panel:

The panel is currently empty and contains only the project start and finish dates. You'll customize the Timeline View by adding tasks and dates to the panel. Add the *Get Supplies*, *Prep House*, *Paint House* and *Apply First Coat* tasks to the Timeline View panel as follows:

1. Select the **Format** tab.

2. Click anywhere in the Timeline panel to display the *Timeline Tools* on the contextual **Timeline Format** tab.

3. In the **Insert** group, select the **Existing Tasks** command to open the *Add Tasks to Timeline* dialog box.

4. In the **Select Tasks** field, select the *Get Supplies*, *Prep House*, *Paint House* and *Apply First Coat* tasks.

5. Select **OK** to close the *Add Tasks to Timeline* dialog box.

The tasks and their start and finish dates should now be added as timeline bars to the Timeline panel. Notice the *Get Supplies* and the *Prep House* timeline bars are shaded in dark blue and have a check mark. This is because these phases are complete.

Next, you'll customize the view and give each timeline bar a unique color, as follows:

1. Select the *Get Supplies* timeline bar.

2. In the **Font** group, from the **Background Color** pick-list, select the **Gold** color.

3. Select the **Prep House** timeline bar.

4. In the **Font** group, from the **Background Color** pick-list, select the **Green** color.

5. Keep the current background color for the *Paint House* and *Apply First Coat* timeline bars.

Since the stakeholders are interested in the start date of the *Apply First Coat* task, you'll display this task as a **Callout Task**, so that it stands out.

To make the Apply First Coat task a Callout task:

1. Right-click the *Apply First Coat* timeline bar.

2. Select **Display as Callout** from the list.

CHECKPOINT: To check your results so far, go to **mspbasics.com**

- Select the **CheckPoint Images** tab.
- Select the version of the book you're using.
- Select **Chapter 17.** Then, go to **Checkpoint Image #4**

Now, you'll use the **Copy Timeline** feature to capture an image of the Timeline view.

1. Select the Timeline panel to display the *Timeline Tools* on the ribbon.

2. In the **Copy** group, from the **Copy Timeline** command pick-list, select **For Presentation**.

3. The Timeline view will be copied to the clipboard. You can now paste the image into a PowerPoint slide or another application to share your timeline. **NOTE:** When pasting the timeline image, select the **Picture** paste option.

Use the Built-In Reports to Share Project Status

You'll now generate the **Project Overview** report to share with your stakeholders.

1. On the **View** tab, in the **Split View** group, uncheck the **Timeline** checkbox to hide the Timeline view panel (to remove the panel from the report).

2. Select the **Report** tab.

3. In the **View Reports** group, from the **Dashboards** pick-list, select the **Project Overview** report.

CHECKPOINT: To check your results so far, go to **mspbasics.com**

- Select the **CheckPoint Images** tab.
- Select the version of the book you're using.
- Select **Chapter 17.** Then, go to **Checkpoint Image #5**

4. The *Report Tools* will be displayed on the **Report Design** contextual Format tab. In the **Report** group, select the **Copy Report** command to copy the report to the clipboard.

5. Paste the report into a PowerPoint slide. **NOTE:** When pasting the report image, select **Picture** for the paste option.

CHECKPOINT: To check your results so far, go to **mspbasics.com**

- Select the **CheckPoint Images** tab.
- Select the version of the book you're using.
- Select **Chapter 17.** Then, go to **Checkpoint Image #6**

You've now created status reports to share project information. You used the Timeline view, the Copy features and the Built-in reports to create dynamic status reports!

[illegible] [illegible] [illegible] results [illegible]

[illegible] fixed-width images [illegible]

[illegible] [illegible] image [illegible]

[illegible] [illegible] [illegible] image [illegible]

[illegible]

Export [illegible] Make the copy [illegible]

[illegible] [illegible] [illegible] [illegible]

[illegible] [illegible] color [illegible]

[illegible]

Select [illegible]

[illegible]

Select [illegible] [illegible] [illegible]

[illegible] [illegible] [illegible] [illegible]

[illegible] [illegible] [illegible]

Chapter 18 Creating Master Schedules

In the last chapter, you learned to create status reports. You learned to use the Copy and Export features and the built-in reports to share project information. In this chapter, you'll learn to create **Master Schedules**. When you're done, you'll be able to consolidate project plans, create a resource pool and create dependencies between projects.

You'll Learn:

- Reasons to Consolidate Schedules
- To Create a Master Schedule
- To Use Resource Pools
- To Link Schedules
- To Create External Links

Consolidating Project Plans

Project managers often manage several projects at the same time, and in many cases, the project schedules are interdependent. To help you manage multiple projects, Microsoft Project allows you to combine projects into a **Master Schedule** – also known as a **Consolidated Project Plan** or **Master Project**. Master schedules are Microsoft Project files that contain other *Inserted Projects*, also called **Subprojects**. You can insert an unlimited number of subprojects into a master schedule. The inserted project plans aren't saved in the master schedule, they are linked to it. When you save a master schedule, changes you've made to its subprojects are also saved in the source files. Also, if a subproject is updated outside of the master schedule file, the new information will appear in the master schedule the next time it's opened.

Why Create a Master Schedule?

Master Schedules enable you to:

- **Get a Program/Portfolio Level View** – You can see all the projects in a program or portfolio and how they interact with one another in a single view.
- **Manage Resources Across Multiple Projects** – You can identify resource availability and over-allocations across the entire program or portfolio.
- **Gain Program/Portfolio Level Insights** – You can query program-level or portfolio-level information for cost, schedule, and performance metrics.
- **Manage Phased Deployments** – You can manage each phase in a project as its own project, while keeping a view of the overall program or portfolio.
- **View the Critical Path of a Program/Portfolio** – You can gain insights for expediting a program or portfolio by viewing its Critical Path.

Creating a Master Schedule

To create a Master Schedule:

- Open a **Blank Project**.
- Select the **Project** tab. In the **Insert** group, select the **Insert Subproject** command (*Figure 240*).

- Locate and select the Project files you want to insert. Hold down the **Ctrl key** to select multiple files.
- Select **Insert**. Project will create a Master Schedule, containing the plans you've inserted.

Figure 240 below shows the "New Program" master schedule, which contains the "New Product Launch", "Marketing Campaign Planning" and "Customer Service Ramp Up" subprojects.

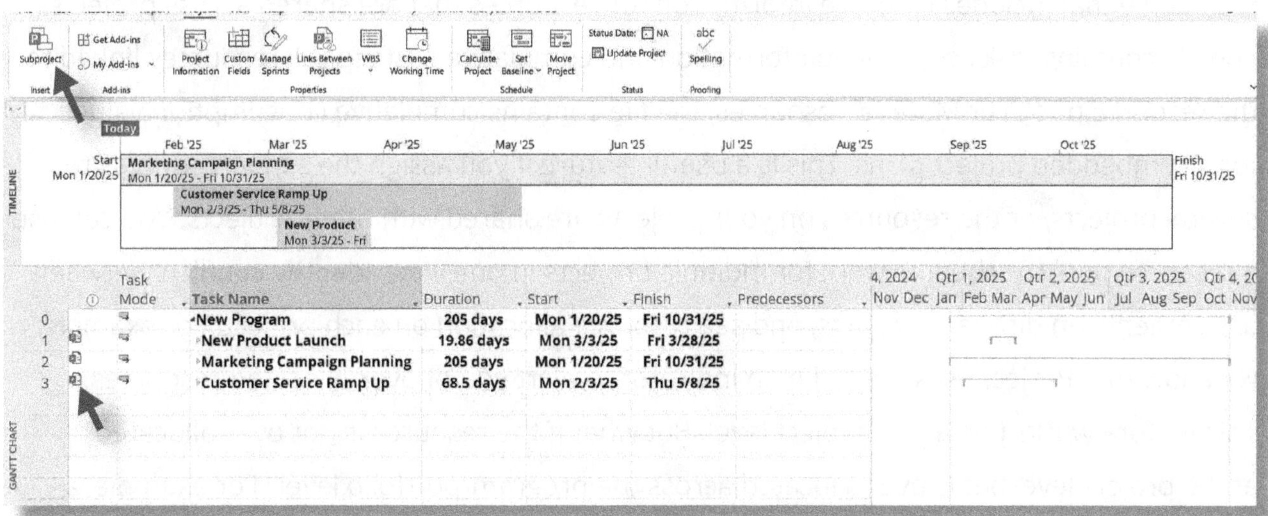

Figure 240 – Create a Master Schedule

In a master schedule, the subprojects are represented as summary tasks in the **Task Name** field and project plan icons in the **Indicators** field. Expand a subproject to view its entire schedule. In the Gantt chart, a summary task bar is shown for each subproject. When the Project Summary Task is displayed, it will display the duration of the master schedule. The start date of the master schedule will be the start date of the earliest subproject. Its finish date will be the finish date of the latest subproject. For example, in *Figure 240* above, the start date of the master schedule coincides with the 1/20/25 start date of the earliest subproject, which is the "Marketing Campaign Planning" project plan. The finish date coincides with the 10/31/25 finish date of the latest subproject, which is also the "Marketing Campaign Planning" plan. The 205-day master schedule duration is automatically calculated from the durations, dependencies, and outline level of its subprojects.

Once you've created a master schedule, you can use the filtering, sorting, and grouping features (Chapter 14) to gain insights at the project, program, and portfolio levels. These insights can help your team make data-driven decisions to help ensure portfolios, programs and projects deliver the value they were intended to deliver.

Managing Resources in a Master Schedule – Creating Resource Pools

When projects are consolidated into a Master Schedule, you can view the resources for each subproject in the Resource Sheet view. However, you can only assign a resource to the tasks in the subproject it came from. To combine resources and make them available across all subprojects, you'll need to create a shared **Resource Pool**. A resource pool is a Microsoft Project file that includes resource information for resources that are shared across projects. The file contains task assignment information and cumulative costs for all resources linked to the resource pool. For Material resources, the file contains cumulative consumption values for all embedded project plans. This is a useful feature if you assign the same resources to several projects, or the resources on your projects are shared with other projects. You can use a resource pool to schedule work for multiple projects in one view, identify conflicts between assignments on different projects, and see resource allocation on each project. For example, we know that Project uses the red man indicator to alert you of over-allocated resources. This feature works fine at the project level. But what if the resource is <u>not</u> over-allocated at the project level but <u>is</u> over-allocated across the program/portfolio level? For example, a resource may show 50% allocated on your project, but they may also be assigned at 50% on three other projects. Resource pools address this issue by allowing you the see how resources are assigned across an entire program/portfolio. To share resources across plans in a master schedule, each plan must be linked to the resource pool. Project plans that are linked to the resource pool are called **Sharer Plans**. Information updated in the resource pool or any of the sharer plans is available to all the linked sharer plans.

To create a Resource Pool:

- Open a **Blank** Project.
- Go to the **Resource Sheet view** to create the resources that will be shared across plans in the master schedule.
- In the Resource Sheet table, enter the resource information. Include any information you want included in the resource pool file (E.g., pay rates if you'll be tracking costs).
  NOTE: If you elect to copy and paste the resource information from other project plans, be sure there are no duplicate resources.
- Save the resource pool file and name it appropriately (E.g., "New Program Resource Pool").

After you create the resource pool file, you'll need to connect the *Sharer Plans* to it. Connecting the sharer plans to the resource pool enables you to see resource allocations across the entire program/portfolio.

To connect Sharer Plans to the Resource Pool:

1. Open the resource pool file.

2. Open the project file (sharer plan) you want to connect to the shared resource pool.

3. In the sharer plan file, select the **Resource** tab.

4. In the **Assignments** group, select **Resource Pool**. Then, select **Share Resources** from the pick-list to open the *Share Resources* dialogue box (*Figure 241* below).

5. Select the **Use resources** option. **NOTE:** This option requires at least one resource pool file to be open. If you have several Project files open and the resource pool file you want isn't populated in the **From** field, you'll need to select it from pick-list.

6. In the **On conflict with calendar or resource information** section, select **Pool takes precedence**. This option tells Project to override any conflicting information from the sharer projects with the resource pool file information. The **Sharer takes precedence** option does the opposite.

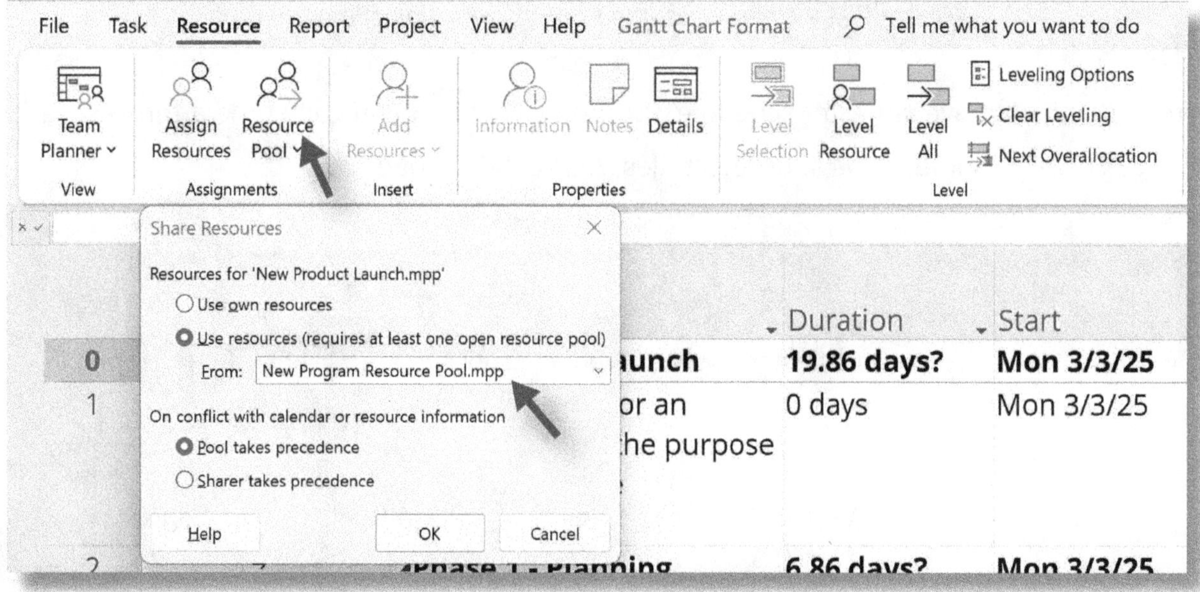

Figure 241 – Create a Resource Pool

7. Select **OK** to close the *Share Resources* dialogue box.

8. Repeat steps 2 through 7 for each sharer plan you want to connect to the resource pool.

9. When all the sharer plans have been connected to the resource pool, save and close all the sharer plan and resource pool files.

When you open a master schedule file after the subprojects have been connected to a resource pool, Project will open the *Open Resource Pool Information* dialogue box (*Figure 242* below) to prompt you that the file shares resources from a resource pool. Select the **Open resource pool to see assignments across all sharer files** option to open the resource pool file. Then, select **OK**.

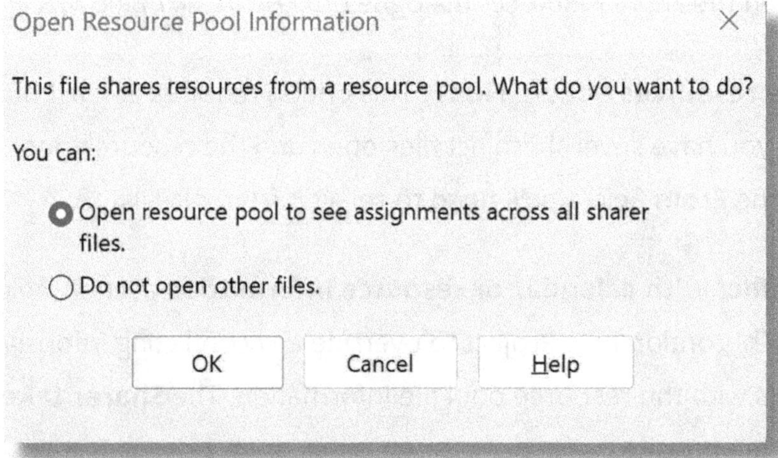

Figure 242 – Open Resource Pool Information Dialogue Box

After you initially save a master schedule, Project will prompt you each time after to save changes to all or some of the subproject files (*Figure 243* below).

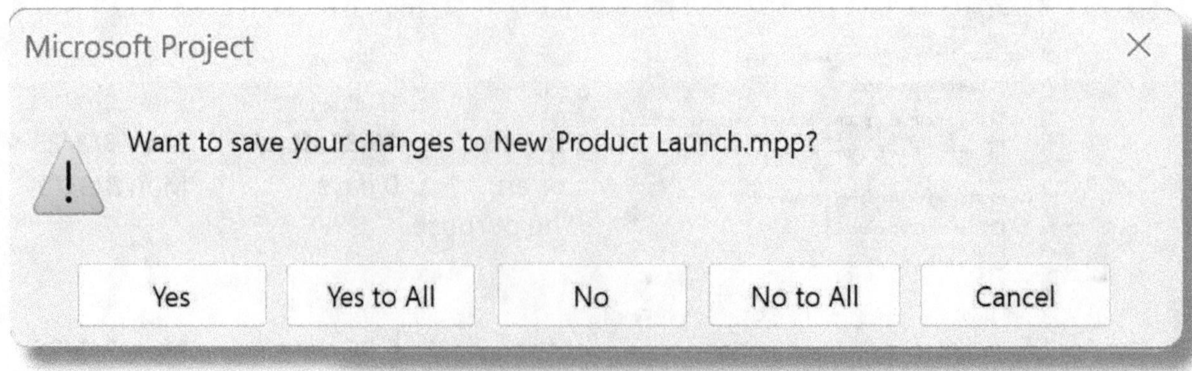

Figure 243 – Saving Master Project Plans

Selecting "Yes to All" tells Project to save changes to all sub-projects in the master project. This is what you'll generally choose. Or, if you haven't made any changes, you can select "No to All". Selecting the "Yes" or "No" option prompts you to save changes for each subproject individually.

Linking Schedules – Creating Inter-Project Dependencies

It's not uncommon for the predecessor of a task to exist in an entirely different project schedule. To address this issue, Project allows you to link two interdependent schedules by creating external predecessors, called **External Links**. Linking schedules enables you to manage inter-project dependencies. For example, a server built on one project may be needed on another project or, a resource may need to finish a task on one project before they can work on a task in a different project. Rather than meeting with the project managers of each inter-dependent project, a dependency can be created between the projects. As a result, changes made to the predecessor task in Project A will be automatically reflected in the successor task in Project B. External tasks can be created between projects in a master schedule or between independent project plans that are not consolidated into a master schedule.

To Link Tasks between Projects in a Master Schedule:

- In the master schedule, select the predecessor task you want to link. Then, holding the **Ctrl key**, select the successor task.
- Select the **Task** tab.
- In the **Schedule** group, select the **Link the selected tasks** command. Project will create a Finish-to-Start task relationship with an external link between the tasks in the plans.

When an external link has been created, Project will insert the external predecessor task into the plan. The task will be grayed out to indicate the external link. The file path to the predecessor's file will be displayed in the Predecessors field of the successor task. Project also inserts the external successor task in the other project plan. The task names will be displayed in grayed-out type, indicating the external links. In *Figure 244*, the *Launch Product* milestone is an external predecessor to the I*nitial Assessment* summary task in the "Customer Service Ramp Up" project.

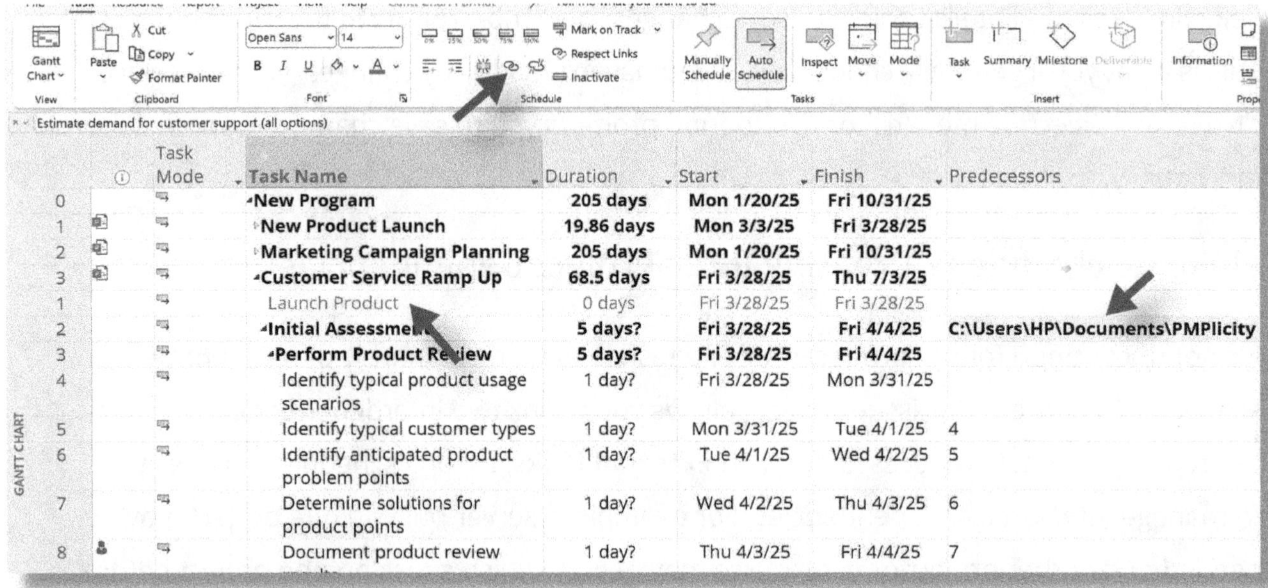

Figure 244 – Creating External Links

NOTE: To create an external link with a task relationship type other than Finish-to-Start, after the file path name, insert the two-letter acronym for the desired task relationship type after the task ID of predecessor in the Predecessors field of the successor task (E.g. SS or FF).

To Link Tasks between Projects in a Non-Consolidated Plan:

- In the plan that contains the successor task, double-click the successor task to open the *Task Information* dialogue box.
- Select the **Predecessors** tab.
- In the **ID** field, select the cell beneath the existing predecessor's task ID.
- Type the **file name** (include the entire file path) of the plan that contains the external predecessor task, then a backslash, then the **Task ID** of the predecessor (*Figure 245*).
- Press the **Tab** key.
- Select **OK** to close the *Task information* dialogue box.

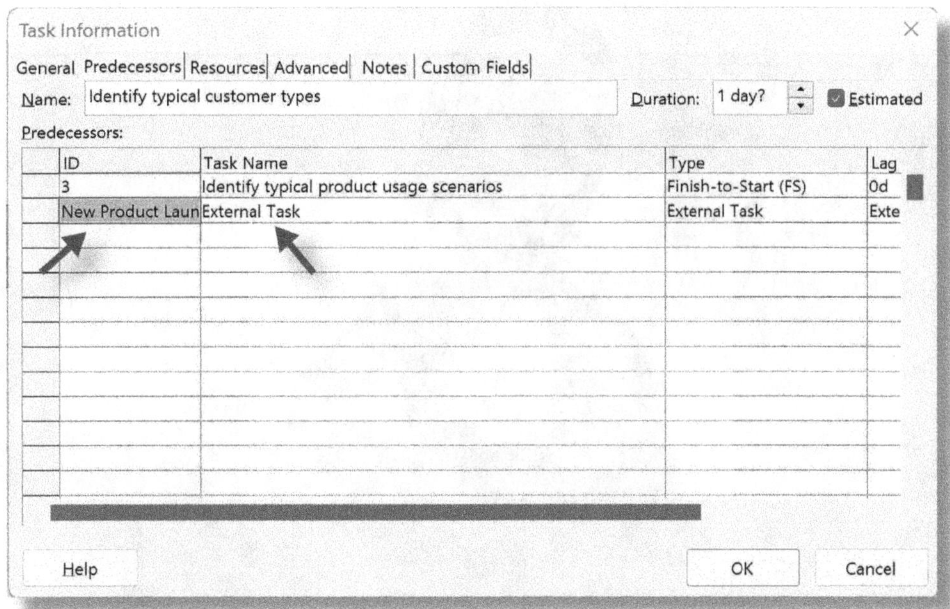

Figure 245 – Creating Inter-Project Dependencies

Project will insert the external predecessor task into the project plan. The task will be displayed in grayed out type to indicate the external link. Project will also create the external successor task in the other plan. It will be displayed in grayed-out type, indicating the external link.

You've now learned to create and use Master Schedules. You've learned to consolidate project plans into a Master Schedule, create a Resource Pool and create dependencies between projects using External Links.

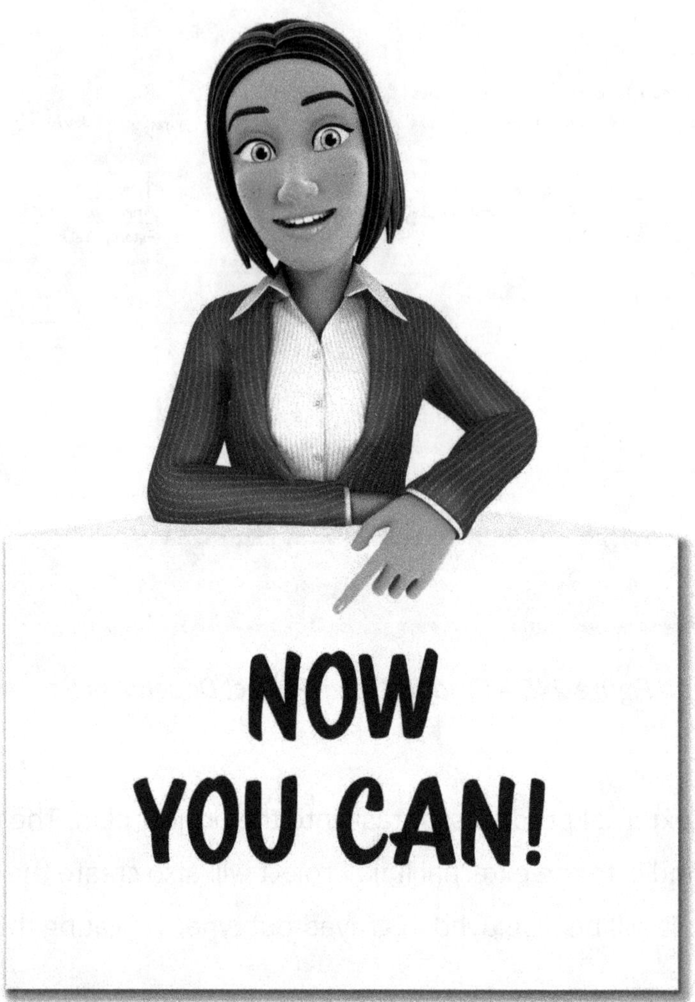

- ✓ Explain when to Consolidate Schedules
- ✓ Create a Master Schedule
- ✓ Use Resource Pools
- ✓ Link Schedules
- ✓ Create External Links

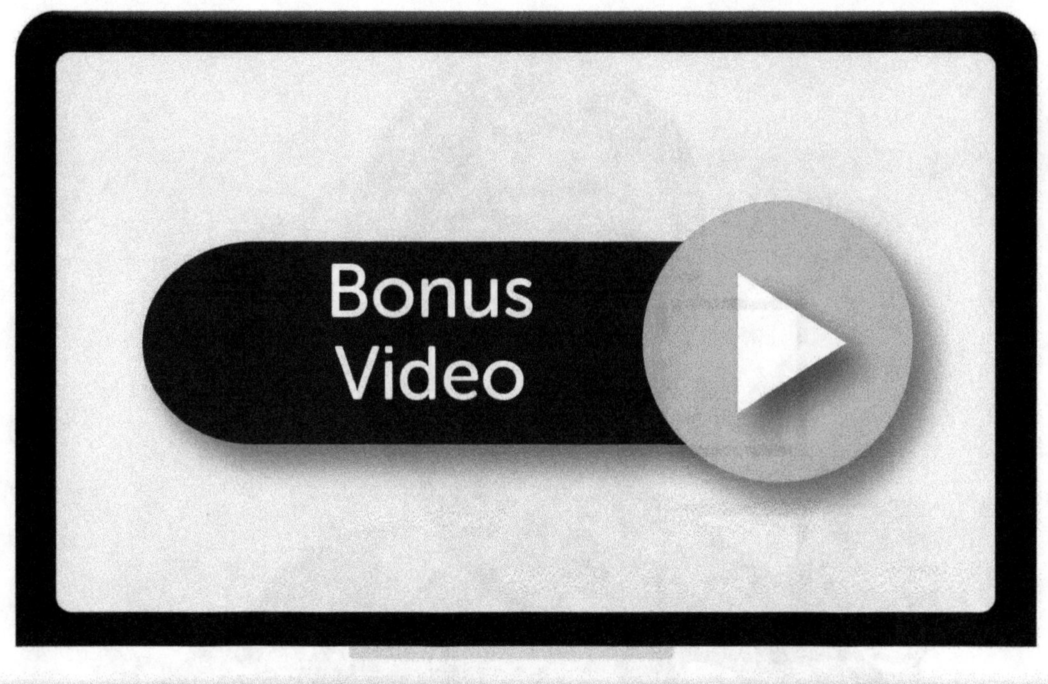

This chapter includes a **BONUS VIDEO** from the "Microsoft Project B.A.S.I.C.S." video course. The videos include tutorials of the information covered in the chapters, software demonstrations and other useful information.

To Watch This Chapter's Video:

✓ Visit mspbasics.com.

✓ Select **CheckPoint Images** from the menu.

✓ Select your version of the book.

✓ Select **Chapter 18.**

✓ Enjoy the video!

Want to watch the entire video course?
visit www.pmplicity.com/store

Chapter 19 Closing Your Project

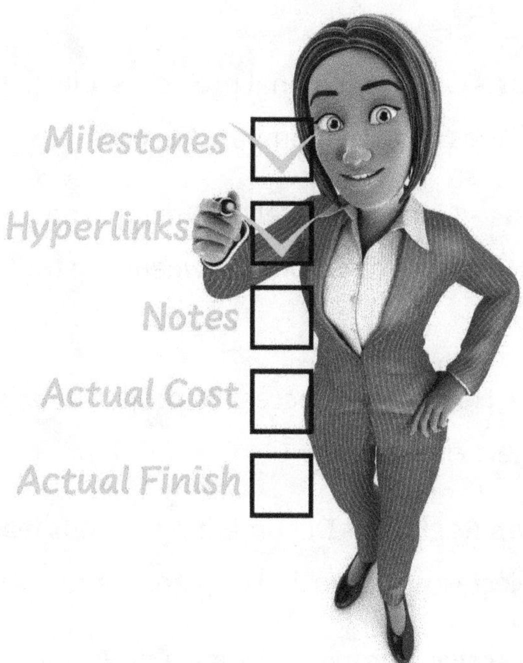

In the last chapter, you learned to consolidate and linked schedules. You learned to inserted sub-projects into a Master Schedule, create a Resource Pool and created dependencies between projects. In this chapter, you'll learn to properly **close a project**. When you're done, you'll be able to use Project to close out a project, compare final results to planned results, and create a template for future projects.

You'll Learn:

- Reasons to Close Your Project
- How to Close Your Project
- How to Compare Planned Estimates to Final Results
- How to Use the Compare Projects Feature
- How to Create a Project Template

Why Close Your Project?

After you've executed your project, it's a good idea to close it properly. Here are some advantages of doing so:

- **Accurate Company Records** – Quantifying final project results (e.g., final project cost or final delivery date) establishes accurate company records.
- **Future Project Negotiations** – Citing historical data from properly closed-out projects informs future negotiations involving trade-offs between constraints such as scope, time and cost.
- **Answer Future Questions** – Having ready access to project details can help explain delays and cost overruns after project closure.
- **Establish a Lessons Learned Register** – Documenting lessons learned with task and resource notes through project closure provides a planning reference for future projects.
- **Comply with PMI® Best Practice** – Properly closing a project is a PMI® best practice.

How to Close Your Project

At the end of your project, complete the following actions to properly close your project:

✓ Add task and resource notes (Ch. 10) to document lessons learned for future projects.

✓ Add hyperlinks to tasks and resources (Ch. 10) for quick access to websites and shared files.

✓ For a Detailed schedule, set the Remaining <u>Work</u> value to zero for all tasks (Ch. 15).

✓ For a Simple schedule, set the Remaining <u>Duration</u> value to zero for all tasks (Ch. 15).

✓ Mark all milestones 100% Complete. **NOTE:** Recall from Chapter 15 that milestones don't automatically get marked complete when their predecessors finish. You can use the **100% Complete** command on the **Task** tab in the **Schedule** group to quickly mark milestones 100% complete.

✓ Record Actual Start and Actual Finish dates as appropriate (Ch. 15).

✓ Record Actual Costs (Ch. 15) as appropriate.

When your project is officially closed out, every task should be marked 100% complete. Each task should have a check mark ✓ in the **Indicators** field. *Figure 246* below shows a properly closed out project.

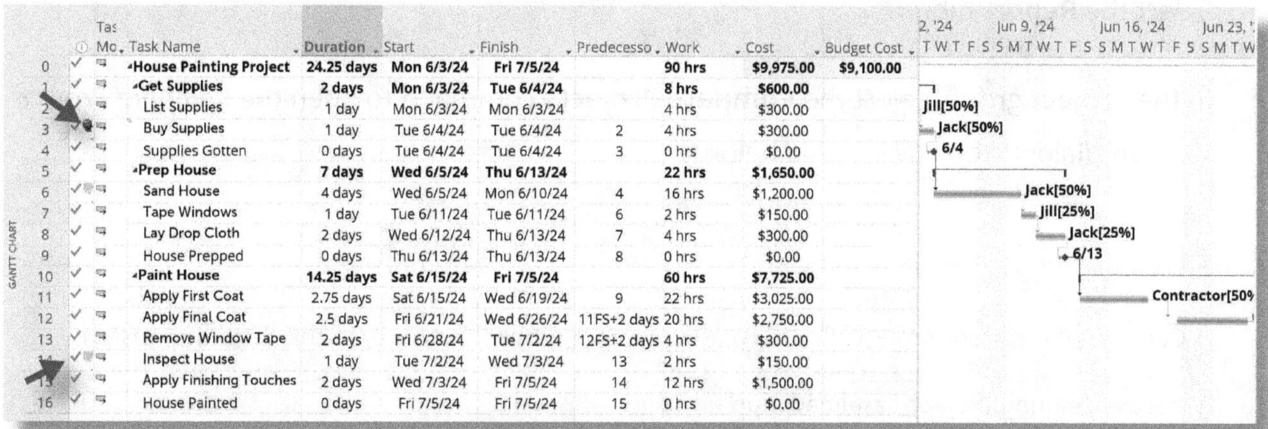

	Task Name	Duration	Start	Finish	Predecessors	Work	Cost	Budget Cost
0	**House Painting Project**	**24.25 days**	**Mon 6/3/24**	**Fri 7/5/24**		**90 hrs**	**$9,975.00**	**$9,100.00**
1	**Get Supplies**	**2 days**	**Mon 6/3/24**	**Tue 6/4/24**		**8 hrs**	**$600.00**	
2	List Supplies	1 day	Mon 6/3/24	Mon 6/3/24		4 hrs	$300.00	
3	Buy Supplies	1 day	Tue 6/4/24	Tue 6/4/24	2	4 hrs	$300.00	
4	Supplies Gotten	0 days	Tue 6/4/24	Tue 6/4/24	3	0 hrs	$0.00	
5	**Prep House**	**7 days**	**Wed 6/5/24**	**Thu 6/13/24**		**22 hrs**	**$1,650.00**	
6	Sand House	4 days	Wed 6/5/24	Mon 6/10/24	4	16 hrs	$1,200.00	
7	Tape Windows	1 day	Tue 6/11/24	Tue 6/11/24	6	2 hrs	$150.00	
8	Lay Drop Cloth	2 days	Wed 6/12/24	Thu 6/13/24	7	4 hrs	$300.00	
9	House Prepped	0 days	Thu 6/13/24	Thu 6/13/24	8	0 hrs	$0.00	
10	**Paint House**	**14.25 days**	**Sat 6/15/24**	**Fri 7/5/24**		**60 hrs**	**$7,725.00**	
11	Apply First Coat	2.75 days	Sat 6/15/24	Wed 6/19/24	9	22 hrs	$3,025.00	
12	Apply Final Coat	2.5 days	Fri 6/21/24	Wed 6/26/24	11FS+2 days	20 hrs	$2,750.00	
13	Remove Window Tape	2 days	Fri 6/28/24	Tue 7/2/24	12FS+2 days	4 hrs	$300.00	
14	Inspect House	1 day	Tue 7/2/24	Wed 7/3/24	13	2 hrs	$150.00	
15	Apply Finishing Touches	2 days	Wed 7/3/24	Fri 7/5/24	14	12 hrs	$1,500.00	
16	House Painted	0 days	Fri 7/5/24	Fri 7/5/24	15	0 hrs	$0.00	

Figure 246 – Closed Out Project

Compare Final Results to Planned Estimates – Using the Compare Projects Feature

Once you've closed your project, you may want to compare your final project results to the planned estimates. You can do this using the **Compare Projects** feature (*Figure 247* below). This feature allows you to compare two versions of a project. When you use this feature, Project will create a "Comparison" report that shows the differences between the two projects.

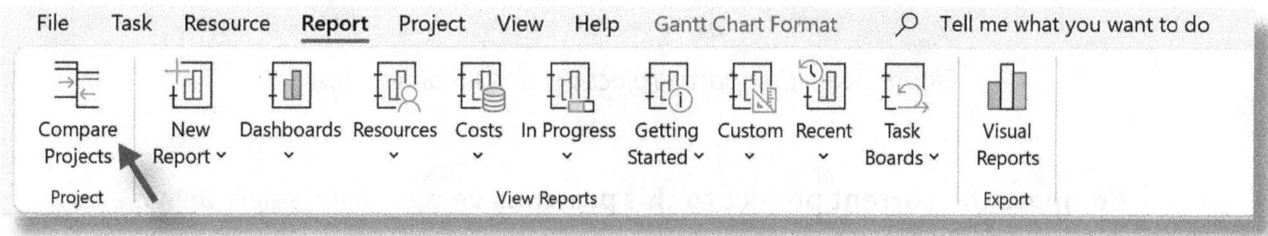

Figure 247 – Compare Projects

IMPORTANT NOTE: To use the Compare Projects feature to compare your planned estimates to your actual results, you'll need to save a copy of your original plan (after baseline and before entering progress data). You'll then need to rename and save a working copy of the file for entering progress data.

To use the Compare Projects feature:

- Open the current version of the project plan you want to compare.
- Select the **Report** tab.
- In the **Project** group, select the **Compare Projects** command to open the *Compare Project Versions* dialogue box (*Figure 248* below).

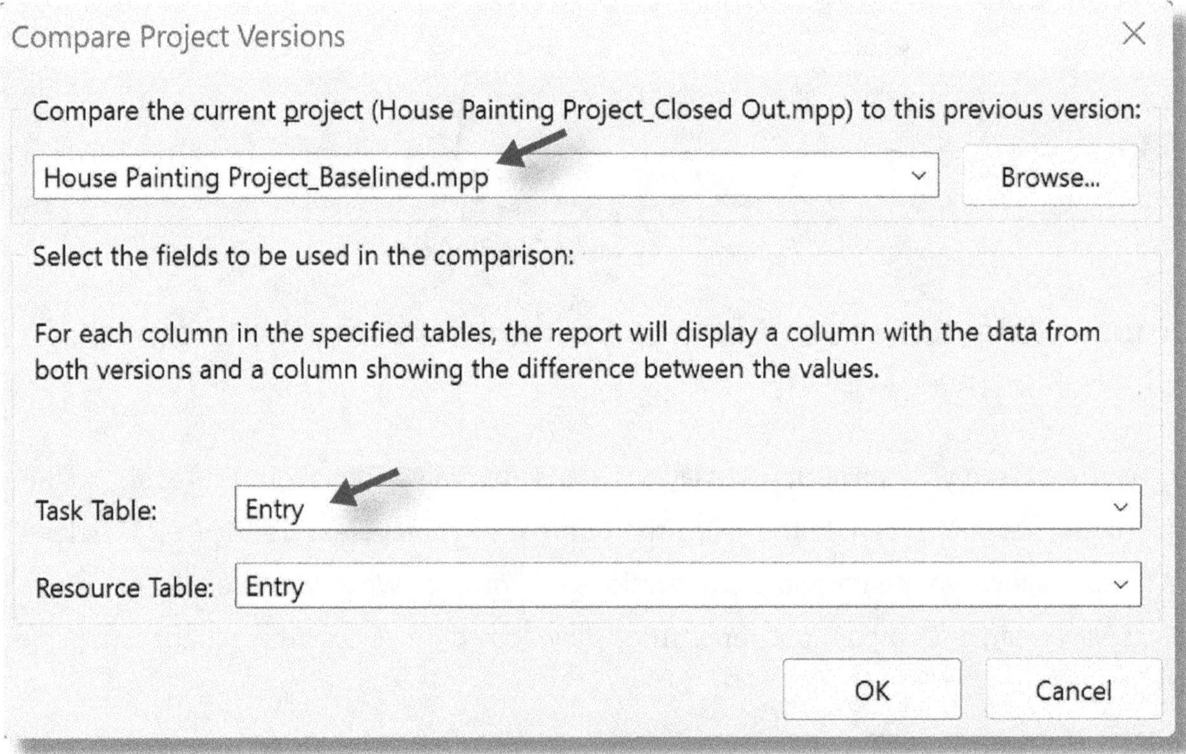

Figure 248 – Compare Project Versions dialogue box

- In the **Compare the current project to this previous version** field, select **Browse** to locate the previous version of the project file.
- In the **Task Table** and **Resource Table** fields, select the table that contains the fields you want to display in the comparison report. For each field in the selected table, the report will display a column with the values from both versions and a column showing the differences between the values.
- Select **OK** to generate the **Comparison Report**.

Figure 249 below shows a Comparison report that compares two versions of a *House Painting* project plan.

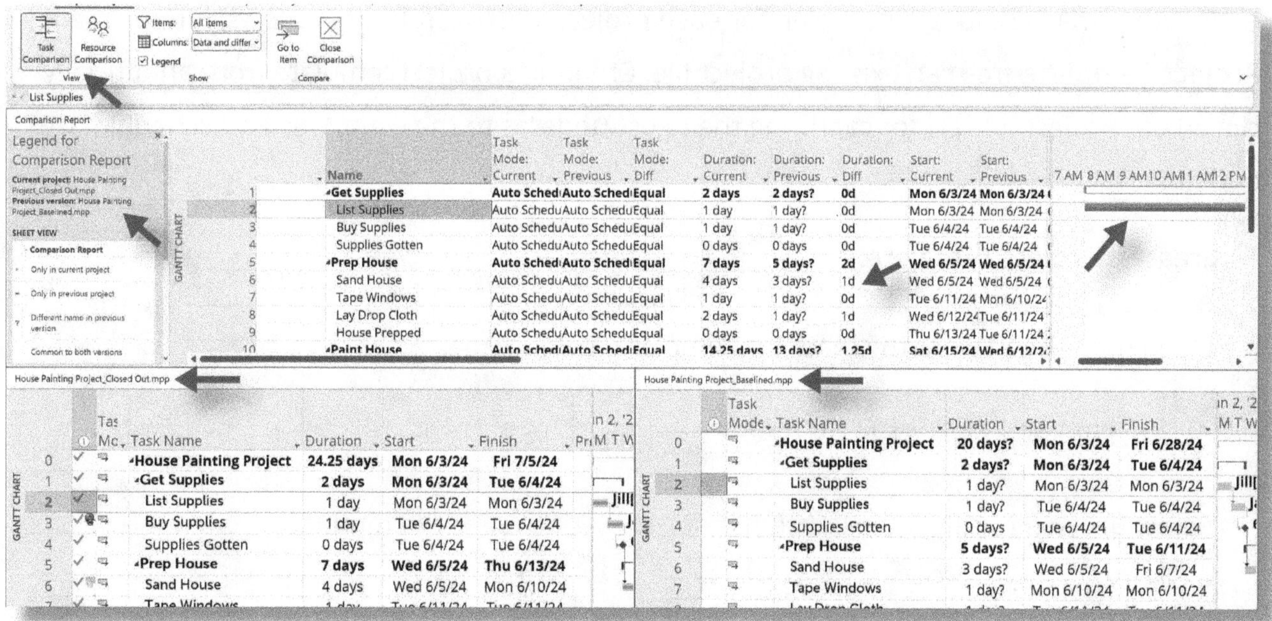

Figure 249 – Comparison Report

In the top left corner, you'll find a legend that describes the various components of the report. In the bottom panel, the two versions of the plan are displayed side by side. In the top panel, for each field of the specified table, Project displays a column with the data from the current version, a column with the data from the previous version and a column showing the differences between the two. The Gantt Chart displays two sets of task bars. The green task bars represent the current version of the project. The purple task bars represent the previous version. When the report is generated, the ribbon includes the **Compare Projects** tab, which contains commands for the report. In the **View** group, to compare tasks, select the **Task Comparison** option to show the task view in all three panes. To compare resources, select the **Resource Comparison** option to show the resource view in all three panes. In the **Show** group, use the **Items** and **Columns** commands to select which items and columns are shown in the report. Use the **Go to Item** command to select an item to display in all three views.

Creating a Project Template

It's not uncommon for the projects in an organization to contain similar project details. In this case, rather than creating a new plan for each project, Microsoft Project allows you to create a **Project Template** from an existing project file. Creating a project template from an officially closed out project is ideal for capturing the latest updates to the estimates and schedule outline.

To Create a Project Template:

- Open the file you want to create the template from.
- On the **File** tab, select **Save As**.
- Select **Browse** to select the location that you want to save the template.
- In the **File name** field of the *Save as* dialogue box, enter a name for the template.
- In the **Save as type** field, select **Project Template** from the pick-list.
- Then, select **Save** to open the *Save As Template* dialogue box (*Figure 250* below).
- Select any data that you want to remove from the template. Then, select **Save**.

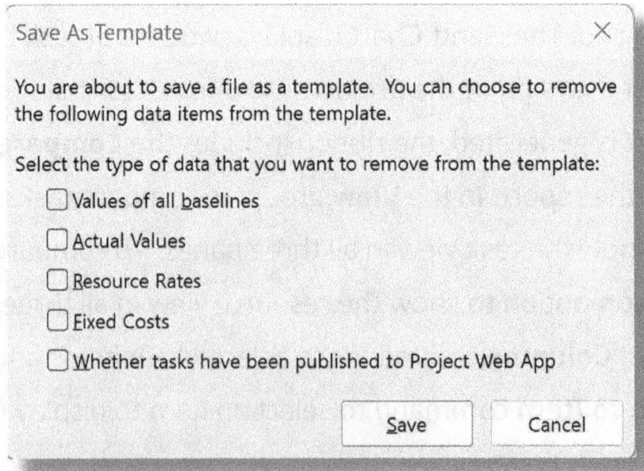

Figure 250 – Save a Project Template

You've now learned to properly close a project in Micrsoft Project. You can also create a Comparison report to compare planned results to final results, and create a project template.

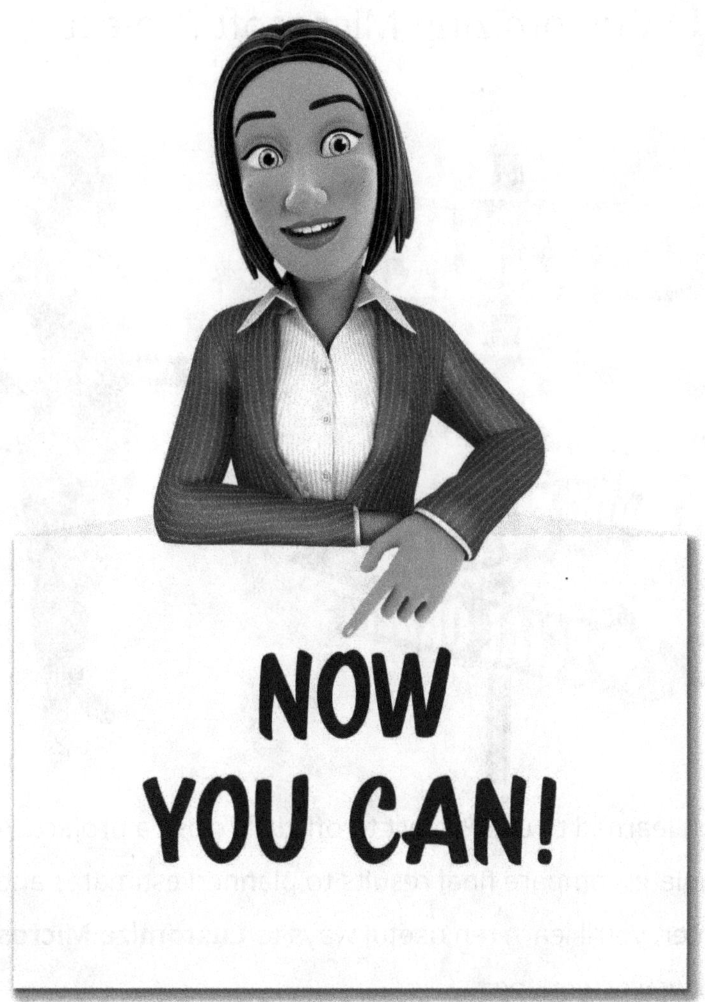

- ✓ Explain Reasons to Close Your Project
- ✓ Close Your Project
- ✓ Compare Planned Estimates to Final Results
- ✓ Use the Compare Projects Feature
- ✓ Create a Project Template

Chapter 20 Customizing Microsoft Project

In the last chapter, you learned to use Project to officially close a project. You learned to set all tasks to 100% complete, compare final results to planned estimates and create a project template. In this chapter, you'll learn ten useful ways to **Customize Microsoft Project** to match your preferred way of working.

You'll Learn To:

- Customize the Quick Access Toolbar
- Customize the Ribbon
- Create a Status Date Indicator
- Customize the Timeline View
- Customize the Gantt Chart Bars
- Customize the Reports
- Create New Reports
- Create a Custom Field
- Create a Lookup Table
- Create a Graphical Indicator

Throughout this book, we've reviewed many Microsoft Project features that can make building and managing your schedule easy and efficient. You can also customize many of the features to match your personal preferences and the way you work. In this chapter, we'll review 10 customizations that can enhance your schedule and help you work more efficiently.

Ten Useful Microsoft Project Customizations

1. Customize the Quick Access Toolbar
2. Customize the Ribbon
3. Create a Status Date Indicator
4. Customize the Timeline View
5. Customize the Gantt Chart Bars
6. Customize the Built-In Reports
7. Create a New Report
8. Create an Open Text Custom Field
9. Create a Look-up Table
10. Create a Graphical Indicator

Customize the Quick Access Toolbar

The **Quick Access Toolbar** (*Figure 251* below), contains frequently used commands to help you quickly navigate the Project interface. By default, some commonly used commands are already added to the toolbar, such as *Save* and *Undo*.

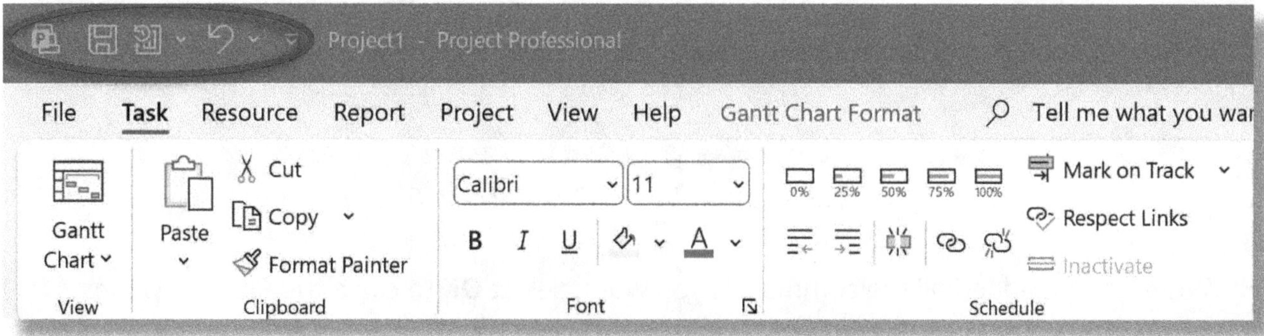

Figure 251 – Quick Access Toolbar

Project allows you to customize the Quick Access toolbar to add the commands you use most.

To add commands to the Quick Access toolbar:

- Select the **File** tab. Then, select **Options** to open the *Project Options* dialogue box.
- Select **Quick Access toolbar** from the options on the far left (*Figure 252* below).
- In the field on the left, you'll find a list of commands that can be added to the toolbar. Select a group of commands from the **Choose commands from** pick-list. The P*opular Commands* group is selected by default. In the field on the right, you'll find the commands that are currently on the Quick Access toolbar.
- Select a command from the pick-list on the left that you want to add to the toolbar, then click **Add**. The command will appear in the field on the right. Repeat for each command you want to add. To remove a command, select the command from the field on the right. Then, select **Remove**.

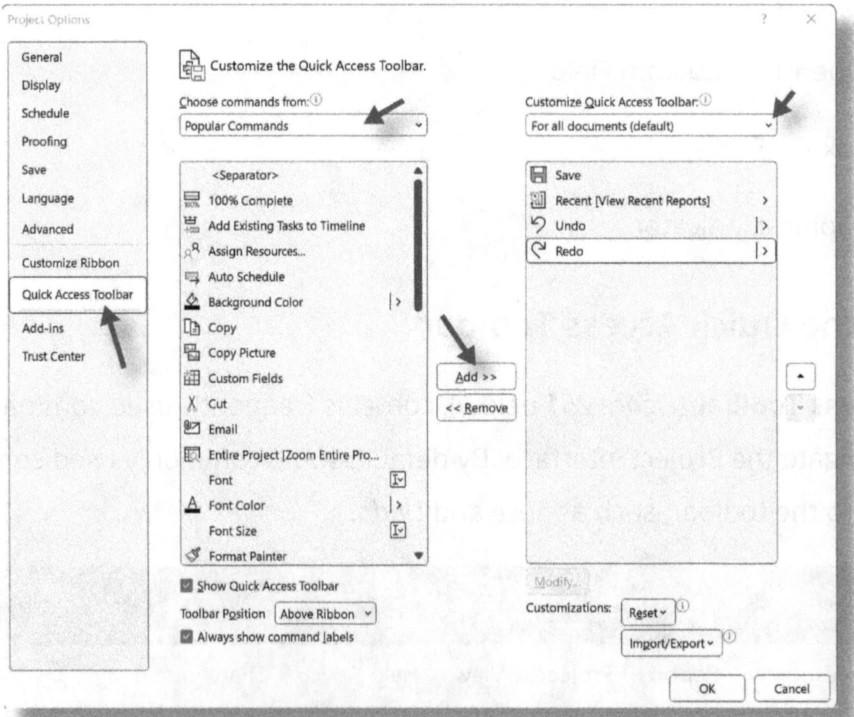

Figure 252 – Customize the Quick Access Toolbar

- When you've added all the commands you want, select **OK** to close the *Project Options* dialogue box. The newly added commands will appear on the Quick Access toolbar.

NOTE: By default, the Quick Access commands you add to the toolbar will appear in all Project documents. To customize the toolbar for the current document only, select that option from the **Customize Quick Access Toolbar** pick-list on the right.

Customize the Ribbon

The **Ribbon** (*Figure 253* below) contains all the commands you need to navigate the Project interface. They are organized on tabs, with relevant commands organized into groups.
By default, the ribbon includes the File, Task, Resource, Report, Project, View and Format tabs. You can customize the ribbon to reorganize, rename, add, or remove tabs, groups, and commands. You can also create custom tabs and groups and include the commands you want.

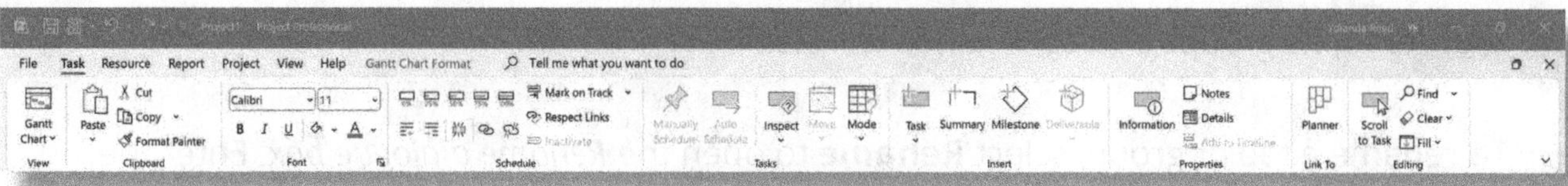

Figure 253 – The Ribbon

To Customize the Ribbon:

- Select the **File** tab. Then, select **Options** to open the *Project Options* dialogue box.
- •Select **Customize Ribbon** from the options on the left (*Figure 254*).

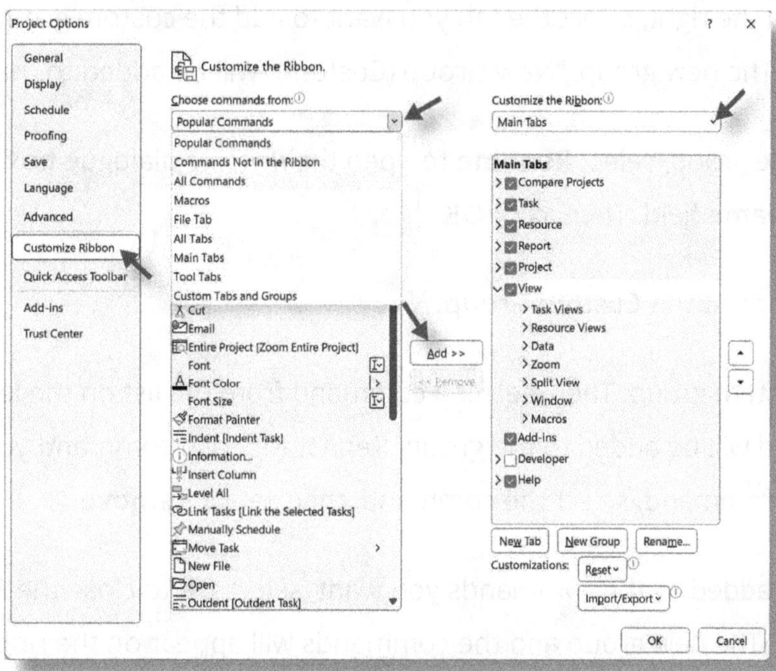

Figure 254 – Customize the Ribbon

- In the field on the left, you'll find a list of commands that can be added to the ribbon. Select a group of commands from the **Choose commands from** pick-list. The *Popular Commands* group is selected by default.

- In the field on the right, you'll find the tabs, groups and commands that are currently on the ribbon. Select the group of tabs you want to customize from the **Customize the Ribbon** pick-list on the top right. Choose from All Tabs, Main Tabs (default) or Tool Tabs.

- To remove a tab, simply uncheck the tab's checkbox. The tab, along with its groups and commands will be removed.

- Use the **Move Up** and **Move Down** arrows on the right to reorder the tabs. When a tab is reordered, its groups and commands will also be reordered.

- To rename a tab or group, select **Rename** to open the *Rename dialogue box*. Enter the name in the **Display name** field, then select **OK**.

To add commands to a tab on the ribbon, you must first create a **Custom Group** and add the commands to the new group.

To Create a Custom Group:

- In the field on the right, select the tab you want to add the custom group to. Then, select **New Group**. The new group, "New Group (Custom)" will be added to the tab.

- To rename the group, select **Rename** to open the *Rename* dialogue box. Enter the name in the **Display name** field. Then, click **OK**.

To Add Commands to the Custom Group:

- Select the custom group. Then, select a command from the list on the left, and select **Add**. The command will be added to the group. Repeat for each command you want to add. To remove a command, select the command, then select **Remove**.

- When you've added all the commands you want, select **OK** to close the *Project Options* dialogue box. The new group and the commands will appear on the ribbon, on the tab you designated.

You can also add a **Custom** tab to the ribbon. This can be helpful if you frequently use commands that are located on various tabs. Creating your own custom tab will allow you to place the commands you use most on one tab.

To Create a Custom Tab:

- On the right, select the tab that you'd like the new tab to follow on the ribbon. New tabs are inserted to the right of the selected tab.
- Select **New Tab**. A new custom tab and group will be added on the right.
- To rename the tab or group, select it, then, select **Rename** to open the *Rename* dialogue box. Enter the name in the **Display name** field, then select **OK**.
- To add additional groups to the tab, select the tab, then select **New Groups**.
- To add commands to a group, select the group. Then, select a command from the list on the left, and select **Add**. Repeat for each command you want to add. To remove a command, select the command, then select **Remove**.
- You can also change the symbol for a command. Select the command, then select **Rename**. In the Rename dialogue box, select the symbol you want, then select **OK**. The new symbol will be displayed with the command on the ribbon.
- When you've added all the groups and commands you want to the custom tab, select **OK** to close the *Project Options* dialogue box. The new tab, groups and commands will appear on the ribbon.

Export/Import Your Customizations

You can export your customized Quick Access toolbar and Ribbon to a file that can be used on other computers. This is a handy feature if you use Project on multiple computers.

To Export Customizations:

- In the Quick Access Toolbar or Customize Ribbon window of the *Project Options* dialogue box, select **Import/Export**. Then, select **Export all customizations**.

- Select the location where you want to save the file, then select **Save**.
- Select **OK** to close the *Project Options* dialogue box.

To Import Customizations:

- In the **Quick Access Toolbar** or **Customize Ribbon** window of the *Project Options* dialogue box, select **Import/Export**. Then, select **Import customization file**.
- Locate the file, then select **Open** to import the customization file.
- Select **OK** to close the *Project Options* dialogue box.

NOTE: When you import a customization file, you will lose all prior customizations. If you think you'll want to revert to prior customizations, you should export the current customizations before you import the new file.

Create a Status Date Indicator

While managing your project, you'll often want to know the last date you updated your schedule. In Project, this date is called the Status Date. To keep track of your latest status date, it's helpful to create a **Status Date Indicator**. A status date indicator is similar to the current date indicator shown in the Gantt chart. Project indicates the current date with a green vertical gridline. A status date indicator is a customized gridline that indicates the project status date.

To create a Status Date Indicator:

- Select the **Format** tab.
- In the **Format** group, select **Gridlines**, then select **Gridlines** again to open the *Gridlines* dialogue box (*Figure 255*).

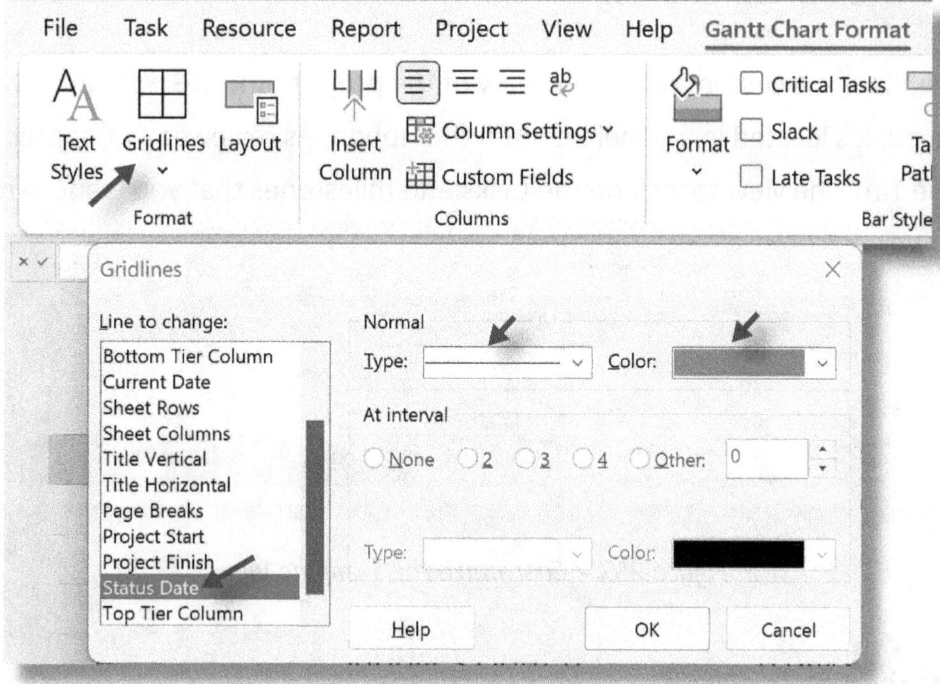

Figure 255 – Create a Status Date Indicator

- In the **Line to change** field, select **Status Date**.
- In the **Normal** section, select a **Type** and **Color** for the gridline from the respective fields.
- Select **OK** to close the *Gridlines* dialogue box. Project will now display a contrasting vertical gridline to indicate the latest status date in your project plan (*Figure 256* below).

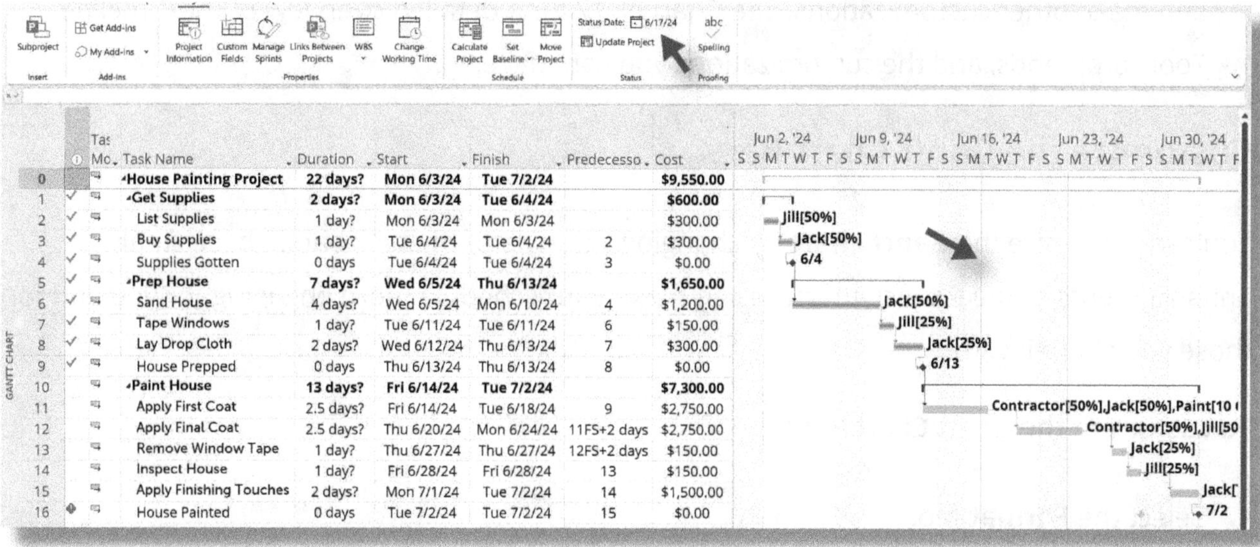

	Task Name	Duration	Start	Finish	Predecessors	Cost
0	House Painting Project	22 days?	Mon 6/3/24	Tue 7/2/24		$9,550.00
1	Get Supplies	2 days?	Mon 6/3/24	Tue 6/4/24		$600.00
2	List Supplies	1 day?	Mon 6/3/24	Mon 6/3/24		$300.00
3	Buy Supplies	1 day?	Tue 6/4/24	Tue 6/4/24	2	$300.00
4	Supplies Gotten	0 days	Tue 6/4/24	Tue 6/4/24	3	$0.00
5	Prep House	7 days?	Wed 6/5/24	Thu 6/13/24		$1,650.00
6	Sand House	4 days?	Wed 6/5/24	Mon 6/10/24	4	$1,200.00
7	Tape Windows	1 day?	Tue 6/11/24	Tue 6/11/24	6	$150.00
8	Lay Drop Cloth	2 days?	Wed 6/12/24	Thu 6/13/24	7	$300.00
9	House Prepped	0 days	Thu 6/13/24	Thu 6/13/24	8	$0.00
10	Paint House	13 days?	Fri 6/14/24	Tue 7/2/24		$7,300.00
11	Apply First Coat	2.5 days?	Fri 6/14/24	Tue 6/18/24	9	$2,750.00
12	Apply Final Coat	2.5 days?	Thu 6/20/24	Mon 6/24/24	11FS+2 days	$2,750.00
13	Remove Window Tape	1 day?	Thu 6/27/24	Thu 6/27/24	12FS+2 days	$150.00
14	Inspect House	1 day?	Fri 6/28/24	Fri 6/28/24	13	$150.00
15	Apply Finishing Touches	2 days?	Mon 7/1/24	Tue 7/2/24	14	$1,500.00
16	House Painted	0 days	Tue 7/2/24	Tue 7/2/24	15	$0.00

Figure 256 – Status Date Indicator

Customize the Timeline View

The **Timeline View** is a customizable summary of the project timeline (*Figure 257* below). When displayed, it's located in a panel beneath the ribbon. As reviewed in Chapter 17, you can customize the Timeline view to include the tasks and milestones that you want to highlight.

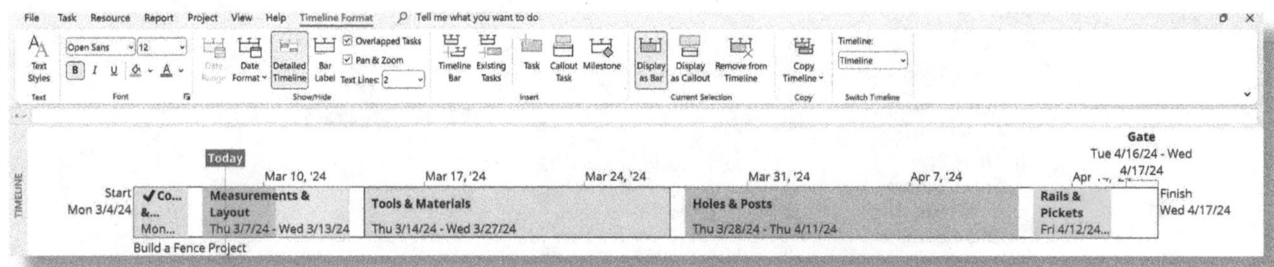

Figure 257 – Customize the Timeline View

To customize the Timeline View:

- Click anywhere in the Timeline view panel to access the **Timeline Tools**.
- In the **Insert** group, select **Existing Tasks** to open the *Add Tasks to Timeline* dialogue box.
- Select the tasks you want to add to the timeline. Then, select **OK**.
- Use the **Timeline Tools** to change the font and color of timeline bars, display Callout tasks and make other customizations. See Chapter 17 for a detailed overview of the Timeline Tool commands, and the customizations you can make.

Customize the Gantt Chart Bars

You can customize the **Gantt chart** by changing the style of the task bars. These small enhancements to the Project interface can make your schedule more engaging for you and for those you share it with.

To customize the Gantt Chart Bars:

- Select the **Format** tab.
- In the **Gantt Chart Style** group, select the bar style you want from the predefined styles (*Figure 258*). You can choose from **Scheduling Styles** or **Presentation Styles**.

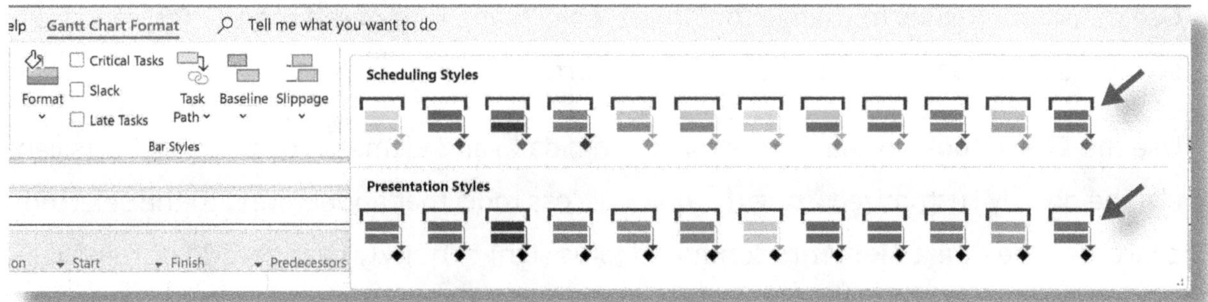

Figure 258 - Customize the Gantt Chart Task Bars

NOTE: If you choose a style from the *Scheduling Styles*, Project will distinguish between Automatic and Manually scheduled tasks. If you select a style from the *Presentation Styles*, these distinctions won't appear.

Customize the Reports

As reviewed in Chapter 17, Project includes a variety of reports that can be used to summarize project information and communicate project status. You can customize the reports to change the data, formatting, and other things.

To Customize a Report:

- To format almost any item on a report, such as a chart or table, select the item. Depending on the item selected, the relevant commands will display on the ribbon, on thecontextual **Design** and **Format** tabs (*Figure 259* below).

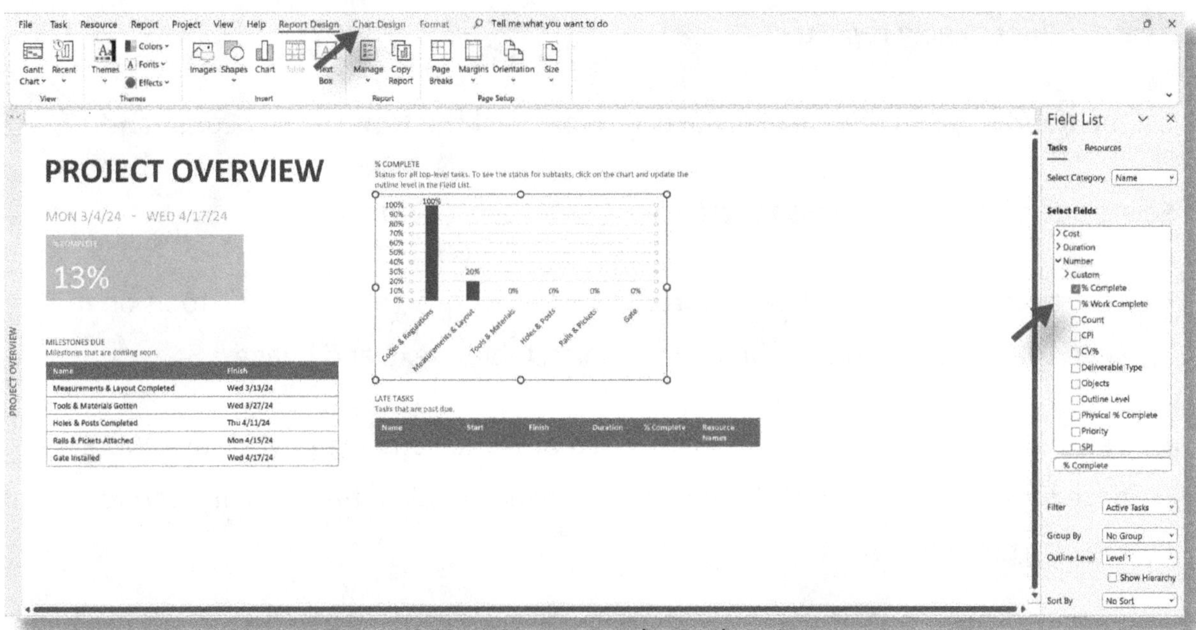

Figure 259 - Customize the Built-In Reports

- Use the **Report Tools** to change the theme, colors, and font of the report. You can also add shapes, charts, tables, and images to the report.
- Use the **Chart Tools** to change the formatting, data, and elements of a chart. Charts can also be quickly customized using the quick access tools that appear next to the selected chart. Use the **Chart Elements** command (plus sign) to quickly change, add or remove chart items such as labels, gridlines, or legends. Use the **Chart Styles** command (paint brush) to change the chart style and color. Use the **Chart Filters** (command funnel) to edit the data points and names that are visible on the report.
- Use the **Table Tools** on the ribbon to change the design and layout of a table.
- Use the **Field List** panel shown on the right to select the fields shown in a chart or table. You can also use the Field List panel to filter, group, and sort information.

NOTE: If the Field List doesn't display, it will have to be manually toggled on. To do this, on the **Table Tools Design** tab, in the **Show/Hide** group, select **Table Data** to toggle the **Field List** panel on or off.

Create a Custom New Report

If you don't find a report you want in the Built-in reports, you can also create your own **custom new report**.

To create a custom new report:

- On the **Report** tab, in the **View Reports** group, select the **New Report** command.
- Select one of the four options for creating a new report *(Figure 260)*:
  - Select **Blank** to create a new report completely from scratch. Use the tools on the *Report Tools Design* Format tab to add charts, tables, text, and images.
  - Select **Chart** to add a chart comparing Actual Work, Remaining Work, and Work as a base for the new report. Use the **Field List** panel to add different fields and to format the chart elements.

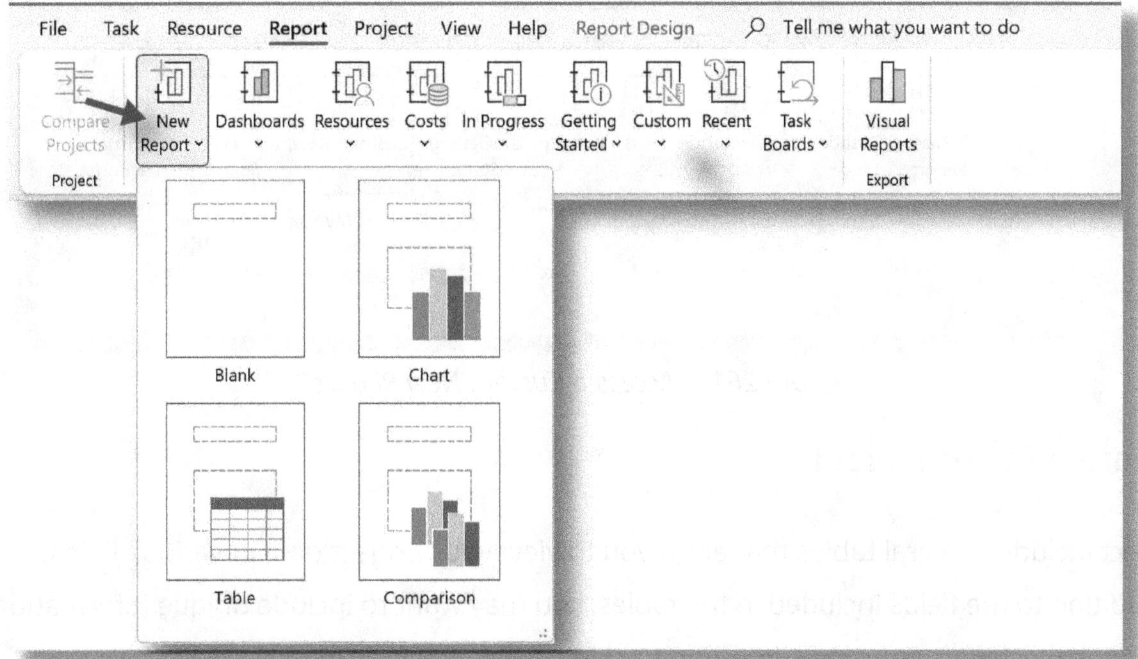

Figure 260 – Create a Custom New Report

- Select **Table** to add a table to the report as a base. Use the **Field List** panel to select the fields you want to display in the table (*Name*, *Start*, *Finish*, and *% Complete* are added by default). Use the **Outline level** box to select the number of levels in the project outline that you want the table to show. Use the *Table Tools* and *Table Tools Layout* tools to customize the look of the table.

- Select **Comparison** to place two charts side-by-side in the new report to compare their data. The charts will contain the same data at first. Select one of the charts and use the **Field List** panel to select the data you want the chart to display. Add the data you want to the second chart to compare the two charts.

- After you select the new report option you want, the *Report Name* dialogue box will open. Enter a name for the report, then select **OK**. Project will generate a base report that you can customize using the various report design tools on the ribbon and the Field List panel options. After your custom new report is created, you can access it using the **Custom Reports** command on the **Report** tab. (*Figure 261*).

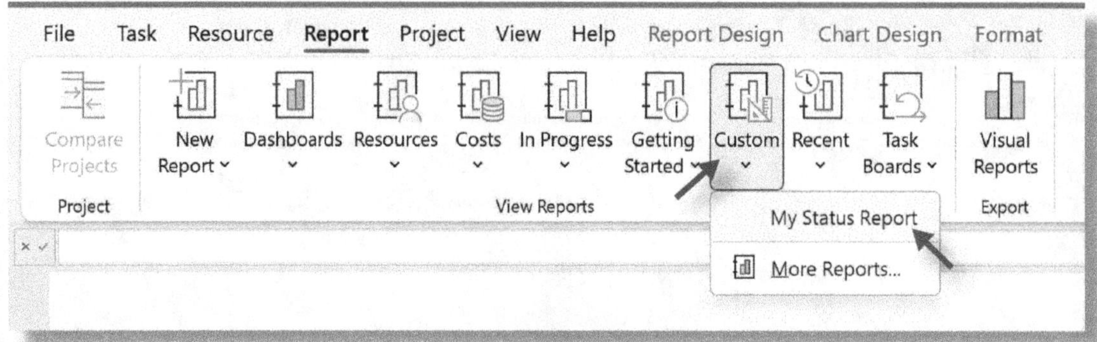

Figure 261 – Access a Custom New Report

Create a Custom Field

Project includes several tables that allow you to view your project data in various fields. In addition to the fields included in the tables, you may want to include unique information in your project plan. For example, when tracking costs, you may want to include resource cost centers next to the tasks they're assigned to. **Custom Fields** are a good way to add additional information to your project plan. Project supports the following nine custom field types: *Cost*, *Date*, *Duration*, *Finish*, *Flag*, *Number*, *Start*, *Text*, and *Outline Code*. You can create up to 30 custom fields for tasks and resources. Most of the custom fields are available for tasks, resources, and assignments. The *Outline Code* field is available for tasks and resources only.

To create a Custom Field:

- Select the **Project** tab. In the **Properties** group, select **Custom Fields** to open the *Custom Fields* dialogue box (*Figure 262*).
- Select **Task** to create a custom field for task-centric views. Select **Resource** to create a custom field for resource-centric views. Select the type of custom field you want to create from the pick-list in the top right corner.
- In the **Field** section, select **Text1** (or the next available custom field), then select **Rename** to name the custom field. The *Rename Field* dialogue box will open.
- In the **New name for** field, enter a name for the custom field, then select **OK**.
- Use the **Import field** option to import a custom field from another open project or from a global master template file. Imported custom fields will include any associated value list, formula, or graphical indicators.

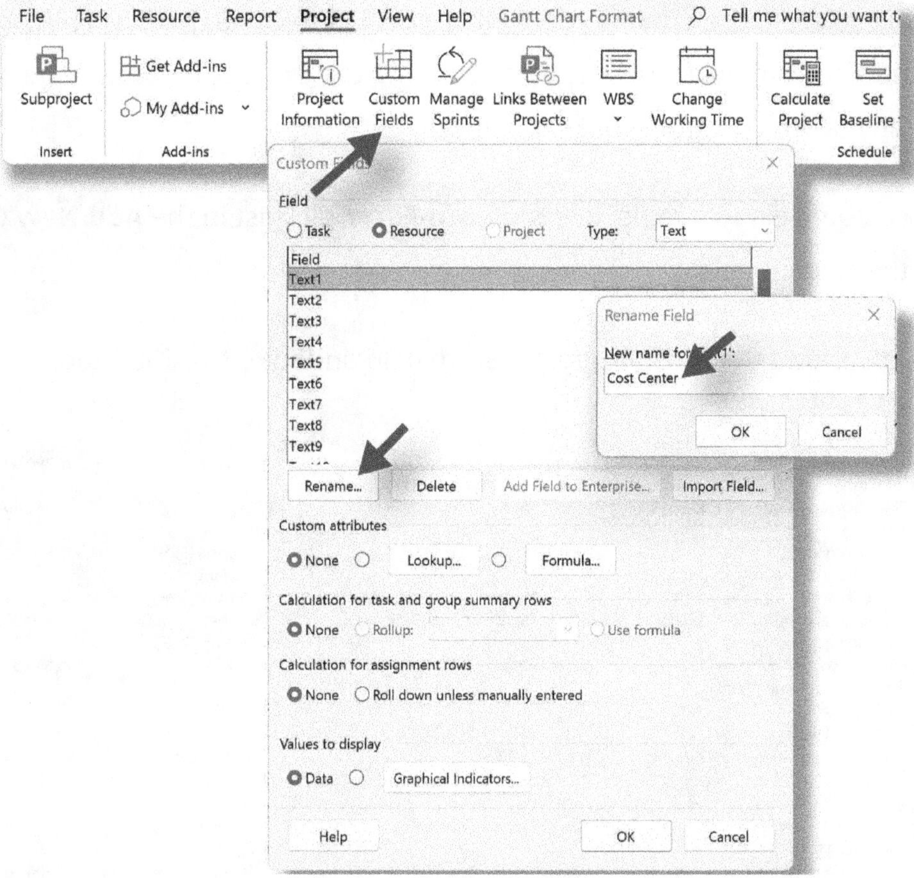

Figure 262 – Custom Fields Dialogue Box

- In the **Custom attributes** section, select **Lookup** to apply a value list for the selected custom field. You'll learn to create a Lookup table later in the chapter. Select **Formula** to apply a formula to calculate the contents of the selected custom field.
- In the **Calculation for tasks and group summary rows** section, select **Roll-up** to specify that the values of the custom field should be rolled up to summary rows. There are several roll-up options to choose from.
- In the **Calculation for assignment rows** section, select **Roll down unless manually entered** if the contents of the custom field are to be distributed across assignments. With this option, the data will be divided among the assignments, unless it's manually entered into an assignment row.
- In the **Values to display** section, select **Data** to display actual data in the field contents. Select **Graphical Indicators** to specify the conditions and related indicators to be displayed in the field instead of data. You'll learn to create Graphical Indicators later in the chapter.

- Once you've selected the options you want, select **OK** to close the *Custom Fields* dialogue box. The new custom field will be included among the existing fields in Project and can be added to any table.

- To add a custom field to a table, use the **Auto-Filter** pick-list in the **Add New Column** field to locate the custom field.

Figure 263 below shows the "Cost Center" custom field added to the Entry table.

	Task Mode	Task Name	Duration	Start	Finish	Predecesso	Resource Names	Cost	Cost Center
0		**Training Rollout Initiative and Plan**	**195 days**	**Mon 1/25/16**	**Fri 10/21/16**		**Budget**	**$88,290.00**	
1		**TRIP - Stage 1 - Project Planning**	**31 days**	**Mon 1/25/16**	**Mon 3/7/16**			**$65,020.00**	
2		Define project objectives and describe mission statement	4 days	Mon 1/25/16	Thu 1/28/16		Sponsor[50%], Training Director[50%]	$15,600.00	199191.01; 199000.01
3		Ensure total participation by training team support	2 days	Mon 1/25/16	Tue 1/26/16		Training Director[25%]	$300.00	199000.01
4		**Identify Departments or End-User Community to be Trained**	**13 days**	**Wed 1/27/16**	**Fri 2/12/16**			**$5,550.00**	
5		Create list of target depart	1 day	Tue 2/9/16	Tue 2/9/16	2	In-House Instructor	$360.00	199000.02
6		Perform departmental trai	7 days	Wed 1/27/16	Thu 2/4/16	3	In-House Instructor	$2,520.00	199000.02
7		Compile results and present findings to	2 days	Fri 2/5/16	Mon 2/8/16	6FS-4 days	In-House Instructor	$720.00	199000.02
8		Prioritize training delivery according to critical need	4 days	Tue 2/9/16	Fri 2/12/16	7	Training Director[25%]	$600.00	199000.0
9		Inform department heads	2 days	Wed 2/10/16	Thu 2/11/16	5	Training Director[25	$300.00	199000.0
10		Determine if training can	3 days	Wed 2/10/16	Fri 2/12/16	5	Training	$1,050.00	199000.0

Figure 263 – Add Custom Fields to the View

NOTE: You'll want to be sure not to use custom fields to enter data that Project also uses to calculate the schedule — namely task durations, predecessors, start and finish dates or resource names. When entering these values, use the default fields already provided in the selected tables, as custom fields have no impact on the schedule.

Rename an Existing Field

You can also rename an existing field, if it already includes the type of data you want to display.

To Rename a Field:

- Right-click the column header for the field that you want to rename. Then, select **Field Settings** to open the *Field Settings* dialogue box.

- Enter the new name in the **Title** field. Select the alignment options you want. Then, select **OK**.

NOTE: If you're a Project Online subscriber, select **Rename** from the column header pick-list. Type the new name, then press **Enter**.

Create a Lookup Table

While managing your project, you may want to monitor certain conditions that affect your project, such as schedule risk. Perhaps, you're unsure if the resources will make their target dates and you'd like them to assign a risk rating to their assigned task. Adding a **Lookup Table** can be useful in this case. Lookup tables can be added to custom fields to apply a value list to the field. For example, if you've created the "Schedule Risk" custom field, you could use a Lookup table to add a risk rating list to the field (E.g., Low, Medium, High).

To add a Lookup Table to a Custom Field:

- Select the **Project** tab. In the **Properties** group, select **Custom Fields** to open the *Custom Fields* dialogue box.
- In the **Field** window, select the custom field you want to add the Lookup table to.
- In the **Custom attributes** section, select **Lookup** to open the *Edit Lookup Table* dialogue box (*Figure 264*).

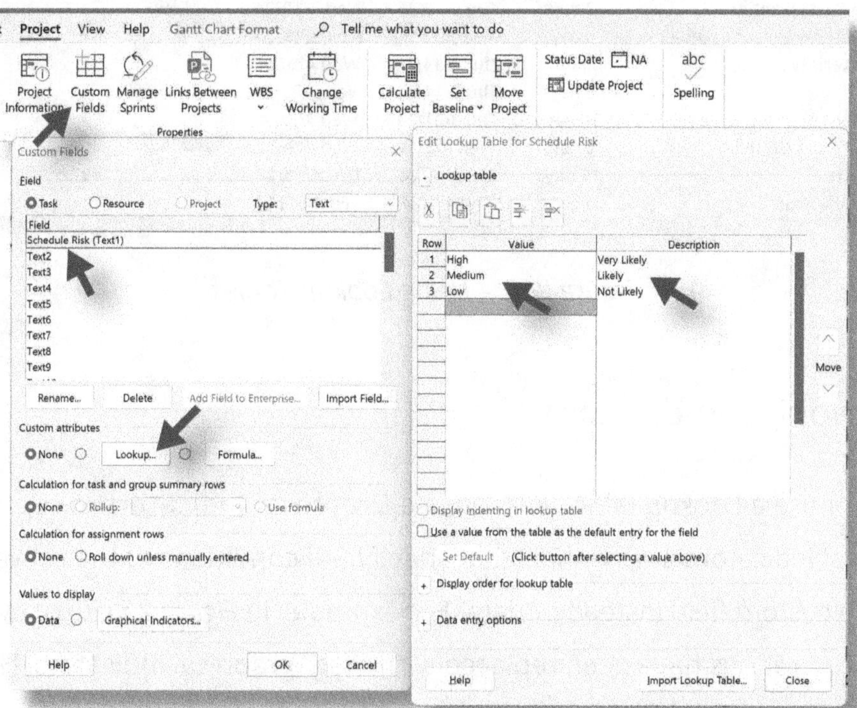

Figure 264 – Create a Lookup Table

- In the first row of the **Value** field, enter the first value you want for the table. Then, enter its **Description** in the adjacent field. In the **Value** field, add the next value and its description in the next row. Repeat for as many values you would like the value list to include, then select **Close** to close the *Edit Lookup Table* dialogue box.

- Select **OK** to close the *Custom Fields* dialogue box. The custom field with the new Lookup table will now be included among the existing fields in Project.

- Use the **Auto-Filter** pick-list in the **Add New Column** field to add the custom field with the Lookup table to the current view.

- You can now select values for specific tasks from the Lookup table in the custom field (*Figure 265* below).

	Task Name	Duration	Start	Finish	Schedule Risk	Predecessors	Resource Names
0	**Look Up Table_Build a Fence**	**38 days?**	**Mon 3/4/24**	**Wed 4/24/24**			
1	**Codes & Regulations**	**3 days**	**Mon 3/4/24**	**Wed 3/6/24**			
2	Check Building Codes	1 day	Mon 3/4/24	Mon 3/4/24	Low		Jack
3	Check & Mark Property Lines	2 days	Tue 3/5/24	Wed 3/6/24	Low	2	Jill
4	Codes & Regulations Checked	0 days	Wed 3/6/24	Wed 3/6/24		3	
5	**Measurements & Layout**	**5 days**	**Thu 3/7/24**	**Wed 3/13/24**		**1**	
6	Measure Fence	1 day	Thu 3/7/24	Thu 3/7/24	Low		Jack
7	Determine Panel Quantity	2 days	Fri 3/8/24	Mon 3/11/24	Low	6	Jack
8	Determine Post Quantity	2 days	Tue 3/12/24	Wed 3/13/24	Low	7	Jack
9	Measurements & Layout Completed	0 days	Wed 3/13/24	Wed 3/13/24		8	
10	**Tools & Materials**	**15 days**	**Thu 3/14/24**	**Wed 4/3/24**		**5**	
11	Get Tools	5 days	Thu 3/14/24	Wed 3/20/24	Medium		Tom
12	Get Materials	10 days	Thu 3/21/24	Wed 4/3/24	High	11	Jerry
13	Tools & Materials Gotten	0 days	Wed 4/3/24	Wed 4/3/24			
14	**Holes & Posts**	**11 days**	**Thu 4/4/24**	**Thu 4/18/24**		**10**	
15	Position Fence Posts	2 days	Thu 4/4/24	Fri 4/5/24			Jill

Figure 265 – Using Lookup Tables

Create a Graphical Indicator

To further customize a Lookup table, you can use **Graphical Indicators** to represent the list values. Graphical Indicators are symbols that specify the conditions of the list values and are displayed in the custom field instead of data. For example, in *Figure 266*, the Low, Medium, and High schedule risk ratings have been replaced with "flag" graphical indicators. Hovering over the indicator will display the conditions for the corresponding text value.

	Task Name	Duration	Start	Finish	Schedule Risk	Predecessors	Resource Names
0	**Look Up Table_Build a Fence**	**38 days?**	**Mon 3/4/24**	**Wed 4/24/24**			
1	**Codes & Regulations**	**3 days**	**Mon 3/4/24**	**Wed 3/6/24**			
2	Check Building Codes	1 day	Mon 3/4/24	Mon 3/4/24			Jack
3	Check & Mark Property Lines	2 days	Tue 3/5/24	Wed 3/6/24		2	Jill
4	Codes & Regulations Checked	0 days	Wed 3/6/24	Wed 3/6/24		3	
5	**Measurements & Layout**	**5 days**	**Thu 3/7/24**	**Wed 3/13/24**		**1**	
6	Measure Fence	1 day	Thu 3/7/24	Thu 3/7/24			Jack
7	Determine Panel Quantity	2 days	Fri 3/8/24	Mon 3/11/24		6	Jack
8	Determine Post Quantity	2 days	Tue 3/12/24	Wed 3/13/24		7	Jack
9	Measurements & Layout Completed	0 days	Wed 3/13/24	Wed 3/13/24		8	
10	**Tools & Materials**	**15 days**	**Thu 3/14/24**	**Wed 4/3/24**		**5**	
11	Get Tools	5 days	Thu 3/14/24	Wed 3/20/24			Tom
12	Get Materials	10 days	Thu 3/21/24	Wed 4/3/24		11	Jerry
13	Tools & Materials Gotten	0 days	Wed 4/3/24	Wed 4/3/24		12	

Figure 266 – Using Graphical Indicators in a Lookup Table

To Create a Graphical Indicator:

1. Select the **Project** tab. In the **Properties** group, select **Custom Fields** to open the *Custom Fields* dialogue box.

2. In the **Field window**, select the custom field you want to add the Graphical Indicators to.

3. In the **Values to display** section, select **Graphical Indicators** to open the *Graphical Indicators* dialogue box (*Figure 267 below*).

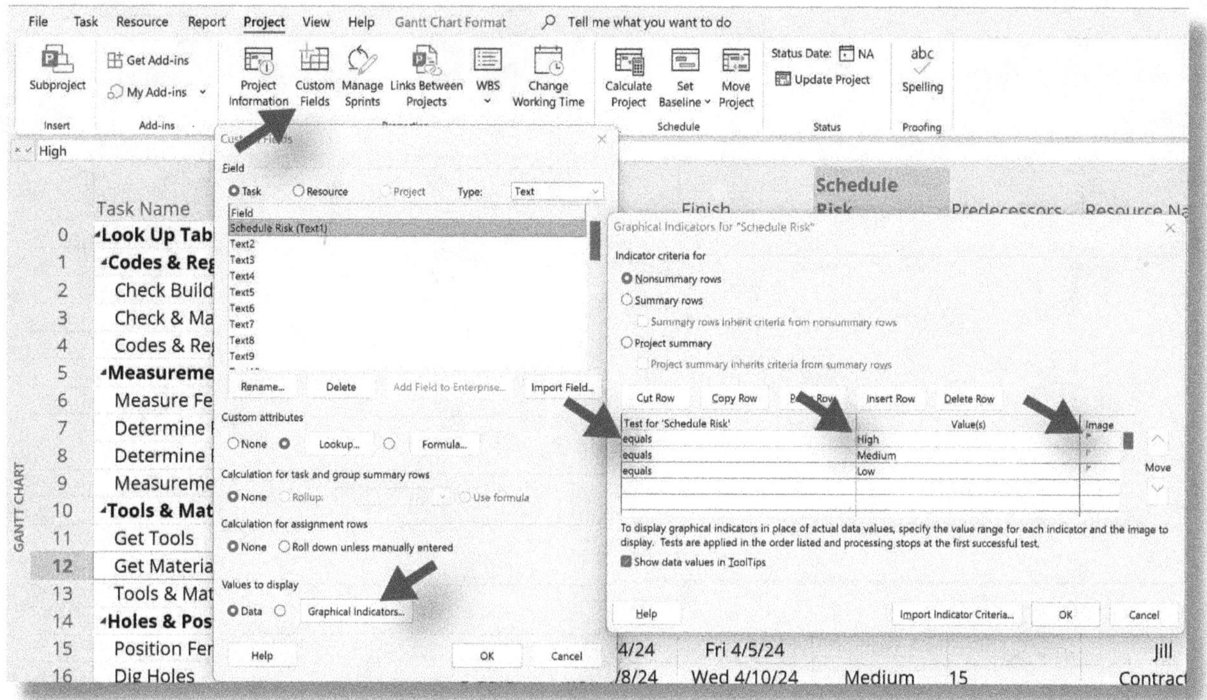

Figure 267 – Graphical Indicators Dialogue Box

4. In the **Test for** field, select **equals** from the pick-list.

5. In the adjacent **Value(s)** field, select the value you want from the pick-list.

6. In the adjacent **Image** field, select the graphical indicator that you want to indicate the value.

7. Repeat steps 4, 5 & 6 for each list value in the Lookup Table, then select **OK**.

You've now learned 10 useful customizations to make the Project fit your personal preferences, enhance your schedule, and help you work more efficiently.

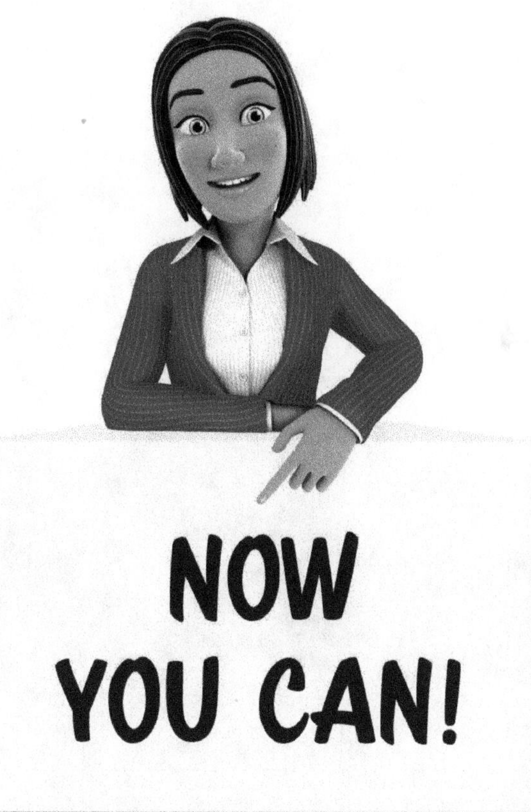

- ✓ Customize the Quick Access Commands
- ✓ Customize the Ribbon
- ✓ Create a Status Date Indicator
- ✓ Customize the Timeline View
- ✓ Customize the Gantt Chart Bars
- ✓ Customize the Reports
- ✓ Create a New Report
- ✓ Create a Custom Field
- ✓ Create a Look-up Table
- ✓ Create a Graphical Indicator

Chapter 21 25 FAQs

In the last chapter, we reviewed 10 useful customizations to make Microsoft Project fit your personal preferences. In this chapter, we'll answer **25 frequently asked questions** about Project and Project for the Web.

In This Chapter:

- 25 Frequently Asked Questions about **Microsoft Project** and **Project for the Web**

25 Frequently Asked Questions about Project and Project for the Web

1 - What Does Microsoft Project Do?

Microsoft Project helps you build, manage and track project schedules. With its powerful scheduling engine, Project generates all the scheduling details you need to manage a successful project. You input project data such as the project start date, task outline, task relationships and durations, and Project calculates your schedule! The more information you provide Project, the more information Project provides you. For example, if you assign resources and include their pay rates, Project will also calculate your total project cost. Project does many other things, like create status reports, such as the Earned Value report. It's the premier scheduling solution across many industries and has benefited from years of user feedback and continuous improvement. **See Chapter 7** for an overview of **B.A.S.I.C.S.**, our 6-step process for building a schedule.

2 - What Can Project Do That Excel Can't?

Microsoft Project builds schedules, calculates project cost, and creates active status reports. It can perform advanced functions like automatically reschedule resources that are over-extended and calculate the Critical Path, so that you can manage your projects with more intelligence. In short, Microsoft Project helps you build a schedule based on task durations and task dependencies. Excel can't do any of these things. **See Chapter 1** for more information.

3 - How Do You Read a Microsoft Project Timeline?

The best way to read a timeline is to zoom in to see the entire timeline. You can do this using the **Entire Project** command (*Figure 268* below). This feature updates the view so that all the Gantt chart bars are visible on the screen.

- On the **View** tab, in **Zoom** group, select **Entire Project**.

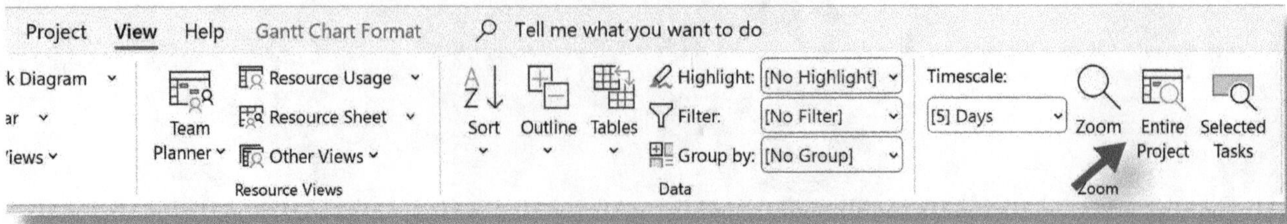

Figure 268 – The Entire Project Command

Figure 269 below shows a schedule for a *New Business* plan, built in Microsoft Project.

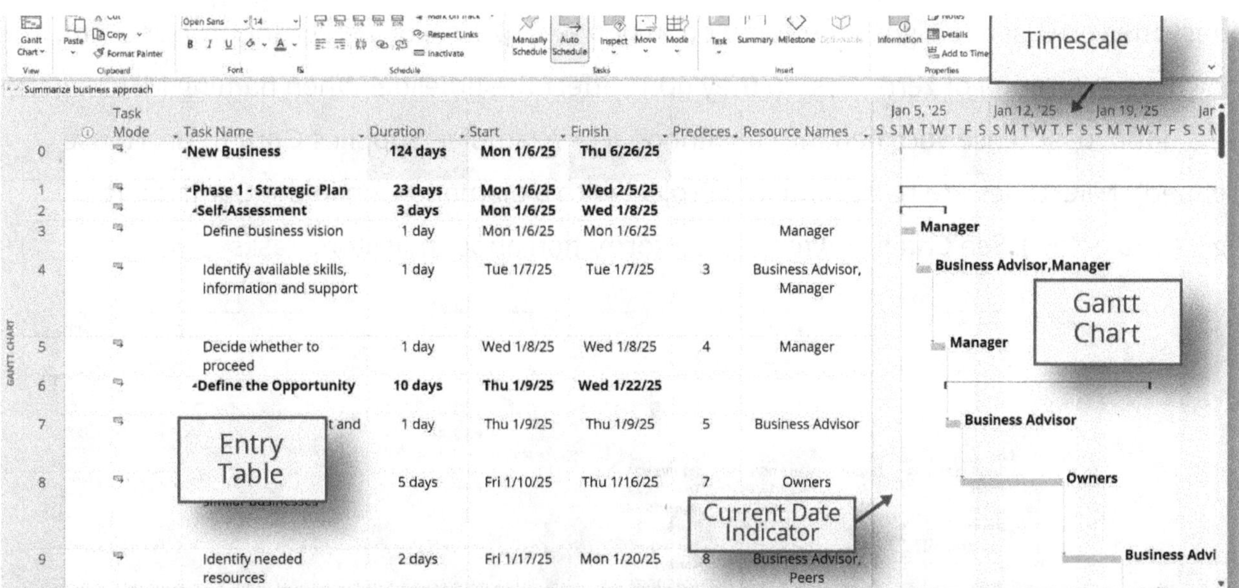

Figure 269 – New Business Project Plan

The area on the left is called the **Entry Table**. It's like an Excel spreadsheet, and it's where you build your schedule. It includes task names, their durations, start and finish dates, predecessors and the resources assigned to them. The graphical chart on the right is called the **Gantt Chart**. It depicts your task durations, start and finish dates and task dependencies. The vertical, green gridline indicates the current date. The gray panel above the Gantt chart is called the **Timescale**. A well-constructed timeline will also include the Project Summary Task (task ID zero). It summarizes the entire project and its duration is the duration of the entire project. In *Figure 269*, the **Project Summary Task** informs us that the project duration is 124 days and it's scheduled to finish on 6/26/25. See **Chapter 2** for more information.

4 - Can I use the newest version of Microsoft Project like I Used the Prior Versions?

Project 2010, 2013, 2016, 2019 and forward include a feature called user-controlled scheduling. This feature allows users to build a schedule in the Automatic or Manual scheduling mode. By default, the program starts in the Manual scheduling mode. To build a schedule the way you did in versions prior to Project 2010, you'll need to work in the Automatic scheduling mode. See the **Chapter 5** for more information.

5 - What is a Milestone?

Milestones are used to signify the completion of a task, phase, or significant project event. They have a duration of zero days, so they don't affect the timeline. When naming Milestones, use a noun, past-tense verb naming convention. For example, "Supplies Gotten" or "House Prepped". Milestones are represented in Project with a diamond icon in the Gantt chart (*Figure 270* below). See **Chapter 4** for more information about milestone tasks.

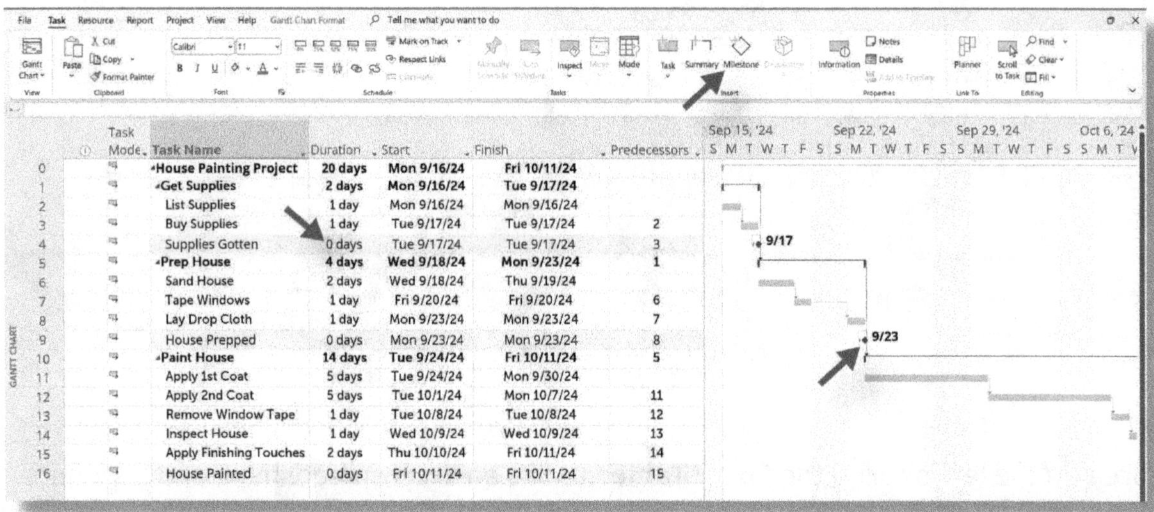

	Task Name	Duration	Start	Finish	Predecessors
0	**House Painting Project**	**20 days**	**Mon 9/16/24**	**Fri 10/11/24**	
1	**Get Supplies**	**2 days**	**Mon 9/16/24**	**Tue 9/17/24**	
2	List Supplies	1 day	Mon 9/16/24	Mon 9/16/24	
3	Buy Supplies	1 day	Tue 9/17/24	Tue 9/17/24	2
4	Supplies Gotten	0 days	Tue 9/17/24	Tue 9/17/24	3
5	**Prep House**	**4 days**	**Wed 9/18/24**	**Mon 9/23/24**	1
6	Sand House	2 days	Wed 9/18/24	Thu 9/19/24	
7	Tape Windows	1 day	Fri 9/20/24	Fri 9/20/24	6
8	Lay Drop Cloth	1 day	Mon 9/23/24	Mon 9/23/24	7
9	House Prepped	0 days	Mon 9/23/24	Mon 9/23/24	8
10	**Paint House**	**14 days**	**Tue 9/24/24**	**Fri 10/11/24**	5
11	Apply 1st Coat	5 days	Tue 9/24/24	Mon 9/30/24	
12	Apply 2nd Coat	5 days	Tue 10/1/24	Mon 10/7/24	11
13	Remove Window Tape	1 day	Tue 10/8/24	Tue 10/8/24	12
14	Inspect House	1 day	Wed 10/9/24	Wed 10/9/24	13
15	Apply Finishing Touches	2 days	Thu 10/10/24	Fri 10/11/24	14
16	House Painted	0 days	Fri 10/11/24	Fri 10/11/24	15

Figure 270 – Milestone Tasks

6 - What are Those Red Men?

This is a powerful feature in Microsoft Project. The "Red Man" icon in the **Indicators** field (*Figure 271* below) alerts you of an over-allocated resource. This means that a resource assigned to the task has exceeded their Maximum Units, which is the maximum number of hours a resource is available to work on any given day. See **Chapter 13** for more information.

	Task Mode	Task Name	Duration	Start	Finish	Predecessors
0		**Commercial Construction**	**344 days**	**Mon 3/11/24**	**Thu 7/3/25**	
1		**General Conditions**	**17 days**	**Mon 3/11/24**	**Tue 4/2/24**	
2		Receive notice to proceed and sign contract	3 days	Mon 3/11/24	Wed 3/13/24	
3		Submit bond and insurance documents	2 days	Thu 3/14/24	Fri 3/15/24	2
4		Prepare and submit project schedule	2 days	Mon 3/18/24	Tue 3/19/24	3
5		Prepare and submit schedule of values	2 days	Wed 3/20/24	Thu 3/21/24	4
6		Obtain building permits	4 days	Thu 3/14/24	Tue 3/19/24	2
7		Submit preliminary shop drawings	2 wks	Wed 3/20/24	Tue 4/2/24	6
8		Submit monthly requests for payment	1 day	Thu 3/14/24	Thu 3/14/24	2

Figure 271 – Over-Allocated Resource Indicator

7 - How Do I Get Rid of Those Question Marks?

The question marks in the Duration field, next to the duration values, indicate that the task duration is estimated. If you don't prefer the question marks, you can remove them.

To remove the question marks:

- Select the **File** tab. Then, select **Options** to open the *Project Options* dialogue box.
- Select **Schedule** from the options on the left.
- In the **Scheduling options for this project** section, uncheck the **show that scheduled tasks have estimated durations** checkbox. This will remove the question marks for the currently scheduled tasks (*Figure 272* below).
- Uncheck the **New scheduled tasks have estimated durations** checkbox. This will remove the question marks for new tasks added to the schedule.
- Select **OK** to close the *Project Options* dialogue box.

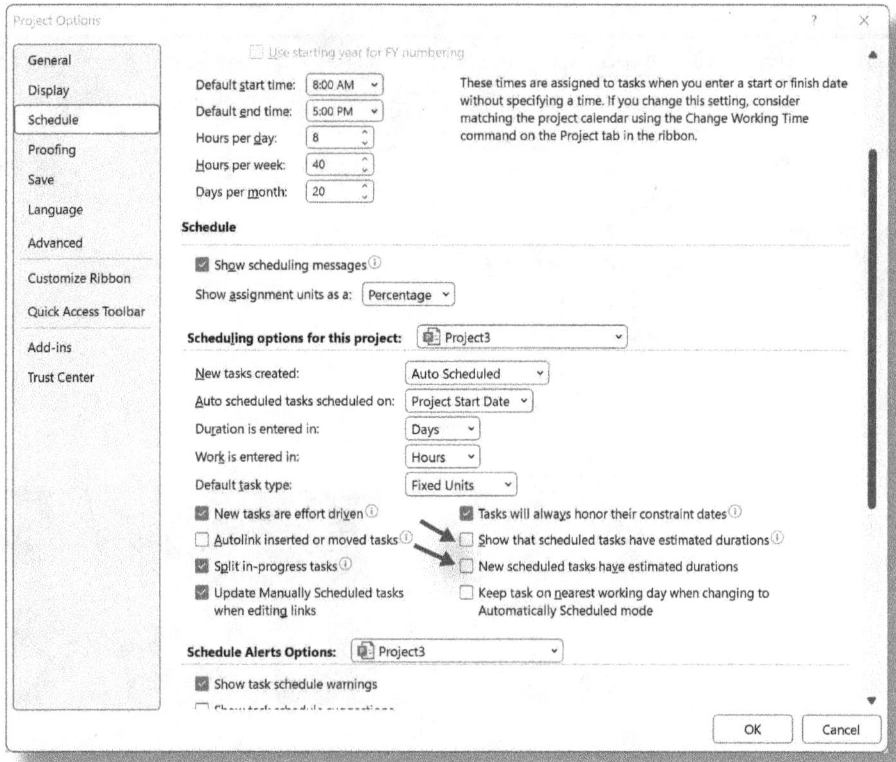

Figure 272 – Remove Estimated Duration Indicators

8 - Should I Enter Start and Finish Dates?

No. Project is designed to calculate start and finish dates after you enter task dependencies and task durations. Manually entering start and finish dates in the Automatic scheduling mode causes Project to apply a *Start No Earlier Than* or *Finish No Earlier Than* scheduling constraint to the task. This limits scheduling flexibility because Project automatically begins each task as soon as possible. If you do want a task constraint in your schedule, you should use the constraint feature. See **Chapter 12** for more information.

9 - How Do I Set the Project Start Date?

To set the Project Start Date:

- Select the **Project** tab. In the **Properties** group, select **Project Information** to open the *Project Information* dialogue box (*Figure 273* below).
- Enter the date in the **Start date** field, or select it from the calendar.
- Select **OK** to close the *Project Information* dialogue box. See **Chapter 7** for more information.

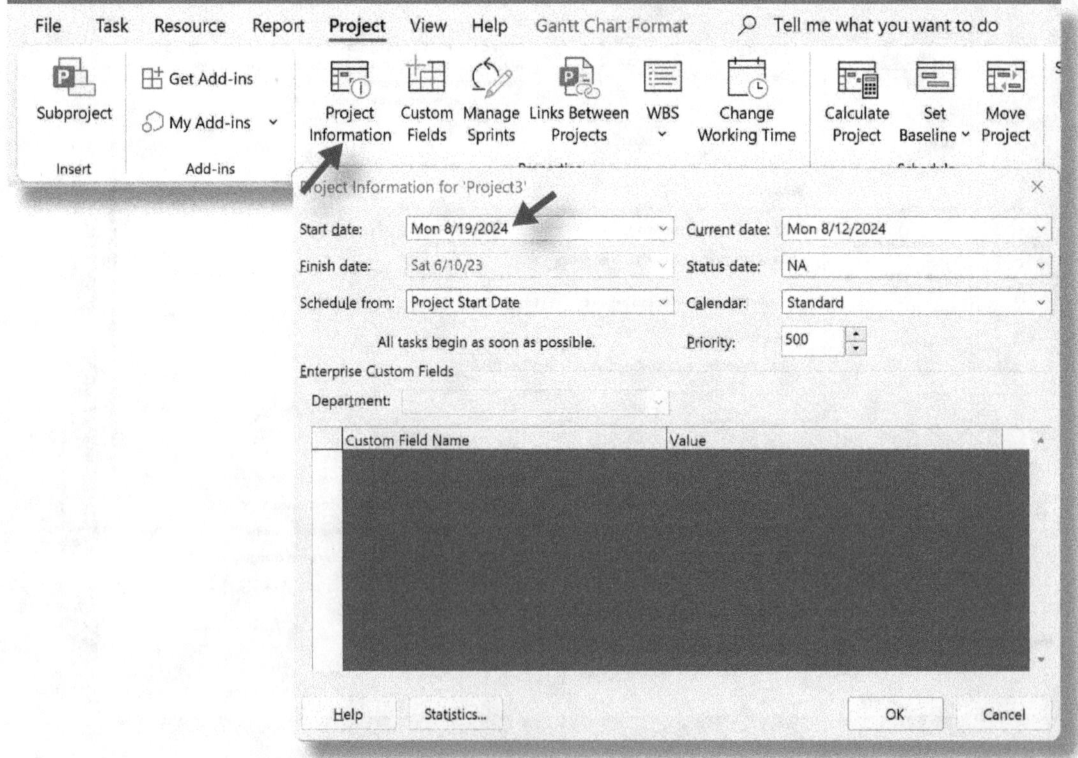

Figure 273 – Set the Project Start Date

10 - Why Do I Get a Constraint Indicator When I Enter a Date?

In the Automatic scheduling mode, entering start or finish dates for tasks creates a *Start No Earlier Than* or *Finish No Earlier Than* constraint respectively. Avoid manually typing in dates unless you want to create either of these constraints. Project is designed to calculate start and finish dates from the task relationships you define in the Predecessors field. See **Chapter 12** for more information.

11 - How Do I Get Rid of a Constraint?

To remove a Constraint:

- Double-click the task name to open the *Task Information* dialogue box (*Figure 274* below).
- Select the **Advanced** tab.
- In the **Constraint type** field, select the default **As Soon As Possible** constraint type.
- Select **OK** to close the *Task Information* dialogue box. See **Chapter 12** for more information.

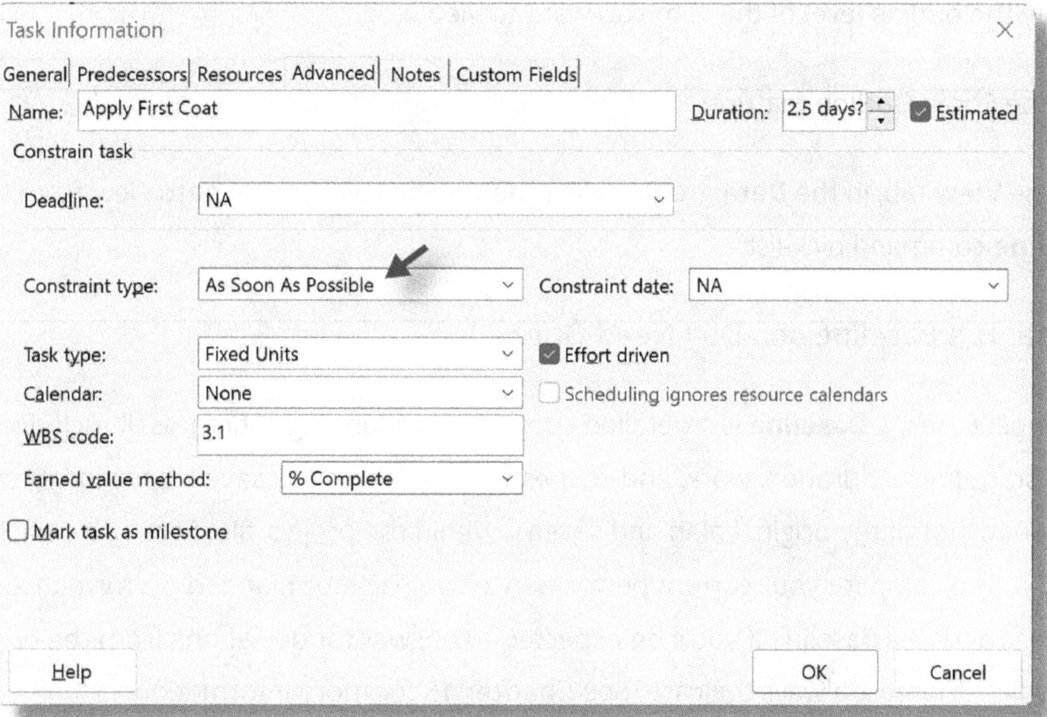

Figure 274 – Remove a Constraint

12 - How Can I Fix My Project Outline?

Use the **Outdent Task** and **Indent Task** commands to outline your schedule. They are located on the **Task** tab, in the **Schedule** group (*Figure 275* below). Promote tasks to create Summary tasks and demote tasks to create subtasks.

TIP: To minimize problems with your outline, enter your entire task list first. Structure the project outline after all the tasks have been entered. This will lead to less re-work. See **Chapter 4** for more information.

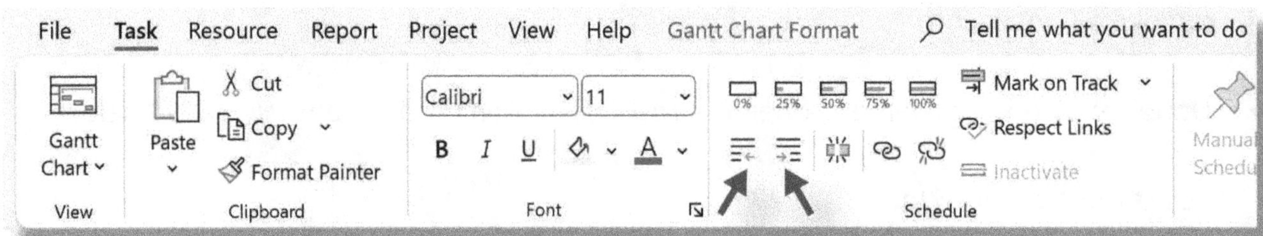

Figure 275 – Structure the Tasks

A handy way to check the outline is to use the **Show Outline** feature. This feature allows you to specify the outline level of the plan you want to view.

To use the Show Outline feature:

- On the **View** tab, in the **Data** group, select the outline level you want to view from the **Outline** command pick-list.

13 - What is a Baseline and Do I Need One?

Yes, in most cases. A **Baseline** is a detailed copy of your planning estimates. It includes the original start, finish, duration, work, and cost estimates. When you save a baseline, Project takes a snapshot of the original plan and saves it within the project file. Setting a Baseline enables you to compare your current performance against your planned performance. It's a good idea to have a baseline if you'll be expected to answer for deviations from the original plan – which is almost always the case. See **Chapter 15** for more information.

To set a Baseline:

- Select the **Project** tab. In the **Schedule** group, select **Set Baseline**, then select **Set Baseline** again to open the *Set Baseline* dialogue box (*Figure 276* below).

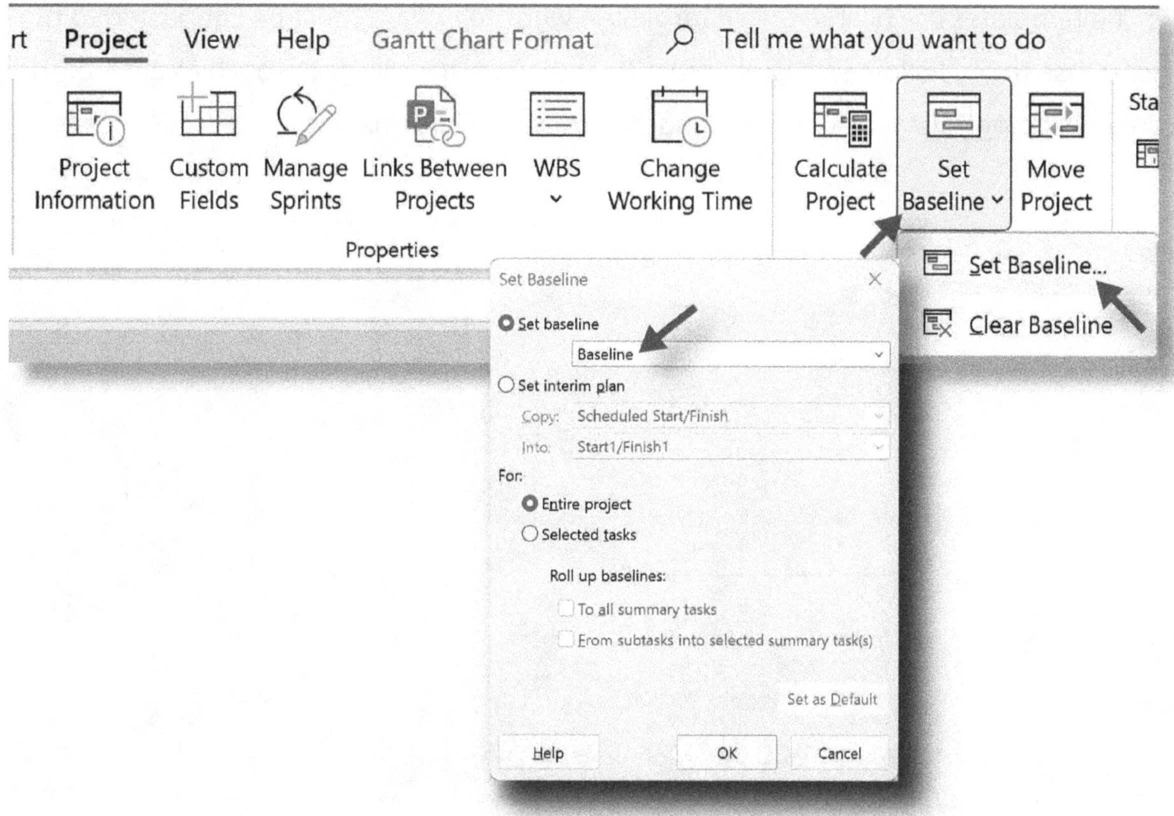

Figure 276 – Set a Baseline

- Be sure the **Set Baseline** option selected. Then, select the baseline you're saving (0 through 10) from the **Set Baseline** pick-list.
- In the **For** section, select **Entire project** to baseline the entire project or select **Selected tasks** to baseline selected tasks.
- Select **OK** to close the *Set Baseline* dialogue box.

14 - How Can I Use the Templates to Get Started Quickly?

The opening view in Project is filled with starter templates for typical business and personal projects (*Figure 277* below).

NOTE: The templates are hosted on a companion website, so you must be connected to the Internet to use them. Follow each step in the B.A.S.I.C.S. scheduling approach to get a quick start on developing your timeline. See Chapter 7 for more information.

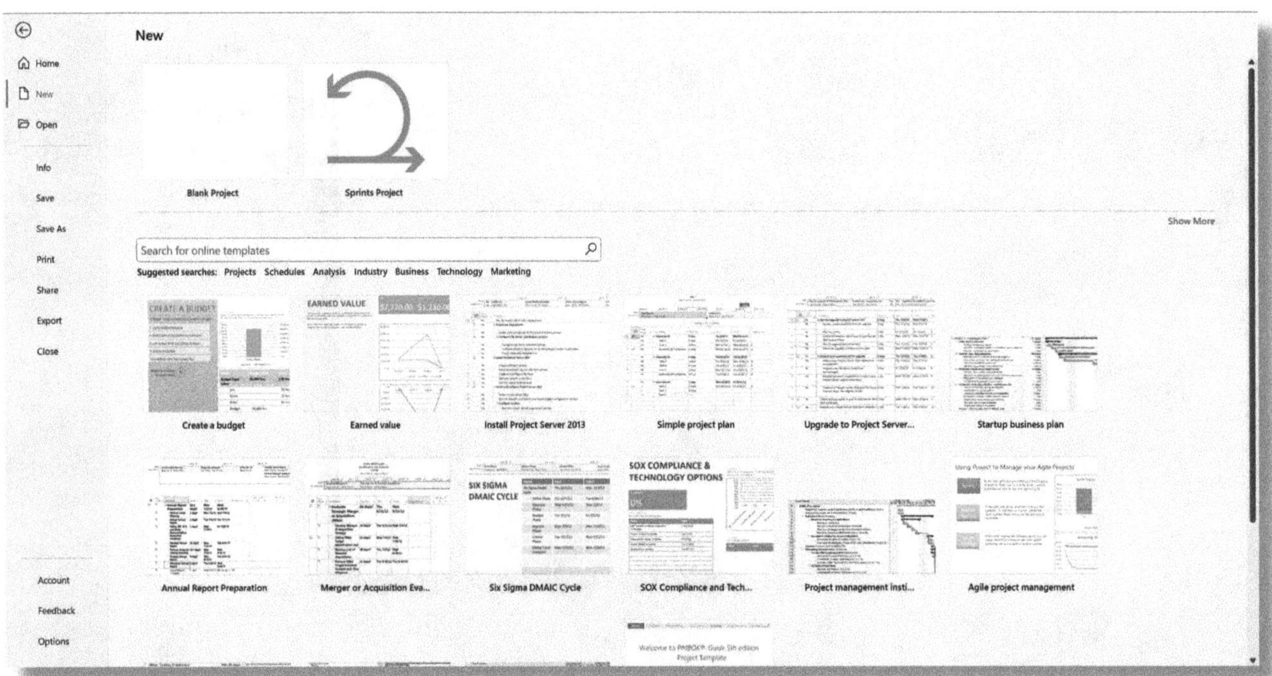

Figure 277 – Project Plan Starter Templates

15 - What is the First Thing I Should Do to Build a Schedule?

The first step is to **Break Down the Project**. That's what the **B** represents in the B.A.S.I.C.S. scheduling process. To perform this step, gather your team (or yourself!), conduct a brainstorming session, use Top-down and Bottom-up planning and create a Work Breakdown Structure. Be sure to follow the 100% Rule and the Exclusivity Rule. See **Chapter 3** for more information.

16 - What is Task Mode

Think of **Task Mode** as the scheduling mode. It determines how Project schedules tasks as you build your schedule. There are two Task Modes (scheduling modes) available in Project — the **Manual** scheduling mode and the **Automatic** scheduling mode. By default, Project schedules new tasks in the Manual scheduling mode. The task mode you choose determines how much control you have over the way tasks are scheduled. In the Manual mode, you can define the task names, start dates, finish dates, and duration values as you like. In the Automatic mode Project automatically calculates start and finish dates based on dependencies, constraints, calendars, and other factors. The ability to toggle between the Manual and Automatic scheduling mode is called **user-controlled scheduling**. The icon in the Task Mode field indicates the task mode you're in. The pushpin icon represents the Manual mode. The task bar icon represents the Automatic mode. See **Chapter 5** for more information.

17 - What Does "New Tasks: Manually Scheduled" Mean?

The *New Tasks: Manually Scheduled* notification on the **Status Bar** means that any new task you create will be **Manually scheduled** and not Automatically scheduled. In the Manual scheduling mode, users have the option of scheduling tasks manually. The scheduling engine is still engaged, but users are less restricted. For example, text entries are allowed in numeric fields like the Duration field. In this mode, you can enter scheduling details as they become available. Some users may find this mode helpful, as it allows a place for rough estimates when planning details are vague. In the Automatic scheduling mode, the scheduling rules are strictly enforced. If you violate them,
you will either get a warning or be switched over to the Manual mode, where such violations are allowed. If you'd like to switch to the Automatic mode, select the "Auto Scheduled" option from the Status Bar pick-list. See **Chapter 5** for more information.

18 - Where Do I Enter Resource Names?

You can enter resource names directly into the **Resource Names** field in the Gantt Chart view. This method works fine if all the resources are "Work" resources and all you're interested in is who's assigned to which task. However, the best place to enter resource names, and other resource information is in the Resource Sheet View (*Figure 278*). See **Chapter 8** for more information.

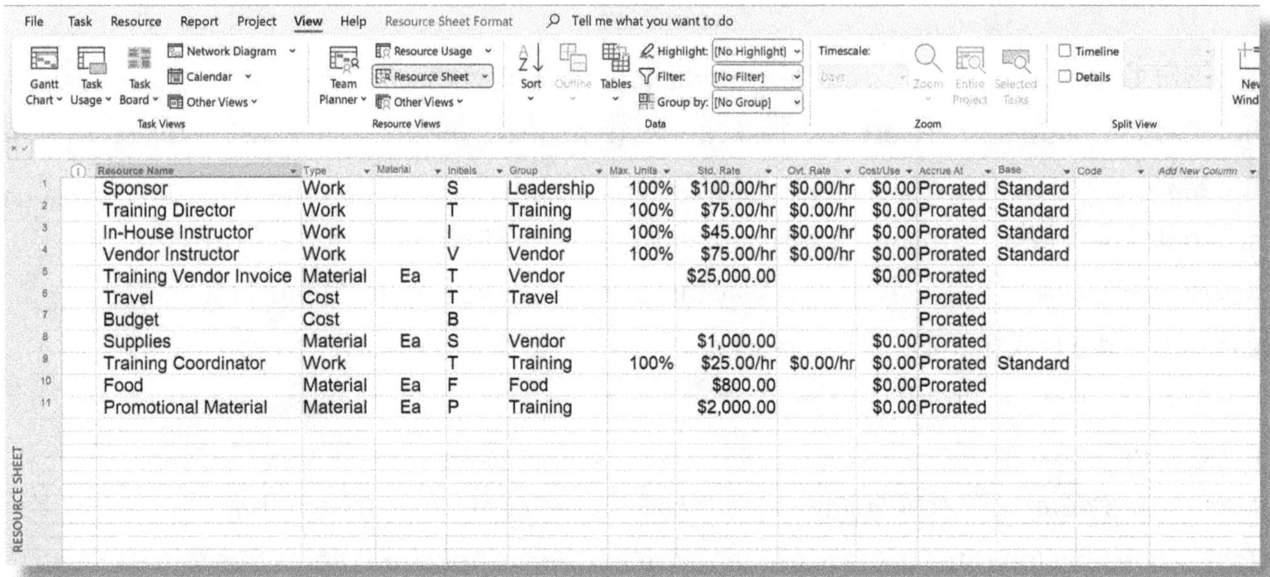

	Resource Name	Type	Material	Initials	Group	Max. Units	Std. Rate	Ovt. Rate	Cost/Use	Accrue At	Base	Code
1	Sponsor	Work		S	Leadership	100%	$100.00/hr	$0.00/hr	$0.00	Prorated	Standard	
2	Training Director	Work		T	Training	100%	$75.00/hr	$0.00/hr	$0.00	Prorated	Standard	
3	In-House Instructor	Work		I	Training	100%	$45.00/hr	$0.00/hr	$0.00	Prorated	Standard	
4	Vendor Instructor	Work		V	Vendor	100%	$75.00/hr	$0.00/hr	$0.00	Prorated	Standard	
5	Training Vendor Invoice	Material	Ea	T	Vendor		$25,000.00		$0.00	Prorated		
6	Travel	Cost		T	Travel					Prorated		
7	Budget	Cost		B						Prorated		
8	Supplies	Material	Ea	S	Vendor		$1,000.00		$0.00	Prorated		
9	Training Coordinator	Work		T	Training	100%	$25.00/hr	$0.00/hr	$0.00	Prorated	Standard	
10	Food	Material	Ea	F	Food		$800.00		$0.00	Prorated		
11	Promotional Material	Material	Ea	P	Training		$2,000.00		$0.00	Prorated		

Figure 278 – The Resource Sheet View

To create Resources in the Resource Sheet View:

- Select the **View** tab. In the **Resource Views** group, select **Resource Sheet**.
- Enter resource names, pay rates and other information into the fields of the table.

19 - What Goes in the Predecessors Field?

The **Predecessors** field is where you define task relationships. A predecessor is a task that drives another task. In the Predecessors field for a given task, enter the task ID number(s) of its predecessor(s). You can also enter task relationship types, Leads and Lags in this field (*Figure 279*). See **Chapter 4** for more information.

	ⓘ	Task Mode	Task Name	Duration	Start	Finish	Predecessors
0			**Build a Fence Project**	**33 days?**	**Mon 3/4/24**	**Wed 4/17/24**	
1			**Codes & Regulations**	**3 days**	**Mon 3/4/24**	**Wed 3/6/24**	
2			Check Building Codes	1 day	Mon 3/4/24	Mon 3/4/24	
3			Check & Mark Property Lines	2 days	Tue 3/5/24	Wed 3/6/24	2
4			Codes & Regulations Checked	0 days	Wed 3/6/24	Wed 3/6/24	3
5			**Measurements & Layout**	**5 days**	**Thu 3/7/24**	**Wed 3/13/24**	**1**
6			Measure Fence	1 day	Thu 3/7/24	Thu 3/7/24	
7			Determine Panel Quantity	2 days	Fri 3/8/24	Mon 3/11/24	6
8			Determine Post Quantity	2 days	Tue 3/12/24	Wed 3/13/24	7
9			Measurements & Layout Completed	0 days	Wed 3/13/24	Wed 3/13/24	8
10			**Tools & Materials**	**10 days**	**Thu 3/14/24**	**Wed 3/27/24**	**5**
11			Get Tools	5 days	Thu 3/14/24	Wed 3/20/24	
12			Get Materials	5 days	Thu 3/21/24	Wed 3/27/24	11
13			Tools & Materials Gotten	0 days	Wed 3/27/24	Wed 3/27/24	12
14			**Holes & Posts**	**11 days**	**Thu 3/28/24**	**Thu 4/11/24**	**10**
15			Position Fence Posts	2 days	Thu 3/28/24	Fri 3/29/24	
16			Dig Holes	3 days	Mon 4/1/24	Wed 4/3/24	15
17			Pour Gravel	2 days	Thu 4/4/24	Fri 4/5/24	16
18			Pour Concrete	1 day	Wed 4/10/24	Wed 4/10/24	17FS+2 days
19			Set Posts	1 day	Thu 4/11/24	Thu 4/11/24	18
20			Holes & Posts Completed	0 days	Thu 4/11/24	Thu 4/11/24	19

GANTT CHART

Figure 279 – Using the Predecessors Field

20 - What are the steps for Building a Schedule in Microsoft Project?

To build a schedule in Project, use our B.A.S.I.C.S. 6-step scheduling process. See **Chapter 7** for more information on each step.

1. First, **Breakdown the project** and organize it into phases.
2. Then, **Adjust the settings** to support the type of schedule you plan to build.
3. Then, **Structure the tasks** into an outline.
4. Then, **Initialize the durations**.
5. Then, **Connect the tasks**.
6. At this point you can **Start the project**.

21 – Can Project for the Web show the Critical Path?

Yes! The ability to show the Critical Path was added to *Project for the Web* between late 2022 and early 2023. See **Chapter 0** for more information.

22 – Does Project for the Web allow you to use all four task relationship types?

Yes! *Project for the Web* allows you to create task relationships using the Finish-to-Start, Start-to-Start, Start-to-Finish and Finish-to-Finish dependency types.

23 – What type of project is best suited for Project for the Web?

Project for the Web is best suited for change-based agile projects and small plan-based projects that require more task tracking than full-scale project management. See **Chapter Zero** for an example of such a project and the characteristics that make it a good fit for *Project for the Web*.

24 – What type of project should not be managed using Project for the Web?

Projects requiring extensive project management would not be a good fit for *Project for the Web*. This would include projects requiring the features that are included with the desktop versions of Project that have been excluded from *Project for the Web.* This includes the ability to baseline a project, track actual and remaining duration and work, track project costs, assign resource calendars and an exhaustive list of additional capabilities.

25 – What can the desktop versions of Project do that Project for the Web can't?

Since new features are continuously being added to *Project for the Web*, the answer to this question changes on a regular basis. However, it's not likely that *Project for the Web* will ever be as robust and full featured as the desktop versions of Project. This would run counter to the design intent of *Project for the Web*, which is to simplify the user experience. The more scheduling features that are added, the less intuitive *Project for the Web* will be. One method you can use to assess the difference in capability is to compare the number of scheduling parameters (I.e., fields) you can add to the *Project for the Web* interface to the number of scheduling parameters you can be add to the Gantt Chart view in Microsoft Project.

At the time of this publication, you can add **less than 10 s**cheduling parameters to the Project for the Web interface. By contrast, you can add **more than 400** scheduling parameters to the Gantt Chart view of any desktop version of Microsoft Project.

START

PART THREE Summary

This concludes Part Three - Executing the Schedule. You learned to execute your schedule and track it to completion. You learned key execution practices, such as capturing your initial scheduling forecast in a baseline, inputting actual performance data, and tracking costs. You also learned to create dynamic status reports, customize the Project interface, and use advanced features, such Earned Value tables and Master schedules to manage projects, programs and portfolios. You concluded with learning guidelines for closing your project.

In Part Four - Executing Agile Schedules, you'll learn to use the Agile features included with the Project Online Desktop Client.

PART FOUR Executing Agile Projects

IN PART FOUR, you'll learn to use the Agile features included with the Project Online Desktop Client. You'll learn to use the Kanban-inspired Task Boards to build and track your agile user stories and tasks. You'll also learn to execute your agile projects using the Scrum-inspired Sprint features. In the final chapter, we'll put all these features to use in a real-world Agile software development project. We'll also review the business drivers behind the Agile movement and key Kanban and Scrum concepts. If you're fuzzy on Agile concepts, this section will sharpen the picture for you. Ideal learners include agile practitioners and anyone managing projects requiring a high level of responsiveness to shifting requirements.

"SOFTWARE IS EATING THE WORLD". This quote, by Marc Andreesson explains what's powering the Agile phenomenon. It's a reference to the disruption caused by software-driven and often digitally native companies. For example, Amazon's disruption of traditional retailers, like Best Buy. In this sense, Amazon has eaten Best Buy. Likewise, Netflix is eating Hollywood, Uber is eating the taxi industry, and Expedia is eating travel agencies. By extension, one can ask whether Agile frameworks are eating Project Management principles. Businesses are looking to Agile methods the way they once looked to Project Management principles for insights into how to deliver better products, faster than their competitors. The Project Management Institute (PMI) has taken definitive steps to disrupt the disrupters by updating its Project Management Body of Knowledge (PMBOK) to be agnostic to a team's preferred way of working. There is now as much focus on change-based agile approaches as there is on plan-based approaches.

Microsoft has also kept pace with this important business trend and now includes a robust set of tools to manage Sprint-based agile projects. In this section, we'll cover those features. We'll review the business drivers behind the Agile movement, key Agile concepts, and use cases for Agile workflows.

Chapter 22 Understanding Agile Projects

In this chapter, we'll give an overview of the **Agile approach to managing projects**. We'll review key aspects of the **Kanban** and **Scrum** Agile frameworks, which you can now apply using the Online Desktop version of Microsoft Project. When you're done, you'll be able to describe the Agile approach, identify its key business drivers, identify distinctions between Kanban and Scrum and select the right approach for your project.

You'll Learn:

- Agile Business Drivers
- Agile Basics
- Kanban Basics
- Scrum Basics
- To Select the Right Agile Approach

Agile Business Drivers

Six business realities are driving the need for new, adaptive approaches to product delivery and schedule management.

1. Uncertainty
2. Unpredictability
3. Fast pace of change
4. Global competition
5. Fuzzy, long-term project scope
6. Shifting plans and priorities

Let's unpackage these new realities - beginning with **uncertainty**. The advent of big data has led to more data-driven decisions, which inherently produce more certainty. But who can be certain what data to collect, or how to interpret the data– especially if it's unstructured data? And if one can't glean the proper insights, how can one forecast properly? And on the topic of **unpredictability**, how much should be invested in emerging technologies, such as A.I.? Who can predict whether new technology is ripe for consumer demand or whether strong demand is further down the road? The answers to these questions are driving the **fast pace of change** in modern business. If your business isn't disrupting itself with innovation, it could quickly fall behind the local and/or **global competitors**. Conversely, if your business becomes an early adopter of new technology, it will need to fail fast enough and learn fast enough to stay ahead of competitors. Therefore, the concept of a progressively elaborated project scope is more relevant now, than ever. For example, suppose your business decides to incorporate cloud-based solutions to save on long-term expenses. At the beginning of the project, it may not be clear which solutions to move to the cloud, the extent those solutions can become fully cloud-based solutions, or what the migration plan should be. This sort of **fuzzy, long-term scope** is unavoidable if you're an early adopter. Furthermore, your **plans and priorities may shift** many times throughout the project life cycle. These modern business realities have fueled a demand for an approach that is adaptive enough to incorporate shifting requirements. The **Agile** approach was designed to accommodate changes and deliver incremental value in time-periods as compressed as two weeks.

The promise of this approach has captured the minds and budgets of business leaders worldwide. In the next section, we'll take a closer look at the Agile approach.

Agile Basics

The Agile movement was formalized in 2001, with the publication of the Agile Manifesto for Agile Software Development. You can read this manifesto at http://agilemanifesto.org. It identifies four values, each of which prioritizes principles that lead to seamless, agile software delivery over things that impede it, such as complex processes and tools and rigid plans. These values are distilled into 12 principles, which emphasize key concepts like *"welcome changing requirements"*, *"deliver working software frequently"* and *"work together daily"*. These principles are realized in several frameworks, including Kanban, Scrum, XP and FDD, to name a few. The new Agile features in Microsoft Project are built around the Kanban and Scrum frameworks. In the next sections, we'll review key aspects of these two approaches.

Kanban and Scrum Basics

The **Kanban** and **Scrum** approaches are based on building and executing an ever-growing "to-do" list. For a software development project, the to-do list would consist of new or changing software features. The to-do list is called a **Backlog**. Each item on the to-do list is called a **User Story**. They're called user stories because they are written by the user, in terms the user can understand. The user who writes the stories and requests the features is called the **Product Owner**. Since the user story is at the heart of either approach, here are two examples to better understand this concept. The following user stories are from a project to build an e-commerce website for a bookseller who wants to expand the reach of their brick-and-mortar business.

User Story 1

A website customer can search for books by author, title or ISBN number.

User Story 2

A website customer can rate and review books.

The Backlog will consist of as many user stories as required to deliver the final product — a working website that meets client expectations. What distinguishes Kanban from Scrum is <u>how</u> these user stories are pulled from the Backlog and delivered to the client as working software features.

Using Kanban

Using the **Kanban** method, the team of developers begin by right-sizing the user stories until each story represents a comparable amount of work. Then, they determine the maximum number of stories they can work on at a time. This is called the **Work-In-Progress (WIP)** limit. The product owner then prioritizes the user stories in the Backlog. This is when execution begins. Respecting the WIP limit, user stories are pulled from the Backlog and placed on a Kanban Board (*Figure 280* below), which is a task board that organizes user stories in columns, such as: Backlog, Next Up, In Progress and Done.

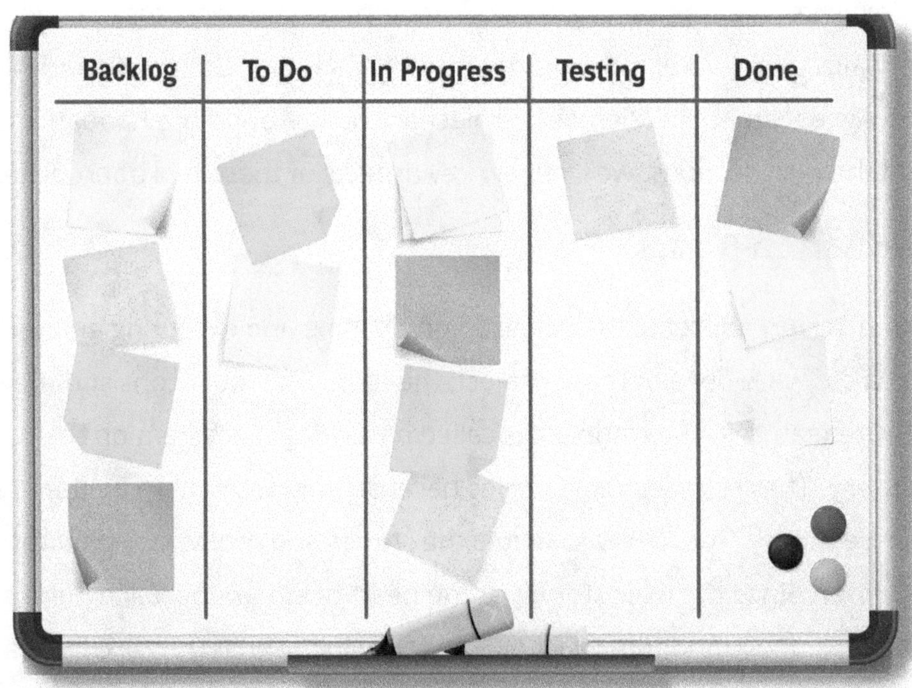

Figure 280 – Kanban Board

The user stories are progressed across the Kanban board from the Backlog column to the Done column. As you may have deduced, Kanban projects are not driven by a predetermined schedule. The schedule is generally reverse-engineered from factors like the size of the Backlog and the WIP limit. The reverse-engineered schedule is an expected outcome of the fourth Agile Manifesto value, which reads *"responding to change over following a plan"*.

If you're an Online Desktop Microsoft Project subscriber, you can work with your projects in an agile way using the different **Task Board views**. *Figure 281* shows the **Backlog Board view**.

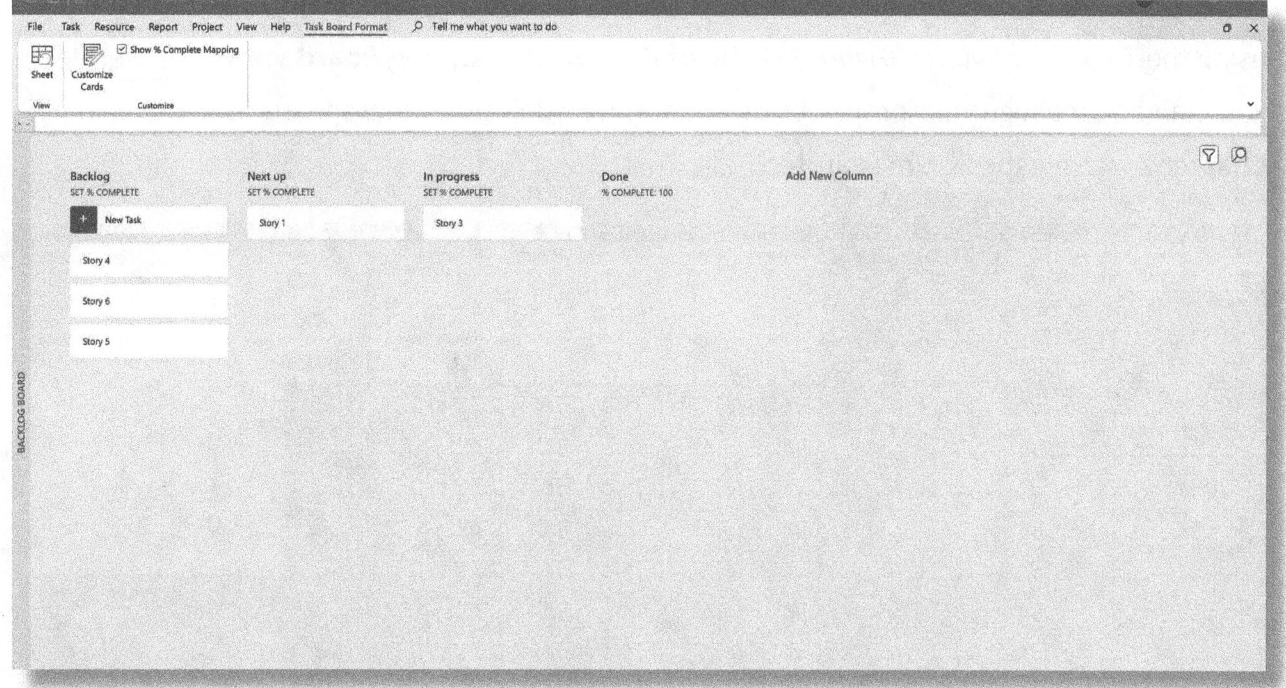

Figure 281 – The Backlog Board View

This view lets you organize and manage projects on a Kanban-style task board. We'll explore these agile features and how to use them in the next chapter.

Using Scrum

Using the **Scrum** method, the team of developers would begin by estimating the amount of work required to deliver each user story. These work estimates are called **Story Points**. The team will then determine how often they can deliver working software to the Product Owner (usually 2 weeks). This 2-week period is called a **Sprint**. Prioritized user stories are then pulled from the Backlog and placed on a **Scrum Board**, which is a task board that includes columns, such as: Sprint 1, Sprint 2, Sprint 3 and so forth. The difference between a Kanban board and a Scrum board is that the Kanban board is used throughout the entire project, whereas a new Scrum board is used after each Sprint. After each Sprint, the client assesses the deliverable and provides feedback. Although there is no schedule at this point, the team will continue to deliver incremental working software every two weeks thereafter. After enough Sprints have gone by, the project manager can determine the team's pace of delivery, which is called **Velocity**. Velocity is the number of Story Points the team can deliver, per Sprint. The schedule can then be forecasted by making projections, based on the team's Velocity.

The Project Online Desktop version also lets you create and manage Sprints-based projects using the Task Board views. *Figure 281* shows the **Sprint Planning Board view**. This view lets you plan and manage your project using sprints. We'll delve into these features in detail in Chapter 24 "Using the Scrum Features".

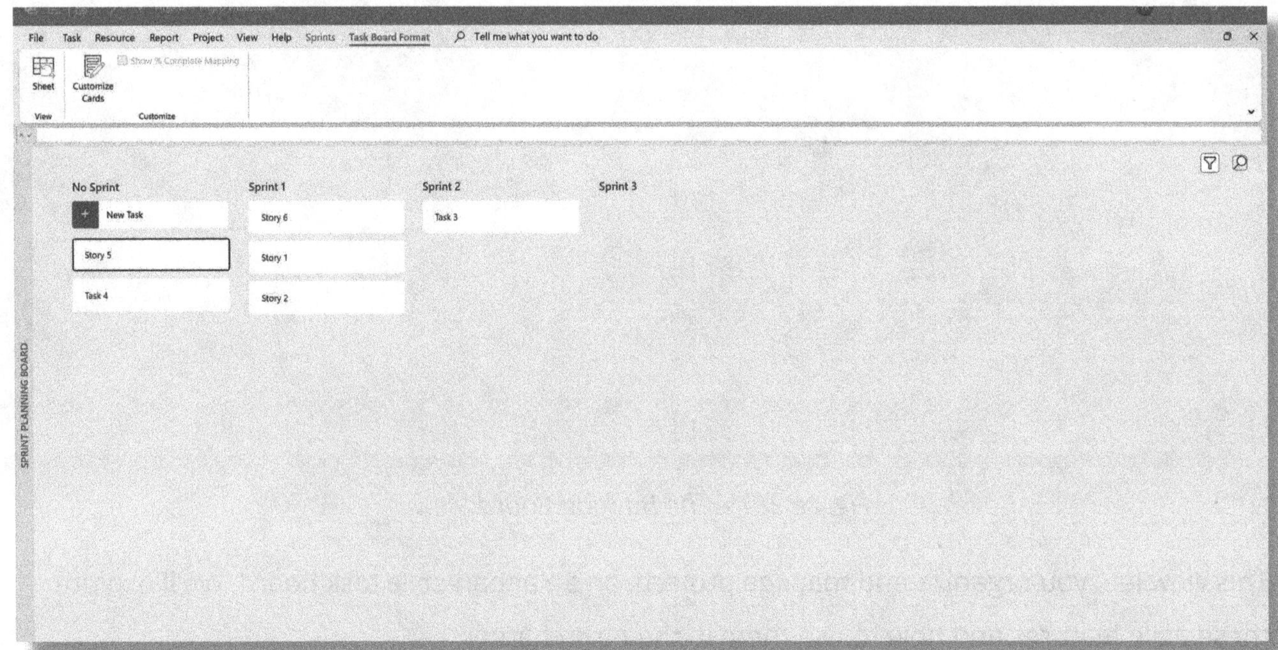

Figure 282 – The Sprints Planning Board View

Selecting the Right Approach

Before selecting a scheduling approach, it's important to determine whether your project warrants a change-based (Agile) or plan-based (Waterfall/Traditional) approach. If your project has never been done before and if the requirements must be determined through trial and error, then it may be a good candidate for an Agile approach. As mentioned earlier, the Agile approach not only allows for scope changes and shifting requirements, but it was also designed to accommodate them. Among the agile approaches available in Project, whether you choose Kanban or Scrum should depend upon the volatility of the requirements. If your requirements are more volatile, consider Kanban. If your requirements are less volatile, consider Scrum. If your requirements are stable, consider the plan-based (Waterfall/Traditional) approach we reviewed in Parts 1, 2 and 3.

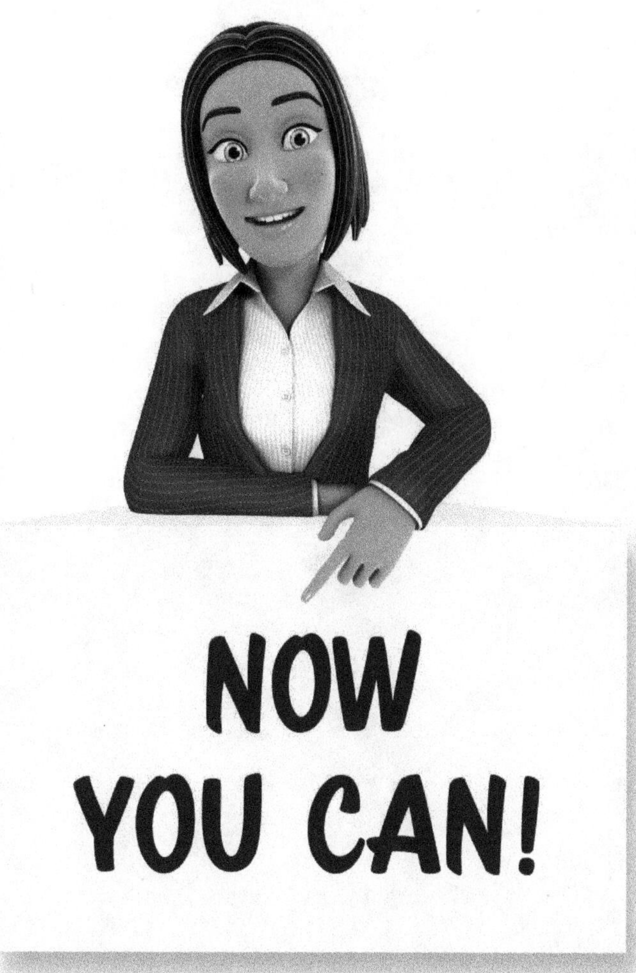

- ✓ Explain Agile Business Drivers
- ✓ Explain the Basics of Agile
- ✓ Explain the Basics of Kanban
- ✓ Explain the Basics of Scrum
- ✓ Select the Right Scheduling Approach

Chapter 23 Using the Kanban Features

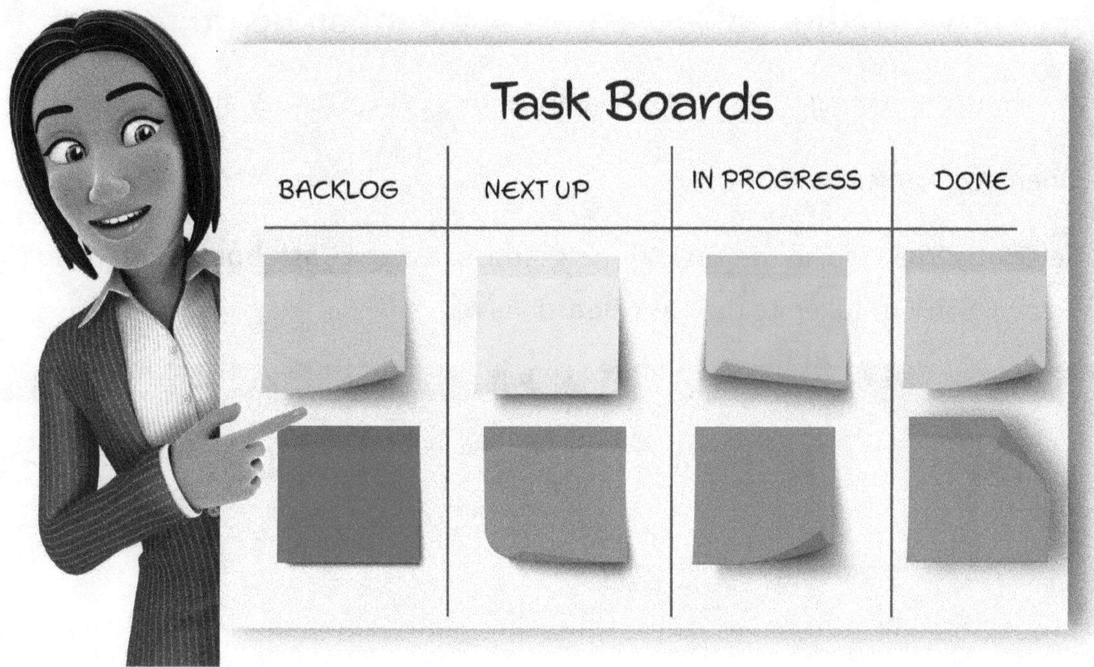

In the last chapter, we reviewed the Agile approach to project management and identified business drivers that contribute to the embrace of this adaptive approach. We reviewed key differences between Kanban and Scrum, and guidelines for selecting the right approach for your project. In this chapter, we'll explore the **Kanban features** available in the Project Online desktop client. When you're done, you'll be able to create a Kanban project, use the Task board view, and use the Agile reports. We'll also look at three contextually different Kanban use cases.

You'll Learn:

- To Create a New Kanban Project
- To Create a Kanban Project from a Waterfall Project
- To Use the Task Board Views
- To Use the Backlog Sheet Views
- To Use the Kanban Reports
- Kanban Project Use Cases

The Project Online Desktop Client includes agile features that let you create and manage your projects after the Kanban framework using the **Task Board views**. You can view and manage a traditional project in a Kanban way, or you can create a new Kanban project.

Work With a Traditional Project using a Kanban Board

To work with an existing traditional or waterfall project in a Task Board view:

- Open your project plan.
- Select the **View** tab. In the **Task Views** group, select the **Task Board** command (*Figure 283* below). You'll be taken to the **Task Board view**.

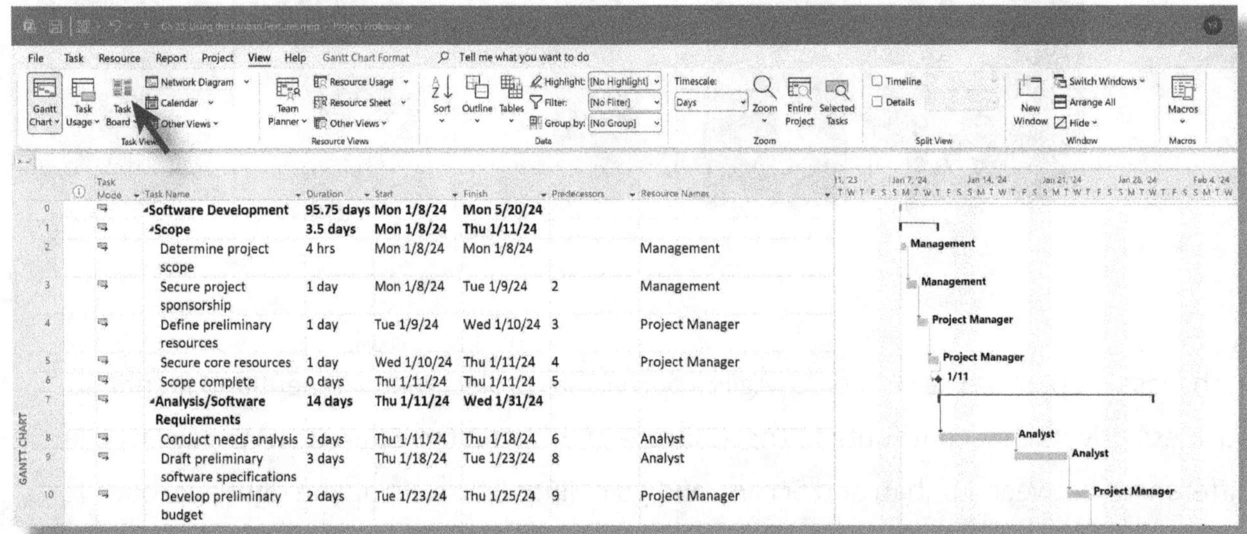

Figure 283 – View Your Project in a Task Board

NOTE: For tasks to display in a Task Board view, the **Show on Board** setting for each task must be set to **Yes** (the default setting).

To change the Show on Board setting for a task or tasks:

- With your project open, go to the Gantt Chart view.
- Using the **Add New Column** field in the Entry table, select **Show on Board** from the pick-list (*Figure 284*).
- The new Show on Board column will display Yes or No for each task.
- Select **Yes** from the toggle list for each task to show it in the Task Board view.

	Mode	Task Name	Duration	Start	Finish	Predecessors	Resource Names	Show on Board
0		**Software Development**	**95.75 days**	**Mon 3/3/25**	**Mon 7/14/25**			**Yes**
1		**Scope**	**3.5 days**	**Mon 3/3/25**	**Thu 3/6/25**			**Yes**
2		Determine project scope	4 hrs	Mon 3/3/25	Mon 3/3/25		Management	Yes
3		Secure project sponsorship	1 day	Mon 3/3/25	Tue 3/4/25	2	Management	Yes
4		Define preliminary resources	1 day	Tue 3/4/25	Wed 3/5/25	3	Project Manager	Yes
5		Secure core resources	1 day	Wed 3/5/25	Thu 3/6/25	4	Project Manager	Yes
6		Scope complete	0 days	Thu 3/6/25	Thu 3/6/25	5		Yes
7		**Analysis/Software Requirements**	**14 days**	**Thu 3/6/25**	**Wed 3/26/25**			**Yes**
8		Conduct needs analysis	5 days	Thu 3/6/25	Thu 3/13/25	6	Analyst	Yes
9		Draft preliminary software specifications	3 days	Thu 3/13/25	Tue 3/18/25	8	Analyst	Yes
10		Develop preliminary budget	2 days	Tue 3/18/25	Thu 3/20/25	9	Project Manager	Yes
11		Review software specifications/budget with	4 hrs	Thu 3/20/25	Thu 3/20/25	10	Project Manager, Analyst	Yes

Figure 284 – Show on Board Column

The Task Board View

The **Task Board view** is the Microsoft Project rendition of a Kanban Board. By default, the board includes the Not Started, Next up, In Progress, and Done columns (*Figure 285* below). You can add new columns using the **Add New Column** command. Simply select the command, type the column name, and press **Enter**. You can add up to six columns. Unlike the Add New Column command in the Gantt Chart view, there is no pick-list of preset columns.

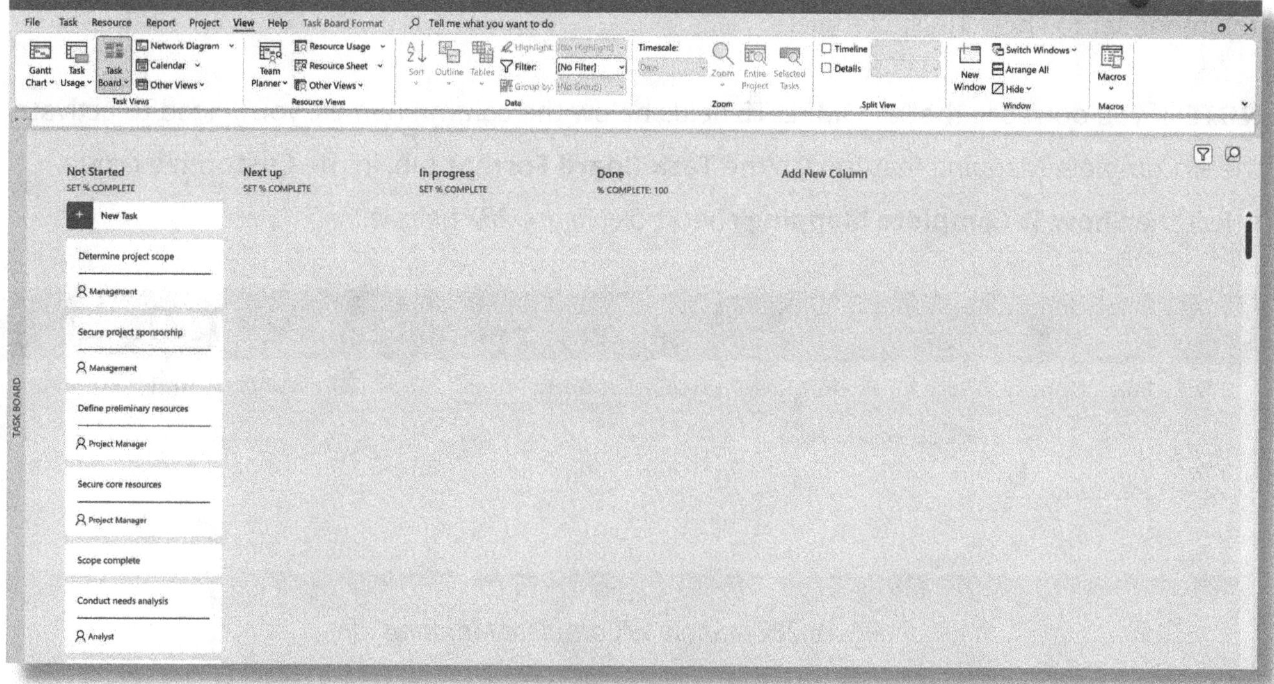

Figure 285 – The Task Board View

By default, tasks are placed in the Not Started column. Each column can be renamed, deleted, or moved to the left or right by right-clicking its column name (*Figure 286* below). The Not Started column can be renamed, but it cannot be deleted or moved.

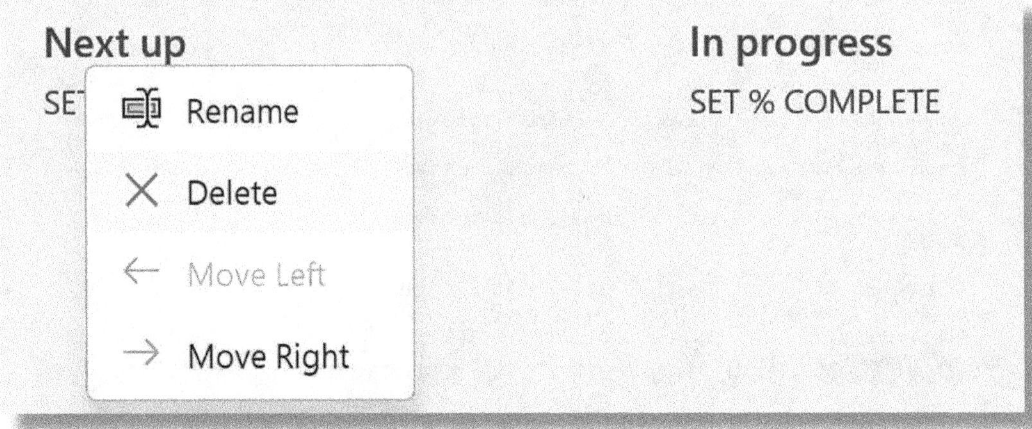

Figure 286 – Customize the Task Board Columns

% Complete Mapping

The **% Complete Mapping** feature lets you dynamically update the percentage complete for a task when they're moved across the columns. Beneath the column names, you'll see the % COMPLETE or SET % COMPLETE dynamic fields. These fields represent the percentage a task is complete when it is moved into that respective column. For example, by default the Done column is set to show 100% complete.

NOTE: If you don't see the % COMPLETE fields below the column names, you'll need to activate the % Complete Mapping feature. On the **Task Board Format** tab, in the **Customize** group, select the **Show % Complete Mapping** checkbox (*Figure 287* below).

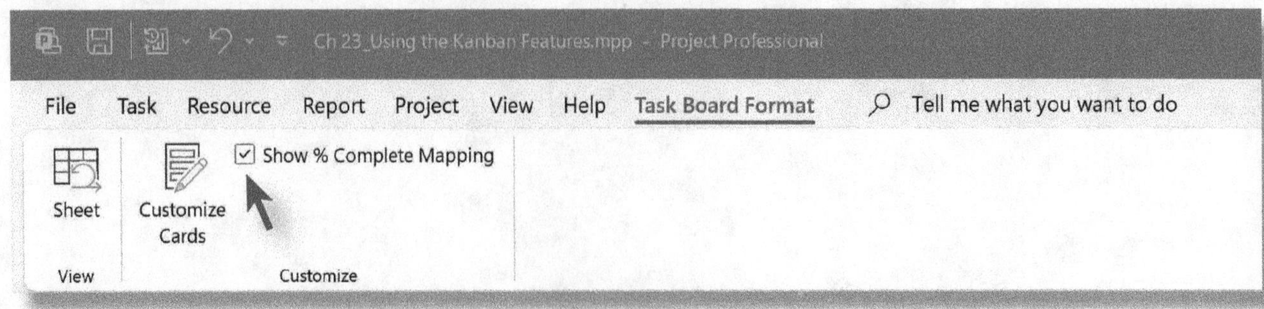

Figure 287 – Show % Complete Mapping

You can set any % Complete value you want for the columns to represent, as follows:

- Select the **SET % COMPLETE** text below the column label.
- Type the value of percentage complete you want the column to represent, and press **ENTER**.

When you move a task into that column, Project will update the task to the respective percent complete.

Task Cards

Project tasks (user stories) are shown on **Task Cards**. By default, the cards display the task name, the resource(s) assigned to it, and a check-mark if the task has been completed. You can customize the cards to show more task information using the **Customize Cards** command, located on the **Task Board Format** tab, in the **Customize** group (*Figure 288* below).

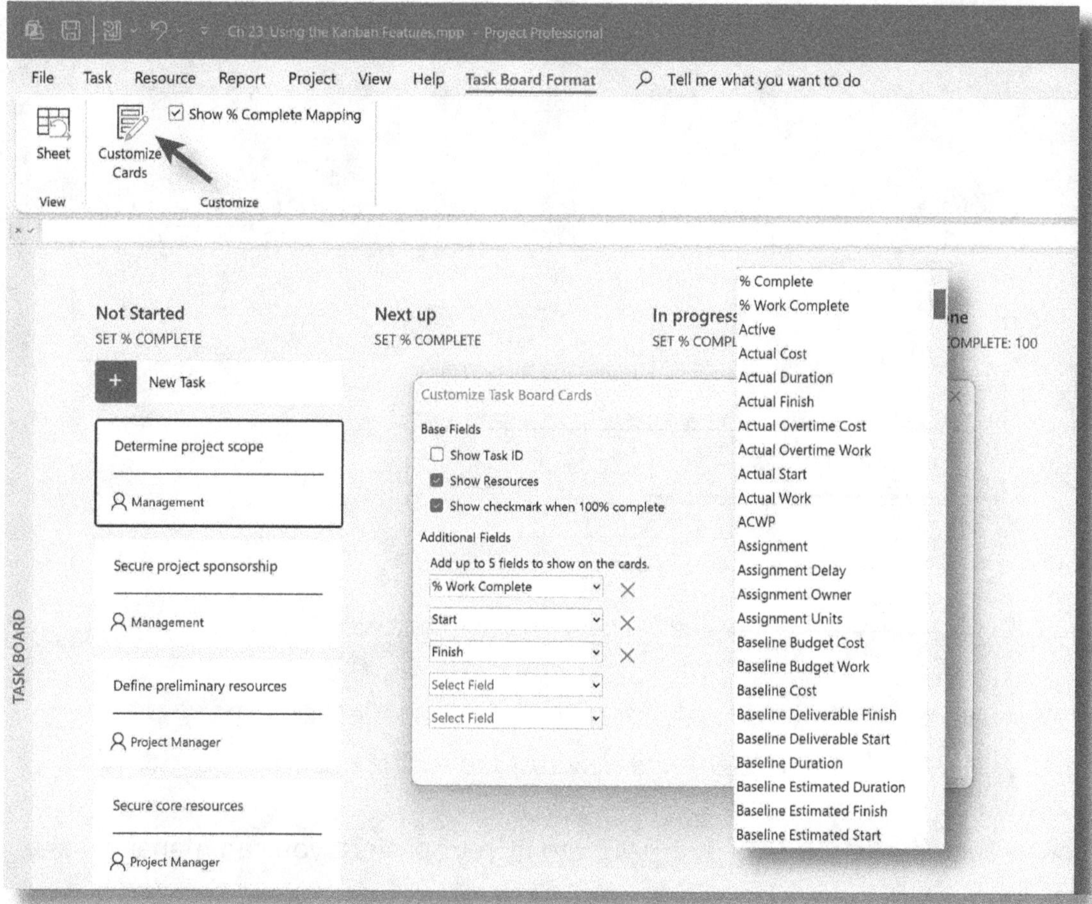

Figure 288 – Customize the Task Cards

In the *Additional Fields* section, you can add up to 5 additional fields of information to the cards from the options in the pick-list. You can also uncheck the options in the *Base Fields* to remove that information from the cards.

NOTE: Task Card customizations are applied to the project in which they were set only. They will need to be customized for each project.

Adding Tasks to the Task Board

To add new tasks to the board, use the **New Task** command (*Figure 289* below). Simply select the plus sign, enter a task name, and select **Add**. The new task will be added to the board in the Not Started column.

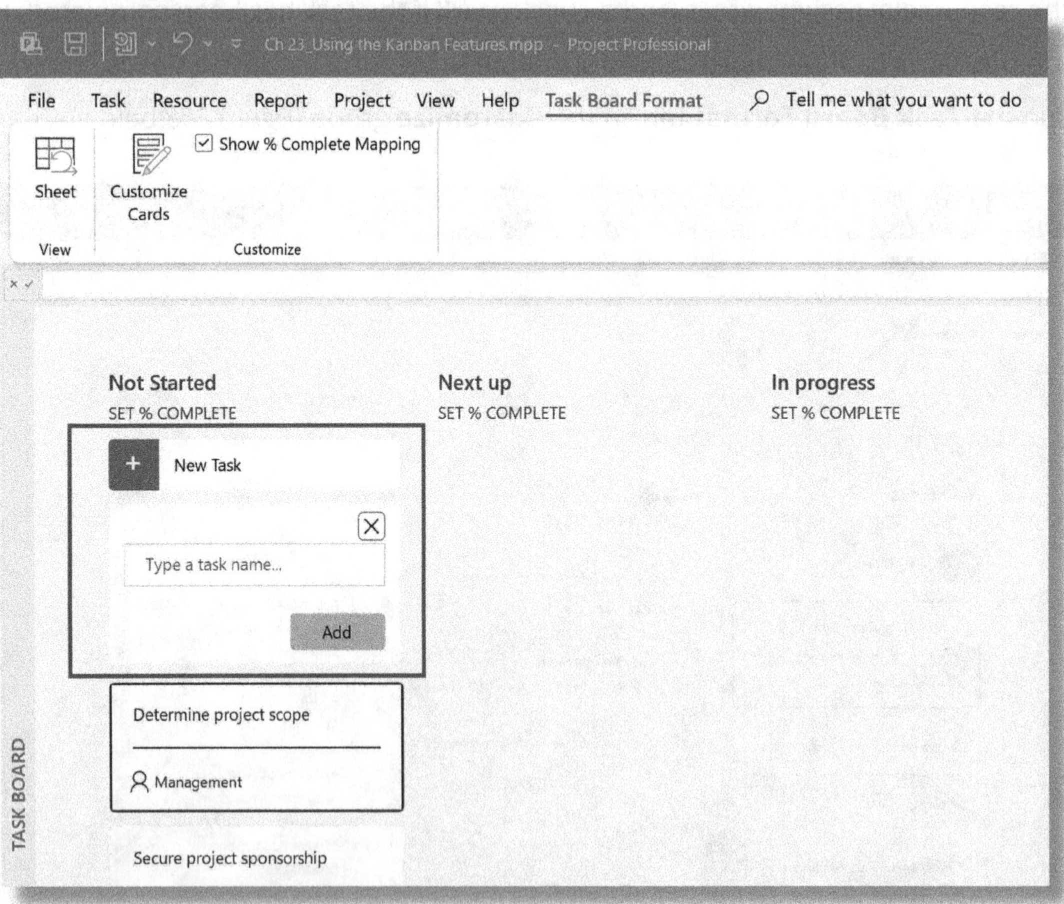

Figure 289 – Add New Tasks to the Task Board

Once you've customized the Task Board view to fit your project, you can manage tasks and update their progress by simply clicking and dragging them across the board to the appropriate columns (*Figure 290*).

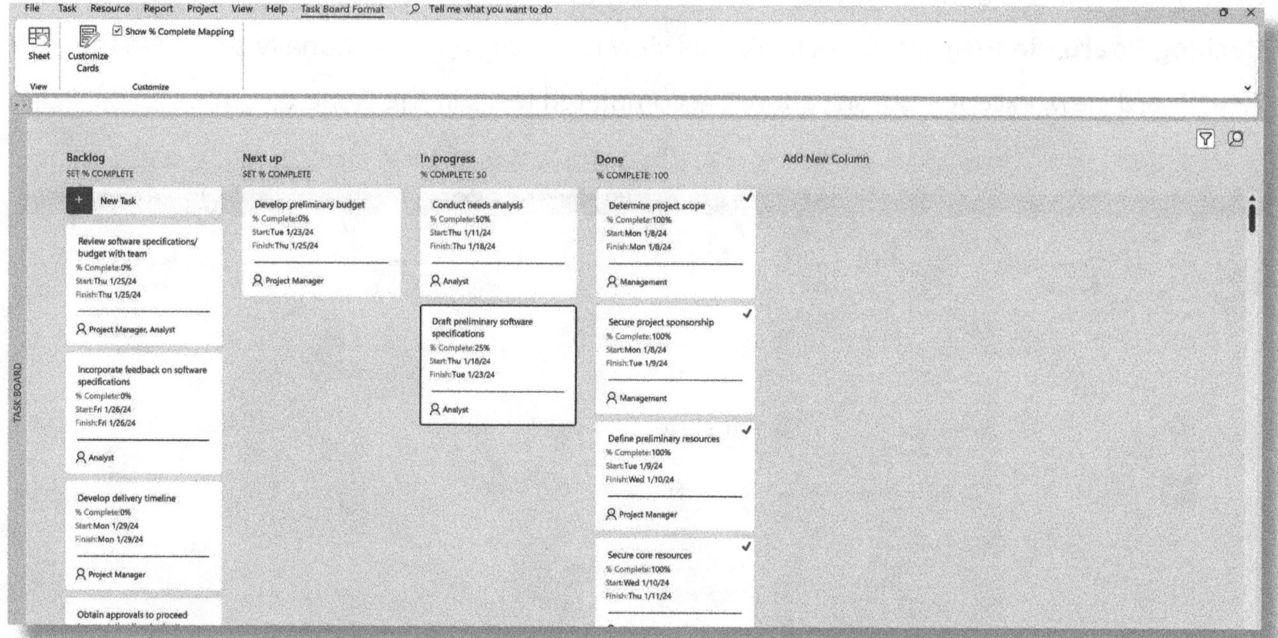

Figure 290 – Progress Tasks Across the Task Board

Filtering Tasks

In the right corner of the board, you'll find the **Filter** and **Search** commands. Use the Filter command to show tasks by their summary tasks or by the resources assigned to them (*Figure 291* below). To use the *Summary Task* option, summary tasks must first be added to the schedule outline in the Gantt chart view. Use the Search command to search for tasks.

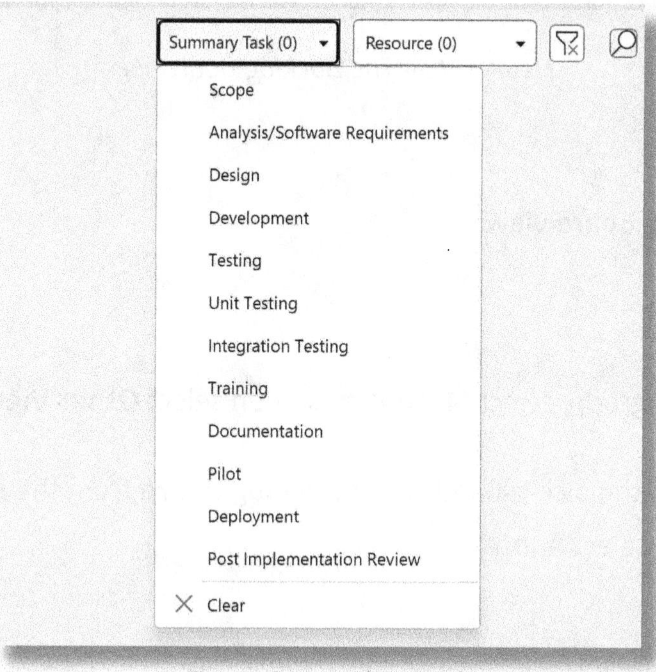

Figure 291 – Filter Tasks

Once your project is underway, you can work with the uncompleted backlog tasks in the **Backlog Board view** (*Figure 292* below). This view is visually and functionally similar to the Task Board view, except it doesn't show the completed tasks in the Done column.

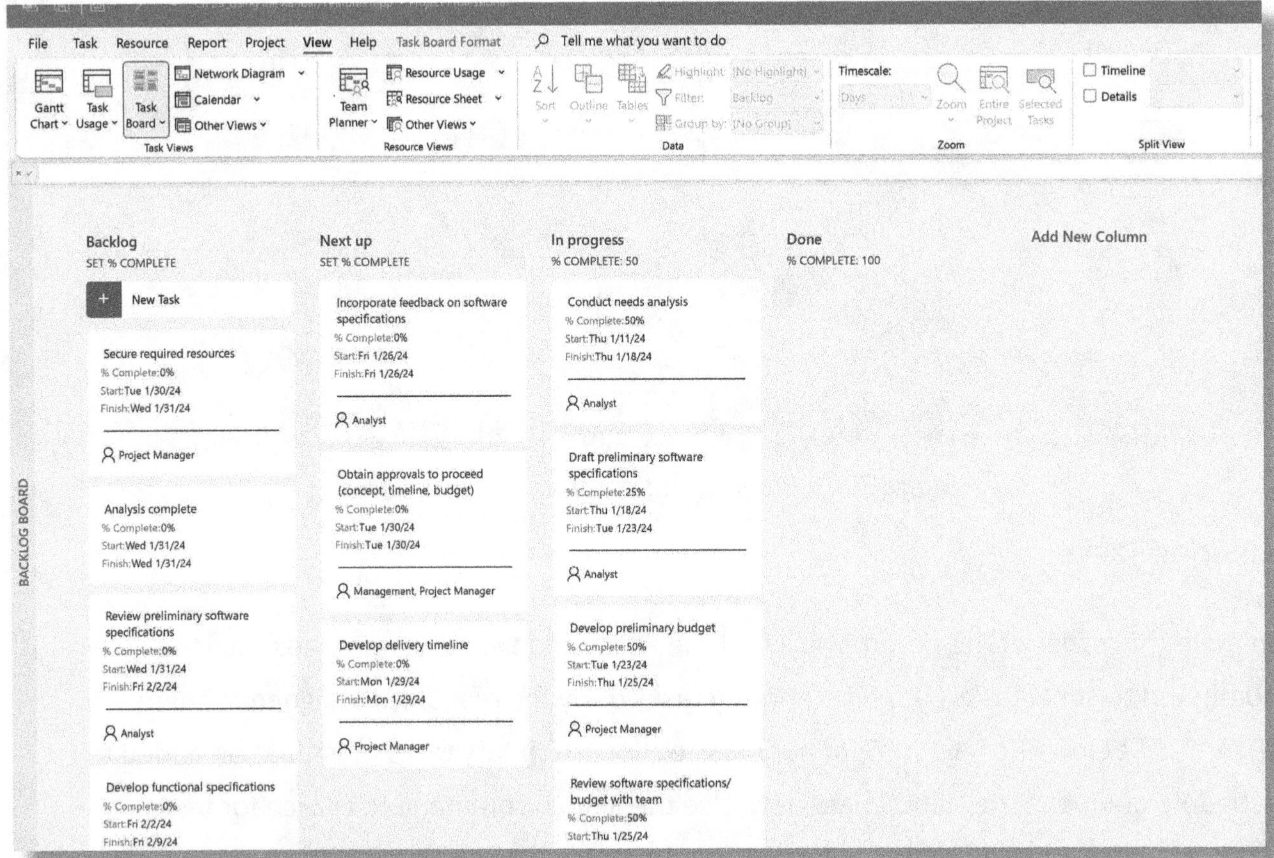

Figure 292 – The Backlog Board View

To access the Backlog Board view:

- Select the **View** tab.
- In the **Task Views** group, select **More Views**, then select **Other Views**.
- Scroll to the top of the pick-list and select **Backlog Board** from the Built-in view options (*Figure 293*). Then, select **Apply**.

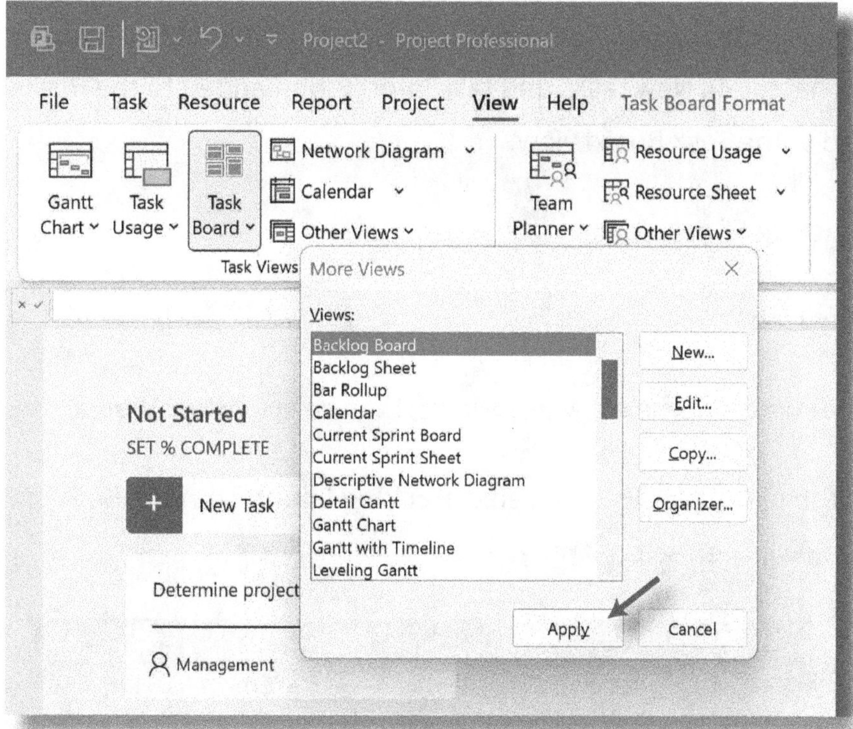

Figure 293 – Access the Backlog Board View

You can also work with incomplete tasks in the **Backlog Sheet view** (*Figure 294* below). In this tabular sheet view, you can update more information for incomplete tasks than is available in the board views. The table shows incomplete tasks and their work hours, board status, resource assignments, deadlines, and the summary tasks (or phases) they're associated with.

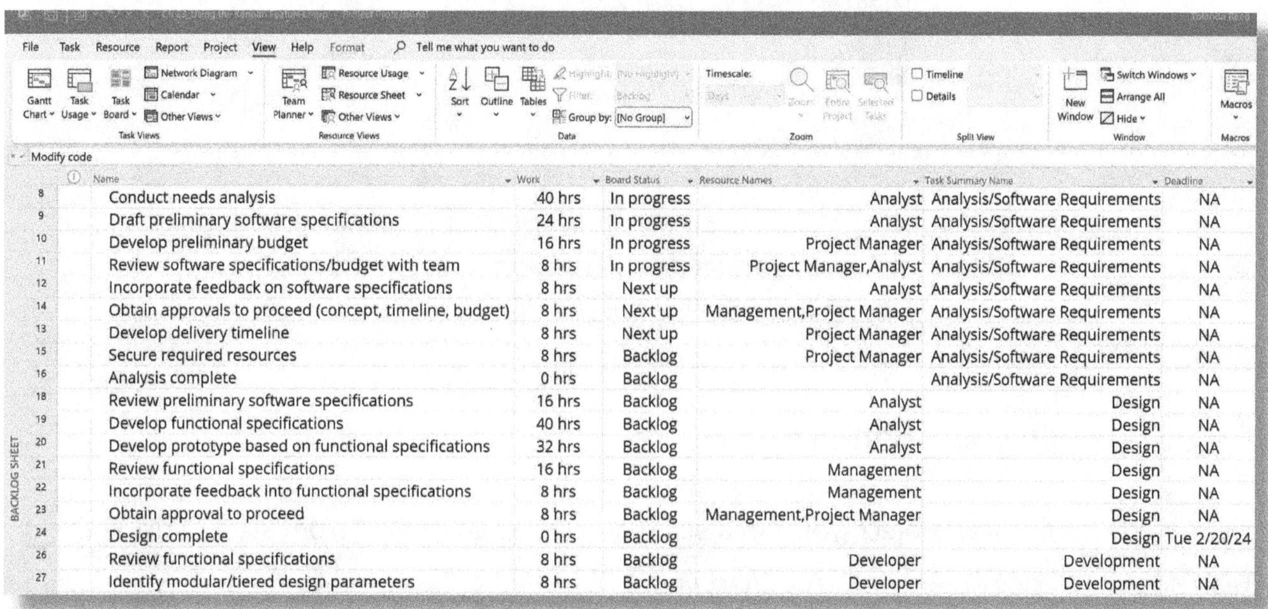

	Name	Work	Board Status	Resource Names	Task Summary Name	Deadline
8	Conduct needs analysis	40 hrs	In progress	Analyst	Analysis/Software Requirements	NA
9	Draft preliminary software specifications	24 hrs	In progress	Analyst	Analysis/Software Requirements	NA
10	Develop preliminary budget	16 hrs	In progress	Project Manager	Analysis/Software Requirements	NA
11	Review software specifications/budget with team	8 hrs	In progress	Project Manager,Analyst	Analysis/Software Requirements	NA
12	Incorporate feedback on software specifications	8 hrs	Next up	Analyst	Analysis/Software Requirements	NA
14	Obtain approvals to proceed (concept, timeline, budget)	8 hrs	Next up	Management,Project Manager	Analysis/Software Requirements	NA
13	Develop delivery timeline	8 hrs	Next up	Project Manager	Analysis/Software Requirements	NA
15	Secure required resources	8 hrs	Backlog	Project Manager	Analysis/Software Requirements	NA
16	Analysis complete	0 hrs	Backlog		Analysis/Software Requirements	NA
18	Review preliminary software specifications	16 hrs	Backlog	Analyst	Design	NA
19	Develop functional specifications	40 hrs	Backlog	Analyst	Design	NA
20	Develop prototype based on functional specifications	32 hrs	Backlog	Analyst	Design	NA
21	Review functional specifications	16 hrs	Backlog	Management	Design	NA
22	Incorporate feedback into functional specifications	8 hrs	Backlog	Management	Design	NA
23	Obtain approval to proceed	8 hrs	Backlog	Management,Project Manager	Design	NA
24	Design complete	0 hrs	Backlog		Design	Tue 2/20/24
26	Review functional specifications	8 hrs	Backlog	Developer	Development	NA
27	Identify modular/tiered design parameters	8 hrs	Backlog	Developer	Development	NA

Figure 294 – The Backlog Sheet View

NOTE: For the summary tasks to populate to this view, tasks must first be structured with summary tasks in your project outline. This is done in the Entry table of the Gantt chart view (as reviewed in Chapter 4). New tasks and task information added to the Backlog Sheet view will be populated to the Task Board view.

To access the Backlog Sheet view:

- Select the **View** tab.
- In the **Task Views** group, select **More Views**, then select **Other Views**.
- Scroll to the top of the pick-list and select **Backlog Sheet** from the Built-in view options (*Figure 295* below). Then select **Apply**.

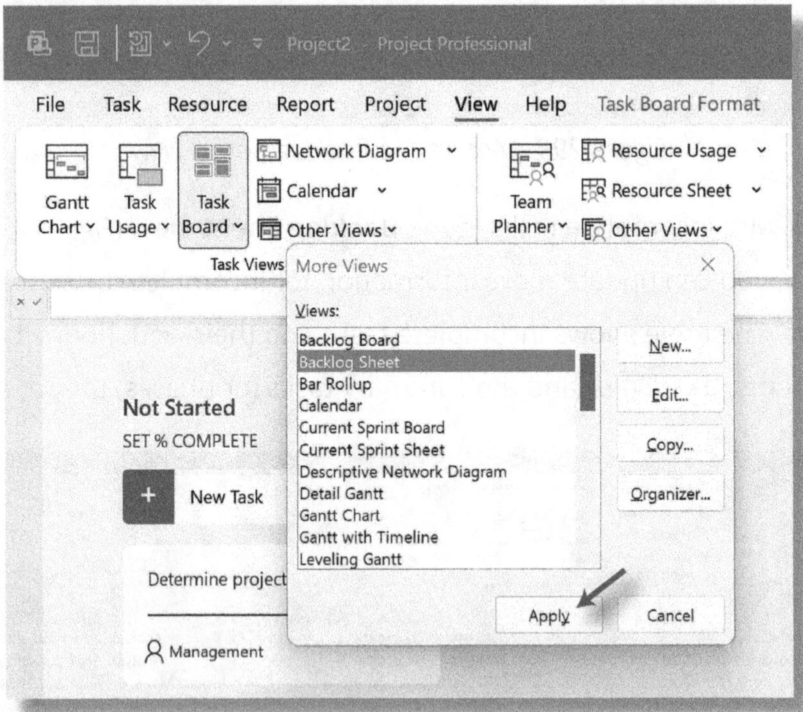

Figure 295 – The Backlog Sheet View

Creating a New Kanban Project

If you're starting a new project, you can also create a Kanban project from scratch using the Task Board, Backlog Sheet, or Gantt Chart views.

To create a new Kanban project in the Task Board view:

- Open a **Blank Project**.
- Select the **View** tab. In the **Task Views** group, select the **Task Board** command to go to the Task Board View. You'll be taken to an empty Kanban Board (*Figure 296* below).

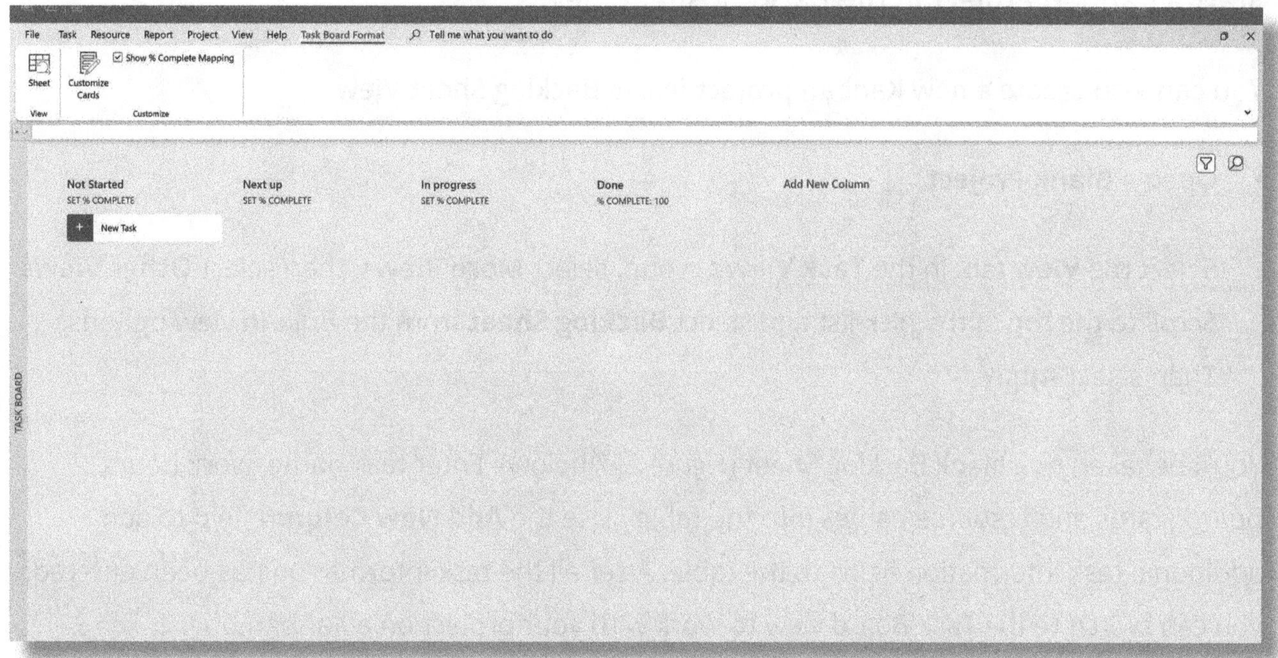

Figure 296 – Create a New Kanban Project in the Task Board View

- Rename, move, add, or delete columns to customize the board to fit your project.
- Use the **New Task** command to add tasks (user stories) to the project.
- Use the **Customize Cards** command on the **Task Board Format** tab, in the **Customize group** to add the information you like to show on the task cards.

Once you've customized the Task Board view to fit your project, and added the tasks (user stories), you can manage tasks and update their progress by dragging them across the board to the appropriate columns.

Start a New Kanban Project in the Gantt Chart View

Another way to create a new Kanban project is to create your schedule outline in the Entry table of the **Gantt Chart View**, and switch to the Task Board view to work with your project using the Kanban features. See Chapter 4 for instructions on creating a schedule outline.

Start a Kanban Project in the Backlog Sheet View

You can also create a new Kanban project in the Backlog Sheet View.

- Open a **Blank Project**.
- Select the **View** tab. In the **Task Views** group, select **More Views**, then select **Other Views**. Scroll to the top of the pick-list and select **Backlog Sheet** from the Built-in view options. Then select **Apply**.

You'll be taken to a blank Backlog Sheet (*Figure 297* below). Enter task name, work hours, board status and resource names into the table. Use the **Add New Column** field to add additional task information fields to the table. After all the task information has been entered, you can switch to the Task Board view to work with your project on a Kanban board.

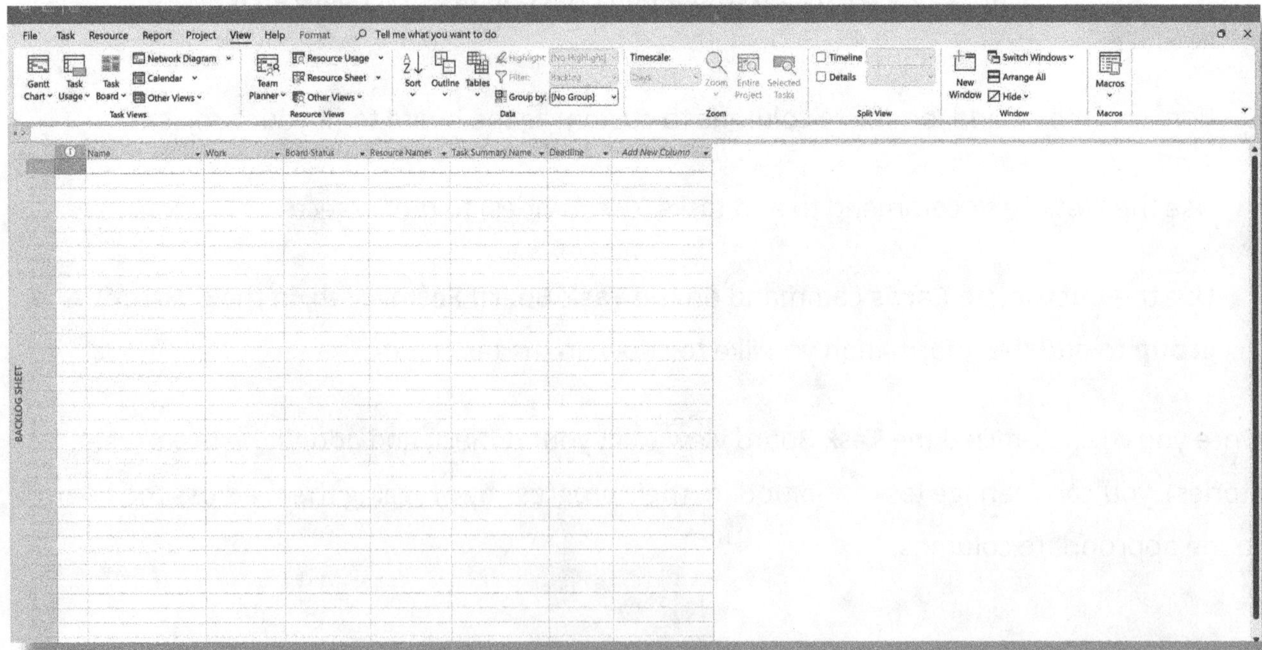

Figure 297 – Start a New Kanban Project in the The Backlog Sheet View

Using the Kanban Reports

In Chapter 17 you learned to use the Report tab to generate dynamic status reports. Project also includes Agile reports. There are two Kanban reports available, the **Boards - Task Status** report and the **Boards - Work Status** report.

Project uses the information from the Task Board and Backlog Sheet views to generate the report. Let's review each report.

The Boards - Task Status Report

To access the report:

- Select the **Report** tab.
- In the **View Reports** group, select the **Task Boards** command. Then, select **Boards - Task Status** from the pick-list (*Figure 298* below).

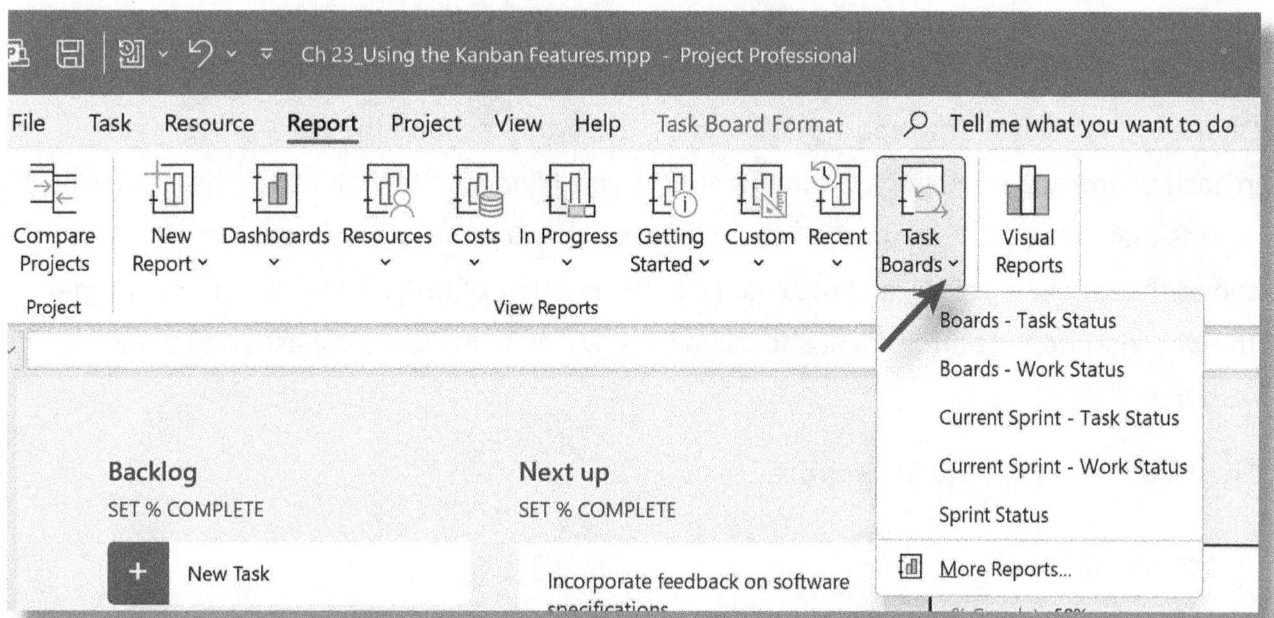

Figure 298 – Access the Task Boards Reports

The Boards – Task Status report consists of charts and tables that show task status information in different categories (*Figure 299* below).

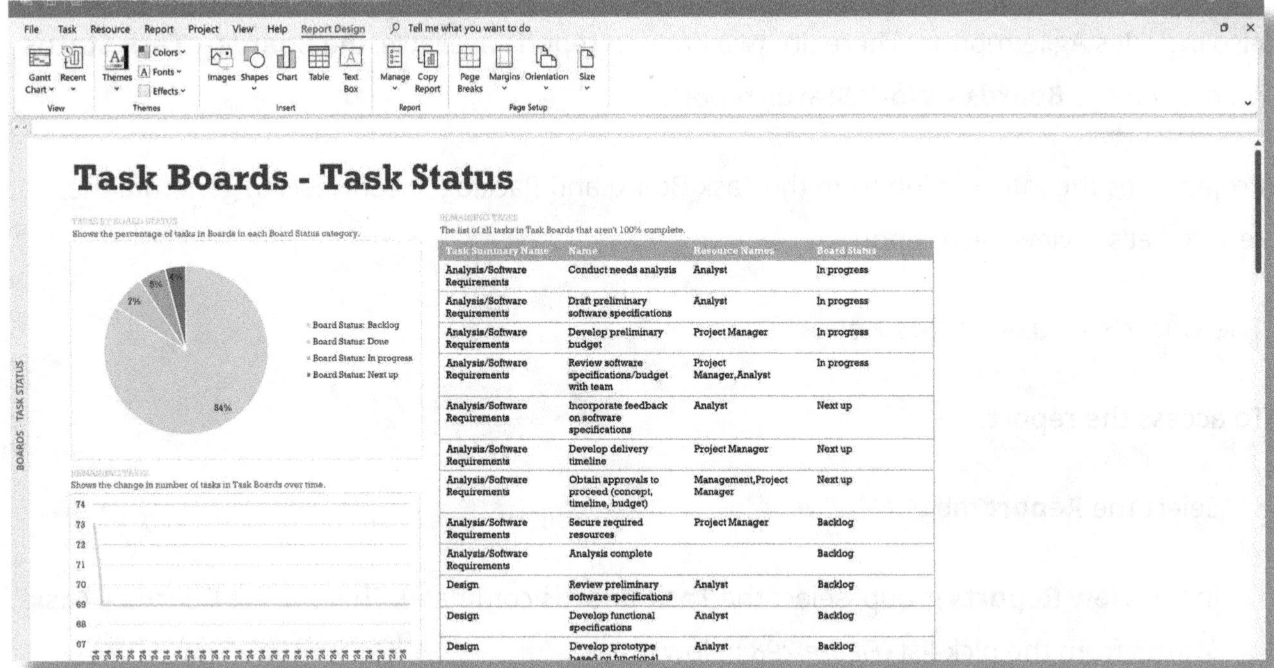

Figure 299 – The Task Boards - Task Status Report

On the top left side of the report, you'll find a pie chart that shows the percentage of tasks in each board status category. On the right side, you'll find a table that lists all tasks in task boards that aren't 100% complete. The burn-down chart on the left, beneath the pie chart, shows the remaining tasks, and the change in the number of tasks in task boards over time. The bar chart on the bottom right shows how many remaining tasks are assigned to each resource.

The Boards – Work Status Report

To access the report:

- Select the **Report** tab.
- In the **View Reports** group, select the **Task Boards** command. Then, select **Boards – Work Status** from the pick-list.

NOTE: To generate this report, you must have assigned resources to the tasks in your project and updated the work hours in either the Backlog Sheet or another resource view.

This report consists of charts and tables that show work status information in different categories (*Figure 300* below).

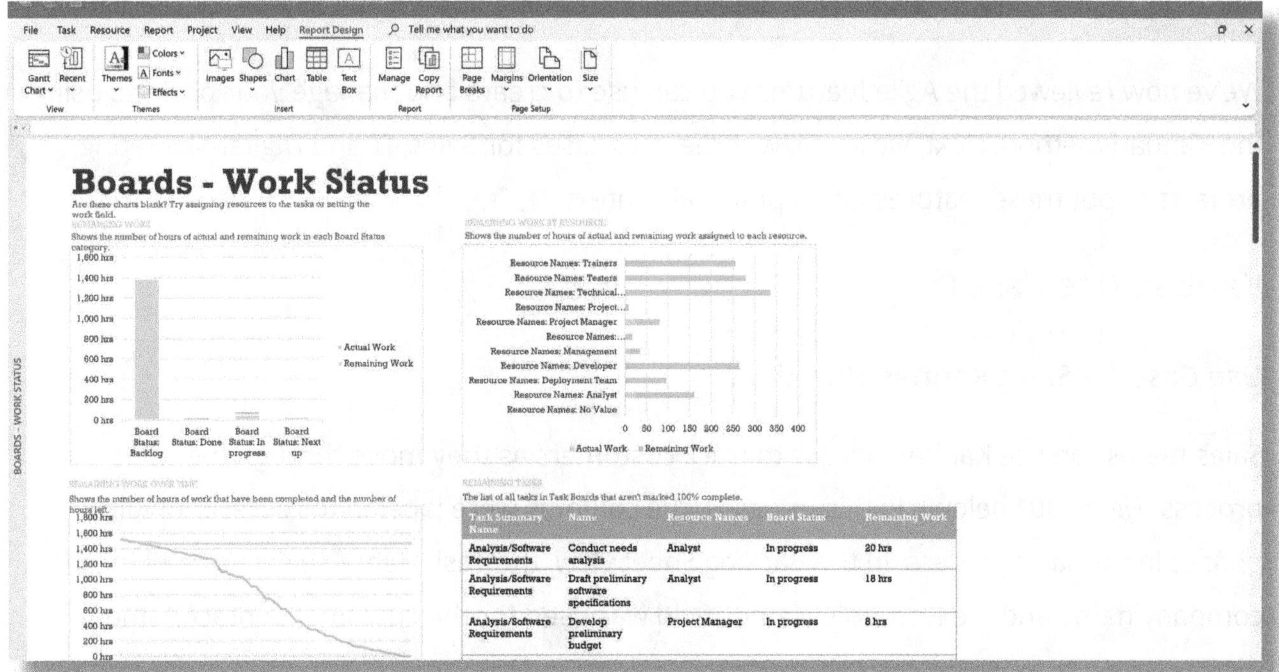

Figure 300 – The Boards - Work Status Report

On the top left side of the report, you'll find a bar chart that shows the number of hours of actual and remaining work in each Board Status category. On the top right, you'll find another bar chart that shows the number of hours of actual and remaining work assigned to each resource. The burn-down chart on the left shows the number of hours of work that have been completed and the number of hours left. Beneath the bar chart on the right, you'll find a table that lists all tasks in task boards that aren't marked 100% complete.

The Report Design Tools

On the ribbon, you'll find a contextual **Report Design** tab with tools for formatting and managing the reports. In the **View** group, you'll find quick access commands to the Gantt Chart view and your most recently viewed reports. In the **Themes** group, you can pick a theme, change the font, and add effects to change the colors and style of the reports.
In the **Insert** group, you can add shapes, tables, charts, text, and images to the report. In the **Report** group, you can rename, delete, or move the report. You can also copy the report to the clipboard to paste into other applications, like Word or PowerPoint documents.

The **Page Setup** group lets you format the page and adjust things like the page size and margins of the report. In addition to the formatting options on the ribbon, if you select certain elements on the report, a panel with additional formatting options will appear on the right.

We've now reviewed the Agile features you can use to create and manage your projects using the Kanban method. Next, we'll review three uses cases for Sales, IT and Digital Marketing projects to put these features into a practical context.

Kanban Use Cases

Use Case 1 – Sales Kanban Board

Sales teams can use Kanban boards to track customers as they move through the sales process (*Figure 301* below). In this use case, the columns were labeled to represent typical phases in the sales process. In the Backlog Sheet view, the Task Name field was used for the company name and the Resource Names field was used for the customer contact name.

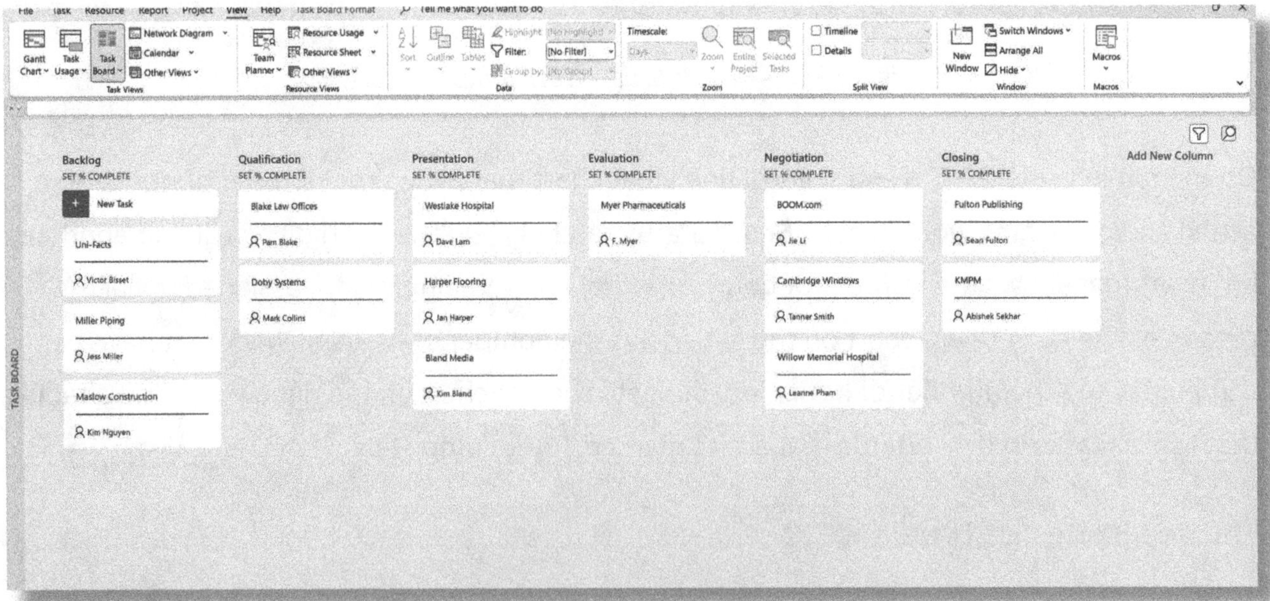

Figure 301 – Sales Project Kanban Board

Use Case 2 – IT Support Kanban Board

IT Support teams can use Kanban boards to track tickets as they move through the resolution process (*Figure 302*). In this example, the columns were labeled to represent typical phases in the ticket resolution process. In the Backlog Sheet view, the Task Name field was used for the ticket issue descriptions and the Resource Names field was used for the assigned support person.

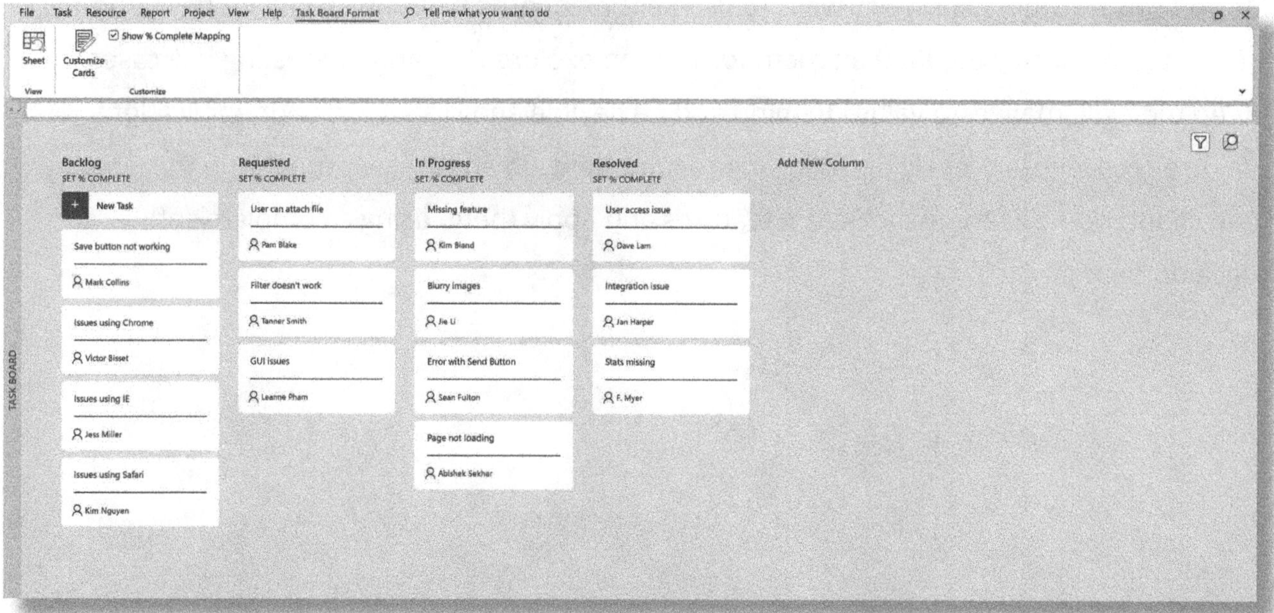

Figure 302 – IT Support Project Kanban Board

Use Case 3 – Digital Marketing Kanban Board

Digital Marketing professionals can use Kanban boards to track action items (*Figure 303* below). In this example, the columns were labeled respectively. In the Backlog Sheet view, the Task Name field was used for action item descriptions and the Resource Names field was used for the assigned action owners.

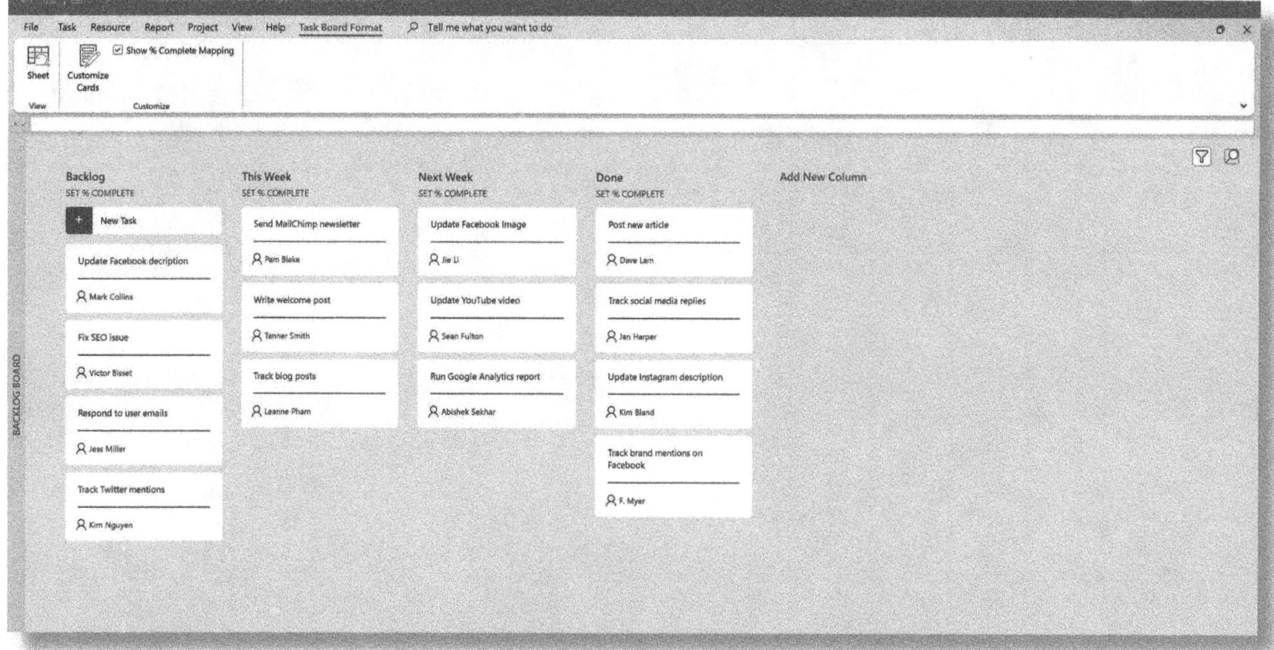

Figure 303 – Digital Marketing Kanban Board

As you can see, there are many ways to use Kanban boards beyond a software development context. When using the Kanban method, you can explore new and interesting use cases. Keep the Agile manifesto values in mind and be flexible and creative in your applications. Value effectiveness over rigidly following requirements in any Agile approach. In the next two chapters, we'll review the Scrum features and apply them, using a complete software development project.

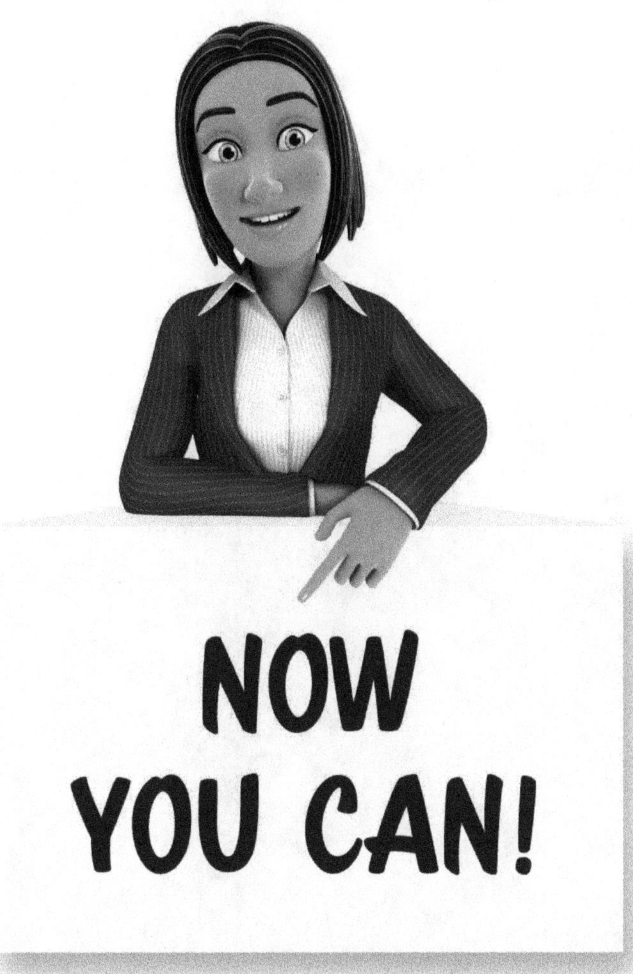

- ✓ Create a New Kanban Project
- ✓ Create a Kanban Project from a Waterfall Project
- ✓ Use the Task Board Views
- ✓ Use the Backlog Sheet Views
- ✓ Use the Kanban Reports

Chapter 24 Using the Scrum Features

In the last chapter, we explored the Kanban features available in Project Online. We then applied those features using three contextually different use cases. In this chapter, we'll explore the **Scrum features**. When you're done, you'll be able to start a Scrum project, use the Sprint Boards and Manage Sprints using the Scrum tools.

You'll Learn To:

- Create Scrum Projects
- Use the Sprint Planning Board
- Use the Sprint Sheet Views
- Use the Sprints Tools
- Manage Sprints
- Use the Sprints Reports

The Project Online Desktop Client includes agile features that let you create and manage your projects after the **Scrum** framework, by creating Sprint-based projects. As reviewed in Chapter 22, a **Sprint** is a short (typically 2 weeks), time-boxed period in which a scrum team works to complete a set amount of work. Sprints are at the core of the Scrum and Agile methodologies.

Starting a New Scrum Project

To start a Scrum project, in the opening view, select the **Sprints Project** command *(Figure 304* below) to open the *Sprints* Project template.

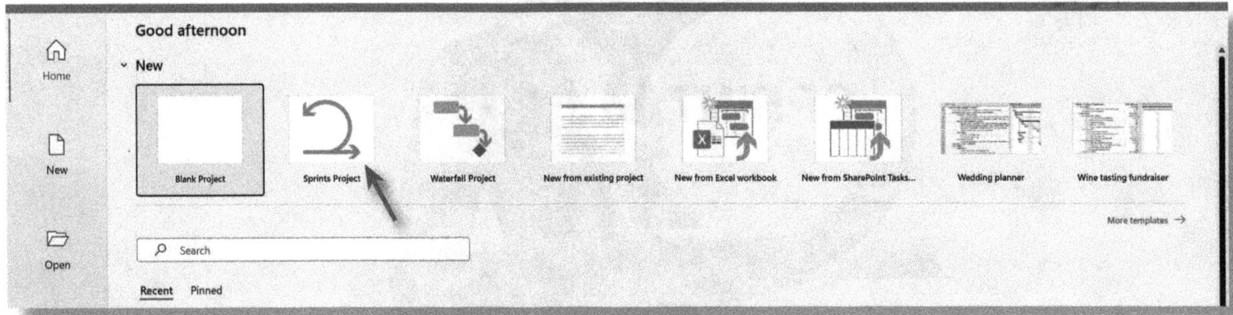

Figure 304 – Start a New Sprints Project

Understanding the Sprint Planning Board

After selecting the **Sprints Project** command, you'll be taken to the **Sprint Planning Board view**, shown in *Figure 305* below.

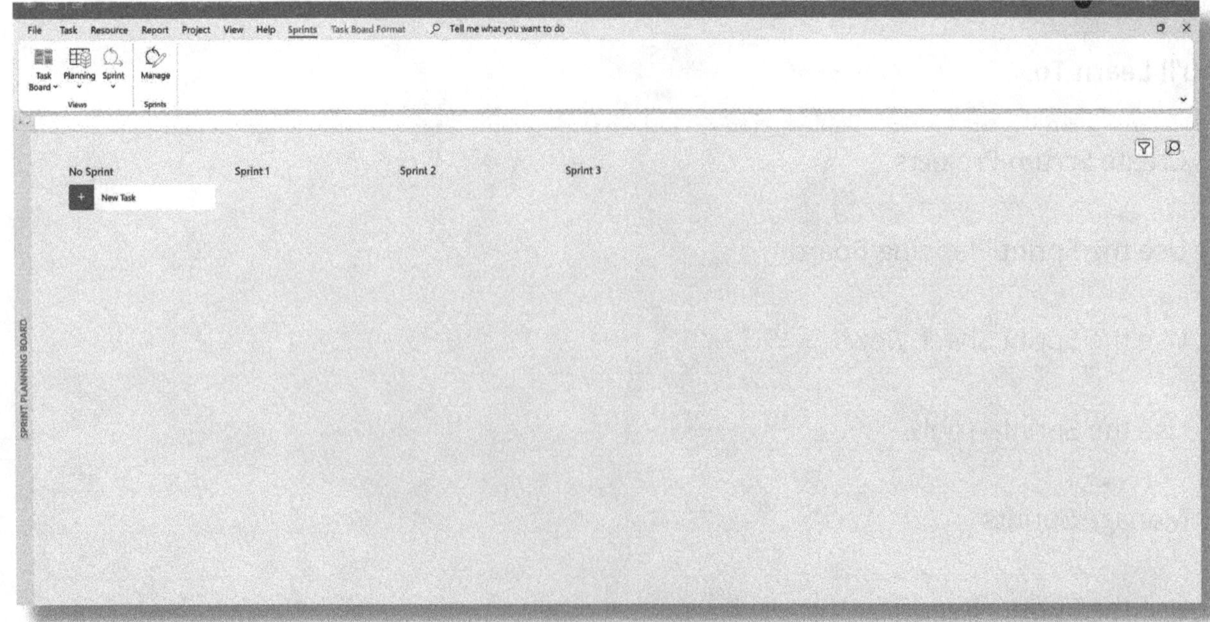

Figure 305 – The Sprint Planning Board

This is where you'll add your tasks and assign them to sprints. The Sprint Planning Board view is similar to the Task Board view, except the board is organized by sprints instead of Board Status categories. By default, there are 4 sprints added to the board – No Sprint, Sprint 1, Sprint 2 and Sprint 3. Before you add tasks to the project, you'll need to define the length and dates for the sprints. This is done using the **Manage Sprints** command located on the **Sprints** contextual tab.

To define Sprint length and dates:

- Select the **Sprints** tab to access the **Sprints tools** on the ribbon.
- In the **Sprints** group, select the **Manage Sprints** command to open the *Manage Sprints* dialogue box (*Figure 306* below).

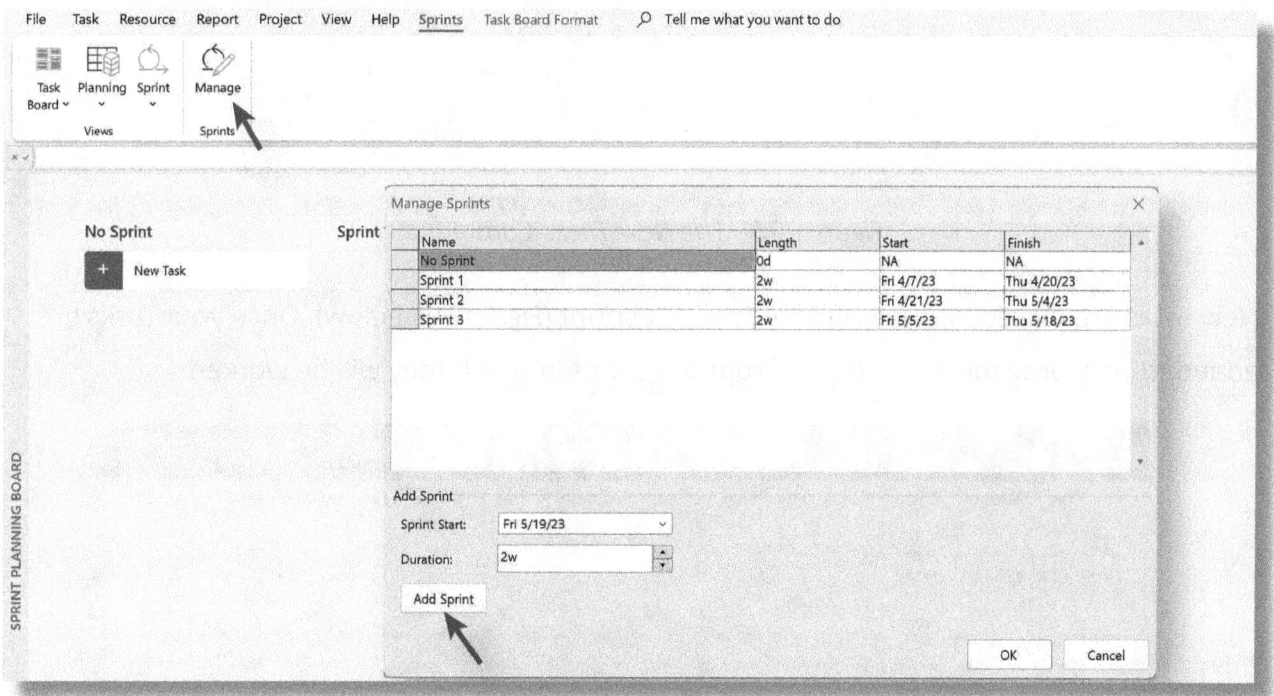

Figure 306 – Manage Sprints

- Starting with Sprint 1, in the **Length** field, enter the duration of the sprint (e.g., 2 weeks or 2w).
- In the **Start** field, enter the date the sprint will start.
- You can also rename the sprints if you'd like (except *No Sprint*).

To add additional sprints to your project:

- In the **Add Sprint** section of the dialogue box, enter the **Sprint Start date** and the **Duration** for the next sprint. Then, select the **Add Sprint** command.
- Add as many sprints as you need and select **OK** to close the *Manage Sprints* dialogue box.

Adding Tasks to your Sprints Project

Use the **New Task** command to add tasks to the project (*Figure 307* below). Simply click the **plus sign**, enter the task name, and select **Add**.

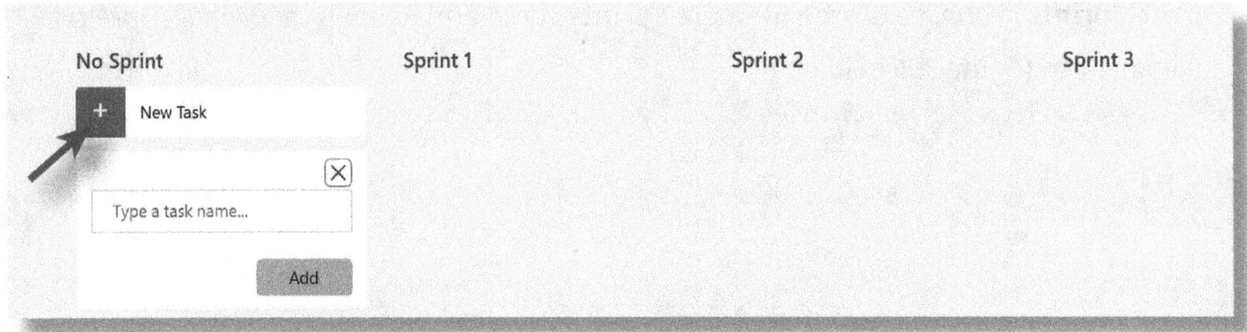

Figure 307 – The New Tasks Command

New tasks are placed into the *No Sprint* default sprint (*Figure 308* below). Once your tasks are added, simply drag them into the appropriate sprint in which they will be worked.

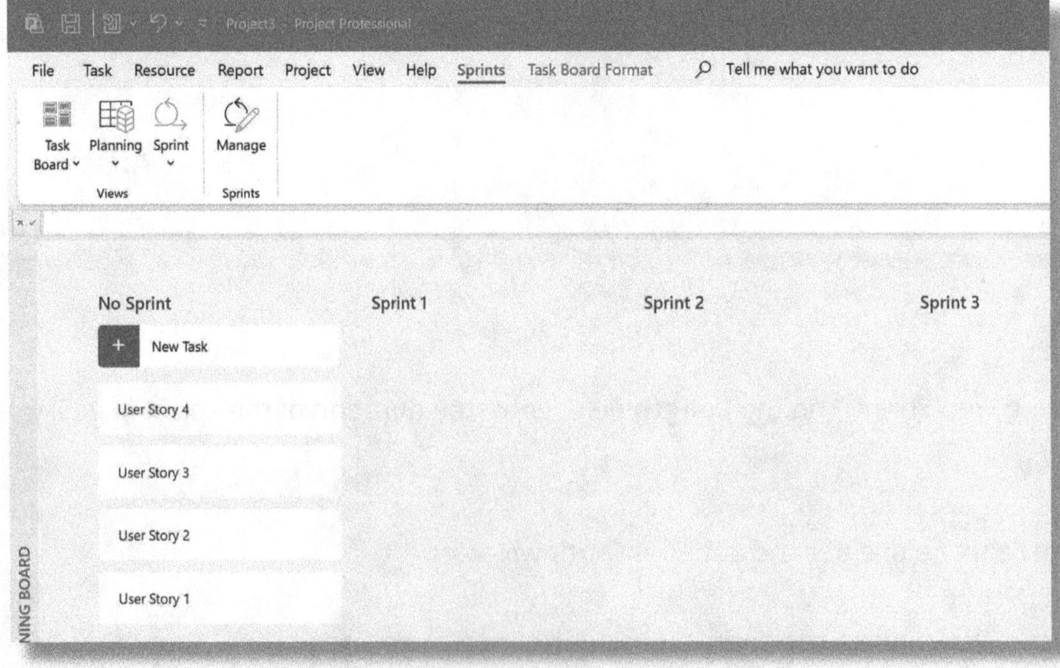

Figure 308 – Adding Tasks to a Sprints Project

Using the Sprint Planning Sheet View

If there are many tasks in your schedule, you can add them to your Sprints project a bit quicker in the *Sprint Planning Sheet* view (*Figure 309* below).

To access this view:

- Select the **Sprints** tab. In the **Views** group, select the **Planning** command.
- From the pick-list, select **Sprint Planning Sheet**.

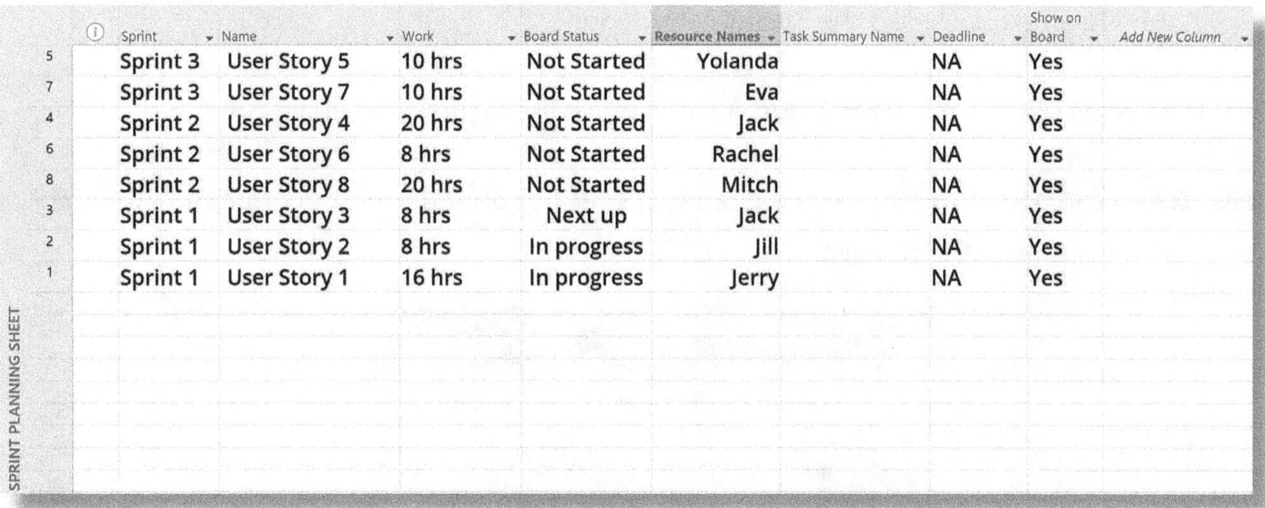

	Sprint	Name	Work	Board Status	Resource Names	Task Summary Name	Deadline	Show on Board	Add New Column
5	Sprint 3	User Story 5	10 hrs	Not Started	Yolanda		NA	Yes	
7	Sprint 3	User Story 7	10 hrs	Not Started	Eva		NA	Yes	
4	Sprint 2	User Story 4	20 hrs	Not Started	Jack		NA	Yes	
6	Sprint 2	User Story 6	8 hrs	Not Started	Rachel		NA	Yes	
8	Sprint 2	User Story 8	20 hrs	Not Started	Mitch		NA	Yes	
3	Sprint 1	User Story 3	8 hrs	Next up	Jack		NA	Yes	
2	Sprint 1	User Story 2	8 hrs	In progress	Jill		NA	Yes	
1	Sprint 1	User Story 1	16 hrs	In progress	Jerry		NA	Yes	

Figure 309 – The Sprint Planning Sheet View

To add a new task, type the task name into the **Name** field. To assign the task to a sprint, in the **Sprint** field, select the appropriate sprint from the pick-list. You can also add work hours, board status, resources, summary tasks, and deadlines. To determine whether a task appears in the boards views, you can toggle its **Show on Board** status. The task information added to this view will populate to the *Sprint Planning Board* view (*Figure 310* below).

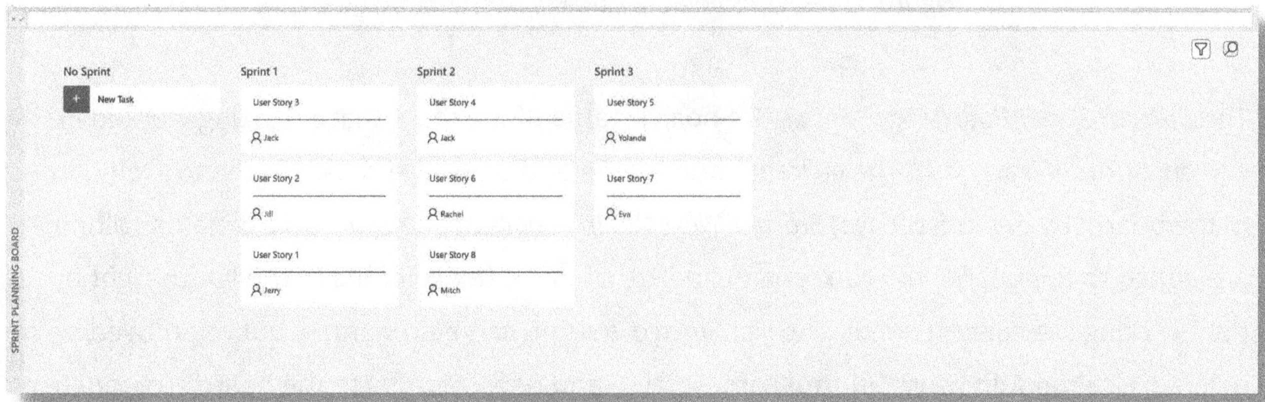

Figure 310 – Viewing Task Information in the Sprint Planning Board View

Using the Current Sprint Board View

After your project is executed and tasks get worked on within their sprints, you can update and track their completion in the **Current Sprint Board view**.

To access this view:

- Select the **Sprints** tab.
- In the **Views** group, select the **Sprint** command.
- Then, select **Current Sprint Board** from the pick-list (*Figure 311* below).

NOTE: You can also view all tasks assigned to a specific sprint using this command. Pick the sprint you want from the pick-list.

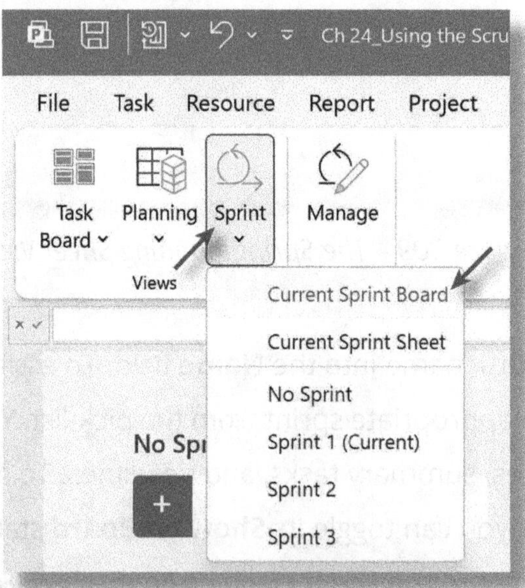

Figure 311 – Accessing the Current Sprint Board View

The *Current Sprint Board* view shows the board status of the tasks that are being worked in the current sprint (*Figure 312*). The current sprint name and dates are shown in the top left corner of the board. By default, the *Not Started, Next Up, In Progress*, and *Done* board status columns are added to the board. You can rename, delete of move the columns to the left or right by right-clicking the column name. The *Not Started* column can be renamed, but not moved or deleted. Use the **Add New Column** command to add new columns to the board. To update a task's progress, simply click and drag the task to the appropriate column.

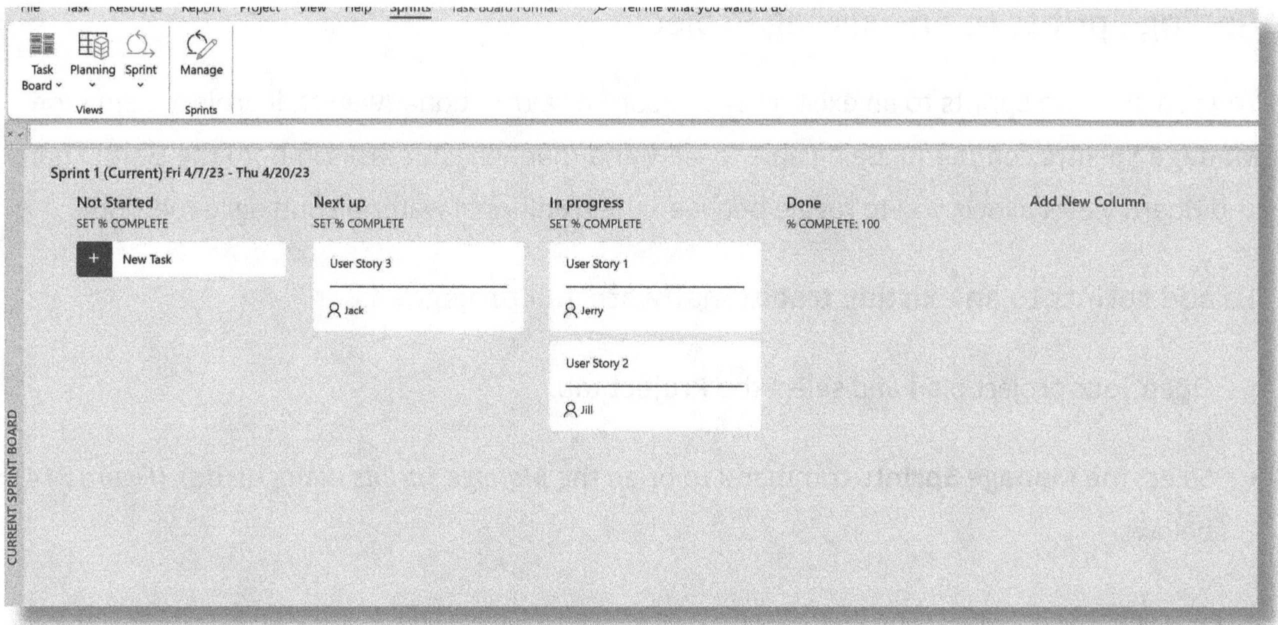

Figure 312 – The Current Sprint Board View

Using the Current Sprint Sheet View

You can also update a task's status in the **Current Sprint Sheet view** (*Figure 313* below). This tabular view also shows task information for tasks that are being worked in the current sprint. It includes additional details that aren't shown in the board views, such as work hours and resource names.

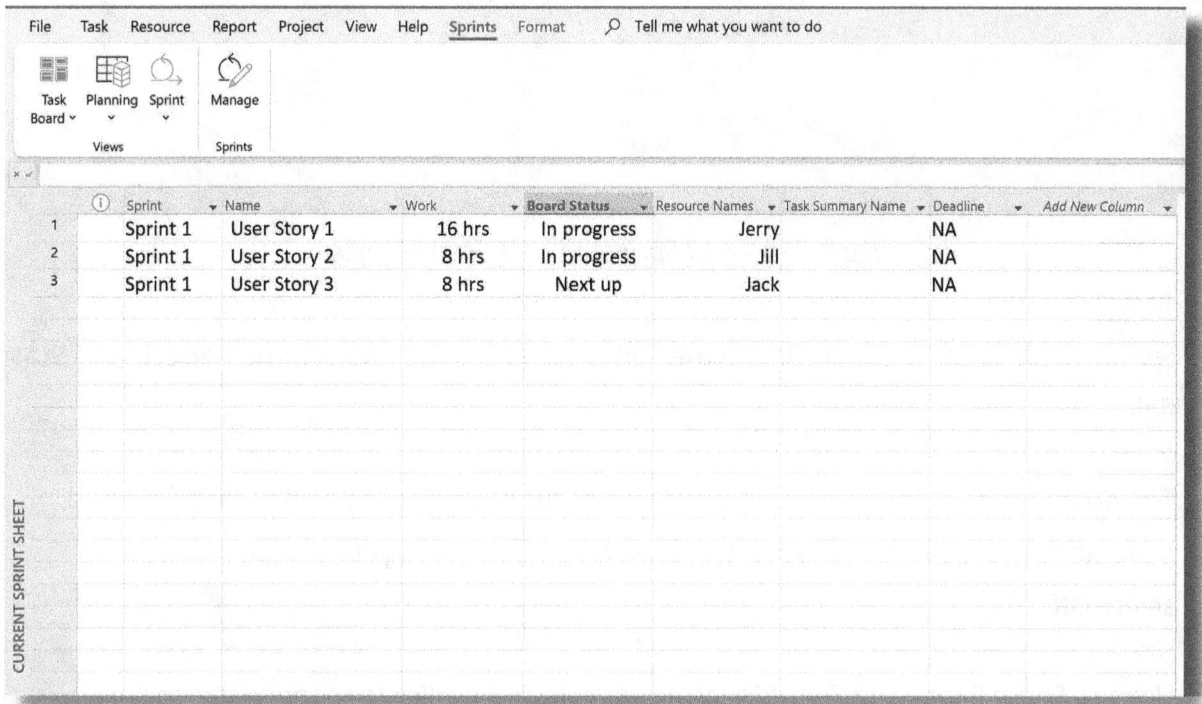

	Sprint	Name	Work	Board Status	Resource Names	Task Summary Name	Deadline	Add New Column
1	Sprint 1	User Story 1	16 hrs	In progress	Jerry		NA	
2	Sprint 1	User Story 2	8 hrs	In progress	Jill		NA	
3	Sprint 1	User Story 3	8 hrs	Next up	Jack		NA	

Figure 313 – The Current Sprint Sheet View

Adding Sprints to an Existing Project

You can also add sprints to an existing Task Board or a traditional/waterfall project, using the **Manage Sprints** command. Being able to view and manage your tasks in both the Gantt chart and Board views allows you to toggle between the traditional waterfall and agile methods.

To add sprints to an existing traditional/waterfall project:

- Open your project plan and select the **Project** tab.
- Select the **Manage Sprints** command to open the *Manage Sprints* dialogue box (*Figure 314* below).

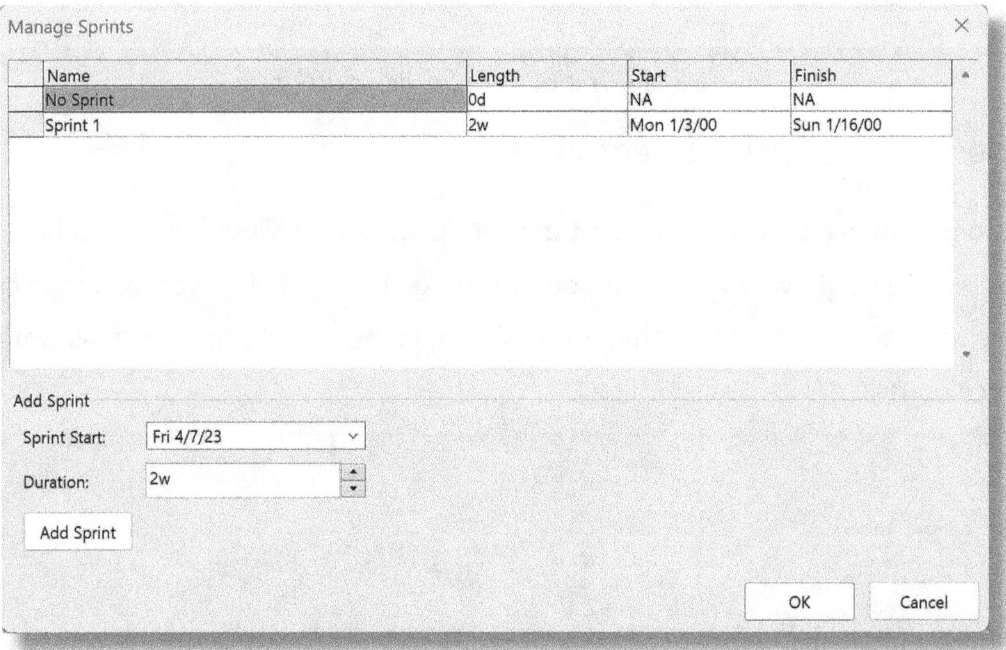

Figure 314 – Add Sprints to an Existing Project

- *Sprint 1* is added by default. Define the sprint duration and dates in the **Length** and **Start** fields.
- To add additional sprints, in the **Add Sprint** section, enter the **Sprint Start** date and **Duration**. Then, select **Add Sprint**. Add as many sprints as your project needs and select **OK**.
- Use the *Sprint Board* and *Sprint Sheet* views reviewed earlier to manage the sprints.

Using the Sprints Reports

There are three Sprints reports available — the **Current Sprint - Task Status** report, the **Current Sprint - Work Status** report, and the **Sprint Status** report. Project uses the information from the *Current Sprint* Board and Sheet views to generate the reports. Let's review each report.

The Current Sprint - Task Status Report

To access the report:

- Select the **Report** tab.
- In the **View Reports** group, select **Task Boards**. Then, select **Current Sprint - Task Status** from the pick-list (*Figure 315* below).

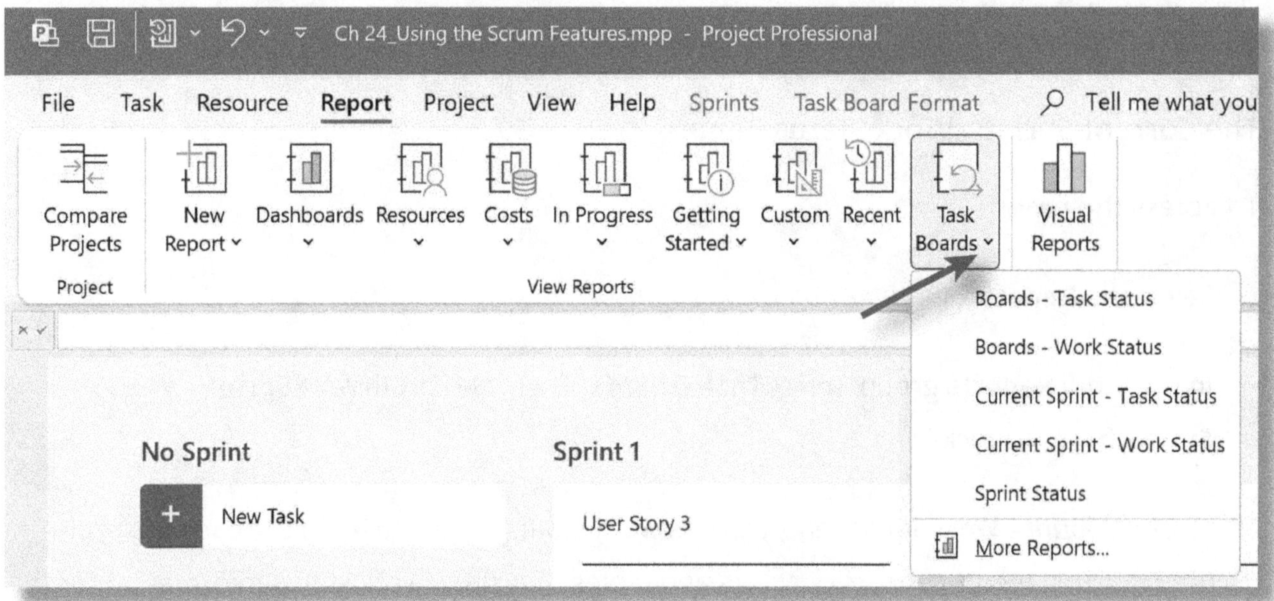

Figure 315 – Access the Sprints Reports

The *Current Sprint – Task Status* report shows status for the tasks in the current sprint in various categories. The report consists of charts and tables that show status information for tasks in the current sprint (*Figure 316*). In the top left, you'll find a pie chart that shows the percentage of the tasks in the current sprint in each Board Status category. The burn-down chart in the middle shows the change in the number of tasks in this current sprint over time.

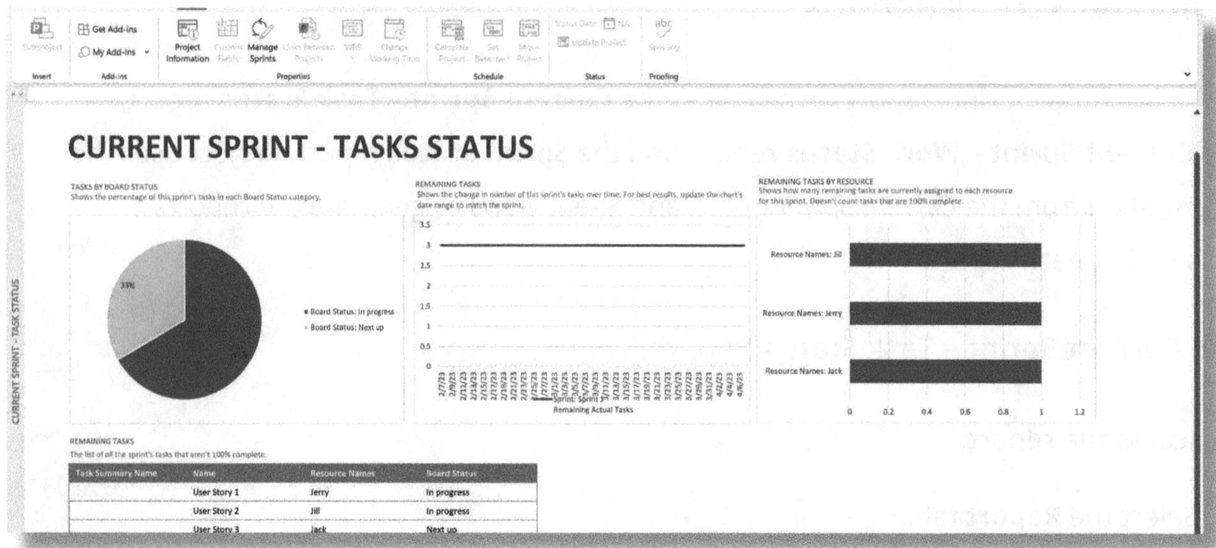

Figure 316 – The Current Sprint – Task Status Report

On the right, you'll find a bar chart that shows the task assignments for the tasks in the current sprint that aren't 100% complete. The table on the bottom shows all the incomplete tasks for the current sprint.

The Current Sprint – Work Status Report

To access the report:

- Select the **Report** tab.
- In the **View Reports** group, select **Task Boards**. Then, select **Current Sprint - Work Status** from the pick-list.

The *Current Sprint - Work Status* report shows work status for the tasks in the current sprint (*Figure 317*). This report consists of charts and tables that show work status information for the current sprint. On the top left side of the report, you'll find a bar chart that shows the number of hours of actual and remaining work in each Board Status category for the current sprint. On the top right, you'll find another bar chart that shows the number of hours of actual and remaining work assigned to each resource for the current sprint. The burn-down chart on the left shows the number of hours of work that have been completed and the number of hours left. Beneath the bar chart on the right, you'll find a table that lists all the incomplete tasks in the current sprint.

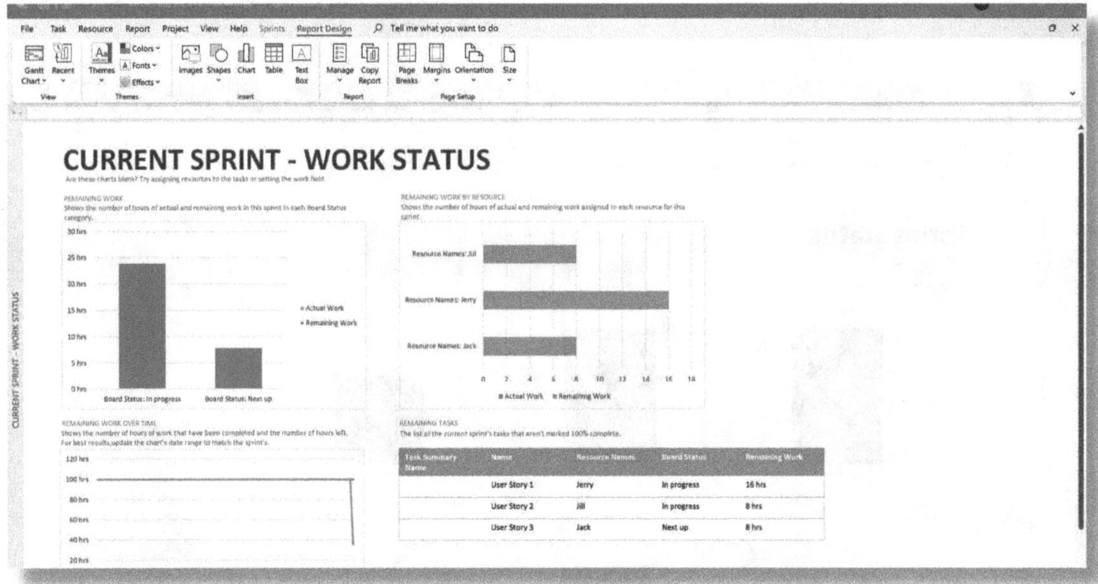

Figure 317 – The Current Sprint – Work Status Report

NOTE: To generate the *Current Sprint - Work Status* report, you must have assigned resources to the tasks in your project and updated the work hours in either the *Sprint Planning sheet* or other resource views.

The Sprint Status Report

To access the report:

- Select the **Report** tab.
- In the **View Reports** group, select **Task Boards**. Then, select **Sprint Status** from the pick-list.

The *Sprint Status* report shows the status of the task and work in each sprint (*Figure 318*). The chart at the top shows how many tasks are in each sprint. The chart on the bottom shows how many hours of work are remaining and completed in each sprint.

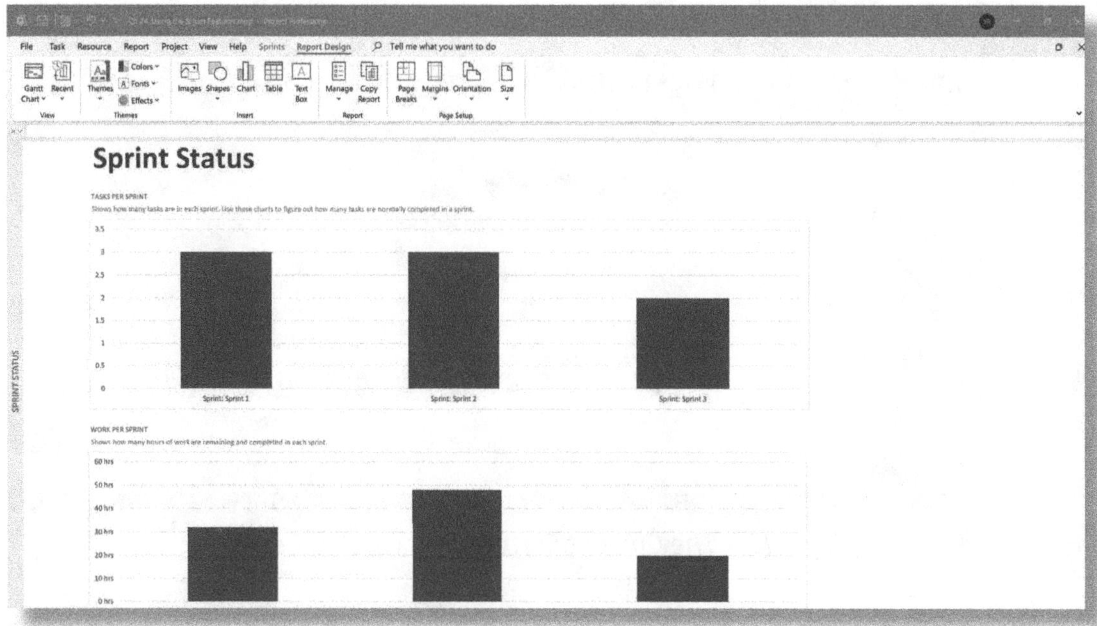

Figure 318 – The Sprint Status Report

The Report Design Tools

On the ribbon, you'll find a contextual **Report Design** tab with tools for formatting and managing the reports. In the **View** group, you'll find quick access commands to the Gantt Chart view and your most recently viewed reports. You can use the tools to format the theme, colors, font, and style of the reports. In addition to the formatting options on the ribbon, if you select certain elements on the report, a panel with additional formatting options will appear on the right.

We've now reviewed the Sprints features you can use to create and manage your projects using the Scrum method. As you can see, the Kanban and Scrum features in Project provide a simple, and useful environment for managing Agile workflows. In the next Chapter, we'll put these features in context on a full-fledged software development project.

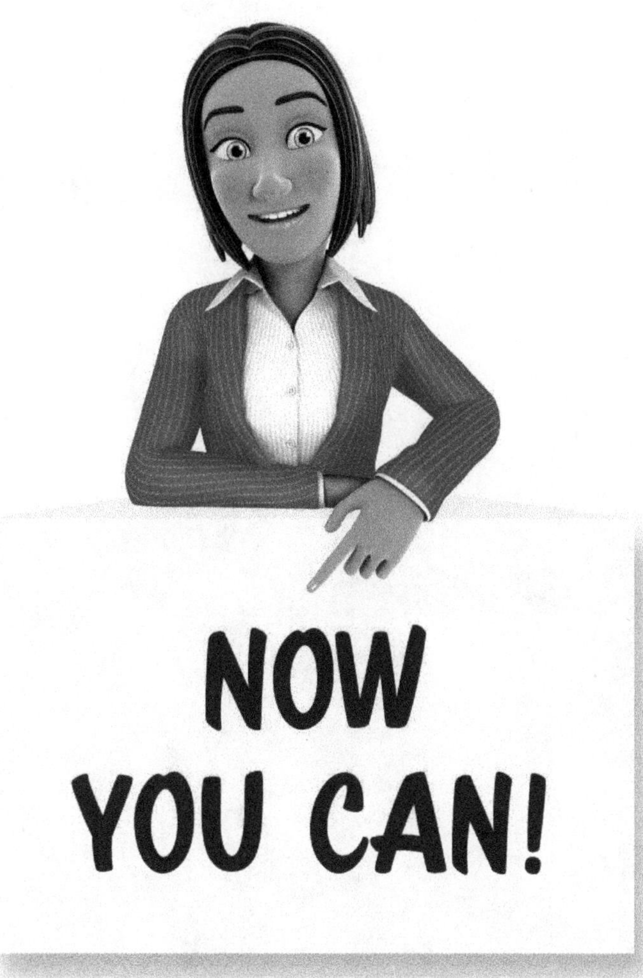

- ✓ Create Scrum Projects
- ✓ Use the Sprint Planning Board
- ✓ Use the Sprint Sheet Views
- ✓ Use the Sprints Tools
- ✓ Mange Sprints
- ✓ Use the Sprints Reports

Chapter 25 An Agile Use Case - Putting It All Together

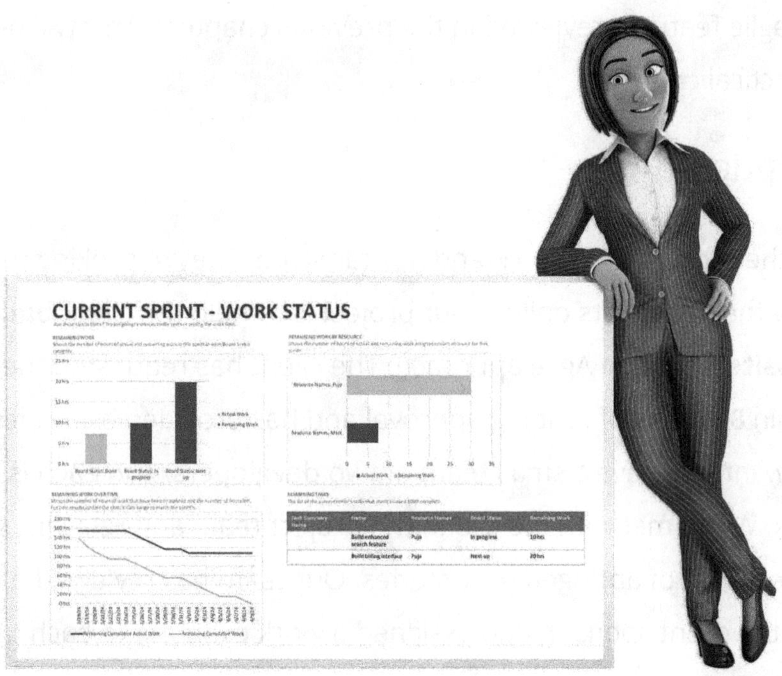

In the last chapter, we explored the Scrum features available in the Project Online desktop client. You learned to create and manage a Scrum project using the Sprint features. In this chapter, we'll put those features to use on a full-fledged software development project. You can work along as we **build and execute an agile project**. We'll enter the project information and progress data and explore each of the Agile reports. Let's get started!

In This Chapter:

- An Agile Use Case – Software Development Project
- Entering Progress Data for Agile Projects
- Using the Agile Reports

Build and Execute a Software Development Project

In this chapter, we will guide you through building and executing a software development project using the agile features reviewed in the previous chapters. This will help put the features into a practical context.

Project Description

Our client sells niche products in a brick-and mortar store. They're seeking to grow their business by selling their products online. Our project is to help the client **build a custom e-commerce website**, using an Agile approach. The client has requested the site be implemented within **8 weeks** of funding approval and has provided examples of the type of online store they want. We have a small team of two developers, and each is only available 20 hours per week. We've met with the client, the project team and relevant stakeholders and have developed a list of abridged user stories. Our team has reviewed each user story, collaborated with the client sponsor, and assigned a work estimate to each user story.

The project inputs are summarized in the following table.

USER STORY	DEVELOPER	WORK (HOURS)
Build Basic Search Feature	Puja	10
Build Shopping Cart	Mark	10
Build Removal from Cart Feature	Mark	7.5
Build Billing Interface	Puja	20
Build Account Set-Up Feature	Puja	20
Build Inventory Add-In Feature	Mark	10
Build Inventory Removal Feature	Mark	7.5
Build Product Editing Feature	Mark	10
Build Enhanced Search Feature	Puja	10
Build Account Editing Feature	Mark	10
Build Recommendation Feature	Mark/Puja	40

Step 1 – Select a Scheduling Methodology

Software development projects are known to have unstable requirements, so we agree with the client's recommendation to use an Agile, rather than a Traditional or Waterfall approach. Since the client has an aggressive deadline (8 weeks) and has provided examples of the type of online store they want, we decide to use Scrum, rather than Kanban.

Here are the reasons:

1. The online store examples will help stabilize requirements, which makes it easier to estimate the work.

2. The use of sprints will help us match the client's schedule requirement to the team's availability, by organizing deliverables into four time-boxed periods, lasting two weeks each.

Step 2 – Start a Scrum Project in Microsoft Project

From the opening view, select the **Sprints Project** template command (*Figure 319* below).

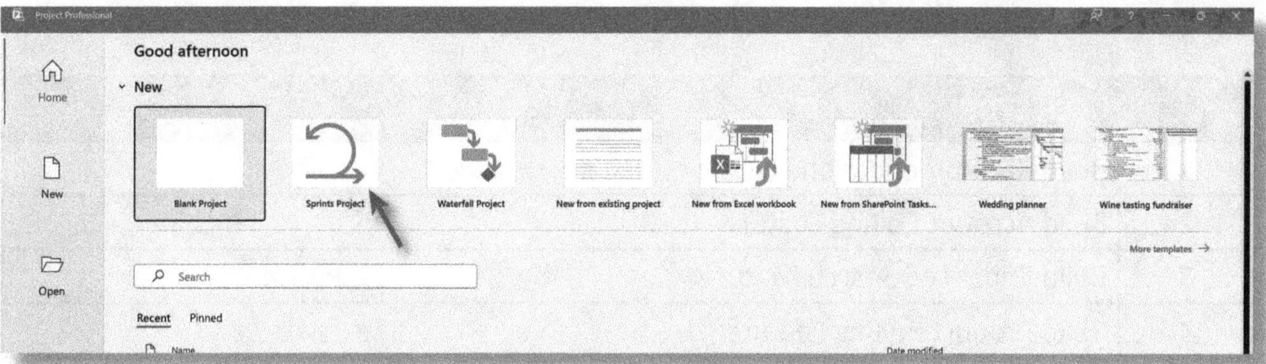

Figure 319 – Start a New Sprints Project

You'll be taken to the **Sprint Planning Board** view (*Figure 320*). By default, there are four sprints added to the board – No Sprint, Sprint 1, Sprint 2 and Sprint 3.

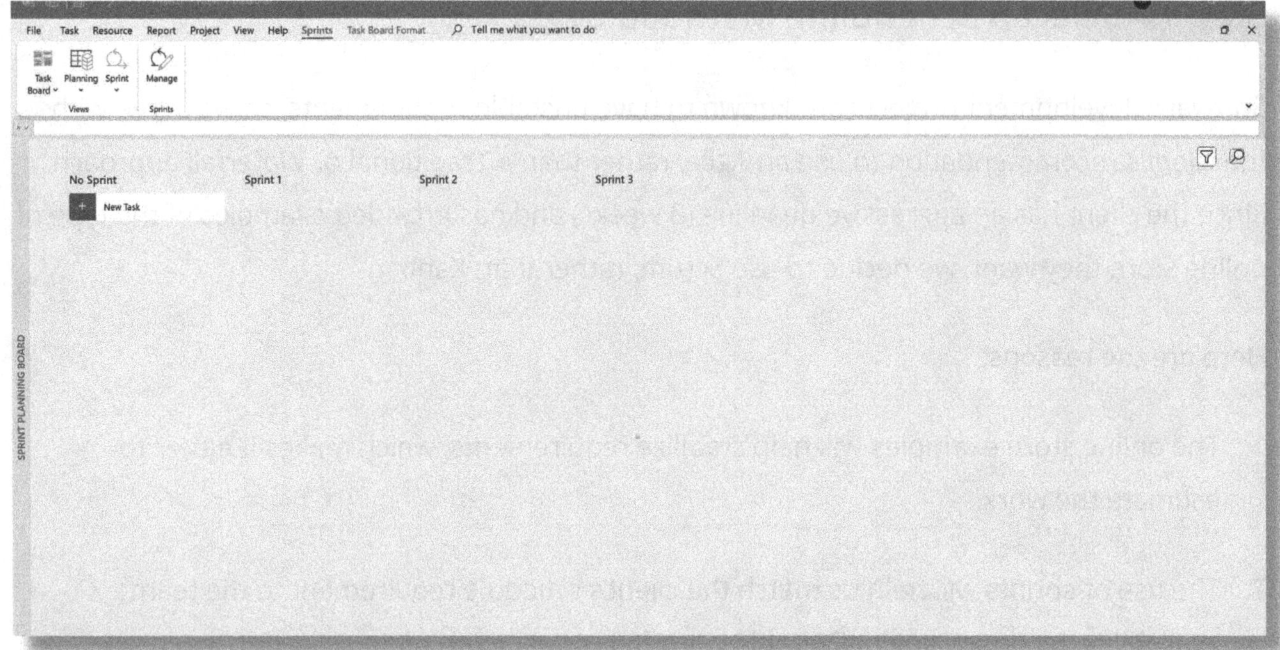

Figure 320 – The Sprint Planning Board View

Step 3 – Enter the Tasks

Use the **New Task** command to enter the following **11 user stories** in the order they're listed.

NOTE: We are entering the tasks out of sequence, starting with the last task. This is so they will appear in the correct sequence on the Sprint Planning Board.

	USER STORY
1	Build Recommendation Feature
2	Build Account Editing Feature
3	Build Enhanced Search Feature
4	Build Product Editing Feature
5	Build Inventory Removal Feature
6	Build Inventory Add-In Feature
7	Build Account Set-Up Feature
8	Build Billing Interface
9	Build Removal From Cart Feature
10	Build Shopping Cart
11	Build Basic Search Feature

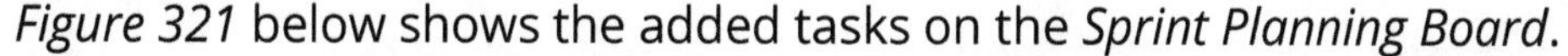

Figure 321 below shows the added tasks on the *Sprint Planning Board*.

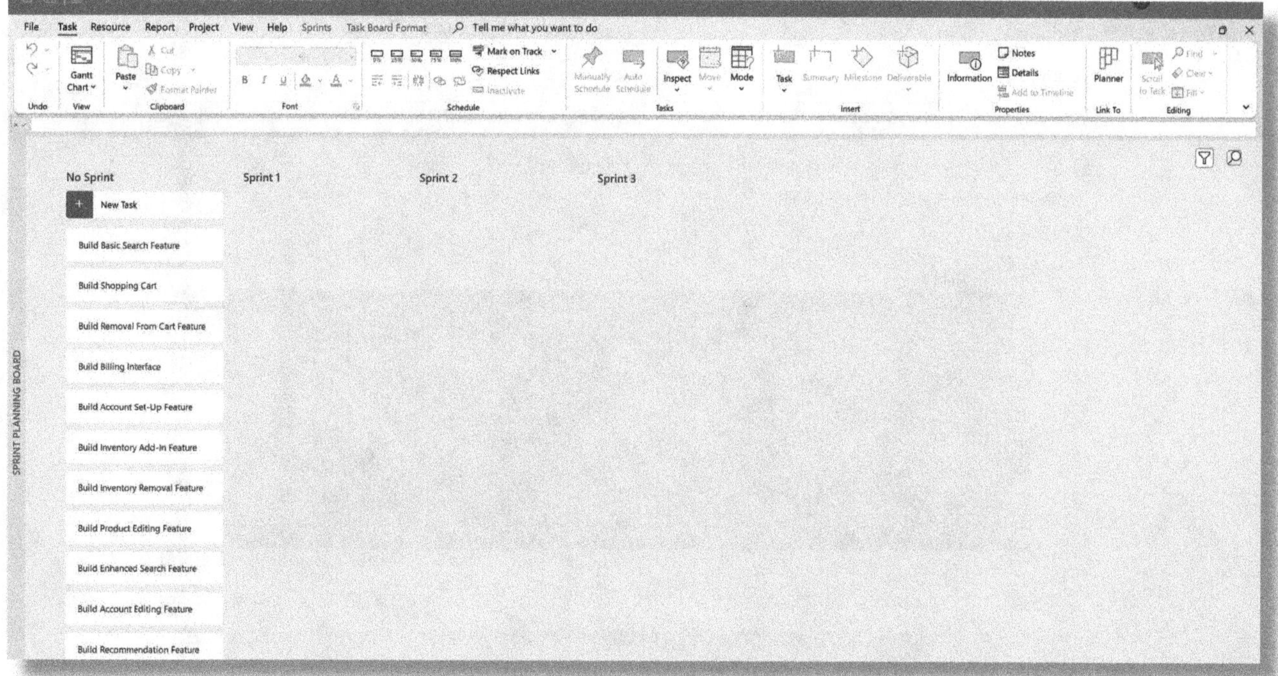

Figure 321 – Tasks Added to the Sprint Planning Board

Step 4 – Set the Project Start Date

The client has informed us that funding will be approved on **3/4/24**. This will be the **Project Start Date**.

To set the project start date:

1. Select the **Project** tab.

2. In the **Properties** group, select the **Project Information** command, to open the *Project Information* dialogue box.

3. Enter **3/4/24** in the **Start date** field. DON'T CLOSE THE DIALOGUE BOX.

4. Since 3/4/24 is not the current date, and we want our project data to reflect this time frame, we will also set **3/4/24** as the "current" date. Enter this date into **Current date** field (*Figure 322*).

5. Select **OK** to close the *Project Information* dialogue box.

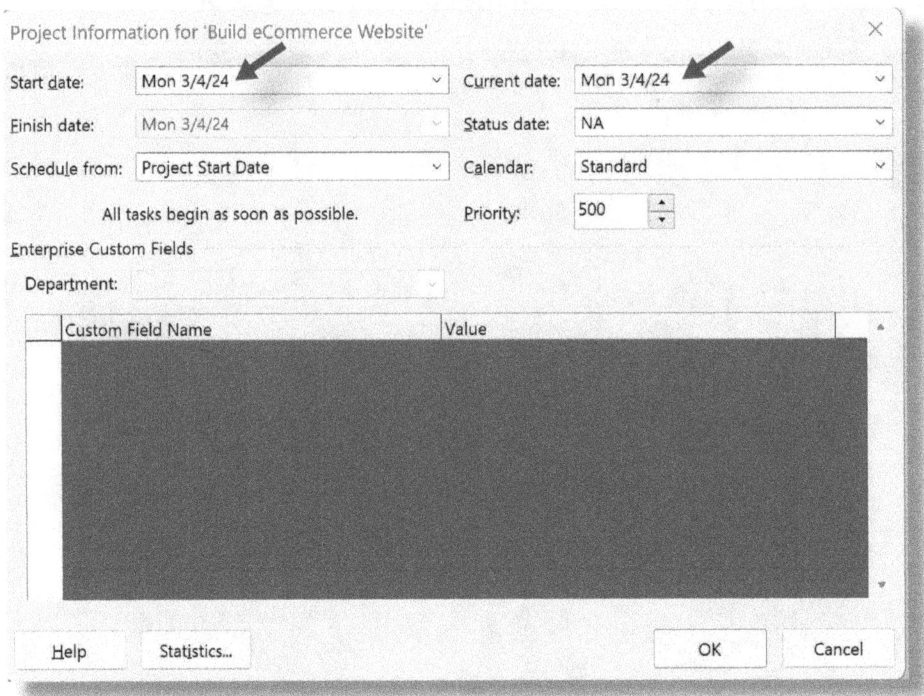

Figure 322 – Set the Project Start Date

Step 5 – Set Sprint Duration and Dates

As mentioned earlier, we will need four 2-week Sprints to complete the project.

The sprint dates are listed in the table below:

SPRINT	DURATION	START DATE	FINISH DATE
SPRINT 1	2 weeks	3/4/24	3/17/24
SPRINT 2	2 weeks	3/18/24	3/31/24
SPRINT 3	2 weeks	4/1/24	4/14/24
SPRINT 4	2 weeks	4/15/24	4/28/24

We'll use the **Manage Sprints** command to set the sprint dates and durations. Also, since Project created only three Sprints (not including the default *No Sprints*), we'll need to add a fourth sprint.

To set sprint durations and dates:

1. Select the **Sprints** tab. In the **Sprints** group, select the **Manage Sprints** command to open the *Manage Sprints* dialogue box.

2. In the **Start** field for Sprint 1, enter **3/4/24**. The finish date for Sprint 1 and the start and finish dates for Sprint 2 and Sprint 3 will automatically update in 2-week intervals.

3. Since the default **Length** is 2 weeks (2w), you don't need to enter the durations. DO NOT CLOSE THE DIALOGUE BOX.

After you enter the start date for Sprint 1, the *Manage Sprints* dialogue box should look like *Figure 323* below.

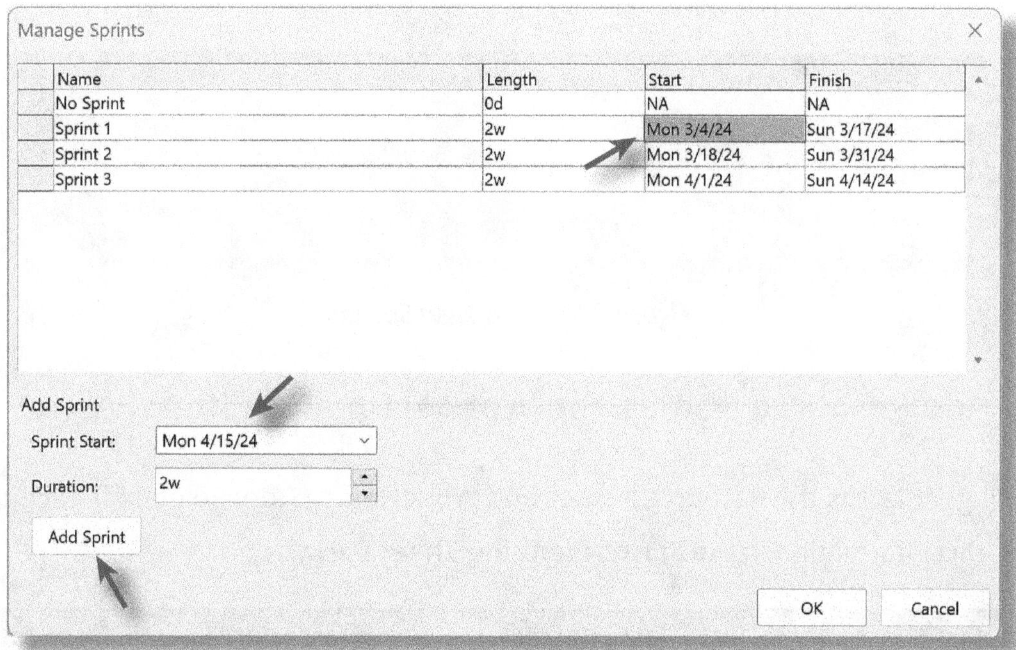

Figure 323 – Set Sprint Dates

Now we'll need to add an additional sprint to the project.

To add a new sprint:

1. In the **Add Sprint** section, the 4/15/24 start date for Sprint 4 should already be populated in the **Sprint Start** field, and 2w should already be populated in the **Duration** field. Since this is correct, select the **Add Sprint** command.

2. Select **OK** to close the *Manage Sprints* dialogue box. A fourth sprint will be added to the *Sprint Planning Board* (*Figure 324*).

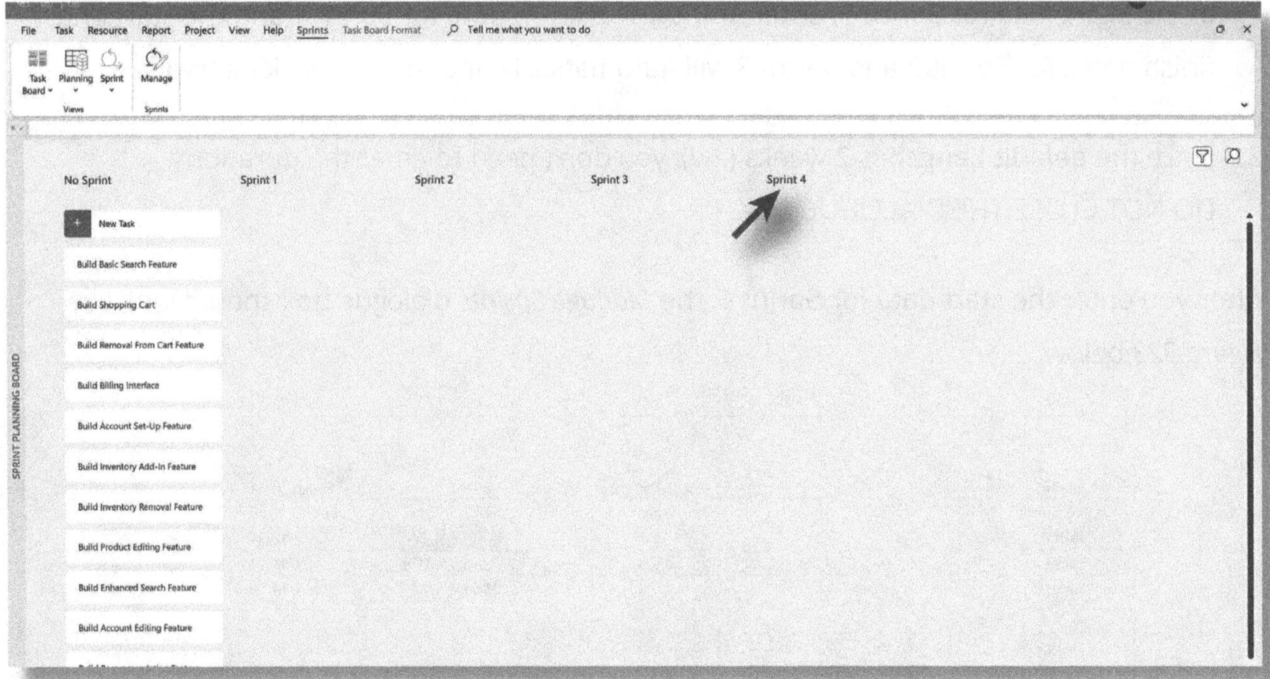

Figure 324 – Add New Sprints

Step 6 – Add Resource Names and Work Estimates (Story Points)

The following table lists the Resource Names and Work Hours (Story Points) for each task. We'll enter this information in the **Sprint Planning Sheet view**.

	TASK NAME	WORK ESTIMATE	RESOURCE NAME
11	Build Basic Search Feature	10	Puja
10	Build Shopping Cart	10	Mark
9	Build Removal Cart Feature	8	Mark
8	Build Billing Interface	20	Puja
7	Build Account Set-Up Feature	20	Puja
6	Build Inventory Add-In Feature	10	Mark
5	Build Inventory Removal Feature	8	Mark
4	Build Product Editing Feature	10	Mark
3	Build Enhanced Search Feature	10	Puja
2	Build Account Editing Feature	10	Mark
1	Build Recommendation Feature	40	Mark, Puja

To switch to the Sprint Planning Sheet view:

1. On the **Sprints** tab, in the **Views** group, select the **Planning** command. Then, select **Sprint Planning Sheet** from the pick-list (*Figure 325* below).

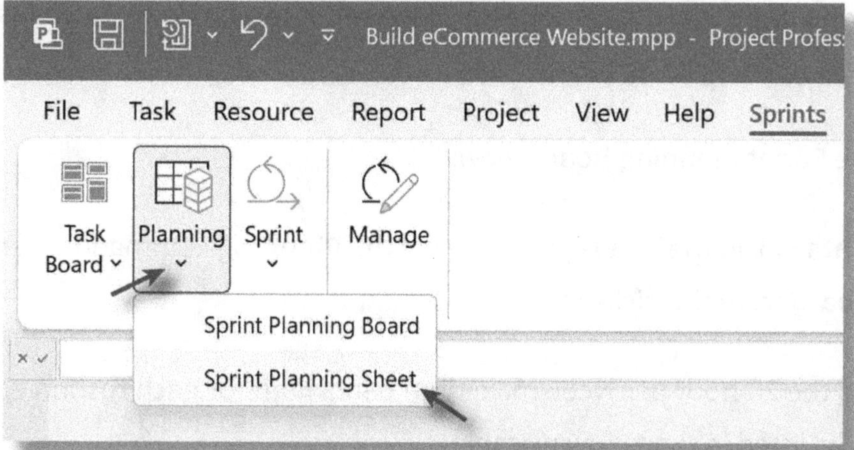

Figure 325 – Access the Sprint Planning Sheet View

To enter the work hours and assign the resources to tasks:

1. In the Sprint Planning Sheet table, enter the work hours into the **Work** field for each task.

2. Type the resource names into the **Resource Names** field for each task.

After the work estimates and resources have been entered, the *Sprint Planning Sheet* should look like *Figure 326* below.

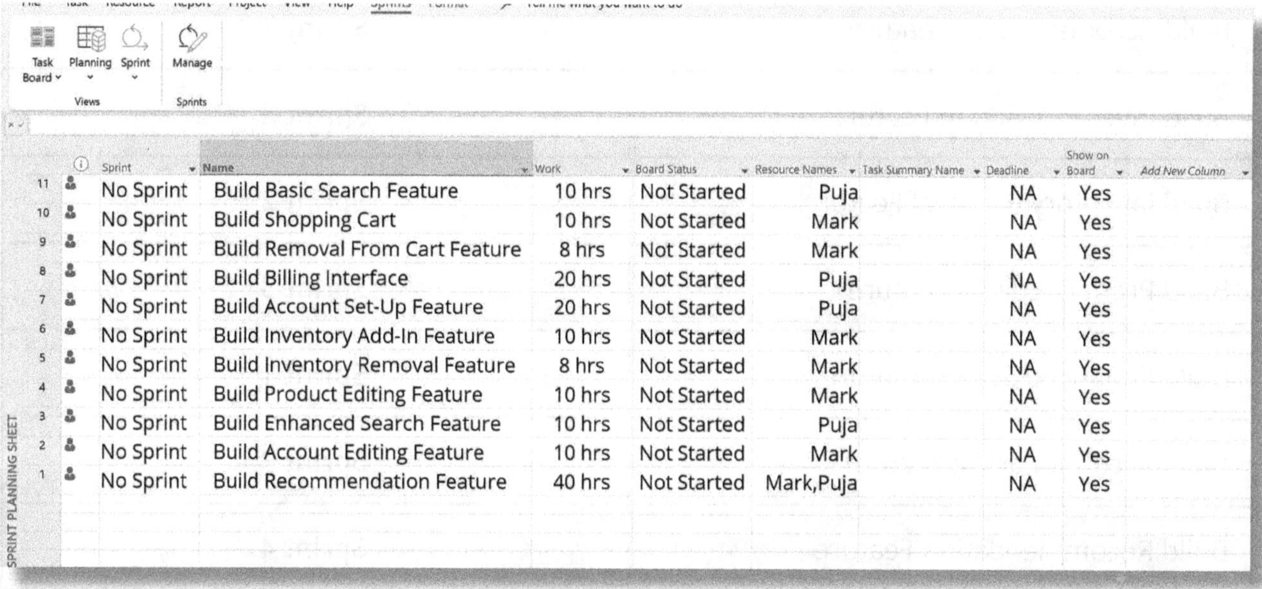

	Sprint	Name	Work	Board Status	Resource Names	Task Summary Name	Deadline	Show on Board	Add New Column
11	No Sprint	Build Basic Search Feature	10 hrs	Not Started	Puja		NA	Yes	
10	No Sprint	Build Shopping Cart	10 hrs	Not Started	Mark		NA	Yes	
9	No Sprint	Build Removal From Cart Feature	8 hrs	Not Started	Mark		NA	Yes	
8	No Sprint	Build Billing Interface	20 hrs	Not Started	Puja		NA	Yes	
7	No Sprint	Build Account Set-Up Feature	20 hrs	Not Started	Puja		NA	Yes	
6	No Sprint	Build Inventory Add-In Feature	10 hrs	Not Started	Mark		NA	Yes	
5	No Sprint	Build Inventory Removal Feature	8 hrs	Not Started	Mark		NA	Yes	
4	No Sprint	Build Product Editing Feature	10 hrs	Not Started	Mark		NA	Yes	
3	No Sprint	Build Enhanced Search Feature	10 hrs	Not Started	Puja		NA	Yes	
2	No Sprint	Build Account Editing Feature	10 hrs	Not Started	Mark		NA	Yes	
1	No Sprint	Build Recommendation Feature	40 hrs	Not Started	Mark,Puja		NA	Yes	

Figure 326 – Enter Work and Assign Resources

Step 7 – Add Tasks to Sprints

Next, we'll switch back to the *Sprint Planning Board* view to add the tasks to their appropriate Sprints. We could do this here in the *Sprint Planning Sheet* by selecting the correct sprint for each task from the pick-list in the Sprint field. However, it can be done much faster (and it's more fun!) on the *Sprint Planning Board*.

To switch to the Sprint Planning Board view:

1. On the **Sprints** tab, in the **Views** group, select the **Planning** command. Then, select **Sprint Planning Board** from the pick-list.

Keeping in mind the 20-hour per week maximum bandwidth for each resource, we will assign tasks to sprints as listed in the following table.

TASK NAME	SPRINT
Build Basic Search Feature	**Sprint 1**
Build Shopping Cart	**Sprint 1**
Build Removal Cart Feature	**Sprint 1**
Build Billing Interface	**Sprint 2**
Build Account Set-Up Feature	**Sprint 3**
Build Inventory Add-In Feature	**Sprint 2**
Build Inventory Removal Feature	**Sprint 2**
Build Product Editing Feature	**Sprint 3**
Build Enhanced Search Feature	**Sprint 1**
Build Account Editing Feature	**Sprint 3**
Build Recommendation Feature	**Sprint 4**

Click and drag the tasks to their appropriate sprint. When you're done, the *Sprint Planning Board* should look like *Figure 327 below*.

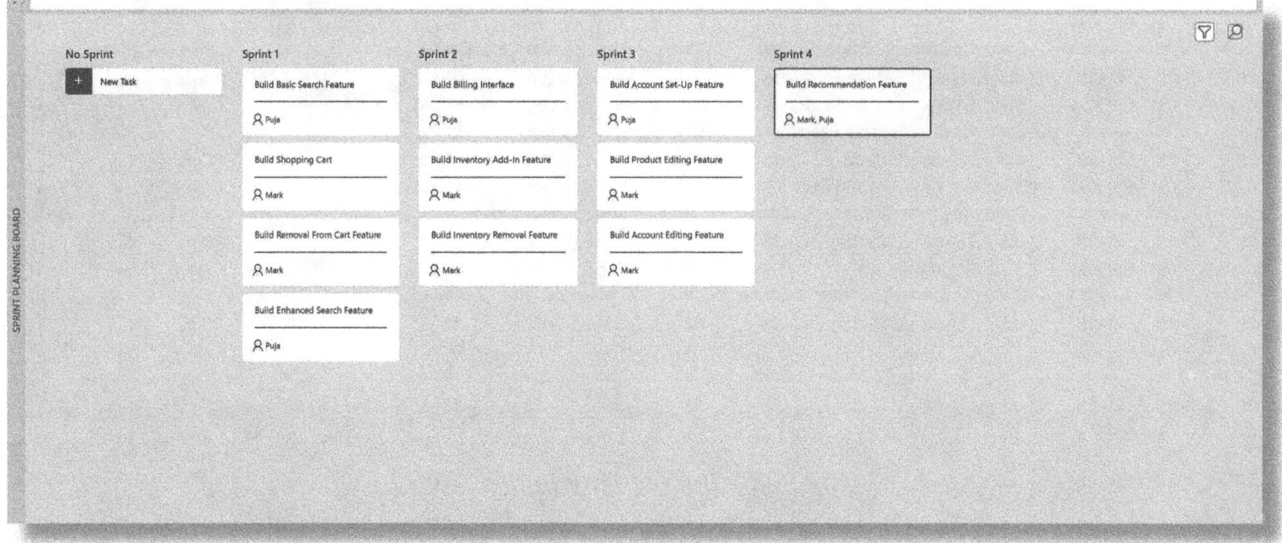

Figure 327 – Add Tasks to Sprints

Step 8 – Update Board Status for the Current Sprint

We're almost ready to present the plan to the client! Before we do, we'll change the **Board Status** for the tasks in Sprint 1 – We'll place 10 hours of work per resource in the *In Progress* column and 10 hours of work per resource in the *Next Up* column.

Let's switch back to the *Sprint Planning Sheet* view to make these updates.

1. On the **Sprints** tab, in the **Views** group, select the **Planning** command. Then, select **Sprint Planning Sheet** from the pick-list.

Notice that the *Sprint* column has been updated, per the sprints we assigned on the Sprints Planning Board.

In the **Board Status** field, update the board status for the sprints in **Sprint 1** as follows:

TASK	BOARD STATUS
Build Basic Search Feature	**In Progress**
Build Shopping Cart	**In Progress**
Build Removal Cart Feature	**Next Up**
Build Enhanced Search Feature	**Next Up**

When you're done, the *Sprint Planning Sheet* should look like *Figure 328* below.

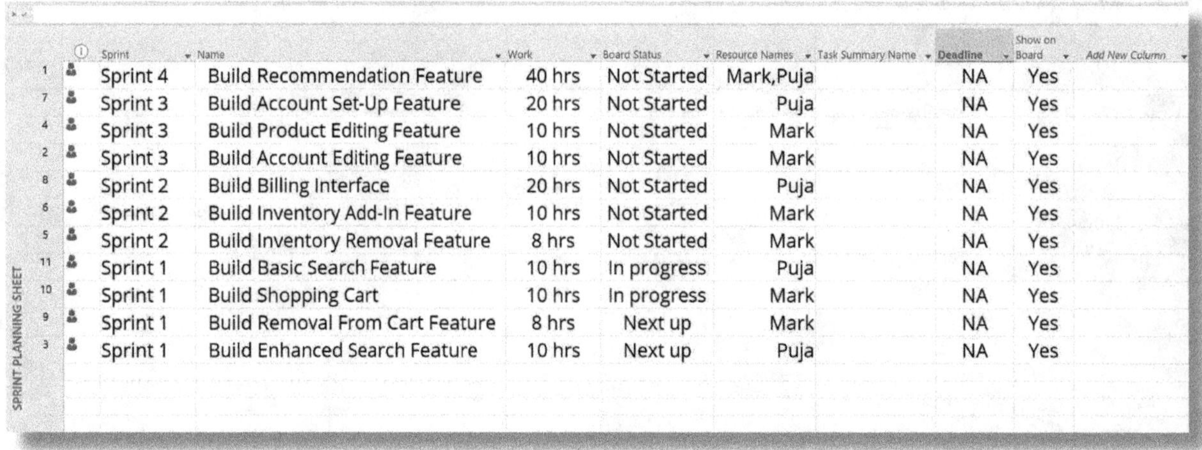

	Sprint	Name	Work	Board Status	Resource Names	Task Summary Name	Deadline	Show on Board	Add New Column
1	Sprint 4	Build Recommendation Feature	40 hrs	Not Started	Mark,Puja		NA	Yes	
7	Sprint 3	Build Account Set-Up Feature	20 hrs	Not Started	Puja		NA	Yes	
4	Sprint 3	Build Product Editing Feature	10 hrs	Not Started	Mark		NA	Yes	
2	Sprint 3	Build Account Editing Feature	10 hrs	Not Started	Mark		NA	Yes	
8	Sprint 2	Build Billing Interface	20 hrs	Not Started	Puja		NA	Yes	
6	Sprint 2	Build Inventory Add-In Feature	10 hrs	Not Started	Mark		NA	Yes	
5	Sprint 2	Build Inventory Removal Feature	8 hrs	Not Started	Mark		NA	Yes	
11	Sprint 1	Build Basic Search Feature	10 hrs	In progress	Puja		NA	Yes	
10	Sprint 1	Build Shopping Cart	10 hrs	In progress	Mark		NA	Yes	
9	Sprint 1	Build Removal From Cart Feature	8 hrs	Next up	Mark		NA	Yes	
3	Sprint 1	Build Enhanced Search Feature	10 hrs	Next up	Puja		NA	Yes	

Figure 328 – Update Task Board Status

To see the effect of these updates, we'll switch to the **Current Sprint Board** view.

1. On the **Sprints** tab, in the **Views** group, select the **Sprint** command. Then, select **Current Sprint Board** from the pick-list.

The Current Sprint Board shows the updated board status of all the tasks in the current Sprint (*Figure 329* below). **NOTE:** if you don't see anything in this view, you'll need to make sure the current start date is set to 3/4/24 in the *Project Options* dialogue box (review "Step 4" for instructions).

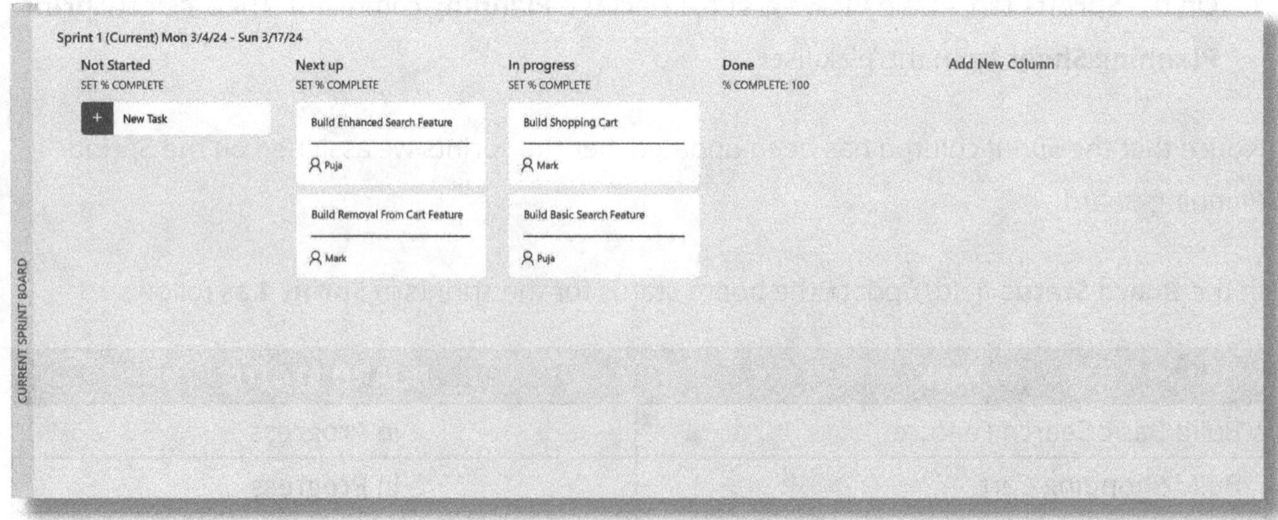

Figure 329 – Current Sprint Board View

Step 9 – Enter Progress data

Mark and Puja, our developers, have each completed 5 hours of work on their *In Progress* tasks in the current sprint. We'll enter this progress data in the *Current Sprint Sheet* view.

1. On the **Sprints** tab, in the **Views** group, select the **Sprint** command. Then, select **Current Sprint Sheet** from the pick-list.

To enter the progress data, we'll first need to add the **Actual Work** column to the table, as follows:

1. Using the **Add New Column** field, add the **Actual Work** column to the table.

2. In the **Actual Work** column for the *Build Shopping Cart* task, enter **5 hrs**.

3. In the **Actual Work** column for the *Build Basic Search Feature* task, enter **5 hrs**.

When you're done, the updated Current Sprint Sheet should look like *Figure 330* below.

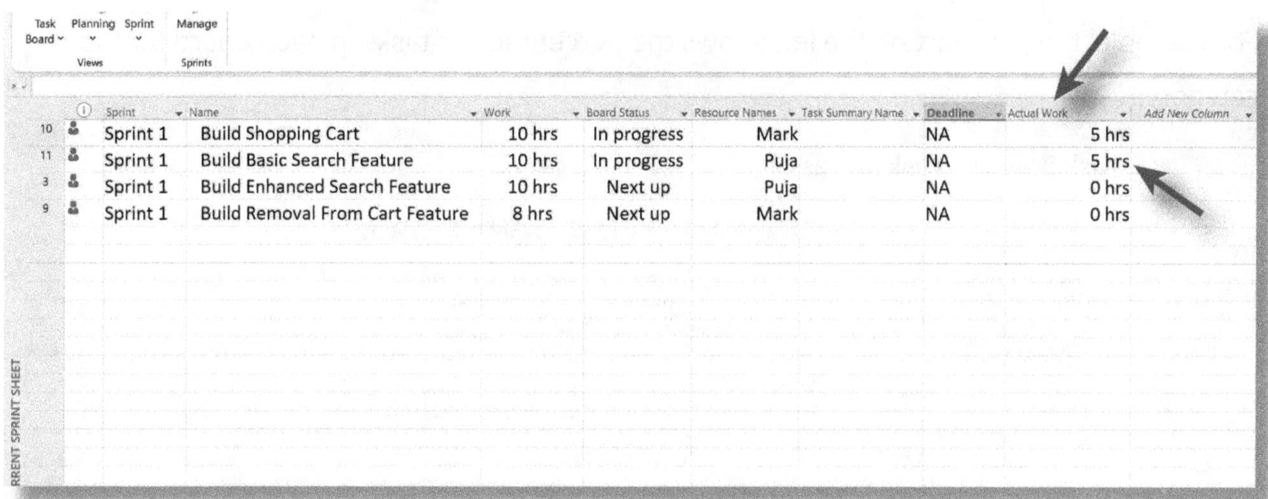

Figure 330 – Enter Progress Data

Step 10 – Generate Agile Reports

We're now ready to show off our work and present our plan to the client! We'll use the Agile reports to make an excellent first impression. Select the **Report** tab to view the reports options on the ribbon. In the **View Reports** group, the Agile reports are accessible under the **Task Boards** group.

There are five Agile reports available – the **Boards - Task Status** report, the **Boards - Work Status** report, the **Current Sprint - Tasks Status** report, the **Current Sprint - Work Status** report, and the **Sprint Status** report (*Figure 331* below). We'll generate each Agile report to send to the client.

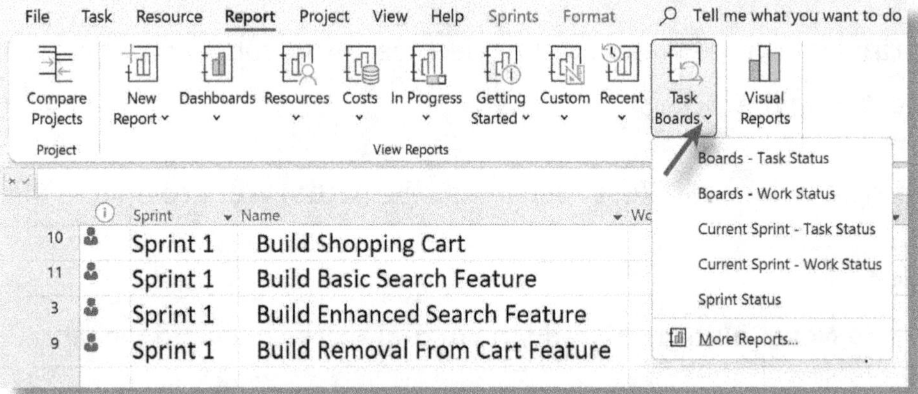

Figure 331 – Access the Agile Reports

Boards – Task Status Report

From the **Task Boards** pick-list, select the **Boards – Task Status** report. This report consists of charts and tables that show task status information in different categories (*Figure 332* below). For example, the pie chart on the left shows the percentage of tasks in each Board Status category.

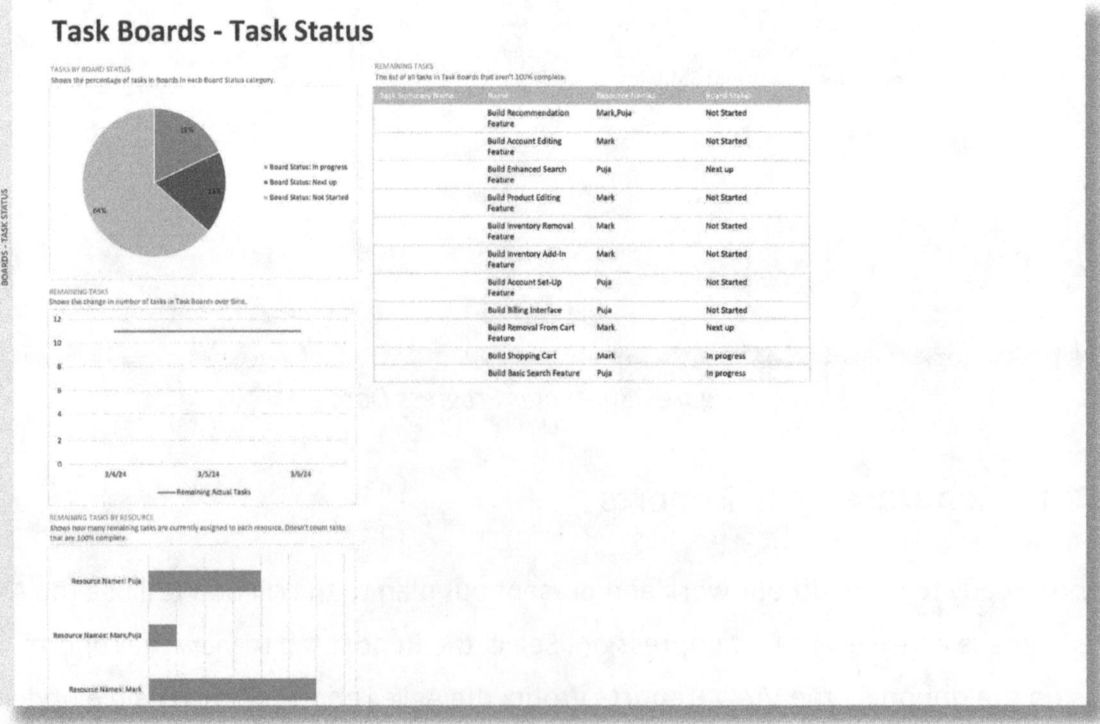

Figure 332 – The Task Boards - Task Status Report

Boards – Work Status Report

Select the **Report** tab. From the **Task Boards** pick-list, select the **Boards – Work Status** report. This report consists of charts and tables that show work status information in different categories (*Figure 333* below). For example, in the bar chart on the top right, we can see the results of the Actual Work progress data we entered for Puja and Mark.

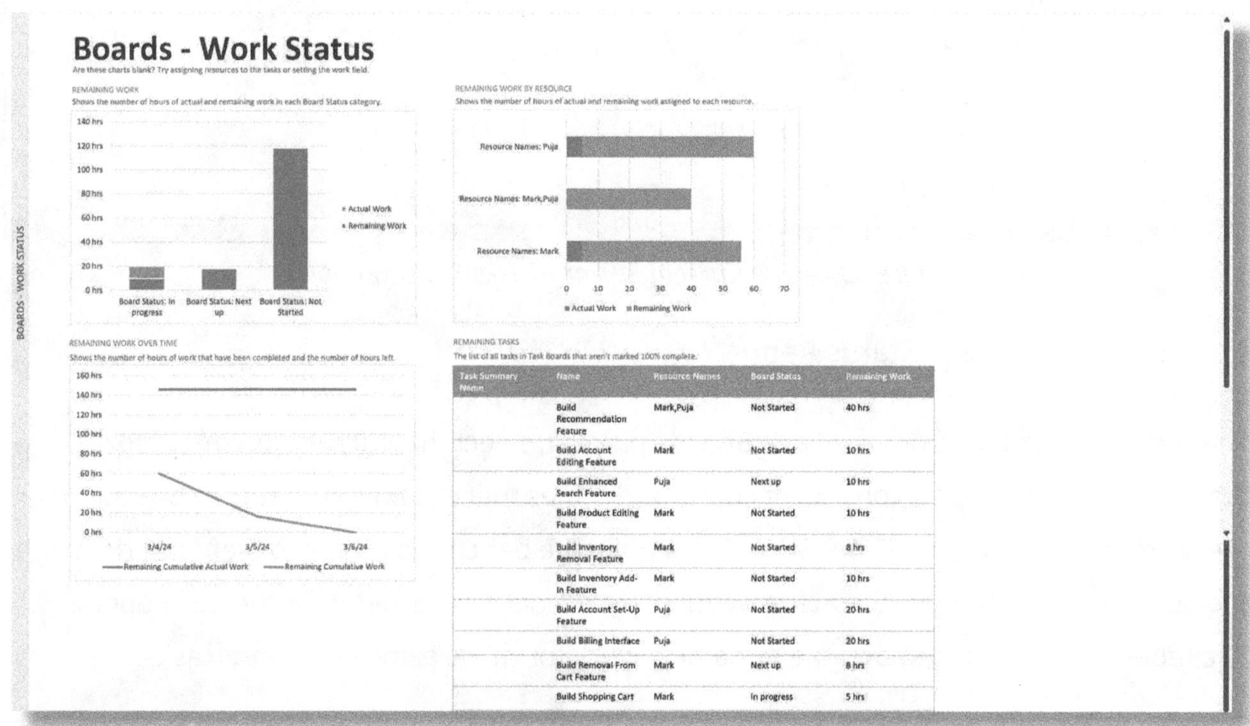

Task Summary Name	Name	Resource Names	Board Status	Remaining Work
	Build Recommendation Feature	Mark,Puja	Not Started	40 hrs
	Build Account Editing Feature	Mark	Not Started	10 hrs
	Build Enhanced Search Feature	Puja	Next up	10 hrs
	Build Product Editing Feature	Mark	Not Started	10 hrs
	Build Inventory Removal Feature	Mark	Not Started	8 hrs
	Build Inventory Add-In Feature	Mark	Not Started	10 hrs
	Build Account Set-Up Feature	Puja	Not Started	20 hrs
	Build Billing Interface	Puja	Not Started	20 hrs
	Build Removal From Cart Feature	Mark	Next up	8 hrs
	Build Shopping Cart	Mark	In progress	5 hrs

Figure 333 – The Boards - Work Status Report

Current Sprint – Task Status Report

Select the **Report** tab. From the **Task Boards** pick-list, select the **Current Sprint – Task Status** report. This report consists of charts and tables that show status information for tasks in the current sprint. (*Figure 334*). For example, this report shows us the results of the Board Status update we entered earlier. We can also see that Mark and Puja have an equal number of remaining tasks in the current sprint.

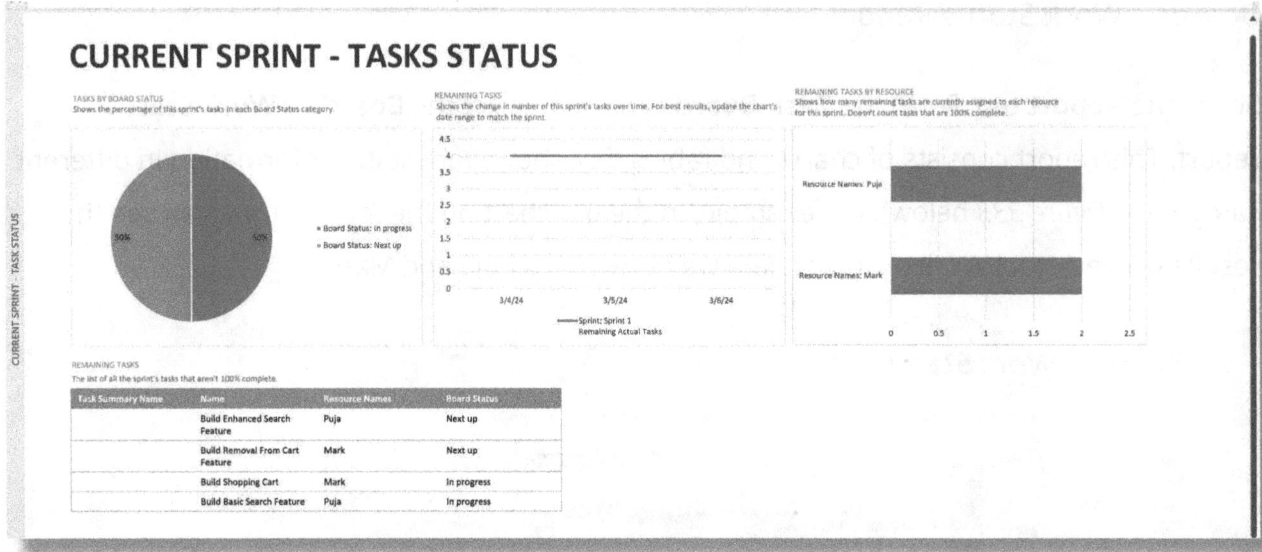

Task Summary Name	Name	Resource Names	Board Status
	Build Enhanced Search Feature	Puja	Next up
	Build Removal From Cart Feature	Mark	Next up
	Build Shopping Cart	Mark	In progress
	Build Basic Search Feature	Puja	In progress

Figure 334 – The Current Sprint - Tasks Status Report

Current Sprint – Work Status Report

Select the **Report** tab. From the **Task Boards** pick-list, select the **Current Sprint – Work Status** report. This report consists of charts and tables that show work status information for the current sprint (*Figure 335* below). For example, the bar charts on the top left and right and the burndown chart reflect the Actual Work progress data we entered for the developers. The table on the bottom shows the remaining work for those same *In Progress* tasks.

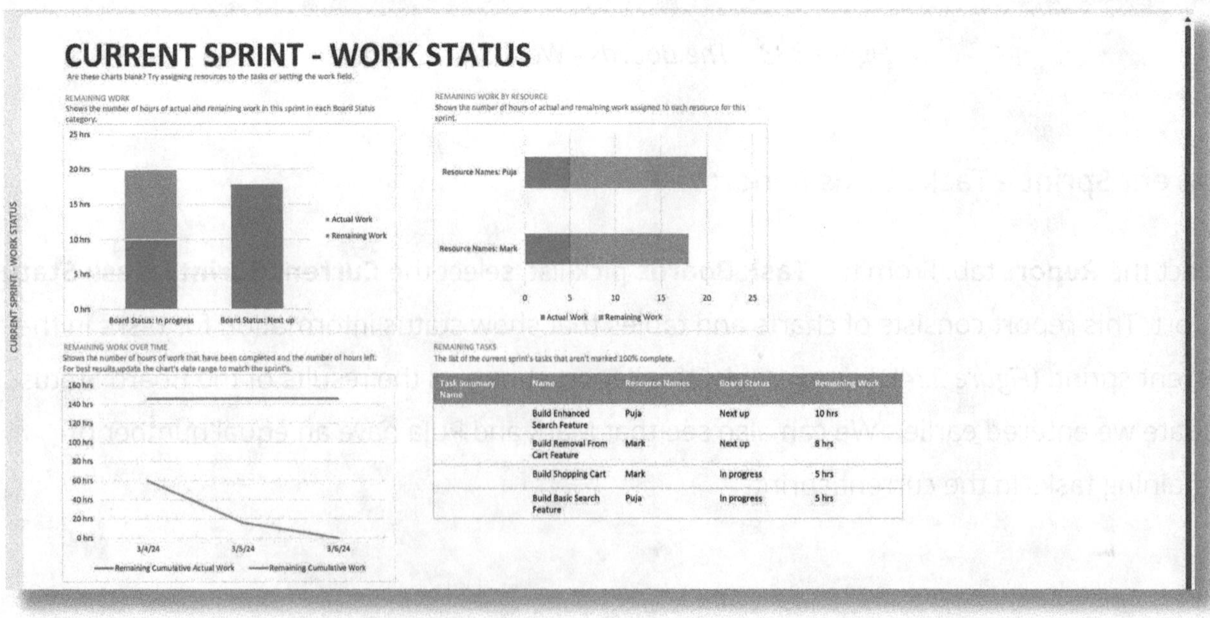

Task Summary Name	Name	Resource Names	Board Status	Remaining Work
	Build Enhanced Search Feature	Puja	Next up	10 hrs
	Build Removal From Cart Feature	Mark	Next up	8 hrs
	Build Shopping Cart	Mark	In progress	5 hrs
	Build Basic Search Feature	Puja	In progress	5 hrs

Figure 335 – The Current Sprint - Work Status Report

Sprint Status Report

Select the **Report** tab. From the **Task Boards** pick-list, select the **Sprint Status** report.

This report shows the status of the task and work in each sprint (*Figure 336* below). The chart at the top shows how many tasks are in each sprint. The chart at the bottom shows how many hours of work are remaining and completed in each sprint.

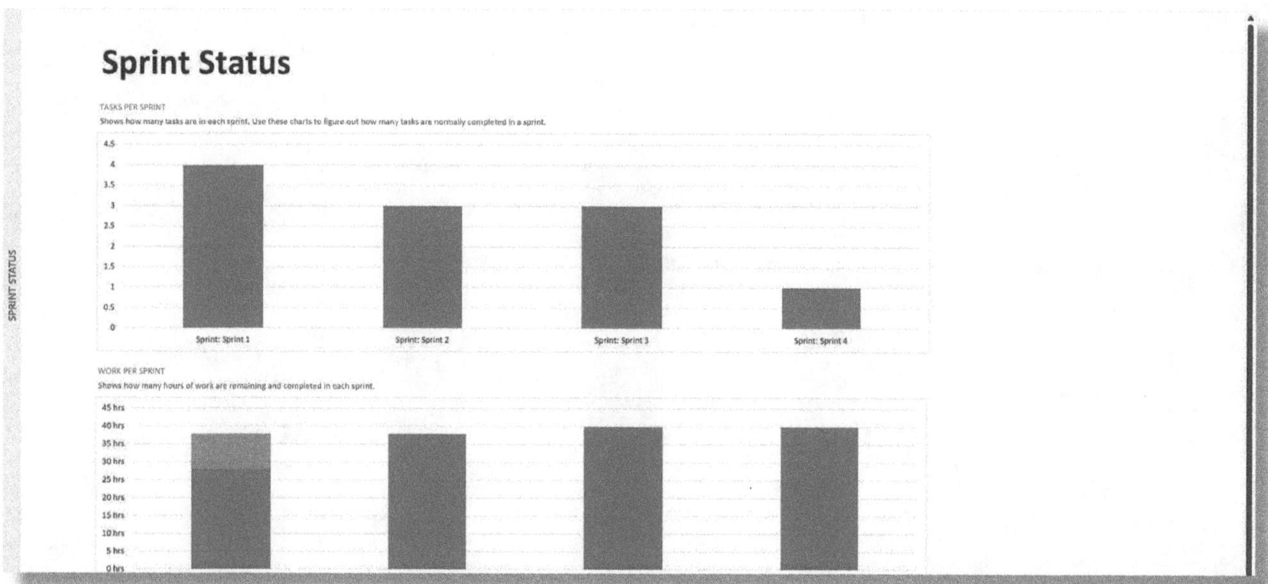

Figure 336 – The Sprint Status Report

We've now applied the Agile features to build and execute a complete software development Sprints project. We also used the Agile reports to show a visual depiction of project status. These reports can make an excellent impression as you work with internal and external clients.

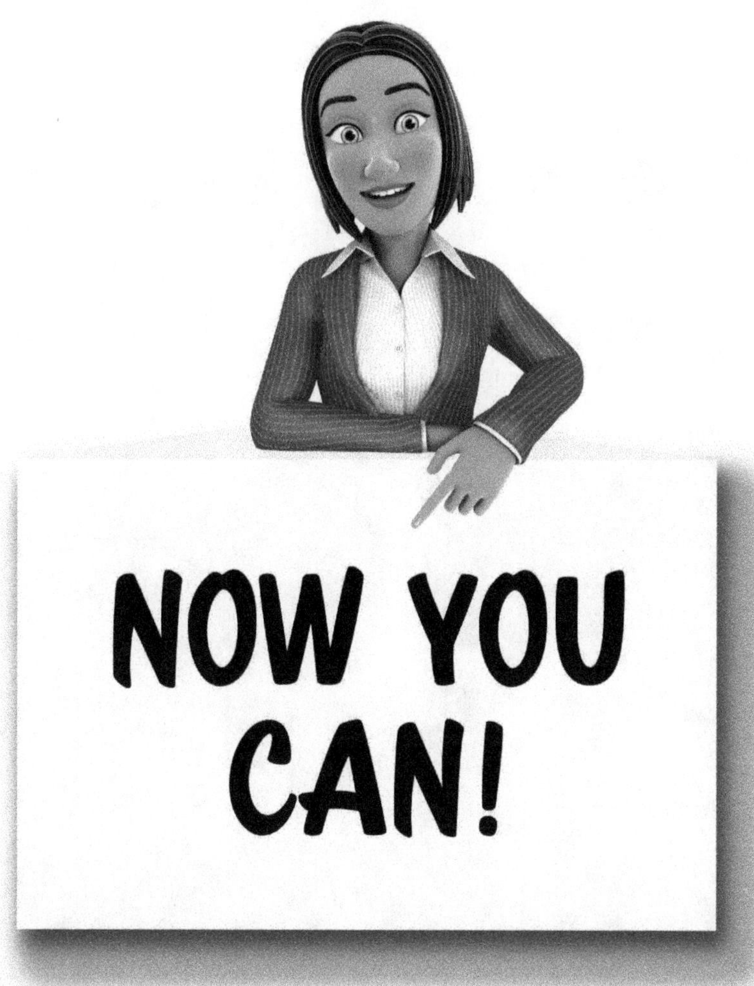

- ✓ Build and Execute a Sprints Project using the Agile Features
- ✓ Enter Progress Data for Agile Projects
- ✓ Use the Boards – Task Status Report
- ✓ Use the Boards – Work Status Report
- ✓ Use the Current Sprint – Tasks Status Report
- ✓ Use the Current Sprint – Work Status Report
- ✓ Use the Sprint Status Report

Part Four Summary

In Part Four - Executing Agile Projects, you learned to use the Agile features included with the Project Online Desktop Client. You learned to use the Kanban-inspired Task Boards to build and track your agile user stories and tasks. You also learned to execute your agile projects using the Scrum-inspired Sprint features.

How to Get the Microsoft Project B.A.S.I.C.S.® On-Demand Course

This book includes a FREE 4-month subscription to the Microsoft Project B.A.S.I.C.S. on-demand course. This video rendition of the Microsoft Project B.A.S.I.C.S. book is a complete course on Microsoft Project, including a comprehensive Project for the Web tutorial. Like the book, you'll be introduced to software features in a meaningful and practical context. You'll also learn to build reliable schedules using the B.A.S.I.C.S. 6-step scheduling process.

It includes:

- A complete course on Microsoft Project
- A video for each chapter of the book
- Work-along software demonstrations
- A comprehensive Project for the Web tutorial
- Stunning, lively graphics

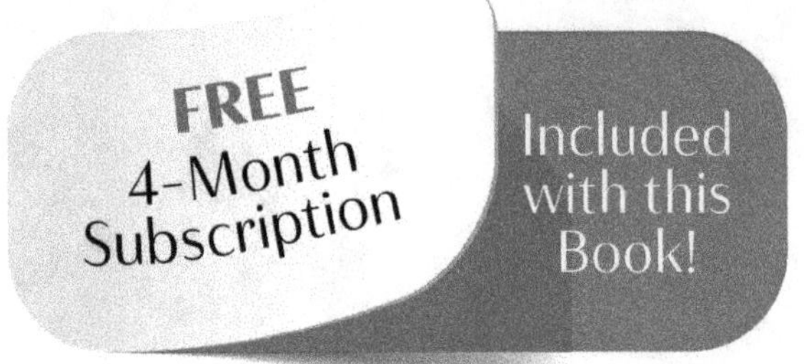

HOW TO GET YOUR 4-MONTH ACCESS LINK TO THE COURSE

If a postcard was included in the cover of your book, follow the instructions included on the postcard.

If your book did not include a postcard, follow the instructions below:

1. Go to **https://www.pmplicity.com/getvideos** to upload proof of purchase of this book. Acceptable forms of proof of purchase include Amazon receipts or screenshots of Amazon order details. Proof of purchase must reflect the Amazon order number, book title (or image) and delivery date. REMOVE ANY PERSONAL INFORMATION, such as your address.

2. Using the contact form, BE SURE TO PROVIDE AN EMAIL ADDRESS to send the access link. After acceptable proof of purchase is received, you'll be emailed a link to access the video course.
   Please note: an email address must be provided or we cannot send you the access link.

More Resources

Be sure to bookmark the companion website for this book — **mspbasics.com**.

You'll find solutions to the Practice Exercises, helpful videos, tips and tools for using Microsoft Project and m.

For more Project Management training, visit **pmplicity.com**.

Errata

We've made every effort to cross every **t** and dot every **i**. But if you should find any errors, please let us know at **mspbasics.com/errata**.

About the Authors

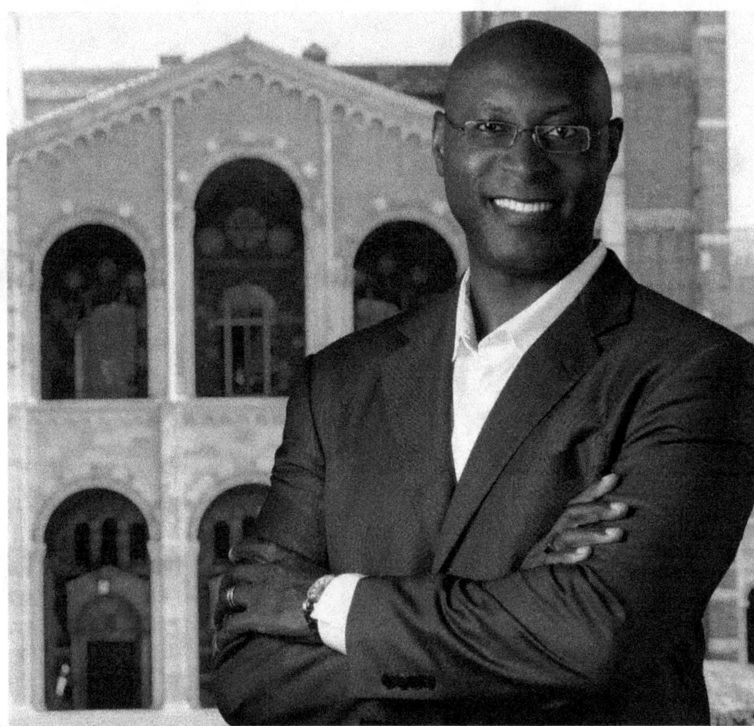

Jerry Reed, Microsoft-Certified Professional, PMP, CSM, EQi 2.0

Jerry Reed is the Co-Founder and President of PMPlicity®. He is a PMI Authorized Training Partner Instructor for the PMP exam. He's an international speaker and an award-winning leadership, project management and agile instructor. He has trained executives, managers, technology workers and individual contributors from AT&T, Optum Rx, Netflix, SpaceX, Google, Boeing, the United Nations, Blizzard, Disney, and several PMI chapters, including the Puget Sound, Los Angeles, Orange County, San Diego, North India, Bangladesh, and UAE (Dubai) chapters. With over 25 years of project management experience, Jerry has successfully delivered over 100 enterprise level projects, using both predictive and agile approaches.

About the Authors

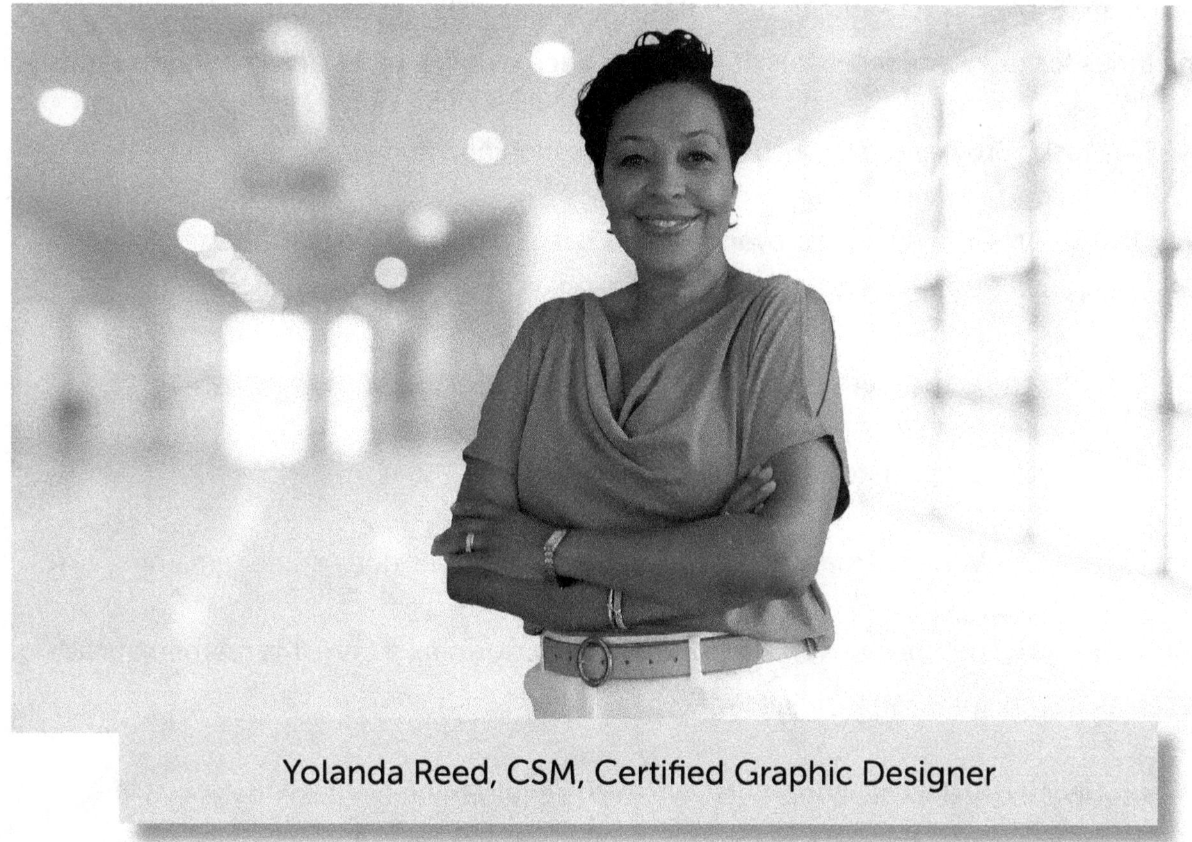

Yolanda Reed, CSM, Certified Graphic Designer

Yolanda Reed is the Co-Founder and Vice President of PMPlicity®. She is a certified Scrum Master, author, editor, graphic designer, and seasoned administrator. She oversees project management, product design and development, and quality assurance. Yolanda is the secret sauce of PMplicity. She maintains strong client relationships and is the primary liaison for PMPlicity partners and distributors, including Amazon, Apple, Barnes and Noble, Follett and UCLA.

Glossary

24-HOURS BASE CALENDAR – one of three Base calendars in Project used to determine working times for tasks and resources. It has no defined working times and runs continuously.

ACTUALS – a task's progress data, such as Actual Duration and Remaining Duration.

ACTUAL DURATION – the number of working days spent performing a task. It is mathematically expressed as – Duration minus Remaining Duration.

ACTUAL FINISH – the actual date the task finished.

ACTUAL START – the actual date the task started.

ACTUAL VARIANCE – Variance that cannot be adjusted, as it does not include remaining cost.

ACTUAL WORK – the number of working hours spent performing a task. It is mathematically expressed as – Work minus Remaining Work.

AGILE – a software development approach, whereby requirements and solutions evolve through the collaborative efforts of a self-organizing, cross functional team consisting of developers, customers, end users, team leaders and project managers.

ASSIGNMENT – the matching of a resource to a task.

ASSIGNMENT UNITS – the percentage of the day resources will work on specific tasks. Assignment Units values are entered in the *Units* field of the *Assign Resources* dialogue box.

AUTOFILTER – a Microsoft Project feature that allows you to quickly sort, group, or filter task or resource data in a table.

AUTOMATIC SCHEDULING MODE – the scheduling mode in which Project automatically calculates the start, finish and duration values for a task, based on dependencies, constraints, calendars and other factors.

AUTOMATIC RESOURCE LEVELING – a feature that allows Project to resolve conflicts or over-allocated resources by delaying or splitting tasks, based on the settings in the *Leveling Options* dialogue box.

BACKSTAGE VIEW – the view accessed from the File tab, where you manage files and adjust project settings.

BACKLOG – a list of all the tasks required to deliver a project. It replaces traditional requirements documentation and consists of user-defined requirements, called user stories.

BASE CALENDAR – the calendar that defines the working and non-working times for the project, tasks and resources. Project includes three base calendars – Standard, Night Shift and 24 hours.

BASELINE – a saved copy of the original schedule. It includes the original start and finish dates and the original duration, work, and cost estimates. It also includes a time-phased distribution of work, duration, cost, and resource allocation.

BOTTOM-UP PLANNING – a method of planning a project, that begins with identifying the tasks in a project, and then organizing them into the major categories or phases of the project.

BUDGET COST RESOURCE – a Cost resource that is used as a placeholder for the Project Budget. It is assigned to the Project Summary Task only and cannot be assigned to individual tasks.

BURNDOWN CHART – a graphical representation of the remaining work on a project, where work is shown on the vertical axis and time is shown on the horizontal axis. For example, if a project requires 400 hours of work, this chart will show the pace at which the work "burns down" to completion across a plot line that descends (or burns down) from left to right.

CHANGE HIGHLIGHTING – a Microsoft Project feature that highlights the values in the schedule that changed due to a schedule edit or update.

CONSTRAINT – a restriction applied to a task that impacts the start or finish date of a task. There are eight constraint types available in Microsoft Project (see Chapter 12 for more details).

COST RESOURCE – a resource type that acts as a placeholder to capture non-recurring cost items that don't accrue via an hourly rate and cannot be classified as consumable. There are two types of Cost resources – Budget and Expense.

CRITICAL PATH – the series of task durations (spanning from the start of the project to the finish of the project) whose collective sum equals the project duration.

DEADLINE – a Microsoft Project feature that allows you to flag a task with the latest date you'd like it to finish.

DETAILED SCHEDULING (also known as effort-driven scheduling) – a method of schedule building in which task durations are determined by estimating task Work and resource availability (Units).

DRIVING PREDECESSORS – predecessor tasks that directly impact or "drive" the start of a successor task.

DURATION – the number of working days estimated to complete a task. It is mathematically expressed as the sum of Actual Duration and Remaining Duration.

DURATION EQUATION – the scheduling formula (Duration = Work / Units) that Microsoft Project uses to calculate duration.

EARNED VALUE – a method of measuring project performance. It indicates how much of the budget and time should have been spent, in view of the amount of work done so far.

EFFORT-DRIVEN SCHEDULING – a Microsoft Project scheduling feature that keeps the work value constant (or fixed) and enables the duration value to increase or decrease as you assign resources to or remove resources from a task.

ELAPSED DURATION – an uninterrupted span of time (24-hour days; 7-day weeks) allotted to complete a task. Elapsed duration is not interrupted by project, resource or task calendars.

ENTRY TABLE – the table in the Gantt Chart view, where scheduling information is entered for the tasks in the schedule.

ESTIMATED VARIANCE – Variance that can be adjusted, as it includes remaining cost.

EXTERNAL LINKS – a link between two interdependent schedules, using external predecessors.

FILTERING – the extraction of task or resource data that meets user-defined criteria.

FIXED CONSUMPTION RATE – the fixed rate at with a Material resource is consumed (e.g. Paint may be consumed at $75 per gallon).

FIXED DURATION – a Task Type setting in which the Duration value is fixed.

FIXED UNITS – a Task Type setting in which the Units value is fixed.

FIXED WORK – a Task Type setting in which the Work value is fixed.

FREE SLACK – the number of days a task can be delayed before it will delay another task(s).

GANTT CHART VIEW – a combination view in Project that includes the Entry table on the left and a graphical chart on the right that depicts the tasks in the schedule, their durations and the how they relate to one another.

GROUPING – the re-sequencing and grouping of task or resource data into a table that summarizes the group values you specify.

INSERTED PLAN (also known as a subproject) – a project plan that is inserted into another project plan to create a Master Project plan.

INTERIM PLAN (also known as an Interim Baseline) – a saved, partial copy of the original schedule. Unlike a full baseline, it only includes the current start and finish dates for all tasks and excludes resource and time-phased values.

KANBAN – an application of the Agile approach that uses a visual system (called a Kanban board) for managing work as it moves through a process.

KANBAN BOARD – a workflow visualization tool that typically uses sticky notes on a whiteboard to communicate status, progress, and issues. Kanban is the Japanese word for "visual signal" or "card."

LAG TIME – the number of days a successor task is delayed after its predecessor finishes. Lag time is entered in the Predecessors field (E.g. 5FS + 2 days).

LEAD TIME – the number of days a successor task can start before its predecessor finishes. Lead time is entered in the Predecessors field (E.g. 5FS – 2 days)

MANUAL SCHEDULING MODE – the scheduling mode in which Project does not automatically calculate the start, finish and duration values for a task. In this mode, users have the option of scheduling tasks manually.

MASTER PROJECT (also called a Consolidated Project Plan) – a Microsoft Project file that contains multiple Inserted Project (subprojects) files consolidated into one project plan.

MATERIAL RESOURCES – consumable supplies that are priced by the amount consumed.

MAXIMUM (MAX.) UNITS – the maximum capacity a resource is available to work on tasks on any given day. This value is entered in the Max. Units field of the Resource Sheet view. The default value is 100%.

MILESTONE – a task that is used to signify the completion of a significant project event. Milestones generally don't include project work, so they have a zero-value duration.

NIGHT SHIFT BASE CALENDAR – one of three Base calendars in Project used to determine working times for tasks and resources. It supports a Monday night thru Saturday morning; 11:00 pm – 8:00 am (1-hour lunch break from 3:00 am to 4:00 am) schedule.

OVER-ALLOCATION – the condition in which a resource is scheduled to work on tasks beyond their maximum capacity (Max. Units value).

PREDECESSOR – a task whose start or finish date determines the start or finish date of another task or tasks.

PROGRESS BAR – a graphical indicator on the task bar in the Gantt Chart that shows how much of a task has been completed.

PROJECT CALENDAR – the Base calendar that defines the working and non-working times for the entire project. One of the three Base calendars in Project is designated as a template for the Project Calendar. It can be modified to reflect the working and non-working times for individual projects.

PROJECT SUMMARY TASK – the summary task that displays the overall values of a project. It's the highest level of the project outline and is assigned task ID zero.

REMAINING DURATION – the number of remaining working days estimated to complete a task. It is mathematically expressed as – Duration minus Actual Duration.

REMAINING WORK – the amount of time still required to complete a task(s). Project calculates Remaining Work as Work – Actual Work.

RESOURCE – a person or thing required to complete a project. In Microsoft Project, there are three types of resources – Work, Material and Cost.

RESOURCE CALENDAR – the Base calendar that is used to define the working and non-working times for a resource.

RESOURCE SHEET VIEW – a view that displays resource information for the entire project in a spreadsheet-like table. It includes information like pay rates and resource groups.

RESOURCE LEVELING – the re-distribution of resource assignments or resource assignment units to resolve (or level) the condition of over-committed (or over-allocated) resources.

RESOURCE POOL – a Microsoft Project file that only includes resource information (in the Resource Sheet view) for resources that are shared across projects.

SCRUM – an application of the Agile approach, whereby teams address complex adaptive problems while delivering incremental value on a continuous delivery cycle (usually 2 weeks).

SHARER PLAN – a project plan that is linked to a resource pool.

SIMPLE SCHEDULING (also known as duration-based scheduling) – a method of schedule building in which task durations are estimated and entered directly into the Duration field.

SLACK (also known as Float) – the number of days a task can be delayed before it will delay another task(s) or the project schedule. There are two types of Slack – Free Slack and Total Slack.

SORTING – the re-sequencing of task or resource data per user-defined criteria.

SPRINT – a time-boxed period (usually 2 weeks), within which to deliver value to a client.

STANDARD BASE CALENDAR – one of three Base calendars in Project used to determine working times for tasks and resources. The "Standard" base calendar is the default calendar in Project. It supports a Monday thru Friday; 8:00 am – 5:00 pm (1-hour lunch break from 12:00 pm to 1:00 pm) schedule.

STATUS DATE – the date on which the latest progress data was collected and entered into Project.

STORY POINTS – a measure of the effort required to implement a User Story. In Microsoft Project, this measure is most like the Work estimate.

SUBTASK – a task demoted beneath a Summary task.

SUCCESSOR – a task whose start or finish date is determined by the start or finish date of another task or tasks.

SUMMARY TASK – a task with subtasks demoted under it. They are represented in Project in bold typeface and are used to group tasks into phases and sub-phases.

TASK – an activity with a unique task ID, indicated numerically in the Entry table of the Gantt chart view. Minimally, it has a duration, a start date, and a finish date.

TASK CALENDAR – the Base calendar that is used to define the working and non-working times for a task.

TASK ID – a unique number that Project assigns to each task in a project plan.

TASK INSPECTOR – a Microsoft Project feature that allows you to view detailed scheduling information for a specific task, including Scheduling Mode, Start and Finish dates, Predecessor information, Calendars and Constraints.

TASK MODE – indicates whether tasks are Automatically or Manually scheduled.

TASK RELATIONSHIP – a dependency (or link) between two or more tasks. There are four task relationship types – Finish-to-Start (FS), Start-to-Start (SS), Finish-to-Finish (FF) and Start-to-Finish (SF).

TASK TYPE – a setting applied to a task that fixes the Work, Units or Duration value, and determines how Project schedules the task. There are three task types available in Project: Fixed Units, Fixed Duration and Fixed Work.

TEMPLATES – the starter project plans included in Project for typical business and personal projects.

TIMELINE VIEW – a customizable view that shows a summary of the project schedule or highlights a selected section of the schedule.

TIMESCALE – a scale shown in views like the Gantt chart view, which depicts units of time, ranging from minutes to years.

TOP-DOWN PLANNING – a method of planning a project that begins with identifying the major categories of work in a project, and then breaking them down into smaller categories or tasks.

TOTAL SLACK – the number of days a task can be delayed before it will delay the project schedule.

TRIPLE CONSTRAINTS – a project management term for the trade-off between scope, schedule and cost when managing a project.

UNITS – the percentage an 8-hour work day a resource is assigned to work on a task.

USER STORY – a tool used in Agile software development to capture a description of a software feature from an end-user perspective. It describes the type of user, what they want and why. It helps to create a simplified description of a requirement.

VARIABLE CONSUMPTION RATE – the rate at with a Material resource is consumed per a specified unit of time (e.g. Paint may be consumed at $75 per Gallon, and at a rate of 1 gallon per hour).

VARIANCE – the difference between the Baseline cost and Total cost for a task, resource, or assignment. Project calculate Cost Variance as Cost – Baseline cost. Therefore, positive variance is unfavorable and negative variance is favorable.

VELOCITY – a key metric in the Scrum methodology that measures the amount of work a team can tackle during a single Sprint. Velocity is calculated at the end of each Sprint by totaling the Story Points for all fully completed User Stories.

WORK – the number of working hours required to complete a task.

WORK BREAKDOWN STRUCTURE – a deliverable-oriented, hierarchical decomposition of the work required to complete a project.

WORK BREAKDOWN STRUCTURE CODING SCHEME – a system of numbering tasks that shows their hierarchical position in the project outline.

WORK IN PROGRESS LIMITS – a limit placed on the work in progress that is determined by the team's development capacity.

WORK RESOURCES – resources that have an hourly rate and a calendar. They can be people, equipment, or rentals, such as a conference room or a crane. They can also be generic, representing a trade or professional group, such as Engineers or Architects.

Index

A

B

C

F

G

H

I

K

L

M

O

P

Q

R

S

INDEX

T

U

V

W

INDEX

Printed in the USA
CPSIA information can be obtained
at www.ICGtesting.com
LVHW072051100124
767851LV00006B/35

2 370011 721781